Race and the Law in the United States

This text explores how the legal history and judicial decisions of the United States contribute to the dynamic societal debates Americans are having around race today. It pairs historical cases and primary sources with contextual commentary to ensure students comprehend how decisions from the past deeply impact the laws they have inherited, as well as shape contemporary issues and political movements. This framework also highlights the distinctive characteristics of the various time periods and how they connect to other eras to provide students with a full appreciation of the events and environments influencing cases. Written in an accessible and engaging style, it avoids the traditional focus of many case-law books and instead promotes a sound understanding of the legal concepts and dynamics that inform current discussions of racial identities, challenging the usual development of doctrinal law and court decisions defining race. An Instructor Manual is available online, with additional teaching resources and assessment materials for each chapter, to foster meaningful class discussions about future choices and how to pursue a more equal nation.

Michelle D. Deardorff is the Adolph S. Ochs Professor of Government at the University of Tennessee at Chattanooga. The co-author of a two-volume constitutional law text and a popular American government text, her career includes decades at a historic Black university, a private college, and a regional public institution. She has served as a Fulbright Senior Specialist, on the governing council of the American Political Science Association, and as co-chair of the APSA Presidential Taskforce on Rethinking Political Science Education. From 1997 to 2017 she was part of the coalition which established the Fannie Lou Hamer National Institute on Citizenship and Democracy, to engage and educate all students and teachers seeking to understand democracy and civil rights in the United States.

"This text is an outstanding resource for teaching race and law in the United States. Designed both to illustrate thematic and group-based concerns and to promote historical understanding, the book covers the breadth of the American experience with race under the law. It provides thoughtfully edited primary sources, including cases, but also legislation, legal commentary, and key movement voices. The explanatory materials provide excellent context for the documents, including outlining the active efforts by people of color and advocacy organizations to promote change. Highly realistic about the potential and limits of law as a tool for reform, this text is an ideal choice for instructors who want to inspire their students to examine legal questions from a richly historical, political, and critical perspective."

Julie Novkov, University at Albany, SUNY

"No one is more qualified to guide students seeking to understand the intersection of law and social justice than Dr. Deardorff. *Race and the Law in the United States* illuminates the intricacies of how the legal system shapes racial identity and lived experiences. This book will be the gold standard for those seeking to foster a deep understanding of how race shapes legal frameworks and perpetuates disparities."

Najja Baptist, University of Arkansas-Fayetteville

"Deardorff's textbook tackles the challenging subject of how to talk about contemporary problems of race and the law. Each chapter couples contextual narratives on discrete topics with cases, legislative documents, and historical sources to explore how the past has shaped the present. Readable and engaging, *Race and the Law in the United States* will encourage robust and critical discussion among students across disciplines and from varying backgrounds."

Jason Gillmer, Gonzaga University

"*Race and the Law in the United States* represents a uniquely comprehensive treatment of the legal concepts and dynamics regarding race and the law in the U.S. Its excellent collection of primary sources will allow students from various backgrounds and perspectives to gain an expansive view of the topic and fuel the development of their own opinions."

Morgan Hazelton, Saint Louis University

Race and the Law in the United States

A Contemporary Perspective

MICHELLE D. DEARDORFF
University of Tennessee at Chattanooga

CAMBRIDGE
UNIVERSITY PRESS

Shaftesbury Road, Cambridge CB2 8EA, United Kingdom

One Liberty Plaza, 20th Floor, New York, NY 10006, USA

477 Williamstown Road, Port Melbourne, VIC 3207, Australia

314–321, 3rd Floor, Plot 3, Splendor Forum, Jasola District Centre, New Delhi – 110025, India

103 Penang Road, #05–06/07, Visioncrest Commercial, Singapore 238467

Cambridge University Press is part of Cambridge University Press & Assessment, a department of the University of Cambridge.

We share the University's mission to contribute to society through the pursuit of education, learning and research at the highest international levels of excellence.

www.cambridge.org
Information on this title: www.cambridge.org/highereducation/isbn/9781009098588

DOI: 10.1017/9781009089715

First published 2025

Cover illustration: Replacing a commemoration of the Confederacy and its leaders, these stained-glass windows in the Washington National Cathedral reflect our nation's complicated past and recognize the perseverance of African Americans in our continuing national struggle to overcome our legacies of racism and slavery. This book explores how the law is used to embed race both into our national identity and in the struggle for human equality. "Now and Forever" windows by Kerry James Marshall, © 2023. Used with permission of Washington National Cathedral.

A catalogue record for this publication is available from the British Library

A Cataloging-in-Publication data record for this book is available from the Library of Congress

ISBN 978-1-009-09858-8 Hardback
ISBN 978-1-009-09636-2 Paperback

Additional resources for this publication at www.cambridge.org/raceandlaw

Cambridge University Press & Assessment has no responsibility for the persistence or accuracy of URLs for external or third-party internet websites referred to in this publication and does not guarantee that any content on such websites is, or will remain, accurate or appropriate.

CONTENTS

PREFACE

Motivation and Aim

The decision to write this book has been driven by my experiences teaching race and law for more than three decades. My career has been spent teaching first- and second-generation students in the Midwest and the South, in both public and private universities, at both historically Black and predominately White campuses. From all of these students, I have learned a great deal about teaching this topic, and those discoveries have helped to frame this text and the approach I take throughout. I believe that the role of the professor – and textbook author – is not one of a provocateur who ends each class session by "dropping the mic," leaving many students stunned because their worldview has been shaken. I see that as the role of guest speakers, a challenging film, or an audacious reading. Some faculty may disagree, but I perceive the primary role of the professor as that of a guide who walks alongside the student, clearing the path of unnecessary obstacles, asking hard questions, providing thoughtful sources for further study, and assisting students as they discover new worlds and begin charting their own course. This text was designed with this approach in mind.

Most constitutional law texts focusing on race and racism emphasize teaching the development of the doctrine of law. Such casebooks typically include a comprehensive selection of cases, discussing both the evolution of the law and distinctions between cases via hypothetical scenarios. This ensures these textbooks are dense and expensive. What is more, many casebooks now focus solely on a single racialized group to ensure that the evolution of the law can be carefully traced and understood. Those that include all racial identities still feature the historical narrative of specific legal topics reflecting the African American experience and then attempt to integrate other races and ethnicities into the narrative or address each racial group separately, pulling them together only in the summative discussion of race or whiteness. While valuable, the focus of these textbooks is limited to cases that have developed around historical doctrinal development or to a single theoretical perspective. Such texts are not designed to equip students to answer a broader range of questions they may have about contemporary topics such as the Black Lives Matter movement, current immigration debates, questions of Native American sovereignty, and the appropriateness of affirmative action.

There is another way to help students wrestle with race and the law that is not predicated on applying the law to scenarios and deciphering doctrine, but instead focuses on instilling an understanding of the legal concepts and dynamics reflected in and contributing to our current societal debates surrounding racial identities. As such, this book is organized by key concepts that contemporary citizens wrestle with in seeking to understand the complexity of the relationship between law and race. It is designed to further class discussions focusing on the limits of the law and not merely the application of the law, exploring how whiteness is a racial identity with repercussions for our society. As a political scientist, I am particularly interested in exploring power dynamics that are controlled, advanced, and mediated by the law. Unlike lawyers, who focus on doctrinal development, or historians, who emphasize the context of the legal decisions, political scientists are focused on exploring key concepts such as federalism, sovereignty, liberty, and equality.

This is a different way of teaching law: not to prepare future lawyers, but to foster citizenship. The Western Interstate Commission for Higher Education (WICHE), using county-level data, predicts a clear decline in White high school graduates applying to college in the next decade (a 17 percent and 26 percent decline, respectively, from those graduating from public and private high schools) and rapid growth in Latino and Latina high school graduates (50 percent) and Asian/Pacific Islander high school graduates (30 percent) (Herman 2019). As our university population changes, the discipline of political science and subsequently, law schools, will be educating a very different student body in the coming decades, necessitating an evolved pedagogy and curricula that reflect their interests and needs (McGee 2015; Nunn 2019). One change that several of my colleagues and I have already observed are the expectations that theory is always clearly related to practice, and that discussions of history relate clearly to current events. Students increasingly insist upon wrestling with current ideas and claims, seeking to understand the relationship of law to other manifestations of state power. They are less interested in merely learning about the development of legal doctrine. The cases in *Race and Law in the United States: A Contemporary Perspective* were selected to help students develop their own critical thinking surrounding the relationship of law and race. The text emphasizes questions designed to expand student understanding of the potential of the law – and its limits – in resolving ongoing dilemmas surrounding our treatment of race in the United States.

Approach and Pedagogy

Currently I teach in Tennessee; I have students from the more liberal and diverse cities of Memphis, Nashville, Chattanooga, and Knoxville, some from wealthy but isolated suburbs, as well as those from the more traditional and conservative regions of Appalachia. These parochial worldviews collide in the classroom. I want all my students to join me on the journey of discovery, regardless of the difficulty and foreign nature of the content. To accomplish this, in each chapter of this book I provide historical context for the selected cases, followed by several challenging questions to explore. Citations to relevant literature allowing students to engage in further personal research to better engage with the book's contentions are included. Primary documents carry much of the intellectual weight of the argument because students find them harder to challenge as being "just an opinion." I avoid loaded language that may be perceived as partisan and try to not take a position on policy issues, although my perspective becomes clear to students during our discussions. I think all Americans – liberal, progressive, conservative, and libertarian – need to participate in this national conversation, and I have found this approach can engage every student in real, meaningful discourse.

With my pedagogical choices in mind, this text has several limitations. It does not try to demonstrate the doctrinal development of every issue that has impacted all racialized groups in the United States. Instead, I see this book as a springboard to further discussions, recognizing that diverse institutions, disciplines, student bodies, and moments in time will focus on discrete questions. As a political scientist who studies public law, I have kept this book focused on questions of power and our democratic state that have clear connections to points of current disagreement.

This book is an entry point for classroom discussions and assignments and not the last word. I take a conversational tone – which is not the norm in legal texts – to make it more accessible to diverse student bodies. I do not make assumptions about what they know, but I do presume that they are intelligent. I ask many questions to encourage critical thinking and to help guide class discussions. All of the cases have been chosen because they can be easily connected to contemporary issues, including ones that the law has not yet addressed.

Outline of Chapters

In Chapter 1, "Race, the Constitution, and Slavery," the text helps students ask *what role did the Constitution play in upholding slavery, and how have our political values informed these decisions?* This chapter highlights the differences between global and contemporary slavery versus the chattel slavery seen in the United States and in the Americas/Caribbean, exploring the question of how the nation can be founded on competing legal claims of equality and liberty while denying personhood under the law. We will also explore how free African Americans, and some Whites, challenged these conflicting notions, and in what ways the law – in upholding property as a key liberty – also created and maintained slavery and racial distinctions. Students will see that slavery in the United States has not been a static concept, and how the law itself embedded slavery, institutionalizing it as a political structure that continued to evolve after formal emancipation. Finally, competing interpretations of the Constitution continue to impact how the nation evaluates its capacity to engage with robust and equitable definitions of liberty and equality. Students will consider what might be the best interpretation of the Constitution's engagement with slavery and why competing definitions matter.

Chapter 2, "Race, Citizenship, and Sovereignty," explores *how racial classifications have affected who gets to vote, immigrate to the United States, self-govern, or become citizens?* This chapter addresses current questions related to immigration and paths to citizenship, and also focuses on the criteria that have been used to determine both the qualifications for citizenship and the rights and obligations that come with it. For indigenous peoples, sovereignty and the ability to self-govern is the core question. The ways in which whiteness shaped the definition and exercise of citizenship and sovereignty will emerge in subsequent chapters. The debates explored in Chapter 2 also show the centrality of the demand for assimilation into "American culture," and how consistent this demand has been throughout our history, with the concomitant justification of excluding those who cannot match our expectations of citizenship due to stereotypes of their culture and "race." Students will reckon with the intention behind the framing of a singular "American culture," and the ongoing demands and costs of racial and cultural assimilation.

In Chapter 3, "Race and Segregation," struggles with *how have some people been geographically separated from Whites or divided within communities based on skin color, language, or cultural markers?* This chapter explores how housing and education opportunities continue to be distinct today for different racialized communities, and the legal actions that have resulted in people living in segregated communities in the United States. Building on some of the most recent research on the relationships between law and segregation, the cases and excerpts in this chapter will explore the role the law played in forcing people to live in isolated communities that resulted in the depression of income for some and limited the accumulation of wealth over generations based on race. Students will consider the ways in which local, state, and federal governments are responsible for ongoing inequities in the United States based on race, and the implications of such accountability.

Chapter 4, "Race and State Obligation," examines *what does it mean when the state does not protect the security of people within its realm because of their race, and how does this intersect with the criminal justice system?* The chapter focuses on current arguments surrounding Black Lives Matter and similar movements in Latino and Native communities regarding state violence against communities of color. The primary sources examine several criminal justice protections provided under the Constitution, consider the Fourteenth Amendment's requirements of state and federal governments, and question how the government protects the people against itself and White majorities. Students will engage with the continuing debates around the responsibility of governments to ensure that policing is not racialized and consider the most just specific policies or legal interpretations focusing on the accountability of state actors.

These first four chapters of the book examine how the law has imagined, defined, and maintained the concept of "race" in the United States, with a consideration of the repercussions today. In the next section of the book, we will begin to examine ways in which the law has tried to rectify the failures of the past, and its limitations in fostering a democracy undamaged by its historic commitments to White supremacy. We will see how the law has attempted to challenge these structures – to provide greater equity and to clarify the status of individuals based on race – and see where the law may be incapable or unwilling to provide answers to the questions the courts have raised.

In Chapter 5, "Race, Culture, and Identity," the text queries *how do cultural and community identities intersect with issues of race?* Here students will explore how the law wrestles with the question of the relationship between laws and cultural customs and norms. Should the law treat discrimination against cultural expressions frequently connected to race, like hair style or language, with the same scrutiny as racial discrimination? Scholars and the courts have disagreed about the relationship between the two and the text engages this debate by presenting different scholarly attempts to resolve this conflict. In this chapter students will explore the ability of Native communities to privilege the adoption of children of indigenous descent into Native families over White families. Another significant question emerges from this discussion: are Native tribal communities in the United States racial or political entities? Conversations related to this question impact core questions of political autonomy and sovereignty, as well as the social constructions of other racial identities.

In Chapter 6, "Race and Constructing Democracy," students investigate *what options does the law provide to correct historic approaches to race, allowing us to more closely align with our national ideals of democracy?* Over time, the different branches of government have worked to develop specific approaches to try and ameliorate the damage of institutionalized racism. However, the courts have wrestled with the question of how these remedies might reify race – making it more central to American life – or destroy the unique aspects of these communities, forged by their shared experiences, in an effort to provide greater equality. Does the law and the Constitution require public institutions to be color-blind in their treatment of race, or does the racial history of the nation demand color-conscious remedies? More specifically, the chapter traces the evolution of affirmative action, especially in education, as a means of compensating for historic generational exclusion. The chapter then focuses on the treatment of U.S. territories that have not been granted statehood, where the majority of the population are people of color. Finally, the chapter explores recent extensions to Native sovereignty and asks readers to consider the impact such protections might have on Native equality.

In Chapter 7, "Race and the Limits of the Law," the text asks, *how can the law address evolving and ongoing concepts such as intentionality, intersectionality, and multiracial identities? If the law does not address these concerns, what options remain for communities of color that experience oppression?* As the law surrounding race in the United States has evolved, it has become clear that legal precedents are static even though public understanding of race in society has expanded dramatically. This chapter explores the historic requirement to demonstrate evidence of an intent to discriminate to justify intervention by the law. This emerged from a traditional understanding of racism as personal and purposeful. As comprehension of the potential harm of neutral policies creating disparate damages in racialized communities has expanded, this barrier to governmental action, and its concomitant justification for neglect, is significant. Students will also explore the inability of the law to address multiple identities simultaneously and the legal consequences of ignoring intersectionality. A proposal to address these two limitations in the statutory law is also considered and evaluated. Finally, the law's hesitance to address multiracial identities is explored, raising the question of whether the current structure of the law is adequate to address our contemporary understanding of racism and racial discrimination.

The Conclusion to the book introduces two new metaphors that force students to consider their own personal and collective responsibility in addressing the relationship between race and the law in the United States. Students should leave the text, and the course, with a clearer personal understanding of the national dynamics around racial discourse in the United States and ideally a personal perspective on both the potential and the limitations of the law in solving societal problems within a democratic system.

Online Resources

The heart of this text is in the pedagogical materials available to instructors at www.cambridge.org/raceandlaw, conveniently compiled into a single Instructor Manual organized by chapter. There, you will find many resources to help your students engage in contemporary debates around race, to focus on the racialized community most relevant to them, and to deepen their understanding of the role of law in our collective interpretations of race.

- *Class Discussion Questions* are more broadly focused than those embedded in the book, allowing a class to pull together themes and encouraging students to extract evidence for their position from the class materials.
- *"Engaging the Argument"* resources are shorter assignments that force students to think more deeply about current manifestations of the themes. They may include reading two different positions on a topic (law reviews, primary documents, or news articles) and then evaluating and assessing the two positions, resolving in a conclusion with a justification.
- *"Furthering the Research"* are questions that address gaps in the literature, incorporate the chapter-level questions, or ask students to independently explore the literature and answer a clear research question suitable for a senior undergraduate or graduate-level term paper.
- *Documentaries* provide two or three different perspectives, digging more deeply into a historical manifestation of one of the elements from the chapter or exploring contemporary challenges arising from these precedents. Discussion questions connecting the documentary to the themes in the chapter are provided in the event that students are assigned to watch a documentary and comment on it independently.
- *Additional Materials* are also provided for the main chapters. These include links to other useful resources such as articles, books, and presentations, or primary sources that can be found, in an edited form, on the accompanying website. Many of these sources are typically taught in political science courses, or demonstrate a premise or concept presented herein.

Each chapter in the book also includes materials that can be used to create assessments for a course.

- *Case Questions* evolve from the individual case or document and can be assigned as part of the brief or in lieu of briefing the case.
- *Chapter-level Questions* are integrated into the introduction and conclusions of each section of the chapter and are designed to help begin and conclude the discussion of a particular subject.

ACKNOWLEDGEMENTS

I would like to thank quite a few people for their deep and meaningful contributions to my thinking regarding the relationship between race and law. Of course, any errors in this text are mine and are not a reflection on the views or interpretations of my generous colleagues.

- From 1991 to 2003, the students at Millikin University in Decatur, Illinois, wrestled through these issues with me in an *African Americans and the Constitution* course and an *Honors Seminar on Civil Rights in the U.S.*
- From 2003 to 2013, graduate and undergraduate students at Jackson State University (JSU) in Mississippi helped me refine my thinking in the courses *Contemporary Issues in the Law* and *Civil Rights and Affirmative Action Law.*
- From 2013 to the present, students at the University of Tennessee at Chattanooga (UTC) have helped me to expand my thinking much more broadly in my *Race and the Law* course.
- The late Professor Augustus J. Jones, Jr. not only introduced me to law as an intellectual passion but showed me how it could reframe my questions around the race and law. Most of all, he saw me – the first woman in my extended family to earn a bachelor's degree and the only one to pursue doctoral-level studies – as an academic and an intellectual. For this I am grateful.
- My colleagues in the Fannie Lou Hamer National Institute on Citizenship and Democracy (1997–2017) are historians and political scientists of different races, generations, and gender identities. They have had the most profound impact on my mind and my heart. I am so grateful to Leslie Burl McLemore, Jeff Kolnick, Thandekile R. M. Mvusi, David Dennard, and our project managers David Deardorff and Keith McMillian as well as our numerous graduate assistants over the years, especially Michael Morris, Janelle Hannah Jefferson, Tameka Yates, Tyrone Hendrix, and Ebou Sowe. I would be remiss not to thank the numerous scholars and activists who contributed to our programming and challenged my thinking in many ways: Emilye Crosby, Tiyi Morris, Daphne Chamberlain, Charles McLaurin, Russ Wigginton, Hollis Watkins, Charles McKinney, Robby Luckett, Charlie Cobb, Mary Delorse Coleman, L. C. Dorsey, Charles Payne, Jimmy Travis, and John Dittmer, among so many others. Plus, I must thank the hundreds of K-12 teachers and students, community college and university faculty, as well as community members who participated in our programs and enjoyed our museum, all made possible by generous funding from the Mississippi Humanities Council, the National Endowment for the Humanities (NEH), the Small Business Administration, and the Kellogg Foundation, among others.

- All of the Hamer Institute's founding members met and organized at the NEH's 1997 Summer Institute, "Teaching the Southern Civil Rights Movement" sponsored by Patricia Sullivan, Waldo Martin, and Henry Louis Gates. It was a watershed experience in my academic life as a young professor, turning my eyes toward the impact of scholarly engagement in public programming. I am grateful to Tim Huebner, Rickey Hill, Renee Romano, and Lee Formwalt for the friendships which have extended long beyond this experience.

In thinking about race and in writing this manuscript, many colleagues – and students – have informed my thinking on both the subject and its relationship to pedagogy. I would like to thank:

- The Hamer faculty, especially Leslie Burl McLemore and Jeff Kolnick and the Jackson Public School history teachers who worked with me on the Teaching American History Project funded by the Department of Education (2008–2013).
- The 120 faculty and staff at UTC who trusted me in 2020–2022 to work through and practice talking about race in meaningful ways, in small ten-person working groups.
- The participants and leaders in the American Political Science Association's (APSA) "Race, Ethnicity, and Politics Teaching and Learning Symposium" in 2022. I want to particularly thank my small group Linda Hasunuma and Julie Lee Merseth for some wonderfully insightful discussions and for helping me think through Asian American and Pacific Islander law and politics resources.
- The participants and leaders in the NYU–Yale American Indian Sovereignty Project and Institute for Constitutional Studies Seminar on "Native Peoples, American Colonialism, and the U.S. Constitution" in 2022. I especially want to thank Maeva Marcus, Ned Blackhawk, Gregory Ablavsky, and Maggie Blackhawk for such an incredible and thought-provoking program.
- The students at UTC who took *Race and the Law* using drafts of this book and its resources during some very difficult semesters during the COVID pandemic. I would like to also thank my Brock Fellow Undergraduate Research Assistants, Grey Warren and Abbi Lowrey, and my graduate assistant Ashley West. Ashley was my first reader and helped me more clearly understand the emotional challenge this material presents for White students new to this history.
- The women of the National Science Foundation ADVANCE projects at JSU and the University of Texas at Rio Grande Valley. Of note, JSU was the first historically Black institution to be awarded an ADVANCE grant. Deep thanks to Loretta A. Moore, Alisa Mosely, Angela Mae Kupenda, ConSandra McNeal, Evelyn Leggette, Leniece T. Smith, and the late Kristi Lowe for supporting and valuing my work and giving me the space and the time for thinking about writing, meaning, and research.

I would like to thank the many anonymous reviewers who provided feedback on this material for Cambridge University Press and the Africana Studies faculty at UTC, for providing feedback on drafts of this text as well as Jeff Kolnick, Angela Mae Kupenda, and David Deardorff, for their comments and for being people who always speak the truth to me (even when I don't want to hear it). At Cambridge University Press, I would like to thank Melanie McFayden, the Politics editor; Melissa Shivers, the development editor, for keeping me on schedule, and the content manager Rachel Norridge, and copy editor Lyn Flight for helping move this book to completion.

Space limitations prevent me from acknowledging every political scientist who has taught me about pedagogy and gave me grace and time to learn and mature. I have been blessed with many wonderful, committed colleagues at Millikin, JSU, and UTC. I also benefit from having a tremendous community of teacher-scholars in APSA's Political Science Education Section. I hope they know how grateful I truly am.

I want to especially thank Angela Mae Kupenda, law professor extraordinaire and emerita, for her friendship, hours, and years of soul-sustaining discussion. Distance and time have not separated us.

Deep appreciation is also given to my parents, Earl and Fonda Donaldson for showing me that doing the right thing is not always easy, and that personal comfort should never be the goal of a meaningful life.

Finally, I owe profound gratitude to David Deardorff, provider of the best and hardest critique. Thank you for thirty-six years of marriage, for challenging me, and for walking with me into uncomfortable but meaningful places.

TABLE OF CASES

TABLE OF STATUTES

Introduction
The Legal Construction and Development of Race

When I was a young girl, my grandparents rented a house with a front yard surrounded by a chain-link fence near which an oak tree grew. As I matured, so did the tree. The fence was so close that the chain links gradually became embedded in the trunk as the tree continued to grow. Over the years, the tree pulled the fence-posts out of the ground. When the landlord finally addressed the problem, the fence had to be cut out of the bark of the tree. To this day, the tree bears the scar of its engagement with the metal fence, and those scars are a lasting reminder of the landlord's neglect.

Race is like this in the United States. The old belief that White[1] people are superior to people of color was a fence that was formally enmeshed into laws and policies before we were our nation. The tree, like the ideal of representative democracy, was planted by people who came long before us. Likewise, we didn't erect the fence. Today's generation has inherited the property and must decide how to maintain it for future generations. Even though the people of the United States have torn down many of the nation's explicitly racist policies and laws, creating formal equality through constitutional amendments and statutory laws, the tree of our democracy has been permanently disfigured by its encounter with legal racism. Just as the tree in my grandparents' yard continued to bear the record of the embedded fence even after the chain links were removed, so does our democracy continue to bear the fresh scars of White supremacy.

Unless we carefully remove all traces of racism from our laws and work to heal our democracy, our past will continue to be reflected in our present practices and will not accurately mirror our ideals of democracy. While extricating the fence from the tree is a necessary first step, it does not repair the damage that was done to the tree or change the beliefs of those who historically or currently have been in the fence-building business. When the United States ended slavery, its political leaders did not repair the economic or social damage of generations of enslavement. When the nation ended segregation, its power structure did not scrutinize all the other enacted laws or the philosophical assumptions made by those who adhered to segregation. Instead, many people assumed that laws that did not directly mandate segregation or did not explicitly reference race were fair because they were neutral. Such political actors do not perceive their choices as having a racial impact, without a racist intent. The problem is that structures and policies that are presumed to be racially neutral by their creators may actually generate

---

[1] In this book, you will see that while race is not a matter of biological differences, the concept was in large part created and reinforced by law. "White" is not a biological classification of people, but one created for social, political, economic, and particularly, legal reasons.

consequences that are unfair or unduly burdensome to subsections of the population. The legal system refers to these burdens as "disparate impacts."

Institutional/Systemic Racism

Disparate impacts can have consequences invisible to the White majority. For instance, a bank may require a family seeking a mortgage to purchase a home to provide bank account records as evidence of how much money comes in and out of the household each month. This policy has a neutral impact on the evaluation of mortgage applicants who maintain bank accounts. However, some communities of color do not have banks in their neighborhoods or do not feel safe using them. Thus, they pay all of their bills using money orders. A presumably neutral and logical requirement to review a checking account to observe monthly cash flow could create a barrier for some people to access mortgages that they are otherwise qualified to obtain. For those in power – bank and mortgage companies, boards, and lenders – the policy seems fair and neutral. Such arbiters are still majority White and likely to be financially secure, as well as comfortable using traditional banking tools. For those who live in communities where contemporary and historical realities do not include a safe, trustworthy banking option – typically African American, Latino,[2] or newer immigrant neighborhoods – such a neutral policy may feel racist in its impact. In this way, universal practices implemented with no racist intent can have the impact of replicating racist patterns (Berry 1994). As we will see in Chapter 6, the question of whether an intent to discriminate is necessary in determining if a policy or action is unlawful racial discrimination has immense significance in our quest to heal our democracy.

Historically, many White Americans have defined racism as hateful personal attitudes toward other people based on their skin color. But as this book will help us understand, racism in the American legal system reflects remnants of policies developed during our racially structured past that have never been reassessed or reimagined in our modern world. As we wrestle with what a just, equitable, and

---

[2] In this book, I will typically use "Latino" and "Latina" to reference communities of Latin American descent, including those from indigenous communities. These individuals are from many different racial and cultural identities but share experiences of immigration, migration, and struggles to be recognized as citizens (Kolnick 2022). Some academics and individuals prefer "Latinx" as the defining term, as it recognizes gender diversity more than "Latino/Latina" does. However, a significant majority of members of this ethnicity do not recognize the term "Latinx," and many are concerned that it erases the specific gendered nature of the Spanish language (see Neo-Bustamante, Mora, and Lopez 2020). There is a nascent movement to embrace "Latine" as a gender-neutral term which still respects the traditions of the Spanish language, but this term does not yet have the recognition of a majority of those who identify with this community. "Hispanic" is a popular term, but it focuses on the shared language of Spanish and not cultural experiences; some are bothered by the inherent reference to the colonial presence of Spain in their categorization. This is the term the government historically uses in demographic measurements.

inclusive American democracy could and should look like, these past debates and values continue reverberating and influencing our present. This book is framed around the key questions of our day, such as "How are our contemporary questions and dilemmas informed by precedent?" and is intended to encourage new thinking, new solutions, and new analyses of problems and injustices that have haunted us from our very origins.

Defining Structural Racism

In considering the legal history of race in America, we see the ways in which the early establishment of chattel slavery, the values of westward expansion and economic development, the need for extremely cheap labor for tending crops and laying railroad track, and the expectation of visible domestic service as a marker of social success resulted in the structured, formal exploitation of many people on the basis of race. While immigrant status and poverty may have initially made the cost of these changes cross-racial, lawmakers' deep national belief in White supremacy and the resulting assumption of the inferiority of other races was embedded in our laws and policies. While we have pulled out the links comprising the fence of explicit White supremacy from most of our institutions, the scars and patterns remained etched in our policies, processes, assumptions, and values. We cannot edit them out of or ignore their presence in our founding documents, our court precedents, or our legislative justifications merely because they make people with twenty-first-century sensibilities uncomfortable. Instead, we must work to repair the damage and improve our democratic system. We will disagree about the optimal form of a just system, but our differences in ideology, political perspectives, and policy priorities will ensure our discussions are robust and nuanced as we work toward a more inclusive democratic republic.

The Individual versus the Systemic

Oppression can occur in many forms, but in the United States when we discuss race, we often perceive racism to be an individual attitude that "bad" people hold toward others of a different race. However, racism is much more complicated and can take many forms beyond individual bad actors. There are personal or individual activities that, on a collective level, are oppressive. Collective actions such as the use of slave patrols, communities deciding to underpay domestic workers, the growth of White supremacist terrorist organizations like the Ku Klux Klan or the Knights of the White Camelia, adoption of derogatory names for an entire community of people, targeted racial violence or hate speech, or the accepted use of humor to belittle and dehumanize others can all foster and maintain oppression without governmental involvement.

Such systemic means of oppression often require collaboration by institutions, including governmental agencies, to ensure that targeted groups of individuals are prevented from fully engaging in society. Changing immigration laws to exclude specific races and ethnicities from our nation, taking children from families to force a culture to assimilate to "American" norms, requiring only English to be spoken, denying residents their constitutional rights, and Supreme Court cases like *Plessy* v. *Ferguson* (1896) can all be ways of legally excluding others. We may disagree over the role that the government and the legal process should play in preventing and repairing individual acts of oppression, yet we must consider whether governmental refusal to protect people from individual oppression is a passive form of governmental action that runs contrary to our democratic ideals.

Resisting Oppression

It is important not to think of the oppressed only as victims, but to also be mindful of the many ways in which people challenge and resist threats to their engagement in democracy. Since the beginning of our democracy – as soon as slavery had a foothold – resistance began. One of the early revolts, Bacon's Rebellion (1676–1677), originated as an attempt by settlers to exterminate Native peoples and expanded to a rebellion against the Virginian colonial government and planter elite. The resulting collaborations of White and Black indentured servants in support of Bacon raised lasting concerns for those with economic and political power (Rice 2012).

Resistance can also provoke a backlash. According to Edmund S. Morgan, Bacon's Rebellion caused wealthy elites to realize that "resentment of an alien race might be more powerful than an upper class" (Morgan 1975, 269–270; Rice 2012, 220). These elites responded by hardening the institution of slavery, designing it to be only for those of Black descent, for the remainder of their natural lives, and as a condition that their children would inherit. These responses to resistance culminated in the Virginia Slave Codes of 1709, which guaranteed that the conditions of White indentured servants and enslaved Blacks were so distinct that the two groups would be less likely to collaborate in future resistance (Morgan 1975).

Forms of Political Resistance

The political resistance we see manifested throughout history takes many forms. We are used to the traditional means of running for office, lobbying and advocacy for policy changes, and voting for like-minded candidates. But people whose beliefs do not have political authority to compel elected officials to listen to them have fewer options. Two options that most free people can exercise are determining to whom they sell their labor, and from whom they buy their goods and services. Consequently, strikes and boycotts are evident throughout our nation's history – well before the 1950s. Others who believe policies are unjust might also exercise civil disobedience by breaking a challenged law, but subsequently accepting the state's punishment for the transgression. In such cases, the law, not the legitimacy of the overall political system, is perceived to be the problem.

Rebellion, on the other hand, is exercised when people seek to overthrow not merely an unfair policy but an unjust system that they believe to be illegitimate and incapable of change. The question thus stands: will the institutions and actors that fill the political void be better or worse for the dispossessed than the stability that the flawed status quo provides?

Role of Law in Making Change

The legal process is another way by which people challenge oppression. They may seek to change unjust laws to something more equitable by engaging with the legislative process, or they may choose to challenge policies they find unfair through litigation. All of these approaches occur at every level of government and in local communities.

Many years ago, I met with a group of Black high school students in Jackson, Mississippi to discuss the role of law in U.S. society. I opened the door to the classroom and asked the students if they believed that the law served as a lock or a key for our democracy. Did law serve as a mechanism for barring people from entering and engaging in our democratic processes, or is it a form of resistance, unlocking the door and allowing those previously excluded to enter and engage in our democratic enterprise? One student quickly argued that the law can be a barrier to entering – preventing people from exercising first-class citizenship and from participating in our democracy. We think of *Dred Scott* v. *Sandford* (1857), in which the U.S. Supreme Court prohibited the enslaved Dred Scott and his family from even bringing a federal claim for freedom to the Court. The justices determined that because Scott was a Black man, "he had no rights the Supreme Court was bound to protect." The law could not see beyond his race and used his race as a justification to lock the door of democracy against him.

Another student immediately spoke up, claiming "but the law is a key." Think of all the litigants over the years who came before the courts seeking assistance. In many cases, relief was granted. For example, in *Melendez* v. *Westminster* (1946), a federal appellate court found that the forced segregation of Mexican American students in public schools was unconstitutional and required the district to dismantle this dual system of learning. And eventually, *Dred Scott* was explicitly overturned by the ratification of the Fourteenth Amendment.

We see this "lock or key" paradox reflected in state and local courts and in legislatures at all levels of governance. Laws and policies can inhibit the exercise of rights and preclude access, or they can open doors and include people. While law does inherently uphold the status quo (as do all societal and political institutions) and rewards stasis, it also can be a tool for the expansion or denial of constitutional rights. It requires people – citizens, lawyers, legislatures, judges, and juries – in order to operate, and people will disagree on the best policies and approaches, often based on their ideologies or their own racial experiences in the world. This book will explore the ways in which the law has both functioned to oppress and to provide meaningful relief from oppression.

The Social Construction of Race and Its Evolution

Social Construction is the theory that our understanding of human beings and how they engage in their environments is not given, natural, or inherent, but the product of historical relationships and events. While there are obvious differences in physical appearance, as well as our experiences and realities, because of race/ethnicity or gender, the meaning we create about these differences is significant. It is natural to observe differences between groups, the variations between cultures, and the biological differences of sex. The issue begins when those perceived differences lead to "othering," when we believe these observable attributes result in a group being of less worth or inherently limited in their capacities.

Defining "Social Construction"

The concept of social construction asserts that our assumptions about race and gender are not innate or immutable. Race, as a concept, is not biological; it is, in fact, socially constructed. The concept of race was created over time in response to societal, cultural, and economic needs and demands. This framework can help us to understand power relationships and their physical or material consequences, as well as how individual characters and personalities are shaped by these relationships. Humans developed the idea of race based on skin color and then organized many societies around this notion, benefiting some and harming others. However, it was not always this way. Determining when race and racism begins in human history is a complicated and contested question (Seth 2020).

In *The Subjection of Women*, English political philosopher John Stuart Mill stated that we ought:

> not to ordain that to be born a girl instead of a boy, any more than to be born black instead of white, or a commoner instead of a nobleman, shall decide the person's position through all of life ... [We should end barriers which] take persons at their birth, and ordain that they shall never in all their lives be allowed to compete for certain things. (Mill 1869)

The idea of social constructs is a very old one. As Christopher Lebron reminds us, "[b]eyond setting the parameters for persons' appropriate roles and self-understanding, social construction motivates normative beliefs about others and ourselves on account of the lessons we learn with respect to the place we occupy in the social scheme" (Lebron 2013, 63).

As Mill notes, social construction also impacts societal understanding of race, gender, and class, and today we also consider sexual identity and orientation along with other aspects of identity. Social constructs affect how people frame the world, perceive others and themselves, and structure society. Because social construction is so fundamental to our understanding of the world and the way we explain our own experiences, its functioning may be difficult to perceive, creating challenges for us in intellectually and emotionally confronting our assumptions. Socially constructed views and beliefs become imbedded into our institutions and structures, a part of our cultural socialization, and so can seem natural and inherent. This book explores how the construction of race was developed in the United States and imbedded into our legal structure, and the myriad ways it influences how we both understand race today and choose to respond to racial inequities. Despite the challenges that come with social constructs of race, the good news is that social constructions developed by humans can likewise be dismantled and replaced by humans.

Evolution of Race as a Concept

In focusing on African Americans and Native people, one of the earliest scholars on the development of the idea of race in America, Winthrop D. Jordan, found that Whites' negative ideas and prejudices about these groups developed and formed over time in response to social and economic changes. Jordan argued that the desire or perceived economic imperative to enslave African peoples to provide labor in the New Worlds created the need and impetus to reframe Africans as a race worthy of enslavement (Jordan 1968). He found that "white American attitudes towards blacks have done a great deal to shape and condition American responses to other racial minorities" (Jordan 1974, viii).

Other scholars have considered how race in America provided a means by which a common "White" culture was created slowly, and through which "whiteness" eventually became equivalent to "American." "Fighting, fearing, and hating Indians had helped forge a common identity among white peoples before; [after the Revolution] the shared experiences of Scots, Irish, Germans, English, and others in fighting and dispossessing Indians helped forge a common bond as Americans" (Calloway 2018, 12). As immigrant groups and indigenous populations were willing or able to assimilate, they became "White" and reaped the economic benefits (Ignatiev 1995; Roediger 2007). Being different from other culturally distinct groups that were perceived as threatening helped to define the meaning of whiteness (Silver 2008). As we will see in Chapter 2, the pressure on racial and ethnic groups to assimilate has motivated many policies and statutory laws.

A complicating factor in the construction of race is that it is only in the United States and other settler societies where *our* specific racial categories exist. Kongo, Mbundu, Igbo, and Tikar peoples brought from Africa and sold in the colonies spoke different languages and practiced different customs, but through a common experience of slavery became "American" (Huggins 1977). Native and indigenous peoples that have seen themselves as unique cultures and nations (e.g., Choctaw, Yavapai, Ho-Chunk, Cherokee, or Penobscot tribes) have now been assigned a common identity based solely on their shared history of oppression. Before coming to the United States, Asian Americans were Chinese and Thai, Japanese and Korean, Indian and Pakistani, Vietnamese and Laotian, with different languages, religions, customs, and long histories of conflict. In the United States, they are treated as a single interchangeable racial group – Asian American – with shared interests and issues. The same is true for Latino peoples; while they may share a language, their racial categorization as a single entity means that the political and cultural differences between Cubans and Mexicans, Peruvians and Puerto Ricans, Bolivians and Nicaraguans are dissipated and replaced by a newly constructed racial identity (Molina 2014). This is complicated by the fact that people can be of different racial descent (Afro-Latino, Asian-Latina, White Latino, Indigenous-Latina, or multiracial) and still share a common Hispanic identity. Yet other groups morph in and out of whiteness (i.e., Arabic people originally from North Africa and the Middle East) depending on our geopolitical fears and their reflection in immigration policy (Lopez 1996). As we will see in later chapters, the idea of "whiteness" has been socially constructed as clearly as all of these other racialized identities.

This book seeks to help us understand the implications of these ideas as we continue to address racial oppression and wrestle with what a just democracy could look like. As you engage with the questions posed by the primary documents provided in this book and challenge your understanding of the role of law, know you are engaging in righteous work, an effort to pursue "a more perfect union" that all denizens of the United States should pursue.

1 Race, the Constitution, and Slavery

The origins of racism in the United States can be difficult to discern as it was formed in a multiracial context. In the Americas, Europeans became "White," as opposed to English, Scottish, or German. The numerous tribes of Africa became "Negro" and then "Black," and the many indigenous peoples of the continents became "Indian." We know that some of the earliest forms of forced labor in the colonies came from indentured servants who were bound to labor for a predetermined amount of time, after which they were to be set free with some contractual settlement (generally land or money). Children born to women while indentured might similarly be bound until they hit the age of majority, depending on the local law and custom. Indentured servants came from Europe and Africa or were indigenous people – some consenting to their status, others filling criminal sentences, and still others were compelled to serve. The laws governing this contract varied immensely, as did its enforcement and colonial protections for the vulnerable. Indigenous peoples were the earliest slaves in the New World with over a million having their labor bought and sold by the colonizers and colonists, reflecting a tradition that had existed before Whites arrived on the continent (Reseñdez 2016; Blackhawk 2023). The transition to race-based institutionalized slavery of Africans was gradual, but Virginia's history demonstrates its evolution in the colonies.

For Virginia, the transition accelerated in 1676 due to Bacon's Rebellion, with similar stories playing out throughout the colonies. The cooperation of White and Black indentured servants in joining Bacon's challenge to Virginia's political structure concerned the power elite. The eventual response was to increase the debited time owed by White rebels and to convert Black servitude to a lifetime sentence, with the children's status following the mother. Elected leaders wrote Native slavery into colonial law, but gradually replaced it with African chattel slavery; this policy quickly was adopted by other communities and became the legal norm.

> The implications of this new social order penetrated into almost every part of life. Racial slavery and white populism – white tribalism, one might say – forced Indians and Africans to shoulder the burden of resolving these tensions and divisions within colonial society ... As the slave population increased, even the poorest, unhappiest white Virginians were lifted further from the bottom of society ... All white men were at least "potential patriarchs." (Rice 2012, 221)

While Native enslavement and peonage would continue external to the law, classified by racial identity, race was becoming central to the legal process (Morgan 1975).

The evolving connection between slavery and race changed the status of Free Blacks into a "social anomaly," contradicting the assumed dual race system (Jordan 1968, 134). Consequently, many freed peoples lost their political agency (Malone 2008) and multi-race individuals were categorized as simply "Black." Native peoples were also distinguished from African Americans by virtue of slavery but were still perceived as alien from White colonists. Over the centuries, slavery would impact all racialized peoples – either by forms of slavery that would control their bodies (e.g., Chinese women in bordellos, Siler 2019) or through unenforced or exploited labor contracts (consider native Hawaiians, indigenous peoples, or Mexican workers) (Glenn 2002; Reséndez 2016). Slavery constructed and framed our understanding of race in the United States for its first 200 years.

1.1 Ancient, Neo-, and Modern Slavery

Chattel slavery is a form of coerced labor in which human beings are owned as property, bought and sold on an open market, inherited and given to others, and otherwise treated as personal property by the owner. In distinguishing race-based chattel slavery from other forms of slavery, we do not dismiss the inherent destructiveness of slavery, for as Orlando Patterson notes, "slavery is the permanent, violent domination of natally alienated and generally dishonored persons" (1982, 13). Historic, race-based chattel slavery in the United States differed greatly from the economic and sexual exploitation seen today in human trafficking. The difference is not in the specific abuses – chattel slavery in the United States was both economic and sexual in its harm to those entrapped and used violence to maintain control. Contemporary trafficking in the United States differs in that it is not state-sanctioned; the government does not regulate, protect, or enforce the claims of the slaver. It is also not race-based, as the institution of trafficking is not designed to control the labor and bodies of a single race of people. Instead, human trafficking consists of webs of individuals collaborating to use the most vulnerable for personal economic gain; people are not currently bought and sold in the public market, and the state does not sustain those contracts as legitimate (Winterdyk 2019). Our nation's current economic system is not dependent upon – although it certainly benefits from – the coerced and unpaid labor of others.

1.1.1 Ancient Slavery

Chattel slavery in the United States also differs from the traditions of slavery that have existed around the world. Many economic systems around the globe and throughout time have been dependent on slavery and their governments have endorsed the generational slaveries of people from other cultures. Classical slavery, for instance, often derived from the enslavement of a vanquished enemy (who might or might not have been of the same race or ethnicity) or as a result of poverty, where such status was inherited by the next generation (Pomeroy 1995; Dubois 2003). While nations depended upon slavery to maintain their economic and social authority, it was often a more porous structure allowing people to leave or enter enslavement as a result of changes in their fortunes. Even indigenous peoples in North America utilized slavery as a means of controlling vanquished enemies from different tribal groups. Unlike chattel slavery, these forms of slavery were not posited upon a multinational structure, endorsed by multiple religious and governmental institutions, or designed to control the labor and bodies of people from another continent, lasting for centuries.

After the Civil War and the passage of the Thirteenth Amendment, slavery and involuntary servitude officially ended in the United States except as a statutory punishment for crime. Chattel slavery, as initially developed and maintained, ceased and new forms of neo-slavery emerged. Peonage allowed Whites to force labor and bodily control over those who owed them debts, which were often contrived and without external oversight (Daniel 1990). As with sharecropping, perpetual debt was the justification for the exploitation of peonage. The White landowner kept the books, recorded the debt, determined the compensation, and often paid in script – forcing the indebted to purchase supplies from the landowner and paying his set prices. Convict leasing was similarly devised to replace slavery in the South as a means of labor and racial control. With a corrupt legal system conspiring with plantation owners, poor men, especially Black men, could be easily charged with nebulous crimes like vagrancy and loitering, assessed fines they could not pay, and then had their labor sold to owners of mines, plantations, railroad companies, and turpentine farms. Without any systemic accountability or supervision, people disappeared and died at alarming rates (Oshinsky 1996; Blackmon 2008).

Slavery originated as a system of cheap labor and then evolved into a system of racial control. But in all of its manifestations the intent of profiting from the undercompensated labor of people of color remains central to slavery's design. So, while there are many forms of slavery, and historically the peoples of our nation used all these modalities, it is the unique characteristics of chattel slavery that has most indelibly impacted our political identity and legal systems.

1.1.2 Race and Chattel Slavery

Under chattel race-based slavery, which extended throughout Latin America, the Caribbean, United States, and much of Europe, race became the determinant of a person's perceived humanity (Thomas 1997). The loss of personhood, culture, identity – the individual deliberately being broken of all sense of self and sold to other continents – and the denial of legal rights outside the inherent value of being physical property, made chattel slavery unique. Consequently, those who benefited from slavery deliberately decimated individual personhood, and an entire race was perceived as being constituted of lesser persons unworthy of freedom. Once the United States ceased the legal importation of slaves from Africa, the demand for new labor was met through forced breeding programs and slave owners reproducing with the women they enslaved (Morgan 2004), as well as natural population growth (Hacker 2020). Scholars estimate that between 1619–1865 "approximately 10 million slaves lived in the United States, where they contributed 410 billion hours of labor" (Hacker 2020, 840). For this kind of slavery – rooted in the U.S. economic system – to have existed in a democratic nation based on the principle of individual liberty and in a country where Christianity with its value of "brotherly love" was culturally embedded, those enslaved had to be dehumanized (Jordan 1968). The various institutions of our society – educational, religious, economic, political, and social – all had to twist and change in order to accept chattel slavery and its horrors as embedded in American democracy.

1.2 Embedding Slavery into Law

The resulting contradictions in these values are all reflected in our political socialization, historical documents, laws, and Constitution. After Bacon's Rebellion, the colonies began crafting Slave Codes that clearly delineated "activities that slaves and indentured servants cannot do, must do, or cannot do with whites, the things that whites cannot do with slaves, and that blacks cannot do even if free" (Bush 1997, 392). These codes further racialized the labor structure and formalized racial boundaries under the law, over time controlling both free Blacks and those enslaved (Smith 1997, 253). Because these social stratifications and racial identities were being legislatively constructed, enforcement was problematic.

The effort it required to construct and maintain these racial identities is clearly seen in the 1723 revisions of the Slave Codes in Virginia. Not only did this law focus on defining the social expectations within a racialized community of Whites, Natives, and Blacks, but it compelled slave owner and overseers; sheriffs, judges and justices of the peace; ministers and church warden; as well as jurors to uphold the Slave Codes or be punished by a personal fine. What is particularly interesting is that the fine is payable to the person who reports the infraction of the law, building an economy of informers. Social construction of a racial identity required coercion and incentives for those who did not economically benefit directly from slavery to support this new system. If laws tell us how the powerful perceive the actions of subordinated populations and what people with power fear – and it can be hard to tell the difference – what were lawmakers in Virginia addressing? What does this tell us about what was required to embed racialized slavery permanently in the culture?

SLAVE LAWS IN VIRGINIA, MAY 1723

An Act directing the trial of Slaves, committing capital crimes; and for the more effectual punishing conspiracies and insurrections of them; and for the better government of Negros, Mulattos, and Indians, bond or free.

I. WHEREAS the laws now in force, for the better ordering and governing of slaves, and for the speedy trial of such of them as commit capital crimes, are found insufficient to restrain their tumultuous and unlawful meetings, or to punish the secret plots and conspiracies carried on amongst them, and known only to such, as by the laws now established, are not accounted legal evidence: And it being found necessary, that some further provision be made, for detecting and punishing all such dangerous combinations for the future.

II. Be it enacted ... That if any number of negros, or other slaves, exceeding five, shall at any time hereafter consult, advise, or conspire, to rebel or make insurrection, or plot or conspire the murder of any person or persons whatsoever, every such consulting, plotting, or conspiring, shall be adjudged and deemed felony; and the slave or slaves convicted thereof ... shall suffer death, and be utterly excluded the benefit of clergy ...

V. ... That at every such trial of slaves committing capital offences, the person who shall be first named in the commission, sitting on such trial, shall, before the examination of every Negro, Mulatto, or Indian, not being a Christian, charge such evidence to declare the truth; which charge shall be in the words following, viz:

> YOU are brought hither as a witness; and, by the direction of the law, I am to tell you, before you give your evidence, that you must tell the truth, the whole truth, and nothing but the truth; and that if it be found hereafter, that you tell a lie, and give false testimony in this matter, you must, for so doing, have both your ears nailed to the pillory, and cut off, and receive thirty-nine lashes on your bare back, well laid on, at the common whipping-post.

VIII. And whereas many inconveniences have arisen, by the meetings of great numbers of negros and other slaves: ... from henceforth no meetings of negros, or other slaves be allowed, on any pretence whatsoever. And that every master, owner, or overseer of any plantation, who shall, knowingly or willingly, permit any such meetings, or suffer more than five negros or slaves, other than the negros or slaves belonging to his, her, or their plantations or quarters, to be and remain upon any plantation or quarter, at any one time, shall forfeit and pay the sum of five shillings, or fifty pounds of tobacco, for each negro or slave, over and above such number, that shall at any time hereafter so unlawfully meet or assemble, on his, her, or their plantation, to the informer ...

X. ... That if any white person, free negro, mulatto, or Indian, shall at any time hereafter be found in company with any such slaves, at any such unlawful meetings, as aforesaid, or harbor or entertain any negro, or other slave whatsoever, without the consent of their owners ... shall forfeit and pay the sum of fifteen shillings, or one hundred and fifty pounds of tobacco, to the informer ... and upon failure to make present paiment, shall have and receive, on his, her, or their bare backs, for every such offence, twenty lashes, well laid on. And every negro, mulatto, or indian slave, shall ... receive, on his or her bare back, any number of lashes, not exceeding thirty-nine.

XI. ... That every justice of the peace of any county wherein such unlawful meetings shall happen ... upon information thereof to him made, within ten days after such offence committed, shall forthwith issue his warrant to apprehend all such persons, who so met or assembled, and cause such offenders to be brought before him, or some other justice, who shall fail in his duty herein, shall forfeit and pay the sum of fifty shillings, or five hundred pounds of tobacco, for every such offence.

XII. ... That every sheriff ... shall fail forthwith to endeavour to suppress and disperse the same, and to carry the offenders before some justice of the peace, in order for the said offenders to receive due punishment, the sheriff, for every offence by him committed, shall forfeit and pay the sum of fifty shillings, or five hundred pounds of tobacco: Both which ... shall be to the informer ... And the under sheriff, or constable, failing to perform his or their duty herein ... shall forfeit and pay twenty shillings, or two hundred pounds of tobacco, to the informer ...

XVII. And be it further enacted, by the authority aforesaid, That no negro, mullatto, or indian slaves, shall be set free, upon any pretence whatsoever, except for some meritorious services, to be adjudged and allowed by the governor and council ...

XIX. ... That if any slave shall happen to die by means of such dismembring, by order of the county court, or for or by reason of any stroke or blow given, during his or her correction; ... no person concerned in such dismembring correction, or accidental homicide, shall undergo any prosecution or punishment for the same; unless ... it shall be proved ... that such slave was killed wilfully, maliciously, or designedly; neither shall any person whatsoever, who shall be indicted for the murder of any slave, and upon trial, shall be found guilty only of manslaughter, incur any forfeiture or punishment for such offence or misfortune.

XX. Provided always, That nothing herein contained, shall be construed, deemed, or taken, to defeat or barr the action of any person or persons, whose slave or slaves shall happen to be killed by any other person whatsoever, or whose slaves shall happen to die thro' the negligence of any surgeon, or other person, undertaking the dismembring or cure of such slave, liable to such punishment by this act: But that all and every owner or owners of such slave or slaves, shall and may bring his or her action, for recovery of damages for such slave or slaves so killed or dying, as if this act had never been made.

XXII. ... That where any female mullatto, or indian, by law obliged to serve 'till the age of thirty or thirty-one years, shall during the time of her servitude, have any child born of her body, every such child shall serve the master or mistress of such mullatto or indian, until it shall attain the same age the mother of such child was obliged by law to serve unto.

XXIII. ... That no free negro, mullatto, or indian whatsoever, shall hereafter have any vote at the election of burgesses, or any other election whatsoever.

XXIV. ... That the churchwardens of each parish, within this his Majesty's colony and dominion, at the charge of their parish, shall provide a true copy of this act, and cause entry thereof to be made in the register book of each parish; and shall, on some Sunday in the months of April and October, yearly, after divine service ended, at the door of every church and chapel in their parish, publicly read the same. And the sheriff of each county shall, at the court held for the county, in the months of June or July, yearly, publish this act, at the door of the courthouse of the said county. And every churchwarden and sheriff making default herein, shall, for each time so offending, forfeit and pay five hundred pounds of tobacco, to the informer... And the minister or reader making default herein, shall, for each time so offending, forfeit and pay two hundred pounds of tobacco, to the informer ...

1. How does the slave state evolve and how does the law enforce its existence?
2. If laws demonstrate what lawmakers' fear, what were the lawmakers concerned about in Virginia in 1723?
3. Does this law demonstrate wide societal support of slavery or the contrary? Why or why not? (Think about whose behavior the law controls and the role of informers.)
4. How does the law render those enslaved as property?
5. What do these laws tell us about how the enslaved and free Black populations were challenging their conditions?

In North Carolina's Supreme Court decision *State* v. *Mann* (1829) we see the violence required to maintain this structure of slavery in the United States. While Justice Ruffin may regret his decision to allow owners of enslaved individuals the authority to force labor from those who "toil that another may reap the fruits," he is compelled by "[t]he established habits and uniform practice of the country." But these are practices and habits that had been deliberately coerced by the enforcement of the Slave Codes, not an inherent status. In this decision we see the transition of a human being to legally constructed property designed to be bought, used, disciplined, and controlled (Wynn 2009). Justice Ruffin addresses his own moral qualms in rendering this decision but seems to believe that in expressing such trepidations he is outside the expectations of the law and his society. After the creation of the United States in 1776 and the ratification of the Constitution in 1789, slavery was slowly abolished in many of the northern states. However, by the early 1830s, the institution of slavery became more stringent in the South, with firmer laws and controls. In 1829, an enslaved woman named Lydia was hired by John Mann from Elizabeth Jones, Lydia's owner. After Lydia fled from punishment for a minor offense, John Mann shot and wounded her. A lower court found Mann guilty of inflicting cruel and disproportionate punishment. Mann then appealed to the North Carolina Supreme Court.

STATE OF NORTH CAROLINA v. MANN, 13 N.C. 263 (1829)

Justice Thomas Ruffin Delivered the Opinion

A Judge cannot but lament, when such cases as the present are brought into judgment ... The struggle, too, in the Judge's own breast between the feelings of the man, and the duty of the magistrate is a severe one, presenting strong temptation to put aside such questions, if it be possible. It is useless however, to complain of things inherent in our political state. And it is criminal in a Court to avoid any responsibility which the laws impose. With whatever reluctance therefore it is done, the Court is compelled to express an opinion upon the extent of the dominion of the master over the slave in North Carolina.

... [U]pon the general question, whether the owner is answerable ... for a battery upon his own slave, or other exercise of authority or force, not forbidden by statute, the Court entertains but little doubt.

... The established habits and uniform practice of the country in this respect, is the best evidence of the portion of power, deemed by the whole community, requisite to the preservation of the master's dominion ... This has indeed been assimilated at the bar to the other domestic relations; and arguments drawn from the well established principles, which confer and restrain the authority of the parent over the child, the tutor over the pupil, the master over the apprentice, have been pressed on us. The Court does not recognise their application. There is no likeness between the cases. They are in opposition to each other, and there is an impassable gulf between them. The difference is that which exists between freedom and slavery – and a greater cannot be imagined. In the one, the end in view is the happiness of the youth, born to equal rights with that governor, on whom the duty devolves of training the young to usefulness, in a station which he is afterwards to assume among freemen. To such an end, and with such a subject, moral and intellectual instruction seem the natural means; and for the most part, they are found to suffice. Moderate force is superadded, only to make the others effectual. If that fail, it is better to leave the party to his own headstrong passions, and the ultimate correction of the law, than to allow it to be immoderately inflicted by a private person. With slavery it is far otherwise. The end is the profit of the master, his security and the public safety; the subject, one doomed in his own person, and his posterity, to live without knowledge, and without the capacity to make anything his own, and to toil that another may reap the fruits. What moral considerations shall be addressed to such a being, to convince him what, it is impossible but that the most stupid must feel and know can never be true – that he is thus to labour upon a principle of natural duty, or for the sake of his own personal happiness, such services can only be expected from one who has no will of his own; who surrenders his will in implicit obedience to that of another.

Such obedience is the consequence only of uncontrolled authority over the body. There is nothing else which can operate to produce the effect. The power of the master must be absolute, to render the submission of the slave perfect. I most freely confess my sense of the harshness of this proposition, I feel it as deeply as any man can. And as a principle of moral right, every person in his retirement must repudiate it. But in the actual condition of things, it must be so. There is no remedy. This discipline belongs to the state of slavery. They cannot be disunited, without abrogating at once the rights of the master, and absolving the slave from his subjection. It constitutes the curse of slavery to both the bond and free portions of our population. But it is inherent in the relation of master and slave.

That there may be particular instances of cruelty and deliberate barbarity, where, in conscience the law might properly interfere, is most probable. The difficulty is to determine, where a Court may properly begin. Merely in the abstract it may well be asked, which power of the master accords with right. The answer will probably sweep away all of them. But we cannot look at the matter in that light. The truth is, that we are forbidden to enter upon a train of general reasoning on the subject. We cannot allow the right of the master to be brought into discussion in the Courts of Justice. The slave, to remain a slave, must be made sensible, that there is no appeal from his master; that his power is in no instance, usurped; but is conferred by the laws of man at least, if not by the law of God. The danger would be great indeed, if the tribunals of justice should be called on to graduate the punishment appropriate to every temper, and every dereliction of menial duty. No man can anticipate the many and aggravated provocations of the master, which the slave would be constantly stimulated by his own passions, or the instigation of others to give; or the consequent wrath of the master, prompting him to bloody vengeance, upon the turbulent traitor – a vengeance generally practised with impunity, by reason of its privacy. The Court therefore disclaims the power of changing the relation in which these parts of our people stand to each other.

We are happy to see, that there is daily less and less occasion for the interposition of the Courts. The protection already afforded by several statutes, that all powerful motive, the private interest of the owner, the benevolences towards each other, seated in the hearts of those who have been born and bred together, the frowns and deep execrations of the community upon the barbarian, who is guilty of excessive and brutal cruelty to his unprotected slave, all combined, have produced a mildness of treatment, and attention to the comforts of the unfortunate class of slaves, greatly mitigating the rigors of servitude, and ameliorating the condition of the slaves. The same causes are operating, and will continue to operate with increased action, until the disparity in numbers between the whites and blacks, shall have rendered the latter in no degree dangerous to the former, when the police now existing may be further relaxed. This result, greatly to be desired, may be much more rationally expected from the events above alluded to, and now in progress, than from any rash expositions of abstract truths, by a Judiciary tainted with a false and fanatical philanthropy, seeking to redress an acknowledged evil, by means still more wicked and appalling than even that evil.

I repeat, that I would gladly have avoided this ungrateful question. But being brought to it, the Court is compelled to declare, that while slavery exists amongst us in its present state, or until it shall seem fit to the Legislature to interpose express enactments to the contrary, it will be the imperative duty of the Judges to recognise the full dominion of the owner over the slave, except where the exercise of it is forbidden by statute. And this we do upon the ground, that this dominion is essential to the value of slaves as property, to the security of the master, and the public tranquility, greatly dependent upon their subordination; and in fine, as most effectually securing the general protection and comfort of the slaves themselves. Let the judgment below be reversed, and judgment entered for the Defendant.

As you answer these questions consider the differences between Virginia and North Carolina and how the concerns surrounding slavery change over time.

1. In *State* v. *Mann*, how does the judge understand the difference between slavery and freedom?
2. What are the consequences for a society that values freedom?
3. The judge notes the need for decreasing intervention by the courts into the institution of slavery – compare this with the specificity of the earlier Virginia law – what might explain this difference?
4. How do both the 1723 Virginia law and the 1829 North Carolina court decision demonstrate the social construction of race? the creation of people into property?

1.3 The Constitution and Slavery

After the American Revolution (1776) and some initial experimentation, the White new citizens of the thirteen states ratified a written governing document called the Constitution (1789) which attempted to provide a clear, shared vision for the operation of the new country. There has been great debate throughout the existence of the United States as to whether the Constitution is a slave document, which allows freedom for some only, or a document of great ideals, which had been perverted to allow for slavery. Scholars such as Derrick Bell (2004) have argued that the Constitution was pro-slavery, noting specific constitutional provisions and the deep compromises made with the slave-holding South for its ratification. Some have argued that it was anti-slavery, and others that it is neutral in its intent, merely waiting for future generations to determine the outcome (Fehrenbacher 2001). A few scholars have read the Constitution through the more radical words of the Declaration of Independence, arguing it is a poor interpretation of the Constitution that leads to conflict with equality (Allen 2014).

Both the abolitionist William Lloyd Garrison and the authors of the Confederacy interpreted the Constitution as strongly advancing the cause of slavery. For Garrison, this amounted to a contract with hell and required nothing less than a new government and founding documents. The compromises with slavery that the ratification of the Constitution required had damned it as a moral document from its very beginning and Garrison could perceive no resolution that did not require its replacement with a governing document with a stated goal of freedom for all of humanity.

WILLIAM LLOYD GARRISON, "THE GREAT CRISIS!" *THE LIBERATOR* VOL. II, NO. 52, DECEMBER 29, 1832: 206–207

There is much declamation about the sacredness of the compact which was formed between the free and slave states, on the adoption of the Constitution. A sacred compact, forsooth! We pronounce it the most bloody and heaven-daring arrangement ever made by men for the continuance and protection of a system of the most atrocious villainy ever exhibited on earth. Yes – we recognize the compact, but with feelings of shame and indignation, and it will be held in everlasting infamy by the friends of justice and humanity throughout the world. It was a compact formed at the sacrifice of the bodies and souls of millions of our race, for the sake of achieving a political object – an unblushing and monstrous coalition to do evil that good might come. Such a compact was, in the nature of things and according to the law of God, null and void from the beginning. No body of men ever had the right to guarantee the holding of human beings in bondage. Who or what were the framers of our government, that they should dare confirm and authorise such high-handed villainy – such flagrant robbery of the inalienable rights of man – such a glaring violation of all the precepts and injunctions of the gospel – such a savage war upon a sixth part of our whole population? – They were men, like ourselves – as fallible, as sinful, as weak, as ourselves. By the infamous bargain which they made between themselves, they virtually dethroned the Most High God, and trampled beneath their feet their own solemn and heaven-attested Declaration, that all men are created equal, and endowed by their Creator with certain inalienable rights – among which are life, liberty, and the pursuit of happiness. They had no lawful power to bind themselves, or their posterity, for one hour – for one moment – by such an unholy alliance. It was not valid then – it is not valid now. Still they persisted in maintaining it – and still do their successors, the people of Massachusetts, of New England, and of the twelve free States, persist in maintaining it. A sacred compact! A sacred compact! What, then, is wicked and ignominious?

This, then, is the relation in which we of New England stand to the holders of slaves at the south, and this is virtually our language toward them – Go on, most worthy associates, from day to day, from month to month, from year to year, from generation to generation, plundering two millions of human beings of their liberty and the fruits of their toil – driving them into the fields like cattle – starving and lacerating their bodies – selling the husband from his wife, the wife from her husband, and children from their parents – spilling their blood – withholding the bible from their hands and all knowledge from their minds – and kidnapping annually sixty thousand infants, the offspring of pollution and shame! Go on, in these practices – we do not wish nor mean to interfere, for the rescue of your victims, even by expostulation or warning – we like your company too well to offend you by denouncing your conduct – although we know that by every principle of law which does not utterly disgrace us by assimilating us to pirates, that they have as good and true a right to the equal protection of the law as we have; and although we ourselves stand prepared to die, rather than submit even to a fragment of the intolerable load of oppression to which we are subjecting them – yet, never mind – let that be – they have grown old in suffering and we iniquity – and we have nothing to do now but to speak *peace, peace*, to one another in our sins. We are too wicked ever to love them as God commands us to do – we are so resolute in our wickedness as not even to desire to do so – and we are so proud in our iniquity that we will hate and revile whoever disturbs us in it. We want, like the devils of old, to be let alone in our sin. We are unalterably determined, and neither God nor man shall move us from this resolution, that our colored fellow subjects never shall be free or happy in their native land. Go on, from bad to worse – add link to link to the chains upon the bodies of your victims – add constantly to the intolerable burdens under which they groan – and if, goaded to desperation by your cruelties; they should rise to assert their rights and redress their wrongs, fear nothing – we are pledged, by a sacred compact, to shoot them like dogs and rescue you from their vengeance! Go on – we never will forsake you, for their is honor among thieves – our swords are ready to leap from their scabbards, and our muskets to pour forth deadly vollies, as soon as you are in danger. We pledge you our physical strength, by the sacredness of the national compact – a compact by which we have enabled you already to plunder, persecute, and destroy two millions of slaves, who now lie beneath the sod; and by which we now give you the same piratical license to prey upon a much larger number of victims and all their posterity. Go on – and by this sacred instrument, the Constitution of the United States, *dripping as it is with human blood*, we solemnly pledge you our lives, our fortunes, and our sacred honor, that we will stand by you to the last.

People of New England, and of the free States! is it true that slavery is no concern of yours? Have you no right even to protest against it, or to seek its removal? Are you not the main pillars of its support? How long do you mean to be answerable to God and the world, for spilling the blood of the poor innocents? Be not afraid to look the monster **Slavery** boldly in the face. He is your implacable foe – the vampyre who is sucking your life-blood – the ravager of a large portion of your country, and the enemy of God and man. Never hope to be a united, or happy, or prosperous people while he exists. He has an appetite like the grave – a spirit as malignant as that of the bottomless pit – and an influence as dreadful as the corruption of death. Awake to your danger! the struggle is a mighty one – it cannot be avoided – it should not be, if it could.

It is said that if you agitate this question, you will divide the Union. Believe it not; but should disunion follow, the fault will not be yours. You must perform your duty, faithfully, fearlessly and promptly, and leave the consequences to God: that duty clearly is, to cease from giving countenance and protection to southern kidnappers. Let them separate, if they can muster courage enough – and the liberation of their slaves is certain. Be assured that slavery will very speedily destroy this Union, *if it be left alone*; but even if the Union can be preserved by treading upon the necks, spilling the blood, and destroying the souls of millions of your race, we say it is not worth a price like this, and that it is in the highest degree criminal for you to continue the present compact. Let the pillars thereof fall – let the superstructure crumble into dust – if it must be upheld by robbery and oppression.

On the other hand, the leaders of the Confederacy saw themselves as restoring the true Constitution – one that would protect Whites as supreme and interpret the Constitution as originally written. Southern leaders agreed with the Constitution as written, "[t]hey simply did not accept what seemed to them loose and radical lines of interpretation" (Kammen 1986, 115). President Jefferson Davis' stated purpose in his inauguration speech before the Congress of the Confederate States of America in 1861 was to restore the Constitution to its prior intent. This is demonstrated in the southern states' individual statements of secession from the federal Union prior to the Civil War. Mississippi's 1861 statement clearly notes their investment in slavery as upholding the true values of the Founding generation.

CONFEDERATE STATES OF AMERICA—*MISSISSIPPI SECESSION*, JANUARY 9, 1861

A Declaration of the Immediate Causes which Induce and Justify the Secession of the State of Mississippi from the Federal Union

In the momentous step which our State has taken of dissolving its connection with the government of which we so long formed a part, it is but just that we should declare the prominent reasons which have induced our course.

Our position is thoroughly identified with the institution of slavery – the greatest material interest of the world. Its labor supplies the product which constitutes by far the largest and most important portions of commerce of the earth. These products are peculiar to the climate verging on the tropical regions, and by an imperious law of nature, none but the black race can bear exposure to the tropical sun. These products have become necessities of the world, and a blow at slavery is a blow at commerce and civilization. That blow has been long aimed at the institution and was at the point of reaching its consummation. There was no choice left us but submission to the mandates of abolition, or a dissolution of the Union, whose principles had been subverted to work out our ruin.

That we do not overstate the dangers to our institution, a reference to a few facts will sufficiently prove.

The hostility to this institution commenced before the adoption of the Constitution, and was manifested in the well-known Ordinance of 1787, in regard to the Northwestern Territory.

It has grown until it denies the right of property in slaves, and refuses protection to that right on the high seas, in the Territories, and wherever the government of the United States had jurisdiction.

It refuses the admission of new slave States into the Union and seeks to extinguish it by confining it within its present limits, denying the power of expansion.

It tramples the original equality of the South under foot.

It has nullified the Fugitive Slave Law in almost every free State in the Union, and has utterly broken the compact which our fathers pledged their faith to maintain.

It advocates negro equality, socially and politically, and promotes insurrection and incendiarism in our midst.

It has enlisted its press, its pulpit and its schools against us, until the whole popular mind of the North is excited and inflamed with prejudice.

It has made combinations and formed associations to carry out its schemes of emancipation in the States and wherever else slavery exists.

It seeks not to elevate or to support the slave, but to destroy his present condition without providing a better.

It has invaded a State and invested with the honors of martyrdom the wretch whose purpose was to apply flames to our dwellings, and the weapons of destruction to our lives.

It has broken every compact into which it has entered for our security.

It has given indubitable evidence of its design to ruin our agriculture, to prostrate our industrial pursuits and to destroy our social system.

It knows no relenting or hesitation in its purposes; it stops not in its march of aggression and leaves us no room to hope for cessation or for pause.

It has recently obtained control of the Government, by the prosecution of its unhallowed schemes, and destroyed the last expectation of living together in friendship and brotherhood.

Utter subjugation awaits us in the Union, if we should consent longer to remain in it. It is not a matter of choice, but of necessity. We must either submit to degradation, and to the loss of property worth four billions of money, or we must secede from the Union framed by our fathers, to secure this as well as every other species of property. For far less cause than this, our fathers separated from the Crown of England.

Our decision is made. We follow their footsteps. We embrace the alternative of separation; and for the reasons here stated, we resolve to maintain our rights with the full consciousness of the justice of our course, and the undoubting belief of our ability to maintain it.

An abolitionist who was formerly enslaved, Frederick Douglass assumes the contrary position, arguing that the Constitution is a document of liberty. Taken at its word and interpreted through the promises of the Declaration of Independence, Douglass finds moral failings in the interpretations of the Constitution but not in the ideals the document itself expresses. While his views on the Constitution's relationship to the slave society changed over time (Buccola 2012), in a debate in Glasgow, Scotland against representatives of the Garrison perspective Douglass carefully enumerated his reasons for viewing the Constitution as a document for freedom before the Scottish Anti-Slavery Society.

FREDERICK DOUGLASS, "THE CONSTITUTION OF THE UNITED STATES: IS IT PRO-SLAVERY OR ANTI-SLAVERY?" MARCH 26, 1860

... [T]he American Government and the American Constitution are spoken of in a manner which would naturally lead the hearer to believe that one is identical with the other; when the truth is, they are distinct in character as is a ship and a compass. The one may point right and the other steer wrong. A chart is one thing, the course of the vessel is another. The Constitution may be right, the Government is wrong. If the Government has been governed by mean, sordid, and wicked passions, it does not follow that the Constitution is mean, sordid, and wicked.

What, then, is the question? I will state it. But first let me state what is not the question. It is not whether slavery existed in the United States at the time of the adoption of the Constitution; it is not whether slaveholders took part in the framing of the Constitution; it is not whether those slaveholders, in their hearts, intended to secure certain advantages in that instrument for slavery; it is not whether the American Government has been wielded during seventy-two years in favour of the propagation and permanence of slavery; it is not whether a pro-slavery interpretation has been put upon the Constitution by the American Courts – all these points may be true or they may be false, they may be accepted or they may be rejected, without in any wise affecting the real question in debate.

The real and exact question ... may be fairly stated thus: – 1st, Does the United States Constitution guarantee to any class or description of people in that country the right to enslave, or hold as property, any other class or description of people in that country? 2nd, Is the dissolution of the union between the slave and free States required by fidelity to the slaves, or by the just demands of conscience? Or, in other words, is the refusal to exercise the elective franchise, and to hold office in America, the surest, wisest, and best way to abolish slavery in America?

To these questions the Garrisonians say Yes. They hold the Constitution to be a slaveholding instrument, and will not cast a vote or hold office, and denounce all who vote or hold office, no matter how faithfully such persons labour to promote the abolition of slavery. I, on the other hand, deny that the Constitution guarantees the right to hold property in man, and believe that the way to abolish slavery in America is to vote such men into power as well use their powers for the abolition of slavery. This is the issue plainly stated, and you shall judge between us ... The American Constitution is a written instrument full and complete in itself. No Court in America,

no Congress, no President, can add a single word thereto, or take a single word thereto. It is a great national enactment done by the people, and can only be altered, amended, or added to by the people ... It should also be borne in mind that the intentions of those who framed the Constitution, be they good or bad, for slavery or against slavery, are so respected so far, and so far only, as we find those intentions plainly stated in the Constitution ...

[The abolitionist who argued against me] doubtless felt some embarrassment from the fact that he had literally to give the Constitution a pro-slavery interpretation; because upon its face it of itself conveys no such meaning, but a very opposite meaning. He thus sums up what he calls the slaveholding provisions of the Constitution. I quote his own words: – "Article 1, section 9, provides for the continuance of the African slave trade for the 20 years, after the adoption of the Constitution. Art. 4, section 9, provides for the recovery from the other States of fugitive slaves. Art. 1, section 2, gives the slave States a representation of the three-fifths of all the slave population; and Art. 1, section 8, requires the President to use the military, naval, ordnance, and militia resources of the entire country for the suppression of slave insurrection, in the same manner as he would employ them to repel invasion." Now any man reading this statement, or hearing it made with such a show of exactness, would unquestionably suppose that he speaker or writer had given the plain written text of the Constitution itself ... The words of the Constitution were before him. Why then did he not give you the plain words of the Constitution? ... It so happens that no such words as "African slave trade," no such words as "slave insurrections," are anywhere used in that instrument. These are the words of that orator, and not the words of the Constitution of the United States ...

Let us look at the objects for which the Constitution was framed and adopted, and see if slavery is one of them. Here are its own objects as set forth by itself:

We, the people of these United States, in order to form a more perfect union, establish justice, ensure domestic tranquility, provide for the common defense, promote the general welfare, and secure the blessings of liberty to ourselves and our posterity, do ordain and establish this Constitution of the United States of America.

The objects here set forth are six in number: union, defence, welfare, tranquility, justice, and liberty. These are all good objects, and slavery, so far from being among them, is a foe of them all. But it has been said that Negroes are not included within the benefits sought under this declaration. This is said by the slaveholders in America – it is said by [some abolitionists] – but it is not said by the Constitution itself. Its language is "we the people;" not we the white people, not even we the citizens, not we the privileged class, not we the high, not we the low, but we the people; not we the horses, sheep, and swine, and wheel-barrows, but we the people, we the human inhabitants; and, if Negroes are people, they are included in the benefits for which the Constitution of America was ordained and established.

But how dare any man who pretends to be a friend to the Negro thus gratuitously concede away what the Negro has a right to claim under the Constitution? Why should such friends invent new arguments to increase the hopelessness of his bondage? This, I undertake to say, as the conclusion of the whole matter, that the constitutionality of slavery can be made out only by disregarding the plain and common-sense reading of the Constitution itself; by discrediting and casting away as worthless the most beneficent rules of legal interpretation; by ruling the Negro outside of these beneficent rules; by claiming that the Constitution does not mean what it says, and that it says what it does not mean; by disregarding the written Constitution, and interpreting it in the light of a secret understanding.

It is in this mean, contemptible, and underhand method that the American Constitution is pressed into the service of slavery. They go everywhere else for proof that the Constitution declares that no person shall be deprived of life, liberty, or property without due process of law; it secures to every man the right of trial by jury, the privilege of the writ of habeas corpus – the great writ that put an end to slavery and slave-hunting in England – and it secures to every State a republican form of government. Anyone of these provisions in the hands of abolition statesmen, and backed up by a right moral sentiment, would put an end to slavery in America.

The Constitution forbids the passing of a bill of attainder: that is, a law entailing upon the child the disabilities and hardships imposed upon the parent. Every slave law in America might be repealed on this very ground. The slave is made a slave because his mother is a slave.

But to all this it is said that the practice of the American people is against my view. I admit it. They have given the Constitution a slaveholding interpretation. I admit it. Thy have committed innumerable wrongs against the Negro in the name of the Constitution. Yes, I admit it all; and I go with him who goes farthest in denouncing these wrongs. But it does not follow that the Constitution is in favour of these wrongs because the slaveholders have given it that interpretation. To be consistent in his logic, [these abolitionists] must follow the example of some of his brothers in America – he must not only fling away the Constitution, but the Bible. The Bible must follow the Constitution, for that, too, has been interpreted for slavery by American divines ...

If the South has made the Constitution bend to the purposes of slavery, let the North now make that instrument bend to the cause of freedom and justice. If 350,000 slaveholders have, by devoting their energies to that single end, been able to make slavery the vital and animating spirit of the American Confederacy for the last 72 years, now let the freemen of the North, who have the power in their own hands, and who can make the American Government just what they think fit, resolve to blot out for ever the foul and haggard crime, which is the blight and mildew, the curse and the disgrace of the whole United States.

A fourth interpretation is found in the words of Supreme Court Justice Thurgood Marshall, who labored against Jim Crow segregation in the federal courts in the mid-twentieth century. In a speech given in Hawaii, to a group of San Francisco Patent and Trademark attorneys during the celebration of the bicentennial of the Constitution, Marshall argues that while the original document was compromised by its acceptance of slavery, it was redeemed by the Reconstruction Amendments, particularly the Fourteenth.

JUSTICE THURGOOD MARSHALL, "REFLECTIONS ON THE BICENTENNIAL OF THE U.S. CONSTITUTION," MAY 6, 1987

1987 marks the 200th anniversary of the United States Constitution ... The focus of this celebration invites a complacent belief that the vision of those who debated and compromised in Philadelphia yielded the "more perfect Union" it is said we now enjoy.

I cannot accept this invitation, for I do not believe that the meaning of the Constitution was forever "fixed" at the Philadelphia Convention. Nor do I find the wisdom, foresight, and sense of justice exhibited by the Framers particularly profound. To the contrary, the government they devised was defective from the start, requiring several amendments, a civil war, and momentous social transformation to attain the system of constitutional government, and its respect for the individual freedoms and human rights, we hold as fundamental today. When contemporary Americans cite "The Constitution," they invoke a concept that is vastly different from what the Framers barely began to construct two centuries ago.

For a sense of the evolving nature of the Constitution we need look no further than the first three words of the document's preamble: "We the People." When the Founding Fathers used this phrase in 1787, they did not have in mind the majority of America's citizens. "We the People" included, in the words of the Framers, "the whole Number of free Persons."

On a matter so basic as the right to vote, for example, Negro slaves were excluded, although they were counted for representational purposes at three-fifths each. Women did not gain the right to vote for over a hundred and thirty years.

These omissions were intentional. The record of the Framers' debates on the slave question is especially clear: The Southern States acceded to the demands of the New England States for giving Congress broad power to regulate commerce, in exchange for the right to continue the slave trade ...

Despite this clear understanding of the role slavery would play in the new republic, use of the words "slaves" and "slavery" was carefully avoided in the original document ... Moral principles against slavery, for those who had them, were compromised, with no explanation of the conflicting principles for which the American Revolutionary War had ostensibly been fought: the self-evident truths "that all men are created equal, that they are endowed by their Creator with certain unalienable Rights, that among these are Life, Liberty and the pursuit of Happiness."

No doubt it will be said, when the unpleasant truth of the history of slavery in America is mentioned during this bicentennial year, that the Constitution was a product of its times, and embodied a compromise which, under other circumstances, would not have been made. But the effects of the Framers' compromise have remained for generations. They arose from the contradiction between guaranteeing liberty and justice to all, and denying both to Negroes.

While the Union survived the civil war, the Constitution did not. In its place arose a new, more promising basis for justice and equality, the 14th Amendment, ensuring protection of the life, liberty, and property of all persons against deprivations without due process, and guaranteeing equal protection of the laws. And yet almost another century would pass before any significant recognition was obtained of the rights of black Americans to share equally even in such basic opportunities as education, housing, and employment, and to have their votes counted, and counted equally. In the meantime, blacks joined America's military to fight its wars and invested untold hours working in its factories and on its farms, contributing to the development of this country's magnificent wealth and waiting to share in its prosperity.

What is striking is the role legal principles have played throughout America's history in determining the condition of Negroes. They were enslaved by law, emancipated by law, disenfranchised and segregated by law; and, finally, they have begun to win equality by law. Along the way, new constitutional principles have emerged to meet the challenges of a changing society. The progress has been dramatic, and it will continue.

The men who gathered in Philadelphia in 1787 could not have envisioned these changes. They could not have imagined, nor would they have accepted, that the document they were drafting would one day be construed by a Supreme Court to which had been appointed a woman and the descendent of an African slave. "We the People" no longer enslave, but the credit does not belong to the Framers. It belongs to those who refused to acquiesce in outdated notions of "liberty," "justice," and "equality," and who strived to better them.

And so we must be careful, when focusing on the events which took place in Philadelphia two centuries ago, that we not overlook the momentous events which followed, and thereby lose our proper sense of perspective. Otherwise, the odds are that for many Americans the bicentennial celebration will be little more than a blind pilgrimage to the shrine of the original document now stored in a vault in the National Archives. If we seek, instead, a sensitive understanding of the Constitution's inherent defects, and its promising evolution through 200 years of history, the celebration ... will, in my view, be a far more meaningful and humbling experience. We will see that the true miracle was not the birth of the Constitution, but its life, a life nurtured through two turbulent centuries of our own making, and a life embodying much good fortune that was not.

Thus, in this bicentennial year, we may not all participate in the festivities with flag-waving fervor. Some may more quietly commemorate the suffering, struggle, and sacrifice that has triumphed over much of what was wrong with the original document, and observe the anniversary with hopes not realized and promises not fulfilled. I plan to celebrate the bicentennial of the Constitution as a living document, including the Bill of Rights and the other amendments protecting individual freedoms and human rights.

Considering the following questions for each of the speeches:

1. How did the author understand the relationship between the Constitution and slavery?
2. What do they understand the relationship between slavery and race to be?
3. What is the purpose of the Constitution, and can the Constitution be altered? Under what circumstances?

The four perspectives presented above answer these questions quite differently. Which perspectives do you find most compelling from your perspective in the twenty-first century? It is worth also considering which viewpoints are currently reflected in our political discourse. Are there other ways of considering the relationship between our Constitution and slavery?

The question of how a nation, ostensibly based on freedom and liberty, was economically and politically rooted in race-based slavery is a complicated one. But this query is central to our understanding of how the United States, and its Constitution, was central to the maintenance of this internal contradiction at the heart of our nation. Throughout this text, we will be examining how this contradiction is manifested in different areas of law, how it is continuously challenged, and how it is sustained.

2 Race, Citizenship, and Sovereignty

One of the difficult challenges in the new nation, based on its residents' assumption of liberty (Rana 2010; Smith 1997), is the question of who would be included the Nation's governance. The notion of popular sovereignty, advanced in the Declaration of Independence and used as a justification for the rebellion against English control, assumed the ability of the people to self-govern. Yet the nation, as it quickly formed, limited the scope of the social contract. As a society settled by colonial forces from Europe, "the need to maintain control over ... a culturally disparate empire directly conflicted with local colonial autonomy, autonomy long enjoyed by settlers and seen as a basic ancestral right" (Rana 2010, 22). To demonstrate this autonomy, White settlers often defined themselves in opposition to others – women, non-Protestants, other immigrants, the enslaved, and Native people – creating secondary citizen status. Consequently, "for over 80 percent of U.S. history, American laws declared most people in the world legally ineligible to become full U.S. citizens solely because of their race, original nationality, or gender" (Smith 1997, 15; see also Erman 2021).

This interpretation has been contested since the beginnings of the Nation, and those excluded from citizenship have insinuated themselves into conversations around the Constitution's meaning. Such research is relatively recent and the political implications have been historically ignored; but there is evidence of the engagement of these divorced voices articulating their perspective and demands for inclusion. If Native and enslaved peoples, women and freed Blacks, poor and indentured Whites saw themselves as having a right to contribute to the constitutional conversations even if they were not formally represented, how does this change our understanding of the meaning of the Constitution and its long-term legitimacy?

These questions of citizenship and sovereignty manifested differently for specific periods of time and for different groups of people. For Native peoples, the tension between independent tribal sovereignty and its conflict with personal citizenship resulted in a century-long focus by the federal government on assimilation and tribal decimation, forcing indigenous people into choices not of their own making. For other groups of people, such as Asian Americans, the relationship between race and citizenship created a new racial category of people who did not share language, religion, or history. However, the treatment of these different national origins as a single community by the law racialized these individuals into a new political and racial category. Finally, for African Americans and Latino/Latina communities, denial of access to the ballot and the long struggle to ensure political representation had unique repercussions for citizenship. This chapter will consider three elements of these questions: sovereignty, citizenship, and voting. By considering how our understanding of these attributes of democracy have evolved over time, we will see the way they also framed our understanding of race in the United States.

2.1 Sovereignty

Sovereignty is the notion that people have the capacity to self-rule without being reliant on the authority of an external authority. In the United States, the concept of the social contract as articulated by John Locke, frames the sovereignty of the nation as relying within the people as a whole. Those who were deemed citizens had the authority to virtually represent others (Gunderson 1987). This interpretation authorized a privileged individual, deemed "the citizen," to articulate and protect the interests of the people who reside within the sphere "he" controlled – his wife, children, tenants, servants, employees, and slaves (Kerber 1997, 262; Deardorff 2014). This created a representative democracy where elected candidates from the people serve as proxy for the public's authority to make and implement the rules for governing. Elections serve as an opportunity for the public to fire the representatives who do not follow the people's will. For Native peoples, who were not determined to be part of the citizenry or protected by citizens, their relationship to the new republic was in flux and initially dependent on legal interpretations.

2.1.1 Sovereignty, the Constitution, and Native Peoples

On February 15, 1830, Cherokee leaders representing 3,025 Native peoples signed a petition that was placed before the House of Representatives then debating legislation that would remove the tribe from their lands and forcibly send them West. The petition was drafted in response to the claim, prominent in the White community, that most Cherokee tribal members endorsed the westward removal but were afraid of the tyranny of their tribal leaders (Saunt 2020). Instead, members of the Cherokee Nation claimed that they had a right to stay under U.S. law. Their argument affirmed the supremacy of U.S. national laws and treaties under the doctrine of federalism, depicting the states' insistence on expansion as problematic.

> The sacredness of treaties, made under the authority of the United States, is paramount and supreme, stronger than the laws and Constitution of any state. The jurisdiction, then of our nation over its soil is settled by the laws, treaties, and Constitution of the United States, and has been exercised from time out of memory.

As the many petitions filed by indigenous communities challenging the federal policies governing them demonstrate, the treatment of Native peoples by the nascent nation was not inevitable. Supreme Court decisions demonstrate the conflicts that existed around their position in the new country. For Native people, the question was not one of citizenship or legal personhood, but of sovereignty. As people who existed prior to the external settlers and who had governed themselves for centuries, their relationship to the new government was unclear.

The land on which they lived, hunted, and based their culture was the very commodity that colonizers, new settlers, local states and communities, as well as the newly formed United States, sought. The wars with the Native peoples informed the structuring of the Constitution (Ablavsky 2014) and defined the early years of the Washington administration (Calloway 2018). Over half the treaties made by the new administration were with Indian tribes, and policies dispossessing Native lands directly influenced the tenfold increase in the war budget and a tremendous growth in the peacetime army (Blackhawk 2019).

For Native people, the question has not been one of citizenship or personhood under the law – as it has been for other racial or ethnic groups – but one of political identity or sovereignty. Do Native people have the right of self-governance and control of their own land? While the United States is the only nation that asserts indigenous sovereignty (Blackhawk 2019) – guaranteed "pre-constitutionally" (Erman 2021, 1242) – such sovereignty has not been consistently respected by the government, nor is self-rule fully realized.

The idea of sovereignty for Native peoples slowly evolved in the early cases by the John Marshall Court (1801–1835). Many of these cases emanated around questions of land ownership and over who had authority to negotiate and purchase from Native peoples. The inconsistencies in these rulings point to debates around how the new nation would engage with indigenous peoples and over Native authority to participate in these determinations. The assumptions regarding the ultimate dispossession of land, the violence it would require, and the fundamental desire for the assimilation of Native peoples are all reflected in these early cases. However, we also see disagreement among the Supreme Court justices regarding how to address competing claims of sovereignty and land ownership, as well as their concerns as to the long-term implications.

After the 1823 decision in *Johnson* v. *M'Intosh*, the federal government defined Native title to land as simply a new right of occupancy, destroying any understanding of Native sovereignty. Although Native people had lived and hunted on this land for many generations, this decision determined that Native people were no longer perceived as owning their land. The rapidly expanding population and the growing desire to possess land, created a larger demand from White farmers pressuring the U.S. government to destroy Native control. In both 1773 and 1775, Thomas Johnson purchased land from the Piankeshaw Native American tribes relying on a 1763 Proclamation by the King of England. William M'Intosh, in 1818, purchased 11,000 acres of the same land from the U.S. Congress. Johnson's heirs, through a speculation company, sued M'Intosh for ownership of the land. The federal District Court found that Johnson's initial purchase and the subsequent title was invalid.

purchased land
1773 + 1775 WI
  1763 Proclamation

purchased land (1818)
from congress

JOHNSON AND BRIGHAM LESSEE v. M'INTOSH, 21 U.S. (8 WHEAT) 543 (1823)

Chief Justice Marshall Delivered the Opinion of the Court

Vote: 6–0

The facts ... show the authority of the chiefs who executed this conveyance so far as it could be given by their own people, and likewise show that the particular tribes for whom these chiefs acted were in rightful possession of the land they sold. The inquiry, therefore, is in a great measure confined to the power of Indians to give, and of private individuals to receive, a title which can be sustained in the courts of this country.

On the discovery of this immense continent, the great nations of Europe were eager to appropriate to themselves so much of it as they could respectively acquire. Its vast extent offered an ample field to the ambition and enterprise of all, and the character and religion of its inhabitants afforded an apology for considering them as a people over whom the superior genius of Europe might claim an ascendency. The potentates of the old world found no difficulty in convincing themselves that they made ample compensation to the inhabitants of the new by bestowing on them civilization and Christianity in exchange for unlimited independence. But as they were all in pursuit of nearly the same object, it was necessary, in order to avoid conflicting settlements and consequent war with each other, to establish a principle which all should acknowledge as the law by which the right of acquisition, which they all asserted should be regulated as between themselves. This principle was that discovery gave title to the government by whose subjects or by whose authority it was made against all other European governments, which title might be consummated by possession.

The exclusion of all other Europeans necessarily gave to the nation making the discovery the sole right of acquiring the soil from the natives and establishing settlements upon it. It was a right with which no Europeans could interfere. It was a right which all asserted for themselves, and to the assertion of which by others all assented.

Those relations which were to exist between the discoverer and the natives were to be regulated by themselves. The rights thus acquired being exclusive, no other power could interpose between them.

In the establishment of these relations, the rights of the original inhabitants were in no instance entirely disregarded, but were necessarily to a considerable extent impaired. They were admitted to be the rightful occupants of the soil, with a legal as well as just claim to retain possession of it, and to use it according to their own discretion; but their rights to complete sovereignty as independent nations were necessarily diminished, and their power to dispose of the soil at their own will to whomsoever they pleased was denied by the original fundamental principle that discovery gave exclusive title to those who made it.

While the different nations of Europe respected the right of the natives as occupants, they asserted the ultimate dominion to be in themselves, and claimed and exercised, as a consequence of this ultimate dominion, a power to grant the soil while yet in possession of the natives. These grants have been understood by all to convey a title to the grantees, subject only to the Indian right of occupancy.

The history of America from its discovery to the present day proves, we think, the universal recognition of these principles.

Thus has our whole country been granted by the Crown while in the occupation of the Indians. These grants purport to convey the soil as well as the right of dominion to the grantees. In those governments which were denominated royal, where the right to the soil was not vested in individuals, but remained in the Crown or was vested in the colonial government, the King claimed and exercised the right of granting lands and of dismembering the government at his will. The grants made out of the two original colonies, after the resumption of their charters by the Crown, are examples of this. The governments of New England, New York, New Jersey, Pennsylvania, Maryland, and a part of Carolina were thus created. In all of them, the soil, at the time the grants were made, was occupied by the Indians. Yet almost every title within those governments is dependent on these grants ...

The United States, then, has unequivocally acceded to that great and broad rule by which its civilized inhabitants now hold this country. They hold and assert in themselves the title by which it was acquired. They maintain, as all others have maintained, that discovery gave an exclusive right to extinguish the Indian title of occupancy either by purchase or by conquest, and gave also a right to such a degree of sovereignty as the circumstances of the people would allow them to exercise.

The title by conquest is acquired and maintained by force. The conqueror prescribes its limits. Humanity, however, acting on public opinion, has established, as a general rule, that the conquered shall not be wantonly oppressed, and that their condition shall remain as eligible as is compatible with the objects of the conquest. Most usually, they are incorporated with the victorious nation, and become subjects or citizens of the government with which they are connected. The new and old members of the society mingle with each other; the distinction between them is gradually lost, and they make one people. Where this incorporation is practicable, humanity demands and a wise policy requires that the rights of the conquered to property should remain unimpaired; that the new subjects should be governed as equitably as the old, and that confidence in their security should gradually banish the painful sense of being separated from their ancient connections, and united by force to strangers.

When the conquest is complete and the conquered inhabitants can be blended with the conquerors or safely governed as a distinct people,

public opinion, which not even the conqueror can disregard, imposes these restraints upon him, and he cannot neglect them without injury to his fame and hazard to his power.

But the tribes of Indians inhabiting this country were fierce savages whose occupation was war and whose subsistence was drawn chiefly from the forest. To leave them in possession of their country was to leave the country a wilderness; to govern them as a distinct people was impossible because they were as brave and as high spirited as they were fierce, and were ready to repel by arms every attempt on their independence.

What was the inevitable consequence of this state of things? The Europeans were under the necessity either of abandoning the country and relinquishing their pompous claims to it or of enforcing those claims by the sword, and by the adoption of principles adapted to the condition of a people with whom it was impossible to mix and who could not be governed as a distinct society, or of remaining in their neighborhood, and exposing themselves and their families to the perpetual hazard of being massacred.

Frequent and bloody wars, in which the whites were not always the aggressors, unavoidably ensued. European policy, numbers, and skill prevailed. As the white population advanced, that of the Indians necessarily receded. The country in the immediate neighborhood of agriculturists became unfit for them. The game fled into thicker and more unbroken forests, and the Indians followed. The soil to which the Crown originally claimed title, being no longer occupied by its ancient inhabitants, was parceled out according to the will of the sovereign power and taken possession of by persons who claimed immediately from the Crown or mediately through its grantees or deputies.

However extravagant the pretension of converting the discovery of an inhabited country into conquest may appear; if the principle has been asserted in the first instance, and afterwards sustained; if a country has been acquired and held under it; if the property of the great mass of the community originates in it, it becomes the law of the land and cannot be questioned. So, too, with respect to the concomitant principle that the Indian inhabitants are to be considered merely as occupants, to be protected, indeed, while in peace, in the possession of their lands, but to be deemed incapable of transferring the absolute title to others. However this restriction may be opposed to natural right, and to the usages of civilized nations, yet if it be indispensable to that system under which the country has been settled, and be adapted to the actual condition of the two people, it may perhaps be supported by reason, and certainly cannot be rejected by courts of justice.

By [the 1763 proclamation by the King of Great Britain], the Crown reserved under its own dominion and protection, for the use of the Indians, "all the land and territories lying to the westward of the sources of the rivers which fall into the sea from the west and northwest," and strictly forbade all British subjects from making any purchases or settlements whatever or taking possession of the reserved lands.

After bestowing on this subject a degree of attention which was more required by the magnitude of the interest in litigation, and the able and elaborate arguments of the bar, than by its intrinsic difficulty, the court is decidedly of opinion, that the plaintiffs do not exhibit a title which can be sustained in the courts of the United States, and that there is no error in the judgment which was rendered against them in the District Court of Illinois.

Judgment affirmed with costs.

1. What is the "doctrine of discovery" and how does it impact Native sovereignty?
2. How does Chief Justice Marshall justify limiting the indigenous people to a "right of occupancy"?
3. What options are provided to Native peoples?
4. Why does the transition from the right of occupancy to the power of conquest cause Chief Justice Marshall concern?

Although British and federal law had prohibited individuals from buying indigenous land, in the *Johnson* decision the Supreme Court allowed Anglo-Americans to buy, sell, and own indigenous land before Native peoples had ceded rights because of their reduced status as occupants (Ablavsky 2021). For Chief Justice Marshall, while Native people had lived on the land, European countries believed in a right of conquest and their dominion over such land destroyed indigenous authority.

The question of Native sovereignty returned to the Supreme Court after the discovery of gold within Cherokee territory, upon which the state of Georgia attempted to claim sole authority over the Cherokee lands within its boundaries. Federal officials had protected Cherokee autonomy and Georgia "decided that it must assert its sovereignty on behalf of the white settlers who were rushing to occupy tribal lands" (Smith 1997, 237). With the presidency of Andrew Jackson, notorious for his violent advocacy of Indian removal, Georgia had reason to believe that the executive branch would support their endeavors.

The Cherokee Nation challenged Georgia's actions before the Supreme Court in *Cherokee Nation* v. *Georgia* (1831). The Nation argued that because they were like a foreign nation in their sovereignty, Georgia had no authority to reappropriate Cherokee land or regulate their nation. Sovereignty then requires that only the federal government can negotiate with the Nation via the treaty process. In this case, the Court internally disagreed over the status of the Cherokee, noting their dependent nature, but unique position in the law.

CHEROKEE NATION v. GEORGIA, 30 U.S. (5 PET.) 1 (1831)

Chief Justice Marshall Delivered the Opinion of the Court

Vote: 5–2

This [legal challenge] is brought by the Cherokee nation, praying an injunction to restrain the state of Georgia from the execution of certain laws of that state, which, as is alleged, go directly to annihilate the Cherokees as a political society, and to seize, for the use of Georgia, the lands of the nation which have been assured to them by the United States in solemn treaties repeatedly made and still in force.

If courts were permitted to indulge their sympathies, a case better calculated to excite them can scarcely be imagined. A people once numerous, powerful, and truly independent, found by our ancestors in the quiet and uncontrolled possession of an ample domain, gradually sinking beneath our superior policy, our arts and our arms, have yielded their lands by successive treaties, each of which contains a solemn guarantee of the residue, until they retain no more of their formerly extensive territory than is deemed necessary to their comfortable subsistence. To preserve this remnant, the present application is made.

... Do the Cherokees constitute a foreign state in the sense of the constitution?

The counsel have shown conclusively that they are not a state of the union, and have insisted that individually they are aliens, not owing allegiance to the United States. An aggregate of aliens composing a state must, they say, be a foreign state. Each individual being foreign, the whole must be foreign.

This argument is imposing, but we must examine it more closely before we yield to it. The condition of the Indians in relation to the United States is perhaps unlike that of any other two people in existence. In the general, nations not owing a common allegiance are foreign to each other. The term foreign nation is, with strict propriety, applicable by either to the other. But the relation of the Indians to the United States is marked by peculiar and cardinal distinctions which exist nowhere else. The Indian territory is admitted to compose a part of the United States. In all our maps, geographical treatises, histories, and laws, it is so considered. In all our intercourse with foreign nations, in our commercial regulations, in any attempt at intercourse between Indians and foreign nations, they are considered as within the jurisdictional limits of the United States, subject to many of those restraints which are imposed upon our own citizens. They acknowledge themselves in their treaties to be under the protection of the United States; they admit that the United States shall have the sole and exclusive right of regulating the trade with them, and managing all their affairs as they think proper; and the Cherokees in particular were allowed by the treaty of Hopewell, which preceded the constitution, "to send a deputy of their choice, whenever they think fit, to congress." ...

Though the Indians are acknowledged to have an unquestionable, and, heretofore, unquestioned right to the lands they occupy, until that right shall be extinguished by a voluntary cession to our government; yet it may well be doubted whether those tribes which reside within the acknowledged boundaries of the United States can, with strict accuracy, be denominated foreign nations. They may, more correctly, perhaps, be denominated domestic dependent nations. They occupy a territory to which we assert a title independent of their will, which must take effect in point of possession when their right of possession ceases. Meanwhile they are in a state of pupilage. Their relation to the United States resembles that of a ward to his guardian.

In [the Constitution's Commerce Clause, Art. I, §8, ¶3, which "empowers Congress to 'regulate commerce with the foreign nations, and among the several states, and with the Indian tribes'",] they are as clearly contradistinguished by a name appropriate to themselves ... The objects, to which the power of regulating commerce might be directed, are divided into three distinct classes-foreign nations, the several states, and Indian tribes. When forming this article, the convention considered them as entirely distinct ...

The court has bestowed its best attention on this question, and, after mature deliberation, the majority is of opinion that an Indian tribe or nation within the United States is not a foreign state in the sense of the constitution, and cannot maintain an action in the courts of the United States ...

If it be true that the Cherokee nation have rights, this is not the tribunal in which those rights are to be asserted. If it be true that wrongs have been inflicted, and that still greater are to be apprehended, this is not the tribunal which can redress the past or prevent the future.

The motion for an injunction is denied.

Justice Baldwin, Concurring

... I concur in the opinion of the court in dismissing the bill, but not for the reasons assigned.

In my opinion there is no plaintiff in this suit; and this opinion precludes any examination into the merits of the bill, or the weight of any minor objections. My judgment stops me at the threshold, and forbids me to examine into the acts complained of.

... [The United States'] jurisdiction over the territory in question is as supreme as that of Congress over what the nation has acquired by cession from the states or treaties with foreign powers, combining the rights of the state and general government. Within her boundaries there can be no other nation, community, or sovereign power, which this department can judicially recognize as a foreign state, capable of demanding or claiming our interposition, so as to enable them to exercise a jurisdiction incompatible with a sovereignty in Georgia, which has been recognized by the constitution, and every department of this government acting under its authority. Foreign states cannot be created by judicial construction; Indian sovereignty cannot

be roused from its long slumber, and awakened to action by our fiat. I find no acknowledgement of it by the legislative or executive power. Till they have done so, I can stretch forth no arm for their relief without violating the constitution ...

Indians have rights of occupancy to their lands as sacred as the fee-simple, absolute title of the whites; but they are only rights of occupancy, incapable of alienation, or being held by any other than common right without permission from the government ...

While the different nations of Europe respected the rights of the natives as occupants, they asserted the ultimate dominion to be in themselves; and claimed and exercised as a consequence of this ultimate dominion, a power to grant the soil while yet in the possession of the natives. These grants have been understood by all to convey a title to the grantees, subject only to the Indian rights of occupancy. The history of America from its discovery to the present day proves, we think, the universal recognition of these principles.

... [T]he judicial power cannot divest the states of rights of sovereignty, and transfer them to the Indians, by decreeing them to be a nation, or foreign state, pre-existing and with rightful jurisdiction and sovereignty over the territory they occupy.

Justice Thompson, Joined by Justice Story, Dissenting

... Every nation that governs itself, under what form soever, without any dependence on a foreign power, is a sovereign state. Its rights are naturally the same as those of any other state. Such are moral persons who live together in a natural society, under the law of nations. It is sufficient if it be really sovereign and independent: that is, it must govern itself by its own authority and laws ... Tributary and feudatory states do not thereby cease to be sovereign and independent states, so long as self government, and sovereign and independent authority is left in the administration of the state.

Testing the character and condition of the Cherokee Indians by these rules, it is not perceived how it is possible to escape the conclusion, that they form a sovereign state. They have always been dealt with as such by the government of the United States; both before and since the adoption of the present constitution. They have been admitted and treated as a people governed solely and exclusively by their own laws, usages, and customs within their own territory, claiming and exercising exclusive dominion over the same; yielding up by treaty, from time to time, portions of their land, but still claiming absolute sovereignty and self government over what remained unsold ... And indeed, I do not understand it is denied by a majority of the court, that the Cherokee Indians form a sovereign state according to the doctrine of the law of nations; but that, although a sovereign state, they are not considered a foreign state within the meaning of the constitution.

That they are entitled to such occupancy, so long as they choose quietly and peaceably to remain upon the land, cannot be questioned. The circumstance of their original occupancy is here referred to, merely for the purpose of showing, that if these Indian communities were then, as they certainly were, nations, they must have been foreign nations, to all the world; not having any connexion, or alliance of any description, with any other power on earth. And if the Cherokees were then a foreign nation; when or how have they lost that character, and ceased to be a distinct people, and become incorporated with any other community?

... Whenever wars have taken place, they have been followed by regular treaties of peace, containing stipulations on each side according to existing circumstances; the Indian nation always preserving its distinct and separate national character. And notwithstanding we do not recognize the right of the Indians to transfer the absolute title of their lands to any other than ourselves; the right of occupancy is still admitted to remain in them, accompanied with the right of self government, according to their own usages and customs; and with the competency to act in a national capacity, although placed under the protection of the whites, and owing a qualified subjection so far as is requisite for public safety. But the principle is universally admitted, that this occupancy belongs to them as matter of right, and not by mere indulgence. They cannot be disturbed in the enjoyment of it, or deprived of it, without their free consent; or unless a just and necessary war should sanction their dispossession.

In this view of their situation, there is as full and complete recognition of their sovereignty, as if they were the absolute owners of the soil ... It is the political relation in which one government or country stands to another, which constitutes it foreign to the other. The Cherokee territory being within the chartered limits of Georgia, does not affect the question ...

The laws of Georgia set out in the bill, if carried fully into operation, go the length of a abrogating all the laws of the Cherokees, abolishing their government, and entirely subverting their national character ... Some of them ... are so directly at variance with these treaties and the laws of the United States touching the rights of property secured to them, that I can perceive no objection to the application of judicial relief ...

1. Why is the denial of foreign nation status so significant for Native tribes?
2. What are the legal implications of this decision?
3. For the dissenting Justices Thompson and Story, the denial of citizenship to the Cherokee renders them a foreign sovereign. Why?

Consequently, the Supreme Court found that representatives of the Cherokee Nation were not eligible (did not have standing) to challenge the Georgia laws as an incursion on their sovereignty in the federal courts. The majority found Native people to be "domestic dependent nations," not external sovereigns or foreign nations. But the Court split on the question; this was unusual for the Marshall Court, which tried to render unanimous opinions. The debating justices either framed indigenous people as having the more limited legal status of "occupants" or, they perceived Native peoples as foreign sovereigns who were constitutionally protected in their right to bring legal challenges against Georgia in the federal courts.

The ambiguity of the Cherokee Nation's position is addressed in *Worchester* v. *Georgia* (1832) where the Court explicitly ruled against Georgia, because unlike the Cherokee, Worchester, as a White citizen from outside Georgia, had standing to bring a federal lawsuit. In this case, Samuel Worchester, a White missionary to the Cherokee Nation from Vermont, was convicted by the State of Georgia of "residing within the limits of the Cherokee Nation without a license" and "without having taken the oath to support and defend the Constitution and laws of the State of Georgia." Worchester was sentenced to four years of hard labor in the Georgia penitentiary. As a citizen of Vermont on Cherokee lands with the permission and approval of the Cherokee Nation, Worchester claimed that the Georgia Acts extending state sovereignty over tribal lands (to regulate residency of Whites on Cherokee lands, allow for Georgia policing of lands, and state enforcement of Georgia law on Cherokee lands) were contrary to the federal treaties with the Cherokee and therefore in violation of the U.S. Constitution.

WORCHESTER v. GEORGIA, 31 U.S. (6 PET.) 515 (1832)

Chief Justice Marshall Delivered the Opinion of the Court

Vote: 5–1

It has been said at the bar that the acts of the Legislature of Georgia seize on the whole Cherokee country, parcel it out among the neighbouring counties of the State, extend her code over the whole country, abolish its institutions and its laws, and annihilate its political existence.

The extraterritorial power of every legislature being limited in its action to its own citizens or subjects, the very passage of this act is an assertion of jurisdiction over the Cherokee Nation, and of the rights and powers consequent on jurisdiction.

The first step, then, in the inquiry which the Constitution and laws impose on this Court is an examination of the rightfulness of this claim.

From the commencement of our government, Congress has passed acts to regulate trade and intercourse with the Indians; which treat them as nations, respect their rights, and manifest a firm purpose to afford that protection which treaties stipulate. All these acts, and especially that of 1802, which is still in force, manifestly consider the several Indian nations as distinct political communities, having territorial boundaries within which their authority is exclusive and having a right to all the lands within those boundaries which is not only acknowledged, but guarantied, by the United States.

The treaties and laws of the United States contemplate the Indian territory as completely separated from that of the States, and provide that all intercourse with them shall be carried on exclusively by the government of the Union.

Is this the rightful exercise of power, or is it usurpation [of the state's sovereignty]?

The Indian nations had always been considered as distinct, independent political communities, retaining their original natural rights as the undisputed possessors of the soil from time immemorial, with the single exception of that imposed by irresistible power, which excluded them from intercourse with any other European potentate than the first discoverer of the coast of the particular region claimed, and this was a restriction which those European potentates imposed on themselves, as well as on the Indians. The very term "nation," so generally applied to them, means "a people distinct from others." The Constitution, by declaring treaties already made, as well as those to be made, to be the supreme law of the land, has adopted and sanctioned the previous treaties with the Indian nations, and consequently admits their rank among those powers who are capable of making treaties. The words "treaty" and "nation" are words of our own language, selected in our diplomatic and legislative proceedings by ourselves, having each a definite and well understood meaning. We have applied them to Indians, as we have applied them to the other nations of the earth. They are applied to all in the same sense.

The Cherokee Nation, then, is a distinct community occupying its own territory, with boundaries accurately described, in which the laws of Georgia can have no force, and which the citizens of Georgia have no right to enter but with the assent of the Cherokees themselves, or in conformity with treaties and with the acts of Congress. The whole intercourse between the United States and this Nation, is, by our Constitution and laws, vested in the Government of the United States.

The act of the State of Georgia, under which the plaintiff in error was prosecuted, is consequently void, and the judgment a nullity. Can this Court revise, and reverse it?

If the objection to the system of legislation lately adopted by the Legislature of Georgia in relation to the Cherokee Nation was confined to its extraterritorial operation, the objection, though complete so far as respected mere right, would give this Court no power over the subject. But it goes much further. If the review which has been taken be correct, and we think it is, the acts of Georgia are repugnant to the Constitution, laws, and treaties of the United States.

They interfere forcibly with the relations established between the United States and the Cherokee Nation, the regulation of which, according to the settled principles of our Constitution, are committed exclusively to the government of the Union.

They are in direct hostility with treaties, repeated in a succession of years, which mark out the boundary that separates the Cherokee country from Georgia, guaranty to them all the land within their boundary, solemnly pledge the faith of the United States to restrain their citizens from trespassing on it, and recognize the preexisting power of the nation to govern itself.

They are in equal hostility with the acts of Congress for regulating this intercourse and giving effect to the treaties.

The forcible seizure and abduction of [Worchester], who was residing in the nation with its permission and by authority of the President of the United States, is also a violation of the acts which authorise the chief magistrate to exercise this authority.

It is the opinion of this Court that the judgment of the Superior Court for the County of Gwinnett, in the State of Georgia, condemning Samuel A. Worcester to hard labour in the penitentiary of the State of Georgia for four years was pronounced by that Court under colour of a law which is void, as being repugnant to the Constitution, treaties, and laws of the United States, and ought, therefore, to be reversed and annulled.

Justice M'Lean, Concurrence

It must be admitted that the Indians sustain a peculiar relation to the United States. They do not constitute, as was decided at the last term, a foreign State so as to claim the right to sue in the Supreme Court of the United States; and yet, having the right of self-government, they, in some sense, form a State. In the management of their internal concerns, they are dependent on no power. They punish offences under their own laws, and, in doing so, they are responsible to no earthly tribunal. They make war and form treaties of peace. The exercise of these and other powers gives to them a distinct character as a people, and constitutes them, in some respects, a state, although they may not be admitted to possess the right of soil.

By various treaties, the Cherokees have placed themselves under the protection of the United States; they have agreed to trade with no other people, nor to invoke the protection of any other sovereignty. But such engagements do not divest them of the right of self-government, nor destroy their capacity to enter into treaties or compacts.

The question may be asked, is no distinction to be made between a civilized and savage people? Are our Indians to be placed upon a footing with the nations of Europe, with whom we have made treaties?

If a tribe of Indians shall become so degraded or reduced in numbers as to lose the power of self-government, the protection of the local law, of necessity, must be extended over them. The point at which this exercise of power by a State would be proper need not now be considered, if indeed it be a judicial question. Such a question does not seem to arise in this case. So long as treaties and laws remain in full force and apply to Indian nations exercising the right of self-government within the limits of a State, the judicial power can exercise no discretion in refusing to give effect to those laws, when questions arise under them, unless they shall be deemed unconstitutional.

The exercise of the power of self-government by the Indians, within a State is undoubtedly contemplated to be temporary. This is shown by the settled policy of the government, in the extinguishment of their title, and especially by the compact with the State of Georgia. It is a question not of abstract right, but of public policy. I do not mean to say that the same moral rule which should regulate the affairs of private life should not be regarded by communities or nations. But a sound national policy does require that the Indian tribes within our States should exchange their territories, upon equitable principles, or eventually consent to become amalgamated in our political communities.

At best, they can enjoy a very limited independence within the boundaries of a State, and such a residence must always subject them to encroachments from the settlements around them, and their existence within a State, as a separate and independent community, may seriously embarrass or obstruct the operation of the State laws. If, therefore, it would be inconsistent with the political welfare of the States and the social advance of their citizens that an independent and permanent power should exist within their limits, this power must give way to the greater power which surrounds it, or seek its exercise beyond the sphere of State authority.

This state of things can only be produced by a cooperation of the State and Federal Governments. The latter has the exclusive regulation of intercourse with the Indians, and, so long as this power shall be exercised, it cannot be obstructed by the State. It is a power given by the Constitution and sanctioned by the most solemn acts of both the Federal and State governments; consequently, it cannot be abrogated at the will of a State. It is one of the powers parted with by the States and vested in the Federal Government. But if a contingency shall occur which shall render the Indians who reside in a State incapable of self-government, either by moral degradation or a reduction of their numbers, it would undoubtedly be in the power of a State government to extend to them the aegis of its laws. Under such circumstances, the agency of the General Government, of necessity, must cease.

Under the administration of the laws of Georgia, a citizen of the United States has been deprived of his liberty, and, claiming protection under the treaties and laws of the United States, he makes the question, as he has a right to make it, whether the laws of Georgia under which he is now suffering an ignominious punishment are not repugnant to the Constitution of the United States and the treaties and laws made under it. This repugnancy has been shown, and it remains only to say what has before been often said by this tribunal of the local laws of many of the States in this Union – that, being repugnant to the Constitution of the United States and to the laws made under it, they can have no force to divest the plaintiff ... of his property or liberty.

Justice Baldwin dissented, ... he said his opinion remained the same as was expressed by him in the case of the *Cherokee Nation* v. *The State of Georgia* at the last term. Justice Baldwin did not provide an opinion.

1. What is the explanation for the difference in decision between *Cherokee Nation* and *Worchester* v. *Georgia* a year later? Does this challenge Chief Justice Marshall's definition of doctrine of discovery in *M'Intosh*?
2. How did the executive branch and the State of Georgia respond to this decision, in light of the decision to drive the Cherokee Nation out of Georgia and further west in 1830?
3. How does the assumption of eventual assimilation of Native people into the White population influence these opinions?

In *Worchester* the Court overturned the doctrine of discovery, finding Native tribes to have "voluntarily agreed to give up a portion of their sovereignty in return for protection by a stronger power. Thus they maintained 'self-government and sovereign and independent authority' in all other respects" (Smith 1997, 239). Consequently, states could not regulate tribes within their borders, and their self-governance could be revoked only by consensual federal treaty. While this decision provided an explicit justification of sovereignty for Native tribes, the response from Southern Whites was fear and deep anger. A committee of citizens from Columbus, Georgia, wrote a response to *Worchester*

> underscoring that "the dearest interest and most sacred right of freedman" – that is, self-government – was at stake. The Supreme Court ought to be respected ... except when its decisions deprived states of "the power of making laws for their own government." In such cases, it was "the duty of the people" to "protect and defend" their sovereignty. The choice before the citizens of Georgia was stark – submit as slaves, or resist and defend their freedom ... It seems not to have occurred to [the committee] that, in defense of self-government, native peoples had the stronger claim. (Saunt 2020, 169–170)

President Jackson ignored the ruling and ordered the removal of most tribes. The result was "[b]y 1850, the United States had removed roughly three-quarters of the Native population living east of the Mississippi in 1830 and had caused great loss of life in doing so" (Ostler 2019, 445). The federal government made the political choices of removal and denial of sovereignty (Saunt 2020, 320) – leaving unresolved the nature of Native sovereignty into the twenty-first century – decisions that would have reverberations to other racialized groups in the Nation.

2.1.2 Native Sovereignty and Citizenship

For Native peoples, the tension between maintaining sovereignty over their own political fate and securing the protections of citizenship was unresolvable. For many Native people, "the tension between individual [citizenship] and group [sovereignty] dwelt at the heart of the fight for U.S. citizenship for American Indians, which seemed to require abjuring tribal life" (Lomawaima 2013, 333). The fear of many indigenous people was that if they accepted citizenship and the right to vote in federal elections – thus helping inform federal policy and the enforcement of Indian law – they would have to give up tribal citizenship and self-governance of their own local communities. In the 1884 case of *Elk* v. *Wilkins* (1884), John Elk, a member of the Winnebago (Ho-Chunk, Wisconsin), severed his tribal relationships and moved to Omaha, Nebraska, where he submitted himself to U.S. jurisdiction, assimilating into the White community. Despite demonstrating residence, Charles Wilkins, the ward registrar in Omaha, refused to register Elk as a voter for the sole reason that he "was an Indian and therefore not a citizen of the United States, and therefore not entitled to a vote, and on account of his race and color ..." The circuit court ruled in favor of Wilkins; Elk claimed the denial of his federal citizenship and right to vote was contrary to the protections of the Constitution's Fourteenth and Fifteenth Amendments. In this case, the Supreme Court had to determine if the Fourteenth Amendment automatically transformed Native people into citizens if they chose assimilation in the hope of citizenship over the promise of sovereignty.

ELK v. WILKINS, 112 U.S. 94 (1884)

Justice Gray Delivered the Opinion of the Court, Joined by Chief Justice Waite and Justices Miller, Field, Bradley, Matthews, and Blatchford

Vote: 7–2

The question, then, is whether an Indian, born a member of one of the Indian tribes within the United States, is, merely by reason of his birth within the United States and of his afterwards voluntarily separating himself from his tribe and taking up his residence among white citizens, a citizen of the United States within the meaning of the first section of the Fourteenth Amendment of the Constitution. Under the Constitution of the United States as originally established, "Indians not taxed" were excluded from the persons according to whose numbers representatives and direct taxes were apportioned among the several states, and Congress had and exercised the power to regulate commerce with the Indian tribes, and the members thereof, whether within or without the boundaries of one of the states of the Union. The Indian tribes, being within the territorial limits of the United States, were not, strictly speaking, foreign states, but they were alien nations, distinct political communities, with whom the United States might and habitually did deal as they thought fit,

either through treaties made by the President and Senate or through acts of Congress in the ordinary forms of legislation. The members of those tribes owed immediate allegiance to their several tribes, and were not part of the people of the United States. They were in a dependent condition, a state of pupilage, resembling that of a ward to his guardian. Indians and their property, exempt from taxation by treaty or statute of the United States, could not be taxed by any state. General acts of Congress did not apply to Indians unless so expressed as to clearly manifest an intention to include them.

The alien and dependent condition of the members of the Indian tribes could not be put off at their own will without the action or assent of the United States. They were never deemed citizens of the United States except under explicit provisions of treaty or statute to that effect either declaring a certain tribe, or such members of it as chose to remain behind on the removal of the tribe westward, to be citizens or authorizing individuals of particular tribes to become citizens on application to a court of the United States for naturalization and satisfactory proof of fitness for civilized life ...

Chief Justice Taney ... in [Dred] Scott v. Sandford, 60 U.S. 404 [(1857)], did not affirm or imply that either the Indian tribes, or individual members of those tribes, had the right, beyond other foreigners, to become citizens of their own will, without being naturalized by the United States. His words were:

They [the Indian tribes] may without doubt, like the subjects of any foreign government, be naturalized by the authority of Congress and become citizens of a state and of the United States, and if an individual should leave his nation or tribe, and take up his abode among the white population, he would be entitled to all the rights and privileges which would belong to an emigrant from any other foreign people.

But an emigrant from any foreign state cannot become a citizen of the United States without a formal renunciation of his old allegiance, and an acceptance by the United States of that renunciation through such form of naturalization as may be required law.

... The main object of the opening sentence of the Fourteenth Amendment was to settle the question, upon which there had been a difference of opinion throughout the country and in this Court, as to the citizenship of free negroes (*Scott* v. *Sandford*, '19 How. 393), and to put it beyond doubt that all persons, white or black, and whether formerly slaves or not, born or naturalized in the United States, and owing no allegiance to any alien power, should be citizens of the United States and of the state in which they reside. *Slaughterhouse Cases*, 16 Wall. 36, 83 U.S. 73 [(1873)]; *Strauder* v. *West Virginia*, 100 U.S. 303 [(1880)].

This section contemplates two sources of citizenship, and two sources only: birth and naturalization. The persons declared to be citizens are "all persons born or naturalized in the United States, and subject to the jurisdiction thereof" ... Persons not thus subject to the jurisdiction of the United States at the time of birth cannot become so afterwards except by being naturalized, either individually, as by proceedings under the naturalization acts, or collectively, as by the force of a treaty by which foreign territory is acquired.

Indians born within the territorial limits of the United States, members of and owing immediate allegiance to one of the Indian tribes (an alien though dependent power), although in a geographical sense born in the United States, are no more "born in the United States and subject to the jurisdiction thereof," within the meaning of the first section of the Fourteenth Amendment, than the children of subjects of any foreign government born within the domain of that government, or the children born within the United States of ambassadors or other public ministers of foreign nations.

This view is confirmed by the second section of the Fourteenth Amendment, which provides that "Representatives shall be apportioned among the several states according to their respective numbers, counting the whole number of persons in each state, excluding Indians not taxed."

Slavery having been abolished, and the persons formerly held as slaves made citizens, this clause fixing the apportionment of representatives has abrogated so much of the corresponding clause of the original Constitution as counted only three-fifths of such persons. But Indians not taxed are still excluded from the count for the reason that they are not citizens. Their absolute exclusion from the basis of representation in which all other persons are now included is wholly inconsistent with their being considered citizens ...

Such Indians, then, not being citizens by birth, can only become citizens in the second way mentioned in the Fourteenth Amendment, by being "naturalized in the United States," by or under some treaty or statute.

Since the ratification of the Fourteenth Amendment, Congress has passed several acts for naturalizing Indians of certain tribes, which would have been superfluous if they were, or might become without any action of the government, citizens of the United States ...

The law upon the question before us has been well stated by Judge Deady in the District Court of the United States for the District of Oregon.

But an Indian cannot make himself a citizen of the United States without the consent and cooperation of the government. The fact that he has abandoned his nomadic life or tribal relations and adopted the habits and manners of civilized people may be a good reason why he should be made a citizen of the United States, but does not of itself make him one. To be a citizen of the United States is a political privilege which no one not born to can assume without its consent in some form. The Indians in Oregon, not being born subject to the jurisdiction of the United States, were not born citizens thereof, and I am not aware of any law or treaty by which any of them have been made so since. *United States* v. *Osborne*, 6 Sawyer 406, 409 [(1880)].

The plaintiff, not being a citizen of the United States under the Fourteenth Amendment of the Constitution, has been deprived of no right secured by the Fifteenth Amendment, and cannot maintain this action. *Judgment affirmed.*

Justice Harlan, Joined by Justice Woods, Dissenting

Justice Woods and myself feel constrained to express our dissent from the interpretation which our brethren give to that clause of the Fourteenth Amendment which provides that "All persons born or naturalized in the United States, and subject to the jurisdiction thereof, are citizens of the United States and of the state wherein they reside."

It is said that the petition contains no averment that Elk was taxed in the state in which he resides, or had ever been treated by her as a citizen. It is evident that the court would not have held him to be a citizen of the United States even if the petition had contained a direct averment that he was taxed, because its judgment, in legal effect, is that, although born within the territorial limits of the United States, he could not, if at his birth a member of an Indian tribe, acquire national citizenship by force of the Fourteenth Amendment, but only in pursuance of some statute or treaty providing for his naturalization. It would therefore seem unnecessary to inquire whether he was taxed at the time of his application to be registered as a voter, for if the words "all persons born ... in the United States and subject to the jurisdiction thereof" were not intended to embrace Indians born in tribal relations, but

who subsequently became *bona fide* residents of the several states, then manifestly the legal status of such Indians is not altered by the fact that they are taxed in those states.

While denying that national citizenship, as conferred by that amendment, necessarily depends upon the inquiry whether the person claiming it is taxed in the state of his residence or has property therein from which taxes may be derived, we submit that the petition does sufficiently show that the plaintiff was taxed – that is, belongs to the class which, by the laws of Nebraska, are subject to taxation ... Further: The plaintiff has become so far incorporated with the mass of the people of Nebraska that being, as the petition avers, a citizen and resident thereof, he constitutes a part of her militia. He may, being no longer a member of an Indian tribe, sue and be sued in her courts. And he is counted in every apportionment of representation in the legislature, for the requirement of her Constitution is that "The legislature shall apportion the Senators and representatives according to the number of inhabitants, excluding Indians not taxed, and soldiers and officers of the United States army."

At the adoption of the Constitution there were, in many of the states, Indians, not members of any tribe, who constituted a part of the people for whose benefit the state governments were established. This is apparent from that clause of Article I, Section 3, which requires, in the apportionment of representatives and direct taxes among the several states "according to their respective numbers," the exclusion of "Indians not taxed." This implies that there were at that time, in the United States, Indians who were taxed – that is, were subject to taxation by the laws of the State of which they were residents. Indians not taxed were those who held tribal relations, and therefore were not subject to the authority of any state, and were subject only to the authority of the United States, under the power conferred upon Congress in reference to Indian tribes in this country. The same provision is retained in the Fourteenth Amendment; for now, as at the adoption of the Constitution, Indians in the several states, who are taxed by their laws, are counted in establishing the basis of representation in Congress.

It seems to us that the Fourteenth Amendment, insofar as it was intended to confer national citizenship upon persons of the Indian race, is robbed of its vital force by a construction which excludes from such citizenship those who, although born in tribal relations, are within the complete jurisdiction of the United States. There were, in some of our states and territories at the time the amendment was submitted by Congress, many Indians who had finally left their tribes and come within the complete jurisdiction of the United States. They were as fully prepared for citizenship as were or are vast numbers of the white and colored races in the same localities. Is it conceivable that the statesmen who framed, the Congress which submitted, and the people who adopted that amendment intended to confer citizenship, national and state, upon the entire population in this country of African descent (the larger part of which was shortly before held in slavery), and, by the same constitutional provision, to exclude from such citizenship Indians who had never been in slavery and who, by becoming *bona fide* residents of states and territories within the complete jurisdiction of the United States, had evinced a purpose to abandon their former mode of life, and become a part of the people of the United States? If this question be answered in the negative, as we think it must be, then we are justified in withholding our assent to the doctrine which excludes the plaintiff from the body of citizens of the United States upon the ground that his parents were, when he was born, members of an Indian tribe, for, if he can be excluded upon any such ground, it must necessarily follow that the Fourteenth Amendment did not grant citizenship even to Indians who, although born in tribal relations, were at its adoption, severed from their tribes, subject to the complete jurisdiction as well of the United States as of the state or territory in which they resided.

Born, therefore, in the territory, under the dominion and within the jurisdictional limits of the United States, plaintiff has acquired, as was his undoubted right, a residence in one of the states, with her consent, and is subject to taxation and to all other burdens imposed by her upon residents of every race. If he did not acquire national citizenship on abandoning his tribe and becoming, by residence in one of the states, subject to the complete jurisdiction of the United States, then the Fourteenth Amendment has wholly failed to accomplish, in respect of the Indian race, what, we think, was intended by it, and there is still in this country a despised and rejected class of persons with no nationality whatever, who, born in our territory, owing no allegiance to any foreign power, and subject, as residents of the states, to all the burdens of government, are yet not members of any political community, nor entitled to any of the rights, privileges, or immunities of citizens of the United States.

1. What are the consequences of this decision for indigenous people?
2. How do the majority and dissent demonstrate different readings of the Fourteenth Amendment?
3. After reading the cases related to Native American sovereignty and citizenship, what is the relationship of a Native American with tribal allegiances to the U.S. government?

The year after the decision in *Elk* v. *Wilkins*, the U.S. Congress passed the Dawes Act in 1885, which authorized the president to allot tribal lands into individual parcels of property to indigenous individuals registered on tribal rolls. By connecting naturalized citizenship with private ownership of land, the Dawes Act used allotment to alter the status of Native peoples from "dependent wards of the federal government into independent, rights-bearing US citizens. But the cost of transformation was high: loss of indigenous culture and dispossession of tribal lands" (Erman 2021, 1233).

The U.S. federal government, via the Indian Citizenship Act, 1924, granted citizenship to all Native peoples regardless of formal membership in sovereign tribes. Again, the tension between individual citizenship and collective sovereignty against the backdrop of expected assimilation becomes clear. As Alexandra Witkin notes (1995), this expectation of citizenship "[f]rom one perspective … can be viewed as granting long-overdue emancipation to Native peoples excluded from the United States political community. From another perspective, shared by many Indians, it can be seen as an ultimate act of domination by a relentless alien power" (353–354). At the time of the Act, approximately 67 percent of Native peoples had become citizens through federal statutes or treaties; the Act itself created a version of dual citizenship by which Native people were U.S. citizens and yet could maintain their tribal citizenship simultaneously (Nackenoff and Novkov 2021, 154). For many Native peoples, this becomes an artificial tension between a pursuit of the rights guaranteed by citizenship and a hope for political power that is protected by sovereignty (Blackhawk 2019).

INDIAN CITIZENSHIP ACT, 1924, 8 USCA §1401

The following shall be nationals and citizens of the United States at birth:

(a) a person born in the United States, and subject to the jurisdiction thereof;

(b) a person born in the United States to a member of an Indian, Eskimo, Aleutian, or other aboriginal tribe: *Provided*, That the granting of citizenship under this subsection shall not in any manner impair or otherwise affect the right of such person to tribal or other property;

(c) a person born outside of the United States and its outlying possessions of parents both of whom are citizens of the United States and one of whom has had a residence in the United States or one of its outlying possessions, prior to the birth of such person;

(d) a person born outside of the United States and its outlying possessions of parents one of whom is a citizen of the United States who has been physically present in the United States or one of its outlying possessions for a continuous period of one year prior to the birth of such person, and the other of whom is a national, but not a citizen of the United States;

(e) a person born in an outlying possession of the United States of parents one of whom is a citizen of the United States who has been physically present in the United States or one of its outlying possessions for a continuous period of one year at any time prior to the birth of such person …

1. How might the idea of "dual citizenship" impact the tension between personal citizenship and tribal sovereignty?
2. Why might Native people want both citizenship and sovereignty?
3. What does citizenship mean without the right to vote?
4. Where do you see the backdrop of the expectation for assimilation in these tensions?

One of the themes seen in all these decisions and Acts is an expectation that Native peoples would eventually choose to give up sovereignty and tribal community to assimilate into the dominant White culture. From the early days of the nation, federal officials perceived assimilation to be the solution to the tensions over Native lands and Native control. Eventually, the government would determine – as seen in later chapters – if the incentive of personal land ownership and U.S. citizenship was insufficient, then violence and coercion might compel assimilation.

2.2 Citizenship

For other racialized groups in America, citizenship was the primary struggle. Hannah Arendt defined citizenship as "a right to have rights (and that means to live in a framework where one is judged by one's actions and opinions) and a right to belong to some kind of organized community" (Arendt 1976, 296–297). However, throughout the life of the nation, the definition of "citizen" has been heavily contested – a battle which continues today. The nature of citizenship is controversial because such status can provide the authority to vote, which in a democratic republic such as the United States means the capacity to govern and rule (Deardorff 2014). Because so many people were excluded from full citizenship in the United States, efforts to include one group risked expanding the definition of citizenship to many other identities.

2.2.1 Rethinking Personhood, Citizenship, and Constitutional Change

In the case of *Dred Scott* v. *Sandford* (1856), the United States wrestled with the appropriate and possible roles of African Americans in the nation. In the mid-nineteenth century, the battles over slavery and its expansion into the territories were hardening. Now considered by most constitutional scholars as the worst decision "ever rendered by the Supreme Court" (Ehrlich 1992; Graber 2006, 15–16), *Dred Scott* was convoluted by nine separate opinions with seven different justifications by the majority. The decision at the time was controversial, as the challenge by Frederick Douglass demonstrates. But was this decision that far outside the mainstream of American constitutional thought in the mid-nineteenth century?

Dred Scott was an enslaved man who sued for freedom because Dr. Emerson – who claimed ownership of him – moved Scott to the free Wisconsin territory where he married his wife Harriet and they later had two daughters, Eliza and Lizzie. Dred Scott asserted this residence in "free territory" emancipated them. After moving them back into slave territory of Louisiana, Dr. Emerson married Irene Sanford,[1] the Scott family sued for freedom in federal court based on their residence in free territory.

---

[1] The Supreme Court misrecorded the name as "Sandford," resulting in references to both spellings.

DRED SCOTT v. SANDFORD, 60 U.S. 393 (1857)

Chief Justice Taney Delivered the Opinion of the Court

Vote: 7–2

The question is simply this: can a negro whose ancestors were imported into this country and sold as slaves become a member of the political community formed and brought into existence by the Constitution of the United States, and as such become entitled to all the rights, and privileges, and immunities, guarantied by that instrument to the citizen, one of which rights is the privilege of suing in a court of the United States in the cases specified in the Constitution?

It will be observed that the plea applies to that class of persons only whose ancestors were negroes of the African race, and imported into this country and sold and held as slaves. The only matter in issue before the court, therefore, is, whether the descendants of such slaves, when they shall be emancipated, or who are born of parents who had become free before their birth, are citizens of a State in the sense in which the word "citizen" is used in the Constitution of the United States. And this being the only matter in dispute on the pleadings, the court must be understood as speaking in this opinion of that class only, that is, of those persons who are the descendants of Africans who were imported into this country and sold as slaves.

The situation of this population was altogether unlike that of the Indian race. The latter, it is true, formed no part of the colonial communities, and never amalgamated with them in social connections or in government. But although they were uncivilized, they were yet a free and independent people, associated together in nations or tribes and governed by their own laws. Many of these political communities were situated in territories to which the white race claimed the ultimate right of dominion. But that claim was acknowledged to be subject to the right of the Indians to occupy it as long as they thought proper, and neither the English nor colonial Governments claimed or exercised any dominion over the tribe or nation by whom it was occupied, nor claimed the right to the possession of the territory, until the tribe or nation consented to cede it. These Indian Governments were regarded and treated as foreign Governments as much so as if an ocean had separated the red man from the white, and their freedom has constantly been acknowledged, from the time of the first emigration to the English colonies to the present day, by the different Governments which succeeded each other. Treaties have been negotiated with them, and their alliance sought for in war, and the people who compose these Indian political communities have always been treated as foreigners not living under our Government. It is true that the course of events has brought the Indian tribes within the limits of the United States under subjection to the white race, and it has been found necessary, for their sake as well as our own, to regard them as in a state of pupilage, and to legislate to a certain extent over them and the territory they occupy. But they may, without doubt, like the subjects of any other foreign Government, be naturalized by the authority of Congress, and become citizens of a State, and of the United States, and if an individual should leave his nation or tribe and take up his abode among the white population, he would be entitled to all the rights and privileges which would belong to an emigrant from any other foreign people.

We proceed to examine the case as presented by the pleadings.

The words "people of the United States" and "citizens" are synonymous terms, and mean the same thing. They both describe the political body who, according to our republican institutions, form the sovereignty and who hold the power and conduct the Government through their representatives. They are what we familiarly call the "sovereign people," and every citizen is one of this people, and a constituent member of this sovereignty. The question before us is whether the class of persons described in the plea ... compose a portion of this people, and are constituent members of this sovereignty? We think they are not, and that they are not included, and were not intended to be included, under the word "citizens" in the Constitution, and can therefore claim none of the rights and privileges which that instrument provides for and secures to citizens of the United States. On the contrary, they were at that time considered as a subordinate and inferior class of beings who had been subjugated by the dominant race, and, whether emancipated or not, yet remained subject to their authority, and had no rights or privileges but such as those who held the power and the Government might choose to grant them.

In discussing this question, we must not confound the rights of citizenship which a State may confer within its own limits and the rights of citizenship as a member of the Union. It does not by any means follow, because he has all the rights and privileges of a citizen of a State, that he must be a citizen of the United States. He may have all of the rights and privileges of the citizen of a State and yet not be entitled to the rights and privileges of a citizen in any other State ...

It is very clear, therefore, that no State can, by any act or law of its own, passed since the adoption of the Constitution, introduce a new member into the political community created by the Constitution of the United States. It cannot make him a member of this community by making him a member of its own. And, for the same reason, it cannot introduce any person or description of persons who were not intended to be embraced in this new political family which the Constitution brought into existence, but were intended to be excluded from it.

The question then arises, whether the provisions of the Constitution, in relation to the personal rights and privileges to which the citizen of a State should be entitled, embraced the negro African race, at that time in this country or who might afterwards be imported, who had then or should afterwards be made free in any State, and to put it in the power of a single State to make him a citizen of the United States and endue him with the full rights of citizenship in every other State without their consent? Does the Constitution of the United States act upon him whenever he shall be made free under the laws of a State, and raised there to the rank of a citizen, and immediately clothe him with all the privileges of a citizen in every other State, and in its own courts.

The court thinks the affirmative of these propositions cannot be maintained. And if it cannot, [Dred Scott] could not be a citizen of the State of Missouri within the meaning of the Constitution of the United States, and, consequently, was not entitled to sue in its courts.

It is true, every person, and every class and description of persons who were, at the time of the adoption of the Constitution, recognised as citizens in the several States became also citizens of this new political body, but none other; it was formed by them, and for them and their posterity, but for no one else ... And it gave to each citizen rights and privileges outside of his State which he did not before possess, and placed him in every other State upon a perfect equality with its own citizens as to rights of person and rights of property; it made him a citizen of the United States.

It becomes necessary, therefore, to determine who were citizens of the several States when the Constitution was adopted ...

In the opinion of the court, the legislation and histories of the times, and the language used in the Declaration of Independence, show that neither the class of persons who had been imported as slaves nor their descendants, whether they had become free or not, were then acknowledged as a part of the people, nor intended to be included in the general words used in that memorable instrument.

It is difficult at this day to realize the state of public opinion in relation to that unfortunate race which prevailed in the civilized and enlightened portions of the world at the time of the Declaration of Independence and when the Constitution of the United States was framed and adopted. But the public history of every European nation displays it in a manner too plain to be mistaken.

They had for more than a century before been regarded as beings of an inferior order, and altogether unfit to associate with the white race either in social or political relations, and so far inferior that they had no rights which the white man was bound to respect, and that the negro might justly and lawfully be reduced to slavery for his benefit. He was bought and sold, and treated as an ordinary article of merchandise and traffic whenever a profit could be made by it. This opinion was at that time fixed and universal in the civilized portion of the white race. It was regarded as an axiom in morals as well as in politics which no one thought of disputing or supposed to be open to dispute, and men in every grade and position in society daily and habitually acted upon it in their private pursuits, as well as in matters of public concern, without doubting for a moment the correctness of this opinion.

And in no nation was this opinion more firmly fixed or more uniformly acted upon than by the English Government and English people. They not only seized them on the coast of Africa and sold them or held them in slavery for their own use, but they took them as ordinary articles of merchandise to every country where they could make a profit on them, and were far more extensively engaged in this commerce than any other nation in the world.

The opinion thus entertained and acted upon in England was naturally impressed upon the colonies they founded on this side of the Atlantic. And, accordingly, a negro of the African race was regarded by them as an article of property, and held, and bought and sold as such, in every one of the thirteen colonies which united in the Declaration of Independence and afterwards formed the Constitution of the United States. The slaves were more or less numerous in the different colonies as slave labor was found more or less profitable. But no one seems to have doubted the correctness of the prevailing opinion of the time.

The legislation of the different colonies furnishes positive and indisputable proof of this fact.

... [I]t is too clear for dispute that the enslaved African race were not intended to be included, and formed no part of the people who framed and adopted this declaration, for if the language, as understood in that day, would embrace them, the conduct of the distinguished men who framed the Declaration of Independence would have been utterly and flagrantly inconsistent with the principles they asserted, and instead of the sympathy of mankind to which they so confidently appealed, they would have deserved and received universal rebuke and reprobation.

Yet the men who framed this declaration were great men – high in literary acquirements, high in their sense of honor, and incapable of asserting principles inconsistent with those on which they were acting. They perfectly understood the meaning of the language they used, and how it would be understood by others, and they knew that it would not in any part of the civilized world be supposed to embrace the negro race, which, by common consent, had been excluded from civilized Governments and the family of nations, and doomed to slavery. They spoke and acted according to the then established doctrines and principles, and in the ordinary language of the day, and no one misunderstood them. The unhappy black race were separated from the white by indelible marks, and laws long before established, and were never thought of or spoken of except as property, and when the claims of the owner or the profit of the trader were supposed to need protection.

This state of public opinion had undergone no change when the Constitution was adopted, as is equally evident from its provisions and language.

The brief preamble sets forth by whom it was formed, for what purposes, and for whose benefit and protection. It declares that it is formed by the people of the United States – that is to say, by those who were members of the different political communities in the several States – and its great object is declared to be to secure the blessings of liberty to themselves and their posterity. It speaks in general terms of the people of the United States, and of citizens of the several States, when it is providing for the exercise of the powers granted or the privileges secured to the citizen. It does not define what description of persons are intended to be included under these terms, or who shall be regarded as a citizen and one of the people ...

No one of that race had ever migrated to the United States voluntarily; all of them had been brought here as articles of merchandise. The number that had been emancipated at that time were but few in comparison with those held in slavery, and they were identified in the public mind with the race to which they belonged, and regarded as a part of the slave population rather than the free. It is obvious that they were not even in the minds of the framers of the Constitution when they were conferring special rights and privileges upon the citizens of a State in every other part of the Union.

Indeed, when we look to the condition of this race in the several States at the time, it is impossible to believe that these rights and privileges were intended to be extended to them.

The legislation of the States ... shows in a manner not to be mistaken the inferior and subject condition of that race at the time the Constitution was adopted and long afterwards, throughout the thirteen States by which that instrument was framed, and it is hardly consistent with the respect due to these States to suppose that they regarded at that time as fellow citizens and members of the sovereignty, a class of beings whom they had thus stigmatized, whom, as we are bound out of respect to the State sovereignties to assume they had deemed it just and necessary thus to stigmatize, and upon whom they had impressed such deep and enduring marks of inferiority and degradation, or, that, when they met in convention to form the Constitution, they looked upon them as a portion of their constituents or designed to include them in the provisions so carefully inserted for the security and protection of the liberties and rights of their citizens. It cannot be supposed that they intended to secure to them rights and privileges and rank, in the new political body throughout the Union which every one of them denied within the limits of its own dominion. More especially, it cannot be believed that the large slaveholding States regarded them as included in the word citizens, or would have consented to a Constitution which might compel them to receive them in that character from another State. For if they were so received, and entitled to the privileges and immunities of citizens, it would exempt them from the operation of the special laws and from the police regulations which they considered to be necessary for their own safety. It would give to persons of the negro race, who were recognised as citizens in any one State of the Union, the right to enter every other State whenever they pleased, singly or in companies, without pass or passport, and without obstruction, to sojourn there as long as they pleased, to go where they pleased at every hour of the day or night without molestation, unless they committed some violation of law for which a white man would be punished; and it would give them the full liberty of speech in public and in private upon all subjects upon which its own citizens might speak; to hold public meetings upon political affairs, and to keep and carry arms wherever they went. And all of this would be done in the face of the subject race of the same color, both free and slaves, and inevitably producing discontent and insubordination among them, and endangering the peace and safety of the State.

Undoubtedly a person may be a citizen, that is, a member of the community who form the sovereignty, although he exercises no share of the political power and is incapacitated from holding particular offices. Women and minors, who form a part of the political family, cannot vote, and when a property qualification is required to vote or hold a particular office, those who have not the necessary qualification cannot vote or hold the office, yet they are citizens.

So, too, a person may be entitled to vote by the law of the State, who is not a citizen even of the State itself. And in some of the States of the Union, foreigners not naturalized are allowed to vote. And the State may give the right to free negroes and mulattoes, but that does not make them citizens of the State, and still less of the United States. And the provision in the Constitution giving privileges and immunities in other States does not apply to them.

And, upon a full and careful consideration of the subject, the court is of opinion, that ... Dred Scott was not a citizen of Missouri within the meaning of the Constitution of the United States, and not entitled as such to sue in its courts, and consequently that the Circuit Court had no jurisdiction of the case, and that the judgment on the plea in abatement is erroneous.

Upon these considerations, it is the opinion of the court that the act of Congress which prohibited a citizen from holding and owning property of this kind in the territory of the United States north of the line therein mentioned is not warranted by the Constitution, and is therefore void, and that neither Dred Scott himself nor any of his family were made free by being carried into this territory, even if they had been carried there by the owner with the intention of becoming a permanent resident.

Justice Curtis, Dissenting

To determine whether any free persons, descended from Africans held in slavery, were citizens of the United States under the Confederation, and consequently at the time of the adoption of the Constitution of the United States, it is only necessary to know whether any such persons were citizens of either of the States under the Confederation at the time of the adoption of the Constitution.

Of this there can be no doubt. At the time of the ratification of the Articles of Confederation, all free native-born inhabitants of the States of New Hampshire, Massachusetts, New York, New Jersey, and North Carolina, though descended from African slaves, were not only citizens of those States, but such of them as had the other necessary qualifications possessed the franchise of electors, on equal terms with other citizens.

Did the Constitution of the United States deprive them or their descendants of citizenship?

That Constitution was ordained and established by the people of the United States, through the action, in each State, or those persons who were qualified by its laws to act thereon in behalf of themselves and all other citizens of that State. In some of the States, as we have seen, colored persons were among those qualified by law to act on this subject. These colored persons were not only included in the body of "the people of the United States" by whom the Constitution was ordained and established, but, in at least five of the States, they had the power to act, and doubtless did act, by their suffrages, upon the question of its adoption. It would be strange if we were to find in that instrument anything which deprived of their citizenship any part of the people of the United States who were among those by whom it was established.

I can find nothing in the Constitution which ... deprives of their citizenship any class of persons who were citizens of the United States at the time of its adoption, or who should be native-born citizens of any State after its adoption, nor any power enabling Congress to disfranchise persons born on the soil of any State, and entitled to citizenship of such State by its Constitution and laws. And my opinion is that, under the Constitution of the United States, every free person born on the soil of a State, who is a citizen of that State by force of its Constitution or laws, is also a citizen of the United States.

It has been often asserted that the Constitution was made exclusively by and for the white race. It has already been shown that, in five of the thirteen original States, colored persons then possessed the elective franchise, and were among those by whom the Constitution was ordained and established. If so, it is not true, in point of fact, that the Constitution was made exclusively by the white race. And that it was made exclusively for the white race is, in my opinion, not only an assumption not warranted by anything in the Constitution, but contradicted by its opening declaration that it was ordained and established by the people of the United States, for themselves and their posterity. And as free colored persons were then citizens of at least five States, and so in every sense part of the people of the United States, they were among those for whom and whose posterity the Constitution was ordained and established.

... The Constitution has left to the States the determination what persons, born within their respective limits, shall acquire by birth citizenship of the United States; it has not left to them any power to prescribe any rule for the removal of the disabilities of alienage. This power is exclusively in Congress.

It has been further objected that, if free colored persons, born within a particular State and made citizens of that State by its Constitution and laws, are thereby made citizens of the United States, then, under the second section of the fourth article of the Constitution, such persons would be entitled to all the privileges and immunities of citizens in the several States, and, if so, then colored persons could vote, and be eligible to not only Federal offices, but offices even in those States whose Constitution and laws disqualify colored persons from voting or being elected to office.

But this position rests upon an assumption which I deem untenable. Its basis is that no one can be deemed a citizen of the United States who is not entitled to enjoy all the privileges and franchises which are conferred on any citizen. That this is not true under the Constitution of the United States seems to me clear.

It may be further objected that, if free colored persons may be citizens of the United States, it depends only on the will of a master whether he will emancipate his slave and thereby make him a citizen. Not so. The master is subject to the will of the State ... Under the Constitution of the United States, each State has retained this power of determining the political status of its native-born inhabitants, and no exception thereto can be found in the Constitution. And if a master in a slaveholding State should carry his slave into a free State, and there emancipate him, he would not thereby make him a native-born citizen of that State, and consequently no privileges could be claimed by such emancipated salve as a citizen of the United States ...

... The conclusions at which I have arrived on this part of the case are:

First. That the free native-born citizens of each State are citizens of the United States.

Second. That, as free colored persons born within some of the States are citizens of those States, such persons are also citizens of the United States.

Third. That every such citizen, residing in any State, has the right to sue and is liable to be sued in the Federal courts, as a citizen of that State in which he resides.

Fourth. That, as the plea to the jurisdiction in this case shows no facts, except that the plaintiff was of African descent, and his ancestors were sold as slaves, and as these facts are not inconsistent with his citizenship of the United States and his residence in the State of Missouri, the plea to the jurisdiction was bad, and the judgment of the Circuit Court overruling it was correct.

I dissent, therefore, from that part of the opinion of the majority of the court in which it is held that a person of African descent cannot be a citizen of the United States....

1. How does Chief Justice Taney interpret the Constitution in relationship to the status of African Americans? Native peoples? How does he justify the difference?
2. To what extent does the *Dred Scott* decision impact those who are enslaved and those of African American descent, regardless of status of servitude?
3. How does the dissenting opinion by Justice Curtis interpret the Constitution in relationship to the status of African Americans?
4. Mark Graber (2006) argues that the Constitution was a compromise between pro-slavery and anti-slavery forces and the *Dred Scott* decision was the "constitutional evil" that resulted. How might this argument be made?
5. How does this case parallel and differ from *Elk* v. *Wilkins* (1884)? For extra credit, incorporate Kelley (1929).

While the majority was so fractured in its reasoning that it is unclear how much of Chief Justice Taney's decision is *obiter dictum* (or non-binding legal reasoning) (Maltz 2007; Graber 2006), the impact of the ruling was clear. The decision denied citizenship to African Americans who were enslaved or free in the United States, arguing that none were seen as citizens at the Founding. So, without explicit federal action, they could not be citizens of the federal government capable of accessing the federal courts. The Court ruled that states could make differing determinations either extending citizenship to those of African descent or not. By clearly distinguishing between state and federal authority over issues of citizenship – a form of dual federalism – the Court replicated claims made by the South in their constitutional interpretation (Finkelman 1996). This distinction would impact women and many racialized groups as they sought full citizenship in the decades ahead. Although the Fourteenth Amendment in overturning *Dred Scott* expanded federal citizenship more broadly, Native peoples were explicitly excluded from the Amendment unless they were willing to assimilate into the White community and pay taxes.

It is significant that this case is not based on Dred Scott's status as a "slave," but based on his descent from Africans brought unwillingly to the United States or to the colonies. If he had been a freed man, seeking to sue on behalf of his family for another reason, the decision would have been the same. The decision in *Dred Scott* is based on race, not a condition of servitude. According to Rogers Smith (1997), Chief Justice Taney:

> ... clearly wanted to block off every possible legal route for recognizing either constitutional citizenship for blacks or federal power to ban slavery ... His waving of the specter of black civic equality thus seems designed chiefly to enable him to rule that blacks were not and could not be U.S. citizens in any sense. (265)

Frederick Douglass, in his 1857 speech to the American Anti-Slavery Society in New York, responded to the *Dred Scott* decision critically. In this speech, he echoed many of his earlier arguments about the nature of the Constitution from his debates with the Garrisonians. However, he particularly focuses on Chief Justice Taney's claims about the nature of the Founding and historic views of citizenship for both free and enslaved Blacks. The decision in *Dred Scott* denied him federal citizenship too and prohibited him access to the federal courts and constitutional protections. He claimed that an interpretation of the Constitution of demanding liberty and equality demonstrates that the decision of the Court does not reflect the wisdom of the Constitution. As he argues:

> It may be said that it is quite true that the Constitution was designed to secure the blessings of liberty and justice to the people who made it, and to the posterity of the people who made it, but was never designed to do any such thing for the colored people of African descent. This is Judge Taney's argument, and it is Mr. Garrison's argument, but it is not the argument of the Constitution. (Douglass 1857)

How might the debate between Frederick Douglass and William Lloyd Garrison of the Constitution in the definition of slavery connect to the arguments in *Dred Scott*?

2.2.2 The Reconstruction Amendments

In the years immediately following the Civil War (1861–1865), called the Reconstruction Era (1863–1877), Congress passed three constitutional amendments. Often referred to as the "Reconstruction Amendments," the constitutional emendations were designed to respond to the needs of the newly freed peoples and incorporate them into the governance of the nation. The Thirteenth Amendment explicitly ended slavery throughout the nation, as opposed to the Emancipation Proclamation which only freed those held in the seceding states not under Union control. While the Thirteenth Amendment banned slavery, the need for unregulated cheap labor resulted in long, unprotected contracts for many racialized groups, convict leasing, peonage and sharecropping (see Chapter 1).

RECONSTRUCTION AMENDMENTS

Thirteenth Amendment, 1865

Section 1

Neither slavery nor involuntary servitude, except as a punishment for crime whereof the party shall have been duly convicted, shall exist within the United States, or any place subject to their jurisdiction.

Section 2

Congress shall have power to enforce this article by appropriate legislation.

Fourteenth Amendment, 1868

Section 1

All persons born or naturalized in the United States and subject to the jurisdiction thereof, are citizens of the United States and of the State wherein they reside. No State shall make or enforce any law which shall abridge the privileges or immunities of citizens of the United States; nor shall any State deprive any person of life, liberty, or property, without due process of law; nor deny to any person within its jurisdiction the equal protection of the laws.

Section 5

The Congress shall have power to enforce, by appropriate legislation, the provisions of this article.

Fifteenth Amendment, 1870

Section 1

The right of citizens of the United States to vote shall not be denied or abridged by the United States or by any State on account of race, color, or previous condition of servitude.

Section 2

The Congress shall have power to enforce this article by appropriate legislation.

The Fourteenth Amendment implicitly overturned the *Dred Scott* v. *Sandford* (1856) decision by granting citizenship to all who had been born in the United States (birthright citizens) or had immigrated to the United States and become a citizen of a state. What was left unanswered is what would happen to those sold in the slave trade after the Constitution banned it in 1808 – who had not been born in the United States and could not be naturalized. The Fifteenth Amendment was the third of the Reconstruction era constitutional transformations. This amendment guaranteed the right to vote to the newly freed peoples and to free Blacks. It only prevented the federal and state governments from curtailing voting rights based on race, color, or prior condition of servitude. While it prevented explicit racial barriers, it "left the states power to enact many other restrictions, including property qualifications and exclusions from office holding that could negate the formal political rights of Blacks and many other citizens as well" (Smith 1997, 314). The right to vote was not extended to women, regardless of racial identity.

Despite this initial emphasis on the expansion of citizenship, soon after the passage of the Reconstruction Acts, the Nation will go quickly into a period in which these promises of the expansion of citizenship were quickly retracted. The nation entered an

> era of Chinese exclusion, the anti-tribal Dawes Act, stagnation in the women's suffrage campaign, the rise of Jim Crow segregation and disenfranchisement, the emergence of the literacy test and other proposals to curb non-Nordic immigration, resurgent anti-Catholicism, and finally the racially justified imposition of colonial rule over Latinos and Asians via the Spanish-American War. (Smith 1997, 348)

The justification for these policies will sound familiar to us today: the fear of the alien culture, mass immigration, and the desire for all to assimilate to "Americans," as well as the continuous need for cheap controllable labor may resonate with twenty-first-century citizens.

2.3 Asian Americans and Citizenship

The Reconstruction Amendments with their extension of citizenship to Black Americans did not alter the perspective of many that the United States was a White nation. With the ending of slavery, the United States was seeking other sources of inexpensive labor and worried about the loss of its historic identity as waves of new immigrants entered the country (Shklar 1991; Walzer 1992). By century's end, the United States "simultaneously embrace[d] a broad, universal definition of national membership based on native birth and voluntary allegiance and an exclusionary policy of Asiatic racial differentiation" (Wong 2015, 11). This conflict between identifying who are "real Americans" with the self-identified label of an immigrant nation continues today unabated.

The highlighted immigration of Chinese workers to the West Coast challenged broad definitions of citizenship that were initially defined by western European immigrants. Between 1848 and 1852, 35,000 Chinese arrived in California, soon constituting 10 percent of the state population (Nackenoff and Novkov 2021, 30) and generating in the White population a fear of "replacement," a conspiracy theory still promoted today. By the 1870s, anti-Chinese violence was so extreme that a massacre in Los Angeles in 1871 resulted in the annihilation of a tenth of the Chinese population (72–73). New state legislation was implemented to prevent property being transferred to Asian ownership, and laws were being interpreted in discriminatory ways. The question of the proper application of the Fourteenth Amendment to these laws rose quickly to the Supreme Court, culminating with the 1886 decision in *Yick Wo* v. *Hopkins* (1886). San Francisco passed Order No. 156 in 1880, which required all laundries housed in wooden structures to obtain a permit from local officials. Although 89 percent of laundry operators were of Chinese descent and 95 percent of the city's laundries were in wooden buildings, only one Chinese owner and all but one non-Chinese launderers were granted a permit under this policy. Yick Wo and Wo Lee were fined $10 for operating a laundry after being denied a permit and were imprisoned by the San Francisco sheriff, Peter Hopkins, when they would not pay the fine. They sued for a violation of the *writ of habeas corpus* and argued that the ordinance's discriminatory enforcement violated the Fourteenth Amendment's Equal Protection Clause. The lower state courts ruled the law was neutral and racially nondiscriminatory, finding for Sheriff Hopkins.

YICK WO v. *HOPKINS*, 118 U.S. 356 (1886)

Justice Matthews Delivered the Opinion of the Court

Vote: 9–0

We … differ from the Supreme Court of California upon the real meaning of the ordinances in question. That court considered these ordinances as vesting in the board of supervisors a not unusual discretion in granting or withholding their assent to the use of wooden buildings as laundries, to be exercised in reference to the circumstances of each case with a view to the protection of the public against the dangers of fire. We are not able to concur in that interpretation of the power conferred upon the supervisors. There is nothing in the ordinances which points to such a regulation of the business of keeping and conducting laundries. They seem intended to confer, and actually do confer, not a discretion to be exercised upon a consideration of the circumstances of each case, but a naked and arbitrary power to give or withhold consent not only as to places, but as to persons … The power given to them is not confided to their discretion in the legal sense of that term, but is granted to their mere will. It is purely arbitrary, and acknowledges neither guidance nor restraint.

The ordinance drawn in question in the present case … does not prescribe a rule and conditions for the regulation of the use of property for laundry purposes to which all similarly situated may conform. It allows without restriction the use for such purposes of buildings of brick or stone, but, as to wooden buildings, constituting nearly all those in previous use, it divides the owners or occupiers into two classes, not having respect to their personal character and qualifications for the business, nor the situation and nature and adaptation of the buildings themselves, but merely by an arbitrary line, on one side of which are those who are permitted to pursue their industry by the mere will and consent of the supervisors, and on the other those from whom that consent is withheld at their mere will and pleasure ...

The rights of the petitioners, as affected by the proceedings of which they complain, are not less because they are aliens and subjects of the Emperor of China. By the third article of the [November 17, 1880] treaty between this Government and that of China ... it is stipulated:

> If Chinese laborers, or Chinese of any other class, now either permanently or temporarily residing in the territory of the United States, meet with ill treatment at the hands of any other persons, the Government of the United States will exert all its powers to devise measures for their protection, and to secure to them the same rights, privileges, immunities and exemptions as may be enjoyed by the citizens or subjects of the most favored nation, and to which they are entitled by treaty.

The Fourteenth Amendment to the Constitution is not confined to the protection of citizens. It says:

> Nor shall any State deprive any person of life, liberty, or property without due process of law; nor deny to any person within its jurisdiction the equal protection of the laws.

These provisions are universal in their application to all persons within the territorial jurisdiction, without regard to any differences of race, of color, or of nationality, and the equal protection of the laws is a pledge of the protection of equal laws ...

The questions we have to consider and decide in these cases, therefore, are to be treated as invoking the rights of every citizen of the United States equally with those of the strangers and aliens who now invoke the jurisdiction of the court.

It is contended on the part of the petitioners that the ordinances for violations of which they are severally sentenced to imprisonment are void on their face as being within the prohibitions of the Fourteenth Amendment, and, in the alternative, if not so, that they are void by reason of their administration, operating unequally so as to punish in the present petitioners what is permitted to others as lawful, without any distinction of circumstances – an unjust and illegal discrimination, it is claimed, which, though not made expressly by the ordinances, is made possible by them.

When we consider the nature and the theory of our institutions of government, the principles upon which they are supposed to rest, and review the history of their development, we are constrained to conclude that they do not mean to leave room for the play and action of purely personal and arbitrary power. Sovereignty itself is, of course, not subject to law, for it is the author and source of law; but, in our system, while sovereign powers are delegated to the agencies of government, sovereignty itself remains with the people, by whom and for whom all government exists and acts. And the law is the definition and limitation of power. It is, indeed, quite true that there must always be lodged somewhere, and in some person or body, the authority of final decision, and in many cases of mere administration, the responsibility is purely political, no appeal lying except to the ultimate tribunal of the public judgment, exercised either in the pressure of opinion or by means of the suffrage. But the fundamental rights to life, liberty, and the pursuit of happiness, considered as individual possessions, are secured by those maxims of constitutional law which are the monuments showing the victorious progress of the race in securing to men the blessings of civilization under the reign of just and equal laws, so that, in the famous language of the Massachusetts Bill of Rights, the government of the commonwealth "may be a government of laws, and not of men." For the very idea that one man may be compelled to hold his life, or the means of living, or any material right essential to the enjoyment of life at the mere will of another seems to be intolerable in any country where freedom prevails, as being the essence of slavery itself.

... In the present cases, we are not obliged to reason from the probable to the actual, and pass upon the validity of the ordinances complained of, as tried merely by the opportunities which their terms afford, of unequal and unjust discrimination in their administration. For the cases present the ordinances in actual operation, and the facts shown establish an administration directed so exclusively against a particular class of persons as to warrant and require the conclusion that, whatever may have been the intent of the ordinances as adopted, they are applied by the public authorities charged with their administration, and thus representing the State itself, with a mind so unequal and oppressive as to amount to a practical denial by the State of that equal protection of the laws which is secured to the petitioners, as to all other persons, by the broad and benign provisions of the Fourteenth Amendment to the Constitution of the United States. Though the law itself be fair on its face and impartial in appearance, yet, if it is applied and administered by public authority with an evil eye and an unequal hand, so as practically to make unjust and illegal discriminations between persons in similar circumstances, material to their rights, the denial of equal justice is still within the prohibition of the Constitution.

The present cases, as shown by the facts disclosed in the record, are within this class. It appears that both petitioners have complied with every requisite deemed by the law or by the public officers charged with its administration necessary for the protection of neighboring property from fire or as a precaution against injury to the public health. No reason whatever, except the will of the supervisors, is assigned why they should not be permitted to carry on, in the accustomed manner, their harmless and useful occupation, on which they depend for a livelihood. And while this consent of the supervisors is withheld from them and from two hundred others who have also petitioned, all of whom happen to be Chinese subjects, eighty others, not Chinese subjects, are permitted to carry on the same business under similar conditions. The fact of this discrimination is admitted. No reason for it is shown, and the conclusion cannot be resisted that no reason for it exists except hostility to the race and nationality to which the petitioners belong, and which, in the eye of the law, is not justified. The discrimination is, therefore, illegal, and the public administration which enforces it is a denial of the equal protection of the laws and a violation of the Fourteenth Amendment of the Constitution. The imprisonment of the petitioners is, therefore, illegal, and they must be discharged.

1. What does the Fourteenth Amendment protect?
2. What does the Court say about the application of the Fourteenth Amendment to non-citizens?
3. What relationship does the Court see between race and the exercise of arbitrary power?
4. Can a neutral rule still be discriminatory? Why or why not?

2.3.1 Chinese Exclusion Laws

At the end of the nineteenth century, the meaning of citizenship was again challenged as African Americans, who were initially included in the federal Republic, then saw their political power restrained. As Justice Harlan in his famed *Plessy* v. *Ferguson* (1896) (see Chapter 3) dissent argued for a color-blind Constitution to protect citizenship and constitutional equality for African Americans, he simultaneously rejected these rights for Chinese immigrants and citizens. As the one Justice arguing for a "color-blind Constitution," he finds Chinese Americans and Chinese immigrants alike to be inherently alien, unable to assimilate and thereby unable to become citizens. Similar conflicts appeared in Congress and in the national discourse (Wong 2015). Do we welcome all or only Europeans? If we want the inexpensive labor of others, do we welcome them as citizens or should we use their labor and ship them home? What does it mean to be "American"?

In 1868, the Burlingame Treaty provided China most-favored-nation status and encouraged Chinese citizens to come and work in the United States. While male Chinese laborers were welcome to work in the goldfields, laying rail lines, and on the farmlands of the Northwest, immigrating Chinese women were given limited entrance to the United States. There were few intact Chinese families who could live in the United States and subsequently laborers returned frequently to China to marry and visit their families. Consequently, the mostly male Chinese communities were often seen as aberrant and not adaptable to the local culture. Fear arose, as rising numbers of immigrants were non-Christians, they were labeled as heathens, as parodied by Chinese American journalist and activist Wong Chin Foo in his 1887 essay "Why Am I a Heathen?" and deemed incapable of assimilating appropriately to American values.

The treaty was amended in 1880 to suspend further Chinese immigration. In 1882, the Chinese Exclusion Act was passed preventing further immigration of labor to the United States but protecting the rights of immigrants already living here. The Act was later altered to require Chinese nationals in the United States who wanted to temporarily leave the country to have a reentry permit. Chae Chan Ping was a Chinese citizen, living in San Francisco, who had worked in California from 1875 to 1887 when he wanted to visit China to see his family. He obtained the necessary reentry permit before he left the United States. During his absence, Congress passed the Scott Act, 1888, which prohibited Chinese workers abroad from returning to the United States and stranded tens of thousands of Chinese outside the United States. Chae Chan Ping was interviewed upon his arrival, the immigration officer did not accept his reentry certification and denied him access to the United States.

CHAE CHAN PING v. UNITED STATES, 130 U.S. 581 (1889), (CHINESE EXCLUSION CASE)

Justice Field Delivered the Opinion of the Court

Vote: 8–0

The validity of the [Scott Act of 1888] is assailed as being in effect an expulsion from the country of Chinese laborers, in violation of existing treaties between the United States and the government of China, and of rights vested in them under the laws of Congress.

The discovery of gold in California in 1848, as is well known, was followed by a large immigration thither from all parts of the world, attracted not only by the hope of gain from the mines, but from the great prices paid for all kinds of labor. The news of the discovery penetrated China, and laborers came from there in great numbers, a few with their own means, but by far the greater number under contract with employers for whose benefit they worked. These laborers readily secured employment, and, as domestic servants, and in various kinds of outdoor work, proved to be exceedingly useful. For some years little opposition was made to them except when they sought to work in the mines, but, as their numbers increased, they began to engage in various mechanical pursuits and trades, and thus came in competition with our artisans and mechanics, as well as our laborers in the field ... They were generally industrious and frugal. Not being accompanied by families except in rare instances, their expenses were small and they were content with the simplest fare, such as would not suffice for our laborers and artisans. The competition between them and our people was for this reason altogether in their favor, and the consequent irritation, proportionately deep and bitter, was followed, in many cases, by open conflicts, to the great disturbance of the public peace.

The differences of race added greatly to the difficulties of the situation. Notwithstanding the favorable provisions of the new articles of the treaty of 1868, by which all the privileges, immunities, and exemptions were extended to subjects of China in the United States which were accorded to citizens or subjects of the most favored nation, they remained strangers in the land, residing apart by themselves and adhering to the customs and usages of their own country. It seemed impossible for them to assimilate with our people or to make any change in their habits or modes of living. As they grew in numbers each year, the people of the coast saw, or believed they saw, in the facility of immigration and in the crowded millions of China, where population presses upon the means of subsistence, great danger that at no distant day that portion of our country would be overrun by them unless prompt action was taken to restrict their immigration. The people there accordingly petitioned earnestly for protective legislation.

In December, 1878, the [California Constitutional Convention petitioned] Congress upon it, setting forth in substance that the presence of Chinese laborers had a baneful effect upon the material interests of the state, and upon public morals; that their immigration was in numbers approaching the character of an Oriental invasion, and was a menace to our civilization; that the discontent from this cause was not confined to any political party, or to any class or nationality, but was well nigh universal; that they retained the habits and customs of their own country, and in fact constituted a Chinese settlement within the state, without any interest in our country or its institutions, and praying Congress to take measures to prevent their further immigration. This memorial was presented to Congress in February, 1879. So urgent and constant were the prayers for relief against existing and anticipated evils, both from the public authorities of the Pacific coast and from private individuals that Congress was impelled to act on the subject. Many persons, however, both in and out of Congress, were of opinion that so long as the treaty remained unmodified, legislation restricting immigration would be a breach of faith with China. A statute was accordingly passed appropriating money to send commissioners to China to act with our minister there in negotiating and concluding by treaty a settlement of such matters of interest between the two governments ...

The government of China ... agreed that notwithstanding the stipulations of former treaties, the United States might regulate, limit, or suspend the coming of Chinese laborers, or their residence therein, without absolutely forbidding it, whenever in their opinion the interests of the country... might require such action. Legislation for such regulation, limitation, or suspension was entrusted to the discretion of our government, with the condition that it should only be such as might be necessary for that purpose, and that the immigrants should not be maltreated or abused ...

The same difficulties and embarrassments continued with respect to the proof of their former residence. Parties were able to pass successfully the required examination as to their residence before November 17, 1880, who, it was generally believed, had never visited our shores. To prevent the possibility of the policy of excluding Chinese laborers being evaded, the [Scott] Act of October 1, 1888, the validity of which is the subject of consideration in this case, was passed ...

The validity of this act, as already mentioned, is assailed as being in effect an expulsion from the country of Chinese laborers in violation of existing treaties between the United States and the government of China and of rights vested in them under the laws of Congress ... By the Constitution, laws made in pursuance thereof, and treaties made under the authority of the United States, are both declared to be the supreme law of the land, and no paramount authority is given to one over the other ...

✶ There being nothing in the treaties between China and the United States to impair the validity of the act of Congress of October 1, 1888, was it on any other ground beyond the competency of Congress to pass it? If so, it must be because it was not within the power of Congress to prohibit Chinese laborers who had at the time departed from the United States, or should subsequently depart, from returning to the United States. Those laborers are not citizens of the United States; they are aliens. That the government of the United States, through the action of the legislative department, can exclude aliens from its territory is a proposition which we do not think open to controversy. Jurisdiction over its own territory to that extent is an incident of every independent nation. It is a part of its independence.

If it could not exclude aliens, it would be to that extent subject to the control of another power.

While under our Constitution and form of government the great mass of local matters is controlled by local authorities, the United States, in their relation to foreign countries and their subjects or citizens, are one nation, invested with powers which belong to independent nations, the exercise of which can be invoked for the maintenance of its absolute independence and security throughout its entire territory. The powers to declare war, make treaties, suppress insurrection, repel invasion, regulate foreign commerce, secure republican governments to the states, and admit subjects of other nations to citizenship are all sovereign powers, restricted in their exercise only by the Constitution itself and considerations of public policy and justice which control, more or less, the conduct of all civilized nations.

The power of the government to exclude foreigners from the country whenever in its judgment the public interests require such exclusion has been asserted in repeated instances, and never denied by the executive or legislative departments.

The power of exclusion of foreigners being an incident of sovereignty belonging to the government of the United States as a part of those sovereign powers delegated by the Constitution, the right to its exercise at any time when, in the judgment of the government, the interests of the country require it, cannot be granted away or restrained on behalf of anyone.

... Whatever license, therefore, Chinese laborers may have obtained, previous to the Act of October 1, 1888, to return to the United States after their departure is held at the will of the government, revocable at any time at its pleasure. Whether a proper consideration by our government of its previous laws or a proper respect for the nation whose subjects are affected by its action ought to have qualified its inhibition and made it applicable only to persons departing from the country after the passage of the act are not questions for judicial determination. If there be any just ground of complaint on the part of China, it must be made to the political department of our government, which is alone competent to act upon the subject.

Order affirmed.

✶ Upheld the Scott Act of 1888

1. How does the Court dictate the scope of judicial authority in this case? How is it justified?
2. Are there constitutional limitations of congressional authority to regulate immigration?
3. What are the legal implications for Chinese immigrants?
4. Can you think of other times when immigration limitations were based on racial concerns – not necessarily based on foreign policy objectives? What might be the difference?

✶ Court ruled that ~~the~~ Congress had the inherent power to regulate immigration ✶

Similar cases also impacted birthright citizens in the United States – those whose citizenships were based on being born in the United States – such as in *United States* v. *Ju Toy*, 198 U.S. 253 (1905). Ju Toy was born in the United States and of Chinese descent. Because he was a U.S. citizen, he assumed the Chinese Exclusion laws did not apply to him. After visiting China, he returned home to San Francisco but was not allowed to disembark and an immigration official ordered deportation, despite his citizenship status. He filed a *writ of habeas corpus* in the federal District Court, demanding that the government justify his detention, the court found Ju Toy to be a citizen and ordered his release; the U.S. government appealed. As the case demonstrates, many exclusion cases were litigated by Chinese immigrants and citizens, especially those who were separated from their families (Nackenoff and Novkov 2021).

✳ affirmed the power of congress to delegate immigration

UNITED STATES v. JU TOY, 198 U.S. 253 (1905)

Justice Holmes Delivered the Opinion of the Court, Joined by Chief Justice Fuller, and Justices Harlan, Brown, White, and McKenna

Vote: 6–3

The broad question is presented whether or not the decision of the Secretary of Commerce and Labor is conclusive. It was held in *United States* v. *Sing Tuck*, that the Act of August 18, 1894 purported to make it so, but whether the statute could have that effect constitutionally was left untouched, except by a reference to cases where an opinion already had been expressed. To quote the latest first, in *The Japanese Immigrant Case*, 189 U.S. 86 [1903] it was said:

> That Congress may exclude aliens of a particular race from the United States, prescribe the terms and conditions upon which certain classes of aliens may come to this country, establish regulations for sending out of the country such aliens as come here in violation of law, and commit the enforcement of such provisions, conditions, and regulations exclusively to executive officers, without judicial intervention are principles firmly established by the decisions of this Court.

In *Fok Young Yo* v. *United States*, 185 U.S. 296 [1902], it was held that the decision of the collector of customs on the right of transit across the territory of the United States was conclusive, and, still more to the point, in *Lem Moon Sing* v. *United States*, 158 U.S. 538 [1895], where the petitioner for *habeas corpus* alleged facts which, if true, gave him a right to enter and remain in the country, it was held that the decision of the collector was final as to whether or not he belonged to the privileged class.

It is true that it may be argued that these cases are not directly conclusive of the point now under decision. It may be said that the parties concerned were aliens, and that, although they alleged absolute rights, and facts which it was contended went to the jurisdiction of the officer making the decision, still their rights were only treaty or statutory rights, and therefore were subject to the implied qualification imposed by the later statute, which made the decision of the collector with regard to them final ...

It is established, as we have said, that the act purports to make the decision of the Department final, whatever the ground on which the right to enter the country is claimed – as well when it is citizenship as when it is domicile – and the belonging to a class excepted from the exclusion acts. It also is established by the former case and others which it cites that the relevant portion of the Act of August 18, 1894 is not void as a whole. The statute has been upheld and enforced. But the relevant portion being a single section, accomplishing all its results by the same general words, must be valid as to all that it embraces, or altogether void. An exception of a class constitutionally exempted cannot be read into those general words merely for the purpose of saving what remains. That has been decided over and over again.

... The petitioner, although physically within our boundaries, is to be regarded as if he had been stopped at the limit of our jurisdiction, and kept there while his right to enter was under debate. If, for the purpose of argument, we assume that the Fifth Amendment applies to him, and that to deny entrance to a citizen is to deprive him of liberty, we nevertheless are of opinion that with regard to him due process of law does not require judicial trial. That is the result of the cases which we have cited, and the almost necessary result of the power of Congress to pass exclusion laws. That the decision may be entrusted to an executive officer, and that his decision is due process of law, was affirmed and explained in *Nishimura Ekiu* v. *United States*, 142 U. S. 651 [1892], and in *Fong Yue Ting* v. *United States* ...

Justice Brewer, Joined by Justice Peckham, Dissenting

I am unable to concur in the views expressed in the foregoing opinion, and, believing the matter of most profound importance, I give my reasons therefor.

The proposition ... is that, unless the petitioner for a *writ of habeas corpus* shows that the immigration officers have been guilty of unlawful action or abuse of their discretion or powers, the writ must be denied, and the petitioner banished from the country. In order to see what action is lawful, I refer to the rules prescribed under the authority hereinafter referred to.

It will be seen that, under these rules, it is the duty of the immigration officer to prevent communication with the Chinese seeking to land by anyone except his own officers. He is to conduct a private examination, with only the witnesses present whom he may designate. His counsel, if, under the circumstances, the Chinaman has been able to procure one, is permitted to look at the testimony, but not to make a copy of it. He must give notice of appeal, if he wishes one, within two days, and within three days thereafter the record is to be sent to the Secretary at Washington, and every doubtful question is to be settled in favor of the government. No provision is made for summoning witnesses from a distance or for taking depositions, and, if, for instance, the person landing at San Francisco was born and brought up in Ohio, it may well be that he would be powerless to find any testimony in San Francisco to prove his citizenship. If he does not happen to have money, he must go without the testimony, and when the papers are sent to Washington (3,000 miles away from the port, which, in this case, was the place of landing), he may no have the means of employing counsel to present his case to the Secretary. If this be not a star-chamber proceeding of the most stringent sort, what more is necessary to make it one?

I do not see how anyone can read those rules and hold that they constitute due process of law for the arrest and deportation of a citizen of the United States. If they do in proceedings by the United States, they will also in proceedings instituted by a state, and an obnoxious class may be put beyond the protection of the Constitution by ministerial officers of a state, proceeding in strict accord with exactly similar rules.

It will be borne in mind that the petitioner has been judicially determined to be a free-born American citizen, and the contention of the government, sustained by the judgment of this Court, is that a citizen, guilty of no crime – for it is no crime for a citizen to come back to his native land – must, by the action of a ministerial officer, be punished by deportation and banishment, without trial by jury and without judicial examination.

Such a decision is, to my mind, appalling. By all the authorities the banishment of a citizen is punishment, and punishment of the severest kind ...

President Madison, in his report on the Virginia resolutions concerning the alien and sedition laws, said, referring to the possibilities which attend a removal from the country, "if a banishment of this sort be not a punishment, and among the severest of punishments, it will be difficult to imagine a doom to which the name can be applied."

It is true in this case the petitioner was returning to San Francisco from China. Whether his absence from this country had been for a few weeks or a few years is not shown, nor does it matter. The right of a citizen is not lost by a temporary absence from his native land, and when he returns he is entitled to all the protection which he had when he left.

Summing this up, banishment is a punishment, and of the severest sort. There can be no punishment except for crime. This petitioner has been guilty of no crime, and so judicially determined. Yet, in defiance of this adjudication of innocence, with only an examination before a ministerial officer, he is compelled to suffer punishment as a criminal, and is denied the protection of either a grand or petit jury.

But, it is said, that he did not prove his innocence before the ministerial officer. Can one who judicially establishes his innocence of any offense be punished for crime by the action of a ministerial officer? Can he be punished because he has failed to show to the satisfaction of that officer that he is innocent of an offense? The Constitution declares that "the privilege of the writ of habeas corpus shall not be suspended, unless when, in cases of invasion or rebellion, the public safety may require it." There is no rebellion or invasion. Can a citizen be deprived of the benefit of that so much vaunted writ of protection by the action of a ministerial officer?

So it appears that this Court discharged from the custody of the immigration officers a person of Chinese descent on the ground that he was a citizen of the United States, doing this upon the concession of the government that, if he was a citizen, the exclusion acts had no application to him; that Congress in terms makes the decision of the immigration officer final only when the party is an alien, and that the rules prescribed by the proper department exclude from the operation of the law citizens of the United States of Chinese descent. Yet, in spite of all this, it is held that this citizen of the United States must, by virtue of the ruling of a ministerial officer, be banished from the country of which he is a citizen. And this upon the ground that such officer has a right to decide whether he is or is not a citizen, and his decision on the question excludes all judicial examination.

... [I]t is said that the exclusion acts speak of Chinese persons, and that such term includes citizens as well as aliens, and therefore Congress has given power to the immigration officers to banish citizens of the United States if they happen to be of Chinese descent. But obviously the statutes refer to citizens of China, and not to citizens of the United States. The treaty of 1894, in execution of which most of these statutes were passed, speaks, on the one hand, of Chinese subjects in the United States, and, on the other, of citizens of the United States in China. The treaty declared the rights and burdens of Chinese citizens in the United States, as well as the rights and burdens of citizens of the United States in China. The treaty, then, placing Chinese subjects over against American citizens, must have had in mind citizenship, and not race. The legislation carrying that treaty into effect must be interpreted in the light of that fact. The statutes of the United States expressly limit the finality of the determination of the immigration officers to the case of aliens. It has been conceded by the government that these statutes do not apply to citizens, and this Court made a most important decision based upon that concession. The rules of the Department declare that the statutes do not apply to citizens, and yet, in the face of all this, we are told that they may be enforced against citizens, and that Congress so intended. Banishment of a citizen not merely removes him from the limits of his native land, but puts him beyond the reach of any of the protecting clauses of the Constitution. In other words, it strips him of all the rights which are given to a citizen. I cannot believe that Congress intended to provide that a citizen, simply because he belongs to an obnoxious race, can be deprived of all the liberty and protection which the Constitution guarantees, and if it did so intend, I do not believe that it has the power to do so.

1. How should citizenship status matter in this situation?
2. On what grounds should a citizen be precluded from returning to their home country? How did the majority justify this decision?
3. On what grounds did the dissent challenge this decision?

The Chinese were the only racialized group that had immigration legislation written specifically regarding their treatment (Barde 2004), most legislation focused on limiting access by country. Just as African Americans used litigation as an organized approach to challenge legalized segregation in the twentieth century (see Chapter 3), Chinese Americans used a similar approach against the Exclusion Laws. One scholar estimates that "Chinese litigants filed at least seven thousand appeals in the first ten years of the Exclusion Act's operation, and between 1891 and 1905 there were another twenty-six hundred" (referenced by Nackenoff and Novkov 2021, 43). It was not until 1922, in *Ng Fung Ho* v. *White* (259 U.S. 276) that the Supreme Court overturned this decision, allowing for a judicial hearing for U.S. citizens of Chinese descent who file a *habeas corpus* claim.

2.3.2 Defining "Race" for Citizenship

The construction of racial classifications such as "Asian American" also raised questions of what is "White" and later, what is "colored?" These definitions became significant in terms of deciding who can immigrate to the United States. The construction of "whiteness" transformed, depending on national interests and political agendas (Lopez 1996), heightening during the era of state-sanctioned Jim Crow segregation (see Chapter 3 and *Gong Lum* v. *Rice* (1927) and *Westminster* v. *Mendez* (1947)). For instance, in the case of *United States* v. *Bhagat Singh Thind* (1923), Bhagat Singh Thind was from the far northwestern regions of India where he had been classified as "Caucasian" or "Aryan" under some racial classifications. He sought to become a U.S. naturalized citizen under the Naturalization Act, 1906, which extended citizenship only to "free white persons" and persons of African descent. For this reason, the Court had to determine if he would be classified as "White" in the United States.

UNITED STATES v. *BHAGAT SINGH THIND*, 261 U.S. 204 (1923)

Justice Sutherland Delivered the Unanimous Opinion of the Court

Vote: 9–0

This cause is here upon a certificate from the Circuit Court of appeals requesting the instruction of this Court in respect of the following questions:

1. Is a high-caste Hindu, of full Indian blood, born at Amritsar, Punjab, India, a white person within the meaning of § 2169, Revised Statutes?

2. Does the Act of February 5, 1917 (39 Stat. 875, § 3) disqualify from naturalization as citizens those Hindus now barred by that act

who had lawfully entered the United States prior to the passage of said act?

Section 2169 provides that the provisions of the Naturalization Act "shall apply to aliens being free white persons and to aliens of African nativity and to persons of African descent."

If the applicant is a white person within the meaning of this section, he is entitled to naturalization; otherwise not. In *Ozawa* v. *United States*, 260 U.S. 178 [(1922)], we had occasion to consider the application of these words to the case of a cultivated Japanese, and were constrained to hold that he was not within their meaning. As there pointed out, the provision is not that any particular class of persons shall be excluded, but it is, in effect, that only white persons shall be included within the privilege of the statute.

Following a long line of decisions of the lower federal courts, we held that the words imported a racial, and not an individual, test, and were meant to indicate only persons of what is popularly known as the Caucasian race. But, as there pointed out, the conclusion that the phrase "white persons" and the word "Caucasian" are synonymous does not end the matter ... Mere ability on the part of an applicant for naturalization to establish a line of descent from a Caucasian ancestor will not ... necessarily conclude the inquiry ...

They imply, as we have said, a racial test; but the term "race" is one which, for the practical purposes of the statute, must be applied to a group of living persons now possessing in common the requisite characteristics, not to groups of persons who are supposed to be or really are descended from some remote common ancestor, but who, whether they both resemble him to a greater or less extent, have at any rate ceased altogether to resemble one another. It may be true that the blond Scandinavian and the brown Hindu have a common ancestor in the dim reaches of antiquity, but the average man knows perfectly well that there are unmistakable and profound differences between them today, and it is not impossible, if that common ancestor could be materialized in the flesh, we should discover

that he was himself sufficiently differentiated from both of his descendants to preclude his racial classification with either. The question for determination is not, therefore, whether, by the speculative processes of ethnological reasoning, we may present a probability to the scientific mind that they have the same origin, but whether we can satisfy the common understanding that they are now the same or sufficiently the same to justify the interpreters of a statute – written in the words of common speech, for common understanding, by unscientific men – in classifying them together in the statutory category as white persons ...

The eligibility of this applicant for citizenship is based on the sole fact that he is of high-caste Hindu stock, born in Punjab, one of the extreme northwestern districts of India, and classified by certain scientific authorities as of the Caucasian or Aryan race. The Aryan theory, as a racial basis, seems to be discredited by most, if not all, modern writers on the subject of ethnology.

The term "Aryan" has to do with linguistic, and not at all with physical, characteristics, and it would seem reasonably clear that mere resemblance in language, indicating a common linguistic root buried in remotely ancient soil, is altogether inadequate to prove common racial origin. There is, and can be, no assurance that the so-called Aryan language was not spoken by a variety of races living in proximity to one another. Our own history has witnessed the adoption of the English tongue by millions of negroes, whose descendants can never be classified racially with the descendants of white persons, notwithstanding both may speak a common root language.

The word "Caucasian" is in scarcely better repute. It is, at best, a conventional term, with an altogether fortuitous origin, which, under scientific manipulation, has come to include far more than the unscientific mind suspects. [I]t includes not only the Hindu, but some of the Polynesians (that is, the Maori, Tahitians, Samoans, Hawaiians, and others), the Hamites of Africa, upon the ground of the Caucasic cast of their features, though in color they range from brown to black. We venture to think that the average well informed white American would learn with some degree of astonishment that the race to which he belongs is made up of such heterogeneous elements.

It may be, therefore, that a given group cannot be properly assigned to any of the enumerated grand racial divisions. The type may have been so changed by intermixture of blood as to justify an intermediate classification. Something very like this has actually taken place in India.

We are unable to agree with the district court, or with other lower federal courts, in the conclusion that a native Hindu is eligible for naturalization under § 2169. The words of familiar speech, which were used by the original framers of the law, were intended to include only the type of man whom they knew as white. The immigration of that day was almost exclusively from the British Isles and Northwestern Europe, whence they and their forebears had come. When they extended the privilege of American citizenship to "any alien being a free white person," it was these immigrants – bone of their bone and flesh of their flesh – and their kind whom they must have had affirmatively in mind. The succeeding years brought immigrants from Eastern, Southern and Middle Europe, among them the Slavs and the dark-eyed, swarthy people of Alpine and Mediterranean stock, and these were received as unquestionably akin to those already here and readily amalgamated with them. It was the descendants of these, and other immigrants of like origin, who constituted the white population of the country when § 2169, reenacting the naturalization test of 1790, was adopted, and, there is no reason to doubt, with like intent and meaning.

What we now hold is that the words "free white persons" are words of common speech, to be interpreted in accordance with the understanding of the common man, synonymous with the word "Caucasian" only as that word is popularly understood. As so understood and used, whatever may be the speculations of the ethnologist, it does not include the body of people to whom the appellee belongs. It is a matter of familiar observation and knowledge that the physical group characteristics of the Hindus render them readily distinguishable from the various groups of persons in this country commonly recognized as white. The children of English, French, German, Italian, Scandinavian, and other European parentage quickly merge into the mass of our population and lose the distinctive hallmarks of their European origin. On the other hand, it cannot be doubted that the children born in this country of Hindu parents would retain indefinitely the clear evidence of their ancestry. It is very far from our thought to suggest the slightest question of racial superiority or inferiority. What we suggest is merely racial difference, and it is of such character and extent that the great body of our people instinctively recognize it and reject the thought of assimilation.

It is not without significance in this connection that Congress, by the Act of February 5, 1917, has now excluded from admission into this country all natives of Asia within designated limits of latitude and longitude, including the whole of India. This not only constitutes conclusive evidence of the congressional attitude of opposition to Asiatic immigration generally, but is persuasive of a similar attitude toward Asiatic naturalization as well, since it is not likely that Congress would be willing to accept as citizens a class of persons whom it rejects as immigrants.

It follows that a negative answer must be given to the first question, which disposes of the case and renders an answer to the second question unnecessary, and it will be so certified.

1. Why is the Court concerned about Bhagat Singh Thind's religious background and caste status in India in making this determination?
2. How might this decision, and decisions like this one, explain to us the legal construction of race in the United States?
3. What might this case tell us about the "scientific racism" of the nineteenth century?

Ian Haney Lopez, in his work *White by Law*, demonstrates:

... law constructs race, of course it does so within the larger context of society, and so law is only one of many institutions and a force implicated in the formation of races ... [Law] does more than simply codify race in the limited senses of merely giving legal definition to pre-existing social categories. Instead, legislatures and courts have served not only to fix the boundaries of race in the forms we recognize today, but also to define the content of racial identities and specify their relative privilege or disadvantage in U.S. society. (Lopez 1996, 10)

For Lopez and other scholars, these cases demonstrate that not only does the law construct the meaning of Asian American or Hispanic, but they also help to define the identity of "White" (Ignatiev 1995; Roediger 2007).

This question reappears *In re Ah Yup* (1878) where Ah Yup, a native of China, sought U.S. citizenship. His was the first request by a Chinese individual for naturalization – he met all legal qualifications and only the question of eligibility based on race remained. In this case, we see the federal court rely on common knowledge and scientific claims to justify their definition of the compass of "whiteness." The Supreme Court eventually relied on common understandings as legally defining race demonstrates "racial classification finds its origins in social practice" (Lopez 1996, 6). The result of this decision was that Indian Americans, even those who were naturalized citizens, lost their citizenship status after this decision.

IN RE AH YUP, 5 SAWY. 155, CIRCUIT CT, D. CAL. (1878)

Circuit Judge Sawyer Delivered the Decision

In all the acts of congress relating to the naturalization of aliens, from that of April 14, 1802, down to the Revised Statutes, the language has been "that any alien, being a free white person, may be admitted to become a citizen," etc. After the adoption of the thirteenth and fourteenth amendments to the national constitution; the former prohibiting slavery, and the latter declaring who shall be citizens, congress in the act of July 14, 1870, amending the naturalization laws, added the following provision: "That the naturalization laws are hereby extended to aliens of African nativity, and to persons of African descent."

The questions are: 1. Is a person of the Mongolian race a "white person" within the meaning of the statute? 2. Do these provisions exclude all but white persons and persons of African nativity or African descent? Words in a statute, other than technical terms, should be taken in their ordinary sense. The words "white person," as well argued by petitioner's counsel, taken in a strictly literal sense, constitute a very indefinite description of a class of persons, where none can be said to be literally white and those called white may be found of every shade from the lightest blonde to the most swarthy brunette. But these words in this country, at least, have undoubtedly acquired a well settled meaning in common popular speech, and they are constantly used in the sense so acquired in the literature of the country, as well as in common parlance. As ordinarily used everywhere in the United States, one would scarcely fail to understand that the party employing the words "white person" would intend a person of the Caucasian race.

In speaking of the various classifications of races, Webster in his dictionary says, "The common classification is that of Blumenbach, who makes five. 1. The Caucasian, or white race, to which belong the greater part of the European nations and those of Western Asia; 2. The Mongolian, or yellow race, occupying Tartary, China, Japan, etc.; 3. The Ethiopian or Negro (black) race, occupying all Africa, except the north; 4. The American, or red race, containing the Indians of North and South America; and, 5. The Malay, or Brown race, occupying the islands of the Indian Archipelago," etc. This division ... is founded on the combined characteristics of complexion, hair and skull. Linnaeus makes four divisions, founded on the color of the skin: "1. European, whitish; 2. American, coppery; 3. Asiatic, tawny; and, 4. African, black." Cuvier makes three: Caucasian, Mongol, and Negro. Others make many more, but no one includes the white, or Caucasian, with the Mongolian or yellow race; and no one of those classifications recognizing color as one of the distinguishing characteristics includes the Mongolian in the white or whitish race.

Neither in popular language, in literature, nor in scientific nomenclature, do we ordinarily, if ever, find the words "white person" used in a sense so comprehensive as to include an individual of the Mongolian race. Yet, in all, color, notwithstanding its indefiniteness as a word of description, is made an important factor in the basis adopted for the distinction and classification of races. I am not aware that the term "white person," as used in the statutes as they have stood from 1802 till the late revision, was ever supposed to include a Mongolian. While I find nothing in the history of the country, in common or scientific usage, or in legislative proceedings, to indicate that congress intended to include in the term "white person" any other

than an individual of the Caucasian race, I do find much in the proceedings of congress to show that it was universally understood in that body, in its recent legislation, that it excluded Mongolians. At the time of the amendment, in 1870, extending the naturalization laws to the African race, [Senator Charles] Sumner made repeated and strenuous efforts to strike the word "white" from the naturalization laws, or to accomplish the same object by other language. It was opposed on the sole ground that the effect would be to authorize the admission of Chinese to citizenship. Every senator, who spoke upon the subject, assumed that they were then excluded by the term "white person," and that the amendment would admit them, and the amendment was advocated on the one hand, and opposed on the other, upon that single idea. Senator Morton, in the course of the discussion said: "This amendment involves the whole Chinese problem. The country has just awakened to the question and to the enormous magnitude of the question, involving a possible immigration of many millions, involving another civilization; involving labor problems that no intellect can solve without study and time. Are you now prepared to settle the Chinese problem, thus in advance inviting that immigration?" Senator Sumner replied: "Senators undertake to disturb us in our judgment by reminding us of the possibility of large numbers swarming from China; but the answer to all this is very obvious and very simple. If the Chinese come here they will come for citizenship, or merely for labor. If they come for citizenship then in this desire do they give a pledge of loyalty to our institutions, and where is the peril in such vows? They are peaceful and industrious; how can their citizenship be the occasion of solicitude?"

... It is clear, from these proceedings that congress retained the word "white" in the naturalization laws for the sole purpose of excluding the Chinese from the right of naturalization ... Thus, whatever latitudinarian construction might otherwise have been given to the term "white person," it is entirely clear that congress intended by this legislation to exclude Mongolians from the right of naturalization. I am, therefore, of the opinion that a native of China, of the Mongolian race, is not a white person within the meaning of the act of congress.

The second question is answered in the discussion of the first ... It was certainly intended to have some operation, or it would not have been adopted. The purpose undoubtedly was to restore the law to the condition in which it stood before the revision, and to exclude the Chinese. It was intended to exclude some classes, and as all white aliens and those of the African race are entitled to naturalization under other words, it is difficult to perceive whom it could exclude unless it be the Chinese. It follows that the petition must be denied, and it is so ordered.

1. How does this case parallel *Dred Scott, Bhagat Singh Thind*, and *Elk* v. *Wilkins*? In what ways does it differ?
2. What do these cases tell us about the debates around citizenship and race/ethnicity?
3. How do we see these debates reemerging in the twenty-first century?
4. How does the question of assimilation undergird this policy of racialization?

These same questions were raised for the Latino community in the case of *In re Rodríguez* (1897). Ricardo Rodríguez, born in Mexico, lived in San Antonio, Texas, for ten years and came before the federal District Court for final confirmation of his U.S. citizenship. The consequence of this action was an unsuccessful attempt in the federal courts to disenfranchise all Texas-Mexicans (Tejanos) (Molina 2014). At issue was the 1872 federal law requiring that U.S. citizenship only be granted to Whites, Africans, and those of African descent.

IN RE RODRÍGUEZ, 81 F. 337 U.S. D.C., W.D. TEX. (1897)

District Judge Maxey, after stating the Case, Delivered the following Opinion

... The contention is that, by the letter of the statute, a Mexican citizen, answering to the description of the applicant, is, because of his color, denied the right to become a citizen of the United States by naturalization; and, in support of this view, the following authorities are relied upon: *In re Ah Yup* (decided by Judge Sawyer in 1878) 5 Sawy. 155, 1 Fed. Cas. 223 (1878); *In re Camille* (decided by Judge Deady in 1880) 6 Fed. 256; *In re Kanaka Nian* (decided by the Supreme Court of Utah in 1889) 21 Pac. 993; *In re Saito* (decided by Judge Colt in 1894) 62 Fed. 126; and 2 Kent, Comm. 73, when the learned chancellor expresses a doubt in these words:

> Perhaps there might be difficulties also as to the copper-colored natives of American, or the yellow or tawny races of Asiatics, and it may well be doubted whether any of them are white persons, within the purview of the law.

Of the four cases above cited, *In re Ah Yup* is the first in point of time, and the leading one. The four applications were denied, Ah Yup being a native of China, Camille a native of British Columbia, and of half Indian and half white blood, Nian a native of the Hawaiian Islands, whose ancestors were Kanakas, and Saito a native of Japan. When the Case of Ah Yup was decided, the Chinese question was flagrant on the Pacific slope, and Judge Sawyer seemed to think, predicating his conclusion upon the debates in congress, that the purpose of the amendment extending the right of naturalization to Africans and persons of African descent was to exclude Chinese from the benefits of naturalization. To quote his own language:

> ... The purpose [of § 2169] undoubtedly was to restore the law to the condition in which it stood before the revision, and to exclude the Chinese. It was intended to exclude some classes, and, as all white aliens and those of the African race are entitled to naturalization under other words, it is difficult to perceive whom it could exclude, unless it be the Chinese.

The opinion of Judge Sawyer is by no means decisive of the present question, as his language may well convey the meaning that the amendment of the naturalization statutes referred to by him was intended solely as a prohibition against the naturalization of members of the Mongolian race. The naturalization of Chinese is, however, no longer an open question, as section 14 of the act of May 6, 1882, expressly provides "that hereafter no state court or court of the United States shall admit Chinese to citizenship; and all laws in conflict with this act are hereby repealed."

If Chinese were denied the right to become naturalized citizens under laws existing when *In re Ah Yup* was decided, why did congress subsequently enact the prohibitory statute above quoted? Indeed, it is a debatable question whether the term "free white person," as used in the original act of 1790, was not employed for the sole purpose of withholding the right of citizenship from the black or African race and the Indians then inhabiting this country. But it is not necessary to enter upon a discussion of that question; nor is it deemed material to inquire to what race ethnological writers would assign the present applicant. If the strict scientific classification of the anthropologist should be adopted, he would probably not be classed as white. It is certain he is not an African, nor a person of African descent. According to his own statement, he is a "pure-blooded Mexican," bearing no relation to the Aztecs or original races of Mexico. Being, then, a citizen of Mexico, may he be naturalized pursuant to the laws of congress? If debarred by the strict letter of the law from receiving letters of citizenship, is he embraced within the intent and meaning of the statute? If he falls within the meaning and intent of the law, his application should be granted, notwithstanding the letter of the statute may be against him.

A reference to the constitution of the republic of Texas and the constitution, laws, and treaties of the United States will disclose that both that republic and the United States have freely, during the past 60 years, conferred upon Mexicans the rights and privileges of American citizenship, not individually, it is true, but by various collective acts of naturalization ...

It is said by Mr. Justice McLean, in his dissenting opinion in *Scott v. Sandford*, 21 U.S. (8 Wheat.) 393 (1856), that:

> On the question of citizenship it must be admitted that we have not been very fastidious. Under the late treaty with Mexico, we have made citizens of all grades, combinations, and colors. The same was done in the admission of Louisiana and Florida. No one over doubted, and no court ever held, that the people of these territories did not become citizens under the treaty. They have exercised all the rights of citizens, without being naturalized under the acts of congress.

On September 9, 1850, congress passed three acts having more or less bearing upon the question under discussion, to wit, the act for the admission of California into the Union, and the acts establishing territorial governments for New Mexico and Utah. By the act admitting California, Mexicans who were recognized as citizens by the treaty of Guadalupe-Hidalgo became citizens of the new state ...

It has been shown that Mexicans (and the term includes all Mexicans, without discrimination as to color) who remained in the ceded territory, and who failed to declare their intention within one year to remain Mexican citizens, became, by virtue of the stipulations of the treaty of February 2, 1848, citizens of the United States ...

The next act affecting the question of citizenship to which attention will be directed is the Fourteenth Amendment of the Constitution, declared to be part of the organic law, by resolution of Congress, July 21, 1868. By this amendment, which completely overthrew the last remaining vestige of the doctrine announced in *Scott* v. *Sandford*, 21 U.S. (8 Wheat.) 393 (1856), touching the question of citizenship of the African, and invested the native-born negro with the rights of an American citizen (*Slaughterhouse Cases*, 83 U.S. (16 Wall.) 36 (1973); *Elk* v. *Wilkins*, 112 U.S. 94 (1884); *Strauder* v. *West Virginia*, 100 U.S. 303 (1880); ... it is provided: "All persons born or naturalized in the United States, and subject to the jurisdiction thereof, are citizens of the United States and of the state wherein they reside."

While this amendment, as held in the authorities last cited, was intended primarily for the benefit of the negro race, it also confers the right of citizenship upon persons of all other races, white, yellow, or red, born or naturalized in the United States, and "subject to the jurisdiction thereof." The language has been held to embrace even Chinese, to whom the laws of naturalization do not extend. Mexicans, therefore, born in the United States, and who, at the date of birth, were subject to the jurisdiction of our government ... are citizens of the United States and of the state wherein they reside. The intimation in some of the briefs of counsel that *Elk* v. *Wilkins*, 112 U.S. 94 (1884), excludes Mexicans from citizenship, is not maintainable. That case refers exclusively to tribal Indians born and residing within the territory forming a part of the United States ...

When all the foregoing laws, treaties, and constitutional provisions are considered, which either affirmatively confer the rights of citizenship upon Mexicans, or tacitly recognize in them the right of individual naturalization, the conclusion forces itself ... that citizens of Mexico are eligible to American citizenship, and may be individually naturalized by complying with the provisions of our laws ...

1. This case was written by a federal district judge, what kind of precedental authority does it possess and to whom does it apply?
2. How does it engage the prior precedents on citizenship we have discussed?
3. Why would the United States worry more about the racial classifications of citizens, than the country from which they are emigrating?

Legislative (demonstrated through immigration laws), presidential (through treaties), and judicial concerns regarding the racial backgrounds of potential U.S. citizens has spanned generations. We have a history of focusing more on the race of new citizens than the country of origin from which they emigrate. In the process of defining "citizenship" the nation was also defining and creating new racial groups many of which were largely only relevant in the United States and other immigrant nations.

How does this pattern help to explain many of the current debates we see around immigration today? If biology has shown us that racial categories are essentially meaningless in a physical sense, and our understanding of culture demonstrates racial categories confound many distinct communities, how should we determine who should immigrate to the United States in the twenty-first century?

2.3.3 Japanese Internment and Rights of Citizenship

During the years of the Second World War (1939–1945) when the United States and its allies were at war with Germany, Italy, and Japan, just as in other times of instability, fear of "the other" resulted in policies targeted against despised racial communities. After Japan's bombing of the U.S. Naval Base in Pearl Harbor, Hawai'i, fear of a direct attack by Japan on the western coast of the United States impacted policymaking. The presence of a large Japanese American population in California and throughout the Northwest heightened these fears. In response, President Franklin Roosevelt signed Executive Order No. 9066, which provided broad powers to the military on the west coast to protect against espionage, sabotage, and agents of the emperor of Japan. Similar federal policies were passed impacting citizens of German or Italian descent but selectively applied.

While many Japanese Americans in the region were American citizens and had lived in the United States for generations, even with children serving in the U.S. military, they were an easily identifiable community. After the military successfully enforced a curfew order for people of Japanese descent, this was expanded to an exclusion order: all families were given a limited amount of time to sell what they owned, and were then allowed to bring only what they could carry to an evacuation center. They were then forcibly moved to internment camps throughout the Southwest, without any prior determination of disloyalty to the country. Fred Korematsu defied the exclusion order, claiming that as a citizen of the United States such a denial of due process of law was a violation of the Constitution. The Court had to decide whether this was evidence of unlawful racial bias or a reasonable restriction of personal liberty during a time of war.

KOREMATSU v. *UNITED STATES*, 323 U.S. 214 (1944)

Justice Black Delivered the Opinion of the Court

Vote: 6–3

It should be noted, to begin with, that all legal restrictions which curtail the civil rights of a single racial group are immediately suspect. That is not to say that all such restrictions are unconstitutional. It is to say that courts must subject them to the most rigid scrutiny. Pressing public necessity may sometimes justify the existence of such restrictions; racial antagonism never can.

Exclusion Order No. 34, which the petitioner knowingly and admittedly violated was one of a number of military orders and proclamations, all of which were substantially based upon Executive Order No. 9066. That order, issued after we were at war with Japan, declared that "the successful prosecution of the war requires every possible protection against espionage and against sabotage to national-defense material, national-defense premises, and national-defense utilities ..."

One of the series of orders and proclamations, a curfew order, which like the exclusion order here was promulgated pursuant to Executive Order 9066, subjected all persons of Japanese ancestry in prescribed West Coast military areas to remain in their residences from 8 p.m. to 6 a.m. As is the case with the exclusion order here, that prior curfew order was designed as a "protection against espionage and against sabotage." In *Kiyoshi Hirabayashi* v. *United States*, 320 U.S. 81 [(1943) we sustained a conviction obtained for violation of the curfew order. The *Hirabayashi* conviction and this one thus rest on the same 1942 Congressional Act and the same basic executive and military orders, all of which orders were aimed at the twin dangers of espionage and sabotage.

The 1942 Act was attacked in the *Hirabayashi* case as an unconstitutional delegation of power ... We upheld the curfew order as an exercise of the power of the government to take steps necessary to prevent espionage and sabotage in an area threatened by Japanese attack.

In the light of the principles we announced in the *Hirabayashi* case, we are unable to conclude that it was beyond the war power of Congress and the Executive to exclude those of Japanese ancestry from the West Coast war area at the time they did. True, exclusion from the area in which one's home is located is a far greater deprivation than constant confinement to the home from 8 p.m. to 6 a.m. Nothing short of apprehension by the proper military authorities of the gravest imminent danger to the public safety can constitutionally justify either. But exclusion from a threatened area, no less than curfew, has a definite and close relationship to the prevention of espionage and sabotage. The military authorities, charged with the primary responsibility of defending our shores, concluded that curfew provided inadequate protection and ordered exclusion. They did so, as pointed out in our *Hirabayashi* opinion, in accordance with Congressional authority to the military to say who should, and who should not, remain in the threatened areas.

In this case the petitioner challenges the assumptions upon which we rested our conclusions in the *Hirabayashi* case. He also urges that by May 1942, when Order No. 34 was promulgated, all danger of Japanese invasion of the West Coast had disappeared. After careful consideration of these contentions we are compelled to reject them.

Here, as in ... *Hirabayashi*,

> ... we cannot reject as unfounded the judgment of the military authorities and of Congress that there were disloyal members of that population, whose number and strength could not be precisely and quickly ascertained. We cannot say that the war-making branches of the Government did not have ground for believing that in a critical hour such persons could not readily be isolated and separately dealt with, and constituted a menace to the national defense and safety, which demanded that prompt and adequate measures be taken to guard against it.

Like curfew, exclusion of those of Japanese origin was deemed necessary because of the presence of an unascertained number of disloyal members of the group, most of whom we have no doubt were loyal to this country. It was because we could not reject the finding of the military authorities that it was impossible to bring about an immediate segregation of the disloyal from the loyal that we sustained the validity of the curfew order as applying to the whole group. In the instant case, temporary exclusion of the entire group was rested by the military on the same ground. The judgment that exclusion of the whole group was for the same reason a military imperative answers the contention that the exclusion was in the nature of group punishment based on antagonism to those of Japanese origin. That there were members of the group who retained loyalties to Japan has been confirmed by investigations made subsequent to the exclusion. Approximately five thousand American citizens of Japanese ancestry refused to swear unqualified allegiance to the United States and to renounce allegiance to the Japanese Emperor, and several thousand evacuees requested repatriation to Japan.

We uphold the exclusion order as of the time it was made and when the petitioner violated it. In doing so, we are not unmindful of the hardships imposed by it upon a large group of American citizens. But hardships are part of war, and war is an aggregation of hardships. All citizens alike, both in and out of uniform, feel the impact of war in greater or lesser measure. Citizenship has its responsibilities as well as its privileges, and in time of war the burden is always heavier. Compulsory exclusion of large groups of citizens from their homes, except under circumstances of direst emergency and peril, is inconsistent with our basic governmental institutions. But when under conditions of modern warfare our shores are threatened by hostile forces, the power to protect must be commensurate with the threatened danger.

It is said that we are dealing here with the case of imprisonment of a citizen in a concentration camp solely because of his ancestry, without evidence or inquiry concerning his loyalty and good disposition towards the United States. Our task would be simple, our duty clear, were this a case involving the imprisonment of a loyal citizen in a concentration camp because of racial prejudice. Regardless of the true nature of the assembly and relocation centers – and we deem it unjustifiable to call them concentration camps with all the ugly connotations that term implies – we are dealing specifically with nothing but an exclusion order. To cast this case into outlines of racial prejudice, without reference to the real military dangers which were presented, merely confuses the issue. Korematsu was not excluded from the Military Area because of hostility to him or his race. He was excluded because we are at war with the Japanese Empire, because the properly constituted military authorities feared an invasion of our West Coast and felt constrained to take proper security measures, because they decided that the military urgency of the situation demanded that all citizens of Japanese ancestry be segregated from the West Coast temporarily, and finally, because Congress, reposing its confidence in this time of war in our military leaders – as inevitably it must – determined that they should have the power to do just this. There was evidence of disloyalty on the part of some, the military authorities considered that the need for action was great, and time was short. We cannot – by availing ourselves of the calm perspective of hindsight – now say that at that time these actions were unjustified.

Affirmed.

Justice Frankfurter, Concurring

The provisions of the Constitution which confer on the Congress and the President powers to enable this country to wage war are as much part of the Constitution as provisions looking to a nation at peace. And we have had recent occasion to quote approvingly the statement of former Chief Justice Hughes that the war power of the Government is "the power to wage war successfully." Therefore, the validity of action under the war power must be judged wholly in the context of war. That action is not to be stigmatized as lawless because like action in times of peace would be lawless ... The respective spheres of action of military authorities and of judges are of course very different. But within their sphere, military authorities are no more outside the bounds of obedience to the Constitution than are judges within theirs ... To find that the Constitution does not forbid the military measures now complained of does not carry with it approval of that which Congress and the Executive did. That is their business, not ours.

Justice Roberts, Dissenting

I dissent, because I think the indisputable facts exhibit a clear violation of Constitutional rights.

This is not a case of keeping people off the streets at night as was *Kiyoshi Hirabayashi* v. *United States*, 320 U.S. 81 [(1943)], nor a case of temporary exclusion of a citizen from an area for his own safety or that of the community, nor a case of offering him an opportunity to go temporarily out of an area where his presence might cause danger to himself or to his fellows. On the contrary, it is the case of convicting a citizen as a punishment for not submitting to imprisonment in a concentration camp, based on his ancestry, and solely because of his ancestry, without evidence or inquiry concerning his loyalty and good disposition towards the United States. If this be a correct statement of the facts disclosed by this record, and facts of which we take judicial notice, I need hardly labor the conclusion that Constitutional rights have been violated.

Justice Murphy, Dissenting

This exclusion of "all persons of Japanese ancestry, both alien and non-alien," from the Pacific Coast area on a plea of military necessity in the absence of martial law ought not to be approved. Such exclusion goes over "the very brink of constitutional power" and falls into the ugly abyss of racism.

In dealing with matters relating to the prosecution and progress of a war, we must accord great respect and consideration to the judgments of the military authorities who are on the scene and who have full knowledge of the military facts. The scope of their discretion must, as a matter of necessity and common sense, be wide. And their judgments ought not to be overruled lightly by those whose training and duties ill-equip them to deal intelligently with matters so vital to the physical security of the nation.

At the same time, however, it is essential that there be definite limits to military discretion, especially where martial law has not been declared. Individuals must not be left impoverished of their constitutional rights on a plea of military necessity that has neither substance nor support. Thus, like other claims conflicting with the asserted constitutional rights of the individual, the military claim must subject itself to the judicial process of having its reasonableness determined and its conflicts with other interests reconciled. "What are the allowable limits of military discretion, and whether or not they have been overstepped in a particular case, are judicial questions." *Sterling* v. *Constantin*, 287 U.S. 378, 401 [1932]).

The judicial test of whether the Government, on a plea of military necessity, can validly deprive an individual of any of his constitutional rights is whether the deprivation is reasonably related to a public danger that is so "immediate, imminent, and impending" as not to admit of delay and not to permit the intervention of ordinary constitutional processes to alleviate the danger. Civilian Exclusion Order No. 34, banishing from a prescribed area of the Pacific Coast "all persons of Japanese ancestry, both alien and non-alien," clearly does not meet that test. Being an obvious racial discrimination,

the order deprives all those within its scope of the equal protection of the laws as guaranteed by the Fifth Amendment. It further deprives these individuals of their constitutional rights to live and work where they will, to establish a home where they choose and to move about freely. In excommunicating them without benefit of hearings, this order also deprives them of all their constitutional rights to procedural due process. Yet no reasonable relation to an "immediate, imminent, and impending" public danger is evident to support this racial restriction which is one of the most sweeping and complete deprivations of constitutional rights in the history of this nation in the absence of martial law.

It must be conceded that the military and naval situation in the spring of 1942 was such as to generate a very real fear of invasion of the Pacific Coast, accompanied by fears of sabotage and espionage in that area. The military command was therefore justified in adopting all reasonable means necessary to combat these dangers. In adjudging the military action taken in light of the then apparent dangers, we must not erect too high or too meticulous standards; it is necessary only that the action have some reasonable relation to the removal of the dangers of invasion, sabotage and espionage. But the exclusion, either temporarily or permanently, of all persons with Japanese blood in their veins has no such reasonable relation. And that relation is lacking because the exclusion order necessarily must rely for its reasonableness upon the assumption that all persons of Japanese ancestry may have a dangerous tendency to commit sabotage and espionage and to aid our Japanese enemy in other ways. It is difficult to believe that reason, logic or experience could be marshalled in support of such an assumption.

Justification for the exclusion is sought, instead, mainly upon questionable racial and sociological grounds not ordinarily within the realm of expert military judgment, supplemented by certain semi-military conclusions drawn from an unwarranted use of circumstantial evidence. Individuals of Japanese ancestry are condemned because they are said to be "a large, unassimilated, tightly knit racial group, bound to an enemy nation by strong ties of race, culture, custom and religion." They are claimed to be given to '"emperor worshipping ceremonies" and to "dual citizenship." Japanese language schools and allegedly pro-Japanese organizations are cited as evidence of possible group disloyalty, together with facts as to certain persons being educated and residing at length in Japan. It is intimated that many of these individuals deliberately resided "adjacent to strategic points," thus enabling them "to carry into execution a tremendous program of sabotage on a mass scale should any considerable number of them have been inclined to do so." The need for protective custody is also asserted. The report refers without identity to "numerous incidents of violence" as well as to other admittedly unverified or cumulative incidents. From this, plus certain other events not shown to have been connected with the Japanese Americans, it is concluded that the "situation was fraught with danger to the Japanese population itself" and that the general public "was ready to take matters into its own hands." Finally, it is intimated, though not directly charged or proved, that persons of Japanese ancestry were responsible for three minor isolated shellings and bombings of the Pacific Coast area, as well as for unidentified radio transmissions and night signalling.

The military necessity which is essential to the validity of the evacuation order thus resolves itself into a few intimations that certain individuals actively aided the enemy, from which it is inferred that the entire group of Japanese Americans could not be trusted to be or remain loyal to the United States. No one denies, of course, that there were some disloyal persons of Japanese descent on the Pacific Coast who did all in their power to aid their ancestral land. Similar disloyal activities have been engaged in by many persons of German, Italian and even more pioneer stock in our country. But to infer that examples of individual disloyalty prove group disloyalty and justify discriminatory action against the entire group is to deny that under our system of law individual guilt is the sole basis for deprivation of rights. Moreover, this inference, which is at the very heart of the evacuation orders, has been used in support of the abhorrent and despicable treatment of minority groups by the dictatorial tyrannies which this nation is now pledged to destroy. To give constitutional sanction to that inference in this case, however well-intentioned may have been the military command on the Pacific Coast, is to adopt one of the cruelest of the rationales used by our enemies to destroy the dignity of the individual and to encourage and open the door to discriminatory actions against other minority groups in the passions of tomorrow.

I dissent, therefore, from this legalization of racism. Racial discrimination in any form and in any degree has no justifiable part whatever in our democratic way of life. It is unattractive in any setting but it is utterly revolting among a free people who have embraced the principles set forth in the Constitution of the United States. All residents of this nation are kin in some way by blood or culture to a foreign land. Yet they are primarily and necessarily a part of the new and distinct civilization of the United States. They must accordingly be treated at all times as the heirs of the American experiment and as entitled to all the rights and freedoms guaranteed by the Constitution.

Justice Jackson, Dissenting

Korematsu was born on our soil, of parents born in Japan. The Constitution makes him a citizen of the United States by nativity and a citizen of California by residence. No claim is made that he is not loyal to this country. There is no suggestion that apart from the matter involved here he is not law-abiding and well disposed. Korematsu, however, has been convicted of an act not commonly a crime. It consists merely of being present in the state whereof he is a citizen, near the place where he was born, and where all his life he has lived.

Even more unusual is the series of military orders which made this conduct a crime. They forbid such a one to remain, and they also forbid him to leave. They were so drawn that the only way Korematsu could avoid violation was to give himself up to the military authority. This meant submission to custody, examination, and transportation out of the territory, to be followed by indeterminate confinement in detention camps.

A citizen's presence in the locality, however, was made a crime only if his parents were of Japanese birth. Had Korematsu been one of four – the others being, say, a German alien enemy, an Italian alien enemy, and a citizen of American-born ancestors, convicted of treason but out on parole – only Korematsu's presence would have violated the order. The difference between their innocence and his crime would result, not from anything he did, said, or thought, different than they, but only in that he was born of different racial stock.

Much is said of the danger to liberty from the Army program for deporting and detaining these citizens of Japanese extraction. But a judicial construction of the due process clause that will sustain this order is a far more subtle blow to liberty than the promulgation of the order itself. A military order, however unconstitutional, is not apt to last longer than the military emergency. Even during that period a succeeding commander may revoke it all. But once a judicial opinion rationalizes such an order to show that it conforms to the Constitution, or rather rationalizes the Constitution to show that the Constitution sanctions such an order, the Court for all time has validated the principle of racial discrimination in criminal procedure and of transplanting American citizens. The principle then lies about like a loaded weapon ready for the hand of any authority that can bring forward a plausible claim of an urgent need. Every repetition imbeds that principle more deeply in our law and thinking and expands it to new purposes. All who observe the work of courts are familiar with what Judge Cardozo described as "the tendency of a principle to expand itself to the limit of its logic." A military commander may overstep the bounds of constitutionality, and it is an incident. But if we review and approve, that passing incident becomes the doctrine of the Constitution. There it has a generative power of its own, and all that it creates will be in its own image. Nothing better illustrates this danger than does the Court's opinion in this case.

My duties as a justice as I see them do not require me to make a military judgment as to whether General DeWitt's evacuation and detention program was a reasonable military necessity. I do not suggest that the courts should have attempted to interfere with the Army in carrying out its task. But I do not think they may be asked to execute a military expedient that has no place in law under the Constitution. I would reverse the judgment and discharge the prisoner.

1. How does the tension between national security and personal liberty impact this decision?
2. How is the majority able to argue that this decision is not about race?
3. Why does Justice Murphy believe the Japanese were targeted for these policies? Do you find his arguments compelling? Why or why not?
4. What exactly is Jackson's concern about the precedental value of this case? Was he right or wrong in light of future events? Why?

In 1988, the federal government apologized for the internment of Japanese residents and citizens, paying all survivors $20,000 each in reparations. Fred Korematsu's conviction was finally overturned in 1984, the first time a criminal conviction upheld by the Supreme Court was vacated, and in 1998 he was awarded the Medal of Freedom by President Clinton ("Korematsu" 1998). Despite clear evidence accepted by history that the military had no substantial evidence for their claims of internal threats (Irons 1983), Korematsu remained a legitimate precedent. It was finally reconsidered in *Trump* v. *Hawaii* (585 U.S. 667, 2018), upholding the Trump administration's ban against citizens of predominately Muslim nations entering the United States, a policy widely understood as motivated by anti-Muslim bias.

Chief Justice Roberts, in the conclusion of his majority decision, claims to overrule *Korematsu* in the *dicta* of his opinion, as he attempts to distinguish the two cases.

> ... [T]he dissent invokes *Korematsu* v. *United States*, 323 U.S. 214 (1944). Whatever rhetorical advantage the dissent may see in doing so, *Korematsu* has nothing to do with this case ... [I]t is wholly inapt to liken that morally repugnant order to a facially neutral policy denying certain foreign nationals the privilege of admission ... The dissent's reference to *Korematsu*, however, affords this Court the opportunity to make express what is already obvious: *Korematsu* was gravely wrong the day it was decided, has been overruled in the court of history, and – to be clear – "has no place in law under the Constitution (Jackson, J., dissenting)."

But as Louis Fisher argues (2019), does this mean the other Japanese American Second World War cases remain legal precedent and if the case was wrong since its decision, why did it take until 2018 for the Supreme Court to overturn *Korematsu*?

2.4 Voting Rights and Voter Suppression

A long history of state-sanctioned violence (see Chapter 4) and legislative restrictions, meant that despite the passage of the Fifteenth Amendment, access to the ballot was often limited on a racial basis. State laws creating poll taxes, literacy tests, and grandfather clauses (a grandfather who was enslaved precluded a citizen from voting) all racialized the right to vote, especially in the South (Keyssar 2000; Valelly 2004). In Mississippi, for example, in 1965, only 6.7 percent of African Americans were registered to vote (Colby 1986; McMillen 1990). In response to these factors and the organization of citizens, local people, and communities in the mid-twentieth century Civil Rights Movement (Dittmer 1995; Payne 2007), Congress passed the Voting Rights Act, 1965. Today, in some Southern states a greater percentage of African Americans are registered to vote than Whites, yet many of these same states have still not had a Black state-wide elected official since Reconstruction. Why?

VOTING RIGHTS ACT, 1965

AN ACT To enforce the fifteenth amendment to the Constitution of the United States, and for other purposes.

Be it enacted by the Senate and House of Representatives of the United States of America in Congress assembled, That this Act shall be known as the "Voting Rights Act of 1965."

SEC. 2. No voting qualification or prerequisite to voting, or standard, practice, or procedure shall be imposed or applied by any State or political subdivision to deny or abridge the right of any citizen of the United States to vote on account of race or color.

SEC. 4. (a) To assure that the right of citizens of the United States to vote is not denied or abridged on account of race or color, no citizen shall be denied the right to vote in any Federal, State, or local election because of his failure to comply with any test or device in any State with respect to which the determinations have been made under subsection (b) or in any political subdivision with respect to which such determinations have been made as a separate unit ...

(b) The provisions of subsection (a) shall apply in any State or in any political subdivision of a state which (1) the Attorney General determines maintained on November 1, 1964, any test or device, and with respect to which (2) the Director of the Census determines that less than 50 percentum of the persons of voting age residing therein were registered on November 1, 1964, or that less than 50 percentum of such persons voted in the presidential election of November 1964.

A determination or certification of the Attorney General or of the Director of the Census under this section or under section 6 or section 13 shall not be reviewable in any court and shall be effective upon publication in the Federal Register.

(e)(1) Congress hereby declares that to secure the rights under the fourteenth amendment of persons educated in American-flag schools in which the predominant classroom language was other than English, it is necessary to prohibit the States from conditioning the right to vote of such persons on ability to read, write, understand, or interpret any matter in the English language.

SEC. 5. Whenever a State or political subdivision with respect to which the prohibitions set forth in section 4(a) are in effect shall enact or seek to administer any voting qualification or prerequisite to voting, or standard, practice, or procedure with respect to voting different from that in force or effect on November 1, 1964, such State or subdivision may institute an action in the United States District Court for the District of Columbia for a declaratory judgment that such qualification, prerequisite, standard, practice, or procedure does not have the purpose and will not have the effect of denying or abridging the right to vote on account of race or color, and unless and until the court enters such judgment no person shall be denied the right to vote for failure to comply with such qualification, prerequisite, standard, practice, or procedure: Provided, That such qualification, prerequisite, standard, practice, or procedure may be enforced without such proceeding if the qualification, prerequisite, standard, practice, or procedure has been submitted by the chief legal officer or other appropriate official of such State or subdivision to the Attorney General and the Attorney General has not interposed an objection within sixty days after such submission, except that neither the Attorney General's failure to object nor a declaratory judgment entered under this section shall bar a subsequent action to enjoin enforcement of such qualification, prerequisite, standard, practice, or procedure. Any action under this section shall be heard and determined by a court of three judges in accordance with the provisions of section 2284 of title 28 of the United States Code and any appeal shall lie to the Supreme Court.

This law made illegal many of the traditional barriers that states had established to limit voting by stigmatized racial and ethnic groups and required states with a history of such discrimination to seek approval from the federal government before changing any policies affecting voting. This requirement in section 5 of the Act had to be renewed by Congress after an established period of time. This provision was renewed consistently by Congress in the intervening years. In 2013, after the expected renewal of section V, the legitimacy of the section was challenged in the federal courts by Shelby County, Alabama, as no longer being necessary and therefore constitutionally discriminatory.

SHELBY COUNTY, ALABAMA v. HOLDER, 570 U.S. 529 (2013)

Chief Justice Roberts Delivered the Opinion of the Court, Joined by Justices Scalia, Kennedy, Thomas, and Alito

Vote: 5–4

The Voting Rights Act of 1965 employed extraordinary measures to address an extraordinary problem. Section 5 of the Act required States to obtain federal permission before enacting any law related to voting – a drastic departure from basic principles of federalism. And §4 of the Act applied that requirement only to some States – an equally dramatic departure from the principle that all States enjoy equal sovereignty. This was strong medicine, but Congress determined it was needed to address entrenched racial discrimination in voting, "an insidious and pervasive evil which had been perpetuated in certain parts of our country through unremitting and ingenious defiance of the Constitution." *South Carolina v. Katzenbach*, 383 U.S. 301, 309 (1966). As we explained in upholding the law, "exceptional conditions can justify legislative measures not otherwise appropriate." Reflecting the unprecedented nature of these measures, [§§4 and 5] were scheduled to expire after five years.

Nearly 50 years later, they are still in effect; indeed, they have been made more stringent, and are now scheduled to last until 2031. There is no denying, however, that the conditions that originally justified these measures no longer characterize voting in the covered jurisdictions. By 2009, "the racial gap in voter registration and turnout [was] lower in the States originally covered by §5 than it [was] nationwide." *Northwest Austin Municipal Util. Dist. No. One* v. *Holder*, 557 U.S. 193–204 (2009). Since that time, Census Bureau data indicate that African-American voter turnout has come to exceed white voter turnout in five of the six States originally covered by §5, with a gap in the sixth State of less than one half of one percent.

At the same time, voting discrimination still exists; no one doubts that. The question is whether the Act's extraordinary measures, including its disparate treatment of the States, continue to satisfy constitutional requirements. As we put it a short time ago, "the Act imposes current burdens and must be justified by current needs." *Northwest Austin*, 557 U.S., at 203.

II.

In *Northwest Austin [Municipal Utility District No. One]* v. *Holder*, 557 U.S. 1993 (2009), we stated that "the Act imposes current burdens and must be justified by current needs." 557 U.S., at 203. And we concluded that "a departure from the fundamental principle of equal sovereignty requires a showing that a statute's disparate geographic coverage is sufficiently related to the problem that it targets." These basic principles guide our review of the question before us.

A.

The Constitution and laws of the United States are "the supreme Law of the Land." U.S. Const., Art. VI, ¶2. State legislation may not contravene federal law. The Federal Government does not, however, have a general right to review and veto state enactments before they go into effect.

Outside the strictures of the Supremacy Clause, States retain broad autonomy in structuring their governments and pursuing legislative objectives. Indeed, the Constitution provides that all powers not specifically granted to the Federal Government are reserved to the States or citizens.

Not only do States retain sovereignty under the Constitution, there is also a "fundamental principle of equal sovereignty" among the States.

The Voting Rights Act sharply departs from these basic principles.

And despite the tradition of equal sovereignty, the Act applies to only nine States (and several additional counties). While one State waits months or years and expends funds to implement a validly enacted law, its neighbor can typically put the same law into effect immediately, through the normal legislative process.

B.

In 1966, we found these departures from the basic features of our system of government justified. The "blight of racial discrimination in voting" had "infected the electoral process in parts of our country for nearly a century." *Katzenbach*, 383 U.S., at 308. Several States had enacted a variety of requirements and tests "specifically designed to prevent" African-Americans from voting. Case-by-case litigation had proved inadequate to prevent such racial discrimination in voting, in part because States "merely switched to discriminatory devices not covered by the federal decrees," "enacted difficult new tests," or simply "defied and evaded court orders." Shortly before enactment of the Voting Rights Act, only 19.4 percent of African-Americans of voting age were registered to vote in Alabama, only 31.8 percent in Louisiana, and only 6.4 percent in Mississippi. Those figures were roughly 50 percentage points or more below the figures for whites.

In short, we concluded that "[u]nder the compulsion of these unique circumstances, Congress responded in a permissibly decisive manner." We also noted then and have emphasized since that this extra-ordinary legislation was intended to be temporary, set to expire after five years.

At the time, the coverage formula – the means of linking the exercise of the unprecedented authority with the problem that warranted it – made sense. We found that "Congress chose to limit its attention to the geographic areas where immediate action seemed necessary." *Katzenbach*, 383 U.S., at 328.

C.

Nearly 50 years later, things have changed dramatically. Shelby County contends that the preclearance requirement, even without regard to its disparate coverage, is now unconstitutional. Its arguments have a good deal of force ... The tests and devices that blocked access to the ballot have been forbidden nationwide for over 40 years.

Those conclusions are not ours alone. Congress said the same when it reauthorized the Act in 2006, writing that "[s]ignificant progress has been made in eliminating first generation barriers experienced by minority voters, including increased numbers of registered minority voters, minority voter turnout, and minority representation in Congress, State legislatures, and local elected offices." ... That Report also explained that there have been "significant increases in the number of African-Americans serving in elected offices"; more specifically, there has been approximately a 1,000 percent increase since 1965 in the number of African-American elected officials in the six States originally covered by the Voting Rights Act.

There is no doubt that these improvements are in large part because of the Voting Rights Act. The Act has proved immensely successful at redressing racial discrimination and integrating the voting process.

Yet the Act has not eased the restrictions in §5 or narrowed the scope of the coverage formula in §4(b) along the way. Those extraordinary and unprecedented features were reauthorized – as if nothing had changed. In fact, the Act's unusual remedies have grown even stronger.

Respondents do not deny that there have been improvements on the ground, but argue that much of this can be attributed to the deterrent effect of §5, which dissuades covered jurisdictions from engaging in discrimination that they would resume should §5 be struck down. Under this theory, however, §5 would be effectively immune from scrutiny; no matter how "clean" the record of covered jurisdictions, the argument could always be made that it was deterrence that accounted for the good behavior.

The provisions of §5 apply only to those jurisdictions singled out by §4. We now consider whether that coverage formula is constitutional in light of current conditions.

III.

A.

Coverage today is based on decades-old data and eradicated practices. The formula captures States by reference to literacy tests and low voter registration and turnout in the 1960s and early 1970s. But such tests have been banned nationwide for over 40 years. And voter registration and turnout numbers in the covered States have risen dramatically in the years since. Racial disparity in those numbers was compelling evidence justifying the preclearance remedy and the coverage formula. There is no longer such a disparity.

In 1965, the States could be divided into two groups: those with a recent history of voting tests and low voter registration and turnout, and those without those characteristics. Congress based its coverage formula on that distinction. Today the Nation is no longer divided along those lines, yet the Voting Rights Act continues to treat it as if it were.

B.

The Fifteenth Amendment commands that the right to vote shall not be denied or abridged on account of race or color, and it gives Congress the power to enforce that command. The Amendment is not designed to punish for the past; its purpose is to ensure a better future. To serve that purpose, Congress – if it is to divide the States – must identify those jurisdictions to be singled out on a basis that makes sense in light of current conditions. It cannot rely simply on the past. We made that clear in *Northwest Austin*, and we make it clear again today.

C.

In defending the coverage formula, the Government, the intervenors, and the dissent also rely heavily on data from the record that they claim justify disparate coverage. Congress compiled thousands of pages of evidence before reauthorizing the Voting Rights Act. The court below and the parties have debated what that record shows – they have gone back and forth about whether to compare covered to noncovered jurisdictions as blocks, how to disaggregate the data State by State, how to weigh §2

cases as evidence of ongoing discrimination, and whether to consider evidence not before Congress, among other issues. Regardless of how to look at the record, however, no one can fairly say that it shows anything approaching the "pervasive," "flagrant," "widespread," and "rampant" discrimination that faced Congress in 1965, and that clearly distinguished the covered jurisdictions from the rest of the Nation at that time.

But a more fundamental problem remains: Congress did not use the record it compiled to shape a coverage formula grounded in current conditions. It instead reenacted a formula based on 40-year-old facts having no logical relation to the present day. The dissent relies on "second-generation barriers," which are not impediments to the casting of ballots, but rather electoral arrangements that affect the weight of minority votes. That does not cure the problem. Viewing the preclearance requirements as targeting such efforts simply highlights the irrationality of continued reliance on the §4 coverage formula, which is based on voting tests and access to the ballot, not vote dilution. We cannot pretend that we are reviewing an updated statute, or try our hand at updating the statute ourselves, based on the new record compiled by Congress. Contrary to the dissent's contention, we are not ignoring the record; we are simply recognizing that it played no role in shaping the statutory formula before us today.

The dissent also turns to the record to argue that, in light of voting discrimination in Shelby County, the county cannot complain about the provisions that subject it to preclearance. But that is like saying that a driver pulled over pursuant to a policy of stopping all redheads cannot complain about that policy, if it turns out his license has expired. Shelby County's claim is that the coverage formula here is unconstitutional in all its applications, because of how it selects the jurisdictions subjected to preclearance. The county was selected based on that formula, and may challenge it in court.

*   *   *

Striking down an Act of Congress "is the gravest and most delicate duty that this Court is called on to perform." We do not do so lightly. That is why, in 2009, we took care to avoid ruling on the constitutionality of the Voting Rights Act when asked to do so, and instead resolved the case then before us on statutory grounds. But in issuing that decision, we expressed our broader concerns about the constitutionality of the Act. Congress could have updated the coverage formula at that time, but did not do so. Its failure to act leaves us today with no choice but to declare §4(b) unconstitutional. The formula in that section can no longer be used as a basis for subjecting jurisdictions to preclearance.

Our decision in no way affects the permanent, nationwide ban on racial discrimination in voting found in §2. We issue no holding on §5 itself, only on the coverage formula. Congress may draft another formula based on current conditions. Such a formula is an initial prerequisite to a determination that exceptional conditions still exist justifying such an "extraordinary departure from the traditional course of relations between the States and the Federal Government." Our country has changed, and while any racial discrimination in voting is too much, Congress must ensure that the legislation it passes to remedy that problem speaks to current conditions.

Justice Thomas, Concurring

I join the Court's opinion in full but write separately to explain that I would find §5 of the Voting Rights Act unconstitutional as well. The Court's opinion sets forth the reasons.

"The Voting Rights Act of 1965 employed extraordinary measures to address an extraordinary problem." In the face of "unremitting and ingenious defiance" of citizens' constitutionally protected right to vote, §5 was necessary to give effect to the Fifteenth Amendment in particular regions of the country. *South Carolina* v. *Katzenbach*, 383 U.S. 301, 309 (1966). Though §5's preclearance requirement represented a "shar[p] depart[ure]" from "basic principles" of federalism and the equal sovereignty of the States, the Court upheld the measure against early constitutional challenges because it was necessary at the time to address "voting discrimination where it persist[ed] on a pervasive scale."

Today, our Nation has changed. "[T]he conditions that originally justified [§5] no longer characterize voting in the covered jurisdictions." As the Court explains: "[V]oter turnout and registration rates now approach parity. Blatantly discriminatory evasions of federal decrees are rare. And minority candidates hold office at un-precedented levels."

In spite of these improvements, however, Congress increased the already significant burdens of §5. Following its reenactment in 2006, the Voting Rights Act was amended to "prohibit more conduct than before." "Section 5 now forbids voting changes with 'any discriminatory purpose' as well as voting changes that diminish the ability of citizens, on account of race, color, or language minority status, 'to elect their preferred candidates of choice.'" While the pre-2006 version of the Act went well beyond protection guaranteed under the Constitution, it now goes even further.

While the Court claims to "issue no holding on §5 itself," its own opinion compellingly demonstrates that Congress has failed to justify "current burdens" with a record demonstrating "current needs." By leaving the inevitable conclusion unstated, the Court needlessly prolongs the demise of that provision. For the reasons stated in the Court's opinion, I would find §5 unconstitutional.

Justice Ginsburg, with whom Justices Breyer, Sotomayor, and Kagan join, Dissenting

In the Court's view, the very success of §5 of the Voting Rights Act demands its dormancy. Congress was of another mind. Recognizing that large progress has been made, Congress determined, based on a voluminous record, that the scourge of discrimination was not yet extirpated. The question this case presents is who decides whether, as currently operative, §5 remains justifiable, this Court, or a Congress charged with the obligation to enforce the post-Civil War Amendments "by appropriate legislation." With overwhelming support in both Houses, Congress concluded that, for two prime reasons, §5 should continue in force, unabated. First, continuance would facilitate completion of the impressive gains thus far made; and second, continuance would guard against backsliding. Those assessments were well within Congress' province to make and should elicit this Court's unstinting approbation.

I.

"[V]oting discrimination still exists; no one doubts that." But the Court today terminates the remedy that proved to be best suited to block that discrimination. The Voting Rights Act of 1965 (VRA) has worked to combat voting discrimination where other remedies had been tried and failed. Particularly effective is the VRA's requirement of federal preclearance for all changes to voting laws in the regions of the country with the most aggravated records of rank discrimination against minority voting rights.

In the long course of the legislative process, Congress "amassed a sizable record." *Northwest Austin Municipal Util. Dist. No. One* v. *Holder*, 557 U.S. 193, 205 (2009). The House and Senate Judiciary Committees held 21 hearings, heard from scores of witnesses, received a number of investigative reports and other written documentation of continuing discrimination in covered jurisdictions. In all, the legislative record Congress compiled filled more than 15,000 pages. The compilation presents countless "examples of flagrant racial discrimination" since the last reauthorization; Congress also brought to light systematic evidence that "intentional racial discrimination in voting remains so serious and widespread in covered jurisdictions that section 5 preclearance is still needed."

After considering the full legislative record, Congress made the following findings: The VRA has directly caused significant progress in eliminating first-generation barriers to ballot access, leading to a marked increase in minority voter registration and turnout and the number of minority elected officials. But despite this progress, "second generation barriers constructed to prevent minority voters from fully participating in the electoral process" continued to exist, as well as racially polarized voting in the covered jurisdictions, which increased the political vulnerability of racial and language minorities in those jurisdictions. Extensive "[e]vidence of continued discrimination," Congress concluded, "clearly show[ed] the continued need for Federal oversight" in covered jurisdictions. The overall record demonstrated to the federal lawmakers that, "without the continuation of the Voting Rights Act of 1965 protections, racial and language minority citizens will be deprived of the opportunity to exercise their right to vote, or will have their votes diluted, undermining the significant gains made by minorities in the last 40 years."

Based on these findings, Congress reauthorized preclearance for another 25 years, while also undertaking to reconsider the extension after 15 years to ensure that the provision was still necessary and effective. The question before the Court is whether Congress had the authority under the Constitution to act as it did.

II.

In answering this question, the Court does not write on a clean slate. It is well established that Congress' judgment regarding exercise of its power to enforce the Fourteenth and Fifteenth Amendments warrants substantial deference. The VRA addresses the combination of race discrimination and the right to vote, which is "preservative of all rights." *Yick Wo* v. *Hopkins*, 118 U.S. 356, 370 (1886). When confronting the most constitutionally invidious form of discrimination, and the most fundamental right in our democratic system, Congress' power to act is at its height.

In summary, the Constitution vests broad power in Congress to protect the right to vote, and in particular to combat racial discrimination in voting. This Court has repeatedly reaffirmed Congress' prerogative to use any rational means in exercise of its power in this area. And both precedent and logic dictate that the rational-means test should be easier to satisfy, and the burden on the statute's challenger should be higher, when what is at issue is the reauthorization of a remedy that the Court has previously affirmed, and that Congress found, from contemporary evidence, to be working to advance the legislature's legitimate objective.

III.

A.

I begin with the evidence on which Congress based its decision to continue the preclearance remedy. The surest way to evaluate whether that remedy remains in order is to see if preclearance is still effectively preventing discriminatory changes to voting laws. On that score, the record before Congress was huge. In fact, Congress found there were more DOJ objections between 1982 and 2004 than there were between 1965 and the 1982 reauthorization.

All told, between 1982 and 2006, DOJ objections blocked over 700 voting changes based on a determination that the changes were discriminatory. Congress found that the majority of DOJ objections included findings of discriminatory intent, and that the changes blocked by preclearance were "calculated decisions to keep minority voters from fully participating in the political process." On top of that, over the same time period the DOJ and private plaintiffs succeeded in more than 100 actions to enforce the §5 preclearance requirements.

In addition to blocking proposed voting changes through preclearance, DOJ may request more information from a jurisdiction proposing a change. In turn, the jurisdiction may modify or withdraw the proposed change. The number of such modifications or withdrawals provides an indication of how many discriminatory proposals are deterred without need for formal objection. Congress received evidence that more than 800 proposed changes were altered or withdrawn since the last reauthorization in 1982. Congress also received empirical studies finding that DOJ's requests for more information had a significant effect on the degree to which covered jurisdictions "compl[ied] with their obligatio[n]" to protect minority voting rights.

... Surveying the type of changes stopped by the preclearance procedure conveys a sense of the extent to which §5 continues to protect minority voting rights. Set out below are characteristic examples of changes blocked in the years leading up to the 2006 reauthorization:

In 1995, Mississippi sought to reenact a dual voter registration system, "which was initially enacted in 1892 to disenfranchise Black voters," and for that reason, was struck down by a federal court in 1987.

Following the 2000 census, the City of Albany, Georgia, proposed a redistricting plan that DOJ found to be "designed with the purpose to limit and retrogress the increased black voting strength ... in the city as a whole."

In 2001, the mayor and all-white five-member Board of Aldermen of Kilmichael, Mississippi, abruptly canceled the town's election after "an unprecedented number" of African-American candidates announced they were running for office. DOJ required an election, and the town elected its first black mayor and three black aldermen.

In 2006, this Court found that Texas' attempt to redraw a congressional district to reduce the strength of Latino voters bore "the mark of intentional discrimination that could give rise to an equal protection violation," and ordered the district redrawn in compliance with the VRA. *League of United Latin American Citizens* v. *Perry*, 548 U.S. 399, 440 (2006). In response, Texas sought to undermine this Court's order by curtailing early voting in the district, but was blocked by an action to enforce the §5 preclearance requirement.

In 2003, after African-Americans won a majority of the seats on the school board for the first time in history, Charleston County, South Carolina, proposed an at-large voting mechanism for the board. The proposal, made without consulting any of the African-American members of the school board, was found to be an "exact replica" of an earlier voting scheme that, a federal court had determined, violated the VRA.

In 1993, the City of Millen, Georgia, proposed to delay the election in a majority-black district by two years, leaving that district without representation on the city council while the neighboring majority-white district would have three representatives. DOJ blocked the proposal. The county then sought to move a polling place from a predominantly black neighborhood in the city to an inaccessible location in a predominantly white neighborhood outside city limits.

In 2004, Waller County, Texas, threatened to prosecute two black students after they announced their intention to run for office. The county then attempted to reduce the availability of early voting in that election at polling places near a historically black university.

In 1990, Dallas County, Alabama, whose county seat is the City of Selma, sought to purge its voter rolls of many black voters. DOJ rejected the purge as discriminatory, noting that it would have disqualified many citizens from voting "simply because they failed to pick up or return a voter update form, when there was no valid requirement that they do so."

These examples, and scores more like them, fill the pages of the legislative record. The evidence was indeed sufficient to support Congress' conclusion that "racial discrimination in voting in covered jurisdictions [remained] serious and pervasive."

True, conditions in the South have impressively improved since passage of the Voting Rights Act. Congress noted this improvement and found that the VRA was the driving force behind it. But Congress also found that voting discrimination had evolved into subtler second-generation barriers, and that eliminating preclearance would risk loss of the gains that had been made. Concerns of this order, the Court previously found, gave Congress adequate cause to reauthorize the VRA. Facing such evidence then, the Court expressly rejected the argument that disparities in voter turnout and number of elected officials were the only metrics capable of justifying reauthorization of the VRA.

IV.

C.

The Court has time and again declined to upset legislation of this genre unless there was no or almost no evidence of unconstitutional action by States. No such claim can be made about the congressional record for the 2006 VRA reauthorization. Given a record replete with examples of denial or abridgment of a paramount federal right, the Court should have left the matter where it belongs: in Congress' bailiwick.

Instead, the Court strikes §4(b)'s coverage provision because, in its view, the provision is not based on "current conditions." It discounts, however, that one such condition was the preclearance remedy in place in the covered jurisdictions, a remedy Congress designed both to catch discrimination before it causes harm, and to guard against return to old ways. Volumes of evidence supported Congress' de-termination that the prospect of retrogression was real. Throwing out preclearance when it has worked and is continuing to work to stop discriminatory changes is like throwing away your umbrella in a rainstorm because you are not getting wet.

The sad irony of today's decision lies in its utter failure to grasp why the VRA has proven effective. The Court appears to believe that the VRA's success in eliminating the specific devices extant in 1965 means that preclearance is no longer needed. With that belief, and the argument derived from it, history repeats itself. The same assumption – that the problem could be solved when particular methods of voting discrimination are identified and eliminated – was indulged and proved wrong repeatedly prior to the VRA's enactment. Unlike prior statutes, which singled out particular tests or devices, the VRA is grounded in Congress' recognition of the "variety and persistence" of measures designed to impair minority voting rights. In truth, the evolution of voting discrimination into more subtle second-generation barriers is powerful evidence that a remedy as effective as preclearance remains vital to protect minority voting rights and prevent backsliding.

Beyond question, the VRA is no ordinary legislation. It is extraordinary because Congress embarked on a mission long delayed and of extraordinary importance: to realize the purpose and promise of the Fifteenth Amendment. For a half century, a concerted effort has been made to end racial discrimination in voting. Thanks to the Voting Rights Act, progress once the subject of a dream has been achieved and continues to be made.

1. Why did the Court find §4(b) of the Voting Rights Act, 1965, to be unnecessary in 2013 and therefore constitutionally problematic?
2. How does the dissenting opinion challenge this interpretation as a flawed reading of history?
3. Why is this case significant given our current debates over access to the ballot and reapportionment?

The relationship between citizenship and voting has been highly contested in the United States since the Founding. There has been an ongoing historic tension between an understanding of suffrage as being a right of citizenship versus a perception of suffrage being a privilege (Deardorff 2014). Individuals who understand voting as a right secured by residency or citizenship contend that access to the ballot is inherent to democracy, a fundamental right protected by both statutory law and the Constitution. For these advocates, any barrier to voting – whether complicated registration processes, state identification requirements, excessive lines at the polls, or the threat of losing the vote – are all badges of "second-class citizenship" which threaten democracy. People who perceive voting to be a privilege, on the other hand, believe the franchise should be awarded to specific individuals for their civic virtue or community engagement, will find most limitations to the ballot to be appropriate. These advocates will endorse such policies as required to prevent voting fraud and to guarantee that the most well-informed and dedicated citizens will determine the nation's fate. However, political scientists have found no contemporary evidence of systemic voter fraud (Eggers, Garro, and Grimmer 2021).

> These two understandings of citizenship – one as a universal right that should be generally guaranteed regardless of race, gender, religion, or class and the second which limits citizenship to those whom the power elite trust to exercise their authority wisely because of prior demonstrations of responsibility – have differing interpretations of the role of voting. The first vision constructs citizenship in a manner that respects voting as an inherent right all adult inhabitants possess. The second articulation designs these attributes of citizenship to be a privilege, extended with caution and limited to the responsible. (Deardorff 2014, 164)

How might these competing understandings of the role of voting in a democracy today be relevant? Which approach is right for our nation today?

3 Race and Segregation

At the conclusion of the Reconstruction Era (1863–1877), there was a concentrated attempt by members of the former Confederacy to restore political, economic, and social institutions to White control. However, we see evidence of such efforts to control the newly freed people in Southern public spaces as early as the 1870s; similar efforts followed in the Northern states. Ida B. Wells, famed African American anti-lynching activist, lived 10 miles outside Memphis in a neighborhood called Woodstock, commuting to the city for her work. For two years, she purchased a first-class ticket every week reserving herself a seat in the "ladies' section." In the fall of 1883, many towns throughout the South forbade Blacks to ride with Whites on public transportation, even if they had paid for the most expensive seats. Since the mood of the White community, passengers, and conductor determined whether Blacks could stay with Whites in the reserved cars or were forced to relocate to either the smoking (the dirtiest, most crowded cars) or the baggage cars, African Americans could not anticipate their treatment.

Wells had always purchased tickets for the ladies' car and had never experienced previous trouble. On one occasion, however, the conductor told her that she could not ride in the first-class car but had to go to the smoking car. Wells initially ignored him and continued reading. The conductor assumed her umbrella and baggage, telling her that he would treat her like a lady but that she would have to remove herself to the smoking car. Wells refused to move. When the conductor attempted to forcibly move her, Wells held onto her seat, bracing her feet against the row in front of her, and buried her teeth into his hand. Other passengers came to the assistance of the conductor, carried her out of the car, and cheered while she was dumped with her luggage on the platform. She filed a case in the Tennessee courts against the railroad company for violating her right to equal protection of the law. Arguing that transport in a smoking car could not be equivalent to a ticket for a first-class ladies' car, Wells was awarded $500 in damages. In 1887, the Chesapeake, Ohio and Southwestern Railroad appealed to the Tennessee Supreme Court, which ruled that the two cars were appropriately similar in their comfort, safety, and convenience, asserting that Wells' sole intent in filing the suit was to harass the railroad. She was ordered to pay the costs of the lawsuits (Giddings 2008). As Wells noted in her diary:

> I felt so disappointed, because I had hoped such great things from the suit for my people generally. I have firmly believed all along that the law was on our side and would, when we appealed to it, give us justice. I feel shorn of that belief and utterly discouraged, and just now if it were possible would gather my race in my arms and fly far away with them. (Wells, April 11, 1888 (cited in DeCosta-Willis 1995))

Wells was not alone in protesting the emergence of segregation, especially when segregation evolved to be reflected in state law. According to August Meier and Elliott Rudwick (1976), boycotts and protests began as soon as many of the laws were passed, with the first documented protest found in Georgia in 1891. Protests were documented in Atlanta, Rome, Savannah, and Augusta, Georgia; Montgomery, Little Rock, and Mobile, Alabama; New Orleans and Shreveport, Louisiana; Columbia, Missouri; Houston and San Antonio, Texas; Vicksburg and Natchez, Mississippi; Memphis, Nashville, Chattanooga and Knoxville, Tennessee; Pensacola and Jacksonville, Florida; Danville, Indiana; and, Lynchburg, Portsmouth, Norfolk, Newport News, and Richmond, Virginia. Meiers and Rudwick (1976) consider this litany an underestimation – African American boycotts of racially segregated public transportation occurred in every state of the former Confederacy. As detailed by Meiers and Rudwick, the *Mobile Daily Register* observed on May 17, 1905, "In every city where it has been found advisable to separate the races in the street cars the experience has been the same. The Negroes ... have invariably declared a boycott."

3.1 Early Footprints of Segregation

Segregation did not come passively to the South in the post-Reconstruction years, but it was not an alien concept to the nation. One of the earliest cases the Supreme Court decided regarding educational segregation was the case of *Roberts* v. *City of Boston* (1850) before the Civil War. Sarah Roberts, a five-year-old African American girl, and her father, Benjamin, challenged racial school segregation in Boston, relying upon an 1845 Massachusetts state law that allowed children illegally excluded from a public school to sue the city for damages. There were 160 primary schools in Boston of which 158 were allotted to White children. Sarah applied to the schools closest to her home (less than a quarter of a mile) and was denied entry. Instead, she was sent to an African American school – the Smith school – which was very far away from the Roberts home.

ROBERTS v. *CITY OF BOSTON*, 59 MASS. (5 CUSH.) 198 (1850)

Chief Justice Shaw Delivered the Opinion of the Court

Under these circumstances, has the plaintiff been unlawfully excluded from public school instruction? Upon the best consideration we have been able to give the subject, the court are all of opinion that she has not. It will be considered, that this is a question of power, or of the legal authority of the committee entrusted by the city with this department of public instruction; because, if they have the legal authority, the expediency of exercising it in any particular way is exclusively with them.

The great principle, advanced by the learned and eloquent advocate of the plaintiff, is, that by the constitution and laws of Massachusetts, all persons without distinction of age or sex, birth or color, origin or condition, are equal before the law. This, as a broad general principle, such as ought to appear in a declaration of rights, is perfectly sound; it is not only expressed in terms, but pervades and animates the whole spirit of our constitution of free government. But, when this great principle comes to be applied to the actual and various conditions of persons in society, it will not warrant the assertion, that men and women are legally clothed with the same civil and political powers, and that children and adults are legally to have the same functions and be subject to the same treatment; but only that the rights of all, as they are settled and regulated by law, are equally entitled to the paternal consideration and protection of the law, for their maintenance and security. What those rights are, to which individuals, in the infinite variety of circumstances by which they are surrounded in society, are entitled, must depend on laws adapted to their respective relations and conditions.

Conceding, therefore, in the fullest manner, that colored persons, the descendants of Africans, àre entitled by law, in this commonwealth, to equal rights, constitutional and political, civil and social, the question then arises, whether the regulation in question, which provides separate schools for colored children, is a violation of any of these rights.

We must then resort to the law, to ascertain what are the rights of individuals, in regard to the schools ...

[Masschusetts law] ... provides that the inhabitants shall annually choose, by ballot, a school committee, who shall have the general charge and superintendence of all the public schools in towns. There being no specific direction how schools shall be organized; how many schools shall be kept; what shall be the qualifications for admission to the schools; the age at which children may enter; the age to which they may continue; these must all be regulated by the committee, under their power of general superintendence.

The power of general superintendence vests a plenary authority in the committee to arrange, classify, and distribute pupils, in such a manner as they think best adapted to their general proficiency and welfare. If it is thought expedient to provide for very young children, it may be, that such schools may be kept exclusively by female teachers, quite adequate to their instruction, and yet whose services maybe obtained at a cost much lower than that of more highly-qualified male instructors. So if they should judge it expedient to have a grade of schools for children from seven to ten, and another for those from ten to fourteen, it would seem to be within their authority to establish such schools. So to separate male and female pupils into different schools. It has been found necessary, that is to say, highly expedient, at times, to establish special schools for poor and neglected children, who have passed the age of seven, and have become too old to attend the primary school, and yet have not acquired the rudiments of learning, to enable them to enter the ordinary schools. If a class of youth, of one or both sexes, is found in that condition, and it is expedient to organize them into a separate school, to receive the special training, adapted to their condition, it seems to be within the power of the superintending committee, to provide for the organization of such special school.

In the absence of special legislation on this subject, the law has vested the power in the committee to regulate the system of distribution and classification; and when this power is reasonably exercised, without being abused or perverted by colorable pretenses, the decision of the committee must be deemed conclusive. The committee, apparently upon great deliberation, have come to the conclusion, that the good of both classes of schools will be best promoted, by maintaining the separate primary schools for colored and for white children, and we can perceive no ground to doubt, that this is the honest result of their experience and judgment.

It is urged, that this maintenance of separate schools tends to deepen and perpetuate the odious distinction of caste, founded in a deep-rooted prejudice in public opinion. This prejudice, if it exists, is not created by law, and probably cannot be changed by law. Whether this distinction and prejudice, existing in the opinion and feelings of the community, would not be as effectually fostered by compelling colored and white children to associate together in the same schools, may well be doubted; at all events, it is a fair and proper question for the committee to consider and decide upon, having in view the best interests of both classes of children placed under their superintendence, and we cannot say, that their decision upon it is not founded on just grounds of reason and experience, and in the results of a discriminating and honest judgment.

The increased distance, to which the plaintiff was obliged to go to school from her father's house, is not such, in our opinion, as to render the regulation in question unreasonable, still less illegal.

1. How does Chief Justice Shaw justify allowing racial segregation of the Boston public schools in light of his belief in equality under the law?
2. How does this decision help define equality?
3. Chief Justice Shaw claims that racial prejudice "if it exists, is not created by law, and probably cannot be changed by law." Do you agree, why or why not?
4. How does this case challenge our national narrative around racial segregation? Does this case challenge the distinction between *de facto* and *de jure* segregation?

Albeit a fact pattern paralleling what was seen 100 years later in *Brown* v. *Board of Education* (1954), the case varied from *Brown* in several significant ways. First, *Roberts* is situated in the North and not in the South or in a border state. Segregation was a fact of life in the North, as it was throughout the country, in much of the nineteenth century (Kendrick and Kendrick 2006). In other regions of the nation, segregation may have focused on Asian Americans, Pacific Islanders, indigenous peoples, or Latinos, but the practices were very similar (Glenn 2002). Second, this decision to segregate the public schools and provide fewer, less supported options for students of color was not based on state mandates for segregation, but instead based on the local Board of Education's discretion. Finally, in *Roberts*, unlike *Brown*, the Supreme Court legitimated the school board's requirement for racial segregation. The Court found that school boards required discretion to separate students based on academic need and relevant demographic characteristics such as age, gender, or intellectual capacity. They also determined that legislatures appropriately delegate to local school boards the ability to make the best determination for their community. So, if the committee, based on their "experience and judgment," concluded that separate schools based on race is wise, it is a legitimate exercise of discretion. The decision recognizes that integration might or might not improve race relations, but importantly finds it is to be under the provenance of the local governing board.

Roberts v. *City of Boston* is also notable because Chief Justice Shaw, responding to the petitioner's claim that such segregation "tends to deepen and perpetuate the odious caste, founding a deep-rooted prejudice in public opinion," disagreed, noting "[t]his prejudice, if it exists, is not created by law, and probably cannot be changed by law." While segregation after the passage of the Fourteenth Amendment was initially enforced by private citizens and local policies, in many places in the Nation it quickly migrated to the law where it was enforced by the legislature and the courts.

3.2 Traditional Definitions of Segregation

Chief Justice Shaw's claim is significant in that segregation in the Nation would eventually be classified into two categories – *de facto* and *de jure* – with different understandings of governmental accountability for each. *De facto* segregation was popularly understood to be found primarily in the North and in the West and based on the choices of individuals and local practices, but not compelled by law. School segregation in these areas was perceived as consequences of housing choices, personal preferences, and a natural desire to live in communities that reflected personal demographics. Private companies and organizations which practiced racial discrimination were perceived as merely responding to market forces and reacting to the private prejudices and biases in their own communities (Armor 1995; Bell 2004). *De jure* segregation was popularly understood to be mandated by state or local governments and explicitly forbade people of different races from living, working, worshipping, learning, purchasing, or marrying each other. Such coerced segregation resulted in dual systems of education, religion, and society, with African Americans creating parallel institutions where they exercised agency and were treated with respect (Litwack 1998).

This narrative distinguishing between *de jure* Jim Crow segregation in the South from *de facto* housing segregation and neighborhood "preferences" in the North and West, maintained a White/Black binary understanding of racism, and ignored the legal and extra-legal violence used to keep these policies in place across the nation (Finkelman 1992). In addition, as *Roberts* demonstrates, there were many examples of Northern racial segregation also compelled by both law and policy. Because many believe our government is only responsible for repairing or correcting its own fallacies and sins, reparations could not be compelled in many communities for the long-term consequences of self-segregation.

Richard Rothstein in his 2017 study, *The Color of Law: A Forgotten History of How Our Government Segregated America*, demonstrates how housing discrimination was fostered by the federal government's decisions to fund and secure mortgages, finance housing developments, and purchase and zone land based on introducing and maintaining racial segregation. Similarly, Ira Katznelson in *When Affirmative Action was White* (2005) illustrates the means by which seminal New Deal and post-Second World War programs – forming the American middle class by providing access to higher education and home ownership for veterans, as well as developing a social safety net – promoted segregation. These programs were designed to exclude categories of work disproportionately filled by people of color (such as domestic labor and agriculture) and were locally implemented by racially biased community leaders. Both authors carefully document the explicit debates within the federal government regarding the planned structuring of these programs and their anticipated detrimental impact on racial equity in the United States. It is important to note that these questions of racial equality were consistently challenged and debated, as our Nation created the meaning of race.

3.3 The Fourteenth Amendment and Segregation

The passage of the Fourteenth Amendment intended to ensure that the newly freed people had basic equality as citizens and that the states treated their residents fairly; its language, however, was universal and applied to all racial groups. Soon after its ratification, the Southern states were "redeemed" and the former leaders of the Confederacy and its soldiers were able to return to self-governance. As the historian Leon Litwack demonstrates:

> Before the Civil War, when slavery had fixed the status of most blacks, no need was felt for statutory measures segregating the races. The restrictive Black Codes, along with the few segregation laws passed by the first postwar governments, did not survive Reconstruction. What replaced them, however, was not racial integration but an informal code of exclusion and discrimination ... But in the 1890s whites perceived in the behavior of "uppity" (and invariably younger) blacks a growing threat or indifference to the prevailing customs, habits, and etiquette. Over the next two decades, white Southerners would construct in response an imposing and extensive system of legal mechanisms designed to institutionalize the already familiar and customary subordination of black men and women. (Litwack 1998, 229–230)

"Jim Crow" reflected racist social expectations and cultural practices that were translated into state and municipal laws between 1890 and 1915. Similar efforts to control the labor and behavior of people of color echoed throughout the nation (Glenn 2002). As evidenced by cases provided in this chapter, similar policies were adopted on the West Coast for people of Asian descent (Brooks 2009) and in the Southwest for Latinos and Latinas (Strum 2010). Because of the inherently regional nature of these policies, few such cases came to the U.S. Supreme Court and were mostly addressed in the federal circuit and state Supreme Courts. For instance, San Francisco required Chinese students to attend a public segregated Chinese school until 1870, when the city changed policy and no longer allowed children of Chinese descent to be educated in the public schools, forcing parents to pay for private education. In 1882, Congress passed the Chinese Exclusion Act which prevented Chinese immigration and stopped immigrants from gaining naturalized citizenship (see Chapter 2). In 1884, Joseph and Mary Tape, immigrants from China, attempted to register their daughter, Mamie, in a White local school. When Mamie was denied registration, the family sued the San Francisco school board and won; the decision was appealed to the California Supreme Court in the case of *Tape* v. *Hurley* (1885).

TAPE v. HURLEY, 66 CAL. 473 (1885)

Decision by Judge Sharpstein

The main question in this case is whether a child "between six and twenty-one years of age, of Chinese parentage, but who was born and has always lived in the city and county of San Francisco," is entitled to admission in the public school of the district in which she resides. The language of the code is as follows:

> Every school, unless otherwise provided by law, must be open for the admission of all children between six and twenty-one years of age residing in the district; and the board of trustees, or city board of education, have power to admit adults and children not residing in the district, whenever good reasons exist therefore. Trustees shall have the power to exclude children of filthy or vicious habits, or children suffering from contagious or infectious diseases.

As amended, the clause is broad enough to include all children who are not precluded from entering a public school by some provision of law; and we are not aware of any law which forbids the entrance of children of any race or nationality. The legislature not only declares who shall be admitted, but also who may be excluded, and it does not authorize the exclusion of any one on the ground upon which alone the exclusion of the respondent here is sought to be justified. The vicious, the filthy, and those having contagious or infectious diseases, may be excluded, without regard to their race, color or nationality.

This law must be construed as any other would be construed.

"When the law is clear and explicit, and its provisions are susceptible of but one interpretation, its consequences, if evil, can only be avoided by a change of the law itself, to be effected by legislative and not judicial action" (*Bosley* v. *Mattingly*, 14 B. Mon. 73, 1853). This rule is never controverted or doubted, although perhaps sometimes lost sight of. In this case, if effect be given to the intention of the legislature, as indicated by the clear and unambiguous language used by them, respondent here has the same right to enter a public school that any other child has. It is not alleged that she is vicious, or filthy, or that she has a contagious or infectious disease. As the legislature has not denied to the children of any race or nationality the right to enter our public schools, the question whether it might have done so does not arise in this case.

The board of education has power "to make, establish, and enforce all necessary and proper rules and regulations *not contrary to law*," and none other. Teachers cannot justify a violation of law, on the ground that a resolution of the board of education required them to do so. [The decision of the lower court] is affirmed.

1. What does this decision resolve and what does it leave unanswered?
2. Why does the Court give a different ruling to that in *Roberts* v. *City of Boston*? How does the fact pattern vary between the two cases?
3. Does it surprise you that a law establishing segregated schools for students of Chinese descent was passed by the California State Assembly (Bill 268) in 1885? Why or why not?

In the national perception, the laws and Constitution reflected a Black and White binary around segregation into which other ethnicities were inserted (Perea 1998; Brooks and Widner 2010). This legal approach resulted in scenarios like that found in *Gong Lum* v. *Rice* (1927) where an American child of Chinese descent living in Mississippi was required to attend a school designated for African Americans. Such policies across the Nation demonstrated that the goal of segregation was to protect White identity as well as White cultural, political, and economic power with minimal concern for the needs of other racial and ethnic communities (Berard 2016). Gong Lum, a Chinese immigrant and father of nine-year-old Martha, a citizen of the United States, lived in Mississippi which mandated racial segregation of students into schools designated for Black or White pupils. Martha arrived at the Rosedale consolidated high school on the first day of classes but by noon she was notified by the School Board superintendent that the Board of Trustees had excluded her from school because she was of Chinese descent and "not a member of the white or caucasian race." This decision was made in response to instructions from the State Superintendent of Education. There was no school maintained in the district or in Bolivar County for children of Chinese descent and the state law provided for free public schools paid for by taxation. The Lum family sued to allow Martha continued access to her local school, teachers, and playmates (Berard 2016).

GONG LUM v. *RICE*, 275 U.S. 78 (1927)

Chief Justice Taft Delivered the Opinion of the Court

Vote: 9–0

As we have seen, the plaintiffs aver that the Rosedale Consolidated High School is the only school conducted in that district available for Martha Lum as a pupil. They also aver that there is no school maintained in the district of Bolivar County for the education of Chinese children, and none in the county. How are these averments to be reconciled with the statement of the [Mississippi] Supreme Court that colored schools are maintained in every county by virtue of the Constitution? This seems to be explained, in the language of the state Supreme Court, as follows:

By statute it is provided that all the territory of each county of the state shall be divided into school districts separately for the white and colored races; that is to say, the whole territory is to be divided into white school districts, and then a new division of the county for colored school districts ...

We must assume, then, that there are school districts for colored children in Bolivar county, but that no colored school is within the limits of the Rosedale Consolidated High School district. This is not inconsistent with there being at a place outside of that district and in a different district, a colored school which the plaintiff Martha Lum may conveniently attend. If so, she is not denied, under the existing school system, the right to attend and enjoy the privileges of a common school education in a colored school. If it were otherwise, the petition should have contained an allegation showing it. Had the petition alleged specifically that there was no colored school in Martha Lum's neighborhood to which she could conveniently go, a different question would have been presented, and this, without regard to the state Supreme Court's construction of the state Constitution as limiting the white schools provided for the education of children of the white or Caucasian race. But we do not find the petition to present such a situation.

The case then reduces itself to the question whether a state can be said to afford to a child of Chinese ancestry, born in this country and a citizen of the United States, the equal protection of the laws, by giving her the opportunity for a common school education in a school which receives only colored children of the brown, yellow or black races.

The right and power of the state to regulate the method of providing for the education of its youth at public expense is clear. In *Cumming* v. *Richmond County Board of Education*, 175 U.S. 528 (1899), persons of color sued the Board of Education to enjoin it from maintaining a high school for white children without providing a similar school for colored children, which had existed and had been discontinued. Mr. Justice Harlan, in delivering the opinion of the court, said:

> Under the circumstances disclosed, we cannot say that this action of the state court was, within the meaning of the Fourteenth Amendment, a denial by the state to the plaintiffs and to those associated with them of the equal protection of the laws, or of any privileges belonging to them as citizens of the United States. We may add that, while all admit that the benefits and burdens of public taxation must be shared by citizens without discrimination against any class on account of their race, the education of the people in schools maintained by state taxation is a matter belonging to the respective states, and any

interference on the part of federal authority with the management of such schools cannot be justified, except in the case of a clear and unmistakable disregard of rights secured by the supreme law of the land.

The question here is whether a Chinese citizen of the United States is denied equal protection of the laws when he is classed among the colored races and furnished facilities for education equal to that offered to all, whether white, brown, yellow, or black. Were this a new question, it would call for very full argument and consideration; but we think that it is the same question which has been many times decided to be within the constitutional power of the state Legislature to settle, without intervention of the federal courts under the federal Constitution. *Roberts* v. *City of Boston*, 59 Mass. (5 Cush.) 198 (1850).

In *Plessy* v. *Ferguson*, 163 U.S. 537 (1896), in upholding the validity under the Fourteenth Amendment of a statute of Louisiana requiring the separation of the white and colored races in railway coaches, a more difficult question than this, this court, speaking of permitted race separation, said:

> The most common instance of this is connected with the establishment of separate schools for white and colored children, which has been held to be a valid exercise of the legislative power even by courts of states where the political rights of the colored race have been longest and most earnestly enforced.

The case of *Roberts* v. *City of Boston*, in which Chief Justice Shaw, of the Supreme Judicial Court of Massachusetts, announced the opinion of that court upholding the separation of colored and white schools under a state constitutional injunction of equal protection, the same as the Fourteenth Amendment, was then referred to, and this court continued:

> Similar laws have been enacted by Congress under its general power of legislation over the District of Columbia, as well as by the

Legislatures of many of the states, and have been generally, if not uniformly, sustained by the courts' – citing many of the cases above named. Most of the cases cited arose, it is true, over the establishment of separate schools as between white pupils and black pupils; but we cannot think that the question is any different, or that any different result can be reached, assuming the cases above cited to be rightly decided, where the issue is as between white pupils and the pupils of the yellow races. The decision is within the discretion of the state in regulating its public schools, and does not conflict with the Fourteenth Amendment.

1. If the funding is based on tax base and the same schools can be open for longer than others, are the educational schemas equal? What makes for an equal education?
2. Does this case change or challenge the justification for racial segregation as given in *Plessy* v. *Ferguson* (1896)?
3. Why do you think *Tape* v. *Hurley* (1885) is not cited in the Supreme Court's discussions regarding segregation?
4. How does the state justification for school segregation vary over time and region thinking about the earlier cases we have discussed?
5. In the cited state law, Mississippi is constructing two separate school systems to maintain segregation while meeting its obligation to provide public schools. What might be the long-term consequences for Mississippi and other states that pursued the same policy? (see *Fordice* v. *United States* (1992)).

It is in *Plessy* v. *Ferguson* (1896) that the Supreme Court attempted to reconcile the explicit racism inherent in the nascent Jim Crow laws with the broad claims of equal protection under the law found in the Equal Protection Clause of the Fourteenth Amendment. In order to do this, the Court redefines both principles. Segregation is thus articulated as a preference desired by both Blacks and Whites – an expression of personal liberty – that allows both populations to reside more comfortably. After the years of Reconstruction, once the federal government had pulled out of the South and the South began to self-govern, new racial practices emerged that resurrected the Black Codes. For instance, the 1890 Louisiana Separate Car Act required "separate but equal" accommodations in railroad cars based on race and required passengers to occupy only the coach designated to their race, compelling officers of the railroad company to assign passengers to the correct car by race. Rail officials and African Americans alike noted the threat of these policies because of situations such as that of Ida B. Wells. A community organization advocating for the abolition of such laws, found Homer Plessy, who was "seven-eighths Caucasian and one-eights African blood" and could pass as White, to test the new law. Plessy was travelling by rail in Louisiana when he was "assigned by officers to the coach used for the race to which he belonged, but he insisted upon going into a coach used by the race to which he did not belong." Plessy refused to comply, was rejected, and then imprisoned for violation of the Louisiana law.

PLESSY v. FERGUSON, 163 U.S. 537 (1896)

Justice Brown, Delivered the Opinion of the Court, Joined by Chief Justice Fuller, and Justices Field, Gray, Shiras, White, and Peckham

Vote: 7–1

The constitutionality of this act is attacked upon the ground that it conflicts both with the Thirteenth Amendment of the Constitution, abolishing slavery, and the Fourteenth Amendment, which prohibits certain restrictive legislation on the part of the states.

1. That it does not conflict with the Thirteenth Amendment, which abolished slavery and involuntary servitude, except as a punishment for crime, is too clear for argument. Slavery implies involuntary servitude – a state of bondage; the ownership of mankind as a chattel, or, at least, the control of the labor and services of one man for the benefit of another, and the absence of a legal right to the disposal of his own person, property, and services. This amendment was said in the *Slaughter-House Cases*, 16 Wall. 36 (1873), to have been intended primarily to abolish slavery, as it had been previously known in this country, and that it equally forbade Mexican peonage or the Chinese coolie trade, when they amounted to slavery or involuntary servitude, and that the use of the word 'servitude' was intended to prohibit the use of all forms of involuntary slavery, of whatever class or name ...

A statute which implies merely a legal distinction between the white and colored races – a distinction which is founded in the color of the two races, and which must always exist so long as white men are distinguished from the other race by color – has no tendency to destroy the legal equality of the two races, or re-establish a state of involuntary servitude ...

The object of the [Fourteenth] amendment was undoubtedly to enforce the absolute equality of the two races before the law, but, in the nature of things, it could not have been intended to abolish distinctions based upon color, or to enforce social, as distinguished from political, equality, or a commingling of the two races upon terms unsatisfactory to either. Laws permitting, and even requiring, their separation, in places where they are liable to be brought into contact, do not necessarily imply the inferiority of either race to the other, and have been generally, if not universally, recognized as within the competency of the state legislatures in the exercise of their police power. The most common instance of this is connected with the establishment of separate schools for white and colored children, which have been held to be a valid exercise of the legislative power even by courts of states where the political rights of the colored race have been longest and most earnestly enforced.

One of the earliest of these cases is that of *Roberts* v. *City of Boston*, 59 Mass. (5 Cush.) 198 (1850), in which the supreme judicial court of Massachusetts held that the general school committee of Boston had power to make provision for the instruction of colored children in separate schools established exclusively for them, and to prohibit their attendance upon the other schools ... It was held that the powers of the committee extended to the establishment of separate schools for children of different ages, sexes and colors, and that they might also establish special schools for poor and neglected children, who have become too old to attend the primary school, and yet have not acquired the rudiments of learning, to enable them to enter the ordinary schools. Similar laws have been enacted by Congress under its general power of legislation over the District of Columbia, as well as by the legislatures of many of the states, and have been generally, if not uniformly, sustained by the courts.

Laws forbidding the intermarriage of the two races may be said in a technical sense to interfere with the freedom of contract, and yet have been universally recognized as within the police power of the state.

The distinction between laws interfering with the political equality of the negro and those requiring the separation of the two races in schools, theaters, and railway carriages has been frequently drawn by this court. Thus, in *Strauder* v. *West Virginia*, 100 U.S. 303 (1880), it was held that a law of West Virginia limiting to white male persons 21 years of age, and citizens of the state, the right to sit upon juries, was a discrimination which implied a legal inferiority in civil society, which lessened the security of the right of the colored race, and was a step towards reducing them to a condition of servility. Indeed, the right of a colored man that, in the selection of jurors to pass upon his life, liberty, and property, there shall be no exclusion of his race, and no discrimination against them because of color, has been asserted in a number of cases ...

In the *Civil Rights Cases*, 109 U.S. 3 (1883), it was held that an act of Congress entitling all persons within the jurisdiction of the United States to the full and equal enjoyment of the accommodations, advantages, facilities, and privileges of inns, public conveyances, on land or water, theaters, and other places of public amusement, and made applicable to citizens of every race and color, regardless of any previous condition of servitude, was unconstitutional and void, upon the ground that the Fourteenth Amendment was prohibitory upon the states only, and the legislation authorized to be adopted by Congress for enforcing it was not direct legislation on matters respecting which the states were prohibited from making or enforcing certain laws, or doing certain acts, but was corrective legislation, such as might be necessary or proper for counter-acting and redressing the effect of such laws or acts ...

... [W]e think the enforced separation of the races, as applied to the internal commerce of the state, neither abridges the privileges or immunities of the colored man, deprives him of his property without due process of law, nor denies him the equal protection of the laws, within the meaning of the Fourteenth Amendment ...

It is claimed by the plaintiff ... that, in any mixed community, the reputation of belonging to the dominant race, in this instance the white race, is "property," in the same sense that a right of action or of inheritance is property. Conceding this to be so, for the purposes of this case, we are unable to see how this statute deprives him of, or in any way affects his right to, such property. If he be a white man, and assigned to a colored coach, he may have his action for damages against the company for being deprived of his so-called "property." Upon the other hand, if he be a colored man, and be so assigned, he has been deprived of no property, since he is not lawfully entitled to the reputation of being a white man.

In this connection, it is also suggested by the learned counsel for the plaintiff ... that the same argument that will justify the state legislature in requiring railways to provide separate accommodations for the two races will also authorize them to require separate cars to be provided for people whose hair is of a certain color, or who are aliens, or who belong to certain nationalities, or to enact laws requiring colored people to walk upon one side of the street, and white people upon the other, or requiring white men's houses to be painted white, and colored men's black, or their vehicles or business signs to be of different colors, upon the theory that one side of the street is as good as the other, or that a house or vehicle of one color is as good as one of another color. The reply to all this is that every exercise of the police power must be reasonable, and extend only to such laws as are enacted in good faith for the promotion of the public good, and not for the annoyance or oppression of a particular class.

Thus, in *Yick Wo* v. *Hopkins*, 118 U.S. 356 (1886), it was held by this court that a municipal ordinance of the city of San Francisco, to regulate the carrying on of public laundries within the limits of the municipality, violated the provisions of the constitution of the United States, if it conferred upon the municipal authorities arbitrary power, at their own will, and without regard to discretion, in the legal sense of the term, to give or withhold consent as to persons or places, without regard to the competency of the persons applying or the propriety of the places selected for the carrying on of the business. It was held to be a covert attempt on the part of the municipality to make an arbitrary and unjust discrimination against the Chinese race. While this was the case of a municipal ordinance, a like principle has been held to apply to acts of a state legislature passed in the exercise of the police power.

So far, then, as a conflict with the Fourteenth Amendment is concerned, the case reduces itself to the question whether the statute of Louisiana is a reasonable regulation, and with respect to this there must necessarily be a large discretion on the part of the legislature. In determining the question of reasonableness, it is at liberty to act with reference to the established usages, customs, and traditions of the people, and with a view to the promotion of their comfort, and the preservation of the public peace and good order. Gauged by this standard, we cannot say that a law which authorizes or even requires the separation of the two races in public conveyances is unreasonable, or more obnoxious to the Fourteenth Amendment than the acts of Congress requiring separate schools for colored children in the District of Columbia, the constitutionality of which does not seem to have been questioned, or the corresponding acts of state legislatures.

We consider the underlying fallacy of the plaintiff's argument to consist in the assumption that the enforced separation of the two races stamps the colored race with a badge of inferiority. If this be so, it is not by reason of anything found in the act, but solely because the colored race chooses to put that construction upon it. The argument necessarily assumes that if, as has been more than once the case, and is not unlikely to be so again, the colored race should become the dominant power in the state legislature, and should enact a law in precisely similar terms, it would thereby relegate the white race to an inferior position. We imagine that the white race, at least, would not acquiesce in this assumption. The argument also assumes that social prejudices may be overcome by legislation, and that equal rights cannot be secured to the negro except by an enforced commingling of the two races. We cannot accept this proposition. If the two races are to meet upon terms of social equality, it must be the result of natural affinities, a mutual appreciation of each other's merits, and a voluntary consent of individuals. Legislation is powerless to eradicate racial instincts, or to abolish distinctions based upon physical differences, and the attempt to do so can only result in accentuating the difficulties of the present situation. If the civil and political rights of both races be equal, one cannot be inferior to the other civilly or politically. If one race be inferior to the other socially, the constitution of the United States cannot put them upon the same plane.

It is true that the question of the proportion of colored blood necessary to constitute a colored person, as distinguished from a white person, is one upon which there is a difference of opinion in the different states; some holding that any visible admixture of black blood stamps the person as belonging to the colored race; others, that it depends upon the preponderance of blood; and still others, that the predominance of white blood must only be in the proportion of three-fourths. But these are questions to be determined under the laws of each state, and are not properly put in issue in this case. Under the allegations of his petition, it may undoubtedly become a question of importance whether, under the laws of Louisiana, the petitioner belongs to the white or colored race.

Justice Harlan, Dissenting

... [W]e have before us a state enactment that compels, under penalties, the separation of the two races in railroad passenger coaches, and makes it a crime for a citizen of either race to enter a coach that has been assigned to citizens of the other race.

Thus, the state regulates the use of a public highway by citizens of the United States solely upon the basis of race. However apparent the injustice of such legislation may be, we have only to consider whether it is consistent with the Constitution of the United States.

In respect of civil rights, common to all citizens, the Constitution of the United States does not, I think, permit any public authority to know the race of those entitled to be protected in the enjoyment of such rights. Every true man has pride of race, and under appropriate circumstances, when the rights of others, his equals before the law, are not to be affected, it is his privilege to express such pride and to take such action based upon it as to him seems proper. But I deny that any legislative body or judicial tribunal may have regard to the race of citizens when the civil rights of those citizens are involved. Indeed, such legislation as that here in question is inconsistent not only with that equality of rights which pertains to citizenship, national and state, but with the personal liberty enjoyed by every one within the United States ...

The white race deems itself to be the dominant race in this country. And so it is, in prestige, in achievements, in education, in wealth, and in power. So, I doubt not, it will continue to be for all time, if it remains true to its great heritage, and holds fast to the principles of constitutional liberty. But in view of the Constitution, in the eye of the law, there is in this country no superior, dominant, ruling class of citizens. There is no caste here. Our constitution is color-blind, and neither knows nor tolerates classes among citizens. In respect of civil rights, all citizens are equal before the law. The humblest is the peer of the most powerful. The law regards man as man, and takes no account of his surroundings or of his color when his civil rights as guaranteed by the supreme law of the land are involved. It is therefore to be regretted that this high tribunal, the final expositor of the fundamental law of the land, has reached the conclusion that it is competent for a state to regulate the enjoyment by citizens of their civil rights solely upon the basis of race.

The sure guaranty of the peace and security of each race is the clear, distinct, unconditional recognition by our governments, national and state, of every right that inheres in civil freedom, and of the equality before the law of all citizens of the United States, without regard to race. State enactments regulating the enjoyment of civil rights upon the basis of race, and cunningly devised to defeat legitimate results of the war, under the pretense of recognizing equality of rights, can have no other result than to render permanent peace impossible, and to keep alive a conflict of races, the continuance of which must do harm to all concerned ...

There is a race so different from our own that we do not permit those belonging to it to become citizens of the United States. Persons belonging to it are, with few exceptions, absolutely excluded from our country. I allude to the Chinese race. But, by the statute in question, a Chinaman can ride in the same passenger coach with white citizens of the United States, while citizens of the black race in Louisiana, many of whom, perhaps, risked their lives for the preservation of the Union, who are entitled, by law, to participate in the political control of the state and nation, who are not excluded, by law or by reason of their race, from public stations of any kind, and who have all the legal rights that belong to white citizens, are yet declared to be criminals, liable to imprisonment, if they ride in a public coach occupied by citizens of the white race. It is scarcely just to say that a colored citizen should not object to occupying a public coach assigned to his own race. He does not object, nor, perhaps, would he object to separate coaches for his race if his rights under the law were recognized. But he does object, and he ought never to cease objecting, that citizens of the white and black races can be adjudged criminals because they sit, or claim the right to sit, in the same public coach on a public highway.

The arbitrary separation of citizens, on the basis of race, while they are on a public highway, is a badge of servitude wholly inconsistent with the civil freedom and the equality before the law established by the constitution. It cannot be justified upon any legal grounds.

.... We boast of the freedom enjoyed by our people above all other peoples. But it is difficult to reconcile that boast with a state of the law which, practically, puts the brand of servitude and degradation upon a large class of our fellow citizens – our equals before the law. The thin disguise of "equal" accommodations for passengers in railroad coaches will not mislead anyone, nor atone for the wrong this day done.

1. This was a test case in which a railroad company and a local citizens' committee collaborated with Homer Plessy to challenge the law. Why would a railroad company oppose this law?
2. What were the precedential consequences of this decision? Why does it head the list of worst Supreme Court decisions?
3. How could the majority perceive the reputation of a White man as a White man to be property? How is this reconciled with the rejection of segregation as a "badge of inferiority" for a person of color?
4. Justice Harlan's dissent, particularly his argument that "our Constitution is color-blind, and neither knows or tolerates classes among citizens," is highly celebrated and widely quoted by those on both the ideological left and right. Yet in the sentences above he recognizes White supremacy as a tenet of the nation, and after notes social equality is not possible and that those of Chinese descent are truly alien in the U.S. How do you reconcile these apparently contradicting ideas?
5. In light of this history, what does it mean to exert that the Constitution is color-blind? Is this the best way to interpret the Constitution, why or why not?

After *Plessy*, the Supreme Court interpreted equal protection as only requiring that accommodations (access to travel, hotel, shopping, restaurants) and education be available and accessible to both Black and Whites. Quality was not a consideration in gauging equality. With this new vocabulary, the racism of the Jim Crow South could reside with the new promises of the Fourteenth Amendment and the United States could continue the national practice of segregation. Maintenance of this awkward compromise required violence – as the lynching culture that emerged in the early twentieth century (Finkelman 1992; Wood 2009; see Chapter 4) – and continuous legal redefinitions and interpretations. As the long list of cities hosting protests against mandated segregation indicates, the imposition of this system was heavily and strongly contested both on the streets and in the courts long before Rosa Parks and the Montgomery Bus Boycott in 1955.

Americans of Chinese descent in California first overturned the segregation of public schools in *Tape* v. *Hurley* by successfully contesting these policies under state law in 1885, but after *Plessy*, California found new ways to segregate. Just as African Americans challenged Jim Crow in the South through organizations like the NAACP's Inc. Fund, in the Southwest state-mandated segregation of Latinos was challenged in courts by advocacy groups such as the Mexican American Legal Defense and Educational Fund (MALDEF). Mexican American parents successfully challenged their segregated schools in California in 1947 (*Westminster School District of Orange County* v. *Mendez*), but only because the federal appellate court determined that Mexican Americans were "White" according to California law and therefore could not be segregated. In *Westminster*, Latino parents filed a class action lawsuit against California school districts in Orange County on behalf of their children who were eligible to attend public schools. The parents challenged a set of policies and practices that prevented children of "Mexican and Latin descent" from receiving the full benefits of local public education and instead limited them to segregated schools which provided inferior opportunities to the White schools. The federal District Court found that the practiced segregation was "arbitrary and discriminatory and in violation of rights guaranteed to plaintiffs by the Constitution of the United States."

WESTMINSTER SCHOOL DISTRICT OF ORANGE COUNTY v. MENDEZ, 161 F.2D 774, 9TH CIR. (1947)

Circuit Judge Stephens, Delivers the Opinion for Circuit Judges Garrecht, Denman, Mathews, Stephens, Healy, Bone, and Orr

[The petitioners claim] that the State of California ... is denying the school children of Mexican descent, residing in the school districts described, the equal protection of the laws of the State of California and thereby ... are depriving them of their liberty and property without due process of law, as guaranteed by the Fourteenth Amendment of the Constitution of the United States ...

In both written and oral argument our attention has been directed to the cases in which the highest court of the land has upheld state laws providing for limited segregation of the great races of mankind. In *Roberts* v. *City of Boston*, [59 Mass. (5 Cush.) 198 (1850)], a law providing for the segregation of colored school children was held valid ... but that equal facilities must be provided for the use of the colored children ... *Cumming* v. *Board of Education*, 175 U.S. 528 [1899], reaffirmed the principle. In *Gong Lum* v. *Rice*, 275 U.S. 78 [1927], principle of the *Roberts* case was followed in the opinion written by Chief Justice Taft and affirmed ... application of the "colored" school segregation statute to an American citizen of pure Chinese blood. *Plessy* v. *Ferguson*, 163 U.S. 537 [1896], was upon the right of the state to require segregation of colored and white persons in public conveyances, and the act so providing was sustained again

upon the principles expressed by Chief Justice Shaw [in *Roberts*]. This list of cases is by no means complete.

It is argued by appellants that we should reverse the judgment in this case upon the authority of the segregation cases just cited because the Supreme Court has upheld the right of the states to provide for segregation upon the requirement that equal facilities be furnished each segregated group ... Of course, judges as well as all others must keep abreast of the times but judges must ever be on their guard lest they rationalize outright legislation under the too free use of the power to interpret. We are not tempted by the siren who calls to us that the sometimes slow and tedious ways of democratic legislation is no longer respected in a progressive society

In the first place we are aware of no authority justifying any segregation fiat by an administrative or executive decree as every case cited to us is based upon a legislative act. The segregation in this case is without legislative support and comes into fatal collision with the legislation of the state.

The State of California has a state-wide free school system governed by general law, the local application of which by necessity is to a considerable extent, under the direction of district and city school boards or trustees, superintendents and teachers. Section 16601 of the California Educational Code requires the parent of any child between the ages of eight and sixteen years to send him to the full time day school ... There are no exceptions based upon the ancestry of the child other than those contained in [California state law], which includes Indians under certain conditions and children of Chinese, Japanese or Mongolian parentage. As to these, there are laws requiring them in certain cases to attend separate schools. It may appropriately be noted that the segregation so provided for and the segregation referred to in the cited cases includes only children of parents belonging to one or another of the great races of mankind. It is interesting to note at this juncture of the case that the parties stipulated that there is no question as to race segregation in the case ... Nowhere in any California law is there a suggestion that any segregation can be made of children within one of the great races. Thus it is seen that there is a substantial difference in our case from those which have been decided by the Supreme Court, a difference which possibly could be held as placing our case outside the scope of such decisions. However, we are not put to this choice as the state law permits of segregation only as we have stated, that is, it is definitely confined to Indians and certain named Asiatics. That the California law does not include the segregation of school children because of their Mexican blood, is definitely and affirmatively indicated as the trial judge pointed out, by the fact that legislative action has been taken by the State of California to admit to her schools, children citizens of a foreign country, living across the border. Mexico is the only foreign country on any California boundary.

It follows that the acts of respondents were and are entirely without authority of California law, notwithstanding their performance has been and is under color or pretense of California law. Therefore, conceding for the argument that California could legally enact a law authorizing the segregation as practiced, the fact stands out unchallengeable that California has not done so but to the contrary has enacted laws wholly inconsistent with such practice. By enforcing the segregation of school children of Mexican descent against their will and contrary to the laws of California, respondents have violated the federal law as provided in the Fourteenth Amendment to the Federal Constitution by depriving them of liberty and property without due process of law and by denying to them the equal protection of the laws.

1. How did California justify this decision prior to *Brown* v. *Board of Education I* and the reinterpretation of separate but equal?
2. What was accomplished in this decision and what elements of segregation were left unaddressed?
3. What is meant by the "great races" and why is it relevant to these cases?

It would not be until *Keyes* v. *School District No. 1, Denver, Colorado* (413 U.S. 189, 1973) that the Supreme Court determined that so-called *de facto* segregation, in the absence of state-mandated educational segregation, also violated the Equal Protection Clause of the Fourteenth Amendment. This case led to many decisions forcing northern school districts to desegregate (Fine 1986; Formisano 1991; Jacobs 1998).

After numerous cases brought by the NAACP's Legal Defense Fund in the early twentieth century challenging the premise of separate but equal, the Supreme Court decided *Brown* v. *Board of Education* in 1954. The strategy created by Charles Hamilton Houston and his team of lawyers from Howard University was to expand the definition of separate but equal by demanding that school districts equalize their dual systems of education (one with Black schools, teachers, and administration and another with White schools, teachers, and administrators), correcting the significant underfunding of the Black systems compared with the White. Houston and the NAACP knew that equalizing the dual systems would bankrupt Southern school districts (Tushnet 1987). The prosperity and resources of the White systems had been funded through the impoverishment of the Black systems (Greenberg 1994). A second approach was led by Thurgood Marshall and focused on challenging segregation in graduate programs, building a series of precedents the legal team could depend upon when they challenged *Plessy* v. *Ferguson* (Tushnet 1994).

Brown v. *Board* combined litigation against five school districts across the country, where Black parents and students brought lawsuits against their school districts for not providing an equal education compared with White children (Kluger 2004). The Court knew this decision would be very controversial and that it explicitly challenged the supremacy of the White power structure (Klarman 2004). So, the Court patiently held two rounds of oral arguments, focusing on the intent of the legislature in drafting the Fourteenth Amendment and achieved a unanimous decision.

BROWN v. BOARD OF EDUCATION, 347 U.S. 483 (1954)

Chief Justice Warren Delivered the Unanimous Opinion of the Court

Vote: 9–0

These cases come to us from the states of Kansas, South Carolina, Virginia, and Delaware. They are premised on different facts and different local conditions, but a common legal question justifies their consideration together in this consolidated opinion.

In each of the cases, minors of the Negro race, through their legal representatives, seek the aid of the courts in obtaining admission to the public schools of their community on a nonsegregated basis. In each instance, they have been denied admission to schools attended by white children under laws requiring or permitting segregation according to race. This segregation was alleged to deprive the plaintiffs of the equal protection of the laws under the Fourteenth Amendment. In each of the cases other than the Delaware case, a three-judge federal district court denied relief to the plaintiffs on the so-called "separate

but equal" doctrine announced by this Court in *Plessy* v. *Ferguson*, 163 U.S. 537 (1896). Under that doctrine, equality of treatment is accorded when the races are provided substantially equal facilities, even though these facilities be separate. In the Delaware case, the Supreme Court of Delaware adhered to that doctrine, but ordered that the plaintiffs be admitted to the white schools because of their superiority to the Negro schools.

The plaintiffs contend that segregated public schools are not "equal" and cannot be made "equal," and that hence they are deprived of the equal protection of the laws. Because of the obvious importance of the question presented, the Court took jurisdiction.

In the first cases in this Court construing the Fourteenth Amendment, decided shortly after its adoption, the Court interpreted it as proscribing all state-imposed discriminations against the Negro race. The doctrine of "separate but equal" did not make its appearance in this court until 1896 in the case of *Plessy* v. *Ferguson*, involving not education but transportation. American courts have since labored with the doctrine for over half a century. In this Court, there have been six cases involving the "separate but equal" doctrine in the field of public education. In *Cumming* v. *Board of Education of Richmond County*, 175 U.S. 528 (1899), and *Gong Lum* v. *Rice*, 275 U.S. 78 (1927), the validity of the doctrine itself was not challenged. In more recent cases, all on the graduate school level, inequality was found in that specific benefits enjoyed by white students were denied to Negro students of the same educational qualifications. *State of Missouri ex rel. Gaines* v. *Canada*, 305 U.S. 337 (1938); *Sipuel* v. *Board of Regents of University of Oklahoma*, 332 U.S. 631 (1948); *Sweatt* v. *Painter*, 339 U.S. 629 (1950); *McLaurin* v. *Oklahoma State Regents*, 339 U.S. 637 (1950). In none of these cases was it necessary to re-examine the doctrine to grant relief to the Negro plaintiff. And in *Sweatt* v. *Painter*, the Court expressly reserved decision on the question whether *Plessy* v. *Ferguson* should be held inapplicable to public education.

In the instant cases, that question is directly presented. Here, unlike *Sweatt* v. *Painter*, there are findings below that the Negro and white schools involved have been equalized, or are being equalized, with respect to buildings, curricula, qualifications and salaries of teachers, and other "tangible" factors. Our decision, therefore, cannot turn on merely a comparison of these tangible factors in the Negro and white schools involved in each of the cases. We must look instead to the effect of segregation itself on public education.

In approaching this problem, we cannot turn the clock back to 1868 when the Amendment was adopted, or even to 1896 when *Plessy* v. *Ferguson* was written. We must consider public education in the light of its full development and its present place in American life throughout the Nation. Only in this way can it be determined if segregation in public schools deprives these plaintiffs of the equal protection of the laws.

Today, education is perhaps the most important function of state and local governments. Compulsory school attendance laws and the great expenditures for education both demonstrate our recognition of the importance of education to our democratic society. It is required in the performance of our most basic public responsibilities, even service in the armed forces. It is the very foundation of good citizenship. Today it is a principal instrument in awakening the child to cultural values, in preparing him for later professional training, and in helping him to adjust normally to his environment. In these days, it is doubtful that any child may reasonably be expected to succeed in life if he is denied the opportunity of an education. Such an opportunity, where the state has undertaken to provide it, is a right which must be made available to all on equal terms.

We come then to the question presented: Does segregation of children in public schools solely on the basis of race, even though the physical facilities and other "tangible" factors may be equal, deprive the children of the minority group of equal educational opportunities? We believe that it does.

In *Sweatt* v. *Painter*, in finding that a segregated law school for Negroes could not provide them equal educational opportunities, this Court relied in large part on "those qualities which are incapable of objective measurement but which make for greatness in a law school." In *McLaurin* v. *Oklahoma State Regents*, the Court, in requiring that a Negro admitted to a white graduate school be treated like all other students, again resorted to intangible considerations: "... his ability to study, to engage in discussions and exchange views with other students, and, in general, to learn his profession." Such considerations apply with added force to children in grade and high schools. To separate them from others of similar age and qualifications solely because of their race generates a feeling of inferiority as to their status in the community that may affect their hearts and minds in a way unlikely ever to be undone. The effect of this separation on their educational opportunities was well stated by a finding in the Kansas case by a court which nevertheless felt compelled to rule against the Negro plaintiffs:

> Segregation of white and colored children in public schools has a detrimental effect upon the colored children. The impact is greater when it has the sanction of the law; for the policy of separating the races is usually interpreted as denoting the inferiority of the negro group. A sense of inferiority affects the motivation of a

child to learn. Segregation with the sanction of law, therefore, has a tendency to (retard) the educational and mental development of Negro children and to deprive them of some of the benefits they would receive in a racial(ly) integrated school system.

Whatever may have been the extent of psychological knowledge at the time of *Plessy* v. *Ferguson*, this finding is amply supported by modern authority. Any language in *Plessy* v. *Ferguson* contrary to this finding is rejected.

We conclude that in the field of public education the doctrine of "separate but equal" has no place. Separate educational facilities are inherently unequal. Therefore, we hold that the plaintiffs and others similarly situated for whom the actions have been brought are, by reason of the segregation complained of, deprived of the equal protection of the laws guaranteed by the Fourteenth Amendment. This disposition makes unnecessary any discussion whether such segregation also violates the Due Process Clause of the Fourteenth Amendment.

Because these are class actions, because of the wide applicability of this decision, and because of the great variety of local conditions, the formulation of decrees in these cases presents problems of considerable complexity. On reargument, the consideration of appropriate relief was necessarily subordinated to the primary question – the constitutionality of segregation in public education. We have now announced that such segregation is a denial of the equal protection of the laws. In order that we may have the full assistance of the parties in formulating decrees, the cases will be restored to the docket, and the parties are requested to present further argument on Questions 4 and 5 previously propounded by the Court for the reargument this Term. The Attorney General of the United States is again invited to participate. The Attorneys General of the states requiring or permitting segregation in public education will also be permitted to appear as amici curiae upon request to do so by September 15, 1954, and submission of briefs by October 1, 1954. It is so ordered.

1. What is the rationale in overturning the long-lived precedent in *Plessy* v. *Ferguson* (1896)?
2. Why are separate facilities inherently inequal? What are the limits to this ruling?
3. Considering Chief Justice Shaw's claim in *Roberts* v. *City of Boston* (1850) that racial prejudice "if it exists, is not created by law, and probably cannot be changed by law," does *Brown* and its aftermath support or challenge this interpretation?

Bolling v. *Sharpe*, 347 U.S. 497 (1954) was the fifth *Brown* v. *Board of Education* case that the Supreme Court decided, emerging from the Washington, D.C. school district. Because the District of Columbia is not a state, the Fourteenth Amendment's Equal Protection Clause does not apply to its circumstances. In *Bolling*, the Supreme Court found the Due Process Clause within the Fifth Amendment's liberty provision makes the mandatory segregation in D.C. unconstitutional.

The decision in *Brown* weighs the human consequences of racial segregation against the ideals of equality articulated by the Equal Protection Clause, finding that state-mandated segregation – even if all facilities and resources are equitable – cannot provide equal opportunities in education. As a result, *Plessy* v. *Ferguson* was explicitly overturned and no longer serves as legal precedent. In *Brown* v. *Board of Education II* (1955), the Court reconvened to determine the best means of implementing the decision to desegregate schools. The Court had demolished mandated racial segregation of public schools while legislated Jim Crow segregation of public facilities in the South was still in full force.

BROWN v. BOARD OF EDUCATION II, 349 U.S. 294 (1955)

Chief Justice Warren Delivered the Unanimous Opinion of the Court

Vote: 9–0

These cases were decided on May 17, 1954. The opinions of that date, declaring the fundamental principle that racial discrimination in public education is unconstitutional, are incorporated herein by reference. All provisions of federal, state, or local law requiring or permitting such discrimination must yield to this principle. There remains for consideration the manner in which relief is to be accorded.

Because these cases arose under different local conditions and their disposition will involve a variety of local problems, we requested further argument on the question of relief. In view of the nationwide importance of the decision, we invited the Attorney General of the United States and the Attorneys General of all states requiring or permitting racial discrimination in public education to present their views on that question. The parties, the United States, and the States of Florida, North Carolina, Arkansas, Oklahoma, Maryland, and Texas filed briefs and participated in the oral argument.

These presentations were informative and helpful to the Court in its consideration of the complexities arising from the transition to a system of public education freed of racial discrimination. The presentations also demonstrated that substantial steps to eliminate racial discrimination in public schools have already been taken, not only in some of the communities in which these cases arose, but in some of the states appearing as *amici curiae*, and in other states as well. Substantial progress has been made in the District of Columbia and in the communities in Kansas and Delaware involved in this litigation. The defendants in the cases coming to us from South Carolina and Virginia are awaiting the decision of this Court concerning relief.

Full implementation of these constitutional principles may require solution of varied local school problems. School authorities have the primary responsibility for elucidating, assessing, and solving these problems; courts will have to consider whether the action of school authorities constitutes good faith implementation of the governing constitutional principles. Because of their proximity to local conditions and the possible need for further hearings, the courts which originally heard these cases can best perform this judicial appraisal. Accordingly, we believe it appropriate to remand the cases to those courts.

In fashioning and effectuating the decrees, the courts will be guided by equitable principles. Traditionally, equity has been characterized by a practical flexibility in shaping its remedies and by a facility for adjusting and reconciling public and private needs. These cases call for the exercise of these traditional attributes of equity power. At stake is the personal interest of the plaintiffs in admission to public schools as soon as practicable on a nondiscriminatory basis. To effectuate this interest may call for elimination of a variety of obstacles in making the transition to school systems operated in accordance with the constitutional principles set forth in our May 17, 1954, decision. Courts of equity may properly take into account the public interest in the elimination of such obstacles in a systematic and effective manner. But it should go without saying that the vitality of these constitutional principles cannot be allowed to yield simply because of disagreement with them.

While giving weight to these public and private considerations, the courts will require that the defendants make a prompt and reasonable start toward full compliance with our May 17, 1954, ruling. Once such a start has been made, the courts may find that additional time is necessary to carry out the ruling in an effective manner. The burden rests upon the defendants to establish that such time is necessary in the public interest and is consistent with good faith compliance at the earliest practicable date. To that end, the courts may consider problems related to administration, arising from the physical condition of the school plant, the school transportation system, personnel, revision of school districts and attendance areas into compact units to achieve a system of determining admission to the public schools on a nonracial basis, and revision of local laws and regulations which may be necessary in solving the foregoing problems. They will also consider the adequacy of any plans the defendants may propose to meet these problems and to effectuate a transition to a racially nondiscriminatory school system.

During this period of transition, the courts will retain jurisdiction of these cases.

The judgments below ... are accordingly reversed and the cases are remanded to the District Courts to take such proceedings and enter such orders and decrees consistent with this opinion as are necessary and proper to admit to public schools on a racially nondiscriminatory basis with all deliberate speed the parties to these cases. The judgment in the Delaware case – ordering the immediate admission of the plaintiffs to schools previously attended only by white children – is affirmed on the basis of the principles stated in our May 17, 1954, opinion, but the case is remanded to the Supreme Court of Delaware for such further proceedings as that Court may deem necessary in light of this opinion. It is so ordered.

1. If the segregation has been based on local practice and norms, why did the courts send these cases both to local and district federal courts?
2. The lower federal courts are told to open "public schools on a racially nondiscriminatory basis with all deliberate speed." What does it mean to make policy changes with "all deliberate speed"?
3. What guidance does the Court provide for the dismantling of segregation?

The next step was the largest for the legal system, the Court had to decide how to completely dismantle segregated systems of education found throughout the country. Although it is external to the scope of this text, the U.S. Supreme Court and the lower federal courts then generated precedent for the next forty years covering desegregation plans, busing, metropolitan school districts, Northern desegregation cases, charter and magnet schools, and many other similar cases with widespread implications for school districts, students and teachers, and Black communities nationwide (Bass 1981; Pratt 1992; Cecelski 1994; Armor 1995; Bell 2004).

1. Consider the widely available data on wealth (not income) over time by race. How might the segregation practices of our nation in the nineteenth and twentieth centuries impact disparities in the twenty-first century?
2. Consider the construct of *de jure* and *de facto* segregation. Is there a relationship between the law and segregation based on social expectations and norms? Does the distinction between *de jure* and *de facto* have any relevance in the twenty-first century?

3.4 Ending Segregation, Maintaining Segregation

Education was not the only institution in which American lives were segregated by race; however, while *Brown* v. *Board of Education* (1954) overturned *Plessy* v. *Ferguson* (1896) explicitly addressing mandated segregation in education, it was insufficient to create universal formal equality. As long as state laws mandated different treatment on the basis of race and federal laws did not prohibit racial discrimination by public and most private entities, racial equality could not exist. Formal equality – when laws require equal treatment of all citizens regardless of race – was completed with the Civil Rights Act, 1964, the Voting Rights Act, 1965 (see Chapter 2), and the Housing Act, 1968. Substantive equality – the guarantee that opportunities and lived experiences or outcomes are not distributed on the basis of race – would then become the next frontier (Deardorff and Dahl 2016; Fredman 2016).

The Civil Rights Act, 1964, was one of many federal legislative attempts to prohibit racial discrimination in the economic private sector. As Chapter 2 discusses, earlier Acts passed after the Civil War Amendments, which attempted to prohibit similar forms of discrimination were found in the *Civil Rights Cases* (1883) to be unconstitutional under the Supreme Court's interpretation of the Fourteenth Amendment. By 1964, Congress had decided to focus the constitutional power they possess in the Commerce Clause (Article I, §8, ¶3) to regulate interstate commerce. This federal law prohibited discrimination in the public and private sector, including segregation in accommodations (Title II) and racial, ethnic, gender, and religious discrimination in employment decisions (Title VII).

CIVIL RIGHTS ACT, 1964

To enforce the constitutional right to vote, to confer jurisdiction upon the district courts of the United States to provide injunctive relief against discrimination in public accommodations, to authorize the Attorney General to institute suits to protect constitutional rights in public facilities and public education, to extend the Commission on Civil Rights, to prevent discrimination in federally assisted programs, to establish a Commission on Equal Employment Opportunity, and for other purposes.

TITLE II – INJUNCTIVE RELIEF AGAINST DISCRIMINATION IN PLACES OF PUBLIC ACCOMMODATION SEC. 201. (a) All persons shall be entitled to the full and equal enjoyment of the goods, services, facilities, and privileges, advantages, and accommodations of any place of public accommodation, as defined in this section, without discrimination or segregation on the ground of race, color, religion, or national origin.

(b) Each of the following establishments which serves the public is a place of public accommodation within the meaning of this title if its operations affect commerce, or if discrimination or segregation by it is supported by State action:

(1) any inn, hotel, motel, or other establishment which provides lodging to transient guests, other than an establishment located

within a building which contains not more than five rooms for rent or hire and which is actually occupied by the proprietor of such establishment as his residence;

(2) any restaurant, cafeteria, lunchroom, lunch counter, soda fountain, or other facility principally engaged in selling food for consumption on the premises ...;

(3) any motion picture house, theater, concert hall, sports arena, stadium or other place of exhibition or entertainment; ...

(d) Discrimination or segregation by an establishment is supported by State action within the meaning of this title if such discrimination or segregation (1) is carried on under color of any law, statute, ordinance, or regulation; or (2) is carried on under color of any custom or usage required or enforced by officials of the State or political

subdivision thereof; or (3) is required by action of the State or political subdivision thereof.

(e) The provisions of this title shall not apply to a private club or other establishment not in fact open to the public, except to the extent that the facilities of such establishment are made available to the customers or patrons of an establishment within the scope of subsection (b).

SEC. 202. All persons shall be entitled to be free, at any establishment or place, from discrimination or segregation of any kind on the ground of race, color, religion, or national origin, if such discrimination or segregation is or purports to be required by any law, statute, ordinance, regulation, rule, or order of a State or any agency or political subdivision thereof.

→ definition of state action

In *Heart of Atlanta Motel* v. *United States* (1964) the Supreme Court determined that the Commerce Clause allowed federal interventions into the interstate economy, in this case to rebuke racial discrimination's interference with African American's interstate travel and their accompanying commercial activities. The Heart of Atlanta Motel was a large, centrally located hotel, situated off several interstate highways which advertised both broadly and nationally. It had a large convention business and 75 percent of its business was from out-of-state travelers. It was a segregated enterprise, refusing African American guests even after the Civil Rights Act of 1964 prohibited that practice.

facts

HEART OF ATLANTA MOTEL v. UNITED STATES, 379 U.S. 241 (1964)

Justice Clark Delivered the Opinion of the Court

Vote: 9–0

The [Heart of Atlanta Motel] contends that Congress in passing [the Civil Rights Act of 1964] exceeded its power to regulate commerce under Article I, §8, ¶3, of the Constitution of the United States; that the Act violates the Fifth Amendment

because appellant is deprived of the right to choose its customers and operate its business as it wishes, resulting in a taking of its liberty and property without due process of law and a taking of its property without just compensation; and, finally, that by requiring appellant to rent available rooms to Negroes against its will, Congress is subjecting it to involuntary servitude in contravention of the Thirteenth Amendment.

The [federal government] counter[s] that the unavailability to Negroes of adequate accommodations interferes significantly with interstate travel, and that Congress, under the Commerce Clause, has power to remove such obstructions and restraints; that the Fifth Amendment does not forbid reasonable regulation and that consequential damage does not constitute a "taking" within the meaning of that amendment; that the Thirteenth Amendment claim fails because it is entirely frivolous to say that an amendment directed to the abolition of human bondage and the removal of widespread disabilities associated with slavery places discrimination in public accommodations, beyond the reach of both federal and state law ...

2. *The History of the Act.*

Congress first evidenced its interest in civil rights legislation in the Civil Rights or Enforcement Act of April 9, 1866. There followed four Acts, with a fifth, the Civil Rights Act of March 1, 1875, culminating the series. In 1883 this Court struck down the public accommodations sections of the 1875 Act in the *Civil Rights Cases*, 109 U.S. 3 (1883). No major legislation in this field had been enacted by Congress for 82 years when the Civil Rights Act of 1957 became law. It was followed by the Civil Rights Act of 1960. Three years later, on June 19, 1963, the late President Kennedy called for civil rights legislation in a message to Congress to which he attached a proposed bill. Its stated purpose was

> to promote the general welfare by eliminating discrimination based on race, color, religion, or national origin in ... public accommodations through the exercise by Congress of the powers conferred upon it to enforce the provisions of the Fourteenth and Fifteenth Amendments, to regulate commerce among the several States, and to make laws necessary and proper to execute the powers conferred upon it by the Constitution.

... [I]t was not until July 2, 1964, upon the recommendation of President Johnson, that the Civil Rights Act of 1964, here under attack, was finally passed. The Act as finally adopted was most comprehensive, undertaking to prevent through peaceful and voluntary settlement discrimination in voting, as well as in places of accommodation and public facilities, federally secured programs and in employment. Since Title II is the only portion under attack here, we confine our consideration to those public accommodation provisions.

3. *Title II of the [Civil Rights Act of 1964].*

This Title is divided into seven sections beginning with §201(a) which provides that:

> All persons shall be entitled to the full and equal enjoyment of the goods, services, facilities, privileges, advantages, and accommodations of any place of public accommodation, as defined in this section, without discrimination or segregation on the ground of race, color, religion, or national origin.

There are listed ... four classes of business establishments, each of which "serves the public" and "is a place of public accommodation" ... "if its operations affect commerce, or if discrimination or segregation by it is supported by State action."

4. *Application of Title II to Heart of Atlanta Motel.*

It is admitted that the operation of the motel brings it within the provisions ... of the Act and that appellant refused to provide lodging for transient Negroes because of their race or color and that it intends to continue that policy unless restrained.

The sole question posed is, therefore, the constitutionality of the Civil Rights Act of 1964 as applied to these facts. The legislative history of the Act indicates that Congress based the Act on §5 and the Equal Protection Clause of the Fourteenth Amendment as well as its power to regulate interstate commerce under Article I, §8, ¶3, of the Constitution.

The Senate Commerce Committee made it quite clear that the fundamental object of Title II was to vindicate "the deprivation of personal dignity that surely accompanies denials of equal access to public establishments." At the same time, however, it noted that such an objective has been and could be readily achieved "by congressional action based on the commerce power of the Constitution." Our study of the legislative record, made in the light of prior cases, has brought us to the conclusion that Congress possessed ample power in this regard, and we have therefore not considered the other grounds relied upon. This is not to say that the remaining authority upon which it acted was not adequate, a question upon which we do not pass, but merely that since the commerce power is sufficient for our decision here we have considered it alone....

5. *The* Civil Rights Cases, *109 U.S. 3 (1883), and their Application.*

In light of our ground for decision, it might be well at the outset to discuss the *Civil Rights Cases*, which declared provisions of the Civil Rights Act of 1875 unconstitutional. We think that decision inapposite, and without precedential value in determining the constitutionality of the present Act. Unlike Title II of the present legislation, the 1875 Act broadly proscribed discrimination in "inns, public conveyances on land or water, theaters, and other places of public amusement," without limiting the categories of affected businesses to those impinging upon interstate commerce. In contrast, the applicability of Title II is carefully limited to enterprises having a direct and substantial relation to the interstate flow of goods and people, except where state action is involved. Further, the fact that certain kinds of businesses may not in 1875 have been sufficiently involved in interstate commerce to warrant bringing them within the ambit of the commerce power is not necessarily dispositive of the same question today. Our populace had not reached its present mobility, nor were facilities, goods and services circulating as readily in interstate commerce as they are today.... Finally, there is language in the *Civil Rights Cases* which indicates that the Court did not fully consider whether the 1875 Act could be sustained as an exercise of the commerce power....

... We, therefore, conclude that the *Civil Rights Cases* have no relevance to the basis of decision here where the Act explicitly relies upon the commerce power, and where the record is filled with testimony of obstructions and restraints resulting from the discriminations found to be existing ...

6. *The Basis of Congressional Action.*

While the Act as adopted carried no congressional findings the record of its passage through each house is replete with evidence of the burdens that discrimination by race or color places upon interstate commerce. This testimony included the fact that our people have become increasingly mobile with millions of people of all races traveling from State to State; that Negroes in particular have been the subject of discrimination in transient accommodations, having to travel great distances to secure the same; that often they have been unable to obtain accommodations and have had to call upon friends to put them up overnight; and that these conditions had become so acute as to require the listing of available lodging for Negroes in a special guidebook which was itself "dramatic testimony to the difficulties" Negroes encounter in travel. These exclusionary practices were found to be nationwide, the Under Secretary of Commerce testifying that there is "no question that this discrimination in the North still exists to a large degree" and in the West and Midwest as well ...

7. *The Power of Congress Over Interstate Travel.*

In short, the determinative test of the exercise of power by the Congress under the Commerce Clause is simply whether the activity sought to be regulated is "commerce which concerns more States than one" and has a real and substantial relation to the national interest. Let us now turn to this facet of the problem.

The same interest in protecting interstate commerce which led Congress to deal with segregation in interstate carriers and the white-slave traffic has prompted it to extend the exercise of its power to gambling, *Lottery Case (Champion v Ames)*, 188 U.S. 321 (1903); to criminal enterprises, *Brooks* v. *United States*, 267 U.S. 432 (1925); to deceptive practices in the sale of products, *Federal Trade Comm.* v. *Mandel Bros., Inc.*, 359 U.S. 385 (1959); to fraudulent security transactions, *Securities & Exchange Comm.* v. *Ralston Purina Co.*, 346 U.S. 119 (1953); to misbranding of drugs, *Weeks* v. *United States*, 245 U.S. 618 (1918); to wages and hours, *United*

States v. *Darby*, 312 U.S. 100, 657; to members of labor unions, *National Labor Relations Board* v. *Jones & Laughlin Steel Corp.*, 301 U.S. 1 (1937); to crop control, *Wickard* v. *Filburn*, 317 U.S. 111 (1942); to discrimination against shippers, *United States* v. *Baltimore & Ohio R. Co.*, 333 U.S. 169 (1948); to the protection of small business from injurious price cutting, *Moore* v. *Mead's Fine Bread Co.*, 348 U.S. 115 (1954); to resale price maintenance, *Hudson Distributors, Inc.* v. *Eli Lilly & Co.*, 377 U.S. 386 (1964), *Schwegmann Bros. v. Calvert Distillers Corp.*, 341 U.S. 384 (1951); to professional football, *Radovich* v. *National Football League*, 352 U.S. 445 (1957); and to racial discrimination by owners and managers of terminal restaurants, *Boynton* v. *Com. of Virginia*, 364 U.S. 454 (1960).

That Congress was legislating against moral wrongs in many of these areas rendered its enactments no less valid. In framing Title II of this Act Congress was also dealing with what it considered a moral problem. But that fact does not detract from the overwhelming evidence of the disruptive effect that racial discrimination has had on commercial intercourse. It was this burden which empowered Congress to enact appropriate legislation, and, given this basis for the exercise of its power, Congress was not restricted by the fact that the particular obstruction to interstate commerce with which it was dealing was also deemed a moral and social wrong.

Thus the power of Congress to promote interstate commerce also includes the power to regulate the local incidents thereof, including local activities in both the States of origin and destination, which might have a substantial and harmful effect upon that commerce. One need only examine the evidence which we have discussed above to see that Congress may – as it has – prohibit racial discrimination by motels serving travelers, however "local" their operations may appear.

Nor does the Act deprive appellant of liberty or property under the Fifth Amendment. The commerce power invoked here by the Congress is a specific and plenary one authorized by the Constitution itself. The only questions are: (1) whether Congress had a rational basis for

finding that racial discrimination by motels affected commerce, and (2) if it had such a basis, whether the means it selected to eliminate that evil are reasonable and appropriate. If they are, appellant has no "right" to select its guests as it sees fit, free from governmental regulation.

As we have pointed out, 32 States now have such provisions and no case has been cited to us where the attack on a state statute has been successful, either in federal or state courts. Indeed, in some cases the Due Process and Equal Protection Clause objections have been specifically discarded in this Court. *Bob-Lo Excursion Co.* v. *People of State of Michigan*, 333 U.S. 28, 34 (1948). As a result the constitutionality of such state statutes stands unquestioned. "The authority of the Federal government over interstate commerce does not differ," it was held in *United States* v. *Rock Royal Co-op., Inc.*, 307 U.S. 533 (1939), "in extent or character from that retained by the states over intrastate commerce."

It is doubtful if in the long run appellant will suffer economic loss as a result of the Act. Experience is to the contrary where discrimination is completely obliterated as to all public accommodations. But whether this be true or not is of no consequence since this Court has specifically held that the fact that a "member of the class which is regulated may suffer economic losses not shared by others ... has never been a barrier" to such legislation. Likewise in a long line of cases this Court has rejected the claim that the prohibition of racial discrimination in public accommodations interferes with personal liberty. Neither do we find any merit in the claim that the Act is a taking of property without just compensation. The cases are to the contrary.

We find no merit in the remainder of appellant's contentions, including that of "involuntary servitude." As we have seen, 32 States prohibit racial discrimination in public accommodations. These laws but codify the common-law innkeeper rule which long predated the Thirteenth Amendment. It is difficult to believe that the Amendment was intended to abrogate this principle. Indeed, the opinion of the Court in the Civil Rights Cases is to the contrary as we have seen, it having noted with approval the laws of "all the States" prohibiting discrimination. We could not say that the requirements of the Act in this regard are in any way "akin to African slavery."

We, therefore, conclude that the action of the Congress in the adoption of the Act as applied here to a motel which concededly serves interstate travelers is within the power granted it by the Commerce Clause of the Constitution, as interpreted by this Court for 140 years. It may be argued that Congress could have pursued other methods to eliminate the obstructions it found in interstate commerce caused by racial discrimination. But this is a matter of policy that rests entirely with the Congress not with the courts. How obstructions in commerce may be removed – what means are to be employed – is within the sound and exclusive discretion of the Congress. It is subject only to one caveat – that the means chosen by it must be reasonably adapted to the end permitted by the Constitution. We cannot say that its choice here was not so adapted. The Constitution requires no more.

Justice Douglass, Concurring

Though I join the Court's opinions, I am somewhat reluctant here ... to rest solely on the Commerce Clause. My reluctance is not due to any conviction that Congress lacks power to regulate commerce in the interests of human rights. It is rather my belief that the right of people to be free of state action that discriminates against them because of race, like the "right of persons to move freely from State to State," "occupies a more protected position in our constitutional system than does the movement of cattle, fruit, steel and coal across state lines." ...

Hence I would prefer to rest on the assertion of legislative power contained in §5 of the Fourteenth Amendment which states: "The Congress shall have power to enforce, by appropriate legislation, the provisions of this article" – a power which the Court concedes was exercised at least in part in this Act.

A decision based on the Fourteenth Amendment would have a more settling effect, making unnecessary litigation over whether a particular restaurant or inn is within the commerce definitions of the Act or whether a particular customer is an interstate traveler. Under my construction, the Act would apply to all customers in all the enumerated places of public accommodation. And that construction would put an end to all obstructionist strategies and finally close one door on a bitter chapter in American history.

enforcement clause

1. What is the significance of the decision to base the constitutional authority of the Civil Rights Act, 1964, Title II (public accommodation) under the Commerce Clause and not under the Enforcement Clause (§5) of the Fourteenth Amendment? Consider the strengths and weaknesses of both approaches.
2. What does the Court leave unaddressed in this decision which ended the most visible representation of Jim Crow segregation?

After enforcement, this Act invalidated the structure of Jim Crow and *de jure* – explicitly state-mandated segregation – as illegal. However, the problem of culturally embedded racial segregation remained nationally problematic. Even today, with its guarantee of formal equality, ongoing residential segregation impacts educational opportunity, healthcare outcomes, and economic possibilities (Anderson et al. 2021; Wright et al. 2021).

Shelley v. *Kraemer* (1948) demonstrates the complexity of untangling these realities. This case is a challenge against a restrictive covenant created by a neighborhood coalition of private homeowners in St. Louis who, in 1911, agreed to not sell their property to people of African or Asian descent. This pledge was written into the deeds to their houses, ensuring it was binding for decades into the future. Similar covenants, in other parts of the country, targeted other racial, ethnic, and religious groups. While government-mandated restricted housing had been stricken as unconstitutional under the Fourteenth Amendment (*Buchanan v. Warley*, 245 U.S. 60, 1917), prior precedent interpreting the amendment as only prohibiting state acts of discrimination had limited congressional responses to private acts of racial prejudice. In 1945, the Shelley family, who were African American, bought a home and discovered that the previous owners had signed the restricted racial covenant which forbade their purchase of the property. In 1934, petitioners in Detroit bought and moved into a home that was found subject to a 1934 restricted covenant, their ownership was challenged in court. The state Supreme Courts of Missouri and Michigan upheld the legitimacy of the restrictive covenants and ordered the sales nullified. The Supreme Court combined the two cases in their decision.

SHELLEY v. KRAEMER, 334 U.S. 1 (1948)

Chief Justice Vinson Delivered the Unanimous Opinion of the Court

Vote: 6–0

These cases present for our consideration questions relating to the validity of court enforcement of private agreements, generally described as restrictive covenants, which have as their purpose the exclusion of persons of designated race or color from the ownership or occupancy of real property. Basic constitutional issues of obvious importance have been raised.

Petitioners have placed primary reliance on their contentions, first raised in the state courts, that judicial enforcement of the restrictive agreements in these cases has violated rights guaranteed to petitioners by the Fourteenth Amendment of the Federal Constitution and Acts of Congress passed pursuant to that Amendment. Specifically, petitioners urge that they have been denied the equal protection of the laws, deprived of property without due process of law, and have been denied privileges and immunities of citizens of the United States.

I.

Whether the Equal Protection Clause of the Fourteenth Amendment inhibits judicial enforcement by state courts of restrictive covenants based on race or color is a question which this Court has not heretofore been called upon to consider.

It cannot be doubted that among the civil rights intended to be protected from discriminatory state action by the Fourteenth Amendment are the rights to acquire, enjoy, own and dispose of property. Equality in the enjoyment of property rights was regarded by the framers of that Amendment as an essential pre-condition to the realization of other basic civil rights and liberties which the Amendment was intended to guarantee ...

It is likewise clear that restrictions on the right of occupancy of the sort sought to be created by the private agreements in these cases could not be squared with the requirements of the Fourteenth Amendment if imposed by state statute or local ordinance ... In the case of *Buchanan* v. *Warley*, 245 U.S. 60 (1917), a unanimous Court declared unconstitutional the provisions of a city ordinance which denied to colored persons the right to occupy houses in blocks in which the greater number of houses were occupied by white persons, and imposed similar restrictions on white persons with respect to blocks in which the greater number of houses were occupied by colored persons ...

In *Harmon* v. *Tyler*, 273 U.S. 668 (1927), a unanimous court, on the authority of *Buchanan* v. *Warley*, declared invalid an ordinance which forbade any Negro to establish a home on any property in a white community or any white person to establish a home in a Negro community, "except on the written consent of a majority of the persons of the opposite race inhabiting such community or portion of the City to be affected."

The precise question before this Court in both the *Buchanan* and *Harmon* cases, involved the rights of white sellers to dispose of their properties free from restrictions as to potential purchasers based on considerations of race or color. But that such legislation is also offensive to the rights of those desiring to acquire and occupy property and barred on grounds of race or color, is clear ... from the language of the opinion in *Buchanan* v. *Warley* ...

But the present cases, unlike those just discussed, do not involve action by state legislatures or city councils. Here the particular patterns of discrimination and the areas in which the restrictions are to operate, are determined, in the first instance, by the terms of agreements among private individuals. Participation of the State consists in the enforcement of the restrictions so defined. The crucial issue with which we are here confronted is whether this distinction removes these cases from the operation of the prohibitory provisions of the Fourteenth Amendment.

Since the decision of this Court in the *Civil Rights Cases*, 109 U.S. 3 (1883), the principle has become firmly embedded in our constitutional law that the action inhibited by the first section of the Fourteenth Amendment is only such action as may fairly be said to be that of the States. That Amendment erects no shield against merely private conduct, however discriminatory or wrongful.

We conclude, therefore, that the restrictive agreements standing alone cannot be regarded as a violation of any rights guaranteed to petitioners by the Fourteenth Amendment. So long as the purposes of those agreements are effectuated by voluntary adherence to their terms, it would appear clear that there has been no action by the State and the provisions of the Amendment have not been violated.

But here there was more. These are cases in which the purposes of the agreements were secured only by judicial enforcement by state courts of the restrictive terms of the agreements. The respondents urge that judicial enforcement of private agreements does not amount to state action; or, in any event, the participation of the State is so attenuated in character as not to amount to state action within the meaning of the Fourteenth Amendment. Finally, it is suggested, even if the States in these cases may be deemed to have acted in the constitutional sense, their action did not deprive petitioners of rights guaranteed by the Fourteenth Amendment. We move to a consideration of these matters.

II.

The short of the matter is that from the time of the adoption of the Fourteenth Amendment until the present, it has been the consistent ruling of this Court that the action of the States to which the Amendment has reference, includes action of state courts and state judicial officials. Although, in construing the terms of the Fourteenth Amendment, differences have from time to time been expressed as to whether particular types of state action may be said to offend the Amendment's prohibitory provisions, it has never been suggested that state court action is immunized from the operation of those provisions simply because the act is that of the judicial branch of the state government.

III.

Against this background of judicial construction, extending over a period of some three-quarters of a century, we are called upon to consider whether enforcement by state courts of the restrictive agreements in these cases may be deemed to be the acts of those States; and, if so, whether that action has denied these petitioners the equal protection of the laws which the [Fourteenth] Amendment was intended to insure.

We have no doubt that there has been state action in these cases in the full and complete sense of the phrase. The undisputed facts disclose that petitioners were willing purchasers of properties upon which they desired to establish homes. The owners of the properties were willing sellers; and contracts of sale were accordingly consummated. It is clear that but for the active intervention of the state courts, supported by the full panoply of state power, petitioners would have been free to occupy the properties in question without restraint.

These are not cases, as has been suggested, in which the States have merely abstained from action, leaving private individuals free to impose such discriminations as they see fit. Rather, these are cases in which the States have made available to such individuals the full coercive power of government to deny to petitioners, on the grounds of race or color, the enjoyment of property rights in premises which petitioners are willing and financially able to acquire and which the grantors are willing to sell. The difference between judicial enforcement and nonenforcement of the restrictive covenants is the difference to petitioners between being denied rights of property available to other members of the community and being accorded full enjoyment of those rights on an equal footing.

The problem of defining the scope of the restrictions which the Federal Constitution imposes upon exertions of power by the States has given rise to many of the most persistent and fundamental issues which this Court has been called upon to consider. That problem was foremost in the minds of the framers of the Constitution, and since that early day, has arisen in a multitude of forms. The task of determining whether the action of a State offends constitutional provisions is one which may not be undertaken lightly. Where, however, it is clear that the action of the State violates the terms of the fundamental charter, it is the obligation of this Court so to declare.

The historical context in which the Fourteenth Amendment became a part of the Constitution should not be forgotten. Whatever else the framers sought to achieve, it is clear that the matter of primary concern was the establishment of equality in the enjoyment of basic civil and political rights and the preservation of those rights from discriminatory action on the part of the States based on considerations of race or color. Seventy-five years ago this Court announced that the provisions of the Amendment are to be construed with this fundamental purpose in mind. Upon full consideration, we have concluded that in these cases the States have acted to deny petitioners the equal protection of the laws guaranteed by the Fourteenth Amendment. Having so decided, we find it unnecessary to consider whether petitioners have also been deprived of property without due process of law or denied privileges and immunities of citizens of the United States.

For the reasons stated, the judgment of the Supreme Court of Missouri and the judgment of the Supreme Court of Michigan must be reversed. Reversed.

Justices Reed, Jackson, and Rutledge took no part in the consideration or decision of these cases.

1. Do you believe that state enforcement of private action counts as state action in a way that engages §5 (Enforcement Clause) of the Fourteenth Amendment?
2. Should private action be excluded from the Fourteenth Amendment? How did the court conclude this? What are the implications of this decision in light of the *Civil Rights Cases* (1888)?
3. Would the same principle apply in places where the state refuses to act to protect citizens against private acts of racial discrimination, such as violence? Is the failure to act an action under the law?

In *Shelley*, the Court recognized a new form of state action, the role of the judiciary in upholding private acts of racial discrimination through enforcing racially biased contracts. By assisting homeowners in binding future generations to their own prejudices, the judicial branch and therefore the state violated the Equal Protection Clause, triggering section 5 and allowing for constitutional federal intervention in local decisions.

3.5 Impacts on Higher Education

The consequences of segregation have long tendrils that snake into our contemporary political culture. The Court faced similar historic ramifications of state-sanctioned discrimination in *U.S.* v. *Fordice* (1992). Dual (segregated) school systems were created in the South where segregation was mandated by law, as opposed to implemented via pupil assignments to public schools as typically done in the North. The legacy of these Jim Crow structures is evident in Mississippi's system of higher education. In *U.S.* v. *Fordice*, the Court assessed when a state has eliminated all vestiges of segregation and how a state could demonstrate it operates a system of higher education consistent with the principles of equal protection.

Public higher education in Mississippi began in 1848 with the establishment of the University of Mississippi, an institution designed exclusively for White students. By 1950, the state had five exclusively White universities and three solely Black public institutions. Despite *Brown I* and *Brown II*, Mississippi followed a legal-based policy of racial segregation. By 1969, the U.S. Department of Health, Education, and Welfare (HEW) attempted to enforce Title VI of the Civil Rights Act, 1964, requesting the state to create a plan to "disestablish the formerly *de jure* segregated university systems." HEW and the state could not reach an agreement, the plan the state established was not funded until 1978 and then only at a minimal level. Jake Ayers and other petitioners initiated a lawsuit in 1975, arguing that Mississippi maintained a dual system of higher education in violation of the Fourteenth Amendment's Equal Protection Clause and Title VI of the Civil Rights Act, 1964. The parties negotiated for 12 years, but 20 years after *Brown I* the university system was still segregated with 99 percent of White students matriculated at White schools and in the historically Black institutions, African American students composed over 90 percent of the student populations.

UNITED STATES v. *FORDICE/AYERS* v. *ALLAIN*, 505 U.S. 717 (1992)

Justice White Delivered the Opinion of the Court, Joined by Chief Justice Rehnquist, and Justices Blackmun, Stevens, O'Connor, Kennedy, Souter, and Thomas

Vote: 8–1

III.

The District Court, the Court of Appeals, and respondents recognize and acknowledge that the State of Mississippi had the constitutional duty to dismantle the dual school system that its laws once mandated. Nor is there any dispute that this obligation applies to its higher education system. If the State has not discharged this duty, it remains in violation of the Fourteenth Amendment. *Brown* v. *Board of Education* [347 U.S. 74 (1954)] and its progeny clearly mandate this observation. Thus, the primary issue in these cases is whether the State has met its affirmative duty to dismantle its prior dual university system.

Our decisions establish that a State does not discharge its constitutional obligations until it eradicates policies and practices traceable to its prior *de jure* dual system that continue to foster segregation. Thus we have consistently asked whether existing racial identifiability is attributable to the State; and examined a wide range of factors to determine whether the State has perpetuated its formerly *de jure* segregation in any facet of its institutional system.

... [W]e do not disagree with the Court of Appeals' observation that a state university system is quite different in very relevant respects from primary and secondary schools. Unlike attendance at the lower level schools, a student's decision to seek higher education has been a matter of choice. The State historically has not assigned university students to a particular institution. Moreover, like public universities throughout the country, Mississippi's institutions of higher learning are not fungible – they have been designated to perform certain missions. Students who qualify for admission enjoy a range of choices of which institution to attend.

We do not agree with the Court of Appeals or the District Court, however, that the adoption and implementation of race-neutral policies alone suffice to demonstrate that the State has completely abandoned its prior dual system. That college attendance is by choice and not by assignment does not mean that a race-neutral admissions policy cures the constitutional violation of a dual system. In a system based on choice, student attendance is determined not simply by admissions policies, but also by many other factors. Although some of these factors clearly cannot be attributed to state policies, many can be. Thus, even after a State dismantles its segregative *admissions* policy, there may still be state action that is traceable to the State's prior *de jure* segregation and that continues to foster segregation. The Equal Protection Clause is offended by "sophisticated as well as simple-minded modes of discrimination." *Lane* v. *Wilson*, 307 U.S. 268, 275 (1939). If policies traceable to the *de jure* system are still in force and have discriminatory effects, those policies too must be reformed to the extent practicable and consistent with sound educational practices.

IV.

... [T]here are several surviving aspects of Mississippi's prior dual system which are constitutionally suspect; for even though such policies may be race neutral on their face, they substantially restrict a person's choice of which institution to enter, and they contribute to the racial identifiability of the eight public universities. Mississippi must justify these policies or eliminate them ... [W]e address four policies of the present system: admission standards, program duplication, institutional missions assignments, and continued operation of all eight public universities ...

Because the former *de jure* segregated system of public universities in Mississippi impeded the free choice of prospective students, the State in dismantling that system must take the necessary steps to ensure that this choice now is truly free. The full range of policies and practices must be examined with this duty in mind. That an institution is predominantly white or black does not in itself make out a constitutional violation. But surely the State may not leave in place policies rooted in its prior officially segregated system that serve to maintain the racial identifiability of its universities if those policies can practically be eliminated without eroding sound educational policies.

If we understand private petitioners to press us to order the upgrading of Jackson State, Alcorn State, and Mississippi Valley State *solely* so that they may be publicly financed, exclusively black enclaves by private choice, we reject that request. The State provides these facilities for *all* its citizens and it has not met its burden under *Brown* to take affirmative steps to dismantle its prior *de jure* system when it perpetuates a separate, but "more equal" one. Whether such an increase in funding is necessary to achieve a full dismantlement under the standards we have outlined, however, is a different question, and one that must be addressed on remand.

... To the extent that the State has not met its affirmative obligation to dismantle its prior dual system, it shall be adjudged in violation of the Constitution and Title VI and remedial proceedings shall be conducted ...

Justice O'Connor, Concurring

... I write separately to emphasize that it is Mississippi's burden to prove that it has undone its prior segregation, and that the circumstances in which a State may maintain a policy or practice traceable to *de jure* segregation that has segregative effects are narrow. In light of the State's long history of discrimination, and the lost educational and career opportunities and stigmatic harms caused by discriminatory educational systems, the courts below must carefully examine Mississippi's proffered justifications for maintaining a remnant

of *de jure* segregation to ensure that such rationales do not merely mask the perpetuation of discriminatory practices ... In my view, it also follows from the State's obligation to prove that it has "take[n] all steps" to eliminate policies and practices traceable to *de jure* segregation, *Freeman* v. *Pitts*, 503 U.S. 467 (1992), that if the State shows that maintenance of certain remnants of its prior system is essential to accomplish its legitimate goals, then it still must prove that it has counteracted and minimized the segregative impact of such policies to the extent possible. Only by eliminating a remnant that unnecessarily continues to foster segregation or by negating insofar as possible its segregative impact can the State satisfy its constitutional obligation to dismantle the discriminatory system that should, by now, be only a distant memory.

Justice Thomas, Concurring

I agree with the Court that a State does not satisfy its obligation to dismantle a dual system of higher education merely by adopting race-neutral policies for the future administration of that system. Today, we hold that "[i]f policies traceable to the *de jure* system are still in force and have discriminatory effects, those policies too must be reformed to the extent practicable and consistent with sound educational practices." I agree that this statement defines the appropriate standard to apply in the higher education context. I write separately to emphasize that this standard is far different from the one adopted to govern the grade-school context in *Green* v. *School Bd. of New Kent County*, 391 U.S. 430 (1968) and its progeny. In particular, because it does not compel the elimination of all observed racial imbalance, it portends neither the destruction of historically black colleges nor the severing of those institutions from their distinctive histories and traditions.

A challenged policy does not survive under the standard we announce today if it began during the prior *de jure* era, produces adverse impacts, and persists without sound educational justification. When each of these elements has been met, I believe, we are justified in not requiring proof of a present specific intent to discriminate. It is safe to assume that a policy adopted during the *de jure* era, if it produces segregative effects, reflects a discriminatory intent. As long as that intent remains, of course, such a policy cannot continue. And given an initially tainted policy, it is eminently reasonable to make the State bear the risk of nonpersuasion with respect to intent at some future time, both because the State has created the dispute through its own prior unlawful conduct, and because discriminatory intent does tend to persist through time. Although we do not formulate our standard in terms of a burden shift with respect to intent, the factors we do consider – the historical background of the policy, the degree of its adverse impact, and the plausibility of any justification asserted in its defense – are precisely those factors that go into determining intent under *Washington* v. *Davis*, 426 U.S. 229 (1976). Thus, if a policy remains in force, without adequate justification and despite tainted roots and segregative effect, it appears clear-clear enough to presume conclusively – that the State has failed to disprove discriminatory intent.

In particular, we do not foreclose the possibility that there exists "sound educational justification" for maintaining historically black colleges *as such*. Despite the shameful history of state-enforced segregation, these institutions have survived and flourished. Indeed, they have expanded as opportunities for blacks to enter historically white institutions have expanded. Between 1954 and 1980, for example, enrollment at historically black colleges increased from 70,000 to 200,000 students, while degrees awarded increased from 13,000 to 32,000. These accomplishments have not gone unnoticed:

> I think it undisputable that these institutions have succeeded in part because of their distinctive histories and traditions; for many, historically black colleges have become "a symbol of the highest attainments of black culture." Obviously, a State cannot maintain such traditions by closing particular institutions, historically white or historically black, to particular racial groups. Nonetheless, it hardly follows that a State cannot operate a diverse assortment of institutions – including historically black institutions – open to all on a race-neutral basis, but with established traditions and programs that might disproportionately appeal to

one race or another. No one, I imagine, would argue that such institutional *diversity* is without "sound educational justification," or that it is even remotely akin to program *duplication*, which is designed to separate the races for the sake of separating the races ... Although I agree that a State is not constitutionally *required* to maintain its historically black institutions as such, I do not understand our opinion to hold that a State is *forbidden* to do so. It would be ironic, to say the least, if the institutions that sustained blacks during segregation were themselves destroyed in an effort to combat its vestiges.

Justice Scalia, Concurring in the Judgment in part and Dissenting in part

II.

It is my view that the requirement of compelled integration (whether by student assignment, as in *Green* v. *School Bd. of New Kent County*, 391 U.S. 430 (1968) itself, or by elimination of non-integrated options, as the Court today effectively decrees) does not apply to higher education. Only one aspect of a historically segregated university system need be eliminated: discriminatory admissions standards. The burden is upon the formerly *de jure* system to show that that has been achieved. Once that has been done, however, it is not just unprecedented, but illogical as well, to establish that former *de jure* States continue to deny equal protection of the law to students whose choices among public university offerings are unimpeded by discriminatory barriers. Unless one takes the position that *Brown I* required States not only to provide equal access to their universities but also to correct lingering disparities between them, that is, to remedy institutional noncompliance with the "equal" requirement of *Plessy* [v. *Ferguson, 163 U.S. 537 (1896)*], a State is in compliance with *Brown I* once it establishes that it has dismantled all discriminatory barriers to its public universities. Having done that, a State is free to govern its public institutions of higher learning as it will, unless it is convicted of discriminating anew-which requires both discriminatory intent and discriminatory causation.

III.

I must add a few words about the unanticipated consequences of today's decision. Among petitioners' contentions is the claim that the Constitution requires Mississippi to correct funding disparities between its HBI's and HWI's. The Court rejects that, as I think it should, since it is students and not colleges that are guaranteed equal protection of the laws. But to say that the Constitution does not *require* equal funding is not to say that the Constitution *prohibits* it. The citizens of a State may conclude that if certain of their public educational institutions are used predominantly by whites and others predominantly by blacks, it is desirable to fund those institutions more or less equally.

Ironically enough, however, today's decision seems to prevent adoption of such a conscious policy. What the Court says about duplicate programs is as true of equal funding: The requirement "was part and parcel of the prior dual system." Moreover, equal funding, like program duplication, facilitates continued segregation – enabling students to attend schools where their own race predominates without paying a penalty in the quality of education. Nor could such an equal-funding policy be saved on the basis that it serves what the Court calls a "sound educational justification." The only conceivable *educational* value it furthers is that of fostering schools in which blacks receive their education in a "majority" setting; but to acknowledge that as a "value" would contradict the compulsory-integration philosophy that underlies *Green*. Just as vulnerable, of course, would be all other programs that have the effect of facilitating the continued existence of predominantly black institutions: elevating

an HBI to comprehensive status where the Court inexplicably suggests that this action may be required; offering a so-called Afrocentric curriculum, as has been done recently on an experimental basis in some secondary and primary schools; preserving eight separate universities, which is perhaps Mississippi's single policy most segregative in effect; or providing funding for HBI's as HBI's, which does just that.

But this predictable impairment of HBI's should come as no surprise: for incidentally facilitating – indeed, even tolerating – the continued existence of HBI's is not what the Court's test is about ... What the Court's test is designed to achieve is the elimination of predominantly black institutions. While that may be good social policy, the present petitioners, I suspect, would not agree ... But whether or not the Court's antagonism to unintegrated schooling is good policy, it is assuredly not good constitutional law. There is nothing unconstitutional about a "black" school in the sense, not of a school that blacks *must* attend and that whites *cannot*, but of a school that, as a consequence of private choice residence or in school selection, contains, and has long contained, a large black majority. In a perverse way, in fact, the insistence, whether explicit or implicit, that such institutions not be permitted to endure perpetuates the very stigma of black inferiority that *Brown I* sought to destroy. Not only Mississippi, but Congress itself, seems out of step with the drum that the Court beats today, judging by its passage of an Act entitled "Strengthening Historically Black Colleges and Universities," which authorizes the Education Department to provide money grants to historically black colleges ...

1. How does the court distinguish between the requirements of *Brown* v. *Board of Education* (1954) for primary and secondary education versus the constitutional expectations for higher education?
2. What concern does the concurrence have for historically Black colleges and universities (HBCUs)? Where do Justices Thomas and Scalia differ?
3. Does equality require equivalent funding of institutions? What is the historic concern here?
4. How might admissions standards, program duplication, as well as institutional missions and operations be vestiges of *de jure* segregation in institutions of higher education?

In the mid-2020s, Mississippi has a population of slightly less than 3 million people of which only 28.8 percent attend a minimum of two years of college and only 13.5 percent earn a bachelor's degree; however, there are thirty-seven colleges and universities, of which eight are public four-year institutions (five predominately White (PWI) and three are historically Black (HBCU)) and fifteen are community colleges. Two of the four-year schools, a PWI and an HBCU are located 30 miles apart in the Delta and some of the community colleges are sited within the same metropolitan area. The reason for this is Mississippi's long history of a dual system of education at all levels. If the state was to consolidate their education systems to save resources and improve quality, which schools should be closed or consolidated?

A similar question is raised in the Texas case of *Richards* v. *League of United Latin American Citizens* (LULAC) (1994) where Mexican Americans living in the border counties of Texas brought a class action lawsuit arguing that the Texas history of racial discrimination has resulted in fewer advanced educational opportunities in their region. The plaintiffs claim that resources are less accessible to them, but Texas asserted that educational funding is based on "facially neutral formulas" and so extant disparities are not based on racial discrimination, instead the border region demonstrates less demand or need for higher education than other parts of the state. For the plaintiffs, a history of limited opportunities and economic barriers constrained the educational aspirations of the region and then those lowered expectations justified Texas' lesser investment. Texas believes they respond to the need, fulfilling 93 percent of resource requests from the border region as compared with 79 percent elsewhere in the state. But when historic realities frame current scenarios, do neutral policies adequately provide for racial equality? What should states be expected to do to advance equality, considering the historical contexts?

RICHARDS v. LEAGUE OF UNITED LATIN AMERICAN CITIZENS (LULAC), 868 S.W.2D 306, TEXAS S.CT. (1994)

Justice Thomas R. Phillips, Delivered the Opinion of the Court

This class action challenges the constitutionality of the Texas system of higher education. Plaintiffs contend that the policies and practices of defendants, who are State officials and regents of public universities, have denied Mexican Americans who reside in the border area of Texas participation in quality higher education programs and access to equal higher education resources. The trial court rendered a declaratory judgment that the higher education system was unconstitutional under the Texas Constitution and enjoined defendants from giving any force or effect to the higher education appropriation acts of the Texas Legislature ...

I.

Nine Mexican American organizations and fifteen Mexican American individual plaintiffs filed this action on behalf of a class later certified as follows: All persons of Mexican – (Hispanic) ancestry who reside in the Border Area consisting of these forty-one contiguous counties along the border in Texas and who are now or will be students at Texas public senior colleges and universities ...

Plaintiffs alleged discrimination in the allocation of resources in undergraduate, graduate, and professional programs to the border area schools. Specifically, they contended that defendants have placed academic programs and physical facilities where they were largely inaccessible to border area residents and have funded the institutions in the border area at lower levels than other institutions. This conduct, they charged, violates ... the Texas Constitution, and [Texas statutory code].

[T]he trial court granted plaintiffs' motions for instructed verdict and for uncontroverted fact findings on certain statistical matters. Among these were the following: (1) about 20% of all Texans live in the border area, yet only about 10% of the State funds spent for public universities are spent on public universities in that region; (2) about 54% of the public university students in the border area are Hispanic, as compared to 7% in the rest of Texas; (3) the average public college or university student in the rest of Texas must travel 45 miles from his or her home county to the nearest public university offering a broad range of masters and doctoral programs, but the average border area student must travel 225 miles; (4) only three of the approximately 590 doctoral programs in Texas are at border area universities; (5) about 15% of the Hispanic students from the border area who attend a Texas public university are at a school with a broad range of masters and doctoral programs, as compared to 61% of public university students in the rest of Texas; (6) the physical plant value per capita and number of library volumes per capita for public universities in the border area are approximately one-half of the comparable figures for non-border universities; and (7) these disparities exist against a history of discriminatory treatment of Mexican Americans in the border area (with regard to education and otherwise), and against a present climate of economic disadvantage for border area residents.

Defendants presented uncontroverted evidence that funding of higher education in Texas is currently based on facially neutral formulas ... Defendants also presented evidence that the course offerings of the various universities, which result in disparate levels of funding under the formula, are not the product of discrimination against border area schools. After the faculty, administration, and board of regents of a university decide that the school ought to offer a particular program of study, the university submits a proposal to the Board. The Board makes a determination based on need for the program ... cost, and any arrangement the university has made for start-up funding. Since its inception, the Board has approved 93.6% of the programs requested by schools in the border area, compared to only 79.5% of requests from schools in the rest of the State.

II.

As under the Fourteenth Amendment, equal protection challenges under the Texas Constitution are reviewed under a multi-tiered system. Generally, we require only that the classification under challenge be rationally related to a legitimate state purpose. The general rule gives way, however, when the classification impinges on the exercise of a fundamental right, or when the classification distinguishes between people, in terms of any right, on a "suspect" basis such as race or national origin. In those instances, the state action is subjected to strict scrutiny, requiring that the classification be narrowly tailored to serve a compelling government interest.

B.

... [I]nsofar as the [trial court] judgment in this case purports to find an equal rights violation simply because defendants "expend[] less state resources on higher education in the border area of Texas ... than its population would warrant," it cannot be sustained. In this case, if the state has made a geographical classification, defendants need only show that the system of allocating educational resources is rationally related to a legitimate purpose, which they have done under this record. Attempting to ensure that the State's limited higher education budget is wisely and efficiently spent on necessary and non-redundant programs is clearly a legitimate goal, and the State's system for coordinating these requests is a rational means of furthering that purpose.

C.

Both the federal and Texas constitutions safeguard against invidious discrimination between classes of persons. It is not necessary that the law classify by its terms or that the discrimination be overt. Neutral classifications unevenly applied can violate the constitutional guarantee. See, e.g., *Yick Wo* v. *Hopkins*, 118 U.S. 356 (1886). Also, even a facially neutral law that is applied evenhandedly can be attacked as in substance a device to impose unequal burdens on different classes of persons according to illegitimate criteria.

Although neutral classifications can be attacked as unconstitutional on the basis of uneven application or unequal burdens, we hold as a matter of law that plaintiffs here have failed to establish that the Texas university system policies and practices are in substance a device to impose unequal burdens on Mexican Americans living in the border region.

Before a neutral classification is found to be in fact a racial classification which violates the federal constitutional guarantee of equal protection, a showing of both disproportionate impact and discriminatory intent or purpose is required. "Official action will not be held unconstitutional solely because it results in a racially disproportionate impact ... Proof of racially discriminatory intent or purpose is required to show a violation of the

Equal Protection Clause." *Arlington Heights* v. *Metropolitan Housing Development Corp.*, 429 U.S. 252 (1977), citing *Washington* v. *Davis*, 426 U.S. 229 (1976).

State courts have not unequivocally interpreted their constitutional equal protection guarantees to require intentional discrimination. Some have relied upon the federal line of cases demanding proof of such intent, while others may suggest that claims alleging unintentional discrimination having a disparate impact on suspect classes will be allowed, especially in certain contexts.

There is no direct evidence in this case of an intent to discriminate against Mexican-Americans in the border area on the part of the defendants. Thus, if intent is required to establish a violation of the Texas equal rights clause, plaintiffs must show a sufficiently high level of disparate impact, either alone or in conjunction with other factors, to raise an inference of intent. They have not done so here. Even if intent is not required under the Texas equal rights clause, the evidence of impact in this case simply does not rise to an adequate level to show discrimination ...

Furthermore, there is considerable evidence in the record of the Board's efforts to increase educational opportunities for minority students in Texas.

D.

Plaintiffs nevertheless argue that they are entitled to prevail on this record because higher education should be recognized as a "fundamental right" under the Texas constitution, necessitating strict scrutiny of any law that impinges on the exercise of the right ... The United States Supreme Court has applied heightened scrutiny to laws restricting the right to travel, *Shapiro* v. *Thompson*, 394 U.S. 618 (1969), the right to vote, *Bullock* v. *Carter*, 405 U.S. 134 (1972), [and] the right to marry, *Zablocki* v. *Redhail*, 434 U.S. 374 (1978) ... The Court, however, has expressly declined to include education among that list of fundamental constitutional rights. *San Antonio Independent School District* v.

Rodriguez, 411 U.S. 1 (1973) ... However, in *Stout* v. *Grand Prairie I.S.D.*, 733 S.W.2d 290, 294 (Tex. App., 1987), the court, in another context, asserted that "public education is a fundamental right guaranteed by the Texas Constitution."

The only textual basis, either express or implied, asserted by plaintiffs for the fundamental status of higher education under the Texas Constitution is article VII, § 1. [T]he constitutional directive to maintain "an efficient system of public free schools" does not apply to higher education as that term is used in this case. Therefore, plaintiffs' reliance on that language to argue that higher education is a fundamental right secured by the Texas Constitution must fail.

E.

Finally, plaintiffs rely on *United States* v. *Fordice*, 112 S. Ct. 2727 (1992), for the proposition that adoption and implementation of race-neutral polices does not alone discharge the State's constitutional duty to eliminate segregated university education, so that lack of discrimination by defendants does not absolve them of a constitutional violation.

Whether to negate the requirement that intent be shown or to advance a different standard of requisite impact to establish an equal protection violation, plaintiffs' reliance on *Fordice* in this context is misplaced.

The Supreme Court in *Fordice* assessed Mississippi's steps to dismantle its "prior de jure segregated system" of university education. The Court began from the premise that when a state has operated a legally mandated dual education system in violation of the Equal Protection Clause, it does not suffice for the state simply to abandon the particular laws and policies that are overtly discriminatory and leave in place the system those laws have created. The Court's equal protection decisions dictate that "a State does not discharge its constitutional obligations until it eradicates policies and practices traceable to its prior de jure dual system that continue to foster segregation."

The duty addressed in *Fordice*, therefore, is a remedial one applicable when the state has operated an educational system in violation of the Equal Protection Clause under *Brown* v. *Board of Education*, 347 U.S. 483 (1954), and the duty applies to the vestiges of such *de jure* segregation. Although Texas formerly operated a higher education system in which black students were segregated by law, plaintiffs have not shown that the policies and practices attacked in this suit – i.e., the placement of institutions in regions other than the border area and the allocation of resources to nonborder area schools – are in any way traceable to that *de jure* system of segregation.

1. Why doesn't the Texas Supreme Court find *U.S.* v. *Fordice* (1992) applicable to higher education in Texas?
2. Under this ruling, how can litigants demonstrate sufficient impact to reach a constitutional violation?
3. Is access to education a fundamental right? Should it be? What are the implications for K-12? For higher education? The Civil Rights Act of 1964?

Mississippi and Texas responded differently to their litigation challenges. In addition to a settlement that provided additional funding to HBCUs, the Mississippi Legislature created the Jake Ayers fund (named after the primary litigant in the *Fordice* case) endowment to help equalize public education. However, the endowment was never seeded, although public HBCUs in Mississippi received compensatory funding for a period of time. Texas, while winning their litigation, created the University of Texas Rio Grande Valley in 2013, combining a community college and four-year institution, to provide a medical school and graduate education opportunities along the border with Mexico.

The consequences of centuries of segregation policy are evident today in our public schools – at all levels – housing, and in economic inequality. While formal inequality under the law has been achieved, it is clear by most statistical measurements of outcomes, substantive equality does not exist. What obligation, if any, do you believe that our federal and state governments have to address these inequities and why?

4 Race and State Obligation

Although the cry of "Black Lives Matter" has been traced to 2013 after the acquittal of George Zimmerman for the murder of seventeen-year-old Trayvon Martin (Lebron 2017), the claim that the state (at all levels of governance) has an obligation to respect the lives of its Black citizens and residents has a long and deep history. The devaluing of Black life is a concern that traces its roots to the years after slavery – once African Americans could no longer be legally considered property. The question of how they could be valued as humans and not just a source of cheap labor continues (Oshinsky 1996). If the government – at any level – was unwilling to intercede in the violence of slavery, lynching, sharecropping, peonage, and convict leasing, then how could Black lives be valued as citizens and residents – sovereigns – of the state? Since similar patterns of violence and state complicity existed for other communities of color in the United States, then the claim of "Brown Lives Matter" should not be unexpected. Counter-slogans of "All Lives Matter" and "Blue Lives Matter" often miss the centuries-long concerns and unique history of the relationship between our federal and local governments and people of color.

4.1 Collective Violence and State Obligation

While the state (federal and local/regional governments) reflects the people and, according to western social contract theory, is designed to protect the life, liberty, and property of its residents from the violence of others and itself, this is not always the reality. In fact, the prelude of the Constitution notes:

> We the People of the United States, in Order to form a more perfect Union, establish Justice, insure domestic Tranquility, provide for the common defense, promote the general Welfare, and secure the Blessings of Liberty to ourselves and our Posterity, do ordain and establish this Constitution for the United States of America.

Yet for many people, especially communities of color, the state has not provided these protections.

4.1.1 Lynchings and Black America

The later years of Reconstruction, when the leaders of the Confederacy attempted to regain political and economic power in the South, were particularly violent

(Foner 1990). Mob violence controlled African American voting behavior resulting in the development of a lynching culture; in response, new institutional forms of resistance emerged (e.g., National Association for the Advancement of Colored People (NAACP) and an expanded Black press).

The traditional definition of lynching contains four primary characteristics: lynching is lethal; it has "three or more perpetrators;" "the victim or victims are alleged to have committed a crime or broken a social code;" and, "the killings are extra-legal" or committed outside the legal process (Allen 2000). The heart of the traditional definition of a lynching is that the "broad base of community support ... [make] murders possible. They were not committed in wartime by a foreign enemy, nor were they the result of a single hate group, or a lone killer. They were citizen perpetrated and overwhelmingly motivated by race" (*Without Sanctuary* 2004). The distinction between a lynching and a simple murder is significant. A lynching requires the support of the community and exists for the purpose of maintaining the societal control of the oppressor (Brundage 2006). For those involved in the freedom struggle, however, lynching was always a clear means of racial control. Mary Church Terrell, for example, found lynching to be an expression of racial hatred, "the hatred of a stronger people toward a weaker, once held as slaves" (Williams 2002/2003, 11).

Lynchings are designed to convince every person in the community – regardless of race or gender – that if they step outside the norms constructed for appropriate racial behavior, they too may be destroyed. James C. Scott, in the preface to his classic work *Domination and the Arts of Resistance*, notes that certain elements of the treatment of the subordinate hold commonalities across cultures and chronology:

> ... [R]elations between the master and slave, the landlord and the serf, the high caste Hindu and the untouchable are forms of personal rule providing great latitude for arbitrary and capricious behavior by the superior. An element of personal terror invariably infuses these relations – a terror that may take the form of arbitrary beatings, sexual brutality, insults, and public humiliations. A particular slave, for example, may be lucky enough to escape such treatment but the sure knowledge that it could happen to her pervades the entire relationship. (Scott 1990, xi)

It is this notion of a common experience that can define not only the category of the oppressed, but also the oppressor, by delineating the place and role of both. It may not be solely the communal terror of a mob attacking an individual, or a small group terrorizing, torturing, murdering, and then celebrating that murder, which communicates societal expectations. The lack of prosecution of the perpetrators of extra-legal lynchings sent a powerful message as to the support they had throughout the White community (Wood 2009) and from the government. The lynching culture exists throughout the history of the United States, despite the changing manifestations of the culture. Recent scholarship has also considered the way in which White sexual violence against Black women was also used as a means of social control, this research also considers the way in which African American resistance against said violence helped to motivate many of the institutions that challenged oppression in the modern civil rights movement (McGuire 2010).

The four historical types of lynching begin with the **mob violence** that exploded in the post-Reconstruction era, what is now commonly referred to as the "nadir" of Black history (Logan 1954). Ida B. Wells-Barnett carefully substantiated this first category in her famous works *Southern Horrors* (1892) and *A Red Record* (1895); it is illustrated by public torturing and summary killings by large mobs and is well documented in the scholarly literature (Tolnay and Beck 1995; Patterson 1999; Dray 2003; Wood 2009). The second category, **legal lynching**, expands in the 1920s partly in response to the economic and political pressure orchestrated by Wells-Barnett and others, such as Frederick Douglass, T. Thomas Fortune, Mary Church Terrell, Mary Burnett Talbort, Jessie Daniel Ames, and the NAACP (Zangrando 1980; Hall 1993; Bay 2009; Francis 2011; Blight 2018). One example of this approach is from Arkansas in the early twentieth century. While a group of Black share-croppers and tenant farmers were organizing a union, they were fired upon by Whites; during the subsequent melee, a White man was killed. After the Black men were sentenced to death, the U.S. Supreme Court heard the appeal in *Moore* v. *Dempsey* (1923). Justice Oliver Wendell Holmes, in his majority opinion, noted, "if ... the whole proceeding is a mask – [if] counsel, jury, and judge were swept to the fatal end by an irresistible wave of public passion," then a constitutional violation occurs. In this case, Holmes specifically noted that the jury only deliberated for five minutes after a forty-five-minute trial (Stuntz 2011, 202). Scholars have demonstrated the robustness of the category by documenting the numerous cases where the Supreme Court did not intervene and Justice Holmes' formula was demonstrated (Oshinsky 1996, 205, 208–217; Oshinsky 2010, 7–10).

The third element of this culture of lynching is that of **the disappeared**, in which strategically chosen individuals are seized and executed in private, their bodies frequently never found. Discoveries throughout Latin America, East Asia, and Eastern Europe of mass graves, filled with the bodies of those who had been missing for many years, reinforces the power of state-sanctioned violence and its impact on the communities from where the individuals disappeared (Shestack 1979; Sanford 2004; Feitlowitz 2011). In the United States, local juries demonstrated their compliance by refusing to convict known perpetrators. The lynchings of Emmett Till (1955), the three civil rights workers (James Chaney, Mickey Schwerner, and Andrew Goodman) in Philadelphia, Mississippi (1964), and of Henry Hezekiah Dee and Charles Eddie Moore (1964) are typical of this type. Finally, and more controversially, the **criminal justice system**, especially in terms of the racialized nature of mass incarceration, the disproportionate numbers of racial minorities on death row, and the arbitrariness of its application, have been argued by some as being a contemporary manifestation of our lynching culture (McFeely 1997; Stevenson 2014).

We see similar uses of state-sanctioned private violence or private actions with impunity against other racial groups, in other regions of the country, as discussed in previous chapters. There is evidence of violence throughout our history and even today there are news stories of individuals who are challenging norms – dating cross-racially, attempting to enter the country without documentation, presenting a more fluid sexual identity – being found hanging and claimed as a suicide – or shot and their bodies left to decompose (Lentz 2012; Brown 2021; Allah 2021; Villegas 2023).

4.1.2 Private Violence and State Obligation

What is the role of the state (both federal and state governments) in protecting the individual citizen from other citizens? Does the government have a different role to play when violence is racially targeted? If the purpose of racial violence is to limit the exercise of civil rights, such as the right to vote, do governmental entities have a greater responsibility?

The history of the lynching culture in the United States demonstrates a clear design of limiting the exercise of civil rights. Community groups like the Ku Klux Klan and the Knights of the White Camellia organized to pressure Blacks from exercising the vote or behaving as full citizens; the Republican Congress in 1870 organized to provide the federal government authority to stop such violations through new legislation.

The Civil Rights Act, 1870, was written to enforce the individual right to vote and provide the president with the authority to enforce the voting protections provided to the newly freed peoples in the Fifteenth Amendment. The stated intention of this law was to protect "all persons in their constitutional right to vote without distinction of race, color, or previous condition of servitude." In passing this policy, the legislature perceived a need to federally criminalize attempts to prevent individuals from voting by threats or intimidation and to clarify that groups or organizations that conspire to prevent others from voting are committing a felony. It is notable that Congress explicitly addresses the culpability of state officials – those employed by governments to enforce the law or act "under color of law" – who treat people differently based on race or citizenship status while acting in their official capacity. Two additional Force Acts, also known as the Second and Third Ku Klux Klan Acts, were later passed. The Second Force Act (February 1871) granted the federal government the authority to regulate national elections and supervise local polling sites. The Third Force Act (April 1872) authorized the president to use the military to protect state residents from those who attempted to deny equal protection of the laws and enforce the Acts.

CIVIL RIGHTS ACT, 1870 (ENFORCEMENT ACT OR FIRST KU KLUX KLAN ACT)

CHAP., CXIV., An Act to Enforce the Right of Citizens of the United States to Vote in the Several States of this Union, and for other Purposes

Sec. 4 *And be it further enacted*, That if any person, by force, bribery, threats, intimidation, or other unlawful means, shall hinder, delay, prevent, or obstruct, or shall combine and confederate with others to hinder, delay, prevent, or obstruct, any citizen from doing any act required to be done to qualify him to vote or from voting at any election as aforesaid, such person shall for every such offence forfeit and pay the sum of five hundred dollars to the person aggrieved thereby ... and shall also for every such offence be guilty of a misdemeanor, and shall, on conviction thereof, be fined not less than five hundred dollars, or be imprisoned not less than one month and not more than one year, or both, at the discretion of the court.

Sec. 5 *And be it further enacted*, That if any person shall prevent, hinder, control, or intimidate, or shall attempt to prevent, hinder, control, or intimidate, any person from exercising or in exercising the right of suffrage, to whom the right of suffrage is secured or guaranteed by the fifteenth amendment to the Constitution of the United States, by means of bribery, threats, or threats of depriving such person of employment or occupation, or of ejecting such person from rented house, lands, or other property, or by threats of refusing to renew leases or contracts for labor, or by threats of violence to himself or family, such person so offending shall be deemed guilty of a misdemeanor, and shall, on conviction thereof, be fined not less than five hundred dollars, or be imprisoned not less than one month and not more than one year, or both, at the discretion of the court.

Sec. 6 *And be it further enacted*, That if two or more persons shall band or conspire together, or go in disguise upon the public highway, or upon the premises of another, with intent to violate any provision of this act, or to injure, oppress, threaten, or intimidate any citizen with intent to prevent or hinder his free exercise and enjoyment of any right or privilege granted or secured to him by the Constitution or laws of the United States, or because of his having exercised the same, such persons shall be held guilty of felony, and, on conviction thereof, shall be fined or imprisoned, or both, at the discretion of the court ... and shall, moreover, be thereafter ... disabled from holding, any office or place of honor, profit, or trust created by the Constitution or laws of the United States.

Sec. 8 *And be it further enacted*, That the district courts of the United States, within their respective districts, shall have, exclusively of the courts of the several States, cognizance of all crimes and offenses committed against the provisions of this act, and also, concurrently with the circuit courts of the United States, of all causes, civil and criminal, arising under this act ...

Sec. 16 *And be it further enacted*, That all persons within the jurisdiction of the United Sates shall have the same right in every State and Territory in the United States to make and enforce contracts, to sue, be parties, give evidence, and to the full and equal benefit of all laws and proceedings for the security of person and property as is enjoyed by white citizens, and shall be subject to like punishment, pains, penalties, taxes, licenses, and exactions of every kind, and none other, any law, statue, ordinance, regulation, or custom to the contrary notwithstanding. No tax or charge shall be imposed or enforced by any State upon any person immigrating thereto from a foreign country which is not equally imposed and enforced upon every person immigrating to such State from any other foreign country; and any law of any State in conflict with this provision is hereby declared null and void.

Sec. 17 *And be it further enacted*, That any person who, under color of any law, stature, ordinance, regulation or custom, shall subject, or cause to be subjected, any inhabitant of any State or Territory to the deprivation of any right secured or protected by the last preceding section of this act, or to different punishment, pains, or penalties on account of such person being an alien, or by reason of his color or race, than is prescribed for the punishment of citizens, shall be deemed guilty of a misdemeanor, and, on conviction, shall be punished by fine not exceeding one thousand dollars, or imprisonment not exceeding one year, or both, in the discretion of the court.

1. What does it mean to act under "color of law"?
2. Why would Congress feel the need to recognize this status? What does it mean that the federal government can hold local law enforcement officially criminally accountable? When might that be necessary?

This new law was tested during Reconstruction in the federal Supreme Court case of *U.S.* v. *Cruikshank* (1875). As the former members of the Confederacy sought to take back White authority in the South, there were many violent encounters. One of the bloodiest was in 1872, when a group of Black citizens occupied the courthouse in Colfax, Louisiana, in order to protect Republican officeholders from a private White militia formed of ex-Confederate soldiers and members of the Ku Klux Klan (Lane 2008). An unknown number of African Americans were killed in what was called the Colfax Massacre; the estimates of the number of victims range from sixty to over a hundred and fifty, as the White militiamen hid many of their victims' bodies. The federal government prosecuted a small percentage of the almost a hundred accused perpetrators, claiming that the militia members had denied fundamental constitutional rights protected by the Fourteenth Amendment and the Enforcement Act, 1870 (such as the right to assemble, bear arms, and vote) to the Black citizens they had attacked and killed, three of the 100 were found guilty of some of the charges and they appealed.

UNITED STATES v. CRUIKSHANK, 92 U.S. 542 (1875)

Chief Justice Waite Delivered the Opinion of the Court, Joined by Justices Swayne, Miller, Field, and Strong

Vote: 5–4

… [The case] presents for our consideration an indictment containing sixteen counts, divided into two series of eight counts each, based upon sect. 6 of the Enforcement Act of May 31, 1870.

Citizens are the members of the political community to which they belong. They are the people who compose the community, and who, in their associated capacity, have established or submitted themselves to the dominion of a government for the promotion of their general welfare and the protection of their individual as well as their collective rights. In the formation of a government, the people may confer upon it such powers as they choose. The government, when so formed, may, and when called upon should, exercise all the powers it has for the protection of the rights of its citizens and the people within its jurisdiction; but it can exercise no other. The duty of a government to afford protection is limited always by the power it possesses for that purpose.

Experience made the fact known to the people of the United States that they required a national government for national purposes ... For this reason, the people of the United States,. ordained and established the government of the United States, and defined its powers by a constitution, which they adopted as its fundamental law, and made its rule of action.

The people of the United States resident within any State are subject to two governments: one State, and the other National; but there need be no conflict between the two. The powers which one possesses, the other does not. They are established for different purposes, and have separate jurisdictions. Together they make one whole, and furnish the people of the United States with a complete government, ample for the protection of all their rights at home and abroad ...

We now proceed to an examination of the indictment, to ascertain whether the several rights, which it is alleged the defendants intended to interfere with, are such as had been in law and in fact granted or secured by the constitution or laws of the United States.

The first and ninth counts state the intent of the defendants to have been to hinder and prevent the citizens named in the free exercise and enjoyment of their "lawful right and privilege to peaceably assemble together with each other and with other citizens of the United States for a peaceful and lawful purpose." The right of the people peaceably to assemble for lawful purposes existed long before the adoption of the Constitution of the United States. In fact, it is, and always has been, one of the attributes of citizenship under a free government. It "derives its source," to use the language of Chief Justice Marshall, in *Gibbons* v. *Ogden*, 9 Wheat. 211 (1824), "from those laws whose authority is acknowledged by civilized man throughout the world." It is found wherever civilization exists.

It was not, therefore, a right granted to the people by the Constitution. The government of the United States when established found it in existence, with the obligation on the part of the States to afford it protection. As no direct power over it was granted to Congress, it remains, according to the ruling in *Gibbons* v. *Ogden*, subject to State jurisdiction. Only such existing rights were committed by the people to the protection of Congress as came within the general scope of the authority granted to the national government.

The First Amendment to the Constitution prohibits Congress from abridging "the right of the people to assemble and to petition the government for a redress of grievances." This, like the other amendments proposed and adopted at the same time, was not intended to limit the powers of the State governments in respect to their own citizens, but to operate upon the National government alone ... They left the authority of the States just where they found it, and added nothing to the already existing powers of the United States.

The second and tenth counts are equally defective. The right there specified is that of "bearing arms for a lawful purpose." This is not a right granted by the Constitution. Neither is it in any manner dependent upon that instrument for its existence. The second amendment declares that it shall not be infringed; but this, as has been seen, means no more than that it shall not be infringed by Congress. This is one of the amendments that has no other effect than to restrict the powers of the national government, leaving the people to look for their protection against any violation by their fellow-citizens of the rights it recognizes, to what is called ... the "powers which relate to merely municipal legislation, or what was, perhaps, more properly called internal police," "not surrendered or restrained" by the Constitution of the United States.

The third and eleventh counts are even more objectionable. They charge the intent to have been to deprive the citizens named, they being in Louisiana, "of their respective several lives and liberty of person without due process of law." This is nothing else than alleging a conspiracy to falsely imprison or murder citizens of the United States, being within the territorial jurisdiction of the State of Louisiana. The rights of life and personal liberty are natural rights of man. "To secure these rights," says the Declaration of Independence, "governments are instituted among men, deriving their just powers from the consent of the governed." The very highest duty of the States, when they entered into the Union under the Constitution, was to protect all persons within their boundaries in the enjoyment of these "unalienable rights with which they were endowed by their Creator." Sovereignty, for this purpose, rests alone with the States. It is no more the duty or within the power of the United States to punish for a conspiracy to falsely imprison or murder within a State, than it would be to punish for false imprisonment or murder itself.

The fourth and twelfth counts charge the intent to have been to prevent and hinder the citizens named, who were of African descent and persons of color, in "the free exercise and enjoyment of their several right and privilege to the full and equal benefit of all laws and proceedings, then and there, before that time, enacted or ordained by the said State of Louisiana and by the United States; and then and there, at that time, being in force in the said State and District of Louisiana aforesaid, for the security of their respective persons and property, then and there, at that time enjoyed at and within said State and District of Louisiana by white persons, being citizens of said State of Louisiana and the United States, for the protection of the persons and property of said white citizens." There is no allegation that this was done because of the race or color of the persons conspired against. When stripped of its verbiage, the case as presented amounts to nothing more than that the defendants conspired to prevent certain citizens of the United States, being within the State of Louisiana, from enjoying the equal protection of the laws of the State and of the United States.

The Fourteenth Amendment prohibits a State from denying to any person within its jurisdiction the equal protection of the laws; but this provision does not, any more than the one which precedes it, and which we have just considered, add anything to the rights which one citizen has under the Constitution against another. The equality of the rights of citizens is a principle of republicanism. Every republican government is in duty bound to protect all its citizens in the enjoyment of this principle, if within its power. That duty was originally assumed by the States; and it still remains there. The only obligation resting upon the United States is to see that the States do not deny the right. This the amendment guarantees, but no more. The power of the national government is limited to the enforcement of this guaranty.

The sixth and fourteenth counts state the intent of the defendants to have been to hinder and prevent the citizens named, being of African descent, and colored, "in the free exercise and enjoyment of their several and respective right and privilege to vote at any election to be thereafter by law had and held by the people in and of the said State of Louisiana, or by the people of and in the parish of Grant aforesaid." In *Minor* v. *Happersett*, 85 U.S. 162 (1875), we decided that the Constitution of the United States has not conferred the right of suffrage upon anyone, and that the United States have no voters of their own creation in the States. In *United States* v. *Reese*, 92 U.S. 214 (1876), we hold that the Fifteenth Amendment has invested the citizens of the United States with a new constitutional right, which is, exemption from discrimination in the exercise of the elective franchise on account of race, color, or previous condition of servitude. From this it appears that the right of suffrage is not a necessary attribute of national citizenship; but that exemption from discrimination in the exercise of that right on account of race is. The right to vote in the States comes from the States; but the right of exemption from the prohibited discrimination comes from the United States. The first has not been granted or secured by the Constitution of the United States; but the last has been.

Inasmuch, therefore, as it does not appear in these counts that the intent of the defendants was to prevent these parties from exercising their right to vote on account of their race, it does not appear that it was their intent to interfere with any right granted or secured by the constitution or laws of the United States. We may suspect that race was the cause of the hostility; but it is not so averred. This is material to a description of the substance of the offence, and cannot be supplied by implication. Everything essential must be charged positively, and not inferentially. The defect here is not in form, but in substance.

The seventh and fifteenth counts are no better than the sixth and fourteenth. The intent here charged is to put the parties named in great fear of bodily harm, and to injure and oppress them, because ... they had voted ... There is nothing to show that the elections voted at were any other than State elections, or that the conspiracy was formed on account of the race of the parties against whom the conspirators were to act. The charge as made is really of nothing more than a conspiracy to commit a breach of the peace within a State. Certainly it will not be claimed that the United States have the power or are required to do mere police duly in the States ...

We are, therefore, of the opinion that the first, second, third, fourth, sixth, seventh, ninth, tenth, eleventh, twelfth, fourteenth, and fifteenth counts do not contain charges of a criminal nature made indictable under the laws of the United States, and that consequently they are not good and sufficient in law. They do not show that it was the intent of the defendants, by their conspiracy, to hinder or prevent the enjoyment of any right granted or secured by the Constitution.

The order of the Circuit Court arresting the judgment upon the verdict is, therefore, affirmed; and the cause remanded, with instructions to discharge the defendants.

Justice Clifford, Joined by Justices Davis, Bradley, and Hunt, Concurring and Dissenting

More than one hundred persons were jointly indicted at the April Term, 1873, of the Circuit Court of the United States for the District of Louisiana, charged with offences in violation of the provisions of the Enforcement Act ...

None of the introductory allegations allege that any overt act was perpetrated in pursuance of the alleged conspiracy; but the jurors proceed to present that the unlawful and felonious intent and purpose of the defendants were to prevent and hinder the said citizens of African descent and persons of color, by the means therein described, in the free exercise and enjoyment *of each, every, all, and singular the several rights and privileges* granted and secured to them by the constitution and laws of the United States in common with all other good citizens, without any attempt to describe or designate any particular right or privilege which it was the purpose and intent of the defendants to invade, abridge, or deny.

Certain other causes for arresting the judgment are assigned in the record, which deny the constitutionality of the Enforcement Act; but, having come to the conclusion that the indictment is insufficient, it is not necessary to consider that question.

1. Why does the Court find no protection from the Enforcement Act, 1870, or the Fourteenth Amendment against a racial massacre?
2. Why does the majority begin with a discussion of federalism and the concurring/dissenting opinion question the constitutionality of the Enforcement Act?
3. What remedy might this Court recommend to the victims of racial violence? If the state does not prevent or punish this violence, and the federal government does not have the authority, what options remain?

In *Cruikshank*, the Supreme Court found that the Fourteenth Amendment and the Bill of Rights did not limit the behavior of private (non-state or individual) actors, nor did it compel states to protect the rights of their own citizens. The three men who had been convicted of this mob violence had their sentences overturned. This decision made federal prosecution of crimes against people of color almost impossible and allowed lynch mobs – who were often joined by or condoned by

White elected officials – to do their work without legal challenge. The impact of this decision would reverberate throughout the twentieth century, preventing the federal government from intervening in private acts of violence based on racial animosity absent a national law banning lynching.

Congress, through federal legislation, also tried to prevent the re-establishment of the old Slave Codes as Black Codes. As discussed in Chapter 3, these customs rapidly became laws as White local rule overtook the South and required the maintenance of a racial hierarchy in all elements of life. To limit the legal impact of these customs, the Civil Rights Act, 1875, attempted to prohibit states from providing unequal treatment based on race.

CIVIL RIGHTS ACT, 1875

Whereas it is essential to just government we recognize the equality of all men before the law, and hold that it is the duty of government in its dealings with the people to mete out equal and exact justice to all, of whatever nativity, race, color, or persuasion, religious or political; and it being the appropriate object of legislation to enact great fundamental principles into law: Therefore,

Sec. 1. Be it enacted ... [t]hat all persons within the jurisdiction of the United States shall be entitled to the full and equal enjoyment of the accommodations, advantages, facilities, and privileges of inns, public conveyances on land or water, theaters, and other places of public amusement; subject only to the conditions and limitations established by law, and applicable alike to citizens of every race and color, regardless of any previous condition of servitude.

Sec. 2. That any person who shall violate the foregoing section by denying to any citizen, except for reasons by law applicable to citizens of every race and color, and regardless of any previous condition of servitude, the full enjoyment of any of the accommodations, advantages, facilities, or privileges in said section enumerated, or by aiding or soliciting such denial, shall, for every offence, forfeit and pay the sum of five hundred dollars to the person aggrieved thereby, to be recovered in an action of debt, with full costs; and shall also, for every such offense, be deemed guilty of a misdemeanor, and, upon conviction thereof, shall be fined not less than five hundred nor more than one thousand dollars, or shall be imprisoned not less than thirty days nor more than one year ...

Sec. 3. That the district and circuit courts of the United States shall have, exclusively of the courts of the several States, cognizance of all crimes and offenses against, and violations of, the provisions of this act; and actions for the penalty given by the preceding section may be prosecuted in the territorial, district, or circuit courts of the United States wherever the defendant may be found, without regard to the other party; and the district attorneys, marshals, and deputy marshals of the United States, and commissioners appointed by the circuit and territorial courts of the United States, with powers of arresting and imprisoning or bailing offenders against the laws of the United States, are hereby specially authorized and required to institute proceedings against every person who shall violate the provisions of this act ...

Sec. 4. That no citizen possessing all other qualification which are or may be prescribed by law shall be disqualified for service as grand or petit juror in any court of the United States, or of any State, on account of race, color, or previous condition of servitude; and any officer or other person charged with any duty in the selection or summoning of jurors who shall exclude or fail to summon any citizen for the cause aforesaid shall, on conviction thereof, be deemed guilty of a misdemeanor, and be fined not more than five thousand dollars.

Sec. 5. That all cases arising under the provisions of this act in the courts of the United States shall be reviewable by the Supreme Court of the United States, without regard to the sum in controversy, under the same provisions and regulations as are now provided by law for the review of other causes in said court.

These laws would be tested by the Supreme Court in 1883 in the *Civil Rights Cases*, which combined five separate court cases in which an African American litigant challenged the denial of accommodations (hotel, public transportation, public amusement, etc.) that White customers were granted, in violation of federal protections. While these companies were privately owned, under the Civil Rights Act, 1875, such businesses were classified as having a public function and thus were capable of being publicly regulated by the federal government. The question before the Court was whether the Fourteenth Amendment's Enforcement Clause (§5), which authorizes the federal government – particularly Congress – to pass legislation, ensured the guarantee of due process, equal protection, and privileges and immunities to the residents of states. The Civil Rights Act, 1875, provided federal penalties for those individuals who personally or collectively violated the civil rights of others based on race. This case asks if the Fourteenth Amendment granted such authority to Congress over the sovereignty of the states.

CIVIL RIGHTS CASES, 109 U.S. 3 (1883)

Justice Bradley Delivered the Opinion of the Court, Joined by Chief Justice Waite, and Justices Miller, Field, Bradley, Woods, Matthews, Gray, and Blatchford

Vote: 8–1

The essence of the law is not to declare broadly that all persons shall be entitled to the full and equal enjoyment of the accommodations, advantages, facilities, and privileges of inns, public conveyances, and theatres, but that such enjoyment shall not be subject to any conditions applicable only to citizens of a particular race or color, or who had been in a previous condition of servitude. In other words, it is the purpose of the law to declare that, in the enjoyment of the accommodations ... no distinction shall be made between citizens of different race or color or between those who have, and those who have not, been slaves ... The second section makes it a penal offence in any person to deny to any citizen of any race or color, regardless of previous servitude, any of the accommodations or privileges mentioned in the first section.

Has Congress constitutional power to make such a law? Of course, no one will contend that the power to pass it was contained in the Constitution before the adoption of the last three amendments. The power is sought, first, in the Fourteenth Amendment, and the views and arguments of distinguished Senators, advanced whilst the law was under consideration, claiming authority to pass it by virtue of that amendment, are the principal arguments adduced in favor of the power ...

The first section of the Fourteenth Amendment (which is the one relied on), after declaring who shall be citizens of the United States, and of the several States, is prohibitory in its character, and prohibitory upon the States. It declares that: "No State shall make or enforce any law which shall abridge the privileges or immunities of citizens of the United States; nor shall any State deprive any person of life, liberty, or property without due process of law; nor deny to any person within its jurisdiction the equal protection of the laws."

It is State action of a particular character that is prohibited. Individual invasion of individual rights is not the subject matter of the amendment. It has a deeper and broader scope. It nullifies and makes void all State legislation, and State action of every kind, which impairs the privileges and immunities of citizens of the United States or which injures them in life, liberty or property without due process of law, or which denies to any of them the equal protection of the laws. It not only does this, but, in order that the national will, thus declared, may not be a mere *brutum fulmen* [an empty threat or loud thunder], the last section of the amendment invests Congress with power to enforce it by appropriate legislation. To enforce what? To enforce the prohibition. To adopt appropriate legislation for correcting the effects of such prohibited State laws and State acts, and thus to render them effectually null, void, and innocuous. This is the legislative power conferred upon Congress, and this is the whole of it. It does not invest Congress with power to legislate upon subjects which are within the domain of State legislation, but to provide modes of relief

against State legislation, or State action, of the kind referred to. It does not authorize Congress to create a code of municipal law for the regulation of private rights, but to provide modes of redress against the operation of State laws and the action of State officers executive or judicial when these are subversive of the fundamental rights specified in the amendment. Positive rights and privileges are undoubtedly secured by the Fourteenth Amendment, but they are secured by way of prohibition against State laws and State proceedings affecting those rights and privileges, and by power given to Congress to legislate for the purpose of carrying such prohibition into effect, and such legislation must necessarily be predicated upon such supposed State laws or State proceedings, and be directed to the correction of their operation and effect. A quite full discussion of this aspect of the amendment may be found in *United States* v. *Cruikshank*, 92 U.S. 542 (1875).

... [T]he legislation which Congress is authorized to adopt in this behalf is not general legislation upon the rights of the citizen, but corrective legislation, that is, such as may be necessary and proper for counteracting such laws as the States may adopt or enforce, and which, by the amendment, they are prohibited from making or enforcing, or such acts and proceedings as the States may commit or take, and which, by the amendment, they are prohibited from committing or taking ...

In this connection, it is proper to state that civil rights, such as are guaranteed by the Constitution against State aggression, cannot be impaired by the wrongful acts of individuals, unsupported by State authority in the shape of laws, customs, or judicial or executive proceedings. The wrongful act of an individual, unsupported by any such authority, is simply a private wrong, or a crime of that individual; an invasion of the rights of the injured party, it is true, whether they affect his person, his property, or his reputation; but if not sanctioned in some way by the State, or not done under State authority, his rights remain in full force, and may presumably be vindicated by resort to the laws of the State for redress. An individual cannot deprive a man of his right to vote, to hold property, to buy and sell, to sue in the courts, or to be a witness or a juror; he may, by force or fraud, interfere with the enjoyment of the right in a particular case; he may commit an assault against the person, or commit murder, or use ruffian violence at the polls, or slander the good name of a fellow citizen; but, unless protected in these wrongful acts by some shield of State law or State authority, he cannot destroy or injure the right; he will only render himself amenable to satisfaction or punishment, and amenable therefor to the laws of the State where the wrongful acts are committed. Hence, in all those cases where the Constitution seeks to protect the rights of the citizen against discriminative and unjust laws of the State by prohibiting such laws, it is not individual offences, but abrogation and denial of rights, which it denounces and for which it clothes the Congress with power to provide a remedy. This abrogation and denial of rights for which the States alone were or could be responsible was the great seminal and fundamental wrong which was intended to be remedied. And the remedy to be provided must necessarily be predicated upon that wrong. It must assume that, in the cases provided for, the evil or wrong actually committed rests upon some State law or State authority for its excuse and perpetration.

If the principles of interpretation which we have laid down are correct ... it is clear that the [Civil Rights Act of 1875] cannot be sustained by any grant of legislative power made to Congress by the Fourteenth Amendment ...

When a man has emerged from slavery, and, by the aid of beneficent legislation, has shaken off the inseparable concomitants of that state, there must be some stage in the progress of his elevation when he takes the rank of a mere citizen and ceases to be the special favorite of the laws, and when his rights as a citizen or a man are to be protected in the ordinary modes by which other men's rights are protected. There were thousands of free colored people in this country before the abolition of slavery, enjoying all the essential rights of life, liberty and property the same as white citizens, yet no one at that time thought that it was any invasion of his personal status as a freeman because he was not admitted to all the privileges enjoyed by white citizens, or because he was subjected to discriminations in the enjoyment of accommodations in inns, public conveyances and places of amusement. Mere discriminations on account of race or color were not regarded as badges of slavery. If, since that time, the enjoyment of equal rights in all these respects has become established by constitutional enactment, it is not by force of the Thirteenth Amendment (which merely abolishes slavery), but by force of the Thirteenth and Fifteenth Amendments.

On the whole, we are of opinion that no countenance of authority for the passage of the law in question can be found in either the Thirteenth or Fourteenth Amendment of the Constitution, and no other ground of authority for its passage being suggested, it must necessarily be declared void, at least so far as its operation in the several States is concerned.

Justice Harlan, Dissenting

There seems to be no substantial difference between my brethren and myself as to the purpose of Congress, for they say that the essence of the law is not to declare broadly that all persons shall be entitled to the full and equal enjoyment of the accommodations, advantages, facilities, and privileges of inns, public conveyances, and theatres, but that such enjoyment shall not be subject to conditions applicable only to citizens of a particular race or color, or who had been in a previous condition of servitude. The effect of the statute, the court says, is that colored citizens, whether formerly slaves or not, and citizens of other races shall have the same accommodations and privileges in all inns, public conveyances, and places of amusement as are enjoyed by white persons, and vice versa.

The court adjudges, I think erroneously, that Congress is without power, under either the Thirteenth or Fourteenth Amendment, to establish such regulations, and that the first and second sections of the statute are, in all their parts, unconstitutional and void.

That there are burdens and disabilities which constitute badges of slavery and servitude, and that the power to enforce by appropriate legislation the Thirteenth Amendment may be exerted by legislation of a direct and primary character for the eradication not simply of the institution, but of its badges and incidents, are propositions which ought to be deemed indisputable ...

I am of the opinion that such discrimination practised by corporations and individuals in the exercise of their public or *quasi*-public functions is a badge of servitude the imposition of which Congress may prevent under its power, by appropriate legislation, to enforce the Thirteenth Amendment; and consequently, without reference to its enlarged power under the Fourteenth Amendment, the act of March 1, 1875, is not, in my judgment, repugnant to the Constitution.

But when, under what circumstances, and to what extent may Congress, by means of legislation, exert its power to enforce the provisions of [the Fourteenth Amendment]? The theory of the opinion of the majority of the court – the foundation upon which their reasoning seems to rest – is that the general government cannot, in advance of hostile State laws or hostile State proceedings, actively interfere for the protection of any of the rights, privileges, and immunities secured by the Fourteenth Amendment. It is said that such rights, privileges, and immunities are secured by way of *prohibition* against State laws and State proceedings affecting such rights and privileges, and by power given to Congress to legislate for the purpose of carrying *such prohibition* into effect; also, that congressional legislation must necessarily be predicated upon such supposed State laws or State proceedings, and be directed to the correction of their operation and effect.

The citizenship thus acquired by that race in virtue of an affirmative grant from the nation may be protected not alone by the judicial branch of the government, but by congressional legislation of a primary direct character, this because the power of Congress is not restricted to the enforcement of prohibitions upon State laws or State action. It is, in terms distinct and positive, to enforce "the *provisions of this article*" of amendment; not simply those of a prohibitive character, but the provisions – *all* of the provisions – affirmative and prohibitive, of the amendment. It is, therefore, a grave misconception to suppose that the fifth section of the amendment has reference exclusively to express prohibitions upon State laws or State action. If any right was created by that amendment, the grant of power through appropriate legislation to enforce its provisions authorizes Congress, by means of legislation operating throughout the entire Union, to guard, secure, and protect that right.

My brethren say that, when a man has emerged from slavery, and by the aid of beneficent legislation has shaken off the inseparable concomitants of that state, there must be some stage in the progress of his elevation when he takes the rank of a mere citizen, and ceases to be the special favorite of the laws, and when his rights as a citizen or a man are to be protected in the ordinary modes by which other men's rights are protected. It is, I submit, scarcely just to say that the colored race has been the special favorite of the laws. The statute of 1875, now adjudged to be unconstitutional, is for the benefit of citizens of every race and color. What the nation, through Congress, has sought to accomplish in reference to that race is what had already been done in every State of the Union for the white race – to secure and protect rights belonging to them as freemen and citizens, nothing more. It was not deemed enough "to help the feeble up, but to support him after." The one underlying purpose of congressional legislation has been to enable the black race to take the rank of mere citizens. The difficulty has been to compel a recognition of the legal right of the black race to take the rank of citizens, and to secure the enjoyment of privileges belonging, under the law, to them as a component part of the people for whose welfare and happiness government is ordained.

Today it is the colored race which is denied, by corporations and individuals wielding public authority, rights fundamental in their freedom and citizenship. At some future time, it may be that some other race will fall under the ban of race discrimination. If the constitutional amendments be enforced according to the intent with which, as I conceive, they were adopted, there cannot be, in this republic, any class of human beings in practical subjection to another class with power in the latter to dole out to the former just such privileges as they may choose to grant. The supreme law of the land has decreed that no authority shall be exercised in this country upon the basis of discrimination, in respect of civil rights, against freemen and citizens because of their race, color, or previous condition of servitude. To that decree – for the due enforcement of which, by appropriate legislation, Congress has been invested with express power – everyone must bow, whatever may have been, or whatever now are, his individual views as to the wisdom or policy either of the recent changes in the fundamental law or of the legislation which has been enacted to give them effect.

For the reasons stated, I feel constrained to withhold my assent to the opinion of the court.

1. How do the majority and the dissent construct the meaning of the Fourteenth Amendment differently? Consider specifically the question of the "badges of slavery" and the question of whether African Americans are being treated as "special favorites of the law."
2. What is the significance of the disagreement moving forward in the law?
3. If Justice Harlan's interpretation had been adopted what might have been the consequences?
4. Which approach do you find more persuasive? Why?
5. Consider the decision in *Shelley* v. *Kraemer* (1948). How might that decision impact our interpretation of the *Civil Rights Cases*?

In the majority opinion, the Court found the Civil Rights Act, 1875, and the Enforcement Act, 1870, to be unconstitutional because the Fourteenth Amendment provided Congress with the authority to prevent the states from violating the rights of its residents based on their race or previous condition of servitude. These laws were designed to prevent race-based violence and discrimination against citizens by other citizens. The Court repeatedly found that these acts of private discrimination were outside the scope of congressional authority.

Justice Bradley, speaking for the majority, claimed

> When a man has emerged from slavery, and, by the aid of beneficent legislation, has shaken off the inseparable concomitants of that state, there must be some stage in the progress of his elevation when he takes the rank of a mere citizen and ceases to be the special favorite of the laws, and when his rights as a citizen or a man are to be protected in the ordinary modes by which other men's rights are protected.

How does this claim, and the argument which follows, noting that "free colored people" before slavery enjoyed all of the "essential rights of life, liberty and property" that White citizens enjoyed, correspond with the history that we have examined thus far? At what point has the government corrected past wrongs sufficiently enough that previously discriminated-against groups no longer require additional protections or special prohibitions against racial discrimination? This question has reverberated over time and reappeared in the discussion around the policy of affirmative action. Is formal equality sufficient? Chapter 6 will look at these arguments more closely.

The decision in the *Civil Rights Cases* determined that the federal government could not prevent state-regulated private discrimination. This case is still good law and still stands to today. However, in its aftermath, many have asked: is a state's refusal to protect people from individual oppression a form of governmental action, which could trigger federal involvement?

Soon after this decision, a challenge was brought against the Force Acts – claiming that the federal government had no right to interfere in acts of private violence within the states – even if that violence was designed to limit the civil rights of the victims. In *U.S. v. Harris* (1883), the Supreme Court considered a case where Sheriff R. G. Harris led a lynch mob of nineteen men to a Crockett County, Tennessee, jail to torture four African American men who were imprisoned. Despite the efforts of the local deputy sheriff, the men were taken from the jail, beaten, and one was killed. The federal government charged Harris and his mob with violating §2 of the Third Force Act (Ku Klux Klan Act), 1871. The Supreme Court had to determine whether the Fourteenth Amendment provides the federal government with the authority to regulate criminal behavior of state residents in the absence of state actions. Did the fact that the leader of the lynch mob was a sheriff, an agent of the state, change the nature of federal power?

UNITED STATES v. HARRIS, 106 U.S. 626 (1883)

Justice Woods Delivered the Unanimous Opinion of the Court

Vote: 9–0

[The petitioner] questions the power of Congress to pass the law under which the indictment was found. It is therefore necessary to search the Constitution to ascertain whether or not the power is conferred.

There are only four paragraphs in the Constitution which can in the remotest degree have any reference to the question in hand. These are Section 2 of Article IV of the original Constitution and the [Fourteenth Amendment] ...

It is clear that the Fifteenth Amendment can have no application. That amendment, as was said by this Court in the case of *United States* v. *Reese*, 92 U. S. 214 (1876),

relates to the right of citizens of the United States to vote. It does not confer the right of

suffrage on anyone. It merely invests citizens of the United States with the constitutional right of exemption from discrimination in the enjoyment of the elective franchise on account of race, color, or previous condition of servitude.

It is however strenuously insisted that the legislation under consideration finds its warrant in the first and fifth sections of the Fourteenth Amendment. The first section declares

All persons born or naturalized in the United States and subject to the jurisdiction thereof are citizens of the United States and of the state wherein they reside. No state shall make or enforce any law which shall abridge the privileges or immunities of citizens of the United States, nor shall any state deprive any person of life, liberty, or property without due process of law, nor deny to any person within its jurisdiction the equal protection of the laws.

The fifth section declares "The Congress shall have power to enforce by appropriate legislation the provisions of this amendment."

It is perfectly clear from the language of the first section that its purpose also was to place a restraint upon the action of the states. In the *Slaughterhouse Cases*, 16 Wall. 36 (1875), it was held by the majority of the Court, speaking through Mr. Justice Miller, that the object of the second clause of the first section of the Fourteenth Amendment was to protect from the hostile legislation of the states the privileges and immunities of citizens of the United States, and this was conceded by Mr. Justice Field, who expressed the views of the dissenting Justices in that case. In the same case the Court, referring to the Fourteenth Amendment, said that "if the states do not conform their laws to its requirements, then by the fifth section of the article of amendment Congress was authorized to enforce it by suitable legislation."

The purpose and effect of the two sections of the Fourteenth Amendment above quoted were clearly defined by Mr. Justice Bradley in the case of *United States* v. *Cruikshank*, 1 Woods 316 (1875), as follows:

> It is a guarantee of protection against the acts of the state government itself. It is a guarantee against the exertion of arbitrary and tyrannical power on the part of the government and legislature of the state, not a guarantee against the commission of individual offenses, and the power of Congress, whether express or implied, to legislate for the enforcement of such a guarantee does not extend to the passage of laws for the suppression of crime within the states. The enforcement of the guarantee does not require or authorize Congress to perform the duty that the guarantee itself supposes it to be the duty of the state to perform, and which it requires the state to perform.

When the case of *United States* v. *Cruikshank* came to this Court, the same view was taken here. The Chief Justice, delivering the opinion of the Court in that case, said:

The Fourteenth Amendment prohibits a state from depriving any person of life, liberty, or property without due process of law or from denying to any person the equal protection of the laws, but this provision does not add anything to the rights of one citizen as against another. It simply furnishes an additional guarantee against any encroachment by the states upon the fundamental rights which belong to every citizen as a member of society. The duty of protecting all its citizens in the enjoyment of an equality of rights was originally assumed by the states, and it remains there. The only obligation resting upon the United States is to see that the states do not deny the right. This the amendment guarantees, and no more. The power of the national government is limited to this guarantee.

So, in *Virginia* v. *Rives*, 100 U.S. 313 (1880), it was declared by this Court, speaking through Mr. Justice Strong, that "these provisions of the Fourteenth Amendment have reference to state action exclusively, and not to any action of private individuals."

These authorities show conclusively that the legislation under consideration finds no warrant for its enactment in the Fourteenth Amendment.

The language of the amendment does not leave this subject in doubt. When the state has been guilty of no violation of its provisions; when it has not made or enforced any law abridging the privileges or immunities of citizens of the United States; when no one of its departments has deprived any person of life, liberty, or property without due process of law, or denied to any person within its jurisdiction the equal protection of the laws; when, on the contrary, the laws of the state, as enacted by its legislative and construed by its judicial and administered by its executive departments recognize and protect the rights of all persons, the amendment imposes no duty and confers no power upon Congress.

[The Force Act/Ku Klux Klan Act] is not limited to take effect only in case the state shall abridge the privileges or immunities of citizens of the United States or deprive any person of life, liberty, or property without due process of law or deny to any person the equal protection of the laws. It applies no matter how well the state may have performed its duty. Under it, private persons are liable to punishment for conspiring to deprive anyone of the equal protection of the laws enacted by the state.

In the indictment in this case, for instance, which would be a good indictment under the law if the law itself were valid, there is no intimation that the State of Tennessee has passed any law or done any act forbidden by the Fourteenth Amendment. On the contrary, the gravamen of the charge against the accused is that they conspired to deprive certain citizens of the United States and of the State of Tennessee of the equal protection accorded them by the laws of Tennessee.

As, therefore, the section of the law under consideration is directed exclusively against the action of private persons, without reference to the laws of the states or their administration by the officers of the state, we are clear in the opinion that it is not warranted by any clause in the Fourteenth Amendment to the Constitution.

It was never supposed that the section under consideration conferred on Congress the power to enact a law which would punish a private citizen for an invasion of the rights of his fellow citizen conferred by the State of which they were both residents on all its citizens alike.

We have therefore been unable to find any constitutional authority for the enactment of [The Force Act/Ku Klux Klan Act of 1871]. The decisions of this Court above referred to leave no constitutional ground for the act to stand on.

1. Is the refusal of a state to protect its own citizens from racial violence a state action?
2. Is *U.S.* v. *Harris* consistent in the line of precedent interpreting the Fourteenth Amendment since the *Slaughterhouse Cases*? Why or why not?
3. After these cases, what options did African Americans and other vulnerable groups have to protect themselves from racial violence?

Therefore, according to *U.S.* v. *Harris* (1883), if the state government allowed private violence against its citizens to go unpunished and unsanctioned, the federal government could not interfere. Without a federal lynching law, lynchings of people by private mobs condoned or embraced by the state could not be stopped. Throughout the twentieth century, multiple efforts to pass a federal anti-lynching law would be unsuccessful (Zangrando 1980; Wood 2009; Kato 2016). A federal anti-lynching law was finally signed by President Joe Biden in March 2022, when the Emmitt Till Anti-Lynching Act amended federal code to reclassify lynching as a federal hate crime with a potential sentence of 30 years in prison.

While *U.S.* v. *Harris* (1883) determined that most of the Force Acts were an unconstitutional extension of federal power, one section of the law remains constitutional (good law) and is in force today. This part of the law addresses when state officials – acting in their official capacity (under color of law) – violate the constitutional rights of citizens. In these limited cases, the federal government can intervene and file charges against local police officers or sheriffs who are found to violate the civil rights of the very people they are sworn to protect.

42 U.S. CODE §1983: CIVIL ACTION FOR DEPRIVATION OF RIGHTS

(formerly Civil Rights Act (aka Ku Klux Klan Act/the Force Act) of 1871, §1)

Every person who, under color of any statute, ordinance, regulation, custom, or usage, of any State or Territory or the District of Columbia, subjects, or causes to be subjected, any citizen of the United States or other person within the jurisdiction thereof to the deprivation of any rights, privileges, or immunities secured by the Constitution and laws, shall be liable to the party injured in an action at law, suit in equity, or other proper proceeding for redress, except that in any action brought against a judicial officer for an act or omission taken in such officer's judicial capacity, injunctive relief shall not be granted unless a declaratory decree was violated or declaratory relief was unavailable. For the purposes of this section, any Act of Congress applicable exclusively to the District of Columbia shall be considered to be a statute of the District of Columbia.

Section 1983 was written to grant the federal government the authority to intervene in states when local government actors abused their authority and the state declined to hold them accountable. After the *Civil Rights Cases* (1883), the constitutionality of such federal intervention was in question. These types of federal intervention were tested in the Supreme Court decision of *Screws* v. *U.S.* (1945), where the actions of M. Claude Screws, the sheriff of Baker County, Georgia, were federally challenged. Accompanied by Police Officer Jones and Special Deputy Kelley, both petitioners in this case, Sheriff Screws arrested Robert Hall, a thirty-year-old African American veteran, and a popular leader in the Black community, on a fabricated warrant for stealing a tire. Hall had pressed charges against the sheriff for unlawfully seizing his gun which he had brought back to Georgia from his military service. The three law enforcement officers beat Hall with their fists and an 8-inch blackjack that weighed 2 pounds, claiming that Hall had reached for a gun and used offensive language. Once Hall, still handcuffed, was knocked to the ground outside the courthouse they publicly beat him for 15–30 minutes. Unconscious, they dragged him feet first through the courthouse to the jail where he was left on the floor. An ambulance was called, and Hall was taken to the hospital, where he died without regaining consciousness. Evidence was uncovered that Screws had previously threatened Hall after Hall had filed charges against Screws for the wrongful, prior seizure of his gun. After the state of Georgia refused to hold the officers accountable, the petitioners were prosecuted under §242 of Title 18 of the U.S. Code which, like §1983 of Title 42, proscribed criminal action taken "under color of law" or under the authority of one's position with the government. A federal jury found them guilty, and the Circuit Court affirmed.

SCREWS v. *UNITED STATES*, 325 U.S. 91 (1945)

Justice Douglas Announced the Judgment of the Court and Delivered the Plurality Opinion, Joined by Chief Justice Stone, and Justices Black and Reed

Vote: 5–4

I.

... [Section 242] was enacted to enforce the Fourteenth Amendment. It derives from §2 of the Civil Rights Act of April 9, 1866. Senator Trumbull, chairman of the Senate Judiciary Committee which reported the bill, stated that its purpose was "to protect all persons in the United States in their civil rights, and furnish the means of their vindication." In origin it was an antidiscrimination measure (as its language indicated), framed to protect negroes in their newly won rights ... The requirement for a "willful" violation was introduced by the draftsmen of the Criminal Code of 1909. And we are told "willfully" was added ... in order to make the section "less severe."

II.

... [T]he specific intent required by the Act is an intent to deprive a person of a right which has been made specific either by the express terms of the Constitution or laws of the United States or by decisions interpreting them. Take the case of a local officer who persists in enforcing a type of ordinance which the Court has held invalid as violative of the guarantees of free speech or freedom of worship. Or a local official continues to select juries in manner which flies in the teeth of decisions of the Court. If those acts are done willfully, how can the officer possibly claim that he had no fair warning that his acts were prohibited by the statute? He violates the statute not merely because he has a bad purpose but because he acts in defiance of announced rules of law. He who defies a decision interpreting the Constitution knows precisely what he is doing ...

The difficulty here is that this question of intent was not submitted to the jury with the proper instructions. The court charged that petitioners acted illegally if they applied more force than was necessary to make the arrest effectual or to protect themselves from the prisoner's alleged assault. But in view of our construction of the word "willfully" the jury should have been further instructed that it was not sufficient that petitioners had a generally bad purpose. To convict it was necessary for them to find that petitioners had the purpose to deprive the prisoner of a constitutional right, e.g. the right to be tried by a court rather than by ordeal. And in determining whether that requisite bad purpose was present the jury would be entitled to consider all the attendant circumstance – the malice of petitioners, the weapons used in the assault, its character and duration, the provocation, if any, and the like.

III.

It is said, however, that petitioners did not act "under color of any law" within the meaning of §20 of the Criminal Code. We disagree. We are of the view that petitioners acted under "color" of law in making the arrest of Robert Hall and in assaulting him. They were officers of the law who made the arrest. By their own admissions they assaulted Hall in order to protect themselves and to keep their prisoner from escaping. It was their duty under Georgia law to make the arrest effective. Hence, their conduct comes within the statute.

We agree that when this statute is applied to the action of state officials, it should be construed so as to respect the proper balance between the States and the federal government in law enforcement. Violation of local law does not necessarily mean that federal rights have been invaded. The fact that a prisoner is assaulted, injured, or even murdered by state officials does not necessarily mean that he is deprived of any right protected or secured by the Constitution or laws of the United States. The Fourteenth Amendment did not alter the basic relations between the States and the national government. *United States v. Harris*, 106 U.S. 629 (1883). Our national government is one of delegated powers alone. Under our federal system the administration of criminal justice rests with the States except as Congress, acting within the scope of those delegated powers, has created offenses against the United States ... It is only state action of a "particular character" that is prohibited by the Fourteenth Amendment and against which the Amendment authorizes Congress to afford relief. *Civil Rights Cases*, 109 U.S. 3, 11, 13 (1883). Thus Congress in §20 of the Criminal Code did not undertake to make all torts of state officials federal crimes. It brought within §20 only specified acts done "under color" of law and then only those acts which deprived a person of some right secured by the Constitution or laws of the United States.

Since there must be a new trial, the judgment below is reversed.

Justice Rutledge, Concurring in the Result

The case comes here established in fact as a gross abuse of authority by state officers. Entrusted with the state's power and using it, without a warrant or with one of only doubtful legality they invaded a citizen's home, arrested him for alleged theft of a tire, forcibly took him in handcuffs to the courthouse yard, and there beat him to death. Previously they had threatened to kill him, fortified themselves at a near-by bar, and resisted the bartender's importunities not to carry out the arrest. Upon this and other evidence which overwhelmingly supports the verdict, together with instructions adequately covering an officer's right to use force, the jury found the petitioners guilty.

I.

... They do not come ... as faithful state officers, innocent of crime. Justification has been foreclosed. Accordingly, their argument now admits the offense, but insists it was against the state alone, not the nation. So they have made their case in this Court.

In effect, the position urges it is murder they have done, not deprivation of constitutional right. Strange as the argument is the reason. It comes to this, that abuse of state power creates immunity to federal power. Because what they did violated the state's laws, the nation cannot reach their conduct. It may deprive the citizen of his liberty and his life. But whatever state officers may do in abuse of their official capacity can give this Government and its courts no concern. This, though the prime object of the Fourteenth Amendment and Section 20 was to secure these fundamental rights against wrongful denial by exercise of the power of the states.

The defense is not pretty. Nor is it valid ... The evidence has nullified any pretense that petitioners acted as individuals, about their personal though nefarious business. They used the power of official place in all that was done. The verdict has foreclosed semblance of any claim that only private matters, not touching official functions, were involved. Yet neither was the state's power, they say.

There could be no clearer violation of the Amendment or the statute. No act could be more final or complete, to denude the victim of rights secured by the Amendment's very terms. Those rights so destroyed cannot be restored. Nor could the part played by the state's power in causing their destruction be lessened, though other organs were now to repudiate what was done. The state's law might thus be vindicated. If so, the vindication could only sustain, it could not detract from the federal power. Nor could it restore what the federal power shielded. Neither acquittal nor conviction, though affirmed by the state's highest court, could resurrect what the wrongful use of state power has annihilated. There was in this case abuse of state power, which for the Amendment's great purposes was state action, final in the last degree, depriving the victim of his liberty and his life without due process of law.

Accordingly, I would affirm the judgment.

My convictions are as I have stated them. Were it possible for me to adhere to them in my vote, and for the Court at the same time to dispose of the cause, I would act accordingly. The Court, however, is divided in opinion. If each member accords his vote to his belief, the case cannot have disposition. Stalemate should not prevail for any reason, however compelling, in a criminal cause or, if avoidable, in any other. My views concerning appropriate disposition are more nearly in accord with those stated by Mr. Justice Douglas, in which three other members of the Court concur, than they are with the views of my dissenting brethren who favor outright reversal. Accordingly, in order that disposition may be made of this case, my vote has been cast to reverse the decision of the Court of Appeals and remand the cause to the District Court for further proceedings in accordance with the disposition required by the opinion of Mr. Justice Douglas.

Justice Murphy, Dissenting

I dissent. Robert Hall, a Negro citizen, has been deprived not only of the right to be tried by a court rather than by ordeal. He has been deprived of the right of life itself. That right belonged to him not because he was a Negro or a member of any particular race or creed. That right was his because he was an American citizen, because he was a human being. As such, he was entitled to all the respect and fair treatment that befits the dignity of man, a dignity that is recognized and guaranteed by the Constitution. Yet not even the semblance of due process has been accorded him. He has been cruelly and unjustifiably beaten to death by local police officers acting under color of authority derived from the state. It is difficult to believe that such an obvious and necessary right is indefinitely guaranteed by the Constitution or is foreign to the knowledge of local police officers so as to cast any reasonable doubt on the conviction under [§ 242] of the perpetrators of this "shocking and revolting episode in law enforcement."

It is axiomatic, of course, that a criminal statute must give a clear and unmistakable warning as to the acts which will subject one to criminal punishment. And courts are without power to supply that which Congress has left vague. But this salutary principle does not mean that if a statute is vague as to certain criminal acts but definite as to others the entire statute must fall. Nor does it mean that in the first case involving the statute to come before us we must delineate all the prohibited acts that are obscure and all those that are explicit.

Under these circumstances it is unnecessary to send this case back for a further trial on the assumption that the jury was not charged on the matter of the willfulness of the state officials, an issue that was not raised below or before us. The evidence is more than convincing that the officials willfully, or at least with wanton disregard of the consequences, deprived Robert Hall of his life without due process of law ...

It is an illusion to say that the real issue in this case is the alleged failure of Section [242] fully to warn the state officials that their actions were illegal. The Constitution, Section [242] and their own consciences told them that. They knew that they lacked any mandate or authority to take human life unnecessarily or without due process of law in the course of their duties. They knew that their excessive and abusive use of authority would only subvert the ends of justice. The significant question, rather, is whether law enforcement officers and those entrusted with authority shall be allowed to violate with impunity the clear constitutional rights of the inarticulate and the friendless. Too often unpopular minorities, such as Negroes, are unable to find effective refuge from the cruelties of bigoted and ruthless authority. States are undoubtedly capable of punishing their officers who commit such outrages. But where, as here, the states are unwilling for some reason to prosecute such crimes the federal government must step in unless constitutional guarantees are to become atrophied.

This necessary intervention, however, will be futile if courts disregard reality and misuse the principle that criminal statutes must be clear and definite. Here state officers have violated with reckless abandon a plain constitutional right of an American citizen. The two courts below have found and the record demonstrates that the trial was fair and the evidence of guilt clear. And Section [242] unmistakably outlaws such actions by state officers. We should therefore affirm the judgment.

Justices Roberts, Frankfurter, and Jackson, Dissenting

Of course the petitioners are punishable. The only issue is whether Georgia alone has the power and duty to punish, or whether this patently local crime can be made the basis of a federal prosecution. The practical question is whether the States should be relieved from responsibility to bring their law officers to book for homicide, by allowing prosecutions in the federal courts for a relatively minor offense carrying a short sentence. The legal question is whether, for the purpose of accomplishing this relaxation of State responsibility, hitherto settled principles for the protection of civil liberties shall be bent and tortured.

I.

... The Fourteenth Amendment prohibited a State from so acting as to deprive persons of new federal rights defined by it. Section 5 of the Amendment specifically authorized enabling legislation to enforce that prohibition. Since a State can act only through its officers, Congress provided for the prosecution of any officer who deprives others of their guaranteed rights and denied such an officer the right to defend by claiming the authority of the State for his action. In short, Congress said that no State can empower an officer to commit acts which the Constitution forbade the State from authorizing, whether such unauthorized command be given for the State by its legislative or judicial voice, or by a custom contradicting the written law. The present prosecution is not based on an officer's claim that that for which the United States seeks his punishment was commanded or authorized by the law of his State. On the contrary, the present prosecution is based on the theory that Congress made it a federal offense for a State

officer to violate the explicit law of his State. We are asked to construe legislation which was intended to effectuate prohibitions against States for defiance of the Constitution, to be equally applicable where a State duly obeys the Constitution, but an officer flouts State law and is unquestionably subject to punishment by the State for his disobedience.

II.

In our view then, the Government's attempt to bring an unjustifiable homicide by local Georgia peace officers within the defined limits of the federal Criminal Code cannot clear the first hurdle of the legal requirement that that which these officers are charged with doing must be done under color of Georgia law.

III.

By holding, in this case, that State officials who violate State law nevertheless act "under color of" State law, and by establishing as federal crimes violations of the vast, undisclosed range of the Fourteenth Amendment, this Court now creates new delicate and complicated problems for the enforcement of the criminal law. The answers given to these problems, in view of the tremendous scope of potential offenses against the Fourteenth Amendment, are bound to produce a confusion detrimental to the administration of criminal justice.

That such a pliable instrument of prosecution is to be feared appears to be recognized by the Government. It urges three safeguards against abuse of the broad powers of prosecution for which it contends. (1) Congress it says will supervise the Department's policies and curb excesses by withdrawal of funds. It surely is casting an impossible burden upon Congress to expect it to police the propriety of prosecutions by the Department of Justice. Nor would such detailed oversight by Congress make for the effective administration of the criminal law. (2) The Government further urges that since prosecutions must be brought in the district where the crime was committed the judge and jurors of that locality can be depended upon to protect against federal interference with state law enforcement. Such a suggestion would, for practical purposes, transfer the functions of this Court, which adjudicates questions concerning the proper relationship between the federal and State governments, to jurors whose function is to resolve factual questions. Moreover, if federal and State prosecutions are subject to the same influences, it is difficult to see what need there is for taking the prosecution out of the hands of the State. After all, Georgia citizens sitting as a federal grand jury indicted and other Georgia citizens sitting as a federal trial jury convicted Screws and his associates; and it was a Georgia judge who charged more strongly against them than this Court thinks he should have.

But such a "policy of strict self-limitation" is not accompanied by assurance of permanent tenure and immortality of those who make it the policy. Evil men are rarely given power; they take it over from better men to whom it had been entrusted. There can be no doubt that this shapeless and all-embracing statute can serve as a dangerous instrument of political intimidation and coercion in the hands of those so inclined.

We are told local authorities cannot be relied upon for courageous and prompt action, that often they have personal or political reasons for refusing to prosecute. If it be significantly true that crimes against local law cannot be locally prosecuted, it is an ominous sign indeed. In any event, the cure is a re-invigoration of State responsibility. It is not an undue incursion of remote federal authority into local duties with consequent debilitation of local responsibility.

The complicated and subtle problems for law enforcement raised by the Court's decision emphasize the conclusion that §[242] was never designed for the use to which it has now been fashioned. The Government admits that it is appropriate to leave the punishment of such crimes as this to local authorities. Regard for this wisdom in federal-State relations was not left by Congress to executive discretion. It is, we are convinced, embodied in the statute itself.

1. How do the four different positions (plurality, Justices Rutledge and Murphy, and the other dissenters) frame the question differently? What does each group fear? Whose fears have prevailed in contemporary discourse?
2. Which position do you find more compelling and why? Does it surprise you to see these contrasting positions?

The impact of the federal charges in *Screws* is complex. When the case went back to a jury, all three officers were acquitted on the grounds that while it was murder, accountable under Georgia law, the intent to deny Mr. Hall his civil rights was not demonstrated. In fact, Sheriff Screws himself was subsequently elected a Georgia State Senator by a wide margin. But as Paul Watford (2014) notes, the long-term impact of the *Screws* decision and the survival of federal protections against state and local officials acting under color of law was significant. In this case, §242 (and also §1983), was interpreted in ways that allowed the federal government to intervene in state authority and hold the police accountable for their conduct. In so doing, "the Court made clear that the federal government could play a significant role in forcing Southern states to change practices that seriously disadvantaged minorities" (Watford 2014, 485). *Screws* was one case where the Supreme Court denied the states the power to solely regulate civil rights for their citizens. While it would take many years after 1945 and a massive social movement, the willingness of the federal government to engage in protecting citizens from state abuse of authority tempered state abuses of communities of color.

As we leave the discussion of state obligation against private racial violence, here are some questions to consider as we evaluate the meaning of the Fourteenth Amendment and what obligations the state may have around race.

1. What are the implications of the federal government being constitutionally unable to ban private discrimination in the absence of state protections? What happens next historically?
2. What are the implications of the federal government being constitutionally unable to ban private and collective acts of violence designed to limit citizenship rights (voting, running for office, politically organizing) in the absence of state protections? What happens next historically?
3. How does the ability of the federal government to prosecute state representatives acting under color of law who violate the civil rights of individuals provide some protections?
4. Is the failure of the state to act – for example, to protect its own citizens from criminal violence or punish police officers who commit battery or murder – sufficient for the federal government to intervene? Why or why not?

4.2 State Violence: Excessive Force

The history of the police power of the state and local governments being used to abuse people of color in the United States is a long one, which became more complex after policing forces desegregated in the mid-twentieth century. With people's ability to record quotidian interactions with police as well as the global organizing around the police-caused death of individual citizens – names like Daunte Wright (Brooklyn Center, Minnesota, 2021); George Floyd (Minneapolis, 2020); Breonna Taylor (Louisville, 2020); Philando Castile (Falcon Heights, Minnesota, 2016); Eric Garner (Staten Island, New York, 2014); and, Freddie Gray (Baltimore, 2015) became well-known nationally. Organizing pressure from Black Lives Matter activists, systemic data-collection by advocates, Justice Department investigations, and readily available visuals on social media pressured many police departments to evaluate how their own training contributed to unwarranted fatalities of people of color and to adopt new technologies like body cameras. While in some cases, departments fired police officers and provided financial settlements to bereaved families, in other cases, police departments found no fault on the part of the officers. In such situations, the families had to decide if they wanted to sue the state and the police officers in civil court as a form of structural accountability.

One limitation in holding individual police officers accountable is the Supreme Court's recognition of the qualified immunity of state employers like judges, elected officials, bureaucrats, and police officers against being personally liable for the decisions they make in their occupation. The concern is that professionals, who must exercise their best discretion in daily decisions, will sometimes err and

if they could be found personally responsible for every decision with an unanticipated impact, no one would want to do those jobs. In these occupations there are
professional consequences – such as being fired or demoted – for incompetence;
the question of qualified immunity attempts to encourage the appropriate exercise
of professional discretion by holding abusive individuals personally accountable.
But this is a very complicated balance.

The case of *Pierson* v. *Ray* (1967) is a civil-rights-era Supreme Court decision
that attempted to address this balance by creating the protection of qualified
immunity for police officers. In 1961, an interracial group of priests participated
in a freedom ride from New Orleans to Detroit as a challenge to state-mandated
segregation. When they arrived at the Jackson, Mississippi bus terminal, they
were cautioned and stopped by Jackson police officers David Nichols and Joseph
Griffin and arrested by Captain J. L. Ray. The priests were charged with violating
§2087.5 of the Mississippi Code, which deemed congregating in a public place
where a breach of peace might occur and refusing to disperse upon police order
a misdemeanor offense. Reverend Robert L. Pierson and his colleagues were convicted by municipal police Judge James Spencer and sentenced to four months
in jail and a $200 fine. Upon appeal, the charges were dropped after the Supreme
Court determined the Mississippi law to be unconstitutional in *Thompson* v.
Mississippi (1965). The priests then brought a civil case against the police officers
and the local judge under 42 U.S.C. §1983, seeking damages for false arrest and
imprisonment. After the jury decided in favor of the police, the Court of Appeals
upheld the decision.

PIERSON v. RAY, 386 U.S. 547 (1967)

Chief Justice Warren Delivered the Opinion of Court, Joined by Justices Black, Clark, Fortas, Brennan, White, Stewart, and Harlan

Vote: 8–1

We granted *certiorari* ... to consider whether a
local judge is liable for damages under §1983 for
an unconstitutional conviction and whether the
ministers should be denied recovery against the
police officers if they acted with the anticipation
that they would be illegally arrested. We also
granted the police officers' petition ... to determine if the Court of Appeals correctly held that
they could not assert the defense of good faith
and probable cause to an action under §1983 for
unconstitutional arrest.

We find no difficulty in agreeing with the
Court of Appeals that Judge Spencer is immune
from liability for damages for his role in these
convictions. The record is barren of any proof
or specific allegation that Judge Spencer played
any role in these arrests and convictions other
than to adjudge petitioners guilty when their
cases came before his court. Few doctrines were
more solidly established at common law than
the immunity of judges from liability for damages for acts committed within their judicial
jurisdiction, as this Court recognized when it
adopted the doctrine, in *Bradley* v. *Fisher*, 13

(margin note, left side) Justification for Judge

Wall. 335 (1872). This immunity applies even when the judge is accused of acting maliciously and corruptly, and it "is not for the protection or benefit of a malicious or corrupt judge, but for the benefit of the public, whose interest it is that the judges should be at liberty to exercise their functions with independence and without fear of consequences." *Scott* v. *Stansfield*, 3 L.R. Exch. 220, 223 (1868). It is a judge's duty to decide all cases within his jurisdiction that are brought before him, including controversial cases that arouse the most intense feelings in the litigants. His errors may be corrected on appeal, but he should not have to fear that unsatisfied litigants may hound him with litigation charging malice or corruption. Imposing such a burden on judges would contribute not to principled and fearless decision-making but to intimidation.

The common law has never granted police officers an absolute and unqualified immunity, and the officers in this case do not claim that they are entitled to one. Their claim is rather that they should not be liable if they acted in good faith and with probable cause in making an arrest under a statute that they believed to be valid. Under the prevailing view in this country a peace officer who arrests someone with probable cause is not liable for false arrest simply because the innocence of the suspect is later proved. A policeman's lot is not so unhappy that he must choose between being charged with dereliction of duty if he does not arrest when he has probable cause, and [punished by] damages if he does. Although the matter is not entirely free from doubt, the same consideration would seem to require excusing him from liability for acting under a statute that he reasonably believed to be valid but that was later held unconstitutional, on its face or as applied.

We hold that the defense of good faith and probable cause, which the Court of Appeals found available to the officers in the common-law action for false arrest and imprisonment, is also available to them in the action under §1983. This holding does not, however, mean that the count based thereon should be dismissed. The Court of Appeals ordered dismissal of the common-law count on the theory that the police officers were not required to predict our decision in *Thomas* v. *Mississippi*, 380 U.S. 524 (1965) [holding §2087.5 of the Mississippi Code was unconstitutional]. We agree that a police officer is not charged with predicting the future course of constitutional law. But the petitioners in this case did not simply argue that they were arrested under a statute later held unconstitutional. They claimed and attempted to prove that the police officers arrested them solely for attempting to use the "White Only" waiting room, that no crowd was present, and that no one threatened violence or seemed about to cause a disturbance. The officers did not defend on the theory that they believed in good faith that it was constitutional to arrest the ministers solely for using the waiting room. Rather, they claimed and attempted to prove that they did not arrest the ministers for the purpose of preserving the custom of segregation in Mississippi, but solely for the purpose of preventing violence. They testified, in contradiction to the ministers, that a crowd gathered and that imminent violence was likely. If the jury believed the testimony of the officers and disbelieved that of the ministers, and if the jury found that the officers reasonably believed in good faith that the arrest was constitutional, then a verdict for the officers would follow even though the arrest was in fact unconstitutional. The jury did resolve the factual issues in favor of the officers but, for reasons previously stated, its verdict was influenced by irrelevant and prejudicial evidence. Accordingly, the case must be remanded to the trial court for a new trial.

It is necessary to decide what importance should be given at the new trial to the substantially undisputed fact that the petitioners went to Jackson expecting to be illegally arrested. We do not agree with the Court of Appeals that they somehow consented to the arrest because of their anticipation that they would be illegally arrested, even assuming that they went to the Jackson bus terminal for the sole purpose of testing their rights to unsegregated public accommodations. The case contains no proof or allegation that they in any way tricked or goaded the officers into arresting them. The petitioners had the right to use the waiting room of the Jackson bus terminal, and their deliberate exercise of that right in a peaceful, orderly, and inoffensive manner does not disqualify them from seeking damages under §1983.

The judgment of the Court of Appeals is affirmed in part and reversed in part, and the cases are remanded for further proceedings consistent with this opinion.

It is so ordered.

Justice Douglas, Dissenting

I do not think that all judges, under all circumstances, no matter how outrageous their conduct are immune from suit under 42 U.S.C. § 1983. The Court's ruling is not justified by the admitted need for a vigorous and independent judiciary, is not commanded by the common-law doctrine of judicial immunity, and does not follow inexorably from our prior decisions.

The statute, which came on the books as §1 of the Ku Klux Klan Act of April 20, 1871, provides that "every person" who under color of state law or custom "subjects, or causes to be subjected, any citizen … to the deprivation of any rights, privileges, or immunities secured by the Constitution and laws, shall be liable to the party injured in an action at law, suit in equity, or other proper proceeding for redress." The congressional purpose seems to me to be clear. A condition of lawlessness existed in certain of the States, under which people were being denied their civil rights. Congress intended to provide a remedy for the wrongs being perpetrated. And its members were not unaware that certain members of the judiciary were implicated in the state of affairs which the statute was intended to rectify. It was often noted that "[i]mmunity is given to crime, and the records of the public tribunals are searched in vain for any evidence of effective redress." … The members supporting the proposed measure were apprehensive that there had been a complete breakdown in the administration of justice in certain States and that laws nondiscriminatory on their face were being applied in a discriminatory manner, that the newly won civil rights of the Negro were being ignored, and that the Constitution was being defied. It was against this background that the section was passed, and it is against this background that it should be interpreted.

The section's purpose was to provide redress for the deprivation of civil rights. It was recognized that certain members of the judiciary were instruments of oppression and were partially responsible for the wrongs to be remedied. The parade of cases coming to this Court shows that a similar condition now obtains in some of the States. Some state courts have been instruments of suppression of civil rights. The methods may have changed; the means may have become more subtle; but the wrong to be remedied still exists.

The immunity which the Court today grants the judiciary is not necessary to preserve an independent judiciary. If the threat of civil action lies in the background of litigation, so the argument goes, judges will be reluctant to exercise the discretion and judgment inherent in their position and vital to the effective operation of the judiciary … But, it is argued that absolute immunity is necessary to prevent the chilling effects of a judicial inquiry, or the threat of such inquiry, into whether, in fact, a judge has been unfaithful to his oath of office. Thus, it is necessary to protect the guilty as well as the innocent.

The argument that the actions of public officials must not be subjected to judicial scrutiny because to do so would have an inhibiting effect on their work, is but a more sophisticated manner of saying "The King can do no wrong." …

This is not to say that a judge who makes an honest mistake should be subjected to civil liability. It is necessary to exempt judges from liability for the consequences of their honest mistakes. The judicial function involves an informed exercise of judgment. It is often necessary to choose between differing versions of fact, to reconcile opposing interests, and to decide closely contested issues. Decisions must often be made in the heat of trial. A vigorous and independent mind is needed to perform such delicate tasks. It would be unfair to require a judge to exercise his independent judgment and then to punish him for having exercised it in a manner which, in retrospect, was erroneous. Imposing liability for mistaken, though honest judicial acts, would curb the independent mind and spirit needed to perform judicial functions. Thus, a judge who sustains a conviction on what he forthrightly considers adequate evidence should not be subjected to liability when an appellate court decides that the evidence was not adequate. Nor should a judge who allows a conviction under what is later held an unconstitutional statute.

But that is far different from saying that a judge shall be immune from the consequences of any of his judicial actions, and that he shall not be liable for the knowing and intentional deprivation of a person's civil rights. What about the judge who conspires with local law enforcement officers to "railroad" a dissenter? What about the judge who knowingly turns a trial into a "kangaroo" court? Or one who intentionally flouts the Constitution in order to obtain a conviction? Congress, I think, concluded that the evils of allowing intentional, knowing deprivations of civil rights to go unredressed far outweighed the speculative inhibiting effects which might attend an inquiry into a judicial deprivation of civil rights.

The plight of the oppressed is indeed serious. Under *City of Greenwood, Mississippi* v. *Peacock*, 384 U.S. 808 (1966), the defendant cannot remove to a federal court to prevent a state court from depriving him of his civil rights. And under the rule announced today, the person cannot recover damages for the deprivation.

1. Why do the dissent and majority disagree on the nature of immunity for judges: what are their competing justifications?
2. What are their competing fears?
3. How does the majority's argument over qualified immunity for police officers compare with the criminal liability articulated in *Screws* v. *U.S.*?
4. What are the contemporary implications of this decision?

The *Pierson* decision provided an absolute immunity for judges from civil litigation, although it allowed for federal accountability under §1983. It also provided qualified immunity for police, if an arrest that was found unconstitutional was determined to be made in good faith and with probable cause. This question of qualified immunity for the police has grown in intensity in the twenty-first century, but the Supreme Court has consistently demonstrated a willingness to expand these protections to police officers under a wide net of circumstances. "Although a good faith defense was the impetus for qualified immunity, today officers are entitled to qualified immunity even if they act in bad faith, as long as there is no prior court decision with nearly identical facts" (Schwartz 2023, 71). In two recent cases in which the Supreme Court extended qualified immunity for police officers, the Court rendered *per curiam* opinions. The two cases demonstrating this extension are both *per curiam* opinions, in which no single justice signs their name. In the case of *Kisela* v. *Hughes* (2018) we see the Court articulate some of the key principles as to when qualified immunity should be granted to officers but then disagree in the application to a common set of facts. *Kisela* demonstrates the difficulty the law has in assessing the appropriate use of force under "color of law."

KISELA v. *HUGHES*, 584 U.S. 100 (2018)

Per Curiam

Vote: 8–2

Petitioner Andrew Kisela, a police officer in Tucson, Arizona, shot respondent Amy Hughes. Kisela and two other officers had arrived on the scene after hearing a police radio report that a woman was engaging in erratic behavior with a knife. They had been there but a few minutes, perhaps just a minute. When Kisela fired, Hughes was holding a large kitchen knife, had taken steps toward another woman standing nearby, and had refused to drop the knife after at least two commands to do so. The question is whether at the time of the shooting Kisela's actions violated clearly established law.

The record, viewed in the light most favorable to Hughes, shows the following. In May 2010, somebody in Hughes' neighborhood called 911 to report that a woman was hacking a tree with a kitchen knife. Kisela and another police officer, Alex Garcia, heard about the report over the radio in their patrol car and responded. A few minutes later the person who had called 911 flagged down the officers; gave them a description of the woman with the knife; and told them the woman had been acting erratically. About the same time, a third police officer, Lindsay Kunz, arrived on her bicycle.

Garcia spotted a woman, later identified as Sharon Chadwick, standing next to a car in the driveway of a nearby house. A chain-link fence with a locked gate separated Chadwick from the officers. The officers then saw another woman, Hughes, emerge from the house carrying a large knife at her side. Hughes matched the description of the woman who had been seen hacking a tree. Hughes walked toward Chadwick and stopped no more than six feet from her.

All three officers drew their guns. At least twice they told Hughes to drop the knife. Viewing the record in the light most favorable to Hughes, Chadwick said "take it easy" to both Hughes and

the officers. Hughes appeared calm, but she did not acknowledge the officers' presence or drop the knife. The top bar of the chain-link fence blocked Kisela's line of fire, so he dropped to the ground and shot Hughes four times through the fence. Then the officers jumped the fence, handcuffed Hughes, and called paramedics, who transported her to a hospital. There she was treated for non-life-threatening injuries. Less than a minute had transpired from the moment the officers saw Chadwick to the moment Kisela fired shots.

All three of the officers later said that at the time of the shooting they subjectively believed Hughes to be a threat to Chadwick. After the shooting, the officers discovered that Chadwick and Hughes were roommates, that Hughes had a history of mental illness, and that Hughes had been upset with Chadwick over a $20 debt. In an affidavit produced during discovery, Chadwick said that a few minutes before the shooting her boyfriend had told her Hughes was threatening to kill Chadwick's dog, named Bunny. Chadwick "came home to find" Hughes "somewhat distressed," and Hughes was in the house holding Bunny "in one hand and a kitchen knife in the other." Hughes asked Chadwick if she "wanted [her] to use the knife on the dog." The officers knew none of this, though. Chadwick went outside to get $20 from her car, which is when the officers first saw her. In her affidavit Chadwick said that she did not feel endangered at any time. Based on her experience as Hughes' roommate, Chadwick stated that Hughes "occasionally has episodes in which she acts inappropriately," but "she is only seeking attention."

Hughes sued Kisela under 42 U.S.C. §1983, alleging that Kisela had used excessive force in violation of the Fourth Amendment. The District Court granted summary judgment to Kisela, but the Court of Appeals for the Ninth Circuit reversed.

In one of the first cases on this general subject, *Tennessee* v. *Garner*, 471 U.S. 1 (1985), the Court addressed the constitutionality of the police using force that can be deadly. There, the Court held that "[w]here the officer has probable cause to believe that the suspect poses a threat of serious physical harm, either to the officer or to others, it is not constitutionally unreasonable to prevent escape by using deadly force."

In *Graham* v. *Connor*, 490 U.S. 386, 396 (1989), the Court held that the question whether an officer has used excessive force "requires careful attention to the facts and circumstances of each particular case, including the severity of the crime at issue, whether the suspect poses an immediate threat to the safety of the officers or others, and whether he is actively resisting arrest or attempting to evade arrest by flight." "The 'reasonableness' of a particular use of force must be judged from the perspective of a reasonable officer on the scene, rather than with the 20/20 vision of hindsight." And "[t]he calculus of reasonableness must embody allowance for the fact that police officers are often forced to make split-second judgments – in circumstances that are tense, uncertain, and rapidly evolving – about the amount of force that is necessary in a particular situation."

Here, the Court need not, and does not, decide whether Kisela violated the Fourth Amendment when he used deadly force against Hughes. For even assuming a Fourth Amendment violation occurred – a proposition that is not at all evident – on these facts Kisela was at least entitled to qualified immunity.

"Qualified immunity attaches when an official's conduct does not violate clearly established statutory or constitutional rights of which a reasonable person would have known." *White* v. *Pauly*, 580 U.S. 73 (2017). "Because the focus is on whether the officer had fair notice that her conduct was unlawful, reasonableness is judged against the backdrop of the law at the time of the conduct" *Brasseau* v. *Haugen*, 543 U.S. 194, 198 (2004).

... Use of excessive force is an area of the law "in which the result depends very much on the facts of each case," and thus police officers are entitled to qualified immunity unless existing precedent "squarely governs" the specific facts at issue. Precedent involving similar facts can help move a case beyond the otherwise "hazy border between excessive and acceptable force"

and thereby provide an officer notice that a specific use of force is unlawful.

Kisela says he shot Hughes because, although the officers themselves were in no apparent danger, he believed she was a threat to Chadwick. Kisela had mere seconds to assess the potential danger to Chadwick. He was confronted with a woman who had just been seen hacking a tree with a large kitchen knife and whose behavior was erratic enough to cause a concerned bystander to call 911 and then flag down Kisela and Garcia. Kisela was separated from Hughes and Chadwick by a chain-link fence; Hughes had moved to within a few feet of Chadwick; and she failed to acknowledge at least two commands to drop the knife. Those commands were loud enough that Chadwick, who was standing next to Hughes, heard them. This is far from an obvious case in which any competent officer would have known that shooting Hughes to protect Chadwick would violate the Fourth Amendment.

... [Not] one of the decisions relied on by the Court of Appeals – *Deorle* v. *Rutherford*, 272 F.3d 1272 (CA9 2001), *Glenn* v. *Washington County*, 673 F.3d 864 (CA9 2011), and *Harris* v. *Roderick*, 126 F.3d 1189 (CA9 1997) – supports denying Kisela qualified immunity ... *Deorle* involved a police officer who shot an unarmed man in the face, without warning, even though the officer had a clear line of retreat; there were no bystanders nearby; the man had been "physically compliant and generally followed all the officers' instructions"; and he had been under police observation for roughly 40 minutes. In this case, by contrast, Hughes was armed with a large knife; was within striking distance of Chadwick; ignored the officers' orders to drop the weapon; and the situation unfolded in less than a minute. "Whatever the merits of the decision in *Deorle*, the differences between that case and the case before us leap from the page."

Glenn, which the panel described as "[t]he most analogous Ninth Circuit case," was decided after the shooting at issue here. Thus, *Glenn* "could not have given fair notice to [Kisela]" because a reasonable officer is not required to foresee judicial decisions that do not yet exist in instances where the requirements of the Fourth Amendment are far from obvious ...

The panel's reliance on *Harris* "does not pass the straight-face test." In *Harris*, the Court of Appeals determined that an FBI sniper, who was positioned safely on a hilltop, used excessive force when he shot a man in the back while the man was retreating to a cabin during what has been referred to as the Ruby Ridge stand-off. Suffice it to say, a reasonable police officer could miss the connection between the situation confronting the sniper at Ruby Ridge and the situation confronting Kisela in Hughes' front yard.

For these reasons, the petition for *certiorari* is granted; the judgment of the Court of Appeals is reversed; and the case is remanded for further proceedings consistent with this opinion.

Justice Sotomayor, with Whom Justice Ginsburg joins, Dissenting

Officer Andrew Kisela shot Amy Hughes while she was speaking with her roommate, Sharon Chadwick, outside of their home. The record, properly construed at this stage, shows that at the time of the shooting: Hughes stood stationary about six feet away from Chadwick, appeared "composed and content," and held a kitchen knife down at her side with the blade facing away from Chadwick. Hughes was nowhere near the officers, had committed no illegal act, was suspected of no crime, and did not raise the knife in the direction of Chadwick or anyone else. Faced with these facts, the two other responding officers held their fire, and one testified that he "wanted to continue trying verbal command[s] and see if that would work." But not Kisela. He thought it necessary to use deadly force, and so, without giving a warning that he would open fire, he shot Hughes four times, leaving her seriously injured.

If this account of Kisela's conduct sounds unreasonable, that is because it was. And yet, the Court today insulates that conduct from liability under the doctrine of qualified immunity, holding that Kisela violated no "clearly established" law. I disagree. Viewing the facts in the light most favorable to Hughes, as the Court must at summary judgment, a jury could find that Kisela violated Hughes' clearly established Fourth Amendment rights by needlessly resorting to lethal force. In holding otherwise, the Court

misapprehends the facts and misapplies the law, effectively treating qualified immunity as an absolute shield. I therefore respectfully dissent.

II.

Police officers are not entitled to qualified immunity if "(1) they violated a federal statutory or constitutional right, and (2) the unlawfulness of their conduct was 'clearly established at the time.'" *District of Columbia* v. *Wesby*, 583 U.S. 48 (2018). Faithfully applying that well-settled standard, the Ninth Circuit held that a jury could find that Kisela violated Hughes' clearly established Fourth Amendment rights. That conclusion was correct.

A.

I begin with the first step of the qualified-immunity inquiry: whether there was a violation of a constitutional right. Hughes alleges that Kisela violated her Fourth Amendment rights by deploying excessive force against her. In assessing such a claim, courts must ask "whether the officers' actions are 'objectively reasonable' in light of the facts and circumstances confronting them." *Graham* v. *Connor*, 490 U.S. 386, 397 (1989). That inquiry "requires careful attention to the facts and circumstances of each particular case, including the severity of the crime at issue, whether the suspect poses an immediate threat to the safety of the officers or others, and whether he is actively resisting arrest or attempting to evade arrest by flight." All of those factors (and others) support the Ninth Circuit's conclusion that a jury could find that Kisela's use of deadly force was objectively unreasonable. Indeed, the panel's resolution of this question was so convincing that not a single judge on the Ninth Circuit, including the seven who dissented from denial of rehearing en banc, expressly disputed that conclusion. Neither does the majority here, which simply assumes without deciding that "a Fourth Amendment violation occurred."

B.

Rather than defend the reasonableness of Kisela's conduct, the majority sidesteps the inquiry altogether and focuses instead on the "clearly established" prong of the qualified-immunity analysis ... That standard is not as onerous as the majority makes it out to be. As even the majority must acknowledge, this Court has long rejected the notion that "an official action is protected by qualified immunity unless the very action in question has previously been held unlawful," *Anderson* [v. *Creighton*, 83 U.S. 635, 640 (1987)]. "[O]fficials can still be on notice that their conduct violates established law even in novel factual circumstances." *Hope* v. *Pelzer*, 536 U.S. 730, 741 (2002). At its core, then, the "clearly established" inquiry boils down to whether Kisela had "fair notice" that he acted unconstitutionally.

The answer to that question is yes. This Court's precedents make clear that a police officer may only deploy deadly force against an individual if the officer "has probable cause to believe that the [person] poses a threat of serious physical harm, either to the officer or to others." *Tennessee* v. *Garner*, 471 U.S. 1, 11 (1985). It is equally well established that any use of lethal force must be justified by some legitimate governmental interest. Consistent with those clearly established principles, and contrary to the majority's conclusion, Ninth Circuit precedent predating these events further confirms that Kisela's conduct was clearly unreasonable. Because Kisela plainly lacked any legitimate interest justifying the use of deadly force against a woman who posed no objective threat of harm to officers or others, had committed no crime, and appeared calm and collected during the police encounter, he was not entitled to qualified immunity.

The Ninth Circuit's opinion in *Deorle* v. *Rutherford*, 272 F.3d 1272 (2001) proves the point. In that case, the police encountered a man who had reportedly been acting "erratically." The man was "verbally abusive," shouted "kill me" at the officers, screamed that he would "kick [the] ass" of one of the officers, and "brandish[ed] a hatchet at a police officer," ultimately throwing it "into a clump of trees when told to put it down." The officers also observed the man carrying an unloaded crossbow in one hand and what appeared to be "a can or a bottle of lighter fluid in the other." The man discarded the crossbow when instructed to do so by the police and then steadily

walked toward one of the officers. In response, that officer, without giving a warning, shot the man in the face with beanbag rounds. The man suffered serious injuries, including multiple fractures to his cranium and the loss of his left eye.

*   *   *

In sum, precedent existing at the time of the shooting clearly established the unconstitutionality of Kisela's conduct. The majority's decision, no matter how much it says otherwise, ultimately rests on a faulty premise: that those cases are not identical to this one. But that is not the law, for our cases have never required a factually identical case to satisfy the "clearly established" standard. It is enough that governing law places "the constitutionality of the officer's conduct beyond debate." Because, taking the facts in the light most favorable to Hughes, it is "beyond debate" that Kisela's use of deadly force was objectively unreasonable, he was not entitled to summary judgment on the basis of qualified immunity.

III.

This unwarranted summary reversal is symptomatic of "a disturbing trend regarding the use of this Court's resources" in qualified-immunity cases. As I have previously noted, this Court routinely displays an unflinching willingness "to summarily reverse courts for wrongly denying officers the protection of qualified immunity" but "rarely intervene[s] where courts wrongly afford officers the benefit of qualified immunity in these same cases." Such a one-sided approach to qualified immunity transforms the doctrine into an absolute shield for law enforcement officers, gutting the deterrent effect of the Fourth Amendment.

The majority today exacerbates that troubling asymmetry. Its decision is not just wrong on the law; it also sends an alarming signal to law enforcement officers and the public. It tells officers that they can shoot first and think later, and it tells the public that palpably unreasonable conduct will go unpunished. Because there is nothing right or just under the law about this, I respectfully dissent.

1. According to the *per curiam* and the dissent, what are the agreed upon tests regarding the appropriate denial of qualified immunity for police officers who cause physical harm?
2. Why do the dissent and *per curiam* disagree in the application of this test in the *Kisela* case?
3. How would you have decided this case based on the record provided, in light of the guidelines around qualified immunity?

In *Tahlequah, Oklahoma* v. *Bond* (2021), the Court, in another *per curiam* opinion, clarified their understanding of the application of qualified immunity. In this case, police officers responded to a 911 call from a woman whose ex-husband, Dominic Rollice, was in her garage, clearly intoxicated, and unwilling to leave. The officers stood in the doorway of the garage and Rollice became agitated because he did not want to go to jail.

CITY OF TAHLEQUAH, OKLAHOMA v. AUSTIN P. BOND, 595 U.S. 9 (2021)

Per Curiam

Police body-camera video captured what happened next. As the conversation continued, Officer Girdner gestured with his hands and took one step toward the doorway, causing Rollice to take one step back. Rollice, still conversing with the officers, turned around and walked toward the back of the garage where his tools were hanging over a workbench. Officer Girdner followed, the others close behind. No officer was within six feet of Rollice. The video is silent, but the officers stated that they ordered Rollice to stop. Rollice kept walking. He then grabbed a hammer from the back wall over the workbench and turned around to face the officers. Rollice grasped the handle of the hammer with both hands, as if preparing to swing a baseball bat, and pulled it up to shoulder level. The officers backed up, drawing their guns. At this point the video is no longer silent, and the officers can be heard yelling at Rollice to drop the hammer.

He did not. Instead, Rollice took a few steps to his right, coming out from behind a piece of furniture so that he had an unobstructed path to Officer Girdner. He then raised the hammer higher back behind his head and took a stance as if he was about to throw the hammer or charge at the officers. In response, Officers Girdner and Vick fired their weapons, killing Rollice.

Rollice's estate filed suit against, among others, Officers Girdner and Vick, alleging that the officers were liable under 42 U.S.C. §1983, for violating Rollice's Fourth Amendment right to be free from excessive force. The officers moved for summary judgment, both on the merits and on qualified immunity grounds. The District Court granted their motion. The officers' use of force was reasonable, it concluded, and even if not, qualified immunity prevented the case from going further.

A panel of the Court of Appeals for the Tenth Circuit reversed. The Court began by explaining that Tenth Circuit precedent allows an officer to be held liable for a shooting that is itself objectively reasonable if the officer's reckless or deliberate conduct created a situation requiring deadly force. Applying that rule, the Court concluded that a jury could find that Officer Girdner's initial step toward Rollice and the officers' subsequent "cornering" of him in the back of the garage recklessly created the situation that led to the fatal shooting, such that their ultimate use of deadly force was unconstitutional. As to qualified immunity, the Court concluded that several cases, most notably *Allen* v. *Muskogee*, 119 F.3d 837 (CA10 1997), clearly established that the officers' conduct was unlawful ...

We need not, and do not, decide whether the officers violated the Fourth Amendment in the first place, or whether recklessly creating a situation that requires deadly force can itself violate the Fourth Amendment. On this record, the officers plainly did not violate any clearly established law.

The doctrine of qualified immunity shields officers from civil liability so long as their conduct "does not violate clearly established statutory or constitutional rights of which a reasonable person would have known." *Pearson* v. *Callahan*, 555 U.S. 223, 231 (2009). As we have explained, qualified immunity protects "all but the plainly incompetent or those who knowingly violate the law." *District of Columbia* v. *Wesby*, 583 U.S. 48 (2018).

We have repeatedly told courts not to define clearly established law at too high a level of generality. It is not enough that a rule be suggested by then-existing precedent; the "rule's contours must be so well defined that it is 'clear to a reasonable officer that his conduct was unlawful in the situation he confronted.'" *Wesby*, 583 U.S., at 51. Such specificity is "especially important in the Fourth Amendment context," where it is "sometimes difficult for an officer to determine how the relevant legal doctrine, here excessive force, will apply to the factual situation the officer confronts." *Mullenix* v. *Luna*, 577 U.S. 7, 12 (2015).

The Tenth Circuit contravened those settled principles here. Not one of the decisions relied upon by the Court of Appeals – *Estate of Ceballos* v. *Husk*, 919 F.3d 1204 (CA10 2019),

Hastings v. *Barnes*, 252 Fed. Appx. 197 (CA10 2007), *Allen* v. *Muskogee*, 119 F.3d 837 (1997), and *Sevier* v. *Lawrence*, 60 F.3d 695 (CA10 1995) – comes close to establishing that the officers' conduct was unlawful. The Court relied most heavily on *Allen*. But the facts of *Allen* are dramatically different from the facts here. The officers in *Allen* responded to a potential suicide call by sprinting toward a parked car, screaming at the suspect, and attempting to physically wrest a gun from his hands. Officers Girdner and Vick, by contrast, engaged in a conversation with Rollice, followed him into a garage at a distance of 6 to 10 feet, and did not yell until after he picked up a hammer. We cannot conclude that *Allen* "clearly established" that their conduct was reckless or that their ultimate use of force was unlawful.

The other decisions relied upon by the Court of Appeals are even less relevant. As for *Sevier*, that decision merely noted in *dicta* that deliberate or reckless preseizure conduct can render a later use of force excessive before dismissing the appeal for lack of jurisdiction. To state the obvious, a decision where the court did not even have jurisdiction cannot clearly establish substantive constitutional law. Regardless, that formulation of the rule is much too general to bear on whether the officers' particular conduct here violated the Fourth Amendment. *Estate of Ceballos*, decided after the shooting at issue, is of no use in the clearly established inquiry. And *Hastings*, an unpublished decision, involved officers initiating an encounter with a potentially suicidal individual by chasing him into his bedroom, screaming at him, and pepper-spraying him. Suffice it to say, a reasonable officer could miss the connection between that case and this one.

Neither the panel majority nor the respondent have identified a single precedent finding a Fourth Amendment violation under similar circumstances. The officers were thus entitled to qualified immunity.

The petition for certiorari and the motions for leave to file briefs *amici curiae* are granted, and the judgment of the Court of Appeals is reversed.

1. How is this case similar to the 2018 *Kisela* v. *Hughes* decision and how is it distinguished?
2. Is Justice Sotomayor's dissent's explanation of the Supreme Court's practice in qualified immunity cases, supported in this decision?
3. How would you respond to this case, in light of the *Kisela* precedent? Have the guidelines for applying qualified immunity to officers accused of excessive force changed in this decision?

Over the last half century, the Supreme Court has clearly noted that the intent of an officer in exercising discretion (such as self-defense, racism, protecting public safety, or brutality) is not relevant to the granting of qualified immunity. The Court instead has promised qualified immunity to all officers as long as they are not in violation of clearly established law, which precedent clearly indicates is defined solely by previous Court decisions that "are so similar to the facts in the present case that every reasonable officer would know what one was doing was wrong" (Schwartz 2023, 76). The question of qualified immunity of police officers and the exercise of excessive force against the public is one that has only grown more intense over time. How does the question of race in the United States complicate this issue?

4.3 Jury Representation as Protection from State

One of the principles of basic due process and of the rule of law – when the government accuses an individual of a crime in which a penalty could take away a person's life, liberty, or property – is the right to have the case heard before a jury of one's peers (Eberle 1987). This protection is designed to prevent governmental abuse of power by allowing citizens to limit the state's authority by making all determinations public. The capacity to have a hearing by a jury ensures those who are not dependent on the government for their paycheck supervise the decisions of those employees. A question that frequently arises is what categories – for instance, race, sex, class, age – determine one's peers? Recognizing the power of a sympathetic jury, many states banned the testimony of people of color in the courtroom and restricted juries to White men with property only. Many Whites were socialized (as the prior chapters demonstrate) to see people of different racial communities as politically and economically incompetent and therefore incapable of providing the citizenship functions of a juror. It would not be until the passage of the Fourteenth Amendment that the Supreme Court would reevaluate the assumption that only White men could legitimately serve on the juries (*Strauder* v. *West Virgina*, 1880). Taylor Strauder, a formerly enslaved man, was charged with murdering his wife, Anna, after an argument over alleged infidelity. The murder was witnessed by Anna's daughter, Fannie Green. After his trial in West Virginia, Strauder appealed and asked for his case to be moved to federal courts, because he could not be tried fairly before a jury of his peers in West Virginia, as African American males were barred from jury service. The state denied his appeal and all subsequent ones.

STRAUDER v. WEST VIRGINIA, 100 U.S. 303 (1880)

Justice Strong Delivered the Opinion of the Court, Joined by Chief Justice Waite and Justices Swayne, Miller, Bradley, Hunt, and Harlan

Vote: 7–2

... [T]he controlling question underlying [is] whether, by the Constitution and laws of the United States, every citizen of the United States has a right to a trial of an indictment against him by a jury selected and impaneled without discrimination against his race or color ...

It is to be observed that the first of these questions is not whether a colored man, when an indictment has been preferred against him, has a right to a grand or a petit jury composed in whole or in part of persons of his own race or color, but it is whether, in the composition or selection of juror by whom he is to be indicted or tried, all persons of his race or color may be excluded by law solely because of their race or color, so that by no possibility can any colored man sit upon the jury.

This is one of a series of constitutional provisions having a common purpose – namely, securing to a race recently emancipated, a race that, through many generations, had been held in slavery, all the civil rights that the superior race enjoy. The true spirit and meaning of the amendments, as we said in the *Slaughterhouse Cases*, 16 Wall. 36 (1876), cannot be understood without keeping in view the history of the times when they were adopted and the general objects they plainly sought to accomplish. At the time when they were incorporated into the Constitution, it required little knowledge of human nature to anticipate that those who had long been regarded as an inferior and subject race would, when suddenly raised to the rank of citizenship, be looked upon with jealousy and positive dislike, and that State laws might be enacted or enforced to perpetuate the distinctions that had before existed. discriminations against them had been habitual. It was well known that, in some States, laws making such discrimination then existed, and others might well be expected. The colored race, as a race, was abject and ignorant, and in that condition was unfitted to command the respect of those who had superior intelligence. Their training had left them mere children, and, as such, they needed the protection which a wise government extend to those who are unable to protect themselves. They especially needed protection against unfriendly action in the States where they were resident. It was in view of these considerations the Fourteenth Amendment was framed and adopted. It was designed to assure to the colored race the enjoyment of all the civil rights that, under the law, are enjoyed by white persons, and to give to that race the protection of the general government in that enjoyment whenever it should be denied by the States. It not only gave citizenship and the privileges of citizenship to persons of color, but it denied to any State the power to withhold from them the equal protection of the laws, and authorized Congress to enforce its provisions by appropriate legislation.

... What is this but declaring that the law in the States shall be the same for the black as for the white; that all persons, whether colored or white, shall stand equal before the laws of the States, and, in regard to the colored race, for whose protection the amendment was primarily designed, that no discrimination shall be made against them bar law because of their color? The words of the amendment, it is true, are prohibitory, but they contain a necessary implication of a positive immunity, or right, most valuable to the colored race – the right to exemption from unfriendly legislation against them distinctively as colored – exemption from legal discriminations, implying inferiority in civil society, lessening the security of their enjoyment of the rights which others enjoy, and discriminations which are steps towards reducing them to the condition of a subject race.

That the West Virginia statute respecting juries – the statute that controlled the selection of the grand and petit jury in the case of the plaintiff ... – is such a discrimination ought not to be doubted. Nor would it be if the persons excluded by it were white men. If, in those States where the colored people constitute a majority of the entire population, a law should be enacted excluding all white men from jury service, thus denying to them the privilege of participating fully with the blacks in the administration of justice, we apprehend no one would be heard to claim that it would not be a denial to white men of the equal protection of the laws. Nor, if a law should be passed excluding all naturalized Celtic Irishmen, would there be any doubt of its inconsistency with the spirit of the amendment. The very fact that colored people are singled out and expressly denied by a statute all right to participate in the administration of the law as jurors because of their color, though they are citizens and may be in other respects fully qualified, is practically a brand upon them affixed by the law, an assertion of their inferiority, and a stimulant to that race prejudice which is an impediment to securing to individuals of the race that equal justice which the law aims to secure to all others.

The right to a trial by jury is guaranteed to every citizen of West Virginia by the Constitution of that State, and the constitution of juries is a very essential part of the protection such a mode of trial is intended to secure. The very idea of a jury is a body of men composed of the peers or equals of the person whose rights it is selected or summoned to determine – that is, of his neighbors, fellows, associates, persons having the same legal status in society as that which he holds ...

It is also guarded by statutory enactments intended to make impossible what Mr. Bentham called "packing juries." It is well known that prejudices often exit against particular classes in the community which sway the judgment of jurors and which therefore operate in some cases to deny to persons of those classes the full enjoyment of that protection which others enjoy. Prejudice in a local community is held to be a reason for a change of venue. The framers of the constitutional amendment must have known full well the existence of such prejudice and its likelihood to continue against the manumitted slaves and their race, and that knowledge was doubtless a motive that led to the amendment. By their manumission and citizenship, the colored race became entitled to the equal protection of the laws of the States in which they resided, and the apprehension that, through prejudice, they might be denied that equal protection, that is, that there might be discrimination against them, was the inducement to bestow upon the national government the power to enforce the provision that no State shall deny to them the equal protection of the laws. Without the apprehended existence of prejudice, that portion of the amendment would have been unnecessary, and it might have been left to the States to extend equality of protection.

In view of these considerations, it is hard to see why the statute of West Virginia should not be regarded as discriminating against a colored man when he is put upon trial for an alleged criminal offence against the State. It is not easy to comprehend how it can be said that, while every white man is entitled to a trial by a jury selected from persons of his own race or color, or, rather, selected without discrimination against his color, and a negro is not, the latter is equally protected by the law with the former. Is not protection of life and liberty against race or color prejudice a right, a legal right, under the constitutional amendment? And how can it be maintained that compelling a colored man to submit to a trial for his life by a jury drawn from a panel from which the State has expressly excluded every man of his race, because of color alone, however well qualified in other respects, is not a denial to him of equal legal protection?

We do not say that, within the limits from which it is not excluded by the amendment, a State may not prescribe the qualifications of its jurors, and, in so doing, make discriminations. It may confine the selection to males, to freeholders, to citizens, to persons within certain ages, or to persons having educational qualifications. We do not believe the Fourteenth Amendment was ever intended to prohibit this. Looking at its history, it is clear it had no such purpose. Its aim was against discrimination because of race or color. As we have said more than once, its design was to protect an emancipated race, and to strike down all possible legal discriminations against those who belong to it …

We are not now called upon to affirm or deny that it had other purposes.

The Fourteenth Amendment makes no attempt to enumerate the rights it designed to protect. It speaks in general terms, and those are as comprehensive as possible. Its language is prohibitory, but every prohibition implies the existence of rights and immunities, prominent among which is an immunity from inequality of legal protection either for life, liberty, or property. Any State action that denies this immunity to a colored man is in conflict with the Constitution.

Concluding, therefore, that the statute of West Virginia, discriminating in the selection of jurors, as it does, against negroes because of their color, amounts to a denial of the equal protection of the laws to a colored man when he is put upon trial for an alleged offence against the State....

The judgment of the Supreme Court of West Virginia will be reversed, and the case remitted with instructions to reverse the judgment of the Circuit Court of Ohio county, and it is so ordered.

Justice Field, Dissenting and Joined by Justice Clifford, that pulls from his Opinion in *Ex parte Virginia*, 100 U.S. 339 (1880)

The government created by the Constitution was not designed for the regulation of matters of purely local concern. The States required no aid from any external authority to manage their domestic affairs. They were fully competent to provide for the due administration of justice between their own citizens in their own courts; and they needed no directions in that matter from any other government, any more than they needed directions as to their highways and schools, their hospitals and charitable institutions, their public libraries, or the magistrates they should appoint for their towns and counties. It was only for matters which concerned all the States, and which could not be managed by them in their independent capacity, or managed only with great difficulty and embarrassment, that a general and common government was desired. Whilst they retained control of local matters, it was felt necessary that matters of general and common interest, which they could not wisely and efficiently manage, should be intrusted to a central authority. And so to the common government which grew out of this prevailing necessity was granted exclusive jurisdiction over external affairs, including the great powers of declaring war, making peace, and concluding treaties; but only such powers of internal regulation were conferred as were essential to the successful and efficient working of the government established – to facilitate intercourse and commerce between the people of the different States and secure to them equality of protection in the several States.

Nothing, in my judgment, could have a greater tendency to destroy the independence and autonomy of the States, reduce them to a humiliating and degrading dependence upon the central government, engender constant irritation, and destroy that domestic tranquillity which it was one of the objects of the Constitution to insure than the doctrine asserted in this case – that Congress can exercise coercive authority over judicial officers of the States in the discharge of their duties under State laws. It will be only another step in the same direction towards consolidation, when it assumes to exercise similar coercive authority over governors and legislators of the States.

I cannot think I am mistaken in saying that a change so radical in the relation between the Federal and State authorities as would justify legislation interfering with the independent action of the different departments of the State governments in all matters over which the States retain jurisdiction was never contemplated by the recent amendments.

The people, in adopting them, did not suppose they were altering the fundamental theory of their dual system of governments ... It was intended to render everyone within the domain of the republic a freeman, with the right to follow the ordinary pursuits of life without other restraints than such as are applied to all others, and to enjoy equally with them the earnings of his labor. But it confers no political rights; it leaves the States free as before its adoption to determine who shall hold their offices and participate in the administration of their laws. A similar prohibition of slavery and involuntary servitude was in the Constitution of several States previous to its adoption by the United States, and it was never held to confer any political rights.

... In the consideration of questions growing out of these amendments, much confusion has arisen from a failure to distinguish between the civil and the political rights of citizens. Civil rights are absolute and personal. Political rights, on the other hand, are conditioned and dependent upon the discretion of the elective or appointing power, whether that be the people acting through the ballot or one of the departments of their government. The civil rights of the individual are never to be withheld, and may be always judicially enforced. The political rights which he may enjoy, such as holding office and discharging a public trust, are qualified because their possession depends on his fitness, to be adjudged by those whom society has clothed with the elective authority. The Thirteenth and Fourteenth Amendments were designed to secure the civil rights of all persons, of every race, color, and condition; but they left to the States to determine to whom the possession of political powers should be intrusted. This is manifest from the fact that when it was desired to confer political power upon the newly made citizens of the States, as was done by inhibiting the denial to them of the suffrage on account of race, color, or previous condition of servitude, a new amendment was required.

... [I]f it can make the exclusion of persons from jury service on account of race or color a criminal offence, it can make their exclusion from office on that account also criminal, and, adopting the doctrine of the district judge in this case, the failure to appoint them to office will be presumptive evidence of their exclusion on that ground. To such a result are we logically led. The legislation of Congress is founded, and is sustained by this court, as it seems to me, upon a theory as to what constitutes the equal protection of the laws which is purely speculative, not warranted by any experience of the country, and not in accordance with the understanding of the people as to the meaning of those terms since the organization of the government.

1. Why is having a jury of your peers seen as so significant in protecting due process and equal protection of the laws?
2. On what specific point does the majority and dissent disagree?
3. Why might this ruling surprise you in light of some of the other rulings on extension of rights?
4. Do you agree with the dissent that there is a distinction between civil and political rights? Why or why not?

It would be seventy years later before the Court would extend *Strauder* to apply to Latinos and another decade before women of any race would receive similar protections. In *Hernandez* v. *Texas* (1954), Pete Hernandez was indicted, convicted, and sentenced to life imprisonment for the murder of Joe Espinosa by grand and trial juries constituted by a Texas system that systematically excluded all jurors of Mexican descent, such as Hernandez. He claimed that the exclusion of fully qualified Latino jurors resulted in his denial of the Fourteenth Amendment's guarantee of equal protection.

HERNANDEZ v. *TEXAS*, 347 U.S. 79 (1954)

Chief Justice Warren Delivered the Opinion of the Court

Vote: 9–0

In numerous decisions, this Court has held that it is a denial of the equal protection of the laws to try a defendant of a particular race or color under an indictment issued by a grand jury, or before a petit jury, from which all persons of his race or color have, solely because of that race or color, been excluded by the State, whether acting through its legislature, its courts, or its executive or administrative officers. Although the Court has had little occasion to rule on the question directly, it has been recognized since *Strauder* v. *West Virginia*, 100 U.S. 303 (1880), that the exclusion of a class of persons from jury service on grounds other than race or color may also deprive a defendant who is a member of that class of the constitutional guarantee of equal protection of the laws. The State of Texas would have us hold that there are only two classes – white and Negro – within the contemplation of the Fourteenth Amendment. The decisions of this Court do not support that view. And, except where the question presented involves the exclusion of persons of Mexican descent from juries, Texas courts have taken a broader view of the scope of the equal protection clause.

Throughout our history, differences in race and color have defined easily identifiable groups which have at times required the aid of the courts in securing equal treatment under the laws. But community prejudices are not static, and, from time to time, other differences from the community norm may define other groups which need the same protection. Whether such a group exists within a community is a question of fact. When the existence of a distinct class is demonstrated, and it is further shown that the laws, as written or as applied, single out that class for different treatment not based on some reasonable classification, the guarantees of the Constitution have been violated. The Fourteenth Amendment is not directed solely against discrimination due to a "two-class theory" – that is, based upon differences between "white" and Negro.

As the petitioner acknowledges, the Texas system of selecting grand and petit jurors by the use of jury commissions is fair on its face and capable of being utilized without discrimination. But, as this Court has held, the system is susceptible to abuse, and can be employed in a discriminatory manner. The exclusion of otherwise eligible persons from jury service solely because of their ancestry or national origin is discrimination prohibited by the Fourteenth Amendment. The Texas statute makes no such discrimination, but the petitioner alleges that those administering the law do.

The petitioner's initial burden in substantiating his charge of group discrimination was to prove that persons of Mexican descent constitute a separate class in Jackson County, distinct from "whites." One method by which this may be demonstrated is by showing the attitude of the community. Here, the testimony of responsible officials and citizens contained the admission that residents of the community distinguished between "white" and "Mexican." The participation of persons of Mexican descent in business and community groups was shown to be slight. Until very recent times, children of Mexican descent were required to attend a segregated school for the first four grades. At least one restaurant in town prominently displayed a sign announcing "No Mexicans Served." On the courthouse grounds at the time of the hearing, there were two men's toilets, one unmarked, and the other marked "Colored Men" and "Hombres Aqui" ("Men Here"). No substantial evidence was offered to rebut the logical inference to be drawn from these facts, and it must be concluded that petitioner succeeded in his proof.

Having established the existence of a class, petitioner was then charged with the burden of proving discrimination. To do so, he relied on the pattern of proof established by *Norris* v. *Alabama*, 294 U.S. 587 (1935). In that case, proof that Negroes constituted a substantial segment of the population of the jurisdiction, that some Negroes were qualified to serve as jurors, and that none had been called for jury service over an extended period of time, was held to constitute *prima facie* proof of the systematic exclusion of Negroes from jury service. This holding, sometimes called the "rule of exclusion," has been applied in other cases, and it is available in supplying proof of discrimination against any delineated class.

The petitioner established that 14% of the population of Jackson County were persons with Mexican or Latin American surnames, and that 11% of the males over 21 bore such names. The County Tax Assessor testified that 6 or 7 percent of the freeholders on the tax rolls of the County were persons of Mexican descent. The State of Texas stipulated that, "for the last twenty-five years, there is no record of any person with a Mexican or Latin American name having served on a jury commission, grand jury or petit jury in Jackson County."

The parties also stipulated that "there are some male persons of Mexican or Latin American descent in Jackson County who, by virtue of being citizens, freeholders, and having all other legal prerequisites to jury service, are eligible to serve as members of a jury commission, grand jury and/or petit jury."

The petitioner met the burden of proof imposed in *Norris* v. *Alabama*. To rebut the strong *prima facie* case of the denial of the equal protection of the laws guaranteed by the Constitution thus established, the State offered the testimony of five jury commissioners that they had no discriminated against persons of Mexican or Latin American descent in selecting jurors. They stated that their only objective had been to select those whom they thought were best qualified. This testimony is not enough to overcome the petitioner's case. As the Court said in *Norris* v. *Alabama:*

> That showing as to the long-continued exclusion of negroes from jury service, and as to the many negroes qualified for that service, could not be met by mere generalities. If, in the presence of such testimony as defendant adduced, the mere general assertions by officials of their performance of duty were to be accepted as an adequate justification for the complete exclusion of negroes from jury service, the constitutional provision ... would be but a vain and illusory requirement.

The same reasoning is applicable to these facts.

Circumstances or chance may well dictate that no persons in a certain class will serve on a particular jury or during some particular period. But it taxes our credulity to say that mere chance resulted in their being no members of this class among the over six thousand jurors called in the past 25 years. The result bespeaks discrimination, whether or not it was a conscious decision on the part of any individual jury commissioner. The judgment of conviction must be reversed.

To say that this decision revives the rejected contention that the Fourteenth Amendment requires proportional representation of all the component ethnic groups of the community on every jury ignores the facts. The petitioner did not seek proportional representation, nor did he claim a right to have persons of Mexican descent sit on the particular juries which he faced. His only claim is the right to be indicted and tried by juries from which all members of his class are not systematically excluded – juries selected from among all qualified persons regardless of national origin or descent. To this much he is entitled by the Constitution.

Reversed.

1. How did the protection of African American rights under the Constitution create a legal pattern other communities were able to use to extend their constitutional rights?
2. How might you explain the broad expanse of time between *Strauder* and *Hernandez*?

Making a jury pool more racially universal does not guarantee a jury of one's peers. While this may provide formal equality to the accused (the law treating everyone the same regardless of racial identity), there are many other barriers to fair trials. One such example is the exercise of the peremptory challenge by prosecuting attorneys. In the process of empaneling a jury (*voir dire*), the competing attorneys question the members of the jury pool to ensure the selected members of the jury are not inherently biased and thereby incapable of objectively weighing the evidence presented. This power of the attorney to reject – without a justification or explanation – a potential member of the jury has existed since the beginnings of our western common law. But what happens when these exclusions are used to empanel an all-White jury?

In *Batson* v. *Kentucky* (1986) the Supreme Court addressed this question of the potential of peremptory challenges being used to hinder the right to due process and equal protection for citizens of color. James Kirkland Batson, was indicted in Louisville, Kentucky, for second-degree burglary and receipt of stolen goods. In the *voir dire* portion of his trial, the prosecutor, Joe Gutman, struck all Black potential jurors and left an all-White jury. When challenged, the judge ruled that the attorneys could use peremptory challenges to "strike anybody they want to," denying Batson's motion. The jury convicted Batson on both counts. Batson appealed to the Kentucky Supreme Court claiming a violation of the Sixth Amendment of the Constitution. The Kentucky high court upheld the conviction.

BATSON v. *KENTUCKY*, 476 U.S. 79 (1986)

Justice Powell Delivered the Opinion of the Court, Joined by Justices Brennan, White, Marshall, Blackmun, Stevens, and O'Connor

Vote: 7–2

II.

In *Swain* v. *Alabama*, 380 U.S. 202 (1965), this Court recognized that a "State's purposeful or deliberate denial to Negroes on account of race of participation as jurors in the administration of justice violates the Equal Protection

Clause." This principle has been "consistently and repeatedly" reaffirmed, numerous decisions of this Court both preceding and following *Swain*. We reaffirm the principle today.

A.

More than a century ago, the Court decided that the State denies a black defendant equal protection of the laws when it puts him on trial before a jury from which members of his race have been purposefully excluded. *Strauder* v. *West Virginia*, 100 U.S. 303 (1880). That decision laid the foundation for the Court's unceasing efforts to eradicate racial discrimination in the procedures used to select the venire from which individual jurors are drawn. In *Strauder*, the Court explained that the central concern of the recently ratified Fourteenth Amendment was to put an end to governmental discrimination on account of race. Exclusion of black citizens from service as jurors constitutes a primary example of the evil the Fourteenth Amendment was designed to cure.

In holding that racial discrimination in jury selection offends the Equal Protection Clause, the Court in *Strauder* recognized, however, that a defendant has no right to a "petit jury composed in whole or in part of persons of his own race." "The number of our races and nationalities stands in the way of evolution of such a conception" of the demand of equal protection. *Akins* v. *Texas*, 325 U.S. 398 (1945). But the defendant does have the right to be tried by a jury whose members are selected pursuant to nondiscriminatory criteria. *Martin* v. *Texas*, 200 U.S. 316 (1906); *Ex parte Virginia*, 100 U.S. 339 (1880). The Equal Protection Clause guarantees the defendant that the State will not exclude members of his race from the jury venire on account of race, or on the false assumption that members of his race as a group are not qualified to serve as jurors, *see Norris* v. *Alabama*, 294 U.S. 587 (1935).

Purposeful racial discrimination in selection of the venire violates a defendant's right to equal protection, because it denies him the protection that a trial by jury is intended to secure ...

Racial discrimination in selection of jurors harms not only the accused whose life or liberty they are summoned to try. Competence to serve as a juror ultimately depends on an assessment of individual qualifications and ability impartially to consider evidence presented at a trial. A person's race simply "is unrelated to his fitness as a juror." As long ago as *Strauder*, therefore, the Court recognized that, by denying a person participation in jury service on account of his race, the State unconstitutionally discriminated against the excluded juror.

The harm from discriminatory jury selection extends beyond that inflicted on the defendant and the excluded juror to touch the entire community. Selection procedures that purposefully exclude black persons from juries undermine public confidence in the fairness of our system of justice.

B.

In *Strauder*, the Court invalidated a state statute that provided that only white men could serve as jurors. We can be confident that no State now has such a law. The Constitution requires, however, that we look beyond the face of the statute defining juror qualifications, and also consider challenged selection practices to afford "protection against action of the State through its administrative officers in effecting the prohibited discrimination." *Norris* v. *Alabama* at 589; see *Hernandez* v. *Texas*, 347 U.S. 475 (1954). Thus, the Court has found a denial of equal protection where the procedures implementing a neutral statute operated to exclude persons from the venire on racial grounds, and has made clear that the Constitution prohibits all forms of purposeful racial discrimination in selection of jurors. While decisions of this Court have been concerned largely with discrimination during selection of the venire, the principles announced there also forbid discrimination on account of race in selection of the petit jury. Since the Fourteenth Amendment protects an accused throughout the proceedings bringing him to justice, the State may not draw up its jury lists pursuant to neutral procedures, but then resort to discrimination at "other stages in the selection process," *Avery* v. *Georgia*, 345 U.S. 559, 562 (1953).

Accordingly, the component of the jury selection process at issue here, the State's privilege to strike individual jurors through peremptory challenges, is subject to the commands of the Equal Protection Clause. Although a prosecutor ordinarily is entitled to exercise permitted peremptory challenges "for any reason at all, as long as that reason is related to his view concerning the outcome" of the case to be tried, *United States* v. *Robinson*, 421 F. Supp. 467, 473 (Conn. 1976). [T]he Equal Protection Clause forbids the prosecutor to challenge potential jurors solely on account of their race or on the assumption that black jurors as a group will be unable impartially to consider the State's case against a black defendant.

III.

The principles announced in *Strauder* never have been questioned in any subsequent decision of this Court.

Rather, the Court has been called upon repeatedly to review the application of those principles to particular facts. A recurring question in these cases, as in any case alleging a violation of the Equal Protection Clause, was whether the defendant had met his burden of proving purposeful discrimination on the part of the State. That question also was at the heart of the portion of *Swain* v. *Alabama* we reexamine today.

A.

Swain required the Court to decide, among other issues, whether a black defendant was denied equal protection by the State's exercise of peremptory challenges to exclude members of his race from the petit jury. The record in *Swain* showed that the prosecutor had used the State's peremptory challenges to strike the six black persons included on the petit jury venire. While rejecting the defendant's claim for failure to prove purposeful discrimination, the Court nonetheless indicated that the Equal Protection Clause placed some limits on the State's exercise of peremptory challenges.

The Court sought to accommodate the prosecutor's historical privilege of peremptory challenge free of judicial control, and the constitutional prohibition on exclusion of persons from jury service on account of race. While the Constitution does not confer a right to peremptory challenges, those challenges traditionally have been viewed as one means of assuring the selection of a qualified and unbiased jury. To preserve the peremptory nature of the prosecutor's challenge, the Court in *Swain* declined to scrutinize his actions in a particular case by relying on a presumption that he properly exercised the State's challenges.

The Court went on to observe, however, that a State may not exercise its challenges in contravention of the Equal Protection Clause. It was impermissible for a prosecutor to use his challenges to exclude blacks from the jury "for reasons wholly unrelated to the outcome of the particular case on trial," or to deny to blacks "the same right and opportunity to participate in the administration of justice enjoyed by the white population." Accordingly, a black defendant could make out a *prima facie* case of purposeful discrimination on proof that the peremptory challenge system was "being perverted" in that manner. For example, an inference of purposeful discrimination would be raised on evidence that a prosecutor,

> in case after case, whatever the circumstances, whatever the crime and whoever the defendant or the victim may be, is responsible for the removal of Negroes who have been selected as qualified jurors by the jury commissioners and who have survived challenges for cause, with the result that no Negroes ever serve on petit juries.

Evidence offered by the defendant in *Swain* did not meet that standard. While the defendant showed that prosecutors in the jurisdiction had exercised their strikes to exclude blacks from the jury, he offered no proof of the circumstances under which prosecutors were responsible for striking black jurors beyond the facts of his own case.

A number of lower courts following the teaching of *Swain* reasoned that proof of repeated striking of blacks over a number of cases was necessary to establish a violation of the Equal Protection Clause. Since this interpretation of *Swain* has placed on defendants a crippling burden of proof, prosecutors' peremptory challenges are now largely immune from constitutional scrutiny. For reasons that follow, we reject this evidentiary formulation as inconsistent with standards that have been developed since *Swain* for assessing a *prima facie* case under the Equal Protection Clause.

B.

Since the decision in *Swain*, we have explained that our cases concerning selection of the venire reflect the general equal protection principle that the "invidious quality" of governmental action claimed to be racially discriminatory "must ultimately be traced to a racially discriminatory purpose." *Washington* v. *Davis*, 426 U.S. 229, 240 (1976). As in any equal protection case, the "burden is, of course," on the defendant who alleges discriminatory selection of the venire "to prove the existence of purposeful discrimination." In deciding if the defendant has carried his burden of persuasion, a court must undertake "a sensitive inquiry into such circumstantial and direct evidence of intent as may be available." *Arlington Heights* v. *Metropolitan Housing Development Corp.*, 429 U.S. 252, 266 (1977). Circumstantial evidence of invidious intent may include proof of disproportionate impact. *Washington* v. *Davis* at 242. We have observed that, under some circumstances, proof of discriminatory impact "may, for all practical purposes, demonstrate unconstitutionality because, in various circumstances, the discrimination is very difficult to explain on nonracial grounds."

Moreover, since *Swain*, we have recognized that a black defendant alleging that members of his race have been impermissibly excluded from the venire may make out a *prima facie* case of purposeful discrimination by showing that the totality of the relevant facts gives rise to an inference of discriminatory purpose. Once the defendant makes the requisite showing, the burden shifts to the State to explain adequately the racial exclusion. The State cannot meet this burden on mere general assertions that its officials did not discriminate, or that they properly performed their official duties. Rather, the State must demonstrate that "permissible racially neutral selection criteria and procedures have produced the monochromatic result."

The showing necessary to establish a *prima facie* case of purposeful discrimination in selection of the venire may be discerned in this Court's decisions. The defendant initially must show that he is a member of a racial group capable of being singled out for different treatment. In combination with that evidence, a defendant may then make a *prima facie* case by proving that, in the particular jurisdiction, members of his race have not been summoned for jury service over an extended period of time. Proof of systematic exclusion from

the venire raises an inference of purposeful discrimination, because the "result bespeaks discrimination." *Hernandez* v. *Texas* at 482.

Since the ultimate issue is whether the State has discriminated in selecting the defendant's venire, however, the defendant may establish a *prima facie* case "in other ways than by evidence of long-continued unexplained absence" of members of his race "from many panels." *Cassell* v. *Texas*, 339 U.S. 282, 290 (1950). In cases involving the venire, this Court has found a *prima facie* case on proof that members of the defendant's race were substantially underrepresented on the venire from which his jury was drawn, and that the venire was selected under a practice providing "the opportunity for discrimination." This combination of factors raises the necessary inference of purposeful discrimination because the Court has declined to attribute to chance the absence of black citizens on a particular jury array where the selection mechanism is subject to abuse. When circumstances suggest the need, the trial court must undertake a "factual inquiry" that "takes into account all possible explanatory factors" in the particular case.

Thus, since the decision in *Swain*, this Court has recognized that a defendant may make a *prima facie* showing of purposeful racial discrimination in selection of the venire by relying solely on the facts concerning its selection *in his case*.

C.

In deciding whether the defendant has made the requisite showing, the trial court should consider all relevant circumstances. For example, a "pattern" of strikes against black jurors included in the particular venire might give rise to an inference of discrimination. Similarly, the prosecutor's questions and statements during *voir dire* examination and in exercising his challenges may support or refute an inference of discriminatory purpose. These examples are merely illustrative. We have confidence that trial judges, experienced in supervising *voir dire*, will be able to decide if the circumstances concerning the prosecutor's use of peremptory challenges creates a *prima facie* case of discrimination against black jurors.

Once the defendant makes a *prima facie* showing, the burden shifts to the State to come forward with a neutral explanation for challenging black jurors. Though this requirement imposes a limitation in some cases on the full peremptory character of the historic challenge, we emphasize that the prosecutor's explanation need not rise to the level justifying exercise of a challenge for cause. But the prosecutor may not rebut the defendant's *prima facie* case of discrimination by stating merely that he challenged jurors of the defendant's race on the assumption – or his intuitive judgment – that they would be partial to the defendant because of their shared race. Just as the Equal Protection Clause forbids the States to exclude black persons from the venire on the assumption that blacks as a group are unqualified to serve as jurors, so it forbids the States to strike black veniremen on the assumption that they will be biased in a particular case simply because the defendant is black. The core guarantee of equal protection, ensuring citizens that their State will not discriminate on account of race, would be meaningless were we to approve the exclusion of jurors on the basis of such assumptions, which arise solely from the jurors' race. Nor may the prosecutor rebut the defendant's case merely by denying that he had a discriminatory motive or "affirm[ing] [his] good faith in making individual selections." If these general assertions were accepted as rebutting a defendant's *prima facie* case, the Equal Protection Clause "would be but a vain and illusory requirement." The prosecutor therefore must articulate a neutral explanation related to the particular case to be tried. The trial court then will have the duty to determine if the defendant has established purposeful discrimination.

IV.

The State contends that our holding will eviscerate the fair trial values served by the peremptory challenge. Conceding that the Constitution does not guarantee a right to peremptory challenges and that *Swain* did state that their use ultimately is subject to the strictures of equal protection, the State argues that the privilege of unfettered exercise of the challenge is of vital importance to the criminal justice system.

While we recognize, of course, that the peremptory challenge occupies an important position in our trial procedures, we do not agree that our decision today will undermine the contribution the challenge generally makes to the administration of justice. The reality of practice, amply reflected in many state and federal court opinions, shows that the challenge may be, and unfortunately at times has been, used to discriminate against black jurors. By requiring trial courts to be sensitive to the racially discriminatory use of peremptory challenges, our decision enforces the mandate of equal protection and furthers the ends of justice. In view of the heterogeneous population of our Nation, public respect for our criminal justice system and the rule of law will be strengthened if we ensure that no citizen is disqualified from jury service because of his race.

V.

In this case, petitioner made a timely objection to the prosecutor's removal of all black persons on the venire. Because the trial court flatly rejected the objection without requiring the prosecutor to give an explanation for his action, we remand this case for further proceedings. If the trial court decides that the facts establish, *prima facie*, purposeful discrimination and the prosecutor does not come forward with a neutral explanation for his action, our precedents require that petitioner's conviction be reversed. *It is so ordered.*

Justice White, Concurring

The Court overturns the principal holding in *Swain* v. *Alabama*, 380 U.S. 202 (1965), that the Constitution does not require in any given case an inquiry into the prosecutor's reasons for using his peremptory challenges to strike blacks from the petit jury panel in the criminal trial of a black defendant, and that, in such a case, it will be presumed that the prosecutor is acting for legitimate trial-related reasons. The Court now rules that such use of peremptory challenges in a given case may, but does not necessarily, raise an inference, which the prosecutor carries the burden of refuting, that his strikes were based on the belief that no black citizen could be a satisfactory juror or fairly try a black defendant.

I agree that, to this extent, *Swain* should be overruled. I do so because *Swain* itself indicated that the presumption of legitimacy with respect to the striking of black venire persons could be overcome by evidence that, over a period of time, the prosecution had consistently excluded blacks from petit juries. This should have warned prosecutors that using peremptories to exclude blacks on the assumption that no black juror could fairly judge a black defendant would violate the Equal Protection Clause.

It appears, however, that the practice of peremptorily eliminating blacks from petit juries in cases with black defendants remains widespread, so much so that I agree that an opportunity to inquire should be afforded when this occurs ...

The Court emphasizes that using peremptory challenges to strike blacks does not end the inquiry; it is not unconstitutional, without more, to strike one or more blacks from the jury....

Much litigation will be required to spell out the contours of the Court's equal protection holding today, and the significant effect it will have on the conduct of criminal trials cannot be gainsaid. But I agree with the Court that the time has come to rule as it has, and I join its opinion and judgment.

Justice Marshall, Concurring

I join Justice Powell's eloquent opinion for the Court, which takes a historic step toward eliminating the shameful practice of racial discrimination in the selection of juries ... The decision today will not end the racial discrimination that peremptories inject into the jury selection process. That goal can be accomplished only by eliminating peremptory challenges entirely.

I.

Misuse of the peremptory challenge to exclude black jurors has become both common and flagrant. Black defendants rarely have been able to compile statistics showing the extent of that practice, but the few cases setting out such figures are instructive. See *United States* v. *Carter*, 528 F.2d 844, 848 (CA8 1975) (in 15 criminal cases in 1974 in the Western District of Missouri involving black defendants, prosecutors peremptorily challenged 81% of black jurors); *United States* v. *McDaniels*, 379 F. Supp. 1243 (ED La. 1974) (in 53 criminal cases in 1972–1974 in the Eastern District of Louisiana involving black defendants, federal prosecutors used 68.9% of their peremptory challenges against black jurors, who made up less than one-quarter of the venire); *McKinney* v. *Walker*, 394 F. Supp. 1015 (SC 1974) (in 13 criminal trials in 1970–1971 in Spartansburg County, South Carolina, involving black defendants, prosecutors peremptorily challenged 82% of black jurors). Prosecutors have explained to courts that they routinely strike black jurors. An instruction book used by the prosecutor's office in Dallas County, Texas, explicitly advised prosecutors that they conduct jury selection so as to eliminate "any member of a minority group." 100 felony trials in Dallas County in 1983–1984, prosecutors peremptorily struck 405 out of 467 eligible black jurors; the chance of a qualified black sitting on a jury was 1 in 10, compared to 1 in 2 for a white.

III.

The inherent potential of peremptory challenges to distort the jury process by permitting the exclusion of jurors on racial grounds should ideally lead the Court to ban them entirely from the criminal justice system.

I believe that this case presents just such a choice, and I would resolve that choice by eliminating peremptory challenges entirely in criminal cases.

Justice O'Connor, Concurring

I concur in the Court's opinion and judgment, but also agree with the views of the Chief Justice and Justice White that today's decision does not apply retroactively.

Chief Justice Burger, Joined by Justice Rehnquist, Dissenting

I.

Today the Court sets aside the peremptory challenge, a procedure which has been part of the common law for many centuries and part of our jury system for nearly 200 years. It does so on the basis of a constitutional argument that was rejected, without a single dissent, in *Swain* v. *Alabama*, 380 U.S. 202 (1965). Reversal of such settled principles would be unusual enough on its own terms, for only three years ago we said that "*stare decisis*, while perhaps never entirely persuasive on a constitutional question, is a doctrine that demands respect in a society governed by the rule of law." *Akron* v. *Akron Center for Reproductive Health, Inc.*, 462 U.S. 416, 420 (1983). What makes today's holding truly extraordinary is that it is based on a constitutional argument that the petitioner has *expressly* declined to raise, both in this Court and in the Supreme Court of Kentucky.

Petitioner has not suggested any barrier prevented raising an equal protection claim in the Kentucky courts. In such circumstances, review of an equal protection argument is improper in this Court ...

II.

Because the Court nonetheless chooses to decide this case on the equal protection grounds not presented, it may be useful to discuss this issue as well ... Long ago, it was recognized that "[t]he right of challenge is almost essential for the purpose of securing perfect fairness and impartiality in a trial." The peremptory challenge has been in use without scrutiny into its basis for nearly as long as juries have existed.

IV.

An institution like the peremptory challenge that is part of the fabric of our jury system should not be casually cast aside, especially on a basis not raised or argued by the petitioner. As one commentator aptly observed: "The real question is whether to tinker with a system, be it of jury selection or anything else, that has done the job for centuries. We stand on the shoulders of our ancestors, as Burke said. It is not so much that the past is always worth preserving, he argued, but rather that ... it is with infinite caution that any man ought to venture upon pulling down an edifice, which has answered in any tolerable degree for ages the common purposes of society ..."

At the very least, this important case reversing centuries of history and experience ought to be set for reargument next Term.

Justice Rehnquist, with whom the Chief Justice joins, Dissenting

The Court states, in the opening line of its opinion, that this case involves only a reexamination of that portion of *Swain* v. *Alabama*, 380 U.S. 202 (1965), concerning "the evidentiary burden placed on a criminal defendant who claims that he has been denied equal protection through the State's use of peremptory challenges to exclude members of his race from the petit jury."

But in reality the majority opinion deals with much more than "evidentiary burden[s]." With little discussion and less analysis, the Court also overrules one of the fundamental substantive holdings of *Swain*, namely, that the State may use its peremptory challenges to remove from the jury, on a case-specific basis, prospective jurors of the same race as the defendant. Because I find the Court's rejection of this holding both ill-considered and unjustifiable under established principles of equal protection, I dissent.

I cannot subscribe to the Court's unprecedented use of the Equal Protection Clause to restrict the historic scope of the peremptory challenge, which has been described as "a necessary part of trial by jury." In my view, there is simply nothing "unequal" about the State's using its peremptory challenges to strike blacks from the jury in cases involving black defendants, so long as such challenges are also used to exclude whites in cases involving white defendants, Hispanics in cases involving Hispanic defendants, Asians in cases involving Asian defendants, and so on. This case-specific use of peremptory challenges by the State does not single out blacks, or members of any other race for that matter, for discriminatory treatment. Such use of peremptories is, at best, based upon seat-of-the-pants instincts, which are undoubtedly crudely stereotypical and may in many cases be hopelessly mistaken. But as long as they are applied across-the-board to jurors of all races and nationalities, I do not see – and the Court most certainly has not explained – how their use violates the Equal Protection Clause.

Nor does such use of peremptory challenges by the State infringe upon any other constitutional interests. The Court does not suggest that exclusion of blacks from the jury through the State's use of peremptory challenges results in a violation of either the fair-cross-section or impartiality component of the Sixth Amendment. And because the case-specific use of peremptory challenges by the State does not deny blacks the right to serve as jurors in cases involving nonblack defendants, it harms neither the excluded jurors nor the remainder of the community.

The use of group affiliations, such as age, race, or occupation, as a "proxy" for potential juror partiality, based on the assumption or belief that members of one group are more likely to favor defendants who belong to the same group, has long been accepted as a legitimate basis for the State's exercise of peremptory challenges. Indeed, given the need for reasonable limitations on the time devoted to *voir dire*, the use of such "proxies" by both the State and the defendant may be extremely useful in eliminating from the jury persons who might be biased in one way or another. The Court today holds that the State may not use its peremptory challenges to strike black prospective jurors on this basis without violating the Constitution. But I do not believe there is anything in the Equal Protection Clause, or any other constitutional provision, that justifies such a departure from the substantive holding contained in Part II of *Swain*. Petitioner in the instant case failed to make a sufficient showing to overcome the presumption announced in *Swain* that the State's use of peremptory challenges was related to the context of the case. I would therefore affirm the judgment of the court below.

1. What is the significance of peremptory challenges? Consider the difficulty in accounting for the role of discretion (police, judge, prosecutor) in trying to eradicate discrimination.
2. Would barring all peremptory challenges or all forms of discretion make a more just system (per Justice Marshall)? What other costs might result?
3. How do you explain the difference in tone and structure between this case and the early cases addressing fair juries?
4. Do you agree with the dissenters' portrayal of the majority opinion? Does making an absolute power challengeable destroy it?

The power of the state to deprive people of their life, liberty, and property – by direct action, the decision of governmental agents, or by ignoring the actions of private citizens – was a key concern of the Founding generation. Many constitutional protections, including due process and equal protection were designed to provide limits to the actions of governments. But the history of the United States clearly demonstrates that many communities, because of their perceived race, were deliberately excluded from these central protections. This history has parallels for most racialized groups in the United States. For example, in the 1850s, twenty-three states authorized their settler militias to "hunt Indians" and steal their land and livestock (Blackhawk 2023). The state (federal and local) used violence directly to advance its own agendas and ignored the use of violence by private citizens.

Even after the Fourteenth Amendment explicitly extended these rights to all individuals regardless of race – excluding sovereign Native peoples – it took most of the twentieth century to ensure this formal equality was understood as applying to all racialized groups. For instance, while access to serving on a jury was a key element for holding the state accountable to the racialized violence conducted under federal and state governmental auspices, the expansion of this right to all communities has taken many court cases and significant coordinated political action. The challenge in the twenty-first century has been evaluating policies that are racially neutral as written (e.g., peremptory strikes and qualified immunity), but have disparate impact on some racial groups and determining the constitutionality of these governmental powers as they are practiced and implemented.

In the context of the protests of 2020 and the long history of state violence (and state-sanctioned private violence) against communities of color, why do you believe the qualified immunity standard remains so contested? What does this tell you about the responses of "Blue Lives Matter" or "All Lives Matter" to the cry of "Black Lives Matter"? It is easy to see the history of the United States as being one of extensive oppression of people based on their perceived racial identity, but continuous resistance and legal challenges to this oppression is evidenced in our history of litigation. Considering the threat of violence evident in these cases, how do you see these precedents as exuding resistance?

5 Race, Culture, and Identity

In the fall of 2023, Darryl George, spent a month in daily detention in part because his hair was deemed to be in violation of the school's dress code. George, a Black student who wears his hair in locs, was told because his hair fell below his eyebrows and earlobes, even though he wore his hair twisted and up, it violated school guidelines. By the time his family filed a federal lawsuit, the junior had missed 86 percent of instructional days. The family notes that men in their family have worn their hair in locs for generations and the hair style – natural for George's hair – has religious and cultural importance for his family (Mumphrey and Ma 2023). A similar scenario occurred that same term when a Native student, a member of the Wyandotte tribe, was also forced to cut his hair on threat of suspension despite his religious and cultural claims (ACLU 2023).

In prior chapters of this book, we have explored how the law has created and enforced the concept of "race" in the United States. We have also seen how these definitions directly impact our current political and social debates surrounding race. In this chapter, we will ask: how do cultural and community identities intersect with issues of race? By focusing on several current issues with which our society is struggling – the adoption of Native American children by White families and their subsequent assimilation; the regulation of Spanish and other languages in the workplace; and the protection of hairstyles of racial significance – we will consider how cultural elements of specific racial communities act as signifiers of identity. The protection of cultural norms has not been guaranteed by the courts. Instead, these cultural aspects challenge the extent to which the law can and should address questions of race and how the parameters of legal protections against racial discrimination help us determine the role of law.

While race in all of its manifestations is constructed socially, its impact on our lives and how many people fashion their identity in the United States is still very real. Communities have formed around shared experiences and cultures have emerged. For many people, their understanding or framing of their race is based on their cultural identity. But should the law protect people's cultural experience as an extension of their racial identity?

5.1 Hairstyles and Community Values in the Workplace

One classic example of this tension is found in the discussion of employment and educational discrimination around specific hairstyles. For many women of African descent, employment in a professional workplace requires them to use harsh chemical relaxers and heating appliances to create a hairstyle that meets the dominant culture's expectations of "professionalism." The use of traditional protective hair-styles (braids, for instance) or natural hairstyles (such as an afro) untreated with heat or chemicals, are often deemed inappropriate or grounds for dismissal. There has been a long tradition of students being punished for wearing braids or dreadlocks to school, and employees denied promotions or fired because of their desire to wear their hair naturally. For many schools and employers, natural hair (such as locs, twists, or afros) was perceived to be "messy," "unkempt," and "unprofessional," and so students and employees are instructed to alter their naturally textured hair or told to "cut it off" (Greene 2017). While these forms of cultural discrimination have been upheld by courts, bans on prescribed hair coverings related to religious beliefs (such as hijabs, yarmulke, or turbans) were at times found to be judicially problematic on the basis of religious discrimination. Why might religious expressions related to hair be protected when cultural expressions of race would not?

In 2017, the 11th Circuit in *Equal Employment Opportunity Commission* v. *Catastrophe Management Solutions* addressed this specific question, debating the role that the law should play in protecting potential cultural manifestations of racial identity. Chastity Jones, a Black woman who was a candidate for a position as a customer service representative for Catastrophe Management Solutions, was told she would be hired only if she would cut off her short dreadlocks. The company based its decision on an internal policy banning "excessive hair-styles" and Ms. Jones' hiring manager interpreted the guideline as banning all forms of dreadlocks regardless of length or "neatness." The Equal Employment Opportunity Commission (EEOC), the federal agency investigating employment discrimination claims, filed a lawsuit against the company for discriminating against Ms. Jones based on race. The EEOC's complaint claimed that "dreadlocks are black hair in its natural unmanipulated state, and that the natural texture of black hair carries with it a deeply entrenched racial stereotype that sees black people as 'unprofessional,' 'extreme,' and 'not neat'" (as explained by Judge Martin, in her dissenting opinion).

EEOC v. *CATASTROPHE MANAGEMENT SOLUTIONS*, 852 F.3D 1018, 11TH CIR. (2016)

Circuit Judge Jordan

III.

The EEOC claimed in its proposed amended complaint that a "prohibition of dreadlocks in the workplace constitutes race discrimination because dreadlocks are a manner of wearing the hair that is physiologically and culturally associated with people of African descent." So, according to the EEOC, the decision of [Catastrophe Management Solutions (CMS)] to "interpret its race-neutral written grooming policy to ban the wearing of dreadlocks constitutes an employment practice that discriminates on the basis of race."

The district court dismissed the initial complaint, and concluded that the proposed amended complaint was futile, because "Title VII prohibits discrimination on the basis of immutable characteristics, such as race, color, or natural origin," and "[a] hairstyle, even one more closely associated with a particular ethnic group, is a mutable characteristic." The district court was not swayed by the EEOC's contention that the allegations were sufficient because "hairstyle can be a determinant of racial identity," explaining that other courts had rejected that argument. The district court also declined the EEOC's invitation to discard the immutable/mutable distinction for Title VII race discrimination claims.

The EEOC advances a number of arguments on appeal in support of its position that denying a black person employment on the basis of her dreadlocks through the application of a race-neutral grooming policy constitutes intentional discrimination on the basis of race in violation of Title VII. The arguments, which build on each other, are that dreadlocks are a natural outgrowth of the immutable trait of black hair texture; that the dreadlocks hairstyle is directly associated with the immutable trait of race; that dreadlocks can be a symbolic expression of racial pride; and that targeting dreadlocks as a basis for employment can be a form of racial stereotyping.

IV.

The question in a disparate treatment case is "whether the protected trait actually motivated the employer's decision." Generally speaking, "[a] plaintiff can prove disparate treatment ... by direct evidence that a workplace policy, practice, or decision relies expressly on a protected characteristic, or ... by [circumstantial evidence] using the burden-shifting framework set forth in *McDonnell Douglas* [*Corp. v. Green*, 411 U.S. 792, 1973]."

Title VII does not define the term "race." And, in the more than 50 years since Title VII was enacted, the EEOC has not seen fit to issue a regulation defining the term. This appeal requires us to consider, at least in part, what "race" encompasses under Title VII because the EEOC maintains that "if ... individual expression

is tied to a protected trait, such as race, discrimination based on such expression is a violation of the law."

A.

There is little support for the position of the EEOC that the 1964 Congress meant for Title VII to protect "individual expression ... tied to a protected race." Indeed, from a legal standpoint, it appears that "race" was then mostly understood in terms of inherited physical characteristics.

It may be that today "race" is recognized as a "social construct," rather than an absolute biological truth. But our possible current reality does not tell us what the country's collective zeitgeist was when Congress enacted Title VII half a century ago.

B.

If we assume, however, that the quest for the ordinary understanding of "race" in the 1960s does not have a clear winner, then we must look for answers elsewhere. Some cases from the former Fifth Circuit provide us with binding guidance, giving some credence to Felix Frankfurter's adage that "[n]o judge writes on a wholly clean slate." As we explain below, those cases teach that Title VII protects against discrimination based on immutable characteristics. In *Willingham* v. *Macon Tel. Publ'g Co.*, 507 F.2d 1084 (5th Cir. 1975) we addressed a Title VII sex discrimination claim by a male job applicant who was denied a position because his hair was too long. Although the employer interpreted its neutral dress/grooming policy to prohibit the wearing of long hair only by men, and although the plaintiff argued that he was the victim of sexual stereotyping (i.e., the view that only women should have long hair), we affirmed the grant of summary judgment in favor of the employer.

We held in *Willingham* that "[e]qual employment opportunity," which was the purpose of Title VII, "may be secured only when employers are barred from discriminating against employees on the basis of immutable characteristics, such as race and national origin. Similarly, an employer cannot have one hiring policy for men and another for women *if* the distinction is based on some fundamental right. But a hiring policy that distinguishes on some other ground, such as grooming or length of hair, is related more closely to the employer's choice of how to run his business than equality of employment opportunity." We "adopt[ed] the view ... that distinctions in employment practices between men and women on the basis of something other than immutable or protected characteristics do not inhibit employment *opportunity* in violation of [Title VII]." And we approved the district court's alternative ground for affirming the grant of summary judgment in favor of the employer – that because grooming and hair standards were also imposed on female employees, men and women were treated equally. In closing, we reiterated that "[p]rivate employers are prohibited from using different hiring policies for men and women only when the distinctions used relate to immutable characteristics or legally protected rights." *Willingham* involved hair length in the context of a sex discrimination claim, but in *Garcia* v. *Gloor*, 618 F.2d 264, 5th Cir. (1980), we applied the immutable characteristic limitation to national origin, another of Title VII's protected categories. In *Garcia*, a bilingual Mexican-American employee who worked as a salesperson was fired for speaking Spanish to a co-worker on the job in violation of his employer's English-only policy, and he alleged that his termination was based on his national origin in violation of Title VII. We affirmed the district court's judgment in favor of the employer following a bench trial. We noted that an expert witness called by the employee had "testified that the Spanish language is the most important aspect of ethnic identification for Mexican-Americans, and it is to them what skin color is to others," and that testimony formed part of the basis for the claim that the employer's policy was unlawful. Although the district court had found that there were other reasons for the employee's dismissal, we assumed that the use of Spanish was a significant factor in the employer's decision.

We explained that neither Title VII nor common understanding "equates national origin with the language that one chooses to speak," and noted that the English-only rule was not applied to the employee as a "covert basis for national origin discrimination." Though the employee argued that he was discriminated against on the basis of national origin "because national origin influences or determines his language preference," we were unpersuaded because the employee was bilingual and was allowed to speak Spanish during breaks. And even if the employer had no genuine business need for the English-only policy, we said that "[n]ational origin must not be confused with ethnic or sociocultural traits or an unrelated status, such as citizenship or alienage." Citing *Willingham*, we emphasized that Title VII "focuses its laser of prohibition" on discriminatory acts based on matters "that are either beyond the victim's power to alter, or that impose a burden on an employee on one of the prohibited bases."

The employee in *Garcia* also argued that the employer's English-only policy was "discriminatory in impact, even if that result was not intentional, because it was likely to be violated only by Hispanic-Americans and that, therefore, they ha[d] a higher risk of incurring penalties." We rejected this argument as well because "there is no disparate impact if the rule is one that the affected employee can readily observe and nonobservance is a matter of individual preference," and Title VII "does not support an interpretation that equates the language an employee prefers to use with his national origin."

What we take away from *Willingham* and *Garcia* is that, as a general matter, Title VII protects persons in covered categories with respect to their immutable characteristics, but not their cultural practices. And although these two decisions have been criticized by some, we are not free, as a later panel, to discard the immutable/mutable distinction they set out.

We recognize that the distinction between immutable and mutable characteristics of race can sometimes be a fine (and difficult) one, but it is a line that courts have drawn. So, for example, discrimination on the basis of black hair texture (an immutable characteristic) is prohibited by Title VII, while adverse action on the basis of black hairstyle (a mutable choice) is not. Critically, the EEOC's proposed amended complaint did not allege that dreadlocks themselves are an immutable characteristic of black persons, and in fact stated that black persons choose to wear dreadlocks because that hairstyle is historically, physiologically, and culturally associated with their race. That dreadlocks are a "natural outgrowth" of the texture of black hair does not make them an immutable characteristic of race. Under *Willingham* and *Garcia*, the EEOC failed to state a plausible claim that CMS intentionally discriminated against Ms. Jones on the basis of her race by asking her to cut her dreadlocks pursuant to its race-neutral grooming policy. The EEOC's allegations – individually or collectively – do not suggest that CMS used that policy as proxy for intentional racial discrimination.

D.

We would be remiss if we did not acknowledge that, in the last several decades, there have been some calls for courts to interpret Title VII more expansively by eliminating the biological conception of "race" and encompassing cultural characteristics associated with race. But even those calling for such an interpretive change have different visions (however subtle) about how "race" should be defined.

Yet the call for interpreting "race" as including culture has not been unanimous. This is in part because culture itself is (or can be) a very broad and ever-changing concept. Assuming that general definitional consensus could be achieved among those who advocate the inclusion of culture within the meaning of "race," and that courts were willing to adopt such a shared understanding of Title VII, that would only be the beginning of a difficult interpretive battle, and there would be other very thorny issues to confront, such as which cultural characteristics or traits to protect. There would also be the related question of whether cultural characteristics or traits associated with one racial group can be absorbed by or transferred to members of a different racial group. At oral argument, for example, the EEOC asserted that if a white person chose to wear dreadlocks as a sign of racial support for her black colleagues, and the employer applied its dreadlocks ban to that person, she too could assert a race-based disparate treatment claim.

The resolution of these issues, moreover, could itself be problematic. Even if courts prove sympathetic to the "race as culture" argument, and are somehow freed from current precedent, how are they to choose among the competing definitions of "race"? How are they (and employers, for that matter) to know what cultural practices are associated with a particular "race"? And if cultural characteristics and practices are included as part of "race," is there a principled way to figure out which ones can be excluded from Title VII's protection?

... [L]aw prohibits discrimination on the basis of race – something it can do without knowing what race is and indeed without accepting that race is something that is knowable. To prohibit discrimination on the basis of race, we need only know that there is a set of ideas about race that many people accept and decide to prohibit them from acting on the basis of these ideas.

Our point is not to take a stand on any side of this debate – we are, after all, bound by *Willingham* and *Garcia* – but rather to suggest that, given the role and complexity of race in our society, and the many different voices in the discussion, it may not be a bad idea to try to resolve through the democratic process what "race" means (or should mean) in Title VII.

V.

Ms. Jones told CMS that she would not cut her dreadlocks in order to secure a job, and we respect that intensely personal decision and all it entails. But, for the reasons we have set out, the EEOC's original and proposed amended complaint did not state a plausible claim that CMS intentionally discriminated against Ms. Jones because of her race. The district court therefore did not err in dismissing the original complaint and in concluding that the proposed amended complaint was futile. **Affirmed.**

This case was appealed to be heard en banc by the entire circuit, when the Appellate Court refused to rehear the case (876 F.3d 1273, 11th Cir. (2017)).

Circuit Judge
Beverly Martin, with whom Judges Robin Rosenbaum and Jill Pryor join, dissenting from the denial of rehearing en banc.

The panel held that the complaint failed to state a claim because Title VII prohibits only discrimination based on "immutable traits" and dreadlocks are not "an immutable characteristic of black persons." The panel said our decision in *Willingham* v. *Macon Tel. Publ'g Co.*, 507 F.2d 1084 (5th Cir. 1975), dictates this conclusion. I cannot agree. By resting its decision on *Willingham*'s mutable/immutable distinction, the panel ... a doctrine the Supreme Court invalidated more than twenty-five years ago in *Price Waterhouse* v. *Hopkins*, 490 U.S. 228 (1989). Even if *Willingham*'s immutable-trait requirement survived *Price Waterhouse*, the allegations the EEOC made ... are sufficient to satisfy that requirement and state a Title VII disparate treatment claim.

II. Discussion

A.

Willingham's immutable-trait requirement is no longer good law, and [the appellate court] was wrong to invoke it. The Supreme Court's 1989 decision in *Price Waterhouse* made clear that Title VII's prohibition against discrimination on the basis of a statutorily protected class is not limited to protecting only those characteristics of the class that may be deemed "immutable." Because *Price Waterhouse* undermined *Willingham*'s immutable-trait requirement "to the point of abrogation," the panel should not have relied on it to dismiss Ms. Jones's claim. *Price Waterhouse* addressed sex discrimination. Ann Hopkins alleged that her employer, the accounting firm Price Waterhouse, refused to allow her to become a partner in the firm because her gender presentation defied the firm's view of how a woman should look and act. One partner described her as "macho." Another advised

her to take "a course at charm school." But the "coup de grace," to use the Supreme Court's term, came from a partner who told Ms. Hopkins she needed to "walk more femininely, talk more femininely, dress more femininely, wear make-up, have her hair styled, and wear jewelry."

The Supreme Court held that these comments showed Price Waterhouse discriminated against Ms. Hopkins on the basis of her sex in violation of Title VII. None of the traits the employer identified as its reasons for not promoting Ms. Hopkins were immutable. Nonetheless, the Supreme Court held that discrimination on the basis of these traits, which Ms. Hopkins *could* but did not change, constituted sex discrimination. The Court explained that discrimination on the basis of these mutable characteristics – how a woman talks, dresses, or styles her hair – showed discrimination on the basis of sex. In asking Ms. Hopkins to make these aspects of her "deportment" more feminine, Price Waterhouse required her to conform to "the stereotype associated with" her sex ...

The lesson of *Price Waterhouse* is clear. An employment decision based on a stereotype associated with the employee's protected class may be disparate treatment under Title VII even when the stereotyped trait is not an "immutable" biological characteristic of the employee. As this Court has recognized, "Title VII bar[s] not just discrimination because of biological sex, but also gender stereotyping – failing to *act and appear* according to expectations defined by gender."

Thus, after *Price Waterhouse*, Title VII's protections clearly extend beyond *Willingham*'s requirement that a plaintiff show discrimination based on an immutable trait. In *Willingham*, the plaintiff, who was denied employment solely because he did not have the short haircut required of male employees, argued that "since short hair is stereotypically male, requiring it of all male applicants violates [Title VII]." Mr. Willingham raised the gender-stereotyping argument, so the court necessarily and expressly considered whether "sexual stereotypes violate [Title VII]." Our court concluded they do not. In rejecting the gender-stereotyping theory of liability, the *Willingham* court held that the "objective" of "eliminating sexual stereotypes ... may not be read into the Civil Rights Act of 1964 without further Congressional action." "Congress," the court reasoned, "did not intend for its proscription of sexual discrimination to have [such] significant and sweeping implications." But of course this is precisely what the Supreme Court in *Price Waterhouse* told us Congress intended. Commentators have long noted that this Court's decision in *Willingham* "predate[s] the Supreme Court's more expansive prohibitions of sexual stereotyping [in *Price Waterhouse*] and thus relied on reasoning that is no longer good law."

When a "direct conflict" like this arises between our prior precedent and a later decision of the Supreme Court, it is our obligation to leave our precedent behind and respect the Supreme Court's pronouncement. By applying *Willingham* to dismiss Ms. Jones's case, our Court has shirked its obligation.

B.

In *Garcia* v. *Gloor*, 618 F.2d 264, 5th Circuit (1980), the former Fifth Circuit applied the immutable-trait requirement to a claim of national-origin discrimination, upholding an employer's English-only policy. But the court said nothing about applying the requirement in the context of race discrimination. Rather, as far as race is concerned, *Garcia* made only the same point as *Willingham* – that the racial classifications themselves are immutable and therefore protected.

It isn't hard to see why an immutable-trait requirement has no place in the race-discrimination context. The doctrine presumes that there *are* immutable, or naturally-occurring physical differences between racial groups. This, even though both the academy and the courts have long rejected the notion that racial divisions are based on biological differences.

The supposed distinction between an "immutable" racial trait and a "mutable" one is illusory. Is the color of an employee's hair an immutable trait? What about the shape of an employee's nose? It seems to me that employers could use the panel's rule to argue that any case in which the employer hasn't overtly discriminated on the basis of skin color itself falls outside of Title VII's protections. And even that may be questionable, because with modern medicine skin color can be changed too.

The panel opinion itself shows us that the notion of an "immutable" racial characteristic is fiction. In an effort to give lower courts an example of "the distinction between immutable and mutable characteristics of race," the panel draws a bright line between dreadlocks and an Afro. The panel actually says that while dreadlocks, a "black hairstyle," is a "mutable choice" and therefore not protected, an Afro, "black hair texture," is an "immutable characteristic" and is therefore protected. This distinction is nonsense. If an immutable trait is something that is "beyond the [plaintiff]'s power to alter" then neither dreadlocks nor Afros are immutable traits of black people. Like any hair style, both can be altered.

The discriminatory animus that motivates an employer to ban dreadlocks offends the antidiscrimination principle embodied in Title VII just as much as the discriminatory animus motivating a ban on Afros. Both are distinctly African-American racial traits. So, when an employer refuses to hire or promote a black employee on the basis of one of those traits, there is a strong indication that the employee's race motivated the decision. In other words, when an aspect of a person's appearance marks her as a member of a protected class and her employer then cites that racial marker as the reason for taking action against her, the employee's race probably had something to do with it. Whether that racialized aspect of her appearance is "immutable" such as skin color or "mutable" such as hair is beside the point. Either way, the employer's action based on a racial identifier is an action based on the employee's race.

III. Conclusion

"[T]he very purpose of [T]itle VII is to promote hiring on the basis of job qualifications, rather than on the basis of race or color." *Griggs* v. *Duke*

Power Co., 401 U.S. 424, 434 (1971). Although instances of open and obvious racial discrimination in the workplace still exist, intentional discrimination may now take on more subtle forms. In many cases an employer's racial preference will be camouflaged by policies that appear facially neutral. That is what the EEOC alleged happened to Ms. Jones. A ban on "all" applicants with dreadlocks is about as race-neutral as a ban on "all" applicants with dark-colored skin.

The panel's conclusion that, as a matter of law, a blanket ban on dreadlocks does not violate Title VII's prohibition on disparate treatment is simply wrong. And so is the immutable-trait requirement the panel used to get there. If Title VII prohibits an employer from rescinding a job offer because it perceives a female applicant's appearance to be insufficiently feminine (or overly masculine), it must also prohibit an employer from rescinding an offer because it perceives a black applicant's appearance to be insufficiently white (or overly black) ...

There was a time in our nation's history when a person's legal status was dictated by whether she was white or black. Courts frequently adjudicated the physical features that "[n]ature has stampt upon the African and his descendants." Today we count those decisions among the most shameful in the history of our courts. And, of course, Congress's purpose in passing Title VII was to eliminate one of the many stubborn vestiges of that era. Our task, in applying that statute today, is to be true to that most important goal. The panel opinion is not. Rather, in holding that certain physical features are immutable traits of the different racial groups, this Court legitimizes the very categories that Title VII was intended to dismantle.

–

I respectfully dissent.

1. Do you find the majority decision or the dissenting opinion by Judge Martin to be more compelling? Why? What are the implications of that position for racial discrimination law or judicial authority? What about for the other position?
2. Are certain hairstyles a proxy for race? Can you think of other examples of where culture might be a proxy for race?
3. Why might this be such a difficult question for the law and courts to address? Any solutions come to mind?

This case was appealed to the Supreme Court, which declined to hear the case. This refusal is not meaningful. Although between 7,000 and 8,000 cases are appealed to the Supreme Court annually, the Court hears oral argument for under a hundred cases. However, the decision in *Catastrophe Management* remains good precedent in the 11th Circuit and similar cases have continuously been brought to the EEOC for evaluation (Johnson 2020). While the Supreme Court was unwilling to address the question of banning specific cultural traditions of hair as a manifestation of racial discrimination, this topic gained a lot of public visibility. Over the next several years, stories of children of color – particularly of African descent – being expelled or suspended, having their hair forcibly cut, or being prohibited from participating in sporting events proliferated on social media. Social pressure grew to challenge this form of discrimination by passing state laws. In 2019, states began deliberating around a proposed CROWN Act (Creating a Respectful and Open Workplace for Natural Hair), which is a model law prohibiting race-based hair discrimination in the workplace and educational settings. Interestingly, this model legislation was advanced by several public interest groups as well as corporations. Initially adopted by the state of California, versions have been ratified by many local communities and by approximately half of the states (by 2024), and versions of the CROWN Act have been introduced in all but five of the remaining state legislatures. There have been repeated efforts in the U.S. House of Representatives to pass a federal version of the Crown Act but these have thus far been unsuccessful.

CREATING A RESPECTFUL AND OPEN WORKPLACE FOR NATURAL HAIR (CROWN) ACT, 2019

An act to amend Section 212.1 of the Education Code, and to amend Section 12926 of the Government Code, relating to discrimination. California State Law [The CROWN Act amends the definition of race in California's Fair Employment and Housing Act and Education Code to include traits historically connected with race, such as hair texture and hairstyles designed to protect that texture.]

THE PEOPLE OF THE STATE OF CALIFORNIA DO ENACT AS FOLLOWS:
SECTION. 1
The Legislature finds and declares all of the following:

(a) The history of our nation is riddled with laws and societal norms that equated "blackness," and the associated physical traits, for example, dark skin, kinky and curly hair to a badge of inferiority, sometimes subject to separate and unequal treatment.

(b) This idea also permeated societal understanding of professionalism. Professionalism was, and still is, closely linked to European features and mannerisms, which entails that those who do not naturally fall into Eurocentric norms must alter their appearances, sometimes drastically and permanently, in order to be deemed professional.

(c) Despite the great strides American society and laws have made to reverse the racist ideology that Black traits are inferior, hair remains a rampant source of racial discrimination with serious economic and health consequences, especially for Black individuals.

(d) Workplace dress code and grooming policies that prohibit natural hair, including afros, braids, twists, and locks, have a disparate impact on Black individuals as these policies are more likely to deter Black applicants and burden or punish Black employees than any other group.

(e) Federal courts accept that Title VII of the Civil Rights Act of 1964 prohibits discrimination based on race, and therefore protects against discrimination against afros. However, the courts do not understand that afros are not the only natural presentation of Black hair. Black hair can also be naturally presented in braids, twists, and locks.

(f) In a society in which hair has historically been one of many determining factors of a person's race, and whether they were a second class citizen, hair today remains a proxy for race. Therefore, hair discrimination targeting hairstyles associated with race is racial discrimination.

(g) Acting in accordance with the constitutional values of fairness, equity, and opportunity for all, the Legislature recognizes that continuing to enforce a Eurocentric image of professionalism through purportedly race-neutral grooming policies that disparately impact Black individuals and exclude them from some workplaces is in direct opposition to equity and opportunity for all.

SECTION. 2

Section 212.1 of the Education Code is amended to read:

(a) "Race or ethnicity" includes ancestry, color, ethnic group identification, and ethnic background.
(b) "Race" is inclusive of traits historically associated with race, including, but not limited to, hair texture and protective hairstyles.
(c) "Protective hairstyles" includes, but is not limited to, such hairstyles as braids, locks, and twists.

SECTION. 3

Section 12926 of the Government Code is amended to read:

As used in this part in connection with unlawful practices, unless a different meaning clearly appears from the context ...

(w) "Race" is inclusive of traits historically associated with race, including, but not limited to, hair texture and protective hairstyles.
(x) "Protective hairstyles" includes, but is not limited to, such hairstyles as braids, locks, and twists.

As many states have adopted this legislation, debates have exploded over how such policies can be implemented in school districts and by employers. Local restrictions over the length of hair, the scope of "protective legislation," and other questions of implementation continue to be contested in public discourse, as evidenced by the experience of Darryl George, whose story introduced this chapter. While the courts were unwilling to extend legal or statutory protections to hairstyles under the category of "race," activists were successful in directly changing policy through legislative lobbying.

1. Are there hairstyles that act as a proxy for race? Why or why not? Can you think of other examples where culture might represent racial identity?
2. What is the difference between an act of discrimination being addressed by the judiciary or by legislatures? Is one a greater protection? Why or why not?
3. If most states and many larger cities pass this legislation, would a federal law be necessary?
4. Has the passage of these laws addressed this question completely? Why or why not?
5. How do you understand the relationship between race and culture as demonstrated by this new area of activism?

5.2 Protection of Language of Culture

Racial proxies – like some hair styles – which are elements of people's identities related to specific racial cultures, are complicated. Such proxies are not applicable to *all* individuals who identify with a race or ethnicity, but they can be significant to many in a given racial community. Language may be a clarifying example. The classification of "Latino" or "Latina" is seen as an "ethnicity," not a race; people who share this identity can emerge from diverse cultures, faith traditions, even racial backgrounds. It is possible to be Afro-Latino, Anglo-Latina, or indigenous-Hispanic, for example. Yet, as the previous chapters on citizenship and segregation have demonstrated, this ethnicity was legally constructed as "racial." So, what do members of the Latino and Latina communities have in common or are perceived to hold in common? As you can see, when we discuss race and discrimination, the perception of others regarding racial identity may be as significant as that within the racial group. This leads us to the question of language.

Many people who identify as Latino – or who are so perceived – speak Spanish, but certainly not all. Are English-only laws a form of racial discrimination or only in certain circumstances? How do we make that determination? The EEOC is highly invested in trying to parse out the appropriateness of English-only rules and identify when they serve discriminatory purposes. Without the binding authority to decide these conflicts between employees and employers, instead the EEOC offers guidance as to how courts may interpret federal law. The EEOC has determined that since primary language is an immutable characteristic, it should be protected under Title VII of the Civil Rights Act, 1964, which prevents employment discrimination on the basis of race or ethnicity.

EEOC ENFORCEMENT GUIDANCE ON NATIONAL ORIGIN DISCRIMINATION, NOVEMBER 2016

V. Language Issues

As the U.S. labor force has grown more ethnically diverse, the number of workers who are not native English speakers has increased. Between 2010 and 2014, an average of 20.9 percent of the population spoke a language other than English at home. This represents an increase from 17.9 percent in 2000 and 13.8 percent in 1990.

Employers may have legitimate business reasons for basing employment decisions on linguistic characteristics. However, because linguistic characteristics are closely associated with national origin, it is important to carefully scrutinize employment decisions that are based on language to ensure that they do not violate Title VII. The subsections below provide guidance on how Title VII applies to employment decisions that are based on accent, English fluency, and restrictive workplace language policies.

A. Accent Discrimination

An accent can reflect whether a person lived in a different country or grew up speaking a language other than English. National origin and accent are therefore intertwined, and employment decisions or harassment based on accent may violate Title VII. Due to the link between accent and national origin, courts take a "very searching look" at an employer's reasons for using accent as a basis for an adverse employment decision. Courts require employers to provide evidence – as opposed to unsupported assertions – to explain such actions.

Under Title VII, an employment decision may legitimately be based on an individual's accent if the accent "interferes materially with job performance." To meet this standard, an employer must provide evidence showing that: (1) effective spoken communication in English is required to perform job duties; *and* (2) the individual's accent materially interferes with his or her ability to communicate in spoken English.

Where the evidence shows that an individual has a good command of spoken English or satisfactorily performs his job when speaking accented English, courts have ruled against employers under Title VII.

Example 22. National Origin Discrimination Involving Accent

Chinasa, an experienced retail professional who works for National Retailer, speaks English with a Nigerian accent. National Retailer selects Chinasa for a Regional Loss Prevention Manager position. An executive who will oversee Chinasa's work approaches her immediately after the promotion and comments, "I bet this is a great achievement considering where you came from. As an African, you must be the first to achieve this much success in your family given your accent." The executive tells Chinasa to "try to speak more like an American" and also to be careful about her demeanor because, in his opinion, "Africans are known to be brash and aggressive." The executive repeats these comments on several occasions during Chinasa's first several months on the job. There is no evidence, however, that staff members misinterpret or do not understand Chinasa's spoken English. In fact, the evidence shows that staff members respond promptly to Chinasa's directions without seeking clarification and provide information that is responsive to her requests. Nonetheless, after nine months, the executive terminates Chinasa's employment, telling her that she is a "poor fit" for the Regional Loss Prevention Manager position. When Chinasa requests further explanation, he cites discomfort with her "thick African accent," asserts that some staff members do not understand her, and laments that she did not speak "more like

an American." Based on these facts, the EEOC finds reasonable cause to believe that National Retailer discriminated against Chinasa because of her national origin.

In assessing whether an individual's accent materially interferes with the ability to perform job duties, the key is to distinguish a merely discernible accent from one that actually interferes with the spoken communication skills necessary for the job. Evidence of an accent materially interfering with job duties may include documented workplace mistakes attributable to difficulty understanding the individual; assessments from several credible sources who are familiar with the individual and the job; or specific substandard job performance that is linked to failures in spoken communication.

Example 23. No National Origin Discrimination Involving Accent: Accent Materially Interferes with Job Performance

Discount Airline needs to hire a customer service agent at a major metropolitan airport to provide in-person assistance for passengers who have missed their connections or whose flights have been cancelled or delayed. This position requires short but effective spoken communication in a noisy environment with a disgruntled public. Romel, who speaks English with a pronounced Filipino accent, applies for the position and is invited for an interview. The interviewing process includes a job simulation during which the applicant responds to customers in an atmosphere that mimics that of a busy airport. Two experienced interviewers who understand the demands of this job are impressed by Romel's calm demeanor and commitment to problem-solving, but they have difficulty understanding Romel's spoken English during the interview process. The interviewers conclude that Romel's pronounced Filipino accent will materially interfere with effective spoken communication in this environment. As a result, Romel is not hired. Romel challenges his rejection as national origin discrimination involving his accent. The EEOC does not find reasonable cause to believe that Romel was subjected to national origin discrimination because effective oral communication is required for this position, and Romel's accent materially interferes with his ability to communicate effectively in the circumstances of this job.

Example 24. National Origin Discrimination Involving Accent: Accent Does Not Materially Interfere with Job Performance

Mariam, who speaks with a discernible Lebanese accent, is an experienced English-language teacher who earned an American graduate degree in education after moving to the United States with her American husband. Mariam's graduate school professors commended her demonstrated ability to engage high school students. High School hired Mariam as a permanent substitute teacher for humanities courses. Teachers at High School specifically requested her as a substitute teacher because it is clear to them that the students learn the assigned material when she teaches.

Mariam subsequently applies and is rejected for three permanent teaching jobs at High School. The School District's hiring official explains that effective communication in English is required for classroom teachers, and Mariam is not qualified because she speaks with a Lebanese accent. Although effective communication in English is required to teach at High School, Mariam's accent does not materially interfere with her ability to do so, as demonstrated by the statements of other High School teachers and her graduate school professors. Mariam states a claim for national origin discrimination involving her accent.

If an employer takes an employment action in response to the discriminatory preferences of others, the employer itself is discriminating. Employers may not rely on coworker, customer, or client discomfort or preference to justify a discriminatory employment action based on accent.

C. English-Only Rules and Other Restrictive Language Policies

Restrictive language policies or practices requiring the use of the English language at work are commonly known as English-only rules. These policies or practices may also involve languages other than English, for example, Spanish-only policies. Restrictive language policies implicate national origin because an individual's primary language is closely tied to his or her cultural and ethnic identity.

1. Policies Adopted for Discriminatory Reasons

As with other workplace policies, a restrictive language policy violates Title VII if it is adopted for discriminatory reasons, such as bias against employees of a particular national origin. Thus, it would be unlawful disparate treatment to implement an English-only rule in order to avoid hearing foreign languages in the workplace, to generate a reason to discipline or terminate people who are not native English speakers, or to create a hostile work environment for certain non-English speaking workers.

Evidence of disparate treatment includes failure to consider whether there are substantial business reasons for the policy. The weaker the business reasons, the more difficult it may be to justify the policy under Title VII.

Example 28. Evidence Establishes that Policy was Adopted for Discriminatory Reasons

John, a Latino man who is bilingual in Spanish and English, works in a warehouse for Factory, Inc. John works on an assembly line and has job duties that do not require him to speak English. Factory decides to adopt a rule that requires all workplace communications to be conducted in English after a complaint is received objecting to John speaking Spanish during a break. In practice, the English-only rule is applied at all times on company property, even though its text says that it should not be applied during breaks and personal time.

John files a Title VII charge challenging the rule. Based on the evidence, the EEOC finds reasonable cause to believe that John was subjected to unlawful disparate treatment. In particular, the evidence reveals that Factory, Inc., had no work-related reasons for the rule, and a manager expressed concern prior to the rule's adoption that other warehouse employees were likely to taunt Latinos if they knew about the rule. Finally, Factory, Inc.'s chief executive referred to the Spanish language as "garbage' in a public interview. The evidence establishes reasonable cause to believe that the English-only rule was adopted because of anti-Latino bias.

2. Policies Applied in a Discriminatory Manner

Regardless of whether a restrictive language policy was adopted for nondiscriminatory reasons, the policy may not be applied differently to employees because of their national origin. For example, if six languages other than English are spoken in a workplace, it would be facially discriminatory to prohibit employees from speaking one of those languages but not the others, e.g., a "no Russian rule," no matter the reason. Title VII also prohibits an employer from enforcing a policy in a discriminatory manner, for example, imposing more severe discipline on Vietnamese employees who violate the policy than on Latino employees with comparable violations. Finally, penalizing employees for minor, inadvertent infractions that do not undermine workplace safety or efficiency may be evidence of intentional discrimination.

3. EEOC Guidelines on English-only Policies

The EEOC's long-standing English-only guidelines, issued in 1980, provide that rules requiring employees to speak English in the workplace at all times will be presumed to violate Title VII.

a. Adverse Effect on National Origin Groups

When an employer imposes an English-only rule, either in limited circumstances or at all times, employees with limited or no English skills and bilingual employees whose primary language is not English may be adversely affected because they are prohibited from communicating at work-including for work-related purposes – in their most effective language. An English-only rule may also adversely impact these employees by subjecting them to discipline and termination

for speaking their most effective language while imposing no comparable risk for native English-speaking employees. Finally, an English-only rule "is likely in itself to 'create an atmosphere of inferiority, isolation, and intimidation' that constitutes a 'discriminatory working environment.'"

b. Policies that Apply at All Times

A restrictive language policy is applied "at all times" when employees are prohibited from speaking their primary language any time they are on duty or in the workplace, including during lunch, breaks, and other personal time while on the employer's premises.

Because language-restrictive policies may be applied only to those specific employment situations for which they are needed to promote safe and efficient job performance or business operations, blanket rules requiring employees to speak English (or another language) at all times are presumptively unlawful.

c. Policies that Apply in Limited Circumstances

The lawfulness of a limited language-restrictive policy – one that does not apply at all times or to all jobs, workplace situations, or locations – depends on whether the evidence shows that the policy is job related and consistent with business necessity. An employer may satisfy this standard by providing detailed, fact-specific, and credible evidence demonstrating that the business purpose of requiring employees to speak a common language is sufficiently necessary to safe and efficient job performance or safe and efficient business operations to override its adverse impact, and that it is narrowly tailored to minimize any discriminatory impact based on national origin.

d. Job Related and Consistent with Business Necessity

Because of the adverse effects of a restrictive language policy on employees with limited or no English skills, and on bilingual employees whose primary language is not English, such a policy is unlawful unless the employer establishes that the policy is job related and consistent with business necessity. It is not sufficient that the policy merely promote business convenience.

To meet the burden of establishing business necessity, the employer must present detailed, fact-specific, and credible evidence showing that the language-restrictive policy is "necessary to safe and efficient job performance" or safe and efficient business operations. This burden cannot be met with conclusory statements or bare assertions about the business need for a language-restrictive policy. It is necessary to analyze the specific circumstances that are presented in each situation. The following general principles provide guidance when evaluating whether a language-restrictive policy is job related for the position in question and consistent with business necessity.

(1) Restrictive Language Policy Effectively Serves Business Needs

Part of establishing business necessity is demonstrating that the language-restrictive policy actually serves the identified business need. The effectiveness of a language-restrictive policy also may hinge on which language is identified as the common language of those performing the work. Sales representatives with monolingual clientele may generate the most sales by speaking the language in which the customer is proficient. Similarly, cooperative work assignments may be completed efficiently when employees use the language in which they are most proficient. If safety considerations constitute the demonstrated business need, employers may assess whether their employees with limited English skills are more likely to understand and relay safety instructions or warnings efficiently and effectively in English or in their shared language.

(2) Restrictive Language Policy is Narrowly Tailored

A language-restrictive policy is narrowly tailored when it applies only to those workers, work areas, circumstances, times, and job duties in which it is necessary to effectively promote safe and efficient business operations. This minimizes the adverse impact.

Example 29. Policy Narrowly Tailored to Promote Safe and Efficient Job Performance

Claudia, a Honduran-born U.S. immigrant who is fluent in Spanish and English, is employed by County hospital as a housekeeper, and she is assigned to clean operating rooms. She files a charge of discrimination alleging that she was subjected to unlawful national origin discrimination when the hospital adopted an English-only rule. The respondent produces evidence showing that the rule applies to all workers, including cleaning staff, but only for job-related discussions when they are working in the operating room. The evidence shows that most of the medical staff in the operating room only speak English.

Clear and precise communication between the medical staff and the cleaning staff is essential in the operating room because cleanliness is of paramount importance to patients' health and safety. The rule only applies to job-related discussions in the operating room and does not apply in any other circumstances. Based on this evidence, the EEOC does not find reasonable cause to believe that County Hospital's English-only rule violates Title VII.

Some employers contend they adopt language-restrictive policies in order to improve interpersonal relationships between employees. If coworkers or customers are concerned about exposure to languages they do not understand, or about gossip in these languages, one approach is to address these concerns on an individualized basis without resorting to language-restrictive policies. A language-restrictive policy that has a disparate impact on a particular group cannot be justified if an employer can effectively promote safe and efficient business operations through a policy that does not disproportionately harm protected national origin groups.

Example 30. English-Only Rule Not Justified

At a management meeting of Athletic Shoe Co., a supervisor proposes that the company adopt an English-only rule to decrease tensions among its ethnically diverse workforce. Two of the employees he supervises, Ann and Vinh, allegedly made derogatory comments in Vietnamese about their coworkers. Managers conclude that this can be addressed effectively under the company's discipline policy and that it would not justify a practice that adversely affects other workers based on their national origin. Therefore, Athletic Shoe decides that the circumstances do not justify adoption of an English-only rule. To reduce the likelihood of future incidents, supervisors are instructed to investigate the allegations and, if necessary, to counsel line employees about appropriate workplace conduct.

4. Notice and Enforcement of Restrictive Language Policy

Employers must provide adequate notice of language-restrictive policies. "Adequate notice" means effectively communicating to employees under what circumstances they will be required to speak a specific or common language and what will happen if they violate the rule. Notice can be provided by any reasonable means under the circumstances, such as explaining the rule

at a meeting, providing personal notice, sending e-mail, or posting the rule. In some circumstances, it may be necessary to provide notice in multiple languages. A grace period before the effective date of the policy generally will be important. Because adequate notice is essential to ensure employee compliance with the policy, "[i]f an employer fails to effectively notify its employees of the rule and makes an adverse employment decision against an individual based on a violation of the rule, the Commission will consider the employer's application of the rule as evidence of discrimination on the basis of national origin."

Managers often benefit from guidance on how to enforce the policy. Employers are strongly discouraged from "draconian" enforcement of language-restrictive policies. By limiting disciplinary measures to willful violations and not penalizing workers for inadvertent violations linked to their protected status, employers will more likely be able to establish business necessity.

1. When does language become a proxy for racial or national origin discrimination, if ever? Why or why not? What about accents?
2. What seems to be the line distinguishing between legitimate and illegitimate banning of second languages in the workplace? Does this seem consistent with the treatment of race or different?
3. Do English-only requirements hide an expectation for whiteness or do these requirements have legitimate purposes? According to the EEOC, how could we know?

5.3 Law and Cultural Discrimination

As demonstrated by discrimination against culturally related hair styles and English-only policies, there are differing perspectives as to how the law should address the relationship between race and culture. Some scholars point to these forms of cultural discrimination and perceive clear expressions of illicit racial discrimination, despite the lack of legal acknowledgement. For instance, Kevin Woodson, in his 2016 law review article "Derivative Racial Discrimination," explored the experiences of African American lawyers in elite predominately White law firms. He found evidence of what he called *cultural homophily* or "the tendency of people to gravitate towards others who possess similar cultural capital" (Woodson 2016, 317). The result in these firms was a "universal intersectional dynamic [that] disadvantages underrepresented minority employees independently of racial bias because of patterns of cultural and social differences between workers of different racial groups" (Woodson 2016, 317).

For Woodson and others, purely focusing on the eradication of illegal racial discrimination in the workplace would not address significant aspects of racial inequities. Woodson calls such cultural points of conflict with the racial majority, like cultural homophily, forms of derivative racial discrimination. As such cultural differences do not explicitly reference racial discrimination, they are not protected as racial differences. Instead, Woodson argues such cultural biases could serve as intentional or inadvertent forms of racial discrimination, even if they are not legally condemned as such. For Woodson and similar scholars, our interpretations of the law must change to protect typical cultural manifestations of race to provide a more equitable, yet diverse, society. In this perspective, the requirement of assimilation to the dominant culture – a price of success for many people of color – is too great a cost for racial equality. If to fit into the dominant culture, individuals from other communities (Woodson, in particular, notes the intersections of race and class in this dilemma) must give up their distinctiveness to reflect the majority or White elite preferences, is the cost of equality too great for communities of color?

Building on social science research, Woodson notes that people hire individuals in whose presence they are most comfortable – those who pass the airport or bar test. In other words, would I want to have a drink with this person or be stuck at an airport with them? While Woodson's research specifically addresses the differences between Black and White lawyers, his argument could apply to any racial minority group in the United States.

> Cultural homophily consistently produces racialized relationship patterns because of the vast cultural differences that emerged between black and white Americans over the course of centuries of racial stratification and separation. Decades after the civil rights revolution brought an end to de jure segregation, Americans remain largely separated by race, structurally and socially. By and large, black and white Americans grew up in different neighborhoods, attend different schools, and develop different social networks. These patterns across the socioeconomic spectrum, even the most affluent black and white Americans lead separate, racially defined social and institutional lives. (Woodson 2016, 349)

If biased treatment based on cultural distinctions have an impact as being a form of derivative racial discrimination, our current approach of addressing each specific form of cultural bias with racial implications through statutory protections (for instance, hair discrimination via state and local CROWN Acts or the EEOC's identification of English-only policies that violate federal statutory protections) may not address the collective implications of workplace environments.

While the pressure of assimilation is one concern, other scholars raise additional queries regarding the close linkage between race and culture. Richard T. Ford, in his 2005 book, *Racial Culture: A Critique*, argues that extending race to include cultural practice has the potential to undermine the stated goal of eliminating racism in the workplace (Deardorff 2005). Ford's opposition to racial discrimination reflects concerns around the development of a new legal category of discrimination based on culture. His primary concern is that the category of "race," which is socially and economically constructed, is granted greater legitimacy through the assumption that every member of a racial community manifests cultural similarities and therefore these cultural artifacts should be protected from discrimination in the same manner as racism:

> Even if one believes that the races are distinguished by cultural differences, one needn't advance an inevitably oversimplified account of such distinctive racial cultures; we can acknowledge the salience of race in order to resist racial status without a substantive cultural account of group difference. (Ford 2005, 92–93)

He provides two examples to illustrate the tension he perceives between racial discrimination laws and cultural protections. The first tells the story of Renee Rogers who worked for American Airlines in the late 1970s and preferred to wear her hair in braids. As an African American woman, she believed her braids reflected her heritage and that it "has been, historically, a fashion and style adopted by Black American women, reflective of cultural, historical essence of the Black woman in American society" (*Renee Rogers* v. *American Airlines*, 527 F. Supp, 1989, quoted in Ford 2005, 229). Rogers claimed that because the braids were an expression of her racial identity, termination based upon hairstyle was a violation of her legal rights to her culture. In the second case, Spun Steak employed thirty-three workers, of whom twenty-four were Spanish-speaking, of whom almost all were Hispanic. In September 1990, the company adopted a policy requiring that only English be spoken during work hours and allowing the employees to speak Spanish during breaks. The impacted employees filed a lawsuit alleging that the new policy violated Title VII by disparately impacting Hispanic workers without an articulated legitimate business justification (*Garcia* v. *Spun Steak*, 998 F.2d 1480, 1993).

Ford argues that while, what he labels as "right to difference," scholars have adopted such issues (hair style and language, among others) as representing the next phase of racial discrimination law, he perceives that these cases demonstrate the pitfalls of this approach. For Ford, right to difference advocates argue that behavioral characteristics – like language and hair style – are merely surrogates for race, and, if racial discrimination is illegal and actionable, bigots will simply shift the basis for their discrimination to new characteristics:

> And in order to capture more subtle cases of discrimination, the law must also prohibit or at least scrutinize discrimination on other bases that might be used as proxies for racial status. But then aren't racially correlated traits – racial cultures – all potentially proxies for racial status? Yes, and when we have reason to believe they are intentionally used as proxies, discrimination based on them should be illegal. But, because the essence of the employment relationship is that employees are expected to conform their behavior to the demands of their employers, it is reasonable to exclude discrimination based on volitional behavior as a general manner and limit the legal protection to characteristics that are not within the control of the potential employee. (Ford 2005, 101)

For Ford and similar scholars, this protection of culture will lead to greater racial discrimination, albeit mostly within the protected community. For example, if hair styles become a proxy for race, what happens to Black individuals who choose not to wear locs or twists or individuals of other ethnic groups who do? What about individuals who identify as Latina but are not Spanish speakers, is the judiciary to determine what defines Latino identity? Should the legal process determine what it means to be Black? White? Latina? Asian? Ford concedes it is likely that American Airlines' policy against braids was a racist policy. Consequently, he argues that there is adequate protection under statutory law, as currently interpreted, to challenge this illegal action in the workplace. Ford was writing long before the CROWN Act movement mobilized.

As *Spun Steak* demonstrates, "right to difference" litigation contains the danger of an increased hostility towards other racial groups. In this case, the employer's justification for the English-only policy was to prevent harassment of non-Spanish-speaking racial minorities employed by the company; in particular, one African American and one Asian American claimed that other employees were making racially derogatory comments about them in Spanish. The company passed the policy to ensure a non-hostile working environment for all their employees. According to Ford, the proper solution to these inevitable conflicts is simple:

> [A]nti-discrimination law should be refined so as to recognize only those differences attributable to the production of formal status hierarchy, for the purpose of eliminating or reducing the ill-effects of such hierarchies. Difference discourse, by metastasizing status into a thick social identity, distracts from and confuses the vital task of correcting status hierarchy. Legal decision makers need to be aware of status differences and castelike social practices in order to correct the injustices that they do. But we should resist the temptation to write a speculative sociology of group difference into law or to enlist the state into a psychotherapeutic quest to validate "repressed" identities. (Ford 2005, 123)

Finally, Richard T. Ford is concerned that by privileging racial culture we foster an environment of conflict and competition, without a thoughtful analysis of which cultures are most worthy of protecting. He asserts that by co-opting cultural discrimination, the law continues to define and shape what it means to be a member of a racial group. If natural hair is an attribute of "blackness" and should be protected as such, Ford asks if the law is saying those of African descent with processed hair are less Black? For Ford, while race is highly relevant as a matter of shared experiences and political solidarity, substituting cultural practices as a proxy for race in the courts may do more societal harm than preventing racial discrimination.

These two positions on the relevance of the cultural manifestations of race to racial discrimination demonstrate the difficulties facing the judiciary in enforcing protections against racial discrimination in the twenty-first century. Woodson and Ford both believe that their approaches are more likely to challenge illegal racial discrimination in its current manifestations, but they disagree on the relationship of culture to the definition of race.

1. How would the Woodson and Ford positions respond to the *EEOC* v. *Catastrophe Management Co.* case? To the CROWN Acts? To the EEOC's position on English-only regulations?
2. Why might cultural proxies be such a difficult question for the law and courts to address?
3. Do you find the Ford or Woodson position more persuasive and why? Or do you perceive another position?
4. Where does this leave you with the question of race proxies in a discussion of culture? How should the law address these kinds of challenges? Or is this best handled by legislation around these specific cultural practices?

5.4 Adoption of Native Children by White Families

The tension between race and culture, and the legal struggle to navigate this conflict, is clear in policies addressing the adoption of Native children by White families. While inconsistent in its protection of tribal communities, the federal government has consistently recognized their sovereignty. The federal government has interpreted its own jurisdiction as a plenary power over Native peoples – an authority that is not limited by the states except in narrow ways explicitly carved out by the Constitution. Instead, over a long painful history multiple layers of law have emerged (Wilkins and Lomawaima 2002). Federal Indian law navigates the relationship of tribes to the states and the federal government and tribal law governs Native people on their own lands. It is beyond our scope to discuss the many conflicts and unresolved difficulties that arise from these overlapping areas of law (for instance, tribal authority over non-Native people who commit crimes on tribal lands), but we will look at one specific issue – that of adoption. This is a complex issue in part because of the difficulties of determining who is a Native person.

Deciphering Native identity is difficult because it is not just one of a racial designation, but it is also a political identity. Someone possessing a Native identity could base it on a racial basis – along with African, Hispanic, or White ancestry. But what percentage of Native ancestry is sufficient and who can make this determination? The colony of Virginia was one of the first governments that tried to determine "who had a high enough degree of Indian blood to be classified as an Indian – and whose rights could be restricted as a result" (Treuer 2019, 378). The 1705 blood quantum law was the first of such policies and they continue today. David Treuer reports that between 1997 and 2017, over fifty tribes nationwide have disenrolled at least 8,000 members for having an insufficient percentage of Native heritage. Because of intermarrying with other communities, some estimate that by 2080 less than 8 percent of indigenous Americans will have "one half or more Indian 'blood'" (Schmidt 2011, 6–7). The use of "blood quantum" as a means of determining identity is controversial. On the one hand, it uses the tool of oppression to define identity, but "[l]ike legal definitions based upon documentary evidence, blood quantum definitions provide a relatively nonsubjective standard amenable to bureaucratic needs" (Garroutte 2003, 53–54).

On the other hand, if race is not a biologically real distinction, are there better ways to define Indian identity? Native identity could be based on one's culture during childhood – is being raised on a reservation or in a tribal community necessary to identify as Native? Is a descendant of a family that assimilated into the White community less Native than a descendant whose family did not? Finally, this identity can be framed as a political identity where one is a registered member of a tribe that had been recognized by the U.S. government. But this requires ancestors who were both able to follow the guidelines to register with their tribe and not be from a tribe that the government at some historical point determined was no longer viable and was therefore not "counted" as indigenous.

5.4.1 Forced Assimilation of Native Peoples

All of this is made more complicated because a primary policy goal of the U.S. government was the total assimilation of Native peoples into White communities. After the 1890s and throughout the twentieth century until the 1970s, "it became federal policy to try and absorb Indians into the mainstream, whether they wanted to be absorbed or not" (Treuer 2019, 254). This process was done through national programs – including relocation or termination of tribes, allotment of tribal land to individual Indians, offering of U.S. citizenship with proof of assimilation, and violence – as well as through boarding and residential schools.

At the beginning of the century, the federal government pushed for the creation of boarding schools for Native children, designed to distance them from their families and culture and to prepare them for assimilation into the White community. Richard Henry Pratt, the founder of the Pennsylvania-located Carlisle Indian Industrial School in 1879 justified this policy:

> ... [A]ll the Indian there is in the race should be dead. Kill the Indian in him, and save the man ... The school at Carlisle is an attempt on the part of the government to do this. Carlisle has always planted treason to the tribe and loyalty to the nation at large. It has preached against colonizing Indians, and in favor of individualizing them. It has demanded for them the same multiplicity of chances which all others in the country enjoy. Carlisle fills young Indians with the spirit of loyalty to the stars and stripes, and then moves them out into our communities to show by their conduct and ability that the Indian is no different from the white or the colored, that he has the inalienable right to liberty and opportunity that the white and the negro have. Carlisle does not dictate to him what line of life he should fill, so it is an honest one. It says to him that, if he gets his living by the sweat of his brow, and demonstrates to the nation that he is a man, he does more good for his race than hundreds of his fellows who cling to their tribal communistic surroundings ... (Pratt 1892)

To make this forced assimilation work, children were deliberately separated from other members of their tribe, including siblings, stripped and shorn of anything that reflected home, were forced to only speak English, and beaten for violating any of these expectations. When families realized the impact of this education on their children and kept them home, the children were forcibly taken.

By the 1890s, the federal Office of Indian Affairs ran approximately twenty boarding schools and many "agency schools," additional institutions were developed by religious organizations. There were systemic programs that removed children from Native homes and placed them in White families without parental consent. The long-term consequences of these policies were devastating. By 1928, "government-sponsored campaigns of child removal from Indian reservation communities resulted in 40 percent of Indian children being forcibly separated from their families and taken to boarding schools" (Blackhawk 2023, 3). In New York, the non-Native rate of children in foster care was one out of every 226 children, but for Native children it was one out of 74.8, with 96.5 percent of Native children placed in non-Indian foster homes. These children were placed in adoptive placements 3.3 times that of non-Native children. Nationwide, in 1969, 85 percent of Indian fostered children were placed in non-Native homes (Turner 2016).

5.4.2 Federal Indian Child Welfare Act, 1978

The Indian Child Welfare Act, 1978 (ICWA), is federal legislation designed to help stabilize Native families by prioritizing the placement of children within the child's extended family or tribal community whenever relocation was necessary. The law was designed, according to the House of Representatives, to protect "the unique values of Indian culture" and is seen as a means of respecting tribal sovereignty (Francis et al. 2023). Tribal government still retained its jurisdiction over child welfare and the ICWA gave Native families and the tribal communities both a mandate and a statutory tool to challenge the forced removal of their children (Hahn, Caldwell, and Sinha 2020). While the ICWA remains intact, the interpretations of the policy are challenged through the courts.

The constitutionality of the ICWA was tested in the 2013 Supreme Court decision in *Adoptive Couple* v. *Baby Girl*, 570 U.S. 637. In this case, the birth mother who identified as Hispanic and the birth father, a member of the Cherokee Nation, had broken up before Baby Girl's birth. When texted by the birth mother if he would prefer to pay child support or relinquish his parental rights, birth father texted he would relinquish his rights believing his daughter would be raised by her mother. Baby Girl was put up for adoption and due to a misspelling of his name and an incorrect birth date, the birth father's membership in the Cherokee Nation was not verified. Four months after the birth of Baby Girl, the biological father was notified of the pending adoption, he signed the agreement and then discovered the adoption to which he had consented. The birth father immediately contacted a lawyer within 24 hours and requested a stay of the adoption. By the time of trial Baby Girl was two years old. Under the ICWA (§1912) the family court awarded custody to the biological father. The state Supreme Court affirmed. The Court was asked to evaluate the constitutionality of the ICWA as it was applied in this specific case.

ADOPTIVE COUPLE v. BABY GIRL, 570 U.S. 637 (2013)

Justice Alito Delivered the Opinion of the Court, Joined by Chief Justice Roberts, Justices Kennedy, Thomas, and Breyer.

Vote: 5–4

I.

"The Indian Child Welfare Act of 1978 (ICWA) was the product of rising concern in the mid-1970s over the consequences to Indian children, Indian families, and Indian tribes of abusive child welfare practices that resulted in the separation of large numbers of Indian children from their families and tribes through adoption or foster care placement, usually in non-Indian homes." *Mississippi Band of Choctaw Indians* v. *Holyfield*, 490 U.S. 30, 32 (1989)

Congress found that "an alarmingly high percentage of Indian families [were being] broken up by the removal, often unwarranted, of their children from them by nontribal public and private agencies." This "wholesale removal of Indian children from their homes" prompted Congress to enact the ICWA, which establishes federal standards that govern state-court child custody proceedings involving Indian children.

Three provisions of the ICWA are especially relevant to this case. *First*, "[a]ny party seeking" an involuntary termination of parental rights to an Indian child under state law must demonstrate that "active efforts have been made to provide remedial services and rehabilitative programs designed to prevent the breakup of the Indian family and that these efforts have proved unsuccessful." *Second*, a state court may not involuntarily terminate parental rights to an Indian child "in the absence of a determination, supported by evidence beyond a reasonable

doubt, including testimony of qualified expert witnesses, that the continued custody of the child by the parent or Indian custodian is likely to result in serious emotional or physical damage to the child." *Third*, with respect to adoptive placements for an Indian child under state law, "a preference shall be given, in the absence of good cause to the contrary, to a placement with (1) a member of the child's extended family; (2) other members of the Indian child's tribe; or (3) other Indian families."

III.

It is undisputed that, had Baby Girl not been 3/256 Cherokee, Biological Father would have had no right to object to her adoption under South Carolina law. The South Carolina Supreme Court held, however, that Biological Father is a "parent" under the ICWA and that two statutory provisions – namely, §1912(f) and §1912(d) – bar the termination of his parental rights ... [W]e hold that neither §1912(f) nor §1912(d) bars the termination of his parental rights.

A.

Section 1912(f) addresses the involuntary termination of parental rights with respect to an Indian child. Specifically, §1912(f) provides that "[n]o termination of parental rights may be ordered in such proceeding in the absence of a determination, supported by evidence beyond a reasonable doubt ... that the *continued custody* of the child by the parent or Indian custodian is likely to result in serious emotional or physical damage to the child." The South Carolina Supreme Court held that Adoptive Couple failed to satisfy §1912(f) because they did not make a heightened showing that Biological Father's "*prospective* legal and physical custody" would likely result in serious damage to the child. That holding was error.

Section 1912(f) conditions the involuntary termination of parental rights on a showing regarding the merits of "*continued* custody of the child by the parent." The adjective "continued" plainly refers to a pre-existing state. As Justice Sotomayor concedes, "continued" means "[c]arried on or kept up without cessation" or "[e]xtended in space without interruption or breach of conne[ct]ion." The phrase "continued custody" therefore refers to custody that a parent already has (or at least had at some point in the past). As a result, §1912(f) does not apply in cases where the Indian parent *never* had custody of the Indian child.

Biological Father's contrary reading of §1912(f) is nonsensical. Pointing to the provision's requirement that "[n]o termination of parental rights may be ordered ... in the absence of a determination" relating to "the continued custody of the child by the parent," Biological Father contends that if a determination relating to "continued custody" is inapposite in cases where there is no "custody," the statutory text *prohibits* termination. But it would be absurd to think that Congress enacted a provision that *permits* termination of a custodial parent's rights, while simultaneously *prohibiting* termination of a noncustodial parent's rights. If the statute draws any distinction between custodial and noncustodial parents, that distinction surely does not provide greater protection for noncustodial parents.

Our reading of §1912(f) comports with the statutory text demonstrating that the primary mischief the ICWA was designed to counteract was the unwarranted *removal* of Indian children from Indian families due to the cultural insensitivity and biases of social workers and state courts. The statutory text expressly highlights the primary problem that the statute was intended to solve: "an alarmingly high percentage of Indian families [were being] broken up by the *removal*, often unwarranted, of their children from them by nontribal public and private agencies." And if the legislative history of the ICWA is thought to be relevant, it further underscores that the Act was primarily intended to stem the unwarranted removal of Indian children from intact Indian families. In sum, when, as here, the adoption of an Indian child is voluntarily and lawfully initiated by a non-Indian parent with sole custodial rights, the ICWA's primary goal of preventing the unwarranted removal of Indian children and the dissolution of Indian families is not implicated.

The dissent fails to dispute that nonbinding guidelines issued by the Bureau of Indian Affairs (BIA) shortly after the ICWA's enactment demonstrate that the BIA envisioned that §1912(f)'s standard would apply only to termination of a *custodial* parent's rights. Specifically, the BIA stated that, under §1912(f), "[a] child may not be *removed* simply because there is someone else willing to raise the child who is likely to do a better job"; instead, "[i]t must be shown that ... it is dangerous for the child to *remain* with his or her *present* custodians." Indeed, the Guidelines recognized that §1912(f) applies only when there is pre-existing custody to evaluate.

Under our reading of §1912(f), Biological Father should not have been able to invoke §1912(f) in this case, because he had never had legal or physical custody of Baby Girl as of the time of the adoption proceedings. As an initial matter, it is undisputed that Biological Father never had *physical* custody of Baby Girl. And as a matter of both South Carolina and Oklahoma law, Biological Father never had *legal* custody either.

In sum, the South Carolina Supreme Court erred in finding that §1912(f) barred termination of Biological Father's parental rights.

IV.

The Indian Child Welfare Act was enacted to help preserve the cultural identity and heritage of Indian tribes, but under the State Supreme Court's reading, the Act would put certain vulnerable children at a great disadvantage solely because an ancestor – even a remote one – was an Indian. As the State Supreme Court read §§1912(d) and (f), a biological Indian father could abandon his child *in utero* and refuse any support for the birth mother – perhaps contributing to the mother's decision to put the child up for adoption – and then could play his ICWA trump card at the eleventh hour to override the mother's decision and the child's best interests. If this were possible, many prospective adoptive parents would surely pause before adopting any child who might possibly qualify as an Indian under the ICWA. Such an interpretation would raise equal protection concerns, but the plain text of §§1912(f) and (d) makes clear that neither provision applies in the present context. Nor do §1915(a)'s rebuttable adoption preferences apply when no alternative party has formally sought to adopt the child. We therefore reverse the judgment of the South Carolina Supreme Court and remand the case for further proceedings not inconsistent with this opinion. It is so ordered.

Justice Thomas, Concurring

I join the Court's opinion in full but write separately to explain why constitutional avoidance compels this outcome. Each party in this case has put forward a plausible interpretation of the relevant sections of the Indian Child Welfare Act (ICWA). However, the interpretations offered by respondent Birth Father and the United States raise significant constitutional problems as applied to this case. Because the Court's decision avoids those problems, I concur in its interpretation.

II.

The ICWA asserts that the Indian Commerce Clause, Art. I, §8, cl. 3, and "other constitutional authority" provides Congress with "plenary power over Indian affairs." The reference to "other constitutional authority" is not illuminating, and I am aware of no other enumerated power that could even arguably support Congress' intrusion into this area of traditional state authority. The assertion of plenary authority must, therefore, stand or fall on Congress' power under the Indian Commerce Clause. Although this Court has said that the "central function of the Indian Commerce Clause is to provide Congress with plenary power to legislate in the field of Indian affairs," *Cotton Petroleum*

Corp. v. *New Mexico*, 490 U.S. 163 (1989), neither the text nor the original understanding of the Clause supports Congress' claim to such "plenary" power.

III.

In light of the original understanding of the Indian Commerce Clause, the constitutional problems that would be created by application of the ICWA here are evident. First, the statute deals with "child custody proceedings," not "commerce." It was enacted in response to concerns that "an alarmingly high percentage of Indian families [were] broken up by the removal, often unwarranted, of their children from them by nontribal public and private agencies." The perceived problem was that many Indian children were "placed in non-Indian foster and adoptive homes and institutions." This problem, however, had nothing to do with commerce.

Second, the portions of the ICWA at issue here do not regulate Indian tribes as tribes. Sections 1912(d) and (f), and §1915(a) apply to all child custody proceedings involving an Indian child, regardless of whether an Indian tribe is involved. This case thus does not directly implicate Congress' power to "legislate in respect to Indian *tribes.*" *United States* v. *Lara*, 541 U.S. 193 (2004). Baby Girl was never domiciled on an Indian Reservation, and the Cherokee Nation had no jurisdiction over her. Although Birth Father is a registered member of The Cherokee Nation, he did not live on a reservation either. He was, thus, subject to the laws of the State in which he resided (Oklahoma) and of the State where his daughter resided during the custody proceedings (South Carolina). Nothing in the Indian Commerce Clause permits Congress to enact special laws applicable to Birth Father merely because of his status as an Indian.

Because adoption proceedings like this one involve neither "commerce" nor "Indian tribes," there is simply no constitutional basis for Congress' assertion of authority over such proceedings. Also, the notion that Congress can direct state courts to apply different rules of evidence and procedure merely because a person of Indian descent is involved raises absurd possibilities. Such plenary power would allow Congress to dictate specific rules of criminal procedure for state-court prosecutions against Indian defendants. Likewise, it would allow Congress to substitute federal law for state law when contract disputes involve Indians. But the Constitution does not grant Congress power to override state law whenever that law happens to be applied to Indians. Accordingly, application of the ICWA to these child custody proceedings would be unconstitutional.

Because the Court's plausible interpretation of the relevant sections of the ICWA avoids these constitutional problems, I concur.

Justice Sotomayor, with whom Justice Ginsburg and Justice Kagan join, and with whom Justice Scalia joins in part, Dissenting

A casual reader of the Court's opinion could be forgiven for thinking this an easy case, one in which the text of the applicable statute clearly points the way to the only sensible result. In truth, however, the path from the text of the Indian Child Welfare Act of 1978 (ICWA) to the result the Court reaches is anything but clear, and its result anything but right.

The reader's first clue that the majority's supposedly straightforward reasoning is flawed is that not all Members who adopt its interpretation believe it is compelled by the text of the statute; nor are they all willing to accept the consequences it will necessarily have beyond the specific factual scenario confronted here. The second clue is that the majority begins its analysis by plucking out of context a single phrase from the last clause of the last subsection of the relevant provision, and then builds its entire argument upon it. That is not how we ordinarily read statutes. The third clue is that the majority openly professes its aversion to Congress' explicitly stated purpose in enacting the statute. The majority expresses concern that reading the Act to mean what it says will make it more difficult to place Indian children in adoptive homes, but the Congress

that enacted the statute announced its intent to stop "an alarmingly high percentage of Indian families [from being] broken up" by, among other things, a trend of "plac[ing] [Indian children] in non-Indian … adoptive homes." Policy disagreement with Congress' judgment is not a valid reason for this Court to distort the provisions of the Act. Unlike the majority, I cannot adopt a reading of ICWA that is contrary to both its text and its stated purpose. I respectfully dissent.

II.

C.

The majority also protests that a contrary result to the one it reaches would interfere with the adoption of Indian children. This claim is the most perplexing of all. A central purpose of ICWA is to "promote the stability and security of Indian … families," in part by countering the trend of placing "an alarmingly high percentage of [Indian] children … in non-Indian foster and adoptive homes and institutions." The Act accomplishes this goal by, first, protecting the familial bonds of Indian parents and children; and, second, establishing placement preferences should an adoption take place. ICWA does not interfere with the adoption of Indian children except to the extent that it attempts to avert the necessity of adoptive placement and makes adoptions of Indian children by non-Indian families less likely.

… ICWA protects not only Indian parents' interests but also those of Indian tribes. A tribe's interest in its next generation of citizens is adversely affected by the placement of Indian children in homes with no connection to the tribe, whether or not those children were initially in the custody of an Indian parent.

Moreover, the majority's focus on "intact" families, begs the question of what Congress set out to accomplish with ICWA. In an ideal world, perhaps all parents would be perfect. They would live up to their parental responsibilities by providing the fullest possible financial and emotional support to their children. They would never suffer mental health problems, lose their jobs, struggle with substance dependency, or encounter any of the other multitudinous personal crises that can make it difficult to meet these responsibilities. In an ideal world parents would never become estranged and leave their children caught in the middle. But we do not live in such a world. Even happy families do not always fit the custodial-parent mold for which the majority would reserve IWCA's substantive protections; unhappy families all too often do not. They are families nonetheless. Congress understood as much. ICWA's definitions of "parent" and "termination of parental rights" provided in §1903 sweep broadly. They should be honored.

D.

... [O]ur precedents ... squarely hold that classifications based on Indian tribal membership are not impermissible racial classifications. See *United States* v. *Antelope*, 430 U.S. 641 (1977); *Morton* v. *Mancari*, 417 U.S. 535 (1974). The majority repeated analytically unnecessary references to the fact that Baby Girl is 3/256 Cherokee by ancestry do nothing to elucidate its intimation that the statute may violate the Equal Protection Clause as applied here. I see no ground for this court to second-guess the membership requirements of federally recognized Indian tribes, which are independent political entities. I am particularly averse to doing so when the federal government requires Indian tribes, as a prerequisite for official recognition, to make "descen[t] from a historical Indian tribe" a condition for membership.

The majority's treatment of this issue, in the end, does no more than create a lingering mood of disapprobation of the criteria for membership adopted by the Cherokee Nation that, in turn, make Baby Girl an "Indian child" under the statute ...

*   *   *

The majority opinion turns §1912 upside down, reading it from bottom to top in order to reach a conclusion that is manifestly contrary to Congress' express purpose in enacting ICWA: preserving the familial bonds between Indian parents and their children and, more broadly,

Indian tribes' relationships with the future citizens who are "vital to [their] continued existence and integrity."

The majority casts Birth Father as responsible for the painful circumstances in this case, suggesting that he intervened "at the eleventh hour to override the mother's decision and the child's best interests." I have no wish to minimize the trauma of removing a 27-month-old child from her adoptive family. It bears remembering, however, that Birth Father took action to assert his parental rights when Baby Girl was four months old, as soon as he learned of the impending adoption ...

The majority's hollow literalism distorts the statute and ignores Congress' purpose in order to rectify a perceived wrong that, while heartbreaking at the time, was a correct application of federal law and that in any case cannot be undone. Baby Girl has now resided with her father for 18 months. However difficult it must have been for her to leave Adoptive Couple's home when she was just over 2 years old, it will be equally devastating now if, at the age of 3½, she is again removed from her home and sent to live halfway across the country. Such a fate is not foreordained, of course. But it can be said with certainty that the anguish this case has caused will only be compounded by today's decision.

I believe that the South Carolina Supreme Court's judgment was correct, and I would affirm it. I respectfully dissent.

Justice Scalia, Dissenting

I join Justice Sotomayor's dissent except as to one detail. I reject the conclusion that the Court draws from the words "continued custody" in 25 U.S. C §1912(f) not because "literalness may strangle meaning," but because there is no reason that "continued" must refer to custody in the past rather than custody in the future. I read the provision as requiring the court to satisfy itself (beyond a reasonable doubt) not merely that initial or temporary custody is not "likely to result in serious emotional or physical damage to the child," but that continued custody is not likely to do so. For the reasons set forth in Justice Sotomayor's dissent, that connotation is much more in accord with the rest of the statute.

While I am at it, I will add one thought. The Court's opinion, it seems to me, needlessly demeans the rights of parenthood. It has been the constant practice of the common law to respect the entitlement of those who bring a child into the world to raise that child. We do not inquire whether leaving a child with his parents is "in the best interest of the child." It sometimes is not; he would be better off raised by someone else. But parents have their rights, no less than children do. This father wants to raise his daughter, and the statute amply protects his right to do so. There is no reason in law or policy to dilute that protection.

1. How do the differing opinions determine or describe the father's and child's Native identity? What is the impact of those choices?
2. What do you perceive to be the implications of Justice Alito's use of the phrase "trump card" in reference to members of registered Native communities in relying on the protections of the ICWA?
3. How do you perceive the historical purpose of the ICWA as impacting how you would resolve this case? Do you agree with the majority or the dissenting opinion? Why?
4. How do you understand Justice Thomas' concurring opinion? This concern will be central to the 2023 challenge to ICWA in *Haaland* v. *Brackeen*.

In this decision, the Supreme Court was concerned that the ICWA could harm Indian children by treating them differently from non-Native children and that federal law (which covered Native children) resulted in different outcomes than the state laws (which impacted non-Native children) (Zug 2021). This raised questions by many opponents that the ICWA was an illicit form of racial discrimination. By treating the racial group of Native Americans differently from non-Native peoples, the ICWA could be perceived as violating the Equal Protection Clause of the United States. On the other hand, many supporters of the protections provided by the ICWA, argued that the distinction between children was not based on racial differences but instead recognized the different political status of tribal members versus the political identity of non-tribal members. The painful circumstances surrounding the appeals to adoption cases motivated challenges to the ICWA.

The case of *Adoptive Couple* raised concern in indigenous communities that the Court was going to undermine the ICWA and that the decision was only the first step in an effort to dismantle tribal protections around custody (Irby 2023). A similar challenge to the ICWA, *Haaland* v. *Brackeen* reached the Supreme Court in 2023 and litigated three separate child custody hearings under the ICWA. All three cases address children of Native descent whose tribes had claimed them but were placed with White families who wished to adopt them. In the case of ALM and the Brackeen family, the Navajo family identified by the Navajo Nation as an alternative placement withdrew from consideration and the Brackeens adopted ALM, but now wish to adopt her biological sister. The Libretti family was selected by her mother to adopt Baby D, a member of the

Ysleta del Sur Pueblo tribe. The tribe eventually withdrew its opposition to the adoption, but the family wants to foster and conceivably adopt Indian children in the future. The Clifford family fostered Child P, whose mother told the Court her daughter was not eligible for tribal membership. The White Earth Band of the Ojibewe Tribe later enrolled the child as a member and the lower court denied the Clifford family's request. These petitions challenge the constitutionality of the ICWA as violating the Tenth Amendment, which reserves power to the states, that Congress lacks the authority to enact the ICWA, and that it delegates too much federal authority to tribes.

HAALAND v. *BRACKEEN*, 599 U.S. 255 (2023)

Justice Barrett Delivered the Opinion of the Court, Joined by Chief Justice Roberts, and Justices Sotomayor, Kagan, Gorsuch, Kavanaugh, and Jackson

Vote: 7–2

I.

A.

In 1978, Congress enacted the Indian Child Welfare Act (ICWA) out of concern that "an alarmingly high percentage of Indian families are broken up by the removal, often unwarranted, of their children from them by nontribal public and private agencies." Congress found that many of these children were being "placed in non-Indian foster and adoptive homes and institutions," and that the States had contributed to the problem by "fail[ing] to recognize the essential tribal relations of Indian people and the cultural and social standards prevailing in Indian communities and families." This harmed not only Indian parents and children, but also Indian tribes. As Congress put it, "there is no resource that is more vital to the continued existence and integrity of Indian tribes than their children." Testifying before Congress, the Tribal Chief of the Mississippi Band of Choctaw Indians was blunter: "Culturally, the chances of Indian survival are significantly reduced if our children, the only real means for the transmission of the tribal heritage, are to be raised in non-Indian homes and denied exposure to the ways of their People."

The Act thus aims to keep Indian children connected to Indian families. "Indian child" is defined broadly to include not only a child who is "a member of an Indian tribe," but also one who is "eligible for membership in an Indian tribe and is the biological child of a member of an Indian tribe." If the Indian child lives on a reservation, ICWA grants the tribal court exclusive jurisdiction over all child custody proceedings, including adoptions and foster care proceedings. For other Indian children, state and tribal courts exercise concurrent jurisdiction, although the state court is sometimes required to transfer the case to tribal court. When a state court adjudicates the proceeding, ICWA governs from start to finish. That is true regardless of whether the proceeding is "involuntary" (one to which the parents do not consent) or "voluntary" (one to which they do).

ICWA's placement preferences, which apply to all custody proceedings involving Indian children, are hierarchical: State courts may only place the child with someone in a lower-ranked group when there is no available placement in a higher-ranked group. For adoption, "a preference shall be given" to placements with "(1) a member of the child's extended family; (2) other members of the Indian child's tribe; or (3) other Indian families." For foster care, a preference is given to (1) "the Indian child's extended family"; (2) "a foster home licensed, approved, or specified by the Indian child's tribe"; (3) "an Indian foster home licensed or approved by an authorized non-Indian licensing authority"; and then (4) another institution "approved by an Indian tribe or operated by an Indian organization which has a program suitable to meet the Indian child's needs." ... Together, these definitions mean that Indians from any tribe (not just the tribe to which the child has a tie) outrank unrelated non-Indians for both adoption and foster care. And for foster care, institutions run or approved by any tribe outrank placements with unrelated non-Indian families. Courts must adhere to the placement preferences absent "good cause" to depart from them.

II.

A.

We begin with petitioners' claim that ICWA exceeds Congress's power under Article I ... The Indian Commerce Clause authorizes Congress "[t]o regulate Commerce ... with the Indian Tribes." We have interpreted the Indian Commerce Clause to reach not only trade, but certain "Indian affairs" too ...

The Treaty Clause [Art. II, §8, ¶2] – which provides that the President "shall have Power, by and with the Advice and Consent of the Senate, to make Treaties" – provides a second source of power over Indian affairs. Until the late 19th century, relations between the Federal Government and the Indian tribes were governed largely by treaties. Of course, the treaty power "does not literally authorize Congress to act legislatively," since it is housed in Article II rather than Article I. Nevertheless, we have asserted that "treaties made pursuant to that power can authorize Congress to deal with 'matters' with which otherwise 'Congress could not deal.'" And even though the United States formally ended the practice of entering into new treaties with the Indian tribes in 1871, this decision did not limit Congress's power "to legislate on problems of Indians" pursuant to pre-existing treaties.

We have also noted that principles inherent in the Constitution's structure empower Congress to act in the field of Indian affairs. At the founding, "Indian affairs were more an aspect of military and foreign policy than a subject of domestic or municipal law." With this in mind, we have posited that Congress's legislative authority might rest in part on "the Constitution's adoption of preconstitutional powers necessarily inherent in any Federal Government, namely, powers that this Court has described as 'necessary concomitants of nationality.'"

Finally, the "trust relationship between the United States and the Indian people" informs the exercise of legislative power. As we have explained, the Federal Government has "charged itself with moral obligations of the highest responsibility and trust" toward Indian tribes. The contours of this "special relationship" are undefined.

In sum, Congress's power to legislate with respect to Indians is well established and broad. Consistent with that breadth, we have not doubted Congress's ability to legislate across a wide range of areas, including criminal law, domestic violence, employment, property, tax, and trade. Indeed, we have only rarely concluded that a challenged statute exceeded Congress's power to regulate Indian affairs.

... Article I gives Congress a series of enumerated powers, not a series of blank checks. Thus, we reiterate that Congress's authority to legislate with respect to Indians is not unbounded. It is plenary within its sphere, but even a sizeable sphere has borders.

B.

Petitioners contend that ICWA exceeds Congress's power. Their principal theory, and the one accepted by both Justice Alito and the dissenters in the Fifth Circuit, is that ICWA treads on the States' authority over family law. Domestic relations have traditionally been governed by state law; thus, federal power over Indians stops where state power over the family begins. Or so the argument goes.

It is true that Congress lacks a general power over domestic relations and, as a result, responsibility for regulating marriage and child custody remains primarily with the States. But the Constitution does not erect a firewall around family law. On the contrary, when Congress validly legislates pursuant to its Article I powers, we "ha[ve] not hesitated" to find conflicting state family law preempted, "[n]otwithstanding the limited application of federal law in the field of domestic relations generally." In fact, we have specifically recognized Congress's power to displace the jurisdiction of state courts in adoption proceedings involving Indian children.

Petitioners are trying to turn a general observation (that Congress's Article I powers rarely touch state family law) into a constitutional carveout (that family law is wholly exempt from federal regulation). That argument is a nonstarter. As James Madison said to Members of the First Congress, when the Constitution conferred a power on Congress, "they might exercise it, although it should interfere with the laws, or even the Constitution of the States." Family law is no exception.

C.

Petitioners come at the problem from the opposite direction too: Even if there is no family law carveout to the Indian affairs power, they contend that Congress's authority does not stretch far enough to justify ICWA. Ticking through the various sources of power, petitioners assert that the Constitution does not authorize Congress to regulate custody proceedings for Indian children. Their arguments fail to grapple with our precedent, and because they bear the burden of establishing ICWA's unconstitutionality, we cannot sustain their challenge to the law.

Take the Indian Commerce Clause, which is petitioners' primary focus. According to petitioners, the Clause authorizes Congress to legislate only with respect to Indian tribes as government entities, not Indians as individuals. But we held more than a century ago that "commerce with the Indian tribes, means commerce with the individuals composing those tribes." So that argument is a dead end.

Petitioners also assert that ICWA takes the "commerce" out of the Indian Commerce Clause.

Their consistent refrain is that "children are not commodities that can be traded." Rhetorically, it is a powerful point – *of course* children are not commercial products. Legally, though, it is beside the point. As we already explained, our precedent states that Congress's power under the Indian Commerce Clause encompasses not only trade but also "Indian affairs." Even the judges who otherwise agreed with petitioners below rejected this narrow view of the Indian Commerce Clause as inconsistent with both our cases and "[l]ongstanding patterns of federal legislation." Rather than dealing with this precedent, however, petitioners virtually ignore it.

... We have often sustained Indian legislation without specifying the source of Congress's power, and we have insisted that Congress's power has limits without saying what they are. Yet petitioners' strategy for dealing with the confusion is not to offer a theory for rationalizing this body of law – that would at least give us something to work with. Instead, they frame their arguments as if the slate were clean. More than two centuries in, it is anything but.

If there are arguments that ICWA exceeds Congress's authority as our precedent stands today, petitioners do not make them. We therefore decline to disturb the Fifth Circuit's conclusion that ICWA is consistent with Article I.

III.

B.

Petitioners also raise a Tenth Amendment challenge to §1915, which dictates placement preferences for Indian children. According to petitioners, this provision orders state agencies to perform a "diligent search" for placements that satisfy ICWA's hierarchy ... Just as Congress cannot compel state officials to search databases to determine the lawfulness of gun sales, petitioners argue, Congress cannot compel state officials to search for a federally preferred placement.

As an initial matter, this argument encounters the same problem that plagues petitioners with respect to §1912: Petitioners have not shown that the "diligent search" requirement, which applies to both private and public parties, demands the use of state sovereign authority. But this argument fails for another reason too: Section 1915 does not require *anyone*, much less the States, to search for alternative placements ... Instead, the burden is on the tribe or other objecting party to produce a higher-ranked placement. So, as it stands, petitioners assert an anticommandeering challenge to a provision that does not command state agencies to do anything.

State courts are a different matter. ICWA indisputably requires them to apply the placement preferences in making custody determinations. Petitioners argue that this too violates the anticommandeering doctrine. To be sure, they recognize that Congress can require state courts, unlike state executives and legislatures, to enforce federal law. But they draw a distinction between requiring state courts to entertain federal causes of action and requiring them to apply federal law to state causes of action. They claim that if state law provides the cause of action – as Texas law does here – then the State gets to call the shots, unhindered by any federal instruction to the contrary.

This argument runs headlong into the Constitution. The Supremacy Clause provides that "the Laws of the United States ... shall be the supreme Law of the Land; and the Judges in every State shall be bound thereby, any Thing in the Constitution or Laws of any state to the Contrary notwithstanding." Art. VI, cl. 2. Thus, when Congress enacts a valid statute pursuant to its Article I powers, "state law is naturally preempted to the extent of any conflict with a federal statute." End of story. That a federal law modifies a state law cause of action does not limit its preemptive effect.

IV.

Petitioners raise two additional claims: an equal protection challenge to ICWA's placement preferences and a nondelegation challenge to the provision allowing tribes to alter the placement preferences. We do not reach the merits of these claims because no party before the Court has standing to raise them. Article III requires a plaintiff to show that she has suffered an injury

in fact that is "fairly traceable to the defendant's allegedly unlawful conduct and likely to be redressed by the requested relief." *California* v. *Texas*, 593 U.S. 659 (2021). Neither the individual petitioners nor Texas can pass that test.

A.

The individual petitioners argue that ICWA injures them by placing them on "[un]equal footing" with Indian parents who seek to adopt or foster an Indian child. Under ICWA's hierarchy of preferences, non-Indian parents are generally last in line for potential placements. According to petitioners, this "erects a barrier that makes it more difficult for members of one group to obtain a benefit than it is for members of another group." The racial discrimination they allege counts as an Article III injury.

But the individual petitioners have not shown that this injury is "likely" to be "redressed by judicial relief." They seek an injunction preventing the federal parties from enforcing ICWA and a declaratory judgment that the challenged provisions are unconstitutional. Yet enjoining the federal parties would not remedy the alleged injury, because state courts apply the placement preferences, and state agencies carry out the court-ordered placements. The state officials who implement ICWA are "not parties to the suit, and there is no reason they should be obliged to honor an incidental legal determination the suit produced." So an injunction would not give petitioners legally enforceable protection from the allegedly imminent harm.

* * *

For these reasons, we affirm the judgment of the Court of Appeals regarding Congress's constitutional authority to enact ICWA. On the equal protection and nondelegation claims, we vacate the judgment of the Court of Appeals and remand with instructions to dismiss for lack of jurisdiction. It is so ordered.

Justice Kavanaugh, Concurring

I join the Court's opinion in full. I write separately to emphasize that the Court today does not address or decide the equal protection issue that can arise when the Indian Child Welfare Act is applied in individual foster care or adoption proceedings. As the Court explains, the plaintiffs in this federal-court suit against federal parties lack standing to raise the equal protection issue. So the equal protection issue remains undecided.

In my view, the equal protection issue is serious. Under the Act, a child in foster care or adoption proceedings may in some cases be denied a particular placement because of the child's race – even if the placement is otherwise determined to be in the child's best interests. And a prospective foster or adoptive parent may in some cases be denied the opportunity to foster or adopt a child because of the prospective parent's race. Those scenarios raise significant questions under bedrock equal protection principles and this Court's precedents. Courts, including ultimately this Court, will be able to address the equal protection issue when it is properly raised by a plaintiff with standing – for example, by a prospective foster or adoptive parent or child in a case arising out of a state-court foster care or adoption proceeding.

Justice Gorsuch, with whom Justice Sotomayor and Justice Jackson join as to Parts I and III, Concurring

In affirming the constitutionality of the Indian Child Welfare Act (ICWA), the Court safeguards the ability of tribal members to raise their children free from interference by state authorities and other outside parties. In the process, the Court also goes a long way toward restoring the original balance between federal, state, and tribal powers the Constitution envisioned. I am pleased to join the Court's opinion in full. I write separately to add some historical context. To appreciate fully the significance of today's decision requires an understanding of the long line of policies that drove Congress to adopt ICWA. And to appreciate why that law surely comports with the Constitution requires a bird's-eye view of how our founding document mediates between competing federal, state, and tribal claims of sovereignty.

I.

The Indian Child Welfare Act did not emerge from a vacuum. It came as a direct response to the mass removal of Indian children from their families during the 1950s, 1960s, and 1970s by state officials and private parties. That practice, in turn, was only the latest iteration of a much older policy of removing Indian children from their families – one initially spearheaded by federal officials with the aid of their state counterparts nearly 150 years ago. In all its many forms, the dissolution of the Indian family has had devastating effects on children and parents alike. It has also presented an existential threat to the continued vitality of Tribes – something many federal and state officials over the years saw as a feature, not as a flaw. This is the story of ICWA.

A.

At first, Indian education typically came in the form of day schools, many of them "established through the ... efforts of missionaries or the wives of Army officers stationed at military reservations in the Indian country." At those day schools, "Indian children would learn English as a second language," along with "math and science." But the children lived at home with their families where they could continue to learn and practice "their languages, beliefs, and traditional knowledge." At least in those "early decades," schooling was "generally ... not compulsory" anyway.

The federal government had darker designs. By the late 1870s, its goals turned toward destroying tribal identity and assimilating Indians into broader society. Achieving those goals, officials reasoned, required the "complete isolation of the Indian child from his savage antecedents." And because "the warm reciprocal affection existing between parents and children" was "among the strongest characteristics of the Indian nature," officials set out to eliminate it by dissolving Indian families. Thus began Indian boarding schools. In 1879, the Carlisle Indian Industrial School opened its doors at the site of an old military base in central Pennsylvania.

Carlisle's head, then-Captain Richard Henry Pratt, summarized the school's mission this way: "[A]ll the Indian there is in the race should be dead. Kill the Indian in him, and save the man." From its inception, Carlisle depended on state support. The school "was deeply enmeshed with local governments and their services," and it was "expanded thanks to the Pennsylvania Legislature." Ultimately, Carlisle became the model for what would become a system of 408 similar federal institutions nationwide. "The essential feature" of each was, in the federal government's own words, "the abolition of the old tribal relations."

Unsurprisingly, "[m]any Indian families resisted" the federal government's boarding school initiative and "refus[ed] to send their children." But Congress would not be denied. It authorized the Secretary of the Interior to "prevent the issuing of rations or the furnishing of subsistence" to Indian families who would not surrender their children. When economic coercion failed, officials sometimes resorted to abduction. As one official later recounted, officers would "visit the [Indian] camps unexpectedly with a detachment of [officers], and seize such children as were proper and take them away to school, willing or unwilling." When parents "hurried their children off to the mountains or hid them away in camp," agents "chase[d] and capture[d] them like so many wild rabbits." Fathers were described as "sullen," mothers "loud in their lamentations," and the children "almost out of their wits with fright."

Upon the children's arrival, the boarding schools would often seek to strip them of nearly every aspect of their identity. The schools would take away their Indian names and give them English ones. The schools would cut their hair – a point of shame in many native communities – and confiscate their traditional clothes. Administrators delighted in the process, describing the "metamorphosis [a]s wonderful," and professing that, in the main, "the little savage seems quite proud of his appearance." After intake, the schools frequently prohibited children from speaking their native language or engaging in customary cultural or religious practices. Nor could children freely associate with members of their own Tribe. Schools would organize dorms by the "[s]ize of cadets, and not their tribal relations," so as to further "br[eak] up tribal associations."

Resistance could invite punishments that included "withholding food" and "whipping." Older boys faced "court-martial," with other Indian children serving as prosecutors and judges. Even compliant students faced "[r]ampant physical, sexual, and emotional abuse; disease; malnourishment; overcrowding; and lack of health care." Given these conditions, it is unsurprising that many children tried (often unsuccessfully) to flee. State officials played a key role in foiling those efforts. "[P]olice from a variety of jurisdictions" assisted in "captur[ing] and return[ing] runaway school children." For "the runaways," school administrators believed "a whipping administered soundly and prayerfully, helps greatly towards bringing about the desired result." As one Commissioner of Indian Affairs put it, while "[t]he first wild redskin placed in the school[s] chafes at the loss of freedom and longs to return to his wildwood home," that resistance would fade "with each successive generation," leaving a "greater desir[e] to be in touch with the dominant race."

In 1928, the Meriam Report, prepared by the Brookings Institution, examined conditions in the Indian boarding schools. It found, "frankly and unequivocally," that "the provisions for the care of the Indian children ... are grossly inadequate." It recommended that the federal government "accelerat[e]" the "mov[e] away from the boarding school" system in favor of "day school or public school facilities." That transition would be slow to materialize, though. As late as 1971, federal boarding schools continued to house "more than 17 per cent of the Indian school-age population."

B.

The transition away from boarding schools was not the end of efforts to remove Indian children from their families and Tribes; more nearly, it was the end of the beginning. As federal boarding schools closed their doors and Indian children returned to the reservations, States with significant Native American populations found themselves facing significant new educational and welfare responsibilities. Around this time, as fate would have it, "shifting racial ideologies and changing gender norms [had] led to an increased demand for Indian children" by adoptive couples. Certain States saw in this shift an opportunity. They could "save ... money" by "promoting the *adoption* of Indian children by private families."

In this respect, "[t]he removal of Indian children by [S]tates ha[d] much in common with Indian boarding schools." Through the 1960s and 1970s, Indian-child removal reached new heights. Surveys conducted in 1969 and 1974 showed that "approximately 25–35 per cent of all Indian children [were] separated from their families." Often, these removals whisked children not only out of their families but out of their communities. Some estimate that "more than 90 per cent of non-related adoptions of Indian children [were] made by non-Indian couples."

These family separations frequently lacked justification. According to one report, only about "1 per cent" of the separations studied involved alleged physical abuse. The other 99 percent? "[V]ague grounds" such "as 'neglect' or 'social deprivation.'" These determinations, often "wholly inappropriate in the context of Indian family life," came mainly from non-Indian social workers, many of whom were "ignorant of Indian cultural values and social norms." They routinely penalized Indian parents for conditions of "[p]overty, poor housing, lack of modern plumbing, and overcrowding." One 3-year-old Sioux child, for instance, was removed from her family on the State's "belief that an Indian reservation is an unsuitable environment for a child." So it was that some Indian families, "forced onto reservations at gunpoint," were later "told that they live[d] in a place unfit for raising their children."

Aggravating matters, these separations were frequently "carried out without due process of law." Children and their parents rarely had counsel. For that matter, few cases saw the inside of a courtroom. Welfare departments knew that they could threaten to withhold benefit payments if Indian parents did not surrender custody. Nor were threats always necessary. After all the Tribes had suffered at the government's hands, many parents simply believed they had no power to resist. One interviewed mother "wept that she did not dare protest the taking of her children for fear of going to jail." For those Indian parents who did resist, "simple abduction" remained an option. Parents were, for instance, sometimes tricked into signing forms that they believed authorized only a brief removal of their children. Only later would they discover that the forms purported to surrender full custody.

Like the boarding school system that preceded it, this new program of removal had often-disastrous consequences. "Because the family is the most fundamental economic, educational, and health-care unit" in society, these "assaults on Indian families" contributed to the precarious conditions that Indian parents and children already faced. Many parents came to "feel hopeless, powerless, and unworthy" – further feeding the cycle of removal. For many children, separation from their families caused "severe distress" that "interfere[d] with their physical, mental, and social growth and development." It appears, too, that Indian children were "significantly more likely" to experience "physical, sexual, [and] emotional" abuse in foster and adoptive homes than their white counterparts.

All that often translated into long-lasting adverse health and emotional effects. As one study warned: "[E]fforts to make Indian children 'white,'" by removing them from their Tribes, "can destroy them."

C.

Eventually, Congress could ignore the problem no longer. In 1978, it responded with the Indian Child Welfare Act. The statute's findings show that Congress was acutely aware of the scope of the crisis.

The statute Congress settled upon contains various provisions aimed at addressing this crisis. At bottom, though, the law's operation is simple. It installs substantive and procedural guardrails against the unjustified termination of parental rights and removal of Indian children from tribal life.

The touchstone of the statute is notice. In any involuntary removal proceeding involving an Indian child, the initiating party must inform (1) the parent or custodian; and (2) the child's Tribe. Either or both can intervene. ICWA also makes it harder for the moving party to win an involuntary removal proceeding. The party must show that "active efforts" have been made to avoid removing the Indian child ...

II.

This history leads us to the question at the heart of today's cases: Did Congress lack the constitutional authority to enact ICWA, as Texas and the private plaintiffs contend? In truth, that is not one question, but many. What authorities do the Tribes possess under our Constitution? What power does Congress have with respect to tribal relations? What does that mean for States? And how do those principles apply in a context like adoption, which involves competing claims of federal, state, *and* tribal authority?

Answering these questions requires a full view of the Indian-law bargain struck in our Constitution. Under the terms of that bargain, Indian Tribes remain independent sovereigns with the exclusive power to manage their internal matters. As a corollary of that sovereignty, States have virtually no role to play when it comes to Indian affairs. To preserve this equilibrium between Tribes and States, the Constitution vests in the federal government a set of potent (but limited and enumerated) powers. In particular, the Indian Commerce Clause gives Congress a robust (but not plenary) power to regulate the ways in which non-Indians may interact with Indians...

D.

Today, the Court takes further steps in the right direction. It recognizes that Congress's powers with respect to the Tribes "derive from the Constitution, not the atmosphere." It engages in a robust history-driven analysis of the various fonts of congressional authority without relying only on platitudes about plenary power. It notes that, as an original matter, the Indian Commerce Clause is "broad" and covers more than garden-variety commercial activity. In the process, it reaffirms that "'commerce with the Indian [T]ribes'" necessarily covers commerce with "Indians as individuals."

No less importantly, the Court acknowledges what the federal government *cannot* do. "Article I gives Congress a series of enumerated powers, not a series of blank checks." And that means that "Congress's authority to legislate with respect to Indians is not unbounded," but instead comes with concrete limitations. To resolve the present dispute, the Court understandably sees no need to demarcate those limitations further. But I hope that, in time, it will follow the implications of today's decision where they lead and return us to the original bargain struck in the Constitution – and, with it, the respect for Indian sovereignty it entails.

III.

By now, the full picture has come into view and it is easy to see why ICWA must stand. Under our Constitution, Tribes remain independent sovereigns responsible for governing their own affairs. And as this Court has long recognized, domestic law arrangements fall within Tribes' traditional powers of self-governance. As "a separate people" Tribes may "regulat[e] their internal and social relations" as they wish. In enacting ICWA, Congress affirmed this understanding. It recognized that "there is no resource that is more vital to the continued existence and integrity of Indian [T]ribes than their children." Yet it also recognized that the mass-removal of Indian children by States and other outsiders threatened the "continued existence and integrity of Indian [T]ribes." By setting out to eliminate that practice, Congress sought to preserve the Indian-law bargain written into the Constitution's text by securing the continued viability of the "third sovereign."

Nor is there any serious question that Congress has the power under the Indian Commerce Clause to enact protections against the removal of Indian children. Thankfully, Indian children are not (these days) units of commerce. But at its core, ICWA restricts how non-Indians (States and private individuals) may engage with Indians. And, as we have seen, that falls in the heartland of Congress's constitutional authority. Recall that the very first Congresses punished non-Indians who "commit[ted] any crime upon [any] friendly Indian." ICWA operates in much the same way. The mass removal of Indian children by States and private parties, no less than a pattern of criminal trespasses by States and private parties, directly interferes with tribal intercourse. More than that, it threatens the Tribes' "political existence." And at the risk of stating the obvious, Indian commerce is hard to maintain if there are no Indian communities left to do commerce with.

IV.

Often, Native American Tribes have come to this Court seeking justice only to leave with bowed heads and empty hands. But that is not because this Court has no justice to offer them. Our Constitution reserves for the Tribes a place – an enduring place – in the structure of American life. It promises them sovereignty for as long as they wish to keep it. And it secures that promise by divesting States of authority over Indian affairs and by giving the federal government certain significant (but limited and enumerated) powers aimed at building a lasting peace. In adopting the Indian Child Welfare Act, Congress exercised that lawful authority to secure the right of Indian parents to raise their families as they please; the right of Indian children to grow in their culture; and the right of Indian communities to resist fading into the twilight of history. All of that is in keeping with the Constitution's original design.

Justice Thomas, Dissenting

These cases concern the Federal Government's attempt to regulate child-welfare proceedings in state courts. That should raise alarm bells. Our Federal "[G]overnment is acknowledged by all to be one of enumerated powers," having only those powers that the Constitution confers expressly or by necessary implication. All other powers (like family or criminal law) generally remain with the States. The Federal Government thus lacks a general police power to regulate state family law.

However, in the Indian Child Welfare Act (ICWA), Congress ignored the normal limits on the Federal Government's power and prescribed rules to regulate state child custody proceedings in one circumstance: when the child involved happens to be an Indian. As the majority acknowledges, ICWA often overrides state family law by dictating that state courts place Indian children with Indian caretakers even if doing so is not in the child's best interest. It imposes heightened standards before removing Indian children from unsafe environments. And it allows tribes to unilaterally enroll Indian children and then intervene in their custody proceedings.

In the normal course, we would say that the Federal Government has no authority to enact any of this. Yet the majority declines to hold that ICWA is unconstitutional, reasoning that the petitioners before us have not borne their burden of showing how Congress exceeded its powers. This gets things backwards. When Congress has so clearly intruded upon a long-standing domain of exclusive state powers, we must ask not whether a constitutional provision prohibits that intrusion, but whether a constitutional provision authorizes it.

The majority and respondents gesture to a smorgasbord of constitutional hooks to support ICWA; not one of them works. First, the Indian Commerce Clause is about commerce, not children. See *Adoptive Couple* v. *Baby Girl*, 570 U.S. 637, 659–665 (2013) (Thomas, J., concurring). Second, the Treaty Clause does not work because ICWA is not based on any treaty. Third, the foreign-affairs powers (what the majority terms "structural principles") inherent in the Federal Government have no application to regulating the domestic child custody proceedings of U.S. citizens living within the jurisdiction of States.

I would go no further. But, as the majority notes, the Court's precedents have repeatedly referred to a "plenary power" that Congress possesses over Indian affairs, as well as a general "trust" relationship with the Indians. I have searched in vain for any constitutional basis for such a plenary power, which appears to have been born of loose language and judicial *ipse dixit*. And, even taking the Court's precedents as given, there is no reason to extend this "plenary power" to the situation before us today: regulating state-court child custody proceedings of U.S. citizens, who may never have even set foot on Indian lands, merely because the child involved happens to be an Indian.

II.

To explain the original understanding of the Constitution's enumerated powers with regard to Indians, I start with our Nation's Founding-era dealings with Indian tribes. Those early interactions underscore that the Constitution conferred specific, enumerated powers on the Federal Government ...

B.

After the Constitution's ratification, the new Federal Government exercised its enumerated powers with regard to Indian tribes. To start, the Government embarked on an era of treaty-making with Indian tribes. That treaty-focused policy reflected the Washington administration's view that Indian tribes were best dealt with as mostly "foreign nations," with an eye towards peace lest frontier conflicts continue to plague the new Nation. Many early treaties thus "were treaties of peace and friendship, often providing for the restoration or exchange of prisoners" or including "mutual assistance pacts." Others dealt with passports and commercial affairs. And many attested to the tribes' status as dependent nations, with the United States sometimes promising to protect the tribe.

III.

A.

As the majority notes, some of the candidates that this Court has suggested as the source of the "plenary power" are the Treaty Clause, the Commerce Clause, and "principles inherent in the Constitution's structure." But each of those powers has clear, inherent limits, and not one suggests any sort of unlimited power over Indian affairs – much less a power to regulate U.S. citizens outside of Indian lands merely because those individuals happen to be Indians ...

IV.

Properly understood, the Constitution's enumerated powers cannot support ICWA. Not one of those powers, as originally understood, comes anywhere close to including the child custody proceedings of U.S. citizens living within the sole jurisdiction of States. Moreover, ICWA has no constitutional basis ... While [precedent has] extended the Federal Government's Indian-related powers beyond the original understanding of the Constitution, this Court has never extended them far enough to support ICWA. Rather, virtually all of this Court's modern Indian-law precedents – upholding laws that regulate tribal lands, tribal governments, and commerce with tribes – can be understood through a core conceptual framework that at least arguably corresponds to Founding-era practices. To extend those cases to uphold ICWA thus would require ignoring the context of those precedents, treating their loose "plenary power" language as talismanic, and transforming that power into the truly unbounded, absolute power that they disclaim. The basic premise that the powers of the Federal Government are limited and defined should counsel against taking that step.

A.

ICWA lacks any foothold in the Constitution's original meaning. Most obviously, ICWA has no parallel from the Founding era; it regulates the child custody proceedings of U.S. citizens in state courts – not on Indian lands – merely because the children involved happen to be Indians. No law from that time even came close to asserting a general police power over citizens who happened to be Indians – by, for example, regulating the acts of Indians who were also citizens and who lived within the sole jurisdiction of States (and not on Indian lands). If nothing else, the dearth of Founding-era laws even remotely similar to ICWA should give us pause.

Nor can ICWA find any support in the Constitution's enumerated powers as originally understood. I take those powers in turn: First, the Property Clause cannot support ICWA because ICWA is not based on the disposition of federal property and is not limited to federal lands; in fact, the Federal Government owns very little Indian land.

Second, the Treaty Clause cannot support ICWA because no one has identified a treaty that governs child custody proceedings – much less a treaty with each of the 574 federally recognized tribes to which ICWA applies ...

Third, the Commerce Clause cannot support ICWA. As originally understood, the Clause confers a power only over buying and selling, not family law and child custody disputes. Even under our more modern, expansive precedents, the Clause is still limited to only "economic activity" and cannot support the regulation of core domestic matters like family or criminal laws ...

Fourth, the Federal Government's foreign-affairs powers cannot support ICWA. For today's purposes, I will assume that some tribes still enjoy the same sort of pre-existing sovereignty and autonomy as tribes at the Founding, thereby establishing the sort of quasi-foreign, government-to-government relationship that appears to have defined those powers at the Founding. Even so, the foreign-affairs powers can operate only *externally*, in the context of lands under the purview of another sovereign (like Indian tribal lands) or in the context of a government-to-government relationship (such as matters of diplomacy or peace). But regulating child custody proceedings of citizens within a State is the paradigmatic *domestic* situation; the Federal Government surely could not apply its foreign-affairs powers to the domestic family-law or criminal matters of any other citizens merely because they happened to have citizenship or ancestral connections with another nation. Apart from the single provision that allows tribal governments jurisdiction over proceedings for Indians on tribal lands, ICWA is

completely untethered from any external aspect of our Nation that could somehow implicate these powers.

That should be the end of the analysis. Again, as the majority notes, our Federal Government has only the powers that the Constitution enumerates. Not one of those enumerated powers justifies ICWA. Therefore, it has no basis whatsoever in our constitutional system.

B.

Even taking our "plenary power" precedents as given (as the majority seems to do for purposes of these cases), nothing in those precedents supports ICWA. To be sure, this Court has repeatedly used loose language concerning a "plenary power" and "trust relationship" with Indians, and that language has been taken by some to displace the normal constitutional rules. But, even taken to their new limits, the Court's precedents have upheld only a variety of laws that either regulate commerce with Indians or deal with Indian tribes and their lands. Despite citing a veritable avalanche of precedents, respondents have failed to identify a single case where this Court upheld a federal statute comparable to ICWA.

[*United States* v.] *Kagama*, [118 U.S. 375 (1886)] was careful to note that the Major Crimes Act at issue was "confined to the acts of an Indian of some tribe, of a criminal character, committed within the limits of the reservation." In that vein, the opinion cited cases arising from congressional regulations of Indian lands located within Federal Territories. In other words, it is possible that *Kagama* viewed Congress as having the power to regulate crimes by Indians on Indian lands because those lands remained in a sense "external" to the Nation's normal affairs and akin to quasi-federal lands.

Accordingly, the context of [our precedents] points to lines that are at least plausibly rooted in Founding-era practices and the text of the Constitution. Congress can regulate commerce with Indian tribes; it may be able to regulate tribal governments and lands ... and it can make treaties, dispose of federal funds, and establish discrete trusts.

ICWA does not remotely resemble those practices. It does not regulate commerce, tribal governments, or tribal lands. Nor is it based on treaties, federal funds, or any discrete trust. By regulating family-law matters of citizens living within the sole jurisdiction of States merely because they happen to be Indians, ICWA stands clearly outside the framework of our Indian-law precedents. To uphold ICWA therefore would drastically expand the context in which we have previously upheld Indian-related laws ...

But, even if that is so, the majority appears to ask "*why* Congress's power is limited to these scenarios." The majority nearly answers itself: because our Constitution is one of enumerated powers, and limiting Congress' authority to those "buckets" would bring our jurisprudence closer to the powers enumerated by the text and original meaning of the Constitution. While I share the majority's frustration with petitioners' limited engagement with the Court's precedents, I would recognize the contexts of those cases and limit the so-called plenary power to those contexts. Such limits would at least start us on the road back to the Constitution's original meaning in the area of Indian law.

*　　*　　*

The Constitution confers enumerated powers on the Federal Government. Not one of them supports ICWA. Nor does precedent. To the contrary, this Court has never upheld a federal statute that regulates the noncommercial activities of a U.S. citizen residing on lands under the sole jurisdiction of States merely because he happens to be an Indian. But that is exactly what ICWA does: It regulates child custody proceedings, brought in state courts, for those who need never have set foot on Indian lands. It is not about tribal lands or tribal governments, commerce, treaties, or federal property. It therefore fails equally under the Court's precedents as it fails under the plain text and original meaning of the Constitution.

... [G]iven ICWA's patent intrusion into the normal domain of state government and clear departure from the Federal Government's enumerated powers, I would hold that Congress lacked any authority to enact ICWA.

I respectfully dissent.

Justice Alito, Dissenting

The first line in the Court's opinion identifies what is most important about these cases: they are "about children who are among the most vulnerable." But after that opening nod, the Court loses sight of this overriding concern and decides one question after another in a way that disserves the rights and interests of these children and their parents, as well as our Constitution's division of federal and state authority.

Decisions about child custody, foster care, and adoption are core state functions. The paramount concern in these cases has long been the "best interests" of the children involved. But in many cases, provisions of the Indian Child Welfare Act (ICWA) compel actions that conflict with this fundamental state policy, subordinating what family-court judges – and often biological parents – determine to be in the best interest of a child to what Congress believed is in the best interest of a tribe.

... Whatever authority Congress possesses in the area of Indian affairs, it does not have the power to sacrifice the best interests of vulnerable children to promote the interests of tribes in maintaining membership. Nor does Congress have the power to force state judges to disserve the best interests of children or the power to delegate to tribes the authority to force those judges to abide by the tribes' priorities regarding adoption and foster-care placement.

II.

Congress's power in the area of Indian affairs cannot exceed the limits imposed by the "system of dual sovereignty between the States and the Federal Government" established by the Constitution. "The powers delegated ... to the federal government are few and defined," while "[t]hose which ... remain in the State governments are numerous and indefinite." The powers retained by the States constitute "'a residuary and inviolable sovereignty,'" secure against federal intrusion. This structural principle, reinforced in the Tenth Amendment, "confirms that the power of the Federal Government is subject to limits that may, in a given instance, reserve power to the States." The corollary is also true: in some circumstances, the powers reserved to the

States inform the scope of Congress's power. This includes in the area of Indian affairs.

The ICWA provisions challenged here do not simply run up against this traditional state authority, they run roughshod over it when the State seeks to protect one of its young citizens who also happens to be a member of an Indian tribe or who is the biological child of a member and eligible for tribal membership, herself. In those circumstances, ICWA requires a State to abandon the carefully-considered judicial procedures and standards it has established to provide for a child's welfare and instead apply a scheme devised by Congress that focuses not solely on the best interest of the child, but also on "the stability and security of Indian tribes." That scheme requires States to invite tribal authorities with no existing relationship to a child to intervene in judicial custody proceedings. It requires States to replace their reasoned standards for termination of parental rights and placement in foster care with standards that favor the interests of an Indian custodian over those of the child. It forces state courts to give Indian couples (even those of different tribes) priority in adoption and foster-care placements, even over a non-Indian couple who would better serve a child's emotional and other needs. And it requires state judges to subordinate the State's typical custodial considerations to a tribe's alternative preference.

It is worth underscoring that ICWA's directives apply even when the child is not a member of a tribe and has never been involved in tribal life, and even when a child's biological parents object. As seen in the cases before us, the sad consequence is that ICWA's provisions may delay or prevent a child's adoption by a family ready to provide her a permanent home.

ICWA's mandates do not simply touch on family matters. They override States' authority to determine – and implement through their courts – the child custody and welfare policies they deem most appropriate for their citizens. And in doing so, the mandates harm vulnerable children and their parents. In my view, the Constitution cannot countenance this result. The guarantee of dual sovereignty embodied in the constitutional structure "is not so ephemeral as to dissipate" simply because Congress invoked a so-called plenary power. The challenged ICWA provisions effectively "nullify" a State's authority to conduct state child custody proceedings in accordance with its own preferred family relations policies, a prerogative that States have exercised for centuries. Congress's Indian affairs power, broad as it is, does not extend that far.

*   *   *

I am sympathetic to the challenges that tribes face in maintaining membership and preserving their cultures. And I do not question the idea that the best interests of children may in some circumstances take into account a desire to enable children to maintain a connection with the culture of their ancestors. The Constitution provides Congress with many means for promoting such interests. But the Constitution does not permit Congress to displace long-exercised state authority over child custody proceedings to advance those interests at the expense of vulnerable children and their families.

Because I would hold that Congress lacked authority to enact the challenged ICWA provisions, I respectfully dissent.

1. What is the concern of the Tribal defendants? The plaintiffs? How does the court attempt to resolve this conflict?
2. How do you think the Court resolved each of the plaintiffs' claims? How might this decision challenge the Supreme Court ruling in *Adoptive Couple* v. *Baby Girl*?
3. How does this decision help further the discussion around the sovereignty of Native tribes in the United States? Should this sovereignty preclude state authority to manage family matters? What about Native people who do not physically reside on tribal lands?

While the Court declined to address the Equal Protection question in this decision, the dissenting opinions of Justices Thomas and Alito, as well as the concurring opinion by Justice Kavanaugh, demonstrate that this question is significant for the Court. Many Native advocates and scholars argue that in light of the sovereignty of Native communities and their independence from the states, possessing an indigenous or Indian identity is political classification, not a racial one.

1. What are the implications of declaring statutes like this that protect Native Americans as "political" classifications instead of "race-based"?
2. Is this kind of legislation distinct from those that protect groups like African Americans, Latinos and Latinas, or Asian Americans who have experienced historical discrimination? Why?
3. Such a political classification would allow tribal members to escape the requirements of the Equal Protection Clause to treat all racial groups the same under most circumstances. How do you see this question of preserving unique cultures and preventing assimilation as applying to the ICWA?
4. In what way might this example challenge your interpretation of the role law should play in engaging cultural communities?

6 Race and Constructing Democracy

As we have seen throughout this text, while the concept of race was created by humans, and clarified and hardened by law in the United States, this depiction has been vigorously debated. Dissenting legal opinions have challenged these policy choices. People whose rights were conscribed by statutory law and judicial interpretations have organized and fought against this construction of race. The question of how best to guarantee the rights of everyone under the law – regardless of racial identity or perception of race – continues to be an ongoing challenge to our society.

What complicates this issue is the nature of law. As a tool, it serves as both a lock and a key. It can be used to bar people from participation – such as limiting access to jobs and education – and it can be used to open new opportunities to previously excluded individuals and groups – as in affirmative action programs. One of the great debates in the twenty-first century has been over the question of whether the law should be color-blind. If one source of injustice in the United States has been color-conscious laws which allow for such race-based inequality as slavery, the denial of citizenship, state-sanctioned violence, and segregation, then is the solution simply to remove color-consciousness from the consideration? Some individuals argue that the only solution to past discrimination is to excise all future references to race from the law and policy. Otherwise, we simply replicate the errors of the past by relying on flawed racial classifications to distribute power and resources. By reifying race and keeping it central to policy decisions, such advocates argue that we trap people in artificially constructed racial paradigms that continue from generation to generation (Cose 1997; Hughes 2024). There are also those who believe that with the end of formal inequality (slavery, segregation, and other forms of mandated racial discrimination), race has ceased to have a significant impact on society that the government is obligated to address (D'Souza 1995). For these individuals, government programs and policies that recognize race violate the promise of the Equal Protection of the laws guaranteed by the Fifth and Fourteenth Amendments and exceed state authority over individual liberty.

Others challenge this notion, arguing that the legal damage has already been structured throughout our society and culture on the basis of racial categories. We see evidence of these structural inequalities in the many racial disparities in affordable housing, quality education, heightened socioeconomic status, and access to power. To merely ignore differences caused by flawed governmental policies without a strong, proactive government intervention – using race as a guide – allows these inequities to remain unchallenged (Golub 2018). Some individuals will be able to extract themselves, but racialized communities which have borne the brunt of this oppression remain trapped by the past. Formal equality is not sufficient, the government and its citizens are obligated to do more considering our own national history. Scholars have also demonstrated that the history of federal governmental programs – in such areas as housing and veteran benefits – were both explicitly and implicitly beneficial to Whites, excluding other racial communities (Katznelson 2005; Rothstein 2017). Such racialized discrimination requires a race-conscious remedy to repair.

How can the law be used to construct a more just democracy? Should we trust in color-conscious remedies, at least until the structures of the past have been dismantled? But how do we know when this will happen? Have we advanced enough as a society that we no longer need to take race into consideration so that individuals rise and fall on their own merit? Or is our merit system still so comprised by our history that our structures must be reevaluated before color-blindness advances equity? Advocates on both sides of this debate rely on the same history, citing identical cases and referencing the same advocates, such as Frederick Douglass (Buccola 2012) and Justice John Harlan (Canellos 2021), to make their point, despite arriving at different conclusions.

In this chapter, we will consider the role of affirmative action as a means of change, the question of statehood for the unincorporated U.S. territories and equal status for their citizens, and the continuous advocacy for the expansion of Native sovereignty. These movements all attempt to correct clear errors of the past using the law as a remedy. In each of these sections, as you read majority and dissenting opinions, consider the role of color-conscious versus color-blind remedies in forcing the United States to adhere to its claims of equality. Try to ignore the partisan noise over these very controversial issues. Do you see how claims for reparations – or the contemporary corrections of historic wrongs – connect to these issues?

6.1 Affirmative Action

Laws reinforcing constitutional guarantees by prohibiting discriminatory treatment are the most common objectives of early civil rights battles. We have called this goal "formal equality" throughout this text. Nevertheless, in the 1960s, Executive Orders from Democratic President Lyndon B. Johnson forced the implementation of policies aimed at reinforcing equal access to employment through mandating recruiting procedures that actively sought to identify qualified minority men for government positions. In 1971, Republican President Richard M. Nixon launched the Philadelphia Plan, which created enforceable goals for federal affirmative action programs. This policy of affirmative action was extended to women in the workplace and to opening educational opportunities (Urofsky 1997; Anderson 2004). While bipartisan in their initial creation, affirmative action policies have been and continue to be very controversial.

Affirmative action programs do not require organizations to select unqualified candidates, nor do they require automatically choosing a qualified minority candidate over a qualified nonminority candidate. Affirmative action does require that an organization make intentional efforts to diversify by providing equality opportunity to classes of people who have been historically, and in many cases are currently, subject to discrimination. These types of program, often called minority set-aside programs, were found to be constitutional by the courts in such cases as *Fullilove* v. *Klutznick*, 448 U.S. 448 (1980). Such policies required federal contractors or private companies who were bidding for federally funded projects to demonstrate that a significant percentage of their subcontractors were minority or female-owned businesses.

6.1.1 Affirmative Action in Higher Education

In the 1970s, institutions of higher education began to adopt intentional efforts to expand educational opportunities for both men and women from various minority groups. In addition, colleges and universities used affirmative action to ensure a student body diverse in race, color, economic status, and other characteristics. These institutions believe that having students on campus representing a wide range of backgrounds and experiences enhance all students' educational experience, equipping them to function successfully in an increasingly diverse nation. Critics argue that any admission decision that significantly considers race is unconstitutional discrimination. Advocates note that at the elite institutions, wealthy and privileged students of color were preferred over working-class, first-generation White students. For those challenging affirmative action, such policies are unfair and unrelated to the goal of democracy without compensating for any barriers confronted by students.

In the important *Regents of University of California* v. *Bakke* decision in 1978, the U.S. Supreme Court found the University of California at Davis' affirmative action plan for admission to its medical school unconstitutional. The UC Davis plan set aside 16 of the 100 seats in its first-year medical school class for racial minorities (specifically, African Americans, Hispanics, Asian Americans, and Native Americans). Justice Powell wrote the plurality opinion (meaning a majority of justices agreed on the outcome but could not agree on the reasoning for the decision. Such a decision has a weaker precedential power). He concluded that schools may take race into consideration as one of several factors for admission but cannot use race as the sole consideration. After *Bakke*, the Supreme Court abdicated its authority and "allowed lower federal courts to make decisions that appeared to eradicate the ruling made in *Bakke*, and by refusing to hear the challenges to these decisions, allowed them to stand" (Jones, Deardorff, and Briscoe 2006, 122).

Opponents have challenged affirmative action in the courts as well as through legislative processes and statewide referendums. In the case of *Richmond* v. *J. A. Croson Co.*, 488 U.S. 469 (1989), the Supreme Court modified its constitutional approach by questioning the validity of affirmative action in dismantling the structures of racism in the United States. In examining the city of Richmond, Virginia's minority set-aside program, the Court's majority held that "the standard of review under the Equal Protection Clause is not dependent on the race of those burdened or benefitted by a particular classification and that the single standard of review for racial classifications should be strict scrutiny." While previous courts were expected to use the highest level of scrutiny only for state actions that were harmful to members of racialized groups which had experienced oppression, after *Croson* all government actions that distinguished individuals based on race were evaluated under this highest standard. Precedent no longer differentiated between color-conscious state actions designed to undo White supremacy and such actions with the clear purpose of harming communities of color. All color-conscious policies were treated identically under the law.

In 2003, the Supreme Court heard two cases that addressed the constitutional use of affirmative action plans in universities and law school admissions. Both cases came from the University of Michigan and the Court upheld one race-conscious policy as constitutional and one as unconstitutional. As frequently occurs (Epstein and Kobylica 1991; Deardorff 1993), the Court justified this differentiation by variances in the fact-patterns facing the courts. In *Grutter* v. *Bollinger*, the Court explored the use of race by the law school in admitting new students. Annually, the university winnows 3,500 applicants down to the 350 students who are deemed "individually and collectively ... among the most capable both in academic success in legal studies" and who demonstrate "a strong likelihood of succeeding in the practice of law and contributing in diverse ways to the well-being of others." The school seeks to have a diverse student body with "varying backgrounds and experiences." To do this, admissions officers use a variety of factors (undergraduate grade point average (GPA), Law School Admissions Test (LSAT) score, personal statements, letters of recommendation, and an essay in which the candidate explains the different ways they would bring diversity to the next class). The petitioner was Barbara Grutter, a White Michigan resident who applied to the law school in 1996 with a 3.8 GPA and a 161 LSAT score (the national average was around 157). She was initially placed on the waitlist and then was denied admission. She claims she was discriminated against on the basis of race in violation of the Fourteenth Amendment and Title VI of the Civil Rights Act of 1964.

GRUTTER v. *BOLLINGER*, 539 U.S. 306 (2003)

Justice O'Connor Delivered the Opinion of the Court, Joined by Justices Stevens, Souter, Ginsberg, and Breyer

Vote: 5–4

This case requires us to decide whether the use of race as a factor in student admissions by the University of Michigan Law School (Law School) is unlawful.

II.

A.

We last addressed the use of race in public higher education over 25 years ago. In the landmark [*Regents of University of California* v. *Bakke*, 438 U.S. 265 (1978)] case, we reviewed a racial set-aside program that reserved 16 out of 100 seats in a medical school class for members of certain minority groups. The decision produced six separate opinions, none of which commanded a majority of the Court. Four Justices would have upheld the program against all attack on the ground that the government can use race to "remedy disadvantages cast on minorities by past racial prejudice." Four other Justices avoided the constitutional question altogether and struck down the program on statutory grounds. Justice Powell provided a fifth vote not only for invalidating the set-aside program, but also for reversing the state court's injunction against any use of race whatsoever. The only holding for the Court in *Bakke* was that a "State has a substantial interest that legitimately may be served by a properly devised admissions program involving the competitive consideration of race and ethnic origin." Thus, we reversed that part of the lower court's judgment that enjoined the university "from any consideration of the race of any applicant."

Since this Court's splintered decision in *Bakke*, Justice Powell's opinion announcing the judgment of the Court has served as the touchstone for constitutional analysis of race-conscious admissions policies. Public and private universities across the Nation have modeled their own admissions programs on Justice Powell's views on permissible race-conscious policies.

B.

The Equal Protection Clause provides that no State shall "deny to any person within its jurisdiction the equal protection of the laws." Because the Fourteenth Amendment "protect[s] *persons*, not *groups*," all "governmental action based on race – a *group* classification long recognized as in most circumstances irrelevant and therefore prohibited – should be subjected to detailed judicial inquiry to ensure that the *personal* right to equal protection of the laws has not been infringed." *Adarand Constructors, Inc.* v. *Peña*, 515 U.S. 200, 227 (1995). We are a "free people whose institutions are founded upon the doctrine of equality." *Loving* v. *Virginia*, 388 U.S. 1, 11 (1967). It follows from that principle that "government may treat people differently because of their race only for the most compelling reasons."

We have held that all racial classifications imposed by government "must be analyzed by a reviewing court under strict scrutiny." This means that such classifications are constitutional only if they are narrowly tailored to further compelling governmental interests. "Absent searching judicial inquiry into the justification for such race-based measures," we have no way to determine what "classifications are 'benign' or 'remedial' and what classifications are in fact motivated by illegitimate notions of racial inferiority or simple racial politics." *Richmond* v. *J. A. Croson Co.*, 488 U.S. 469, 493 (1989). We apply strict scrutiny to all racial classifications to "'smoke out' illegitimate uses of race by assuring that [government] is pursuing a goal important enough to warrant use of a highly suspect tool."

Strict scrutiny is not "strict in theory, but fatal in fact."

Although all governmental uses of race are subject to strict scrutiny, not all are invalidated by it. As we have explained, "whenever the government treats any person unequally because of his or her race, that person has suffered an injury that falls squarely within the language and spirit of the Constitution's guarantee of equal protection." But that observation "says nothing about the ultimate validity of any particular law; that determination is the job of the court applying strict scrutiny." When race-based action is necessary to further a compelling governmental interest, such action does not violate the constitutional guarantee of equal protection so long as the narrow-tailoring requirement is also satisfied.

Context matters when reviewing race-based governmental action under the Equal Protection Clause. In *Adarand Constructors, Inc.* v. *Peña*, we made clear that strict scrutiny must take "'relevant differences' into account." Indeed, as we explained, that is its "fundamental purpose." Not every decision influenced by race is equally objectionable, and strict scrutiny is designed to provide a framework for carefully examining the importance and the sincerity of the reasons advanced by the governmental decisionmaker for the use of race in that particular context.

III.

A.

With these principles in mind, we turn to the question whether the Law School's use of race is justified by a compelling state interest. Before this Court, as they have throughout this litigation, respondents assert only one justification for their use of race in the admissions process: obtaining "the educational benefits that flow from a diverse student body." In other words, the Law School asks us to recognize, in the context of higher education, a compelling state interest in student body diversity.

We first wish to dispel the notion that the Law School's argument has been foreclosed, either expressly or implicitly, by our affirmative-action cases decided since *Bakke*. It is true that some language in those opinions might be read to suggest that remedying past discrimination is the only permissible justification for race-based governmental action. But we have never held that the only governmental use of race that can survive strict scrutiny is remedying past discrimination. Nor, since *Bakke*, have we directly addressed the use of race in the context of public higher education. Today, we hold that the Law School has a compelling interest in attaining a diverse student body.

The Law School's educational judgment that such diversity is essential to its educational mission is one to which we defer. The Law School's assessment that diversity will, in fact, yield educational benefits is substantiated by respondents and their *amici*. Our scrutiny of the interest asserted by the Law School is no less strict for taking into account complex educational judgments in an area that lies primarily within the expertise of the university. Our holding today is in keeping with our tradition of giving a degree of deference to a university's academic decisions, within constitutionally prescribed limits.

We have long recognized that, given the important purpose of public education and the expansive freedoms of speech and thought associated with the university environment, universities occupy a special niche in our constitutional tradition ... Our conclusion that the Law School has a compelling interest in a diverse student body is informed by our view that attaining a diverse student body is at the heart of the Law School's proper institutional mission, and that "good faith" on the part of a university is "presumed" absent "a showing to the contrary."

As part of its goal of "assembling a class that is both exceptionally academically qualified and broadly diverse," the Law School seeks to "enroll a 'critical mass' of minority students." The Law School's interest is not simply "to assure within its student body some specified percentage of a particular group merely because of its race or ethnic origin." That would amount to outright racial balancing, which is patently unconstitutional. Rather, the Law School's concept of critical mass is defined by reference to the educational benefits that diversity is designed to produce.

The Law School does not premise its need for critical mass on "any belief that minority students always (or even consistently) express some characteristic minority viewpoint on any issue." To the contrary, diminishing the force of such stereotypes is both a crucial part of the Law School's mission, and one that it cannot accomplish with only token numbers of minority students. Just as growing up in a particular region or having particular professional experiences is likely to affect an individual's views, so too is one's own, unique experience of being a racial minority in a society, like our own, in which race unfortunately still matters. The Law School has determined, based on its experience and expertise, that a "critical mass" of underrepresented minorities is necessary to further its compelling interest in securing the educational benefits of a diverse student body.

B.

Even in the limited circumstance when drawing racial distinctions is permissible to further a compelling state interest, government is still "constrained in how it may pursue that end: [T]he means chosen to accomplish the [government's] asserted purpose must be specifically and narrowly framed to accomplish that purpose." The purpose of the narrow tailoring requirement is to ensure that "the means chosen 'fit' the compelling goal so closely that there is little or no possibility that the motive for the classification was illegitimate racial prejudice or stereotype."

Since *Bakke*, we have had no occasion to define the contours of the narrow-tailoring inquiry with respect to race-conscious university admissions programs. That inquiry must be calibrated to fit the distinct issues raised by the use of race to achieve student body diversity in public higher education. Contrary to Justice Kennedy's assertions, we do not "abando[n] strict scrutiny." Rather, as we have already explained, we adhere to *Adarand*'s teaching that the very purpose of strict scrutiny is to take such "relevant differences into account."

To be narrowly tailored, a race-conscious admissions program cannot use a quota system – it cannot "insulat[e] each category of applicants with certain desired qualifications from competition with all other applicants." Instead, a university may consider race or ethnicity only as a "'plus' in a particular applicant's file," without "insulat[ing] the individual from comparison with all other candidates for the available seats." In other words, an admissions program must be "flexible enough to consider all pertinent elements of diversity in light of the particular qualifications of each applicant, and to place them on the same footing for consideration, although not necessarily according them the same weight."

We find that the Law School's admissions program bears the hallmarks of a narrowly tailored plan. As Justice Powell made clear in *Bakke*, truly individualized consideration demands that race be used in a flexible, nonmechanical way. It follows from this mandate that universities cannot establish quotas for members of certain racial groups or put members of those groups on separate admissions tracks. Nor can universities insulate applicants who belong to certain racial or ethnic groups from the competition for admission. Universities can, however, consider race or ethnicity more flexibly as a "plus" factor in the context of individualized consideration of each and every applicant.

We are satisfied that the Law School's admissions program, like the Harvard plan described by Justice Powell, does not operate as a quota. Properly understood, a "quota" is a program in which a certain fixed number or proportion of opportunities are "reserved exclusively for certain minority groups." Quotas "impose a fixed number or percentage which must be attained, or which cannot be exceeded," *Sheet Metal Workers* v. *EEOC*, 478 U.S. 421, 495 (1986), and "insulate the individual from comparison with all other candidates for the available seats." In contrast, "a permissible goal ... require[s] only a good-faith effort ... to come within a range demarcated by the goal itself," and permits consideration of race as a "plus" factor in any given case while still ensuring that each candidate "compete[s] with all other qualified applicants," *Johnson* v. *Transportation Agency, Santa Clara Cty., 480* U.S. 616, 638 (1987).

The Chief Justice believes that the Law School's policy conceals an attempt to achieve racial balancing, and cites admissions data to contend that the Law School discriminates among different groups within the critical mass. But, as The Chief Justice concedes, the number of underrepresented minority students who ultimately enroll in the Law School differs substantially from their representation in the applicant pool and varies considerably for each group from year to year.

That a race-conscious admissions program does not operate as a quota does not, by itself, satisfy the requirement of individualized consideration. When using race as a "plus" factor in university admissions, a university's admissions program must remain flexible enough to ensure that each applicant is evaluated as an individual and not in a way that makes an applicant's race or ethnicity the defining feature of his or her application. The importance of this individualized consideration in the context of a race-conscious admissions program is paramount.

Here, the Law School engages in a highly individualized, holistic review of each applicant's file, giving serious consideration to all the ways an applicant might contribute to a diverse educational environment. The Law School affords this individualized consideration to applicants of all races. There is no policy, either *de jure* or *de facto*, of automatic acceptance or rejection based on any single "soft" variable. Unlike the program at issue in *Gratz* v. *Bollinger*, the Law School awards no mechanical, predetermined diversity "bonuses" based on race or ethnicity ...

We acknowledge that "there are serious problems of justice connected with the idea of preference itself." Narrow tailoring, therefore, requires that a race-conscious admissions program not unduly harm members of any racial group. Even remedial race-based governmental action generally "remains subject to continuing oversight to assure that it will work the least harm possible to other innocent persons competing for the benefit." To be narrowly tailored, a race-conscious admissions program must not "unduly burden individuals who are not members of the favored racial and ethnic groups."

We are satisfied that the Law School's admissions program does not. Because the Law School considers "all pertinent elements of diversity," it can (and does) select nonminority applicants who have greater potential to enhance student body diversity over underrepresented minority applicants. As Justice Powell recognized in *Bakke*, so long as a race-conscious admissions program uses race as a "plus" factor in the context of individualized consideration, a rejected applicant "will not have been foreclosed from all consideration for that seat simply because he was not the right color or had the wrong surname ... His qualifications would have been weighed fairly and competitively, and he would have no basis to complain of unequal treatment under the Fourteenth Amendment." We agree that, in the context of its individualized inquiry into the possible diversity contributions of all applicants, the Law School's race-conscious admissions program does not unduly harm nonminority applicants.

In the context of higher education, the durational requirement can be met by sunset provisions in race-conscious admissions policies and periodic reviews to determine whether racial preferences are still necessary to achieve student body diversity. Universities in California, Florida, and Washington State, where racial preferences in admissions are prohibited by state law, are currently engaged in experimenting with a wide variety of alternative approaches. Universities in other States can and should draw on the most promising aspects of these race-neutral alternatives as they develop.

The requirement that all race-conscious admissions programs have a termination point "assure[s] all citizens that the deviation from the norm of equal treatment of all racial and ethnic groups is a temporary matter, a measure taken in the service of the goal of equality itself."

We take the Law School at its word that it would "like nothing better than to find a race-neutral admissions formula" and will terminate its race-conscious admissions program as soon as practicable. It has been 25 years since Justice Powell first approved the use of race to further an interest in student body diversity in the context of public higher education. Since that time, the number of minority applicants with high grades and test scores has indeed increased. We expect that 25 years from now, the use of racial preferences will no longer be necessary to further the interest approved today.

Justice Ginsburg, with whom Justice Breyer Joins, Concurring

The Court's observation that race-conscious programs "must have a logical end point," accords with the international understanding of the office of affirmative action. The International Convention on the Elimination of All Forms of Racial Discrimination, ratified by the United States in 1994, endorses "special and concrete measures to ensure the adequate development and protection of certain racial groups or individuals belonging to them, for the purpose of guaranteeing them the full and equal enjoyment of human rights and fundamental freedoms." But such measures, the Convention instructs, "shall in no case entail as a consequence the maintenance of unequal or separate rights for different racial groups after the objectives for which they were taken have been achieved."

However strong the public's desire for improved education systems may be, it remains the current reality that many minority students encounter markedly inadequate and unequal educational opportunities. Despite these inequalities, some minority students are able to meet the high threshold requirements set for admission to the country's finest undergraduate and graduate educational institutions. As lower school education in minority communities improves, an increase in the number of such students may be anticipated. From today's vantage point, one may hope, but not firmly forecast, that over the next generation's span, progress toward nondiscrimination and genuinely equal opportunity will make it safe to sunset affirmative action.

Justice Scalia, with whom Justice Thomas Joins, Concurring in part and Dissenting in part

I join the opinion of the Chief Justice. As he demonstrates, the University of Michigan Law School's mystical "critical mass" justification for its discrimination by race challenges even the most gullible mind. The admissions statistics show it to be a sham to cover a scheme of racially proportionate admissions.

I also join Parts I through VII of Justice Thomas's opinion. I find particularly unanswerable his central point: that the allegedly "compelling state interest" at issue here is not the incremental "educational benefit" that emanates from the fabled "critical mass" of minority students, but rather Michigan's interest in maintaining a "prestige" law school whose normal admissions standards disproportionately exclude blacks and other minorities. If that is a compelling state interest, everything is.

I add the following: The "educational benefit" that the University of Michigan seeks to achieve by racial discrimination consists, according to the Court, of "cross-racial understanding," and "better prepar[ation of] students for an increasingly diverse workforce and society," all of which is necessary not only for work, but also for good "citizenship." This is not, of course, an "educational benefit" on which students will be graded on their law school transcript (Works and Plays Well with Others: B+) or tested by the bar examiners (Q: Describe in 500 words or

less your cross-racial understanding). For it is a lesson of life rather than law-essentially the same lesson taught to (or rather learned by, for it cannot be "taught" in the usual sense) people three feet shorter and 20 years younger than the full-grown adults at the University of Michigan Law School, in institutions ranging from Boy Scout troops to public-school kindergartens. If properly considered an "educational benefit" at all, it is surely not one that is either uniquely relevant to law school or uniquely "teachable" in a formal educational setting. *And therefore*: If it is appropriate for the University of Michigan Law School to use racial discrimination for the purpose of putting together a "critical mass" that will convey generic lessons in socialization and good citizenship, surely it is no less appropriate – indeed, *particularly* appropriate – for the civil service system of the State of Michigan to do so. There, also, those exposed to "critical masses" of certain races will presumably become better Americans, better Michiganders, better civil servants. And surely private employers cannot be criticized – indeed, should be praised – if they also "teach" good citizenship to their adult employees through a patriotic, all-American system of racial discrimination in hiring. The nonminority individuals who are deprived of a legal education, a civil service job, or any job at all by reason of their skin color will surely understand.

Unlike a clear constitutional holding that racial preferences in state educational institutions are impermissible, or even a clear anti-constitutional holding that racial preferences in state educational institutions are OK, today's *Grutter-Gratz* split double header seems perversely designed to prolong the controversy and the litigation ... The Constitution proscribes government discrimination on the basis of race, and state-provided education is no exception.

Justice Thomas, with whom Justice Scalia Joins as to Parts I–VII, Concurring in part and Dissenting in part

... Because I wish to see all students succeed whatever their color, I share, in some respect, the sympathies of those who sponsor the type of discrimination advanced by the University of Michigan Law School (Law School). The Constitution does not, however, tolerate institutional devotion to the status quo in admissions policies when such devotion ripens into racial discrimination. Nor does the Constitution countenance the unprecedented deference the Court gives to the Law School, an approach inconsistent with the very concept of "strict scrutiny."

No one would argue that a university could set up a lower general admissions standard and then impose heightened requirements only on black applicants. Similarly, a university may not maintain a high admissions standard and grant exemptions to favored races. The Law School, of its own choosing, and for its own purposes, maintains an exclusionary admissions system that it knows produces racially disproportionate results. Racial discrimination is not a permissible solution to the self-inflicted wounds of this elitist admissions policy.

VII.

... I believe the Court's opinion to be, in most respects, erroneous. I do, however, find two points on which I agree.

A.

First, I note that the issue of unconstitutional racial discrimination among the groups the Law School prefers is not presented in this case, because petitioner has never argued that the Law School engages in such a practice, and the Law School maintains that it does not. I join the Court's opinion insofar as it confirms that this type of racial discrimination remains unlawful. Under today's decision, it is still the case that racial discrimination that does not help a university to enroll an unspecified number, or "critical mass," of underrepresented minority students is unconstitutional. Thus, the Law School may not discriminate in admissions between similarly situated blacks and Hispanics, or between whites and Asians. This is so because preferring black to Hispanic applicants, for instance, does nothing to further the interest recognized by the majority today. Indeed, the majority describes

such racial balancing as "patently unconstitutional." Like the Court, I express no opinion as to whether the Law School's current admissions program runs afoul of this prohibition.

B.

The Court also holds that racial discrimination in admissions should be given another 25 years before it is deemed no longer narrowly tailored to the Law School's fabricated compelling state interest. While I agree that in 25 years the practices of the Law School will be illegal, they are, for the reasons I have given, illegal now. The majority does not and cannot rest its time limitation on any evidence that the gap in credentials between black and white students is shrinking or will be gone in that timeframe. In recent years there has been virtually no change, for example, in the proportion of law school applicants with LSAT scores of 165 and higher who are black. In 1993 blacks constituted 1.1% of law school applicants in that score range, though they represented 11.1% of all applicants. In 2000 the comparable numbers were 1.0% and 11.3%. No one can seriously contend, and the Court does not, that the racial gap in academic credentials will disappear in 25 years. Nor is the Court's holding that racial discrimination will be unconstitutional in 25 years made contingent on the gap closing in that time.

Indeed, the very existence of racial discrimination of the type practiced by the Law School may impede the narrowing of the LSAT testing gap. An applicant's LSAT score can improve dramatically with preparation, but such preparation is a cost, and there must be sufficient benefits attached to an improved score to justify additional study. Whites scoring between 163 and 167 on the LSAT are routinely rejected by the Law School, and thus whites aspiring to admission at the Law School have every incentive to improve their score to levels above that range. Blacks, on the other hand, are nearly guaranteed admission if they score above 155. As admission prospects approach certainty, there is no incentive for the black applicant to continue to prepare for the LSAT once he is reasonably assured of achieving the requisite score. It is far from certain that the LSAT test-taker's behavior is responsive to the Law School's admissions policies. Nevertheless, the possibility remains that this racial discrimination will help fulfill the bigot's prophecy about black underperformance – just as it confirms the conspiracy theorist's belief that "institutional racism" is at fault for every racial disparity in our society.

I therefore can understand the imposition of a 25-year time limit only as a holding that the deference the Court pays to the Law School's educational judgments and refusal to change its admissions policies will itself expire. At that point these policies will clearly have failed to "eliminat[e] the [perceived] need for any racial or ethnic" discrimination because the academic credentials gap will still be there. The Court defines this time limit in terms of narrow tailoring, but I believe this arises from its refusal to define rigorously the broad state interest vindicated today. With these observations, I join the last sentence of Part III of the opinion of the Court.

*　　*　　*

For the immediate future, however, the majority has placed its *imprimatur* on a practice that can only weaken the principle of equality embodied in the Declaration of Independence and the Equal Protection Clause. "Our Constitution is color-blind, and neither knows nor tolerates classes among citizens." *Plessy* v. *Ferguson*, 163 U.S. 537, 559 (1896) (Harlan, J., dissenting). It has been nearly 140 years since Frederick Douglass asked the intellectual ancestors of the Law School to "[d]o nothing with us!" and the Nation adopted the Fourteenth Amendment. Now we must wait another 25 years to see this principle of equality vindicated. I therefore respectfully dissent from the remainder of the Court's opinion and the judgment.

Chief Justice Rehnquist, with whom Justices Scalia, Kennedy, and Thomas join, Dissenting

I agree with the Court that, "in the limited circumstance when drawing racial distinctions is permissible," the government must ensure that its means are narrowly tailored to achieve a compelling state interest. I do not believe, however, that the University of Michigan Law School's (Law School) means are narrowly tailored to the interest it asserts. The Law School claims it must take the steps it does to achieve a "critical mass" of underrepresented minority students. But its actual program bears no relation to this asserted goal. Stripped of its "critical mass" veil, the Law School's program is revealed as a naked effort to achieve racial balancing.

As we have explained many times, "[a]ny preference based on racial or ethnic criteria must necessarily receive a most searching examination." *Adarand Constructors, Inc.* v. *Peña*, 515 U.S. 200, 223 (1995). Our cases establish that, in order to withstand this demanding inquiry, respondents must demonstrate that their methods of using race "fit" a compelling state interest "with greater precision than any alternative means."

Before the Court's decision today, we consistently applied the same strict scrutiny analysis regardless of the government's purported reason for using race and regardless of the setting in which race was being used. We rejected calls to use more lenient review in the face of claims that race was being used in "good faith" because "[m]ore than good motives should be required when government seeks to allocate its resources by way of an explicit racial classification system." We likewise rejected calls to apply more lenient review based on the particular setting in which race is being used. Indeed, even in the specific context of higher education, we emphasized that "constitutional limitations protecting individual rights may not be disregarded."

Although the Court recites the language of our strict scrutiny analysis, its application of that review is unprecedented in its deference.

Respondents' asserted justification for the Law School's use of race in the admissions process is "obtaining 'the educational benefits that flow from a diverse student body.'" They contend that a "critical mass" of underrepresented minorities is necessary to further that interest. Respondents and school administrators explain generally that "critical mass" means a sufficient number of underrepresented minority students to achieve several objectives:

> To ensure that these minority students do not feel isolated or like spokespersons for their race; to provide adequate opportunities for the type of interaction upon which the educational benefits of diversity depend; and to challenge all students to think critically and reexamine stereotypes. These objectives indicate that "critical mass" relates to the size of the student body. Respondents further claim that the Law School is achieving "critical mass."

In practice, the Law School's program bears little or no relation to its asserted goal of achieving "critical mass." Respondents explain that the Law School seeks to accumulate a "critical mass" of *each* underrepresented minority group. But the record demonstrates that the Law School's admissions practices with respect to these groups differ dramatically and cannot be defended under any consistent use of the term "critical mass."

From 1995 through 2000, the Law School admitted between 1,130 and 1,310 students. Of those, between 13 and 19 were Native American, between 91 and 108 were African-American, and between 47 and 56 were Hispanic. If the Law School is admitting between 91 and 108 African Americans in order to achieve "critical mass," thereby preventing African-American students from feeling "isolated or like spokespersons for their race," one would think that a number of the same order of magnitude would be necessary to accomplish the same purpose for Hispanics and Native Americans. Similarly, even if all of the Native American applicants admitted in a given year matriculate, which the record demonstrates is not at all the case, how can this possibly constitute a "critical mass" of Native Americans in a class of over 350 students? In order for this pattern of admission to be consistent with the Law School's explanation of "critical mass," one would have to believe that the objectives of "critical mass" offered by respondents are achieved with only half the number of Hispanics and one-sixth the number of Native

Americans as compared to African Americans. But respondents offer no race-specific reasons for such disparities. Instead, they simply emphasize the importance of achieving "critical mass," without any explanation of why that concept is applied differently among the three underrepresented minority groups.

These different numbers, moreover, come only as a result of substantially different treatment among the three underrepresented minority groups ...

... Respondents have *never* offered any race-specific arguments explaining why significantly more individuals from one underrepresented minority group are needed in order to achieve "critical mass" or further student body diversity. They certainly have not explained why Hispanics, who they have said are among "the groups most isolated by racial barriers in our country," should have their admission capped out in this manner. True, petitioner is neither Hispanic nor Native American. But the Law School's disparate admissions practices with respect to these minority groups demonstrate that its alleged goal of "critical mass" is simply a sham. Petitioner may use these statistics to expose this sham, which is the basis for the Law School's admission of less qualified underrepresented minorities in preference to her. Surely strict scrutiny cannot permit these sorts of disparities without at least some explanation.

I do not believe that the Constitution gives the Law School such free rein in the use of race. The Law School has offered no explanation for its actual admissions practices and, unexplained, we are bound to conclude that the Law School has managed its admissions program, not to achieve a "critical mass," but to extend offers of admission to members of selected minority groups in proportion to their statistical representation in the applicant pool. But this is precisely the type of racial balancing that the Court itself calls "patently unconstitutional."

Finally, I believe that the Law School's program fails strict scrutiny because it is devoid of any reasonably precise time limit on the Law School's use of race in admissions. We have emphasized that we will consider "the planned duration of the remedy" in determining whether a race-conscious program is constitutional. Our previous cases have required some limit on the duration of programs such as this because discrimination on the basis of race is invidious.

The Court, in an unprecedented display of deference under our strict scrutiny analysis, upholds the Law School's program despite its obvious flaws. We have said that when it comes to the use of race, the connection between the ends and the means used to attain them must be precise. But here the flaw is deeper than that; it is not merely a question of "fit" between ends and means. Here the means actually used are forbidden by the Equal Protection Clause of the Constitution.

Justice Kennedy, Dissenting

The separate opinion by Justice Powell in *Regents of Univ. of Cal.* v. *Bakke*, 438 U.S. 265, 289–291, 315–318 (1978), is based on the principle that a university admissions program may take account of race as one, non-predominant factor in a system designed to consider each applicant as an individual, provided the program can meet the test of strict scrutiny by the judiciary. This is a unitary formulation. If strict scrutiny is abandoned or manipulated to distort its real and accepted meaning, the Court lacks authority to approve the use of race even in this modest, limited way. The opinion by Justice Powell, in my view, states the correct rule for resolving this case. The Court, however, does not apply strict scrutiny. By trying to say otherwise, it undermines both the test and its own controlling precedents.

To be constitutional, a university's compelling interest in a diverse student body must be achieved by a system where individual

assessment is safeguarded through the entire process. There is no constitutional objection to the goal of considering race as one modest factor among many others to achieve diversity, but an educational institution must ensure, through sufficient procedures, that each applicant receives individual consideration and that race does not become a predominant factor in the admissions decisionmaking. The Law School failed to comply with this requirement, and by no means has it carried its burden to show otherwise by the test of strict scrutiny.

It is difficult to assess the Court's pronouncement that race-conscious admissions programs will be unnecessary 25 years from now. If it is intended to mitigate the damage the Court does to the concept of strict scrutiny, neither petitioner nor other rejected law school applicants will find solace in knowing the basic protection put in place by Justice Powell will be suspended for a full quarter of a century. Deference is antithetical to strict scrutiny, not consistent with it.

It is regrettable the Court's important holding allowing racial minorities to have their special circumstances considered in order to improve their educational opportunities is accompanied by a suspension of the strict scrutiny which was the predicate of allowing race to be considered in the first place. If the Court abdicates its constitutional duty to give strict scrutiny to the use of race in university admissions, it negates my authority to approve the use of race in pursuit of student diversity. The Constitution cannot confer the right to classify on the basis of race even in this special context absent searching judicial review. For these reasons, though I reiterate my approval of giving appropriate consideration to race in this one context, I must dissent in the present case.

1. Why does the majority perceive institutions of higher education to be different from employment contracts? What is the impact of this distortion on the majority opinion?
2. How do the majority, concurrence, and dissenting opinions interpret Justice O'Connor's statement around a 25-year span? Which interpretation do you agree with and why? Why is this significant?
3. Why does the dissenting opinion disagree with the majority? What are the key points of disagreement?

The second case addressing affirmative action programs in admissions at the University of Michigan in 2003 was *Gratz* v. *Bollinger*. This case was brought by Jennifer Gratz and Patrick Hamacher, White Michigan residents who unsuccessfully applied to undergraduate programs at the institution. Both were informed that their high school grades and standardized test scores qualified them for admittance, however, they were less competitive than other students and they were denied admission. Both candidates claimed they were denied admission because of their race in violation of the Equal Protection Clause of the Fourteenth Amendment and of Title VI of the Civil Rights Act of 1964. The undergraduate admissions office at Michigan used such factors as: high school GPA, standardized test scores, quality of the high school, strength of their curriculum, location, relationships with alumni, leadership, as well as race. The university considered African Americans, Latinos/as, and Native Americans to be underrepresented minorities and the plaintiffs demonstrated that every qualified applicant from these groups is admitted to the university. The university created a set of guidelines that determined admissions status of students based on where they fell in the institution's matrix. Students with the same scores and classifications could receive different outcomes from the admissions process, based on their race.

GRATZ v. *BOLLINGER*, 539 U.S. 244 (2003)

Chief Justice Rehnquist Delivered the Opinion of the Court, Joined by Justices O'Connor, Scalia, Kennedy, and Thomas

Vote: 5–4

II.

B.
It is by now well established that "all racial classifications reviewable under the Equal Protection Clause must be strictly scrutinized." *Adarand Constructors, Inc.* v. *Pena*, 515 U.S. 200, 224 (1995). This "standard of review ... is not dependent on the race of those burdened or benefited by a particular classification." Thus, "any person, of whatever race, has the right to demand that any governmental actor subject to the Constitution justify any racial classification subjecting that person to unequal treatment under the strictest of judicial scrutiny."

To withstand our strict scrutiny analysis, respondents must demonstrate that the University's use of race in its current admissions program employs "narrowly tailored measures that further compelling governmental interests." Because "[r]acial classifications are simply too pernicious to permit any but the most exact connection between justification and classification," *Fullilove* v. *Klutznick*, 448 U.S. 448, 537 (1980), our review of whether such requirements have been met must entail "a most searching examination." We find that the University's policy, which automatically distributes 20 points, or one-fifth of the points needed to guarantee admission, to every single "underrepresented minority" applicant solely because of race, is not narrowly tailored to achieve the interest in educational diversity that respondents claim justifies their program.

In [*Regents of the University of California v. Bakke*, 438 U.S. 265 (1978)], Justice Powell reiterated that "[p]referring members of any one group for no reason other than race or ethnic origin is discrimination for its own sake." He then explained, however, that in his view it would be permissible for a university to employ an admissions program in which "race or ethnic background may be deemed a 'plus' in a particular applicant's file." He explained that such a program might allow for "[t]he file of a particular black applicant [to] be examined for his potential contribution to diversity without the factor of race being decisive when compared, for example, with that of an applicant identified as an Italian-American if the latter is thought to exhibit qualities more likely to promote beneficial educational pluralism." Such a system, in Justice Powell's view, would be "flexible enough to consider all pertinent elements of diversity in light of the particular qualifications of each applicant."

Justice Powell's opinion in *Bakke* emphasized the importance of considering each particular applicant as an individual, assessing all of the qualities that individual possesses, and in turn, evaluating that individual's ability to contribute to the unique setting of higher education. The admissions program Justice Powell described, however, did not contemplate that any single characteristic automatically ensured a specific and identifiable contribution to a university's diversity. Instead, under the approach Justice Powell described, each characteristic of a particular applicant was to be considered in assessing the applicant's entire application.

The current [University of Michigan College of Literature, Science, and the Arts (LSA)] policy does not provide such individualized consideration. The LSA's policy automatically distributes 20 points to every single applicant from an "underrepresented minority" group, as defined by the University. The only consideration that accompanies this distribution of points is a factual review of an application to determine whether an individual is a member of one of these minority groups. Moreover, unlike Justice Powell's example, where the race of a "particular

black applicant" could be considered without being decisive, the LSA's automatic distribution of 20 points has the effect of making "the factor of race ... decisive" for virtually every minimally qualified underrepresented minority applicant.

Respondents contend that "[t]he volume of applications and the presentation of applicant information make it impractical for [LSA] to use the ... admissions system" upheld by the Court today in *Grutter*. But the fact that the implementation of a program capable of providing individualized consideration might present administrative challenges does not render constitutional an otherwise problematic system. Nothing in Justice Powell's opinion in *Bakke* signaled that a university may employ whatever means it desires to achieve the stated goal of diversity without regard to the limits imposed by our strict scrutiny analysis.

We conclude, therefore, that because the University's use of race in its current freshman admissions policy is not narrowly tailored to achieve respondents' asserted compelling interest in diversity, the admissions policy violates the Equal Protection Clause of the Fourteenth Amendment. We further find that the admissions policy also violates Title VI and 42 U.S.C. § 1981. Accordingly, we reverse that portion of the District Court's decision granting respondents summary judgment with respect to liability and remand the case for proceedings consistent with this opinion.

It is so ordered.

Justice O'Connor, Concurring

I.

Unlike the law school admissions policy the Court upholds today in *Grutter* v. *Bollinger*, the procedures employed by the University of Michigan's (University) Office of Undergraduate Admissions do not provide for a meaningful individualized review of applicants. The law school considers the various diversity qualifications of each applicant, including race, on a case-by-case basis. By contrast, the Office of Undergraduate Admissions relies on the selection index to assign *every* underrepresented minority applicant the same, *automatic* 20-point bonus without consideration of the particular background, experiences, or qualities of each individual applicant. And this mechanized selection index score, by and large, automatically determines the admissions decision for each applicant. The selection index thus precludes admissions counselors from conducting the type of individualized consideration the Court's opinion in *Grutter*, requires: consideration of each applicant's individualized qualifications, including the contribution each individual's race or ethnic identity will make to the diversity of the student body, taking into account diversity within and among all racial and ethnic groups.

II.

Although the Office of Undergraduate Admissions does assign 20 points to some "soft" variables other than race, the points available for other diversity contributions, such as leadership and service, personal achievement, and geographic diversity, are capped at much lower levels. Even the most outstanding national high school leader could never receive more than five points for his or her accomplishments-a mere quarter of the points automatically assigned to an underrepresented minority solely based on the fact of his or her race. Of course, as Justice Powell made clear in *Bakke*, a university need not "necessarily accor[d]" all diversity factors "the same weight," and the "weight attributed to a particular quality may vary from year to year depending upon the 'mix' both of the student body and the applicants for the incoming class." But the selection index, by setting up automatic, predetermined point allocations for the soft variables, ensures that the diversity contributions of applicants cannot be individually assessed. This policy stands in sharp contrast to the law school's admissions plan, which enables admissions officers to make nuanced judgments with respect to the contributions each applicant is likely to make to the diversity of the incoming class.

For these reasons, the record before us does not support the conclusion that the University's admissions program for its College of Literature,

Science, and the Arts – to the extent that it considers race – provides the necessary individualized consideration. The University, of course, remains free to modify its system so that it does so. But the current system, as I understand it, is a non-individualized, mechanical one. As a result, I join the Court's opinion reversing the decision of the District Court.

Justice Thomas, Concurring

I join the Court's opinion because I believe it correctly applies our precedents, including today's decision in *Grutter* v. *Bollinger*. For similar reasons to those given in my separate opinion in that case, however, I would hold that a State's use of racial discrimination in higher education admissions is categorically prohibited by the Equal Protection Clause.

I make only one further observation. The University of Michigan's College of Literature, Science, and the Arts (LSA) admissions policy that the Court today invalidates does not suffer from the additional constitutional defect of allowing racial "discriminat[ion] among [the] groups" included within its definition of underrepresented minorities, because it awards all underrepresented minorities the same racial preference. The ... policy falls, however, because it does not sufficiently allow for the consideration of nonracial distinctions among underrepresented minority applicants. Under today's decisions, a university may not racially discriminate between the groups constituting the critical mass. An admissions policy, however, must allow for consideration of these nonracial distinctions among applicants on both sides of the single permitted racial classification.

Justice Breyer, Concurring in the Judgment

I concur in the judgment of the Court though I do not join its opinion. I join Justice O'Connor's opinion except insofar as it joins that of the Court. I join Part I of Justice Ginsburg's dissenting opinion, but I do not dissent from the Court's reversal of the District Court's decision. I agree with Justice Ginsburg that, in implementing the Constitution's equality instruction, government decisionmakers may properly distinguish between policies of inclusion and exclusion, for the former are more likely to prove consistent with the basic constitutional obligation that the law respect each individual equally.

Justice Stevens, with whom Justice Souter joins, Dissenting

Petitioners seek forward-looking relief enjoining the University of Michigan from continuing to use its current race-conscious freshman admissions policy. Yet unlike the plaintiff in *Grutter* v. *Bollinger*, the petitioners in this case had already enrolled at other schools before they filed their class-action complaint in this case. Neither petitioner was in the process of reapplying to Michigan through the freshman admissions process at the time this suit was filed, and neither has done so since. There is a total absence of evidence that either petitioner would receive any benefit from the prospective relief sought by their lawyer. While some unidentified members of the class may very well have standing to seek prospective relief, it is clear that neither petitioner does. Our precedents therefore require dismissal of the action.

IV.

As this case comes to us, our precedents leave us no alternative but to dismiss the writ for lack of jurisdiction. Neither petitioner has a personal stake in the outcome of the case, and neither has standing to seek prospective relief on behalf of unidentified class members who may or may not have standing to litigate on behalf of themselves. Accordingly, I respectfully dissent.

Justice Souter, with whom Justice Ginsburg joins as to Part II, Dissenting

II.

The cases now contain two pointers toward the line between the valid and the unconstitutional in race-conscious admissions schemes. *Grutter*

reaffirms the permissibility of individualized consideration of race to achieve a diversity of students, at least where race is not assigned a preordained value in all cases. On the other hand, Justice Powell's opinion in *Regents of Univ. of Cal.* v. *Bakke*, 438 U.S. 265 (1978), rules out a racial quota or set-aside, in which race is the sole fact of eligibility for certain places in a class. Although the freshman admissions system here is subject to argument on the merits, I think it is closer to what *Grutter* approves than to what *Bakke* condemns, and should not be held unconstitutional on the current record.

The record does not describe a system with a quota like the one struck down in *Bakke*, which "insulate[d]" all nonminority candidates from competition from certain seats. The *Bakke* plan "focused *solely* on ethnic diversity" and effectively told nonminority applicants that "[n]o matter how strong their qualifications, quantitative and extracurricular, including their own potential for contribution to educational diversity, they are never afforded the chance to compete with applicants from the preferred groups for the [set-aside] special admissions seats."

The plan here, in contrast, lets all applicants compete for all places and values an applicant's offering for any place not only on grounds of race, but on grades, test scores, strength of high school, quality of course of study, residence, alumni relationships, leadership, personal character, socioeconomic disadvantage, athletic ability, and quality of a personal essay. A nonminority applicant who scores highly in these other categories can readily garner a selection index exceeding that of a minority applicant who gets the 20-point bonus.

The Court nonetheless finds fault with a scheme that "automatically" distributes 20 points to minority applicants because "[t]he only consideration that accompanies this distribution of points is a factual review of an application to determine whether an individual is a member of one of these minority groups." The objection goes to the use of points to quantify and compare characteristics, or to the number of points awarded due to race, but on either reading the objection is mistaken.

The very nature of a college's permissible practice of awarding value to racial diversity means that race must be considered in a way that increases some applicants' chances for admission. Since college admission is not left entirely to inarticulate intuition, it is hard to see what is inappropriate in assigning some stated value to a relevant characteristic, whether it be reasoning ability, writing style, running speed, or minority race. Justice Powell's plus factors necessarily are assigned some values. The college simply does by a numbered scale what the law school accomplishes in its "holistic review," the distinction does not imply that applicants to the undergraduate college are denied individualized consideration or a fair chance to compete on the basis of all the various merits their applications may disclose.

Nor is it possible to say that the 20 points convert race into a decisive factor comparable to reserving minority places as in *Bakke*. Of course we can conceive of a point system in which the "plus" factor given to minority applicants would be so extreme as to guarantee every minority applicant a higher rank than every nonminority applicant in the university's admissions system. But petitioners do not have a convincing argument that the freshman admissions system operates this way ...

Any argument that the "tailoring" amounts to a set-aside, then, boils down to the claim that a plus factor of 20 points makes some observers suspicious, where a factor of 10 points might not. But suspicion does not carry petitioners' ultimate burden of persuasion in this constitutional challenge, and it surely does not warrant condemning the college's admissions scheme on this record ... As the Court indicates, we know very little about the actual role of the review committee. The point system cannot operate as a *de facto* set-aside if the greater admissions process, including review by the committee, results in individualized review sufficient to meet the Court's standards. Since the record is quiet, if not silent, on the case-by-case work of the committee, the Court would be on more defensible ground by vacating and remanding for evidence about the committee's specific determinations.

Without knowing more about how the Admissions Review Committee actually functions, it seems especially unfair to treat the candor of the admissions plan as an Achilles' heel. In contrast to the college's forthrightness in saying just what plus factor it gives for membership in an underrepresented minority, it is worth considering the character of one alternative thrown up as preferable, because supposedly not based on race. Drawing on admissions systems used at public universities in California, Florida, and Texas, the United States contends that Michigan could get student diversity in satisfaction of its compelling interest by guaranteeing admission to a fixed percentage of the top students from each high school in Michigan.

While there is nothing unconstitutional about such a practice, it nonetheless suffers from a serious disadvantage. It is the disadvantage of deliberate obfuscation. The "percentage plans" are just as race conscious as the point scheme (and fairly so), but they get their racially diverse results without saying directly what they are doing or why they are doing it. In contrast, Michigan states its purpose directly and, if this were a doubtful case for me, I would be tempted to give Michigan an extra point of its own for its frankness. Equal protection cannot become an exercise in which the winners are the ones who hide the ball.

Justice Ginsburg, with whom Justice Souter joins, Dissenting

I.

Educational institutions, the Court acknowledges, are not barred from any and all consideration of race when making admissions decisions. But the Court once again maintains that the same standard of review controls judicial inspection of all official race classifications. This insistence on "consistency," would be fitting were our Nation free of the vestiges of rank discrimination long reinforced by law. But we are not far distant from an overtly discriminatory past, and the effects of centuries of law-sanctioned inequality remain painfully evident in our communities and schools.

In the wake "of a system of racial caste only recently ended," large disparities endure. Unemployment, poverty, and access to health care vary disproportionately by race. Neighborhoods and schools remain racially divided. African-American and Hispanic children are all too often educated in poverty-stricken and underperforming institutions. Adult African Americans and Hispanics generally earn less than whites with equivalent levels of education. Equally credentialed job applicants receive different receptions depending on their race. Irrational prejudice is still encountered in real estate markets and consumer transactions. "Bias both conscious and unconscious, reflecting traditional and unexamined habits of thought, keeps up barriers that must come down if equal opportunity and nondiscrimination are ever genuinely to become this country's law and practice."

The Constitution instructs all who act for the government that they may not "deny to any person ... the equal protection of the laws." In implementing this equality instruction, as I see it, government decisionmakers may properly distinguish between policies of exclusion and inclusion. Actions designed to burden groups long denied full citizenship stature are not sensibly ranked with measures taken to hasten the day when entrenched discrimination and its aftereffects have been extirpated.

Our jurisprudence ranks race a "suspect" category, "not because [race] is inevitably an impermissible classification, but because it is one which usually, to our national shame, has been drawn for the purpose of maintaining racial inequality." But where race is considered "for the purpose of achieving equality," no automatic proscription is in order.

For, as insightfully explained: "The Constitution is both color blind and color conscious. To avoid conflict with the equal protection clause, a classification that denies a benefit, causes harm, or imposes a burden must not be based on race. In that sense, the Constitution is color blind. But the Constitution is color conscious to prevent discrimination being perpetuated and to undo the effects of past discrimination." *United States* v. *Jefferson County Bd. of Ed.*, 372 F.2d 836, 876 (CA5 1966) (Wisdom, J.). Contemporary human rights documents draw just this line; they distinguish between policies of oppression and measures designed to accelerate *de facto* equality.

The mere assertion of a laudable governmental purpose, of course, should not immunize a race-conscious measure from careful judicial inspection. Close review is needed "to ferret out classifications in reality malign, but masquerading as benign," and to "ensure that preferences are not so large as to trammel unduly upon the opportunities of others or interfere too harshly with legitimate expectations of persons in once preferred groups."

II.

Examining in this light the admissions policy employed by the University of Michigan's College of Literature, Science, and the Arts (College), and for the reasons well stated by Justice Souter, I see no constitutional infirmity. Like other top-ranking institutions, the College has many more applicants for admission than it can accommodate in an entering class. Every applicant admitted under the current plan, petitioners do not here dispute, is qualified to attend the College. The racial and ethnic groups to which the College accords special consideration (African-Americans, Hispanics, and Native-Americans) historically have been relegated to inferior status by law and social practice; their members continue to experience class based discrimination to this day. There is no suggestion that the College adopted its current policy in order to limit or decrease enrollment by any particular racial or ethnic group, and no seats are reserved on the basis of race. Nor has there been any demonstration that the College's program unduly constricts admissions opportunities for students who do not receive special consideration based on race.

The stain of generations of racial oppression is still visible in our society, and the determination to hasten its removal remains vital. One can reasonably anticipate, therefore, that colleges and universities will seek to maintain their minority enrollment – and the networks and opportunities thereby opened to minority graduates – whether or not they can do so in full candor through adoption of affirmative action plans of the kind here at issue. Without recourse to such plans, institutions of higher education may resort to camouflage. For example, schools may encourage applicants to write of their cultural traditions in the essays they submit, or to indicate whether English is their second language. Seeking to improve their chances for admission, applicants may highlight the minority group associations to which they belong, or the Hispanic surnames of their mothers or grandparents. In turn, teachers' recommendations may emphasize who a student is as much as what he or she has accomplished.

If honesty is the best policy, surely Michigan's accurately described, fully disclosed College affirmative action program is preferable to achieving similar numbers through winks, nods, and disguises.

1. What factors in the undergraduate admissions process led Justices O'Connor and Breyer to find it unconstitutional and the Law School admissions process constitutional?
2. How do the justices in the majority and concurring opinions argue for color-blind policies? How do the dissenting opinions argue for color-conscious policies? Which argument do you find most compelling in the context of higher education?
3. Another factor in elite university admissions that results in lower performing students being admitted over higher performing students is the practice of legacy admissions (automatic acceptance of the children of alumni who are frequently donors); this practice is not unconstitutional but hinders diversity and advances inequality. How should the law address this practice? Is the difference between state and private schools relevant?

In 2023, the Supreme Court returned to the question of the use of affirmative action principles, and its consideration of race, in universities with admissions processes that had a stated goal of expanding racial diversity. It is worth noting, that 80 percent of U.S. college students attend institutions with more open admissions structures where affirmative action is much less relevant in admissions decisions (Niemann and Maruyama 2005). But the elite institutions impacted by the courts' decisions are the gatekeepers to power in institutions public and private – influencing future policy making in the United States. While most of us will not attend these institutions, we are all affected by their graduates.

In the decision in *Students for Fair Admissions* v. *Harvard College* (2023), the Supreme Court evaluated the undergraduate admission systems at both Harvard University and the University of North Carolina; both are considered "elite" institutions and admissions is highly competitive, with only a fraction of applicants admitted. At Harvard, each admissions packet is reviewed by a reader who ranks the application from 1 (high) to 6 (low) on the categories of: academic, extracurricular, athletic, school support, personal, and overall. The first reader may take race into account. From here the package is considered by subcommittees and then the full committee. After all are admitted based on these scores, there is the consideration of who to "lop" off before offers are granted. The "lop list" considers only legacy status, recruited athlete status, financial aid eligibility, and race. The University of North Carolina follows a similar process with initial readers considering academic performance and rigor, standardized testing results, extracurricular involvement, essay quality, personal factors, and student background, as well as race and ethnicity. As these applications go through committee consideration, race may be considered as a factor in the discussion. The petitioner in this case is a nonprofit organization, Students for Fair Admissions (SFFA), which argues that race-based admissions programs violate Title VI of the Civil Rights Act of 1964 and the Equal Protection Clause of the Fourteenth Amendment.

STUDENTS FOR FAIR ADMISSIONS, INC. v. HARVARD COLLEGE, 600 U.S. 181 (2023)

Strict Scrutiny

Chief Justice Roberts Delivered the Opinion of the Court, Joined by Justices Thomas, Alito, Gorsuch, Kavanaugh, and Barrett

Vote: 6–2

III.

A.

In the wake of the Civil War, Congress proposed and the States ratified the Fourteenth Amendment, providing that no State shall "deny to any person ... the equal protection of the laws." Amdt. 14, §1. To its proponents, the Equal Protection Clause represented a "foundation[al] principle" – "the absolute equality of all citizens of the United States politically and civilly before their own laws." The Constitution, they were determined, "should not permit any distinctions of law based on race or color."

At first, this Court embraced the transcendent aims of the Equal Protection Clause. "What is this," we said of the Clause in 1880, "but declaring that the law in the States shall be the same for the black as for the white; that all persons, whether colored or white, shall stand equal before the laws of the States?" *Strauder* v. *West Virginia*, 100 U.S. 303, 307–309. "[T]he

broad and benign provisions of the Fourteenth Amendment" apply "to all persons," we unanimously declared six years later; it is "hostility to ... race and nationality" "which in the eye of the law is not justified." *Yick Wo* v. *Hopkins*, 118 U.S. 356, 368–369, 373–374 (1886).

Despite our early recognition of the broad sweep of the Equal Protection Clause, this Court – alongside the country – quickly failed to live up to the Clause's core commitments. For almost a century after the Civil War, state-mandated segregation was in many parts of the Nation a regrettable norm. This Court played its own role in that ignoble history, allowing in *Plessy* v. *Ferguson* the separate but equal regime that would come to deface much of America. The aspirations of the framers of the Equal Protection Clause, "[v]irtually strangled in [their] infancy," would remain for too long only that – aspirations.

After [*Plessy* v. *Ferguson*, 163 U.S. 537 (1896)], "American courts ... labored with the doctrine [of separate but equal] for over half a century." *Brown* v. *Board of Education*, 347 U.S. 483, 491 (1954). Some cases in this period attempted to curtail the perniciousness of the doctrine by emphasizing that it required States to provide black students educational opportunities equal to – even if formally separate from – those enjoyed by white students. But the inherent folly of that approach – of trying to derive equality from inequality – soon became apparent. As the Court subsequently recognized, even racial distinctions that were argued to have no palpable effect worked to subordinate the afflicted students. By 1950, the inevitable truth of the Fourteenth Amendment had thus begun to reemerge: Separate cannot be equal.

The culmination of this approach came finally in *Brown* v. *Board of Education*. In that seminal decision, we overturned *Plessy* for good and set firmly on the path of invalidating all *de jure* racial discrimination by the States and Federal Government. *Brown* concerned the permissibility of racial segregation in public schools. The school district maintained that such segregation was lawful because the schools provided to black students and white students were of roughly the same quality. But we held such segregation impermissible "*even though* the physical facilities and other 'tangible' factors may be equal." The mere act of separating "children ... because of their race," we explained, itself "generate[d] a feeling of inferiority."

The conclusion reached by the *Brown* Court was thus unmistakably clear: the right to a public education "must be made available to all on equal terms." As the plaintiffs had argued, "no State has any authority under the equal-protection clause of the Fourteenth Amendment to use race as a factor in affording educational opportunities among its citizens." The Court reiterated that rule just one year later, holding that "full compliance" with *Brown* required schools to admit students "on a racially nondiscriminatory basis." *Brown* v. *Board of Education*, 349 U.S. 294, 300–301 (1955). The time for making distinctions based on race had passed. *Brown*, the Court observed, "declar[ed] the fundamental principle that racial discrimination in public education is unconstitutional."

So too in other areas of life. Immediately after *Brown*, we began routinely affirming lower court decisions that invalidated all manner of race-based state action. In *Gayle* v. *Browder*, for example, we summarily affirmed a decision invalidating state and local laws that required segregation in busing. 352 U.S. 903 (1956) (*per curiam*). And in *Mayor and City Council of Baltimore* v. *Dawson*, we summarily affirmed a decision striking down racial segregation at public beaches and bathhouses maintained by the State of Maryland and the city of Baltimore. 350 U.S. 877 (1955) (*per curiam*).

In the decades that followed, this Court continued to vindicate the Constitution's pledge of racial equality. Laws dividing parks and golf courses; neighborhoods and businesses; buses and trains; schools and juries were undone, all by a transformative promise "stemming from our American ideal of fairness": "the Constitution ... forbids ... discrimination by the General Government, or by the States, against any citizen because of his race." *Bolling* v. *Sharpe*, 347 U.S. 497, 499 (1954). As we recounted in striking down the State of Virginia's ban on interracial marriage 13 years after *Brown*, the Fourteenth Amendment "proscri[bes] ... all invidious racial discriminations." *Loving* v. *Virginia*, 388 U.S. 1, 8 (1967). Our cases had thus "consistently denied the constitutionality of measures which restrict the rights of citizens on account of race." See also *Yick Wo*, 118 U.S., at 373–375 (commercial property); *Shelley* v. *Kraemer*, 334 U.S. 1 (1948) (housing covenants); *Hernandez* v. *Texas*, 347 U.S. 475 (1954) (composition of juries); *Dawson*, 350 U.S., at 877 (beaches and bathhouses); *Holmes* v. *Atlanta*, 350 U.S. 879 (1955) (*per curiam*) (golf courses); *Browder*, 352 U.S., at 903 (busing); *New Orleans City Park Improvement Assn.* v. *Detiege*, 358 U.S. 54 (1958) (*per curiam*) (public parks); *Bailey* v. *Patterson*, 369 U.S. 31 (1962) (*per curiam*) (transportation facilities); *Swann* v. *Charlotte-Mecklenburg Bd. of Ed.*, 402 U.S. 1 (1971) (education); *Batson* v. *Kentucky*, 476 U.S. 79 (1986) (peremptory jury strikes).

These decisions reflect the "core purpose" of the Equal Protection Clause: "do[ing] away with all governmentally imposed discrimination based on race." *Palmore* v. *Sidoti*, 466 U.S. 429, 432 (1984). We have recognized that repeatedly.

Eliminating racial discrimination means eliminating all of it. And the Equal Protection Clause, we have accordingly held, applies "without regard to any differences of race, of color, or of nationality" – it is "universal in [its] application." *Yick Wo*, 118 U.S., at 369. For "[t]he guarantee of equal protection cannot mean one thing when applied to one individual and something else when applied to a person of another color." *Regents of Univ. of Cal.* v. *Bakke*, 438 U.S. 265, 289–290 (1978). "If both are not accorded the same protection, then it is not equal."

Any exception to the Constitution's demand for equal protection must survive a daunting two-step examination known in our cases as "strict scrutiny." *Adarand Constructors, Inc.* v. *Peña*, 515 U.S. 200, 227 (1995). Under that standard we ask, first, whether the racial classification is used to "further compelling governmental interests." *Grutter* v. *Bollinger*, 539 U.S. 306, 326 (2003). Second, if so, we ask whether the government's use of race is "narrowly tailored" – meaning "necessary" – to achieve that interest. *Fisher* v. *University of Tex. at Austin*, 570 U.S. 297, 311–312 (2013) (*Fisher I*).

Outside the circumstances of these cases, our precedents have identified only two compelling interests that permit resort to race-based government action. One is remediating specific, identified instances of past discrimination that violated the Constitution or a statute. The second is avoiding imminent and serious risks to human safety in prisons, such as a race riot.

Our acceptance of race-based state action has been rare for a reason. "Distinctions between citizens solely because of their ancestry are by their very nature odious to a free people whose institutions are founded upon the doctrine of equality." That principle cannot be overridden except in the most extraordinary case.

B.

These cases involve whether a university may make admissions decisions that turn on an applicant's race. Our Court first considered that issue in *Regents of University of California* v. *Bakke*, which involved a set-aside admissions program used by the University of California, Davis, medical school.

In a deeply splintered decision that produced six different opinions – none of which commanded a majority of the Court – we ultimately ruled in part in favor of the school and in part in favor of Bakke. Justice Powell announced the Court's judgment, and his opinion – though written for himself alone – would eventually come to "serv[e] as the touchstone for constitutional analysis of race-conscious admissions policies."

Justice Powell began by finding three of the school's four justifications for its policy not sufficiently compelling. The school's first justification of "reducing the historic deficit of traditionally disfavored minorities in medical schools," he wrote, was akin to "[p]referring members of any one group for no reason other than race or ethnic origin." Yet that was "discrimination for its own sake," which "the Constitution forbids." Justice Powell next observed that the goal of "remedying ... the effects of 'societal discrimination'" was also insufficient because it was "an amorphous concept of injury that may be ageless in its reach into the past." Finally, Justice Powell found there was "virtually no evidence in the record indicating that [the school's] special admissions program" would, as the school had argued, increase the number of doctors working in underserved areas.

Justice Powell then turned to the school's last interest asserted to be compelling – obtaining the educational benefits that flow from a racially diverse student body. That interest, in his view, was "a constitutionally permissible goal for an institution of higher education." And that was so, he opined, because a university was entitled as a matter of academic freedom "to make its own judgments as to ... the selection of its student body."

But a university's freedom was not unlimited. "Racial and ethnic distinctions of any sort are inherently suspect," Justice Powell explained, and antipathy toward them was deeply "rooted in our Nation's constitutional and demographic history." A university could not employ a quota system, for example, reserving "a specified number of seats in each class for individuals from the preferred ethnic groups." Nor could it impose a "multitrack program with a prescribed number of seats set aside for each identifiable category of applicants." And neither still could it use race to foreclose an individual "from all consideration ... simply because he was not the right color."

The role of race had to be cabined. It could operate only as "a 'plus' in a particular applicant's file." And even then, race was to be weighed in a manner "flexible enough to consider all pertinent elements of diversity in light of the particular qualifications of each applicant." Justice Powell derived this approach from what he called the "illuminating example" of the admissions system then used by Harvard College. Under that system, as described by Harvard in a brief it had filed with the Court, "the race of an applicant may tip the balance in his favor just as geographic origin or a life [experience] may tip the balance in other candidates' cases." Harvard continued: "A farm boy from Idaho can bring something to Harvard College that a Bostonian cannot offer. Similarly, a black student can usually bring something that a white person cannot offer." The result, Harvard proclaimed, was that "race has been" – and should be – "a factor in some admission decisions."

No other Member of the Court joined Justice Powell's opinion. Four Justices instead would have held that the government may use race for the purpose of "remedying the effects of past societal discrimination." Four other Justices, meanwhile, would have struck down the Davis program as violative of Title VI. In their view, it "seem[ed] clear that the proponents of Title VI assumed that the Constitution itself required a colorblind standard on the part of government." The Davis program therefore flatly contravened a core "principle imbedded in the constitutional *and* moral understanding of the times": the prohibition against "racial discrimination."

C.

In the years that followed our "fractured decision in *Bakke*," lower courts "struggled to discern whether Justice Powell's" opinion constituted "binding precedent." We accordingly took up the matter again in 2003, in the case *Grutter* v. *Bollinger*, which concerned the admissions system used by the University of Michigan law school. There, in another sharply divided decision, the Court for the first time "endorse[d] Justice Powell's view that student body diversity is a compelling state interest that can justify the use of race in university admissions."

The Court's analysis tracked Justice Powell's in many respects. As for compelling interest, the Court held that "[t]he Law School's educational judgment that such diversity is essential to its educational mission is one to which we defer." In achieving that goal, however, the Court made clear – just as Justice Powell had – that the law school was limited in the means that it could pursue. The school could not "establish quotas for members of certain racial groups or put members of those groups on separate admissions tracks." Neither could it "insulate applicants who belong to certain racial or ethnic groups from the competition for admission." Nor still could it desire "some specified percentage of a particular group merely because of its race or ethnic origin."

These limits, *Grutter* explained, were intended to guard against two dangers that all race-based government action portends. The first is the risk that the use of race will devolve into "illegitimate ... stereotyp[ing]." *Richmond* v. *J. A. Croson Co.*, 488 U.S. 469, 493 (1989). Universities were thus not permitted to operate their admissions programs on the "belief that minority students always (or even consistently) express some characteristic minority viewpoint on any issue." The second risk is that race would be used not as a plus, but as a negative – to discriminate *against* those racial groups that were not the beneficiaries of the race-based preference. A university's use of race, accordingly, could not occur in a manner that "unduly harm[ed] nonminority applicants."

But even with these constraints in place, *Grutter* expressed marked discomfort with the use of race in college admissions. The Court stressed the fundamental principle that "there are serious problems of justice connected with the idea of [racial] preference itself." It observed that all "racial classifications, however compelling their goals," were "dangerous." *Grutter*,

539 U.S., at 342. And it cautioned that all "race-based governmental action" should "remai[n] subject to continuing oversight to assure that it will work the least harm possible to other innocent persons competing for the benefit."

To manage these concerns, *Grutter* imposed one final limit on race-based admissions programs. At some point, the Court held, they must end. This requirement was critical, and *Grutter* emphasized it repeatedly. "[A]ll race-conscious admissions programs [must] have a termination point"; they "must have reasonable durational limits"; they "must be limited in time"; they must have "sunset provisions"; they "must have a logical end point"; their "deviation from the norm of equal treatment" must be "a temporary matter." The importance of an end point was not just a matter of repetition. It was the reason the Court was willing to dispense temporarily with the Constitution's unambiguous guarantee of equal protection. The Court recognized as much: "[e]nshrining a permanent justification for racial preferences," the Court explained, "would offend this fundamental equal protection principle."

Grutter thus concluded with the following caution: "It has been 25 years since Justice Powell first approved the use of race to further an interest in student body diversity in the context of public higher education ... We expect that 25 years from now, the use of racial preferences will no longer be necessary to further the interest approved today."

IV.

Twenty years later, no end is in sight. "Harvard's view about when [race-based admissions will end] doesn't have a date on it." Neither does UNC's. Yet both insist that the use of race in their admissions programs must continue.

But we have permitted race-based admissions only within the confines of narrow restrictions. University programs must comply with strict scrutiny, they may never use race as a stereotype or negative, and – at some point – they must end. Respondents' admissions systems – however well- intentioned and implemented in good faith – fail each of these criteria. They

must therefore be invalidated under the Equal Protection Clause of the Fourteenth Amendment.

A.

Because "[r]acial discrimination [is] invidious in all contexts," we have required that universities operate their race-based admissions programs in a manner that is "sufficiently measurable to permit judicial [review]" under the rubric of strict scrutiny, *Fisher* v. *University of Tex. at Austin*, 579 U.S. 365, 381 (2016) (*Fisher II*). "Classifying and assigning" students based on their race "requires more than ... an amorphous end to justify it."

Respondents have fallen short of satisfying that burden. First, the interests they view as compelling cannot be subjected to meaningful judicial review. Harvard identifies the following educational benefits that it is pursuing: (1) "training future leaders in the public and private sectors"; (2) preparing graduates to "adapt to an increasingly pluralistic society"; (3) "better educating its students through diversity"; and (4) "producing new knowledge stemming from diverse outlooks." UNC points to similar benefits, namely, "(1) promoting the robust exchange of ideas; (2) broadening and refining understanding; (3) fostering innovation and problem-solving; (4) preparing engaged and productive citizens and leaders; [and] (5) enhancing appreciation, respect, and empathy, cross-racial understanding, and breaking down stereotypes."

Although these are commendable goals, they are not sufficiently coherent for purposes of strict scrutiny. At the outset, it is unclear how courts are supposed to measure any of these goals. How is a court to know whether leaders have been adequately "train[ed]"; whether the exchange of ideas is "robust"; or whether "new knowledge" is being developed? Even if these goals could somehow be measured, moreover, how is a court to know when they have been reached, and when the perilous remedy of racial preferences may cease? ... Finally, the question in this context is not one of *no* diversity or of *some*: it is a question of degree. How many fewer leaders Harvard would create without racial preferences, or how much poorer the education at Harvard would be, are inquiries no court could resolve.

Second, respondents' admissions programs fail to articulate a meaningful connection between the means they employ and the goals they pursue. To achieve the educational benefits of diversity, UNC works to avoid the underrepresentation of minority groups, while Harvard likewise "guard[s] against inadvertent drop-offs in representation" of certain minority groups from year to year. To accomplish both of those goals, in turn, the universities measure the racial composition of their classes using the following categories: (1) Asian; (2) Native Hawaiian or Pacific Islander; (3) Hispanic; (4) White; (5) African-American; and (6) Native American. It is far from evident, though, how assigning students to these racial categories and making admissions decisions based on them furthers the educational benefits that the universities claim to pursue.

For starters, the categories are themselves imprecise in many ways. Some of them are plainly overbroad: by grouping together all Asian students, for instance, respondents are apparently uninterested in whether *South* Asian or *East* Asian students are adequately represented, so long as there is enough of one to compensate for a lack of the other. Meanwhile other racial categories, such as "Hispanic," are arbitrary or undefined. And still other categories are underinclusive. When asked at oral argument "how are applicants from Middle Eastern countries classified, [such as] Jordan, Iraq, Iran, [and] Egypt," UNC's counsel responded, "[I] do not know the answer to that question."

Indeed, the use of these opaque racial categories undermines, instead of promotes, respondents' goals. By focusing on under-representation, respondents would apparently prefer a class with 15% of students from Mexico over a class with 10% of students from several Latin American countries, simply because the former contains more Hispanic students than the latter. Yet "[i]t is hard to understand how a plan that could allow these results can be viewed as being concerned with achieving enrollment that is 'broadly diverse.'" And given the mismatch between the means respondents employ and the goals they seek,

it is especially hard to understand how courts are supposed to scrutinize the admissions programs that respondents use.

The universities' main response to these criticisms is, essentially, "trust us." None of the questions recited above need answering, they say, because universities are "owed deference" when using race to benefit some applicants but not others. It is true that our cases have recognized a "tradition of giving a degree of deference to a university's academic decisions." ... Universities may define their missions as they see fit. The Constitution defines ours. Courts may not license separating students on the basis of race without an exceedingly persuasive justification that is measurable and concrete enough to permit judicial review. As this Court has repeatedly reaffirmed, "[r]acial classifications are simply too pernicious to permit any but the most exact connection between justification and classification." *Gratz* v. *Bollinger*, 539 U.S. 244, 270 (2003). The programs at issue here do not satisfy that standard.

B.

The race-based admissions systems that respondents employ also fail to comply with the twin commands of the Equal Protection Clause that race may never be used as a "negative" and that it may not operate as a stereotype.

First, our cases have stressed that an individual's race may never be used against him in the admissions process. Here, however, the First Circuit found that Harvard's consideration of race has led to an 11.1% decrease in the number of Asian-Americans admitted to Harvard. And the District Court observed that Harvard's "policy of considering applicants' race ... overall results in fewer Asian American and white students being admitted."

Respondents' admissions programs are infirm for a second reason as well. We have long held that universities may not operate their admissions programs on the "belief that minority students always (or even consistently) express some characteristic minority viewpoint on any issue." That requirement is found throughout our Equal Protection Clause jurisprudence more generally.

Yet by accepting race-based admissions programs in which some students may obtain preferences on the basis of race alone, respondents' programs tolerate the very thing that *Grutter* foreswore: stereotyping. The point of respondents' admissions programs is that there is an inherent benefit in race *qua* race – in race for race's sake. Respondents admit as much. Harvard's admissions process rests on the pernicious stereotype that "a black student can usually bring something that a white person cannot offer." UNC is much the same. It argues that race in itself "says [something] about who you are."

We have time and again forcefully rejected the notion that government actors may intentionally allocate preference to those "who may have little in common with one another but the color of their skin." The entire point of the Equal Protection Clause is that treating someone differently because of their skin color is *not* like treating them differently because they are from a city or from a suburb, or because they play the violin poorly or well.

If all this were not enough, respondents' admissions programs also lack a "logical end point."

Respondents and the Government first suggest that respondents' race-based admissions programs will end when, in their absence, there is "meaningful representation and meaningful diversity" on college campuses. The metric of meaningful representation, respondents assert, does not involve any "strict numerical benchmark," or "precise number or percentage" or "specified percentage." So what does it involve?

Numbers all the same. At Harvard, each full committee meeting begins with a discussion of "how the breakdown of the class compares to the prior year in terms of racial identities." And "if at some point in the admissions process it appears that a group is notably underrepresented or has suffered a dramatic drop off relative to the prior year, the Admissions Committee may decide to give additional attention to applications from students within that group."

The results of the Harvard admissions process reflect this numerical commitment. For the admitted classes of 2009 to 2018, black students represented a tight band of 10.0%–11.7% of the admitted pool. The same theme held true for other minority groups ...

Harvard's focus on numbers is obvious.

UNC's admissions program operates similarly. The University frames the challenge it faces as "the admission and enrollment of underrepresented minorities," a metric that turns solely on whether a group's "percentage enrollment within the undergraduate student body is lower than their percentage within the general population in North Carolina." The University "has not yet fully achieved its diversity-related educational goals," it explains, in part due to its failure to obtain closer to proportional representation.

The problem with these approaches is well established. "[O]utright racial balancing" is "patently unconstitutional." That is so, we have repeatedly explained, because "[a]t the heart of the Constitution's guarantee of equal protection lies the simple command that the Government must treat citizens as individuals, not as simply components of a racial, religious, sexual or national class." By promising to terminate their use of race only when some rough percentage of various racial groups is admitted, respondents turn that principle on its head. Their admissions programs "effectively assure that race will always be relevant ... and that the ultimate goal of eliminating" race as a criterion "will never be achieved."

Respondents' second proffered end point fares no better. Respondents assert that universities will no longer need to engage in race-based admissions when, in their absence, students nevertheless receive the educational benefits of diversity. But as we have already explained, it is not clear how a court is supposed to determine when stereotypes have broken down or "productive citizens and leaders" have been created. Nor is there any way to know whether those goals would adequately be met in the absence of a race-based admissions program. As UNC itself acknowledges, these "qualitative standard[s]" are "difficult to measure."

Third, respondents suggest that race-based preferences must be allowed to continue for at least five more years, based on the Court's statement in *Grutter* that it "expect[ed] that 25 years from now, the use of racial preferences will no longer be necessary." The 25-year mark articulated in *Grutter*, however, reflected only that Court's view that race-based preferences would, by 2028, be unnecessary to ensure a requisite level of racial diversity on college campuses. That expectation was oversold. Neither Harvard nor UNC believes that race-based admissions will in fact be unnecessary in five years, and both universities thus expect to continue using race as a criterion well beyond the time limit that *Grutter* suggested. Indeed, the high school applicants that Harvard and UNC will evaluate this fall using their race-based admissions systems are expected to graduate in 2028 – 25 years after *Grutter* was decided.

Finally, respondents argue that their programs need not have an end point at all because they frequently review them to determine whether they remain necessary. Respondents point to language in *Grutter* that, they contend, permits "the durational requirement [to] be met" with "periodic reviews to determine whether racial preferences are still necessary to achieve student body diversity." But *Grutter* never suggested that periodic review could make unconstitutional conduct constitutional. To the contrary, the Court made clear that race-based admissions programs eventually had to end – despite whatever periodic review universities conducted.

Here, however, Harvard concedes that its race-based admissions program has no end point. And it acknowledges that the way it thinks about the use of race in its admissions process "is the same now as it was" nearly 50 years ago. UNC's race-based admissions program is likewise not set to expire any time soon – nor, indeed, any time at all. The University admits that it "has not set forth a proposed time period in which it believes it can end all race-conscious admissions practices." And UNC suggests that it might soon use race to a *greater* extent than it currently does. In short, there is no reason to believe that respondents will – even acting in good faith – comply with the Equal Protection Clause any time soon.

V.

The dissenting opinions resist these conclusions. They would instead uphold respondents' admissions programs based on their view that the Fourteenth Amendment permits state actors to remedy the effects of societal discrimination through explicitly race-based measures. Although both opinions are thorough and thoughtful in many respects, this Court has long rejected their core thesis.

The principal dissent wrenches our case law from its context, going to lengths to ignore the parts of that law it does not like. The serious reservations that *Bakke*, *Grutter*, and *Fisher* had about racial preferences go unrecognized. The unambiguous requirements of the Equal Protection Clause – "the most rigid," "searching" scrutiny it entails – go without note. *Fisher I*, 570 U.S., at 310. And the repeated demands that race-based admissions programs must end go overlooked – contorted, worse still, into a demand that such programs never stop.

Most troubling of all is what the dissent must make these omissions to defend: a judiciary that picks winners and losers based on the color of their skin. While the dissent would certainly not permit university programs that discriminated *against* black and Latino applicants, it is perfectly willing to let the programs here continue. In its view, this Court is supposed to tell state actors when they have picked the right races to benefit. Separate but equal is "*inherently* unequal," said *Brown*. It depends, says the dissent.

That is a remarkable view of the judicial role – remarkably wrong. Lost in the false pretense of judicial humility that the dissent espouses is a claim to power so radical, so destructive, that it required a Second Founding to undo.

VI.

For the reasons provided above, the Harvard and UNC admissions programs cannot be reconciled with the guarantees of the Equal Protection Clause. Both programs lack sufficiently focused and measurable objectives warranting the use of race, unavoidably employ race in a negative manner, involve racial stereotyping, and lack meaningful end points. We have never permitted admissions programs to work in that way, and we will not do so today.

At the same time, as all parties agree, nothing in this opinion should be construed as prohibiting universities from considering an applicant's discussion of how race affected his or her life, be it through discrimination, inspiration, or otherwise. But, despite the dissent's assertion to the contrary, universities may not simply establish through application essays or other means the regime we hold unlawful today. A benefit to a student who overcame racial discrimination, for example, must be tied to *that student's* courage and determination. Or a benefit to a student whose heritage or culture motivated him or her to assume a leadership role or attain a particular goal must be tied to *that student's* unique ability to contribute to the university. In other words, the student must be treated based on his or her experiences as an individual – not on the basis of race.

Many universities have for too long done just the opposite. And in doing so, they have concluded, wrongly, that the touchstone of an individual's identity is not challenges bested, skills built, or lessons learned but the color of their skin. Our constitutional history does not tolerate that choice.

Justice Jackson took no part in the consideration or decision of the case in No. 20–1199.

Justice Thomas, Concurring

III.

Both experience and logic have vindicated the Constitution's colorblind rule and confirmed that the universities' new narrative cannot stand. Despite the Court's hope in *Grutter* that universities would voluntarily end their race-conscious programs and further the goal of racial equality, the opposite appears increasingly true. Harvard and UNC now forthrightly state that they racially discriminate when it comes to admitting students, arguing that such discrimination is consistent with this Court's precedents. And they, along with today's dissenters, defend that discrimination as *good*. More broadly, it is becoming increasingly clear that discrimination on the basis of race – often packaged as "affirmative action" or "equity" programs – are based on the benighted notion "that it is possible to tell when discrimination helps, rather than hurts, racial minorities."

We cannot be guided by those who would desire less in our Constitution, or by those who would desire more. "The Constitution abhors classifications based on race, not only because those classifications can harm favored races or are based on illegitimate motives, but also because every time the government places citizens on racial registers and makes race relevant to the provision of burdens or benefits, it demeans us all." *Grutter*, 539 U.S. at 353 (opinion of Justice Thomas).

D.

Finally, it is not even theoretically possible to "help" a certain racial group without causing harm to members of other racial groups. "It should be obvious that every racial classification helps, in a narrow sense, some races and hurts others." And, even purportedly benign race-based discrimination has secondary effects on members of other races. The antisubordination view thus has never guided the Court's analysis because "whether a law relying upon racial taxonomy is 'benign' or 'malign' either turns on 'whose ox is gored' or on distinctions found only in the eye of the beholder." Courts are not suited to the impossible task of determining which racially discriminatory programs are helping which members of which races – and whether those benefits outweigh the burdens thrust onto other racial groups.

As the Court's opinion today explains, the zero-sum nature of college admissions – where students compete for a finite number of seats in each school's entering class – aptly demonstrates the point. Petitioner here represents Asian Americans who allege that, at the margins, Asian applicants were denied admission because of their race. Yet, Asian Americans can hardly be described as the beneficiaries of historical racial advantages. To the contrary, our Nation's first immigration ban targeted the Chinese, in part, based on "worker resentment of the low wage rates accepted by Chinese workers."

Given the history of discrimination against Asian Americans, especially their history with segregated schools, it seems particularly incongruous to suggest that a past history of segregationist policies toward blacks should be remedied at the expense of Asian American college applicants. But this problem is not limited to Asian Americans; more broadly, universities' discriminatory policies burden millions of applicants who are not responsible for the racial discrimination that sullied our Nation's past ... Today's 17-year-olds, after all, did not live through the Jim Crow era, enact or enforce segregation laws, or take any action to oppress or enslave the victims of the past. Whatever their skin color, today's youth simply are not responsible for instituting the segregation of the 20th century, and they do not shoulder the moral debts of their ancestors. Our Nation should not punish today's youth for the sins of the past.

Justice Kavanaugh, Concurring

I join the Court's opinion in full. I add this concurring opinion to further explain why the Court's decision today is consistent with and follows from the Court's equal protection precedents, including the Court's precedents on race-based affirmative action in higher education.

Justice Sotomayor, Justice Kagan, and Justice Jackson disagree with the Court's decision. I respect their views. They thoroughly recount the horrific history of slavery and Jim Crow in America, as well as the continuing effects of that history on African Americans today. And they are of course correct that for the last five decades, *Bakke* and *Grutter* have allowed narrowly tailored race-based affirmative action in higher education.

But I respectfully part ways with my dissenting colleagues on the question of whether, under this Court's precedents, race-based affirmative action in higher education may extend indefinitely into the future. The dissents suggest that the answer is yes. But this Court's precedents make clear that the answer is no.

To be clear, although progress has been made since *Bakke* and *Grutter*, racial discrimination still occurs and the effects of past racial discrimination still persist. Federal and state civil rights laws serve to deter and provide remedies for current acts of racial discrimination. And governments and universities still "can, of course, act to undo the effects of past discrimination in many permissible ways that do not involve classification by race."

In sum, the Court's opinion today is consistent with and follows from the Court's equal protection precedents, and I join the Court's opinion in full.

Justice Sotomayor, with whom Justices Kagan and Jackson join, Dissenting

The Equal Protection Clause of the Fourteenth Amendment enshrines a guarantee of racial equality. The Court long ago concluded that this guarantee can be enforced through race-conscious means in a society that is not, and has never been, colorblind. In *Brown* v. *Board of Education*, 347 U.S. 483 (1954), the Court recognized the constitutional necessity of racially integrated schools in light of the harm inflicted by segregation and the "importance of education to our democratic society." For 45 years, the Court extended *Brown*'s transformative legacy to the context of higher education, allowing colleges and universities to consider race in a limited way and for the limited purpose of promoting the important benefits of racial diversity. This limited use of race has helped equalize educational opportunities for all students of every race and background and has improved racial diversity on college campuses. Although progress has been slow and imperfect, race-conscious college admissions policies have advanced the Constitution's guarantee of equality and have promoted *Brown*'s vision of a Nation with more inclusive schools.

Today, this Court stands in the way and rolls back decades of precedent and momentous progress. It holds that race can no longer be used in a limited way in college admissions to achieve such critical benefits. In so holding, the Court cements a superficial rule of colorblindness as a constitutional principle in an endemically segregated society where race has always mattered and continues to matter. The Court subverts the constitutional guarantee of equal protection by further entrenching racial inequality in education, the very foundation of our democratic government and pluralistic society. Because the Court's opinion is not grounded in law or fact and contravenes the vision of equality embodied in the Fourteenth Amendment, I dissent.

I.

B.

Brown was a race-conscious decision that emphasized the importance of education in our society. Central to the Court's holding was the recognition that, as Justice Harlan emphasized in *Plessy* v. *Ferguson*, 163 U.S. 537 (1896), segregation perpetuates a caste system wherein Black children receive inferior educational opportunities "solely because of their race," denoting "inferiority as to their status in the community." Moreover, because education is "the very foundation of good citizenship," segregation in public education harms "our democratic society" more broadly as well. In light of the harmful effects of entrenched racial subordination on racial minorities and American democracy, *Brown* recognized the constitutional necessity of a racially integrated system of schools where education is "available to all on equal terms."

The desegregation cases that followed *Brown* confirm that the ultimate goal of that seminal decision was to achieve a system of integrated schools that ensured racial equality of opportunity, not to impose a formalistic rule of race-blindness. In *Green* v. *School Bd. of New Kent Cty.*, 391 U.S. 430 (1968), for example, the Court held that the New Kent County School Board's "freedom of choice" plan, which allegedly allowed "every student, regardless of race ... 'freely' [to] choose the school he [would] attend," was insufficient to effectuate "the command of [*Brown*]." That command, the Court explained, was that schools dismantle "well-entrenched dual systems" and transition "to a unitary, nonracial system of public education." That the board "opened the doors of the former 'white' school to [Black] children

and the ['Black'] school to white children" on a race-blind basis was not enough. Passively eliminating race classifications did not suffice when *de facto* segregation persisted. Instead, the board was "clearly charged with the affirmative duty to take whatever steps might be necessary to convert to a unitary system in which racial discrimination would be eliminated root and branch." Affirmative steps, this Court held, are constitutionally necessary when mere formal neutrality cannot achieve *Brown*'s promise of racial equality.

In so holding, this Court's post-*Brown* decisions rejected arguments advanced by opponents of integration suggesting that "restor[ing] race as a criterion in the operation of the public schools" was at odds with "the *Brown* decisions." Those opponents argued that *Brown* only required the admission of Black students "to public schools on a racially nondiscriminatory basis." Relying on Justice Harlan's dissent in *Plessy*, they argued that the use of race "is improper" because the "Constitution is colorblind." They also incorrectly claimed that their views aligned with those of the *Brown* litigators, arguing that the *Brown* plaintiffs "understood" that *Brown*'s "mandate" was colorblindness. This Court rejected that characterization of "the thrust of *Brown*." It made clear that indifference to race "is not an end in itself" under that watershed decision. The ultimate goal is racial equality of opportunity.

Those rejected arguments mirror the Court's opinion today. The Court claims that *Brown* requires that students be admitted "on a racially nondiscriminatory basis." It distorts the dissent in *Plessy* to advance a colorblindness theory. The Court also invokes the *Brown* litigators, relying on what the *Brown* "plaintiffs had argued."

If there was a Member of this Court who understood the *Brown* litigation, it was Justice Thurgood Marshall, who "led the litigation campaign" to dismantle segregation as a civil rights lawyer and "rejected the hollow, race-ignorant conception of equal protection" endorsed by the Court's ruling today. Justice Marshall joined the *Bakke* plurality and "applaud[ed] the judgment of the Court that a university may consider race in its admissions process." In fact, Justice Marshall's view was that *Bakke*'s holding should have been even more protective of race-conscious college admissions programs in light of the remedial purpose of the Fourteenth Amendment and the legacy of racial inequality in our society. The Court's recharacterization of *Brown* is nothing but revisionist history and an affront to the legendary life of Justice Marshall, a great jurist who was a champion of true equal opportunity, not rhetorical flourishes about colorblindness.

C.

Two decades after *Brown*, in *Bakke*, a plurality of the Court held that "the attainment of a diverse student body" is a "compelling" and "constitutionally permissible goal for an institution of higher education." Race could be considered in the college admissions process in pursuit of this goal, the plurality explained, if it is one factor of many in an applicant's file, and each applicant receives individualized review as part of a holistic admissions process.

Since *Bakke*, the Court has reaffirmed numerous times the constitutionality of limited race-conscious college admissions. First, in *Grutter* v. *Bollinger*, 539 U.S. 306 (2003), a majority of the Court endorsed the *Bakke* plurality's "view that student body diversity is a compelling state interest that can justify the use of race in university admissions," and held that race may be used in a narrowly tailored manner to achieve this interest.

Later, in the *Fisher* litigation, the Court twice reaffirmed that a limited use of race in college admissions is constitutionally permissible if it satisfies strict scrutiny. In *Fisher* v. *University of Texas at Austin*, 570 U.S. 297 (2013) (*Fisher I*), seven Members of the Court concluded that the use of race in college admissions comports with the Fourteenth Amendment if it "is narrowly tailored to obtain the educational benefits of diversity." Several years later, in *Fisher* v. *University of Texas at Austin*, 579 U.S. 365, 376 (2016) (*Fisher II*), the Court upheld the admissions program at the University of Texas under this framework.

Bakke, *Grutter*, and *Fisher* are an extension of *Brown*'s legacy. Those decisions recognize that "experience lend[s] support to the view that the contribution of diversity is substantial." Racially integrated schools improve cross-racial understanding, "break down racial stereotypes," and ensure that students obtain "the skills needed in today's increasingly global marketplace ... through exposure to widely diverse people, cultures, ideas, and viewpoints." More broadly, inclusive institutions that are "visibly open to talented and qualified individuals of every race and ethnicity" instill public confidence in the "legitimacy" and "integrity" of those institutions and the diverse set of graduates that they cultivate. That is particularly true in the context of higher education, where colleges and universities play a critical role in "maintaining the fabric of society" and serve as "the training ground for a large number of our Nation's leaders." It is thus an objective of the highest order, a "compelling interest" indeed, that universities pursue the benefits of racial diversity and ensure that "the diffusion of knowledge and opportunity" is available to students of all races.

This compelling interest in student body diversity is grounded not only in the Court's equal protection jurisprudence but also in principles of "academic freedom," which "long [have] been viewed as a special concern of the First Amendment." In light of "the important purpose of public education and the expansive freedoms of speech and thought associated with the university environment," this Court's precedents recognize the imperative nature of diverse student bodies on American college campuses. Consistent with the First Amendment, student body diversity allows universities to promote "th[e] robust exchange of ideas which discovers truth out of a multitude of tongues [rather] than through any kind of authoritative selection."...

In short, for more than four decades, it has been this Court's settled law that the Equal Protection Clause of the Fourteenth Amendment authorizes a limited use of race in college admissions in service of the educational benefits that flow from a diverse student body. From *Brown* to *Fisher*, this Court's cases have sought to equalize educational opportunity in a society structured by racial segregation and to advance the Fourteenth Amendment's vision of an America where racially integrated schools guarantee students of all races the equal protection of the laws.

D.

Today, the Court concludes that indifference to race is the only constitutionally permissible means to achieve racial equality in college admissions. That interpretation of the Fourteenth Amendment is not only contrary to precedent and the entire teachings of our history, but is also grounded in the illusion that racial inequality was a problem of a different generation. Entrenched racial inequality remains a reality today. That is true for society writ large and, more specifically, for Harvard and the University of North Carolina (UNC), two institutions with a long history of racial exclusion. Ignoring race will not equalize a society that is racially unequal. What was true in the 1860s, and again in 1954, is true today: Equality requires acknowledgment of inequality.

2.

Both UNC and Harvard have sordid legacies of racial exclusion. Because "[c]ontext matters" when reviewing race-conscious college admissions programs, this reality informs the exigency of respondents' current admissions policies and their racial diversity goals.

*   *   *

These may be uncomfortable truths to some, but they are truths nonetheless. "Institutions can and do change," however, as societal and legal changes force them "to live up to [their] highest ideals." It is against this historical backdrop that Harvard and UNC have reckoned with their past and its lingering effects. Acknowledging the reality that race has always mattered and continues to matter, these universities have established institutional goals of diversity and inclusion. Consistent with equal protection principles and this Court's settled law, their policies use race in a limited way with

the goal of recruiting, admitting, and enrolling underrepresented racial minorities to pursue the well-documented benefits of racial integration in education.

II.

The Court today stands in the way of respondents' commendable undertaking and entrenches racial inequality in higher education. The majority opinion does so by turning a blind eye to these truths and overruling decades of precedent, "content for now to disguise" its ruling as an application of "established law and move on." As Justice Thomas puts it, "*Grutter* is, for all intents and purposes, overruled."

It is a disturbing feature of today's decision that the Court does not even attempt to make the extraordinary showing required by *stare decisis*. The Court simply moves the goalposts, upsetting settled expectations and throwing admissions programs nationwide into turmoil. In the end, however, it is clear why the Court is forced to change the rules of the game to reach its desired outcome: Under a faithful application of the Court's settled legal framework, Harvard and UNC's admissions programs are constitutional and comply with Title VI of the Civil Rights Act of 1964.

III.

The Court concludes that Harvard's and UNC's policies are unconstitutional because they serve objectives that are insufficiently measurable, employ racial categories that are imprecise and overbroad, rely on racial stereotypes and disadvantage nonminority groups, and do not have an end point. In reaching this conclusion, the Court claims those supposed issues with respondents' programs render the programs insufficiently "narrow" under the strict scrutiny framework that the Court's precedents command. In reality, however, "the Court today cuts through the kudzu" and overrules its "higher-education precedents" following *Bakke*.

There is no better evidence that the Court is overruling the Court's precedents than those precedents themselves. "Every one of the arguments made by the majority can be found in the dissenting opinions filed in [the] cases" the majority now overrules. ... see, e.g., *Grutter*, 539 U.S., at 354 (Thomas, J., concurring in part and dissenting in part) ("Unlike the majority, I seek to define with precision the interest being asserted"); *Fisher II*, 579 U.S., at 389 (Thomas, J., dissenting) (race-conscious admissions programs "res[t] on pernicious assumptions about race"); (Alito, J., joined by Roberts, C. J., and Thomas, J., dissenting) (diversity interests "are laudable goals, but they are not concrete or precise"); (race-conscious college admissions plan "discriminates against Asian-American students"); (race-conscious admissions plan is unconstitutional because it "does not specify what it means to be 'African-American,' 'Hispanic,' 'Asian American,' 'Native American,' or 'White'"); (race-conscious college admissions policies rest on "pernicious stereotype[s]").

Lost arguments are not grounds to overrule a case. When proponents of those arguments, greater now in number on the Court, return to fight old battles anew, it betrays an unrestrained disregard for precedent. It fosters the People's suspicions that "bedrock principles are founded ... in the proclivities of individuals" on this Court, not in the law, and it degrades "the integrity of our constitutional system of government." *Vasquez* v. *Hillery*, 474 U.S. 254, 265 (1986). Nowhere is the damage greater than in cases like these that touch upon matters of representation and institutional legitimacy.

The Court offers no justification, much less a "special justification," for its costly endeavor. Nor could it. There is no basis for overruling *Bakke*, *Grutter*, and *Fisher*. The Court's precedents were correctly decided, the opinion today is not workable and creates serious equal protection problems, important reliance interests favor respondents, and there are no legal or factual developments favoring the Court's reckless course. At bottom, the six unelected members of today's majority upend the status quo based on their policy preferences about what race in America should be like, but is not, and their

preferences for a veneer of colorblindness in a society where race has always mattered and continues to matter in fact and in law.

A.

2.

In the end, when the Court speaks of a "colorblind" Constitution, it cannot really mean it, for it is faced with a body of law that recognizes that race-conscious measures are permissible under the Equal Protection Clause. Instead, what the Court actually lands on is an understanding of the Constitution that is "colorblind" *sometimes*, when the Court so chooses. Behind those choices lie the Court's own value judgments about what type of interests are sufficiently compelling to justify race-conscious measures.

Overruling decades of precedent, today's newly constituted Court singles out the limited use of race in holistic college admissions. It strikes at the heart of *Bakke*, *Grutter*, and *Fisher* by holding that racial diversity is an "inescapably imponderable" objective that cannot justify race-conscious affirmative action, even though respondents' objectives simply "mirror the 'compelling interest' this Court has approved" many times in the past. At bottom, without any new factual or legal justification, the Court overrides its longstanding holding that diversity in higher education is of compelling value.

IV.

The use of race in college admissions has had profound consequences by increasing the enrollment of underrepresented minorities on college campuses. This Court presupposes that segregation is a sin of the past and that race-conscious college admissions have played no role in the progress society has made. The fact that affirmative action in higher education "has worked and is continuing to work" is no reason to abandon the practice today.

Experience teaches that the consequences of today's decision will be destructive. The two lengthy trials below simply confirmed what we already knew: Superficial colorblindness in a society that systematically segregates opportunity will cause a sharp decline in the rates at which underrepresented minority students enroll in our Nation's colleges and universities, turning the clock back and undoing the slow yet significant progress already achieved.

The costly result of today's decision harms not just respondents and students but also our institutions and democratic society more broadly. Dozens of *amici* from nearly every sector of society agree that the absence of race-conscious college admissions will decrease the pipeline of racially diverse college graduates to crucial professions. Those *amici* include the United States, which emphasizes the need for diversity in the Nation's military, and in the federal workforce more generally. The United States explains that "the Nation's military strength and readiness depend on a pipeline of officers who are both highly qualified and racially diverse – and who have been educated in diverse environments that prepare them to lead increasingly diverse forces."

Today's decision further entrenches racial inequality by making these pipelines to leadership roles less diverse. A college degree, particularly from an elite institution, carries with it the benefit of powerful networks and the opportunity for socioeconomic mobility. Admission to college is therefore often the entry ticket to top jobs in workplaces where important decisions are made ... A less diverse pipeline to these top jobs accumulates wealth and power unequally across racial lines, exacerbating racial disparities in a society that already dispenses prestige and privilege based on race.

By ending race-conscious college admissions, this Court closes the door of opportunity that the Court's precedents helped open to young students of every race. It creates a leadership pipeline that is less diverse than our increasingly diverse society, reserving "positions of influence, affluence, and prestige in America" for a predominantly white pool of college graduates. At its core, today's decision exacerbates segregation and diminishes the inclusivity of our Nation's institutions in service of superficial neutrality that promotes indifference to inequality and ignores the reality of race.

Justice Jackson, with whom Justices Sotomayor and Kagan join, Dissenting

Gulf-sized race-based gaps exist with respect to the health, wealth, and well-being of American citizens. They were created in the distant past, but have indisputably been passed down to the present day through the generations. Every moment these gaps persist is a moment in which this great country falls short of actualizing one of its foundational principles – the "self-evident" truth that all of us are created equal. Yet, today, the Court determines that holistic admissions programs like the one that the University of North Carolina (UNC) has operated, consistent with *Grutter* v. *Bollinger*, 539 U.S. 306 (2003), are a problem with respect to achievement of that aspiration, rather than a viable solution (as has long been evident to historians, sociologists, and policymakers alike).

Justice Sotomayor has persuasively established that nothing in the Constitution or Title VI prohibits institutions from taking race into account to ensure the racial diversity of admits in higher education. I join her opinion without qualification. I write separately to expound upon the universal benefits of considering race in this context, in response to a suggestion that has permeated this legal action from the start. Students for Fair Admissions (SFFA) has maintained, both subtly and overtly, that it is *unfair* for a college's admissions process to consider race as one factor in a holistic review of its applicants.

This contention blinks both history and reality in ways too numerous to count. But the response is simple: Our country has never been colorblind. Given the lengthy history of state-sponsored race-based preferences in America, to say that anyone is now victimized if a college considers whether that legacy of discrimination has unequally advantaged its applicants fails to acknowledge the well-documented "intergenerational transmission of inequality" that still plagues our citizenry.

It is *that* inequality that admissions programs such as UNC's help to address, to the benefit of us all. Because the majority's judgment stunts that progress without any basis in law, history, logic, or justice, I dissent.

I.

B.

History speaks. In some form, it can be heard forever. The race-based gaps that first developed centuries ago are echoes from the past that still exist today. By all accounts, they are still stark.

Start with wealth and income. Just four years ago, in 2019, Black families' median wealth was approximately $24,000. For White families, that number was approximately eight times as much (about $188,000). These wealth disparities "exis[t] at every income and education level," so, "[o]n average, white families with college degrees have over $300,000 more wealth than black families with college degrees." This disparity has also accelerated over time – from a roughly $40,000 gap between White and Black household median net worth in 1993 to a roughly $135,000 gap in 2019. Median income numbers from 2019 tell the same story: $76,057 for White households, $98,174 for Asian households, $56,113 for Latino households, and $45,438 for Black households.

These financial gaps are unsurprising in light of the link between home ownership and wealth. Today, as was true 50 years ago, Black home ownership trails White home ownership by approximately 25 percentage points. Moreover, Black Americans' homes (relative to White Americans') constitute a greater percentage of household wealth, yet tend to be worth less, are subject to higher effective property taxes, and generally lost more value in the Great Recession.

From those markers of social and financial unwellness flow others. In most state flagship higher educational institutions, the percentage of Black undergraduates is lower than the percentage of Black high school graduates in that State. Black Americans in their late twenties are about half as likely as their White counterparts to have college degrees. And because lower family income and wealth force students to borrow more, those Black students who do graduate college find themselves four years out with about $50,000 in student debt – nearly twice as much as their White compatriots.

As for postsecondary professional arenas, despite being about 13% of the population, Black people make up only about 5% of lawyers. Such disparity also appears in the business realm: Of the roughly 1,800 chief executive officers to have appeared on the well-known Fortune 500 list, fewer than 25 have been Black (as of 2022, only six are Black). Furthermore, as the COVID-19 pandemic raged, Black-owned small businesses failed at dramatically higher rates than White-owned small businesses, partly due to the disproportionate denial of the forgivable loans needed to survive the economic downturn.

Health gaps track financial ones. When tested, Black children have blood lead levels that are twice the rate of White children – "irreversible" contamination working irremediable harm on developing brains. Black (and Latino) children with heart conditions are more likely to die than their White counterparts. Race-linked mortality-rate disparity has also persisted, and is highest among infants.

"Across the board, Black Americans experience the highest rates of obesity, hypertension, maternal mortality, infant mortality, stroke, and asthma." These and other disparities – the predictable result of opportunity disparities – lead to at least 50,000 excess deaths a year for Black Americans vis-à-vis White Americans. That is 80 million excess years of life lost from just 1999 through 2020.

Amici tell us that "race-linked health inequities pervad[e] nearly every index of human health" resulting "in an overall reduced life expectancy for racial and ethnic minorities that cannot be explained by genetics." Meanwhile – tying health and wealth together – while she lays dying, the typical Black American "pay[s] more for medical care and incur[s] more medical debt."

III.

B.

The overarching reason the majority gives for becoming an impediment to racial progress – that its own conception of the Fourteenth Amendment's Equal Protection Clause leaves it no other option – has a wholly self-referential, two-dimensional flatness. The majority and concurring opinions rehearse this Court's idealistic vision of racial equality, from *Brown* forward, with appropriate lament for past indiscretions. But the race-linked gaps that the law (aided by this Court) previously founded and fostered – which indisputably define our present reality – are strangely absent and do not seem to matter.

With let-them-eat-cake obliviousness, today, the majority pulls the ripcord and announces "colorblindness for all" by legal fiat. But deeming race irrelevant in law does not make it so in life. And having so detached itself from this country's actual past and present experiences, the Court has now been lured into interfering with the crucial work that UNC and other institutions of higher learning are doing to solve America's real-world problems.

No one benefits from ignorance. Although formal race-linked legal barriers are gone, race still matters to the lived experiences of all Americans in innumerable ways, and today's ruling makes things worse, not better. The best that can be said of the majority's perspective is that it proceeds (ostrich-like) from the hope that preventing consideration of race will end racism. But if that is its motivation, the majority proceeds in vain. If the colleges of this country are required to ignore a thing that matters, it will not just go away. It will take *longer* for racism to leave us. And, ultimately, ignoring race just makes it matter more.

The only way out of this morass – for all of us – is to stare at racial disparity unblinkingly, and then do what evidence and experts tell us is required to level the playing field and march forward together, collectively striving to achieve true equality for all Americans. It is no small irony that the judgment the majority hands down today will forestall the end of race-based disparities in this country, making the colorblind world the majority wistfully touts much more difficult to accomplish.

1. How do the majority and dissent differ in their understanding of what the law requires to provide equal protection?
2. How does this interpretation impact their expectations of color-blind versus color-conscious policies?
3. What do you believe is the obligation of institutions of higher education in terms of admission policies relative to racial identity?
4. Should there be a different expectation of public and private institutions?

6.1.2 Affirmative Action in K-12 Education

After the Supreme Court decisions in *Grutter* and *Gratz*, some states banned race-conscious admissions and implemented non-race-based remedies to advance diversity in higher education. They used such policies as automatically admitting the top 10 percent of every high school class to their state university, utilizing application criteria that focus on resilience and "overcoming," or emphasizing recruiting and supporting first-generation students. However, racial representation in college did decrease in these states after affirmative action was ended (Mickey-Pabello 2020). The Court soon turned its focus on the use of race-conscious plans in primary and secondary schools as it continued to address the claims of the *Brown* v. *Board of Education* litigation. By the twenty-first century, it was clear that public education was still segregated and access to quality education was also racialized. In *Parents Involved in Community Schools* v. *Seattle School District No. 1* (2007), the U.S. Supreme Court evaluated the constitutionality of school district assignment plans which rely upon race. In the Seattle Washington public schools, students were assigned to oversubscribed high schools based upon whether their racial identity would help to diversify the high school. In the Jefferson County school system, sited in Louisville, Kentucky, race was used to assign some students to elementary schools and transfer students to their new schools. In these districts, the goal was to maintain the racial balance of each school within a range that reflected the overall racial representation within the school district. Parents of affected children claimed such policies violated the Fourteenth Amendment's guarantees of equal protection of the laws. The decision was a plurality opinion in which the five justices disagree as to their reasoning.

PARENTS INVOLVED IN COMMUNITY SCHOOLS v. SEATTLE SCHOOL DISTRICT NO. 1, 551 U.S. 701 (2007)

Chief Justice Roberts Announced the Judgment of the Court and Delivered the Opinion of the Court with Respect to Parts I, II, III-A, and III-C, Joined by Justice Kennedy, and an Opinion with Respect to Parts III-B and IV, in which Justices Scalia, Thomas, and Alito join

Vote: 5–4

I.

Both cases present the same underlying legal question – whether a public school that had not operated legally segregated schools or has been found to be unitary may choose to classify students by race and rely upon that classification in making school assignments ...

III.

A.

It is well established that when the government distributes burdens or benefits on the basis of individual racial classifications, that action is reviewed under strict scrutiny. As the Court recently reaffirmed, "racial classifications are simply too pernicious to permit any but the most exact connection between justification and classification." *Gratz*

v. *Bollinger*, 539 U.S. 244, 270 (2003). In order to satisfy this searching standard of review, the school districts must demonstrate that the use of individual racial classifications in the assignment plans here under review is "narrowly tailored" to achieve a "compelling" government interest.

Without attempting in these cases to set forth all the interests a school district might assert, it suffices to note that our prior cases, in evaluating the use of racial classifications in the school context, have recognized two interests that qualify as compelling. The first is the compelling interest of remedying the effects of past intentional discrimination. See *Freeman* v. *Pitts*, 503 U.S. 467, 494 (1992). Yet the Seattle public schools have not shown that they were ever segregated by law, and were not subject to court-ordered desegregation decrees. The Jefferson County public schools were previously segregated by law and were subject to a desegregation decree entered in 1975. In 2000, the District Court that entered that decree dissolved it, finding that Jefferson County had "eliminated the vestiges associated with the former policy of segregation and its pernicious effects," and thus had achieved "unitary" status. Jefferson County accordingly does not rely upon an interest in remedying the effects of past intentional discrimination in defending its present use of race in assigning students.

Nor could it. We have emphasized that the harm being remedied by mandatory desegregation plans is the harm that is traceable to segregation, and that "the Constitution is not violated by racial imbalance in the schools, without more." *Milliken* v. *Bradley*, 433 U.S. 267, 280, n. 14 (1977). Once Jefferson County achieved unitary status, it had remedied the constitutional wrong that allowed race-based assignments. Any continued use of race must be justified on some other basis.

The second government interest we have recognized as compelling for purposes of strict scrutiny is the interest in diversity in higher education upheld in *Grutter* [v. *Bollinger*, 539 U.S. 306, at 328 (2003)]. The specific interest found compelling in *Grutter* was student body diversity "in the context of higher education." The diversity interest was not focused on race alone but encompassed "all factors that may contribute to student body diversity."

The entire gist of the analysis in *Grutter* was that the admissions program at issue there focused on each applicant as an individual, and not simply as a member of a particular racial group ...

In the present cases, by contrast, race is not considered as part of a broader effort to achieve "exposure to widely diverse people, cultures, ideas, and viewpoints," race, for some students, is determinative standing alone. The districts argue that other factors, such as student preferences, affect assignment decisions under their plans, but under each plan when race comes into play, it is decisive by itself. It is not simply one factor weighed with others in reaching a decision, as in *Grutter*; it is *the* factor ...

Even when it comes to race, the plans here employ only a limited notion of diversity, viewing race exclusively in white/nonwhite terms in Seattle and black/"other" terms in Jefferson County. The Seattle "Board Statement Reaffirming Diversity Rationale" speaks of the "inherent educational value" in "[p]roviding students the opportunity to attend schools with diverse student enrollment." But under the Seattle plan, a school with 50 percent Asian-American students and 50 percent white students but no African-American, Native-American, or Latino students would qualify as balanced, while a school with 30 percent Asian-American, 25 percent African-American, 25 percent Latino, and 20 percent white students would not. It is hard to understand how a plan that could allow these results can be viewed as being concerned with achieving enrollment that is "broadly diverse."

In upholding the admissions plan in *Grutter*, though, this Court relied upon considerations unique to institutions of higher education ... The present cases are not governed by *Grutter*.

B.

Perhaps recognizing that reliance on *Grutter* cannot sustain their plans, both school districts assert additional interests, distinct from the interest upheld in *Grutter*, to justify their race-based assignments. In briefing and argument before this Court, Seattle contends that its use of race helps to reduce racial concentration in schools and to ensure that racially concentrated housing patterns do not prevent nonwhite students from having access to the most desirable schools. Jefferson County has articulated a similar goal, phrasing its interest in terms of educating its students "in a racially integrated environment." Each school district argues that educational and broader socialization benefits flow from a racially diverse learning environment, and each contends that because the diversity they seek is racial diversity – not the broader diversity at issue in *Grutter* – it makes sense to promote that interest directly by relying on race alone.

The plans are tied to each district's specific racial demographics, rather than to any pedagogic concept of the level of diversity needed to obtain the asserted educational benefits ... The plans here are not tailored to achieving a degree of diversity necessary to realize the asserted educational benefits; instead the plans are tailored, in the words of Seattle's Manager of Enrollment Planning, Technical Support, and

Demographics, to "the goal established by the school board of attaining a level of diversity within the schools that approximates the district's overall demographics."

The districts offer no evidence that the level of racial diversity necessary to achieve the asserted educational benefits happens to coincide with the racial demographics of the respective school districts – or rather the white/nonwhite or black/"other" balance of the districts, since that is the only diversity addressed by the plans.

In fact, in each case the extreme measure of relying on race in assignments is unnecessary to achieve the stated goals, even as defined by the districts ... When the actual racial breakdown is considered, enrolling students without regard to their race yields a substantially diverse student body under any definition of diversity.

This working backward to achieve a particular type of racial balance, rather than working forward from some demonstration of the level of diversity that provides the purported benefits, is a fatal flaw under our existing precedent. We have many times over reaffirmed that "[r]acial balance is not to be achieved for its own sake." *Freeman* v. *Pitts*, 503 U.S. 467, at 494 (1992). *Grutter* itself reiterated that "outright racial balancing" is "patently unconstitutional."

Accepting racial balancing as a compelling state interest would justify the imposition of racial proportionality throughout American society, contrary to our repeated recognition that "[a]t the heart of the Constitution's guarantee of equal protection lies the simple command that the Government must treat citizens as individuals, not as simply components of a racial, religious, sexual or national class." *Miller* v. *Johnson*, 515 U.S. 900, 911 (1995). Allowing racial balancing as a compelling end in itself would "effectively assur[e] that race will always be relevant in American life, and that the 'ultimate goal' of 'eliminating entirely from governmental decisionmaking such irrelevant factors as a human being's race' will never be achieved." An interest "linked to nothing other than proportional representation of various races ... would support indefinite use of racial classifications, employed first to obtain the appropriate

mixture of racial views and then to ensure that the [program] continues to reflect that mixture."

The validity of our concern that racial balancing has "no logical stopping point," is demonstrated here by the degree to which the districts tie their racial guidelines to their demographics. As the districts' demographics shift, so too will their definition of racial diversity.

The districts have also failed to show that they considered methods other than explicit racial classifications to achieve their stated goals. Narrow tailoring requires "serious, good faith consideration of workable race-neutral alternatives," and yet in Seattle several alternative assignment plans – many of which would not have used express racial classifications – were rejected with little or no consideration.

IV.

Justice Breyer's dissent takes a different approach to these cases, one that fails to ground the result it would reach in law. Instead, it selectively relies on inapplicable precedent and even dicta while dismissing contrary holdings, alters and misapplies our well-established legal framework for assessing equal protection challenges to express racial classifications, and greatly exaggerates the consequences of today's decision.

Justice Breyer also suggests that other means for achieving greater racial diversity in schools are necessarily unconstitutional if the racial classifications at issue in these cases cannot survive strict scrutiny. These other means – e.g., where to construct new schools, how to allocate resources among schools, and which academic offerings to provide to attract students to certain schools – implicate different considerations than the explicit racial classifications at issue in these cases, and we express no opinion on their validity – not even in *dicta*. Rather, we employ the familiar and well-established analytic approach of strict scrutiny to evaluate the plans at issue today, an approach that in no way warrants the dissent's cataclysmic concerns. Under that approach, the school districts have not carried their burden of showing that the ends they seek justify the particular extreme means they have chosen – classifying individual students on the basis of their race and discriminating among them on that basis.

* * *

If the need for the racial classifications embraced by the school districts is unclear, even on the districts' own terms, the costs are undeniable. Government action dividing us by race is inherently suspect because such classifications promote "notions of racial inferiority and lead to a politics of racial hostility" [*Richmond* v. *Croson*, 488 U.S. 469 (1989)], "reinforce the belief, held by too many for too much of our history, that individuals should be judged by the color of their skin," *Shaw* v. *Reno*, 509 U.S. 630, 657 (1993), and "endorse race-based reasoning and the conception of a Nation divided into racial blocs, thus contributing to an escalation of racial hostility and conflict." ...

All this is true enough in the contexts in which these statements were made – government contracting, voting districts, allocation of broadcast licenses, and electing state officers – but when it comes to using race to assign children to schools, history will be heard. In *Brown* v. *Board of Education*, 347 U.S. 483 (1954) (*Brown I*), we held that segregation deprived black children of equal educational opportunities regardless of whether school facilities and other tangible factors were equal, because government classification and separation on grounds of race themselves denoted inferiority. It was not the inequality of the facilities but the fact of legally separating children on the basis of race on which the Court relied to find a constitutional violation in 1954. The next Term, we accordingly stated that "full compliance" with *Brown I* required school districts "to achieve a system of determining admission to the public schools *on a nonracial basis*." *Brown II*, 349 U.S., at 300–301 (1955).

The parties and their *amici* debate which side is more faithful to the heritage of *Brown*, but the position of the plaintiffs in *Brown* was spelled out in their brief and could not have been clearer: "[T]he Fourteenth Amendment prevents states from according differential treatment to

American children on the basis of their color or race." What do the racial classifications at issue here do, if not accord differential treatment on the basis of race? As counsel who appeared before this Court for the plaintiffs in *Brown* put it: "We have one fundamental contention which we will seek to develop in the course of this argument, and that contention is that no State has any authority under the equal-protection clause of the Fourteenth Amendment to use race as a factor in affording educational opportunities among its citizens." There is no ambiguity in that statement. And it was that position that prevailed in this Court, which emphasized in its remedial opinion that what was "[a]t stake is the personal interest of the plaintiffs in admission to public schools as soon as practicable *on a nondiscriminatory basis*," and what was required was "determining admission to the public schools *on a nonracial basis*." What do the racial classifications do in these cases, if not determine admission to a public school on a racial basis? Before *Brown*, schoolchildren were told where they could and could not go to school based on the color of their skin. The school districts in these cases have not carried the heavy burden of demonstrating that we should allow this once again – even for very different reasons. For schools that never segregated on the basis of race, such as Seattle, or that have removed the vestiges of past segregation, such as Jefferson County, the way "to achieve a system of determining admission to the public schools on a nonracial basis," is to stop assigning students on a racial basis. The way to stop discrimination on the basis of race is to stop discriminating on the basis of race.

Justice Thomas, Concurring

Today, the Court holds that state entities may not experiment with race-based means to achieve ends they deem socially desirable. I wholly concur in The Chief Justice's opinion. I write separately to address several of the contentions in Justice Breyer's dissent. Contrary to the dissent's arguments, resegregation is not occurring in Seattle or Louisville; these school boards have no present interest in remedying past segregation; and these race-based student-assignment programs do not serve any compelling state interest. Accordingly, the plans are unconstitutional. Disfavoring a color-blind interpretation of the Constitution, the dissent would give school boards a free hand to make decisions on the basis of race – an approach reminiscent of that advocated by the segregationists in *Brown* v. *Board of Education*, 347 U.S. 483 (1954). This approach is just as wrong today as it was a half-century ago. The Constitution and our cases require us to be much more demanding before permitting local school boards to make decisions based on race.

III.

Most of the dissent's criticisms of today's result can be traced to its rejection of the color-blind Constitution. The dissent attempts to marginalize the notion of a color-blind Constitution by consigning it to me and Members of today's plurality. But I am quite comfortable in the company I keep. My view of the Constitution is Justice Harlan's view in *Plessy:* "Our Constitution is color-blind, and neither knows nor tolerates classes among citizens." *Plessy* v. *Ferguson*, 163 U.S. 537, 559 (1896) (dissenting opinion). And my view was the rallying cry for the lawyers who litigated *Brown*.

The dissent appears to pin its interpretation of the Equal Protection Clause to current societal practice and expectations, deference to local officials, likely practical consequences, and reliance on previous statements from this and other courts. Such a view was ascendant in this Court's jurisprudence for several decades. It first appeared in *Plessy*, where the Court asked whether a state law providing for segregated railway cars was "a reasonable regulation." The Court deferred to local authorities in making its determination, noting that in inquiring into reasonableness "there must necessarily be a large discretion on the part of the legislature." The Court likewise paid heed to societal practices, local expectations, and practical consequences by looking to "the established usages, customs

and traditions of the people, and with a view to the promotion of their comfort, and the preservation of the public peace and good order." Guided by these principles, the Court concluded: "[W]e cannot say that a law which authorizes or even requires the separation of the two races in public conveyances is unreasonable, or more obnoxious to the Fourteenth Amendment than the acts of Congress requiring separate schools for colored children in the District of Columbia."

What was wrong in 1954 cannot be right today. Whatever else the Court's rejection of the segregationists' arguments in *Brown* might have established, it certainly made clear that state and local governments cannot take from the Constitution a right to make decisions on the basis of race by adverse possession. The fact that state and local governments had been discriminating on the basis of race for a long time was irrelevant to the *Brown* Court. The fact that racial discrimination was preferable to the relevant communities was irrelevant to the *Brown* Court. And the fact that the state and local governments had relied on statements in this Court's opinions was irrelevant to the *Brown* Court. The same principles guide today's decision. None of the considerations trumpeted by the dissent is relevant to the constitutionality of the school boards' race-based plans because no contextual detail – or collection of contextual details – can "provide refuge from the principle that under our Constitution, the government may not make distinctions on the basis of race."

In place of the color-blind Constitution, the dissent would permit measures to keep the races together and proscribe measures to keep the races apart. Although no such distinction is apparent in the Fourteenth Amendment, the dissent would constitutionalize today's faddish social theories that embrace that distinction. The Constitution is not that malleable. Even if current social theories favor classroom racial engineering as necessary to "solve the problems at hand," the Constitution enshrines principles independent of social theories. See *Plessy*, 163 U.S., at 559 (Harlan, J., dissenting) ("The white race deems itself to be the dominant race in this country. And so it is, in prestige, in achievements, in education, in wealth and in power. So, I doubt not, it will continue to be for all time ... But in view of the Constitution, in the eye of the law, there is in this country no superior, dominant, ruling class of citizens. ... Our Constitution is color-blind, and neither knows nor tolerates classes among citizens"). Indeed, if our history has taught us anything, it has taught us to beware of elites bearing racial theories. See, e.g., *Dred Scott* v. *Sandford*, 19 How. 393, 407 (1857) ("[T]hey [members of the "negro African race"] had no rights which the white man was bound to respect"). Can we really be sure that the racial theories that motivated *Dred Scott* and *Plessy* are a relic of the past or that future theories will be nothing but beneficent and progressive? That is a gamble I am unwilling to take, and it is one the Constitution does not allow.

Justice Breyer, with whom Justices Stevens, Souter, and Ginsburg join, Dissenting

These cases consider the longstanding efforts of two local school boards to integrate their public schools. The school board plans before us resemble many others adopted in the last 50 years by primary and secondary schools throughout the Nation. All of those plans represent local efforts to bring about the kind of racially integrated education that *Brown* v. *Board of Education*, 347 U.S. 483 (1954), long ago promised – efforts that this Court has repeatedly required, permitted, and encouraged local authorities to undertake. This Court has recognized that the public interests at stake in such cases are "compelling." We have approved of "narrowly tailored" plans that are no less race-conscious than the plans before us. And we have understood that the Constitution *permits* local communities to adopt desegregation plans even where it does not *require* them to do so.

The plurality pays inadequate attention to this law, to past opinions' rationales, their language, and the contexts in which they arise. As a result, it reverses course and reaches the wrong conclusion. In doing so, it distorts precedent, it misapplies the relevant constitutional principles, it announces legal rules that will obstruct efforts by state and local governments to deal effectively with the growing resegregation of public schools, it threatens to substitute for present calm a disruptive round of race-related litigation, and it undermines *Brown*'s promise of integrated primary and secondary education that local communities have sought to make a reality. This cannot be justified in the name of the Equal Protection Clause.

I.

Facts

The historical and factual context in which these cases arise is critical. In *Brown*, this Court held that the government's segregation of schoolchildren by race violates the Constitution's promise of equal protection. The Court emphasized that "education is perhaps the most important function of state and local governments." 347 U.S., at 493. And it thereby set the Nation on a path toward public school integration.

In dozens of subsequent cases, this Court told school districts previously segregated by law what they must do at a minimum to comply with *Brown*'s constitutional holding. The measures required by those cases often included race-conscious practices, such as mandatory busing and race-based restrictions on voluntary transfers. See, e.g., *Columbus Bd. of Ed.* v. *Penick*, 443 U.S. 449, 455, n. 3 (1979); *Davis* v. *Board of School Comm'rs of Mobile Cty.*, 402 U.S. 33, 37–38 (1971); *Green* v. *School Bd. of New Kent Cty.*, 391 U.S. 430, 441–442 (1968).

Beyond those minimum requirements, the Court left much of the determination of how to achieve integration to the judgment of local communities ...

As a result, different districts – some acting under court decree, some acting in order to avoid threatened lawsuits, some seeking to comply with federal administrative orders, some acting purely voluntarily, some acting after federal courts had dissolved earlier orders – adopted, modified, and experimented with hosts of different kinds of plans, including race-conscious plans, all with a similar objective: greater racial integration of public schools. The techniques that different districts have employed range "from voluntary transfer programs to mandatory reassignment." And the design of particular plans has been "dictated by both the law and the specific needs of the district."

Overall these efforts brought about considerable racial integration. More recently, however, progress has stalled. Between 1968 and 1980, the number of black children attending a school where minority children constituted more than half of the school fell from 77% to 63% in the Nation (from 81% to 57% in the South) but then reversed direction by the year 2000, rising from 63% to 72% in the Nation (from 57% to 69% in the South) ... As of 2002, almost 2.4 million students, or over 5% of all public school enrollment, attended schools with a white population of less than 1%. Of these, 2.3 million were black and Latino students, and only 72,000 were white ... In light of the evident risk of a return to school systems that are in fact (though not in law) resegregated, many school districts have felt a need to maintain or to extend their integration efforts.

The upshot is that myriad school districts operating in myriad circumstances have devised myriad plans, often with race-conscious elements, all for the sake of eradicating earlier school segregation, bringing about integration, or preventing retrogression. Seattle and Louisville are two such districts, and the histories of their present plans set forth typical school integration stories.

I describe those histories at length in order to highlight three important features of these cases. First, the school districts' plans serve "compelling interests" and are "narrowly tailored" on any reasonable definition of those terms. Second, the distinction between *de jure* segregation (caused by school systems) and *de facto* segregation (caused, e.g., by housing patterns or generalized societal discrimination) is meaningless in the present context, thereby dooming the plurality's endeavor to find support for its views in that distinction. Third, real-world efforts to substitute racially diverse for racially segregated schools (however caused) are complex, to the

point where the Constitution cannot plausibly be interpreted to rule out categorically all local efforts to use means that are "conscious" of the race of individuals.

[Discussion of Seattle and Louisville histories]

C.

The histories I have set forth describe the extensive and ongoing efforts of two school districts to bring about greater racial integration of their public schools. In both cases the efforts were in part remedial. Louisville began its integration efforts in earnest when a federal court in 1975 entered a school desegregation order. Seattle undertook its integration efforts in response to the filing of a federal lawsuit and as a result of its settlement of a segregation complaint filed with the federal OCR.

The plans in both Louisville and Seattle grow out of these earlier remedial efforts. Both districts faced problems that reflected initial periods of severe racial segregation, followed by such remedial efforts as busing, followed by evidence of resegregation, followed by a need to end busing and encourage the return of, e.g., suburban students through increased student choice. When formulating the plans under review, both districts drew upon their considerable experience with earlier plans, having revised their policies periodically in light of that experience. Both districts rethought their methods over time and explored a wide range of other means, including non-race-conscious policies. Both districts also considered elaborate studies and consulted widely within their communities.

VI.

Conclusions

... The plans before us satisfy the requirements of the Equal Protection Clause. And it is the plurality's opinion, not this dissent that "fails to ground the result it would reach in law."

Four basic considerations have led me to this view. *First*, the histories of Louisville and Seattle reveal complex circumstances and a long tradition of conscientious efforts by local school boards to resist racial segregation in public schools. Segregation at the time of *Brown* gave way to expansive remedies that included busing, which in turn gave rise to fears of white flight and resegregation. For decades now, these school boards have considered and adopted and revised assignment plans that sought to rely less upon race, to emphasize greater student choice, and to improve the conditions of all schools for all students, no matter the color of their skin, no matter where they happen to reside. The plans under review – which are less burdensome, more egalitarian, and more effective than prior plans – continue in that tradition. And their history reveals school district goals whose remedial, educational, and democratic elements are inextricably intertwined each with the others. *Second*, since this Court's decision in *Brown*, the law has consistently and unequivocally approved of both voluntary and compulsory race-conscious measures to combat segregated schools. The Equal Protection Clause, ratified following the Civil War, has always distinguished in practice between state action that excludes and thereby subordinates racial minorities and state action that seeks to bring together people of all races. From *Swann* [v. *Charlotte-Mecklenberg*, 402 U.S. 1 (1971)] to *Grutter*, this Court's decisions have emphasized this distinction, recognizing that the fate of race relations in this country depends upon unity among our children, "for unless our children begin to learn together, there is little hope that our people will ever learn to live together."

Third, the plans before us, subjected to rigorous judicial review, are supported by compelling state interests and are narrowly tailored to accomplish those goals. Just as diversity in higher education was deemed compelling in *Grutter*, diversity in public primary and secondary schools – where there is even more to gain – must be, *a fortiori*, a compelling state interest. Even apart from *Grutter*, five Members of this Court agree that "avoiding racial isolation" and "achiev[ing] a diverse student population" remain today compelling interests. These interests combine remedial, educational, and democratic objectives. For the reasons discussed above, however, I disagree with Justice Kennedy that Seattle and Louisville have not done enough to demonstrate that their present plans are necessary to continue upon the path set by *Brown*. These plans are *more* "narrowly tailored" than the race-conscious law school admissions criteria at issue in *Grutter*. Hence, their lawfulness follows *a fortiori* from this Court's prior decisions.

Fourth, the plurality's approach risks serious harm to the law and for the Nation. Its view of the law rests either upon a denial of the distinction between exclusionary and inclusive use of race-conscious criteria in the context of the Equal Protection Clause, or upon such a rigid application of its "test" that the distinction loses practical significance. Consequently, the Court's decision today slows down and sets back the work of local school boards to bring about racially diverse schools.

Indeed, the consequences of the approach the Court takes today are serious. Yesterday, the plans under review were lawful. Today, they are not. Yesterday, the citizens of this Nation could look for guidance to this Court's unanimous pronouncements concerning desegregation. Today, they cannot. Yesterday, school boards had available to them a full range of means to combat segregated schools. Today, they do not.

The Court's decision undermines other basic institutional principles as well. What has happened to *stare decisis?* The history of the plans before us, their educational importance, their highly limited use of race – all these and more – make clear that the compelling interest here is stronger than in *Grutter*. The plans here are more narrowly tailored than the law school admissions program there at issue. Hence, applying *Grutter*'s strict test, their lawfulness follows *a fortiori*. To hold to the contrary is to transform that test from "strict" to "fatal in fact" – the very opposite of what *Grutter* said ...

And what of respect for democratic local decisionmaking by States and school boards? For several decades this Court has rested its public school decisions upon *Swann*'s basic view that the Constitution grants local school districts a significant degree of leeway where the inclusive use of race-conscious criteria is at issue. Now localities will have to cope with the difficult problems they face (including resegregation) deprived of one means they may find necessary.

And what of law's concern to diminish and peacefully settle conflict among the Nation's people? Instead of accommodating different good-faith visions of our country and our Constitution, today's holding upsets settled expectations, creates legal uncertainty, and threatens to produce considerable further litigation, aggravating race-related conflict.

And what of the long history and moral vision that the Fourteenth Amendment itself embodies? The plurality cites in support those who argued in *Brown* against segregation, and Justice Thomas likens the approach that I have taken to that of segregation's defenders. But segregation policies did not simply tell schoolchildren "where they could and could not go to school based on the color of their skin;" they perpetuated a caste system rooted in the institutions of slavery and 80 years of legalized subordination. The lesson of history, see *ante*, at 39 (plurality opinion), is not that efforts to continue racial segregation are constitutionally indistinguishable from efforts to achieve racial integration. Indeed, it is a cruel distortion of history to compare Topeka, Kansas, in the 1950's to Louisville and Seattle in the modern day – to equate the plight of Linda Brown (who was ordered to attend a Jim Crow school) to the circumstances of Joshua McDonald (whose request to transfer to a school closer to home was initially declined). This is not to deny that there is a cost in applying "a state-mandated racial label." But that cost does not approach, in degree or in kind, the terrible harms of slavery, the resulting caste system, and 80 years of legal racial segregation.

*   *   *

Finally, what of the hope and promise of *Brown*? For much of this Nation's history, the races remained divided. It was not long ago that people of different races drank from separate fountains, rode on separate buses, and studied in separate schools. In this Court's finest hour, *Brown* v. *Board of Education* challenged this history and helped to change it. For *Brown* held out a promise. It was a promise embodied in three Amendments designed to make citizens of slaves. It was the promise of true racial equality – not as a matter of fine words on paper, but as a matter of everyday life in the Nation's cities and schools. It was about

the nature of a democracy that must work for all Americans. It sought one law, one Nation, one people, not simply as a matter of legal principle but in terms of how we actually live.

Not everyone welcomed this Court's decision in *Brown*. Three years after that decision was handed down, the Governor of Arkansas ordered state militia to block the doors of a white schoolhouse so that black children could not enter. The President of the United States dispatched the 101st Airborne Division to Little Rock, Arkansas, and federal troops were needed to enforce a desegregation decree. Today, almost 50 years later, attitudes toward race in this Nation have changed dramatically. Many parents, white and black alike, want their children to attend schools with children of different races. Indeed, the very school districts that once spurned integration now strive for it. The long history of their efforts reveals the complexities and difficulties they have faced. And in light of those challenges, they have asked us not to take from their hands the instruments they have used to rid their schools of racial segregation, instruments that they believe are needed to overcome the problems of cities divided by race and poverty. The plurality would decline their modest request.

The plurality is wrong to do so. The last half-century has witnessed great strides toward racial equality, but we have not yet realized the promise of *Brown*. To invalidate the plans under review is to threaten the promise of *Brown*. The plurality's position, I fear, would break that promise. This is a decision that the Court and the Nation will come to regret.

I must dissent.

Justice Stevens, Dissenting

While I join Justice Breyer's eloquent and unanswerable dissent in its entirety, it is appropriate to add these words.

There is a cruel irony in The Chief Justice's reliance on our decision in *Brown* v. *Board of Education*, 349 U.S. 294 (1955). The first sentence in the concluding paragraph of his opinion states: "Before *Brown*, schoolchildren were told where they could and could not go to school based on the color of their skin." This sentence reminds me of Anatole France's observation: "[T]he majestic equality of the la[w], forbid[s] rich and poor alike to sleep under bridges, to beg in the streets, and to steal their bread." The Chief Justice fails to note that it was only black schoolchildren who were so ordered; indeed, the history books do not tell stories of white children struggling to attend black schools. In this and other ways, The Chief Justice rewrites the history of one of this Court's most important decisions.

The Chief Justice rejects the conclusion that the racial classifications at issue here should be viewed differently than others, because they do not impose burdens on one race alone and do not stigmatize or exclude. The only justification for refusing to acknowledge the obvious importance of that difference is the citation of a few recent opinions – none of which even approached unanimity – grandly proclaiming that all racial classifications must be analyzed under "strict scrutiny." See, e.g., *Adarand Constructors, Inc.* v. *Peña*, 515 U.S. 200, 227 (1995). Even today, two of our wisest federal judges have rejected such a wooden reading of the Equal Protection Clause in the context of school integration. The Court's misuse of the three-tiered approach to Equal Protection analysis merely reconfirms my own view that there is only one such Clause in the Constitution.

If we look at cases decided during the interim between *Brown* and *Adarand*, we can see how a rigid adherence to tiers of scrutiny obscures *Brown*'s clear message. Perhaps the best example is provided by our approval of the decision of the Supreme Judicial Court of Massachusetts in 1967 upholding a state statute mandating racial integration in that State's school system. See *School Comm. of Boston* v. *Board of Education*, 352 Mass. 693, 227 N.E. 2d 729 [(1967)]. Rejecting arguments comparable to those that the plurality accepts today, that court noted: "It would be the height of irony if the racial imbalance act, enacted as it was with the laudable purpose of achieving equal educational opportunities, should, by prescribing school pupil allocations based on race, founder on unsuspected shoals in the Fourteenth Amendment."

Invoking our mandatory appellate jurisdiction, the Boston plaintiffs prosecuted an appeal in this Court. Our ruling on the merits simply stated that the appeal was "dismissed for want of a substantial federal question." That decision not only expressed our appraisal of the merits of the appeal, but it constitutes a precedent that the Court overrules today ...

The Court has changed significantly since it decided *School Comm. of Boston* in 1968. It was then more faithful to *Brown* and more respectful of our precedent than it is today. It is my firm conviction that no Member of the Court that I joined in 1975 would have agreed with today's decision.

1. According to the majority, what is the difference between higher education's reliance on diversity as an educational goal, and primary/secondary education?
2. One key conflict between the majority and the dissenters is over Chief Justice Rehnquist's reliance on *Brown* v. *Board* and how he draws parallels between the Kansas City (and other school districts') segregation and the Louisville/Seattle's race-conscious assignments. Which do you find to be the more compelling interpretation and why?

The question of race-conscious remedies, as a means of constructing our democracy to make it more racially equitable, versus adherence to color-blind principles is unresolved. In the early part of the twenty-first century, the Supreme Court has explicitly moved to advocating for color-blindness, yet evidence has shown this may result in continued racial disparities in many aspects of life (Kernahan 2016; Penner and Dovidio 2016). How do we resolve this tension? Is color-blindness inherently more fair in a nation that relied on color-conscious policies to distribute resources and structure systems of power? If not, at what point do we move away from race to diminish its constructed import in our lives?

Chief Justice Roberts in his *Parents Involved* majority opinion says, "The way to stop discrimination on the basis of race is to stop discrimination on the basis of race." But is this sufficient? Formal equality says people cannot be prevented from legally participating in public opportunities on the basis of race, but it does not address the 300 years of state-maintained racial inequity. What do you believe is the government's responsibility in providing equitable access? Are there limits to how the government should intervene? If so, what are they?

6.2 Statehood for the Unincorporated Territories

Garment industry workers in American Samoa made a minimum wage of $4.98 in 2024, despite a federal minimum wage of $7.25; however, the completed garments are sold with a "Made in the USA" label. Soldiers from Puerto Rico, Virgin Islands, Guam, American Samoa, and the Northern Mariana Islands all fight for the U.S. military, but in the Olympics their athletes compete for their home countries (Sparrow 2006, 212–213). How do these competing identities coexist? What led to such contradictions?

After the Spanish-American War (1898), political and economic leaders in the United States decided that to remain powerful in the global context, the nation needed to emulate other European nations and seek empire to become a world power. Prior to the settlement of the war by the Treaty of Paris (1899), the United States had grown its borders only via westward expansion and through buying, taking, or conquering indigenous territories contiguous to the new nation. At the beginning of the nineteenth century, the United States newly acquired several island nations, including Puerto Rico, Hawai'i, and the Philippines. Additional island nations were taken in the early twentieth century through treaties with European colonizing countries. The country eventually annexed Hawai'i, providing statehood in 1959; refused to encompass Cuba; and after the U.S. occupation of the Philippines, the Filipino people declared independence in 1946. Despite these alterations, the United States still claimed several territories. Historically, territories in the United States were treated as nascent states being groomed for inclusion and their residents perceived as American citizens with all relevant constitutional protections. However, the reality was not so simple for these new island protectorates.

In a series of Supreme Court decisions from 1901 to 1922, collectively named *The Insular Cases*, the Supreme Court wrestled with the constitutional and statutory protections extended to these new territories and their people, as well as whether Congress had the constitutional authority to claim new territories. These extremely fractured opinions (many were 5–4 opinions, with multiple concurrences and dissents) began by questioning if import taxes could be laid on Puerto Rican products shipped to the United States. In other words, is a territory treated like a sovereign foreign country or like a state within the U.S.? Two decades later, the Supreme Court wrestled with the expansion of the protection of the Bill of Rights to the territories' citizens. In these cases, there were two assertions facing the Supreme Court. The first claim was that territories and their residents have always been treated as citizens prior to receiving statehood. The second claim centered on the Black and Brown peoples of these islands and was based on the – frequently racially motivated – contention that "the people of the new territories were unfit to become citizens, a conclusion that foreclosed the possibility of statehood and relegated the people to permanent territorial status" (Pratt 1992, 434).

The Insular Cases determined that these islands, newly annexed to the United States, both "'belonged' to the United States but were not 'part of it'" (Ponsa 2015, 1). Consequently, denizens of these islands had fewer constitutional protections and no guarantee of eventual statehood. In a federalist system such as ours, where both the national government and the individual states possess enumerated and implied powers, as well as independent sources of sovereignty, people in the new territories were politically disadvantaged. The case of *Hawai'i* v. *Mankichi* (1903) demonstrates the racial implications of this construction of citizenship. After the formal grant of Hawai'ian sovereignty to the United States, Osaki Mankichi, a Japanese citizen, was convicted of manslaughter in the first degree by a Hawai'ian court and sentenced to twenty years of hard labor. Following traditional practice on the island, Mankichi was not indicted by a grand jury and the jury convicted him with a 9–3 vote. Mankichi appealed the decision as violating his Fifth and Sixth Amendments constitutional rights. The federal District Court found that his trial, conviction, sentence, and imprisonment violated the Constitution because there was not an indictment by a grand jury prior to trial, nor was he found guilty by the unanimous verdict of his peers. The question that faced the Court was how to reconcile traditional cultural practices on the island with the U.S. expectations of justice; but the case also raises the question of whether citizens of the territories warrant the same legal and constitutional practices as U.S. citizens who reside in the states.

TERRITORY OF HAWAII v. MANKICHI, 190 U.S. 197 (1903)

Justice Brown Delivered the Opinion of the Court, Joined by Justices White, McKenna, Holmes, and Day

Vote: 5–4

The question involved in this case is an extremely simple one. The difficulty is in fixing upon the principles applicable to its solution. By a joint resolution adopted by Congress, July 7, 1898, known as the Newlands Resolution, and with the consent of the Republic of Hawaii, signified in the manner provided in its Constitution, the Hawaiian islands and their dependencies were annexed "as a part of the Territory of the United States, and subject to the sovereign dominion thereof," with the following condition:

The municipal legislation of the Hawaiian Islands, not enacted for the fulfillment of the treaties so extinguished and not inconsistent with this joint resolution nor contrary to the Constitution of the United States nor to any existing treaty of the United States, shall remain in force until the Congress of the United States shall otherwise determine.

... Under the conditions named in this resolution, the Hawaiian Islands lands remained under the name of the "Republic of Hawaii" until June 14, 1900, when they were formally incorporated by act of Congress under the name of the "Territory of Hawaii." By this act, the Constitution was formally extended to these islands, and special provisions made for empaneling grand juries and for unanimous verdicts of petty juries.

The question is whether, in continuing the municipal legislation of the islands not contrary to the Constitution of the United States, it was intended to abolish at once the criminal procedure theretofore in force upon the islands, and to substitute immediately, and without new legislation, the common law proceedings by grand and petit jury, which had been held applicable to other organized territories, though we have also held that the states, when once admitted as such, may dispense with grand juries, and perhaps also allow verdicts to be rendered by less than a unanimous vote.

In fixing upon the proper construction to be given to this resolution, it is important to bear in mind the history and condition of the islands prior to their annexation by Congress. Since 1847 they had enjoyed the blessings of a civilized government, and a system of jurisprudence modeled largely upon the common law of England and the United States. Though lying in the tropical zone, the salubrity of their climate and the fertility of their soil had attracted thither large numbers of people from Europe and America, who brought with them political ideas and traditions which, about sixty years ago, found expression in the adoption of a code of laws appropriate to their new conditions. Churches were founded, schools opened, courts of justice established, and civil and criminal laws administered, and civil and criminal laws administered upon in the two countries from which most of the immigrants had come. Taking the lead, however, in a change which has since been adopted by several of the United States, no provision was made for grand juries, and criminals were prosecuted upon indictments found by judges. By a law passed in 1847, the number of a jury was fixed at twelve, but a verdict might be rendered upon the agreement of nine jurors. The question involved in this case is whether it was intended that this practice should be instantly changed, and the criminal procedure embodied in the 5th and 6th Amendments to the Constitution be adopted as of August 12, 1898, when the Hawaiian flag was hauled down and the American flag hoisted in its place.

If the words of the Newlands Resolution, adopting the municipal legislation of Hawaii, "not contrary to the Constitution of the United States," be literally applied, the petitioner is entitled to his discharge, since that instrument expressly requires (Amendment 5) that "no person shall be held to answer for a capital or otherwise infamous crime, unless on a presentment or indictment of a grand jury;" and (Amendment 6), that "in all criminal prosecutions the accused shall enjoy the right to a speedy and public trial by an impartial jury of the state and district wherein the crime shall have been committed."

Is there any room for construction in this case, or, are the words of the resolution so plain that construction is impossible? There are many reasons which induce us to hold that the act was not intended to interfere with the existing practice, when such interference would result in imperiling the peace and good order of the islands ... From the terms of this resolution it is evident that it was intended to be merely temporary and provisional; that no change in the government was contemplated, and that, until further legislation, the Republic of Hawaii continued in existence. Even its name was not changed until 1900, when the "territory of Hawaii" was organized. The laws of the United States were not extended over the islands until the organic act was passed on April 30, 1900, when, so careful was Congress not to disturb the existing condition of things any further than was necessary, that it was provided that only "the laws of the United States which are not locally inapplicable shall have the same force and effect within the said territory as elsewhere in the United States."

Of course, under the Newlands Resolution, any new legislation must conform to the Constitution of the United States; but how far the exceptions to the existing municipal legislation were intended to abolish existing laws must depend somewhat upon circumstances. Where the immediate application of the Constitution required no new legislation to take the place of that which the Constitution abolished, it may be well held to have taken immediate effect; but where the application of a procedure hitherto well known and acquiesced in left nothing to take its place, without new legislation, the result might be so disastrous that we might well say that it could not have been within the contemplation of Congress. In all probability the contingency which has actually arisen occurred to no one at the time. If it had, and its consequences were foreseen, it is incredible that Congress should not have provided against it.

If the negative words of the resolution, "nor contrary to the Constitution of the United States," be construed as imposing upon the islands every provision of a Constitution which must have been unfamiliar to a large number of their inhabitants, and for which no previous preparation had been made, the consequences in this particular connection would be that every criminal in the Hawaiian islands convicted of an infamous offense between August 12, 1898, and June 14, 1900, when the act organizing the territorial government took effect, must be set at large; and every verdict in a civil case rendered by less than a unanimous jury held for naught. Surely, such a result could not have been within the contemplation of Congress. It is equally manifest that such could not have been the intention of the Republic of Hawaii in surrendering its autonomy. Until then it was an independent nation, exercising all the powers and prerogatives of complete sovereignty. It certainly could not have anticipated that, in dealing with another independent nation, and yielding up its sovereignty, it had denuded itself, by a negative pregnant, of all power of enforcing its criminal laws according to the methods which had been in vogue for sixty years, and was adopting a new procedure for which it had had no opportunity of making preparation. The legislature of the Republic had just adjourned, not to convene again until some time in 1900, and not actually convening until 1901. The resolution on its face bears evidence of having been intended merely for a temporary purpose, and to give time to the Republic to adapt itself to such form of territorial government as should afterwards be adopted in its organic act.

It is not intended here to decide that the words "nor contrary to the Constitution of the United States" are meaningless. Clearly, they would be operative upon any municipal legislation thereafter adopted, and upon any proceedings thereafter had, when the application of the Constitution would not result in the destruction of existing provisions conducive to the peace and good order of the community. Therefore we should answer without hesitation in the negative the question put by counsel for the petitioner in their brief: "Would municipal statutes of Hawaii, allowing a conviction of treason on circumstantial evidence, or on the testimony of one witness, depriving a person of liberty by the will of the legislature and without process or confiscating private property for public use without compensation, remain in force after an annexation of the territory to the United States, which was conditioned upon the extinction of all legislation contrary to the Constitution?" We would even go farther, and say that most, if not all, the privileges and immunities contained in the Bill of Rights of the Constitution were intended to apply from the moment of annexation; but we place our decision of this case upon the ground that the two rights alleged to be violated in this case are not fundamental in their nature, but concern merely a method of procedure which sixty years of practice had shown to be suited to the conditions of the islands, and well calculated to conserve the rights of their citizens to their lives, their property, and their well being.

The decree of the District Court for the territory of Hawaii must be reversed, and the case remanded to that court, with instructions to dismiss the petition.

Chief Justice Fuller, Joined by Justices Harlan, Brewer, and Peckham, Dissenting

In my opinion, the final order of the district court should be affirmed.

Mankichi was tried on an information filed May 4, 1899, charging him with the commission of the crime of murder on March 26 of that year, and was found guilty of manslaughter in the first degree by the verdict of nine jurors. The statutes of Hawaii prior to July 7, 1898, provided for such trial and conviction.

July 7, 1898, the "Joint Resolution to Provide for Annexing the Hawaiian Islands to the United States" was approved. 30 Stat. at L. 750. Surrender of sovereignty and possession was effected August 12, 1898.

The act "To Provide a Government for the Territory of Hawaii" was approved April 30, 1900. 31 Stat. at L. 141, chap. 339.

If Articles of Amendment 5 and 6 were applicable to the territory of Hawaii after August 12, 1898, the district judge was right, and Mankichi was entitled to be discharged.

By the specific language of this resolution no legislation which was contrary to the Constitution of the United States remained in force.

It was said at the bar that the words "contrary to the Constitution of the United States" were inserted as a declaration that certain "fundamental rights and principles, the basis of all free government, which cannot with impunity be transcended," were to be protected in Hawaii; that certain limitations of the Constitution applied "wherever the jurisdiction of the United States extends." But, in that view, the insertion of the phrase was superfluous and accomplished nothing.

Nor were we informed what those fundamental rights are. This is not a question of natural rights, on the one hand, and artificial rights on the other, but of the fundamental rights of every person living under the sovereignty of the United States in respect of that government. And among those rights is the right to be free from prosecution for crime unless after indictment by a grand jury, and the right to be acquitted unless found guilty by the unanimous verdict of a petit jury of twelve.

Assuming, solely for the sake of argument, that the mere fact of annexation might not in itself have at once extended to the inhabitants of Hawaii all the rights, privileges, and immunities guaranteed by the Constitution,

and that Congress had the power to impose limitations in that regard, I think not only that Congress did not do so in the particulars in question, but that, in re-enacting existing legislation, Congress, by the terms of the resolution, intentionally invalidated so much thereof as in these particulars was inconsistent with the Constitution. The presumptions are all opposed to any capitulation in the matter of common-law institutions.

Justice Harlan, Dissenting

In my opinion, the Constitution of the United States became the supreme law of Hawaii immediately upon the acquisition by the United States of complete sovereignty over the Hawaiian islands, and without any act of Congress formally extending the Constitution to those islands. It then, at least, became controlling, beyond the power of Congress to prevent. From the moment when the government of Hawaii accepted the joint resolution of 1898, by a formal transfer of its sovereignty to the United States – when the flag of Hawaii was taken down, by authority of Hawaii, and in its place was raised that of the United States – every human being in Hawaii charged with the commission of crime there could have rightly insisted that neither his life nor his liberty could be taken, as punishment for crime, by any process, or as the result of any mode of procedure, that was inconsistent with the Constitution of the United States. Can it be that the Constitution is the supreme law in the states of the Union, in the organized territories of the United States, between the Atlantic and Pacific oceans, and in the District of Columbia, and yet was not, prior to the act of 1900, the supreme law in territories and among peoples situated as were the territory and people of Hawaii, and over which the United States had acquired all rights of sovereignty of whatsoever kind? A negative answer to this question, and a recognition of the principle that such an answer involves, would place Congress above the Constitution. It would mean that the benefit of the constitutional provisions designed for the protection of life and liberty may be claimed by some of the people subject to the authority and jurisdiction of the United States, but cannot be claimed by others equally subject to its authority and jurisdiction. It would mean that the will of Congress, not the Constitution, is the supreme law of the land for certain peoples and territories under our jurisdiction. It would mean that the United States may acquire territory be cession, conquest, or treaty, and that Congress may exercise sovereign dominion over it, outside of and in violation of the Constitution, and under regulations that could not be applied to the organized territories of the United States and their inhabitants. It would mean that, under the influence and guidance of commercialism and the supposed necessities of trade, this country had left the old ways of the fathers, as defined by a written constitution, and entered upon a new way, in following which the American people will lose sight of, or become indifferent to, principles which had been supposed to be essential to real liberty. It would mean that, if the principles now announced should become firmly established, the time may not be far distant when, under the exactions of trade and commerce, and to gratify an ambition to become the dominant political power in all the earth, the United States will acquire territories in every direction, which are inhabited by human beings, over which territories, to be called "dependencies" or "outlying possessions," we will exercise absolute dominion, and whose inhabitants will be regarded as "subjects'" or "dependent peoples," to be controlled as Congress may see fit, not as the Constitution requires nor as the people governed may wish. Thus will be engrafted upon our republican institutions, controlled by the supreme law of a written Constitution, a colonial system entirely foreign to the genius of our government and abhorrent to the principles that underlie and pervade the Constitution. It will then come about that we will have two governments over the peoples subject to the jurisdiction of the United States – one, existing under a written Constitution, creating a government with authority to exercise only powers expressly granted and such as are necessary and appropriate to carry into effect those so granted; the other, existing outside of the written Constitution, in virtue of an unwritten law, to be declared from time to time by Congress, which is itself only a creature of that instrument.

I stand by the doctrine that the Constitution is the supreme law in every territory, as soon as it comes under the sovereign dominion of the United States for purposes of civil administration, and whose inhabitants are under its entire authority and jurisdiction. I could not otherwise hold without conceding the power of Congress, the creature of the Constitution, by mere nonaction, to withhold vital constitutional guarantees from the inhabitants of a territory governed by the authority, and only by the authority, of the United States. Such a doctrine would admit of the exercise of absolute, arbitrary legislative power under a written Constitution full of restrictions upon Congress, and designed to limit the separate departments of government to the exercise of only expressly enumerated powers and such other powers as may be implied therefrom – each department always acting in subordination to that instrument as the supreme law of the land. Indeed, it has been announced by some statesmen that the Constitution should be interpreted to mean not what its words naturally, or usually, or even plainly, import, but what the apparent necessities of the hour, or the apparent majority of the people, at a particular time, demand at the hands of the judiciary. I cannot assent to any such view of the Constitution. Nor can I approve the suggestion that the status of Hawaii and the powers of its local government are to be "measured" by the resolution of 1898, without reference to the Constitution. It is impossible for me to grasp the thought that that which is admittedly contrary to the supreme law can be sustained as valid.

1. The tension between cultural traditions and constitutional protections is difficult, especially when parties are unwilling to extend them based on racial assumptions of an inability to self-govern. How would you resolve this tension? Does the motive of the government in making such a policy matter?

2. In the majority opinion, the Court noted that the Hawai'ian people had enjoyed a "civilized" government based on English law as part of their traditional practices. Should the similarities or dissimilarities to U.S. practice be relevant to this decision or not?

The United States now exercises sovereignty over more land "outside of its member states or provinces" than any other nation (Sparrow 2006, 215; see also Smith 2015, 109). These unincorporated territories were never intended to become states, and when given the option, several have rejected the opportunity. While the residents of these territories often have U.S. citizenship, it is a form of "differentiated citizenship" (Young 1999; Smith 2015) that varies from rights and protections held by those in the recognized states. They are frequently not eligible to vote in presidential elections and have no formal representation in Congress; they are not able to reject U.S. citizenship while retaining their territorial citizenship and residence; the ability to automatically provide U.S. citizenship to those born in the territory (Fourteenth Amendment birthright citizenship) is unclear; and "whether the U.S. Constitution, especially its equal protection clause, permits them to maintain forms of owning and transmitting land that accord to traditional customs, even when such land ownership would be deemed impermissible racial 'restrictive covenants' within the States" is still unresolved (Smith 2015, 115). For instance, in some island states, only people who are citizens of the territory can buy land as a means of preventing loss of local political and economic control.

This tension between local traditions in the territories and the protections of U.S. citizenship was most recently addressed by the 10th circuit federal court in the case of *Fitisemanu* v. *United States* in 2021. In 2022, the Supreme Court declined to hear the case, allowing the appellate court decision to stand. In this case, three citizens of American Samoa, a U.S. territory whose citizens have not been considered as U.S. citizens, challenged the determinations of *The Insular Cases*. John Fitisemanu, Pale Tuli, and Rosavita Tuli – who resided in Utah – claim that they were born in the United States on the island of American Samoa but are considered non-citizen "nationals" who cannot vote, run for elective office in Utah, serve as an officer in the military, or serve on a jury. They claim they are U.S. citizens based on their birth in a U.S. territory. On the opposite side, the U.S. government claims the Citizenship Clause of the Fourteenth Amendment does not apply to unincorporated territories, such as American Samoa. In addition, the government of American Samoa argues that their people do not want federal "citizenship by judicial fiat." The district court ruled in favor of the plaintiffs finding U.S. birthright citizenship should be extended to citizens of American Samoa and other unincorporated territories.

FITISEMANU v. UNITED STATES, 1 F.4TH 862 (10 CIR.) (2021)

Senior Circuit Judge Lucero

For over a century, the land of American Samoa has been an American territory, but its people have never been considered American citizens. Plaintiffs, three citizens of American Samoa, asked the district court in Utah to upend this longstanding arrangement and declare that American Samoans have been citizens from the start. The district court agreed and so declared. Appellants, the United States federal government joined by the American Samoan government and an individual representative acting as intervenors, ask us to reverse the district court's decision. We conclude that neither constitutional text nor Supreme Court precedent demands the district court's interpretation of the Citizenship Clause of the Fourteenth Amendment.

We instead recognize that Congress plays the preeminent role in the determination of citizenship in unincorporated territorial lands, and that the courts play but a subordinate role in the process. We further understand text, precedent, and historical practice as instructing that the prevailing circumstances in the territory be considered in determining the reach of the Citizenship Clause. It is evident that the wishes of the territory's democratically elected representatives, who remind us that their people have not formed a consensus in favor of American citizenship and urge us not to impose citizenship on an unwilling people from a courthouse thousands of miles away, have not been taken into adequate consideration. Such consideration properly falls under the purview of Congress, a point on which we fully agree with the concurrence. These circumstances advise against the extension of birthright citizenship to American Samoa. We reverse.

I.

American Samoa is one of several unincorporated territories of the United States. It is the only one whose inhabitants are not birthright American citizens. Congress has conferred American citizenship on the peoples of all other inhabited unincorporated territories – Puerto Rico, Guam, the U.S. Virgin Islands, and others – but not the people of American Samoa. American Samoans are instead designated by statute "nationals, but not citizens, of the United States."

A.

American Samoa encompasses the eastern islands of an archipelago located in the South Pacific, approximately 2,500 miles due south of Hawaii. Its current population is 49,437; another 204,640 individuals of Samoan descent live in the United States. In 1900, its tribal leaders ceded sovereignty to the American government. The documents effectuating this cession did not specify how the territory would be governed, and were silent on whether American Samoans were, or would ever be, American citizens. Since then, American Samoans have owed "permanent allegiance" to the United States but have never been American citizens.

Not unlike other colonial relationships, the nature of the relationship between American Samoa and the United States is contested. The traditional view is that the relationship has been largely amicable. According to this narrative, American Samoa voluntarily ceded sovereignty to the United States, and the United States has since provided protection from external interference while largely staying out of the internal affairs of the territory. More recent scholarship has questioned this account, arguing that the relationship has been built more on domination than friend-ship. Whatever the origin, there is no doubt that the relationship has profoundly influenced the cul-ture of American Samoa. American Samoans have particularly high enlistment rates in the American military, for example, and its constitution recog-nizes freedom of speech, freedom of religion, due process of law, and other basic civil rights.

Notwithstanding these cultural imprints, the people of American Samoa have maintained a traditional and distinctive way of life: the fa'a Samoa. It is this amalgam of customs and prac-tices that Intervenors argue would be threatened if birthright citizenship were imposed. For exam-ple, the social structure of American Samoa is organized around large, extended families called 'aiga. These families are led by matai, holders of hereditary chieftain titles. The matai regulate the village life of their 'aiga and are the only individ-uals permitted to serve in the upper house of the American Samoan legislature. Land ownership is predominantly communal, with more than 90% of American Samoan land belonging to the 'aiga rather than to any one individual. There are also racial restrictions on land ownership requiring landowners to be at least 50% American Samoan. Intervenors worry that these and other traditional elements of the American Samoan culture could run afoul of constitutional protections should the plaintiffs in this case prevail.

Citizenship has been a contested issue in American Samoa since its cession to the United States. When the American Samoan people first learned they were not considered American citi-zens, many advocated for citizenship. This effort culminated in the creation of the American Samoan Commission in 1930, which subse-quently recommended that Congress grant citi-zenship to the people of the territory. The United States Senate passed legislation to this effect, but the effort failed in the House.

Public opinion among American Samoans appears to have shifted, with the elected gov-ernment of American Samoa intervening in this case to argue against "citizenship by judicial fiat." Limited evidence exists regard-ing American Samoan public opinion on the question of birthright citizenship, but what little evidence there is suggests Intervenors are not out of step with the people they represent. The position taken by the American Samoan elected representatives appears to be a reliable expres-sion of their people's attitude toward citizenship.

II.

At the outset, we must decide which of two lines of precedent will guide our analysis. The choices before us are the Insular Cases, a string of Supreme Court decisions issued at the turn of the twentieth century that addressed how the Constitution applies to unincorporated territo-ries, and *United States* v. *Wong Kim Ark*, 169 U.S. 649 (1898), a case in which the Supreme Court considered the Citizenship Clause's guar-antee of birthright citizenship to those born in the United States.

A.

Issued between 1900 and 1922, the Insular Cases were a string of Supreme Court opinions that addressed a basic question: when the American flag is raised over an overseas territory, does the Constitution follow? In his concurrence in what became Insular's seminal case, *Downes* v. *Bidwell*, 182 U.S. 244 (1901), Justice Edward White wrote, "[T]he determination of what particular provision of the Constitution is applicable [in an unincor-porated territory] ... involves an inquiry into the situation of the territory and its relations to the United States." Though not the issue in *Downes*, Justice White specifically mentioned citizenship as the type of constitutional right that should not be extended automatically to unincorporated ter-ritories. This flexible and pragmatic approach to the extension of the Constitution to America's overseas territories "bec[a]me the settled law of the court." *Balzac* v. *Porto Rico*, 258 U.S. 298, 305 (1922). The proposition the Insular Cases came to stand for is that constitutional provisions apply only if the circumstances of the territory warrant their application.

The Insular Cases have become controversial. They are criticized as amounting to a license for further imperial expansion and having been based at least in part on racist ideology. These cases "facilitated the imperial ambitions of turn of the century America while retaining a veneer of commitment to constitutional self-government." This facilitation was an explicit concern of the Court in the Insular Cases.

Not only is the purpose of the Insular Cases disreputable to modern eyes, so too is their reasoning. The Court repeatedly voiced concern that native inhabitants of the unincorporated territories were simply unfit for the American constitutional regime. For example, in *Downes*, Justice White found it self-evident that citizenship could not be automatically extended to "those absolutely unfit to receive it." Justice Brown, meanwhile, suggested that "differences of race" raised "grave questions" about the rights that ought to be afforded to native inhabitants. Plaintiffs and their supporting *amici* view this ignominious history as militating against application of the Insular Cases to the case before us.

Yet the Supreme Court has continued to invoke the Insular framework when it has grappled with questions of constitutional applicability to unincorporated territories ...

Notwithstanding its beginnings, the approach developed in the Insular Cases and carried forward in recent Supreme Court decisions can be repurposed to preserve the dignity and autonomy of the peoples of America's overseas territories. "[S]cholars, and increasingly federal judges, have lately recognized the opportunity to repurpose the [Insular] framework in order to protect indigenous culture from the imposition of federal scrutiny and oversight." The flexibility of the Insular Cases' framework gives federal courts significant latitude to preserve traditional cultural practices that might otherwise run afoul of individual rights enshrined in the Constitution. This same flexibility permits courts to defer to the preferences of indigenous peoples, so that they may chart their own course.

B.

Published just three years before the first of the Insular Cases, *United States* v. *Wong Kim Ark*, 169 U.S. 649 (1898) is the alternative candidate for a governing precedent in this case. *Wong Kim Ark* concerned a man who was born in the state of California to two non-citizen parents who had immigrated from China. After Wong tried to return to San Francisco following a visit to China, he was denied reentry because he was deemed not a citizen on account of his parents' Chinese citizenship. The Supreme Court declared the denial unconstitutional ... Determining Wong was a citizen, the Supreme Court held, "The fourteenth amendment affirms the ancient and fundamental rule of citizenship by birth within the territory, in the allegiance and under the protection of the country ..."

In sum, we interpret *Wong Kim Ark*'s discussion of English common law as an invocation of persuasive authority rather than an incorporation of binding caselaw. We take up *Wong Kim Ark*'s instruction to consider English common law in analyzing the extraterritorial application of the Citizenship Clause, but find little light shed by this endeavor.

C.

Between these competing frameworks, the Insular Cases provide the more relevant, workable, and, as applied here, just standard. This is so for several reasons: 1) the Insular Cases were written with the type of issue presented by this case in mind, whereas *Wong Kim Ark* was not; 2) the district court overread the weight accorded English common law by *Wong Kim Ark*; and 3) the Insular Cases permit this court to respect the wishes of the American Samoan people, whereas *Wong Kim Ark* would support the imposition of citizenship on unwilling recipients.

IV.

... I proceed to the next stage of the Insular analysis: whether citizenship is a "fundamental personal right" as that term is defined by the Insular Cases.

Under the Insular Cases, constitutional provisions that implicate fundamental personal rights apply without regard to local context. "[G]uaranties of certain fundamental personal rights declared in the Constitution" apply "even in unincorporated Territories." But "'[f]undamental' has a distinct and narrow meaning in the context of territorial rights." Even rights that we would normally think of as fundamental, such as the constitutional right to a jury trial, are not "fundamental" under the framework of the Insular Cases. Instead, only those "principles which are the basis of all free government" establish the rights that are "fundamental" for Insular purposes.

... [B]irthright citizenship does not qualify as a fundamental right under the Insular framework. Birthright citizenship, like the right to a trial by jury, is an important element of the American legal system, but it is not a prerequisite to a free government. Numerous free countries do not practice birthright citizenship, or practice it with significant restrictions, including Australia, France, and Germany. The United States, for its part, does not apply birthright citizenship to children of American citizens born abroad. Nor has birthright citizenship proven necessary to safeguard basic human rights in American Samoa, where the rights to freedom of speech, freedom of religion, and due process of law are constitutionally guaranteed. Under the particular definition supplied by the Insular Cases, birthright citizenship is not a fundamental right that would preclude application of the "impracticable and anomalous" standard.

V.

Though its articulation postdates the Insular Cases, the lodestar of the Insular framework has come to be the "impracticable and anomalous" standard. Under this standard, "the question is which guarantees of the Constitution should apply in view of the particular circumstances, the practical necessities, and the possible alternatives which Congress had before it." "In sum, we must ask whether the circumstances are such that recognition of the right to birthright citizenship would prove impracticable and anomalous, as applied to contemporary American Samoa."

Two characteristics of contemporary American Samoa guide my analysis: the expressed preferences of the American Samoan people, and the potential disruption of their way of life by judicial imposition of citizenship.

A.

No circumstance is more persuasive to me than the preference against citizenship expressed by the American Samoan people through their elected representatives.

In the context of citizenship, there can hardly be a more compelling practical concern than that it is not wanted by the people who are to receive it. To impose citizenship in such a situation would violate a basic principle of republican association: that "governments ... deriv[e] their [ ] powers from the consent of the governed."

Respect for this principle should be at its zenith in the case of territories born from American imperial expansion, a project that was always in significant tension with our aspirations toward representative democracy. "The fabric of American empire ought to rest on the solid basis of the consent of the People." *The Federalist* No. 22 (Alexander Hamilton). We have sometimes failed to live up to Hamilton's admonition. It is for this reason "that sovereignty and membership need to be reconceptualized in less rigid terms if we are to establish a political regime that overcomes historical subordination and justly rules over the territory and inhabitants of the United States." Recognizing consent as a cornerstone of a flexible approach to the extension of citizenship to the unincorporated territories is a step toward rectifying those mistakes.

I agree with the representatives of the American Samoan government that "an extension of birthright citizenship without the will of the governed is in essence a form of 'autocratic subjugation' of the American Samoan people." While I am sympathetic to Plaintiffs' desire for citizenship, to accept their position would be to impose citizenship over the expressed preferences of the American Samoan people. Such a result would be anomalous to our history and our understanding of the Constitution.

B.

A further concern of extending birthright citizenship to American Samoa is the tension between individual constitutional rights and the American Samoan way of life (the fa'a Samoa). Fundamental elements of the fa'a Samoa rest uneasily alongside the American legal system. Constitutional provisions such as the Equal Protection Clause, the Takings Clause, and the Establishment Clause are difficult to reconcile with several traditional American Samoan practices, such as the matai chieftain social structure, communal land ownership, and communal regulation of religious practice. "In American Sāmoa's case, 'partial membership' works to protect the customary institutions and traditions, and so a push for full equality [as American citizens] is not readily embraced by the American Sāmoan citizenry."

Required by the Insular framework to weigh the practical considerations concerning the extension of the constitutional right to birthright citizenship to American Samoa, I would hold that the extension of United States birthright citizenship is impracticable and anomalous.

The judgment of the district court is **Reversed**.

Judge Bacharach, Dissenting

As Justice Brandeis once observed, "[t]he only title in our democracy superior to that of President [is] the title of citizen." The district court concluded that this title extends to the people of American Samoa, and I agree.

The Fourteenth Amendment's Citizenship Clause extends birthright citizenship to every person "born ... in the United States." For three reasons, this clause provides citizenship to the three individual plaintiffs.

First, all were born in American Samoa, which is a territory "in the United States." When the Fourteenth Amendment was ratified, courts, dictionaries, maps, and censuses uniformly regarded territories as land "in the United States."

Second, even if the territory of American Samoa lay outside the United States, the Citizenship Clause would apply because citizenship is a fundamental right.

Third, even if the right were not fundamental, applying the Citizenship Clause to the three American Samoan plaintiffs would not be impracticable or anomalous.

Because the plaintiffs are U.S. citizens, I would affirm.

III. The Citizenship Clause unambiguously applies to natives of American Samoa.

The Citizenship Clause of the Fourteenth Amendment provides: "All persons born or naturalized in the United States, and subject to the jurisdiction thereof, are citizens of the United States ..." The threshold issue is the meaning of "in the United States."

IV. Even if the Citizenship Clause did not otherwise extend to American Samoa, this clause would apply because it recognized a fundamental right.

V. Even if citizenship were not a fundamental right, its application in American Samoa would be neither impracticable nor anomalous.

Even when rights aren't fundamental, they presumptively apply in unincorporated territories. So the burden falls on those who would decline to apply a given constitutional right based on impracticability or anomalousness.

The Court has interchangeably used the terms "impracticable" and "impractical" to refer to "[p]ractical considerations." "Impractical" "connotes difficulty of implementation or such a substantial degree of inconvenience that it makes the likelihood of success in realizing such a right very low." So when the Supreme Court has considered the "impracticability" of applying a given right, the Court has focused on the difficulty of applying the right in a given territory.

If it's not impracticable to implement a constitutional right in a territory, the court must do so unless it would be "anomalous." Implementing a right would be "anomalous" only if it deviates from ordinary conditions.

To determine whether extending citizenship to inhabitants of unincorporated territories is "impracticable and anomalous," a court must balance "the particular local setting, the practical necessities, and the possible alternatives" against the seriousness of the right.

A. Citizenship for Everyone Born in American Samoa is Neither Impracticable nor Anomalous

Even if citizenship were not a fundamental right, birthright citizenship for everyone born in American Samoa would be neither impracticable nor anomalous. Even without recognition of citizenship, American Samoans already enjoy the constitutional protections of due process and *Miranda* warnings.

The American Samoan government argues that U.S. citizenship would be impractical because it would lead to recognition of other constitutional rights, like equal protection, that would threaten local cultural traditions. This worry lacks any legal foundation. Equal protection already applies to everyone within the United States' territorial jurisdiction regardless of whether they are citizens. So courts have already applied the right to equal protection to American Samoans even while considering them non-citizens.

And there's no reason to think that citizenship would open the floodgates to other constitutional rights. If another right is asserted, the court would need to separately decide the applicability of that right in American Samoa. This inquiry would turn not on citizenship, but on (1) whether the right is fundamental and (2) if not, whether application of the Citizenship Clause in American Samoa would be impracticable or anomalous.

The American Samoan government argues that birthright citizenship would upend political processes that ensure self-determination ...

First, in my view, the Citizenship Clause currently applies by its own terms. And the Citizenship Clause was meant to "put [the] question of citizenship ... beyond the legislative power" for those to whom it applies. As long as American Samoa remains a U.S. territory, citizenship is not for elected leaders to decide. That responsibility instead falls to the courts.

American Samoa can always choose independence. But while American Samoa remains joined with the United States, birthright citizenship respects the promises underlying the political union with the United States.

A substantial part of American Samoa memorialized in its cession that the United States had promised protection against "discrimination in the suffrages and political privileges between the present residents of said Islands and citizens of the United States dwelling therein." To honor this promise, birthright citizenship ensures that people born in American Samoa and living elsewhere can retain autonomy by deciding whether to consent to the governing laws.

Second, the argument is factually unsupported, for the record says nothing about the preference of a majority in American Samoa. Despite the lack of such evidence, the American Samoan government cites a 2007 report by the American Samoa Future Political Status Study Commission. This report states that among American Samoans who had publicly expressed their views to the Commission, "anti-citizenship attitude remain[s] strong[,] especially among the elders." But the report also observed that "some" American Samoans residing in other parts of the United States had "recommended that American Samoa change to a political status which guarantees U.S. citizenship."

Despite the dearth of evidence reflecting opposition to U.S. citizenship, Judge Lucero elevates the role of consent, insisting that we should confine U.S. citizenship to those who consent. Certainly the three American Samoan plaintiffs consent to U.S. citizenship.

But Judge Lucero's focus on current consent is misguided. Our job is to interpret the Constitution regardless of the popularity of our interpretation in American Samoa, and the application of constitutional rights does not become impracticable or anomalous because of disagreement. As long as America Samoa remains a U.S. territory and the U.S. Constitution contains the Citizenship Clause, consent plays no role in applying the Citizenship Clause under the "impracticable or anomalous" test.

B. Citizenship for the Plaintiffs, who were Born in American Samoa and now Reside in Utah, is Neither Impracticable nor Anomalous

VII. Conclusion

A U.S. territory, like American Samoa, is "in the United States." So the Citizenship Clause unambiguously covers individuals born in American Samoa. Since colonial days, Americans understood that citizenship extended to everyone within the sovereign's dominion. So those in territories like American Samoa enjoy birthright citizenship, just like anyone else born in our country. The plaintiffs are thus U.S. citizens, and I would affirm.

1. Does this decision protect the autonomy of the indigenous people of the unincorporated territories to self-govern or deny the people the protections of the U.S. Constitution? Which of these competing values should be privileged? Why are they in conflict?
2. Should all of the different unincorporated territories be treated the same? Should the people in these nations determine for themselves how they are constitutionally treated? What are the consequences of each position?

In addition to these territories, the United States also has its own internal region – the District of Columbia or Washington, D.C. – which is also not a state. Its residents can be U.S. citizens who pay federal taxes and, since 1964, participate in the electoral college for presidential elections, but they have no formal voice in Congress. They are represented by elected "shadow" delegates. In addition, all the local legislation governing D.C. passed by its city council, including the budget, must be approved by Congress. Like the unincorporated territories, D.C.'s population is predominately people of color (60 percent). However, the city was created by the original Constitution, where even its size was clearly defined, and its governance explicitly determined. Despite lobbying on both sides of the issue since its formation, this question remains unresolved. Are the same issues at play with the territories or is the problem of D.C. statehood fundamentally different? What would be the best solution to the question of statehood for territories and for D.C.? Would the self-determination of these communities resolve the question?

6.3 Expanding Native Sovereignty

While the United States has recognized the sovereignty of Native tribes, the historical policy of forced assimilation through land appropriation, residence schools, the termination of tribal identities, and the concomitant removal of "[a] quarter to a third of all American Indian children" (Blackhawk 2023, 431), have resulted in an unclear definition of Native sovereignty. American Indians have organized and mobilized over land rights, control of their own identity and representation, preservation of cultural practices and language, as well as self-governance. The Indian Gaming Regulatory Act, 1988, a federal law allowing tribal governments to operate casinos on tribal lands with limited regulation by the states, allowed tribes the economic resources to preserve and develop tribal communities (Akee, Spilde, and Taylor 2015). The creation of wealth in Indian Country has generated new pressures to define who are classified tribal members able to gain from the casinos and who are excluded from these profits. These pressures again raise the question of is Native identity a racial identity or a political one?

The legal conflicts between the U.S. government's exercise of its "plenary power" to legislate over Native land and tribal sovereignty, as exercised through tribal governance, have filled many casebooks. While federal law regulating Native tribes, known as "Indian Law," has given Congress unchecked power to regulate Indian Country (Blackhawk 2019, 1819), tribal law has governed the behavior of Native people on Native lands, with many exceptions. Without any explicit form of Native or tribal representation in the federal government, the question of the scope and authority of Native sovereignty remains unanswered. Native lands are located within the boundaries of the states. White people on Native lands are governed by state law and not tribal law, but Indian Country is generally policed by tribal authorities enforced by federal law. This creates many questions of jurisdiction and often results in a lack of enforcement of violent crimes (Washburn 2006; Crepelle 2022).

In the 2020 Supreme Court decision of *McGirt* v. *Oklahoma*, the Court was forced to confront some of these tensions. Jimcy McGirt, an enrolled member of the Seminole Nation of Oklahoma, was convicted by the state of Oklahoma of three sexual offenses against a child, occurring on the Muscogee (Creek) Reservation. McGirt argues that the Major Crimes Act of 1885, which requires federal jurisdiction and trials for Native people committing specific enumerated crimes (murder, assault with bodily injury, and most sexual offenses) on tribal lands, applies to his case. Typically, such crimes are policed by the state governments, accordingly Oklahoma state courts rejected his claim, and he appealed to the U.S. Supreme Court.

MCGIRT v. OKLAHOMA, 591 U.S. 844 (2020)

Justice Gorsuch Delivered the Opinion of the Court, Joined by Justices Ginsburg, Breyer, Sotomayor, and Kagan.

Vote: 5–4

On the far end of the Trail of Tears was a promise. Forced to leave their ancestral lands in Georgia and Alabama, the Creek Nation received assurances that their new lands in the West would be secure forever. In exchange for ceding "all their land, East of the Mississippi river," the U.S. government agreed by treaty that "[t]he Creek country west of the Mississippi shall be solemnly guarantied to the Creek Indians." Treaty With the Creeks, Mar. 24 (1832 Treaty). Both parties settled on boundary lines for a new and "permanent home to the whole Creek nation," located in what is now Oklahoma. The government further promised that "[no] State or Territory [shall] ever have a right to pass laws for the government of such Indians, but they shall be allowed to govern themselves."

Today we are asked whether the land these treaties promised remains an Indian reservation for purposes of federal criminal law. Because Congress has not said otherwise, we hold the government to its word.

I.

Mr. McGirt's appeal rests on the federal Major Crimes Act (MCA). The statute provides that, within "the Indian country," "[a]ny Indian who commits" certain enumerated offenses "against the person or property of another Indian or any other person" "shall be subject to the same law and penalties as all other persons committing any of the above offenses, within the exclusive jurisdiction of the United States." By subjecting Indians to federal trials for crimes committed on tribal lands, Congress may have breached its promises to tribes like the Creek that they would be free to govern themselves. But this particular incursion has its limits – applying only to certain enumerated crimes and allowing only the federal government to try Indians. State courts generally have no jurisdiction to try Indians for conduct committed in "Indian country."

The key question Mr. McGirt faces concerns that last qualification: Did he commit his crimes in Indian country? ... Mr. McGirt submits he can satisfy this condition because he committed his crimes on land reserved for the Creek since the 19th century.

The Creek Nation has joined Mr. McGirt as *amicus curiae*. Not because the Tribe is interested in shielding Mr. McGirt from responsibility for his crimes. Instead, the Creek Nation participates because Mr. McGirt's personal interests wind up implicating the Tribe's. No one disputes that Mr. McGirt's crimes were committed on lands described as the Creek Reservation in an 1866 treaty and federal statute. But, in seeking to defend the state-court judgment below, Oklahoma has put aside whatever procedural defenses it might have and asked us to confirm that the land once given to the Creeks is no longer a reservation today.

At another level, then, Mr. McGirt's case winds up as a contest between State and Tribe. The scope of their dispute is limited; nothing we might say today could unsettle Oklahoma's authority to try non-Indians for crimes against non-Indians on the lands in question. Still, the stakes are not insignificant. If Mr. McGirt and the Tribe are right, the State has no right to prosecute Indians for crimes committed in a portion of Northeastern Oklahoma that includes most of the city of Tulsa. Responsibility to try these matters would fall instead to the federal government and Tribe. Recently, the question has taken on more salience too. While Oklahoma state courts have rejected any suggestion that the lands in question remain a reservation, the Tenth Circuit has reached the opposite conclusion. We granted certiorari to settle the question.

II.

Start with what should be obvious: Congress established a reservation for the Creeks. In a series of treaties, Congress not only "solemnly guarantied" the land but also "establish[ed] boundary lines which will secure a country and permanent home to the whole Creek Nation of Indians." The government's promises weren't made gratuitously. Rather, the 1832 Treaty acknowledged that "[t]he United States are desirous that the Creeks should remove to the country west of the Mississippi" and, in service of that goal, required the Creeks to cede all lands in the East. Nor were the government's promises meant to be delusory. Congress twice assured the Creeks that "[the] Treaty shall be obligatory on the contracting parties, as soon as the same shall be ratified by the United States." Both treaties were duly ratified and enacted as law.

Because the Tribe's move west was ostensibly voluntary, Congress held out another assurance as well. In the statute that precipitated these negotiations, Congress authorized the President "to assure the tribe ... that the United States will forever secure and guaranty to them ... the country so exchanged with them." "[A]nd if they prefer it," the bill continued, "the United States will cause a patent or grant to be made and executed to them for the same; *Provided always*, that such lands shall revert to the United States, if the Indians become extinct, or abandon the same." If agreeable to all sides, a tribe would not only enjoy the government's solemn treaty promises; it would hold legal title to its lands.

It was an offer the Creek accepted.

III.

A.

While there can be no question that Congress established a reservation for the Creek Nation, it's equally clear that Congress has since broken more than a few of its promises to the Tribe. Not least, the land described in the parties' treaties, once undivided and held by the Tribe, is now fractured into pieces. While these pieces were initially distributed to Tribe members, many were sold and now belong to persons unaffiliated with the Nation. So in what sense, if any, can we say that the Creek Reservation persists today?

To determine whether a tribe continues to hold a reservation, there is only one place we may look: the Acts of Congress. This Court long ago held that the Legislature wields significant constitutional authority when it comes to tribal relations, possessing even the authority to breach its own promises and treaties. *Lone Wolf* v. *Hitchcock*, 187 U.S. 553 (1903). But that power, this Court has cautioned, belongs to Congress alone. Nor will this Court lightly infer such a breach once Congress has established a reservation.

Under our Constitution, States have no authority to reduce federal reservations lying within their borders. Just imagine if they did. A State could encroach on the tribal boundaries or legal rights Congress provided, and, with enough time and patience, nullify the promises made in the name of the United States. That would be at odds with the Constitution, which entrusts Congress with the authority to regulate commerce with Native Americans, and directs that federal treaties and statutes are the "supreme Law of the Land." Art. I, §8; Art. VI, cl. 2. It would also leave tribal rights in the hands of the very neighbors who might be least inclined to respect them.

Likewise, courts have no proper role in the adjustment of reservation borders ... "[O]nly Congress can divest a reservation of its land and diminish its boundaries." So it's no matter how many other promises to a tribe the federal government has already broken. If Congress wishes to break the promise of a reservation, it must say so.

B.

In an effort to show Congress has done just that with the Creek Reservation, Oklahoma points to events during the so-called "allotment era." Starting in the 1880s, Congress sought to pressure many tribes to abandon their communal lifestyles and parcel their lands into smaller lots owned by individual tribe members. Some allotment advocates hoped that the policy would create a class of assimilated, landowning, agrarian Native Americans. Others may have hoped that, with lands in individual hands and (eventually)

freely alienable, white settlers would have more space of their own.

Missing in all this, however, is a statute evincing anything like the "present and total surrender of all tribal interests" in the affected lands. Without doubt, in 1832 the Creek "cede[d]" their original homelands east of the Mississippi for a reservation promised in what is now Oklahoma. And in 1866, they "cede[d] and convey[ed]" a portion of that reservation to the United States. But because there exists no equivalent law terminating what remained, the Creek Reservation survived allotment.

C.

If allotment by itself won't work, Oklahoma seeks to prove disestablishment by pointing to other ways Congress intruded on the Creek's promised right to self-governance during the allotment era. It turns out there were many. For example, just a few years before the 1901 Creek Allotment Agreement, and perhaps in an effort to pressure the Tribe to the negotiating table, Congress abolished the Creeks' tribal courts and transferred all pending civil and criminal cases to the U.S. Courts of the Indian Territory. Separately, the Creek Allotment Agreement provided that tribal ordinances "affecting the lands of the Tribe, or of individuals after allotment, or the moneys or other property of the Tribe, or of the citizens thereof" would not be valid until approved by the President of the United States.

Plainly, these laws represented serious blows to the Creek. But, just as plainly, they left the Tribe with significant sovereign functions over the lands in question. For example, the Creek Nation retained the power to collect taxes, operate schools, legislate through tribal ordinances, and, soon, oversee the federally mandated allotment process ... Grave though they were, these congressional intrusions on pre-existing treaty rights fell short of eliminating all tribal interests in the land.

In the years that followed, Congress continued to adjust its arrangements with the Tribe ... But Congress never withdrew its recognition of the tribal government, and none of its adjustments would have made any sense if Congress thought it had already completed that job.

Indeed, with time, Congress changed course completely. Beginning in the 1920s, the federal outlook toward Native Americans shifted "away from assimilation policies and toward more tolerance and respect for traditional aspects of Indian culture." ... Pursuant to this new national policy, in 1936, Congress authorized the Creek to adopt a constitution and bylaws, enabling the Creek government to resume many of its previously suspended functions.

The Creek Nation has done exactly that. In the intervening years, it has ratified a new constitution and established three separate branches of government. Today the Nation is led by a democratically elected Principal Chief, Second Chief, and National Council; operates a police force and three hospitals; commands an annual budget of more than $350 million; and employs over 2,000 people. In 1982, the Nation passed an ordinance reestablishing the criminal and civil jurisdiction of its courts. The territorial jurisdiction of these courts extends to any Indian country within the Tribe's territory as defined by the Treaty of 1866. And the State of Oklahoma has afforded full faith and credit to its judgments since at least 1994.

Maybe some of these changes happened for altruistic reasons, maybe some for other reasons. But whatever the confluence of reasons, in all this history there simply arrived no moment when any Act of Congress dissolved the Creek Tribe or disestablished its reservation. In the end, Congress moved in the opposite direction.

D.

... When interpreting Congress's work in this arena, no less than any other, our charge is usually to ascertain and follow the original meaning of the law before us. That is the only "step" proper for a court of law. To be sure, if during the course of our work an ambiguous statutory term or phrase emerges, we will sometimes consult contemporaneous usages, customs, and practices to the extent they shed light on the meaning of the language in question at the time of enactment. But Oklahoma does not point to any ambiguous language in any of the relevant statutes that could plausibly be read as an Act of disestablishment. Nor may a court favor contemporaneous or later practices *instead of* the laws Congress passed. As *Solem* [v. *Bartlett*, 465 U.S. 463 (1984)] explained, "[o]nce a block of land is set aside for an Indian reservation and no matter what happens to the title of individual plots within the area, the entire block retains its reservation status until Congress explicitly indicates otherwise."

To see the perils of substituting stories for statutes, we need look no further than the stories we are offered in the case before us. Put aside that the Tribe could tell more than a few stories of its own: Take just the evidence on which Oklahoma and the dissent wish to rest their case. First, they point to Oklahoma's long historical prosecutorial practice of asserting jurisdiction over Indians in state court, even for serious crimes on the contested lands. If the Creek lands really were part of a reservation, the argument goes, all of these cases should have been tried in federal court pursuant to the MCA ... Second, they offer statements from various sources to show that "everyone" in the late 19th and early 20th century thought the reservation system – and the Creek Nation– would be disbanded soon. Third, they stress that non-Indians swiftly moved on to the reservation in the early part of the last century, that Tribe members today constitute a small fraction of those now residing on the land, and that the area now includes a "vibrant city with expanding aerospace, healthcare, technology, manufacturing, and transportation sectors." All this history, we are told, supplies "compelling" evidence about the lands in question.

To be fair, Oklahoma is far from the only State that has overstepped its authority in Indian country. Perhaps often in good faith, perhaps sometimes not, others made similar mistakes in the past. But all that only underscores further the danger of relying on state practices to determine the meaning of the federal MCA.

In the end, only one message rings true. Even the carefully selected history Oklahoma and the dissent recite is not nearly as tidy as they suggest. It supplies us with little help in discerning the law's meaning and much potential for mischief.

If anything, the persistent if unspoken message here seems to be that we should be taken by the "practical advantages" of ignoring the written law. How much easier it would be, after all, to let the State proceed as it has always assumed it might. But just imagine what it would mean to indulge that path. A State exercises jurisdiction over Native Americans with such persistence that the practice seems normal. Indian landowners lose their titles by fraud or otherwise in sufficient volume that no one remembers whose land it once was. All this continues for long enough that a reservation that was once beyond doubt becomes questionable, and then even farfetched. Sprinkle in a few predictions here, some contestable commentary there, and the job is done, a reservation is disestablished. None of these moves would be permitted in any other area of statutory interpretation, and there is no reason why they should be permitted here. That would be the rule of the strong, not the rule of law.

VI.

In the end, Oklahoma abandons any pretense of law and speaks openly about the potentially "transform[ative]" effects of a loss today. Here, at least, the State is finally rejoined by the dissent. If we dared to recognize that the Creek Reservation was never disestablished, Oklahoma and dissent warn, our holding might be used by other tribes to vindicate similar treaty promises. Ultimately, Oklahoma fears that perhaps as much as half its land and roughly 1.8 million of its residents could wind up within Indian country.

It's hard to know what to make of this self-defeating argument. Each tribe's treaties must be considered on their own terms, and the only question before us concerns the Creek. Of course, the Creek Reservation alone is hardly insignificant, taking in most of Tulsa and certain neighboring communities in Northeastern Oklahoma. But neither is it unheard of for significant non-Indian populations to live successfully in or near reservations today. Oklahoma replies that its situation is different because the affected population here is large and many of its residents will be surprised to find out they have been living in Indian country this whole time. But we imagine some members of the 1832 Creek Tribe would be just as surprised to find them there.

What are the consequences the State and dissent worry might follow from an adverse ruling anyway? Primarily, they argue that recognizing the continued existence of the Creek Reservation could unsettle an untold number of convictions and frustrate the State's ability to prosecute crimes in the future. But the MCA applies only to certain crimes committed in Indian country by Indian defendants. A neighboring statute provides that federal law applies to a broader range of crimes by or against Indians in Indian country. States are otherwise free to apply their criminal laws in cases of non-Indian victims and defendants, including within Indian country. And Oklahoma tells us that somewhere between 10% and 15% of its citizens identify as Native American. Given all this, even Oklahoma admits that the vast majority of its prosecutions will be unaffected whatever we decide today.

Still, Oklahoma and the dissent fear, "[t]housands" of Native Americans like Mr. McGirt "wait in the wings" to challenge the jurisdictional basis of their state-court convictions. But this number is admittedly speculative, because many defendants may choose to finish their state sentences rather than risk reprosecution in federal court where sentences can be graver. Other defendants who do try to challenge their state convictions may face significant procedural obstacles, thanks to well-known state and federal limitations on postconviction review in criminal proceedings.

In reaching our conclusion about what the law demands of us today, we do not pretend to foretell the future and we proceed well aware of the potential for cost and conflict around jurisdictional boundaries, especially ones that have gone unappreciated for so long. But it is unclear why pessimism should rule the day. With the passage of time, Oklahoma and its Tribes have proven they can work successfully together as partners. Already, the State has negotiated hundreds of intergovernmental agreements with tribes, including many with the Creek. These agreements relate to taxation, law enforcement, vehicle registration, hunting and fishing, and countless other fine regulatory questions. No one before us claims that the spirit of good faith, "comity and cooperative sovereignty" behind these agreements, will be imperiled by an adverse decision for the State today any more than it might be by a favorable one. And, of course, should agreement prove elusive, Congress remains free to supplement its statutory directions about the lands in question at any time. It has no shortage of tools at its disposal.

The federal government promised the Creek a reservation in perpetuity. Over time, Congress has diminished that reservation. It has sometimes restricted and other times expanded the Tribe's authority. But Congress has never withdrawn the promised reservation. As a result, many of the arguments before us today follow a sadly familiar pattern. Yes, promises were made, but the price of keeping them has become too great, so now we should just cast a blind eye. We reject that thinking. If Congress wishes to withdraw its promises, it must say so. Unlawful acts, performed long enough and with sufficient vigor, are never enough to amend the law. To hold otherwise would be to elevate the most brazen and longstanding injustices over the law, both rewarding wrong and failing those in the right.

The judgment of the Court of Criminal Appeals of Oklahoma is Reversed.

Chief Justice Roberts, with whom Justices Alito, Kavanaugh, and Thomas join, Dissenting

In 1997, the State of Oklahoma convicted petitioner Jimcy McGirt of molesting, raping, and forcibly sodomizing a four-year-old girl, his wife's granddaughter. McGirt was sentenced to 1,000 years plus life in prison. Today, the Court holds that Oklahoma lacked jurisdiction to prosecute McGirt – on the improbable ground that, unbeknownst to anyone for the past century, a huge swathe of Oklahoma is actually a Creek Indian reservation, on which the State may not prosecute serious crimes committed by Indians like McGirt. Not only does the Court discover a Creek reservation that spans three million acres and includes most of the city of Tulsa, but the Court's reasoning portends that there are four more such reservations in Oklahoma. The rediscovered reservations encompass the entire eastern half of the State – 19 million acres that are home to 1.8 million people, only 10%–15% of whom are Indians.

Across this vast area, the State's ability to prosecute serious crimes will be hobbled and decades of past convictions could well be thrown out. On top of that, the Court has profoundly destabilized the governance of eastern Oklahoma. The decision today creates significant uncertainty for the State's continuing authority over any area that touches Indian affairs, ranging from zoning and taxation to family and environmental law.

None of this is warranted. What has gone unquestioned for a century remains true today: A huge portion of Oklahoma is not a Creek Indian reservation. Congress disestablished any reservation in a series of statutes leading up to Oklahoma statehood at the turn of the 19th century. The Court reaches the opposite conclusion only by disregarding the "well settled" approach required by our precedents.

Under those precedents, we determine whether Congress intended to disestablish a reservation by examining the relevant Acts of Congress and "all the [surrounding] circumstances," including the "contemporaneous and subsequent understanding of the status of the reservation." Yet the Court declines to consider such understandings here, preferring to examine only individual statutes in isolation.

Applying the broader inquiry our precedents require, a reservation did not exist when McGirt committed his crimes, so Oklahoma had jurisdiction to prosecute him. I respectfully dissent.

I.

The Creek Nation once occupied what is now Alabama and Georgia. In 1832, the Creek were compelled to cede these lands to the United States in exchange for land in present day

Oklahoma. The expanse set aside for the Creek and the other Indian nations that composed the "Five Civilized Tribes" – the Cherokees, Chickasaws, Choctaws, and Seminoles – became known as Indian Territory. Each of the Five Tribes formed a tripartite system of government. They "enact[ed] and execut[ed] their own laws," "punish[ed] their own criminals," and "rais[ed] and expend[ed] their own revenues." The Five Tribes also enjoyed unique property rights. While many tribes held only a "right of occupancy" on lands owned by the United States, *United States v. Creek Nation*, 295 U.S. 103, 109 (1935), each of the Five Tribes possessed title to its lands in communal fee simple, meaning the lands were "considered the property of the whole."

Forever, it turns out, did not last very long, because the Civil War disrupted both relationships and borders. The Five Tribes, whose members collectively held at least 8,000 slaves, signed treaties of alliance with the Confederacy and contributed forces to fight alongside Rebel troops. After the war, the United States and the Tribes formed new treaties, which required each Tribe to free its slaves and allow them to become tribal citizens. The treaties also stated that the Tribes had "ignored their allegiance to the United States" and "unsettled the [existing] treaty relations," thereby rendering themselves "liable to forfeit" all "benefits and advantages enjoyed by them" – including their lands. Due to "said liabilities," the treaties departed from prior promises and required each Tribe to give up the "west half" of its "entire domain." These western lands became the Oklahoma Territory. As before, the new treaties promised that the reduced Indian Territory would be "forever set apart as a home" for the Tribes.

Again, however, it was not to last. In the wake of the war, a renewed "determination to thrust the nation westward" gripped the country. Spurred by new railroads and protected by the repurposed Union Army, settlers rapidly transformed vast stretches of territorial wilderness into farmland and ranches. The Indian Territory was no exception. By 1900, over 300,000 settlers had poured in, outnumbering members of the Five Tribes by over 3 to 1. There to stay, the settlers founded "[f]lourishing towns" along the railway lines that crossed the territory.

Coexistence proved complicated. The new towns had no municipal governments or the things that come with them – laws, taxes, police, and the like. No one had meaningful access to private property ownership, as the unique communal titles of the Five Tribes precluded ownership by Indians and non-Indians alike. Despite the millions of dollars that had been invested in the towns and farmlands, residents had no durable claims to their improvements. Members of the Tribes were little better off, as the Tribes failed to hold the communal lands for the "equal benefit" of all members. Instead, a few "enterprising citizens" of the Tribes "appropriate[d] to their exclusive use almost the entire property of the Territory that could be rendered profitable." As a result, "the poorer class of Indians [were] unable to secure enough lands for houses and farms," and "the great body of the tribe derive[d] no more benefit from their title than the neighbors in Kansas, Arkansas, or Missouri."

Attuned to these new realities, Congress decided that it could not maintain an Indian Territory predicated on "exclusion of the Indians from the whites." Congress therefore set about transforming the Indian Territory into a State.

Congress began by establishing a uniform body of law applicable to all occupants of the territory, regardless of race. To apply these laws, Congress established the U.S. Courts for the Indian Territory. Next Congress systematically dismantled the tribal governments. It abolished tribal courts, hollowed out tribal lawmaking power, and stripped tribal taxing authority. Congress also eliminated the foundation of tribal sovereignty, extinguishing the Creek Nation's title to the lands. Finally, Congress made the tribe members citizens of the United States and incorporated them in the drafting and ratification of the constitution for their new State, Oklahoma.

In taking these transformative steps, Congress made no secret of its intentions. It created a commission tasked with extinguishing the Five Tribes' territory and, in one report after another, explained that it was creating a homogenous population led by a common government. That contemporaneous understanding was shared by the tribal leadership and the State of Oklahoma. The tribal leadership acknowledged that its only remaining power was to parcel out the last of its land, and the State assumed jurisdiction over criminal cases that, if a reservation had continued to exist, would have belonged in federal court.

A century of practice confirms that the Five Tribes' prior domains were extinguished. The State has maintained unquestioned jurisdiction for more than 100 years. Tribe members make up less than 10%–15% of the population of their former domain, and until a few years ago the Creek Nation itself acknowledged that it no longer possessed the reservation the Court discovers today. This on-the-ground reality is enshrined throughout the U.S. Code, which repeatedly terms the Five Tribes' prior holdings the "former" Indian reservations in Oklahoma. As the Tribes, the State, and Congress have recognized from the outset, those "reservations were destroyed" when "Oklahoma entered the Union."

III.

Most immediately, the Court's decision draws into question thousands of convictions obtained by the State for crimes involving Indian defendants or Indian victims across several decades. This includes convictions for serious crimes such as murder, rape, kidnapping, and maiming. Such convictions are now subject to jurisdictional challenges, leading to the potential release of numerous individuals found guilty under state law of the most grievous offenses. Although the federal government may be able to reprosecute some of these crimes, it may lack the resources to reprosecute all of them, and the odds of convicting again are hampered by the passage of time, stale evidence, fading memories, and dead witnesses. No matter, the court says, these concerns are speculative because "many defendants may choose to finish their state sentences rather than risk reprosecution in federal court." Certainly defendants like McGirt – convicted of serious crimes and sentenced to 1,000 years

plus life in prison – will not adopt a strategy of running out the clock on their state sentences. At the end of the day, there is no escaping that today's decision will undermine numerous convictions obtained by the State, as well as the State's ability to prosecute serious crimes committed in the future.

Not to worry, the Court says, only about 10%–15% of Oklahoma citizens are Indian, so the "majority" of prosecutions will be unaffected. But the share of serious crimes committed by 10%–15% of the 1.8 million people in eastern Oklahoma, or of the 400,000 people in Tulsa, is no small number.

Beyond the criminal law, the decision may destabilize the governance of vast swathes of Oklahoma. The Court, despite briefly suggesting that its decision concerns only a narrow question of criminal law, ultimately acknowledges that "many" federal laws, triggering a variety of rules, spring into effect when land is declared a reservation.

State and tribal authority are also transformed. As to the State, its authority is clouded in significant respects when land is designated a reservation. Under our precedents, for example, state regulation of even non-Indians is preempted if it runs afoul of federal Indian policy and tribal sovereignty based on a nebulous balancing test. This test lacks any "rigid rule"; it instead calls for a "particularized inquiry into the nature of the state, federal, and tribal interests at stake," contemplated in light of the "broad policies that underlie" relevant treaties and statutes and "notions of sovereignty that have developed from historical traditions of tribal independence." This test mires state efforts to regulate on reservation lands in significant uncertainty, guaranteeing that many efforts will be deemed permissible only after extensive litigation, if at all.

In addition to undermining state authority, reservation status adds an additional, complicated layer of governance over the massive territory here, conferring on tribal government power over numerous areas of life – including powers over non-Indian citizens and businesses. Under our precedents, tribes may regulate non-Indian conduct on reservation land, so long as the conduct stems from a "consensual relationship with the tribe or its members" or directly affects "the political integrity, the economic security, or the health or welfare of the tribe." Tribes may also impose certain taxes on non-Indians on reservation land, and in this litigation, the Creek Nation contends that it retains the power to tax nonmembers doing business within its borders. No small power, given that those borders now embrace three million acres, the city of Tulsa, and hundreds of thousands of Oklahoma citizens. Recognizing the significant "potential for cost and conflict" caused by its decision, the Court insists any problems can be ameliorated if the citizens of Oklahoma just keep up the "spirit" of cooperation behind existing intergovernmental agreements between Oklahoma and the Five Tribes. But those agreements are small potatoes compared to what will be necessary to address the disruption inflicted by today's decision.

The Court responds to these and other concerns with the truism that significant consequences are no "license for us to disregard the law." Of course not. But when those consequences are drastic precisely because they depart from how the law has been applied for more than a century – a settled understanding that our precedents demand we consider – they are reason to think the Court may have taken a wrong turn in its analysis.

* * *

As the Creek, the State of Oklahoma, the United States, and our judicial predecessors have long agreed, Congress disestablished any Creek reservation more than 100 years ago. Oklahoma therefore had jurisdiction to prosecute McGirt. I respectfully dissent.

1. Does this case advance the cause of Native sovereignty or restrict it? In what way? What could be the implications of this decision for future rulings?
2. Does this decision advance the argument of "Native" serving as a racial identity or a political identity? In what way? What are the implications of both perspectives?

This case expanded the definition of Native land to include ground that was previously ceded to tribes, even if the land was then developed by White communities outside the treaties signed with the federal government. While the decision found that the majority of the city of Tulsa, Oklahoma, was located within the Muscogee (Creek) Nation reservation, some scholars have noted that the decision could apply to the many other Indian nations located within Oklahoma. If this is the case, "nearly one-third to one-half of Oklahoma lands would be part of a reservation" (Blackhawk 2023, 269). *McGirt* v. *Oklahoma* is unique in American law and its power as a precedent has not yet been determined. But if a majority White city is now located within Indian Country that is also governed by tribal law, defining the scope of tribal sovereignty becomes significant beyond those who live in Indian Country. This decision upheld the language of a signed treaty and enforced its promises. The Court made it clear that the federally elected branches of Congress and the Executive had to intervene explicitly "to dispossess further Native nations of land and sovereignty secured by treaty" (Blackhawk 2020, 392) even if it had been done in practice. How might this decision help us address the question of whether Native identity is racial, political, or both? Does this decision actually advance greater power for Native people or will it not change the balance of power in Oklahoma?

Determining the best way for the United States to undo errors of the past – expanding constitutional protections to all citizens – continues to be controversial. Efforts like affirmative action, statehood for unincorporated citizens, and increased tribal sovereignty were initiated by activists hoping to find a solution to the nation's past harm to racialized communities. But all these remedial attempts have been challenged as potentially causing more damage than benefit. Critics of affirmative action worry that the reliance on race to provide resources merely reify racial frameworks, while advocates recognize that ignoring the on-going damage done by race-based slavery, segregation, and state-sanctioned violence does not make such impacts dissipate. Those who seek statehood for the unincorporated territories are challenged by the fear that federal requirements and constitutional guarantees could destroy local cultures and practices. Is a model like Native sovereignty a potential solution? Those that want to expand tribal sovereignty must address the difficulties of integrating a third sovereign entity into a federalist system built upon two. Does moving the discourse away from race towards self-determination help us better rectify the past?

What obligation does the United States have to make right these grievances of the past? What role should the government play in making such changes occur? If humans have socially constructed race then we are capable of dismantling it and creating new identities. While we did not build these structures of inequity, we do have an obligation to tear them down. As Hannah Arendt noted in her analysis after the despair, genocide, and destruction of the Second World War (cited in Ushpiz 2015):

> When you take it upon yourself, as a member of the human society, the burden of what the other did, you don't accept the blame, or absolve him for the blame. Rather you take upon yourself the injustice that occurred in reality. It's a decision to be a partner to the accountability, not at all a partner to the guilt.

7 Race and the Limits of the Law

The U.S. Census has recorded the population's demographics every decade since 1790; while imperfect, the manner by which we have defined race over time provides insight as to our collective understanding of identity. Until 2000, individuals had to select a single race with which they identify. In the first census of the twenty-first century, residents were finally able to define themselves as having multiple racial identities. In 2020, the census allowed people to clarify their race, for instance, one claiming "Asian American" as a racial category, could then denote "Cambodian" descent as their heritage.

Historically, our nation has not been very sophisticated in defining racial identity. The Pew Research Center, in their analysis of census data from 1790 to 2020, found that the United States has altered how it categorizes people who are racially designated "Black" or "White" more than any other racial groups (Brown 2020). These changes paralleled the nation's political, social, and legal thinking on race. Prior to 1960, people could not determine their own racial identity for this federal calculation; instead, federal census-takers were told to make their own determination based on observation. People who were phenotypically more ambiguous as to race or for those of a multiracial identity, this determination was generally assumed to be "not White." For instance, government directions for the 1930 census enumerators stipulated that "a person of mixed White and Negro blood was to be returned as Negro, no matter how small the percentage of Negro blood," a reflection of the "one-drop rule." This construction argued that one Black ancestor, no matter how remote in the distant past, made an individual Black.

As we have seen in the Introduction to this book, race is not a biological reality, but something we have constructed through laws and policies over time. It is worth considering the question of why we continue to enforce these classifications – since they are artificial – through demographic measurements. But how can we know the impact of governmental policies on racialized groups without accurate data? So, we work to better define these categories to help people describe how they define themselves racially. For instance, the community of Asian American and Pacific Islanders encompasses more than fifty distinct ethnic identities – all with unique income levels, health outcomes, and educational attainment (Fong, Percival, and Wolf 2023). Similarly, we have no distinct recognition for those of Middle Eastern and Northern African (MENA) descent, although that may change for the 2030 census; they are expected to self-identify as either "White" or "Black," regardless of their self-perception. Does more accurate assessment of the impact of these identities help us to better understand our society or merely reinforce the power of race within our law?

We often expect the law to provide solutions for all our problems and our system of justice to address all inequities. But the law was constructed to engage problems as they were defined by the powerful in the past. Our common law system, which depends on past precedents for guidance, frequently constrains the judiciary in how it addresses modern problems. For instance, our law constructed race as either/or (the one-drop rule) as opposed to both/many. The legal system assumed people were either Black or White, Native or non-Native, Hispanic or Anglo, Asian/Pacific Islander or Hoale and not a blend of multiple identities. While such simplicity was not most people's realities, the law constructed race with very narrow parameters. Today, people construct their identities in many ways, including their class, sexuality, gender, mental and physical capacities, and racial or ethnic ancestry. The law is not equipped for such complex identities and is consistently being challenged – as by the U.S. Census – to consider these more complex notions of self.

7.1 Intentionality

One of the early assumptions regarding racial discrimination – later applied to gender and other forms of bias (Deardorff 2016) – was that the challenged policy or actions had to be implemented deliberately with the evident purpose of harming the injured party. As you may imagine, it can be very hard in contemporary days to demonstrate an intent to discriminate. There could be a "smoking gun" memo or voice mail that explicitly demonstrates a desire to discriminate by executive leaders. More typically, an organization is charged with ignoring ongoing discriminatory actions by supervisors or allowing abusive workplace conditions to continue unabated despite notification by the plaintiffs. For instance, in 2023 the Equal Employment Opportunity Commission (EEOC) filed a lawsuit against Exxon Mobile Corporation after nooses were hung in the firm's Baton Rouge complex, including at the personal stations of Black employees. There were five incidences reported and the company did nothing to protect Black employees from this traditional symbol of lynching (Chapter 4) and racial hatred against African Americans (EEOC 2023). This lawsuit made the national news cycle because such *explicit* racial discrimination by multinational corporations in the current era is unusual. Why does employment law require such evidence of intentionality to demonstrate unlawful racial discrimination?

The U.S. Supreme Court case of *Washington* v. *Davis* (1976) originated in 1970 after two African American police officers sued the Washington D.C. Chief of Police and other metropolitan and federal government officials for their racially discriminatory promotion policies. Two Black police force applicants, George Harley and John D. Sellers, joined the case arguing that the hiring practices were similarly problematic. Plaintiffs claimed that the District relied on a number of

measures, but specifically a written personnel test that resulted in a disproportionate number of Black applicants being excluded from the hiring pool. The
standards to be admitted to the police force's rigorous seventeen-week training program, included: physical and character tests; a high school diploma or
equivalent; and a 40 out of 80 point score on the Civil Service Test (Test 21).
Test 21 was designed to evaluate federal government employees and examine
their verbal ability, vocabulary, reading, and comprehension. The federal District
Court found that while there was no evidence of purposeful or intentional racial
discrimination on the part of police force leadership, the screening test had no
relationship to the job performance and therefore manifested a clear discriminatory impact. However, the court did not believe this impact was sufficient
to prove racial discrimination against the plaintiffs. The appellate court disagreed, finding that a lack of discriminatory intent in the design or use of the
test was irrelevant, instead the fact that four times as many Blacks failed the
test than White applicants demonstrated unlawful discriminatory impact. This
disproportionate impact – regardless of discriminatory purpose – was sufficient
to demonstrate unconstitutional racial discrimination. The case was appealed to
the Supreme Court.

WASHINGTON v. *DAVIS*, 426 U.S. 229 (1976)

**Justice White Delivered the Opinion of
the Court, Joined by Chief Justice Burger
and Justices Stewart, Blackmun, Powell,
Rehnquist, and Stevens**

Vote: 7–2

II.

The central purpose of the Equal Protection
Clause of the Fourteenth Amendment is the
prevention of official conduct discriminating
on the basis of race. It is also true that the Due
Process Clause of the Fifth Amendment contains an equal protection component prohibiting
the United States from invidiously discriminating between individuals or groups. *Bolling*
v. *Sharpe*, 347 U.S. 497 (1954). But our cases
have not embraced the proposition that a law
or other official act, without regard to whether
it reflects a racially discriminatory purpose, is

unconstitutional solely because it has a racially
disproportionate impact.

Almost 100 years ago, *Strauder* v. *West
Virginia*, 100 U.S. 303 (1880), established
that the exclusion of Negroes from grand and
petit juries in criminal proceedings violated
the Equal Protection Clause, but the fact that
a particular jury or a series of juries does not
statistically reflect the racial composition of
the community does not in itself make out
an invidious discrimination forbidden by the
Clause. "A purpose to discriminate must be
present which may be proven by systematic
exclusion of eligible jurymen of the proscribed
race or by unequal application of the law to
such an extent as to show intentional discrimination." *Akins* v. *Texas*, 325 U.S. 398, 403–404
(1945). A defendant in a criminal case is entitled "to require that the State not deliberately

and systematically deny to members of his race the right to participate as jurors in the administration of justice." *Alexander* v. *Louisiana*, 405 U.S. 625, 628–629 (1972).

The school desegregation cases have also adhered to the basic equal protection principle that the invidious quality of a law claimed to be racially discriminatory must ultimately be traced to a racially discriminatory purpose. That there are both predominantly black and predominantly white schools in a community is not alone violative of the Equal Protection Clause. The essential element of *de jure* segregation is "a current condition of segregation resulting from intentional state action. *Keyes* v. *School Dist. No. 1*, 413 U.S. 189, 205 (1973). The differentiating factor between de jure segregation and so-called de facto segregation ... is Purpose or Intent to segregate." The Court has also recently rejected allegations of racial discrimination based solely on the statistically disproportionate racial impact of various provisions of the Social Security Act because "(t)he acceptance of appellants' constitutional theory would render suspect each difference in treatment among the grant classes, however lacking in racial motivation and however otherwise rational the treatment might be." *Jefferson* v. *Hackney*, 406 U.S. 535, 548 (1972).

This is not to say that the necessary discriminatory racial purpose must be express or appear on the face of the statute, or that a law's disproportionate impact is irrelevant in cases involving Constitution-based claims of racial discrimination. A statute, otherwise neutral on its face, must not be applied so as invidiously to discriminate on the basis of race. *Yick Wo* v. *Hopkins*, 118 U.S. 356 (1886). It is also clear from the cases dealing with racial discrimination in the selection of juries that the systematic exclusion of Negroes is itself such an "unequal application of the law ... as to show intentional discrimination." A prima facie case of discriminatory purpose may be proved as well by the absence of Negroes on a particular jury combined with the failure of the jury commissioners to be informed of eligible

Negro jurors in a community, or with racially non-neutral selection procedures. With a prima facie case made out, "the burden of proof shifts to the State to rebut the presumption of unconstitutional action by showing that permissible racially neutral selection criteria and procedures have produced the monochromatic result." *Alexander*, 405 U.S., at 632.

Necessarily, an invidious discriminatory purpose may often be inferred from the totality of the relevant facts, including the fact, if it is true, that the law bears more heavily on one race than another. It is also not infrequently true that the discriminatory impact in the jury cases for example, the total or seriously disproportionate exclusion of Negroes from jury venires may for all practical purposes demonstrate unconstitutionality because in various circumstances the discrimination is very difficult to explain on nonracial grounds. Nevertheless, we have not held that a law, neutral on its face and serving ends otherwise within the power of government to pursue, is invalid under the Equal Protection Clause simply because it may affect a greater proportion of one race than of another. Disproportionate impact is not irrelevant, but it is not the sole touchstone of an invidious racial discrimination forbidden by the Constitution. Standing alone, it does not trigger the rule, that racial classifications are to be subjected to the strictest scrutiny and are justifiable only by the weightiest of considerations.

As an initial matter, we have difficulty understanding how a law establishing a racially neutral qualification for employment is nevertheless racially discriminatory and denies "any person ... equal protection of the laws" simply because a greater proportion of Negroes fail to qualify than members of other racial or ethnic groups. Had respondents, along with all others who had failed Test 21, whether white or black, brought an action claiming that the test denied each of them equal protection of the laws as compared with those who had passed with high enough scores to qualify them as police recruits, it is most unlikely that their challenge would have been sustained. Test 21, which is administered generally to prospective Government employees, concededly seeks to ascertain whether those who take it have acquired a particular level of verbal skill; and it is untenable that the Constitution prevents the Government from seeking modestly to upgrade the communicative abilities of its employees rather than to be satisfied with some lower level of competence, particularly where the job requires special ability to communicate orally and in writing. Respondents, as Negroes, could no more successfully claim that the test denied them equal protection than could white applicants who also failed. The conclusion would not be different in the face of proof that more Negroes than whites had been disqualified by Test 21. That other Negroes also failed to score well would, alone, not demonstrate that respondents individually were being denied equal protection of the laws by the application of an otherwise valid qualifying test being administered to prospective police recruits.

Nor on the facts of the case before us would the disproportionate impact of Test 21 warrant the conclusion that it is a purposeful device to discriminate against Negroes and hence an infringement of the constitutional rights of respondents as well as other black applicants. As we have said, the test is neutral on its face and rationally may be said to serve a purpose the Government is constitutionally empowered to pursue. Even agreeing with the District Court that the differential racial effect of Test 21 called for further inquiry, we think the District Court correctly held that the affirmative efforts of the Metropolitan Police Department to recruit black officers, the changing racial composition of the recruit classes and of the force in general, and the relationship of the test to the training program negated any inference that the Department discriminated on the basis of race or that "a police officer qualifies on the color of his skin rather than ability."

Under Title VII, Congress provided that when hiring and promotion practices disqualifying substantially disproportionate numbers of blacks are challenged, discriminatory purpose need not be proved, and that it is an insufficient response to demonstrate some rational basis for the challenged practices. It is necessary, in addition, that they be "validated" in terms of job performance in any one of several ways, perhaps by ascertaining the minimum skill, ability, or potential necessary for the position at issue and determining whether the qualifying tests are appropriate for the selection of qualified applicants for the job in question. However this process proceeds, it involves a more probing judicial review of, and less deference to, the seemingly reasonable acts of administrators and executives than is appropriate under the Constitution where special racial impact, without discriminatory purpose, is claimed. We are not disposed to adopt this more rigorous standard for the purposes] of applying the Fifth and the Fourteenth Amendments in cases such as this.

A rule that a statute designed to serve neutral ends is nevertheless invalid, absent compelling justification, if in practice it benefits or burdens one race more than another would be far-reaching and would raise serious questions about, and perhaps invalidate, a whole range of tax, welfare, public service, regulatory, and licensing statutes that may be more burdensome to the poor and to the average black than to the more affluent white.

Given that rule, such consequences would perhaps be likely to follow. However, in our view, extension of the rule beyond those areas where it is already applicable by reason of statute, such as in the field of public employment, should await legislative prescription.

Justices Stewart and Stevens, Concurring

Frequently the most probative evidence of intent will be objective evidence of what actually happened rather than evidence describing the subjective state of mind of the actor. For normally the actor is presumed to have intended the natural consequences of his deeds. This is particularly true in the case of governmental action which is frequently the product of compromise, of collective decisionmaking, and of mixed motivation. It is unrealistic, on the one hand, to require the victim of alleged discrimination to uncover the actual subjective intent of the decisionmaker or, conversely, to invalidate otherwise legitimate action simply because an improper motive affected the deliberation of a participant in the decisional process. A law conscripting clerics should not be invalidated because an atheist voted for it.

My point in making this observation is to suggest that the line between discriminatory purpose and discriminatory impact is not nearly as bright, and perhaps not quite as critical, as the reader of the Court's opinion might assume. I agree, of course, that a constitutional issue does not arise every time some disproportionate impact is shown. On the other hand, when the disproportion is as dramatic as in *Yick Wo* v. *Hopkins*, 118 U.S. 356 (1886), it really does not matter whether the standard is phrased in terms of purpose or effect. Therefore, although I accept the statement of the general rule in the Court's opinion, I am not yet prepared to indicate how that standard should be applied in the many cases which have formulated the governing standard in different language.

Justice Brennan, Joined by Justice Marshall, Dissenting

The [Civil Service Commission (CSC)] standards thus recognize that Test 21 can be validated by a correlation between Test 21 scores and recruits' averages on training examinations only if (1) the training averages predict job performance or (2) the averages are proved to measure performance in job-related training. There is no proof that the recruits' average is correlated with job performance after completion of training. And although a positive relationship to the recruits' average might be sufficient to validate Test 21 if the average were proved to reflect mastery of material on the training curriculum that was

in turn demonstrated to be relevant to job performance, the record is devoid of proof in this regard. First, there is no demonstration by petitioners that the training-course examinations measure comprehension of the training curriculum; indeed, these examinations do not even appear in the record. Furthermore, the Futransky study [which tested the correlation between the applicants' score on Test 21 and success in the police training course] simply designated an average of 85 on the examination as a "good" performance and assumed that a recruit with such an average learned the material taught in the training course. Without any further proof of the significance of a score of 85, and there is none in the record, I cannot agree that Test 21 is predictive of "success in training."

III.

The Court also says that its conclusion is not foreclosed by *Griggs* v. *Duke Power Co.*, 401 U.S. 424 (1971) and *Albemarle Paper Co.* v. *Moody*, 422 U.S. 405 (1975), but today's result plainly conflicts with those cases. *Griggs* held that "(i)f an employment practice which operates to exclude Negroes cannot be shown to be related to job performance, the practice is prohibited." Once a discriminatory impact is shown, the employer carries the burden of proving that the challenged practice "bear(s) a Demonstrable relationship to successful performance of the jobs for which it was used." We observed further:

> Nothing in the Act precludes the use of testing or measuring procedures; obviously they are useful. What Congress has forbidden is giving these devices and mechanisms controlling force unless they are demonstrably a reasonable measure of job performance ... What Congress has commanded is that any tests used must measure the person for the job and not the person in the abstract.

Albemarle read *Griggs* to require that a discriminatory test be validated through proof "by professionally acceptable methods" that it is "predictive of or significantly correlated with *important* elements of work behavior *which comprise or are relevant to the job or jobs* for which candidates are being evaluated." Further, we rejected the employer's attempt to validate a written test by proving that it was related to supervisors' job performance ratings, because there was no demonstration that the ratings accurately reflected job performance. We were unable "to determine whether the criteria Actually considered were sufficiently related to the (employer's) legitimate interest in job-specific ability to justify a testing system with a racially discriminatory impact." To me, therefore, these cases read Title VII as requiring proof of a significant relationship to job performance to establish the validity of a discriminatory test. Petitioners do not maintain that there is a demonstrated correlation between Test 21 scores and job performance. Moreover, their validity study was unable to discern a significant positive relationship between training averages and job performance. Thus, there is no proof of a correlation either direct or indirect between Test 21 and performance of the job of being a police officer.

Finally, it should be observed that every federal court, except the District Court in this case, presented with proof identical to that offered to validate Test 21 has reached a conclusion directly opposite to that of the Court today. Sound policy considerations support the view that, at a minimum, petitioners should have been required to prove that the police training examinations either measure job-related skills or predict job performance. Where employers try to validate written qualification tests by proving a correlation with written examinations in a training course, there is a substantial danger that people who have good verbal skills will achieve high scores on both tests due to verbal ability, rather than "job-specific ability." As a result, employers could validate any entrance examination that measures only verbal ability by giving another written test that measures verbal ability at the end of a training course. Any contention that the resulting correlation between examination scores would be evidence that the initial test is "job related" is plainly erroneous. It seems to me, however, that the Court's holding in this case can be read as endorsing this dubious proposition. Today's result will prove particularly unfortunate if it is extended to govern Title VII cases.

1. Besides "smoking gun" evidence, how else does the Court believe intent to unlawfully discriminate could be determined?
2. Why is the question so significant in employee discrimination cases? How can it be demonstrated?
3. Why do the dissenting justices disagree with the majority? What impact do they anticipate this ruling might have?

Washington v. *Davis* (1976) is still good law, providing guidance to federal courts on evaluating claims of discrimination under the Civil Rights Act, 1964. This rule applies to all forms of unlawful discrimination. For instance, the decision was expanded by the Supreme Court a year later to apply to the Fair Housing Act, 1968, in *Arlington Heights* v. *Metropolitan Housing Development Corporation.* The conflict in this case arose when the nonprofit Metropolitan Housing Development Corporation (MHDC) requested that a local predominately White Illinois community, Arlington Heights, rezone a section of land from single-family to a multiple-family classification. MHDC had hoped to create Lincoln Green, a clustered townhouse community that would provide integrated housing for low- and moderate-income families. Arlington Heights denied the request. MHDC sued in federal court arguing that this denial was racially discriminatory and violated the Fair Housing Act, 1968, and the Fourteenth Amendment. The District Court sided with Arlington Heights and upon appeal, the Court of Appeals in the 7th Circuit found the "ultimate effect" of this denial to be racially discriminatory and therefore the refusal to rezone violated the Fourteenth Amendment.

ARLINGTON HEIGHTS v. *METROPOLITAN HOUSING DEV. CORP.*, 429 U.S. 252 (1977)

Justice Powell Delivered the Opinion of the Court, in which Chief Justice Burger and Justices Stewart, Blackmun, and Rehnquist joined

Vote: 5–3

III.

Our decision last Term, in *Washington* v. *Davis*, 426 U.S. 229 (1976), made it clear that official action will not be held unconstitutional solely because it results in a racially disproportionate impact. "Disproportionate impact is not irrelevant, but it is not the sole touchstone of an invidious racial discrimination." Proof of racially discriminatory intent or purpose is required to show a violation of the Equal Protection Clause. Although some contrary indications may be drawn from some of our cases, the holding in *Davis* reaffirmed a principle well established in a variety of contexts.

Davis does not require a plaintiff to prove that the challenged action rested solely on racially discriminatory purposes. Rarely can it be said that a legislature or administrative body operating under a broad mandate made a decision motivated solely by a single concern, or even that a particular purpose was the "dominant" or "primary" one. In fact, it is because legislators and administrators are properly concerned with balancing numerous competing considerations that courts refrain from reviewing the merits of their decisions, absent a showing of arbitrariness or irrationality. But racial discrimination is not just another competing consideration. When there is a proof that a discriminatory purpose has been a motivating factor in the decision, this judicial deference is no longer justified.

Determining whether invidious discriminatory purpose was a motivating factor demands a sensitive inquiry into such circumstantial and direct evidence of intent as may be available. The impact of the official action – whether it "bears more heavily on one race than another," *Washington* v. *Davis* – may provide an important starting point. Sometimes a clear pattern, unexplainable on grounds other than race, emerges from the effect of the state action even when the governing legislation appears neutral on its face. *Yick Wo* v. *Hopkins*, 118 U.S. 356 (1886); *Gomillion* v. *Lightfoot*, 364 U.S. 339 (1960). The evidentiary inquiry is then relatively easy. But such cases are rare. Absent a pattern as stark as that in *Gomillion* or *Yick Wo*, impact alone is not determinative, and the Court must look to other evidence.

The historical background of the decision is one evidentiary source, particularly if it reveals a series of official actions taken for invidious purposes. The specific sequence of events leading up to the challenged decision also may shed some light on the decisionmaker's purposes. For example, if the property involved here always had been zoned R-5 but suddenly was changed to R-3 when the town learned of MHDC's plan to erect integrated housing, we would have a far different case. Departures from the normal procedural sequence also might afford evidence that improper purposes are playing a role. Substantive departures too may be relevant, particularly if the factors usually considered important by the decision-maker strongly favor a decision contrary to the one reached.

The legislative or administrative history may be highly relevant, especially where there are contemporary statements by members of the decisionmaking body, minutes of its meetings, or reports. In some extraordinary instances, the members might be called to the stand at trial to testify concerning the purpose of the official action, although even then such testimony frequently will be barred by privilege.

IV.

... The impact of the Village's decision does arguably bear more heavily on racial minorities. Minorities constitute 18% of the Chicago area population, and 40% of the income groups said to be eligible for Lincoln Green. But there is little about the sequence of events leading up to the decision that would spark suspicion. The area around the ... property has been zoned R-3 since 1959, the year when Arlington Heights first adopted a zoning map. Single-family homes surround the 80-acre site, and the Village is undeniably committed to single-family homes as its dominant residential land use. The rezoning request progressed according to the usual procedures. The Plan Commission even scheduled two additional hearings, at least in part to accommodate MHDC and permit it to supplement its presentation with answers to questions generated at the first hearing.

The statements by the Plan Commission and Village Board members, as reflected in the official minutes, focused almost exclusively on the zoning aspects of the MHDC petition, and the zoning factors on which they relied are not novel criteria in the Village's rezoning decisions. There is no reason to doubt that there has been reliance by some neighboring property owners on the maintenance of single-family zoning in the vicinity. The Village originally adopted its buffer policy long before MHDC entered the picture, and has applied the policy too consistently for us to infer discriminatory purpose from its application in this case. Finally, MHDC called one member of the Village Board to the stand at trial. Nothing in her testimony supports an inference of invidious purpose.

In sum, the evidence does not warrant overturning the concurrent findings of both courts below. Respondents simply failed to carry their burden of proving that discriminatory purpose was a motivating factor in the Village's decision.

V.

Respondents' complaint also alleged that the refusal to rezone violated the Fair Housing Act of 1968. They continue to urge here that a zoning decision made by a public body may, and that petitioners' action did, violate §3604 or §3617. The Court of Appeals, however, proceeding in a somewhat unorthodox fashion, did not decide the statutory question. We remand the case for further consideration of respondents' statutory claims. *Reversed and remanded.*

Justice Marshall, with whom Justice Brennan joins, Concurring in part and Dissenting in part

... I believe the proper result would be to remand this entire case to the Court of Appeals for further proceedings consistent with *Washington* v. *Davis*, 426 U.S. 229 (1976), and today's opinion. The Court of Appeals is better situated than this Court both to reassess the significance of the evidence developed below in light of the standards we have set forth and to determine whether the interests of justice require further District Court proceedings directed toward those standards.

1. In trying to address the legacy of segregation, what would be the impact of this decision?
2. How does the Court demonstrate how intentionality might be demonstrated as opposed to impact? Why might the Court be afraid to make decisions based on racial discriminatory impact alone?
3. What is the concern articulated by the dissent? Do you find their claims compelling, why or why not?

While the formal equality provided by the Civil Rights Act, 1964, and the Fair Housing Act, 1968, removed the legally explicit (formal) barriers to equality, it did not transform the perspectives and values of the Nation. As the country attempted to eradicate the various manifestations of inequality (substantive equality), the question of when the government can intervene to eradicate racial discrimination becomes significant. Does the long-standing test of intentionality, as opposed to impact, advance or block our quest for a more just society?

The intentionality test not only applies to issues of employment and housing, but permeates many aspects of human existence, limiting the law's ability to challenge and remediate the consequences of generations of racial discrimination. For instance, a decade later the question of the impact of racist beliefs impacting the criminal justice system came before the Supreme Court. One consequence of a long history of policing Black and Brown bodies (see Chapter 4) is their disproportionate representation in the criminal justice system.

In *McCleskey* v. *Kemp* (1987), the Supreme Court tested the necessity for racist intent to invalidate a death penalty in the face of evident racial discriminatory impact. Warren McCleskey was a Black man convicted of murdering a White police officer while committing an armed robbery of a furniture store in Fulton County, Georgia. At the mandated separate penalty hearing, a jury sentenced McCleskey to death; as part of his appeal, McCleskey claimed that the Georgia capital sentencing process was implemented in a racially discriminatory manner. As evidence of his claim, he provided a statistical study conducted by Professors David C. Baldus, Charles Pulaski, and George Woodworth (known as the Baldus Study). This research demonstrates disparity in the application of the death penalty, based on the race of the victim, and less significantly, the race of the defendant. This research project integrated two sophisticated statistical analyses of over 2,000 murder cases in Georgia, which incorporated over 230 variables. They found:

> [d]efendants charged with killing white victims were 4.3 times as likely to receive a death sentence as defendants charged with killing blacks ... black defendants were 1.1 times as likely to receive a death sentence as other defendants (*McCleskey* v. *Kemp*, 481 U.S. 288).

The application of the models in the Baldus Study indicated that Black defendants who kill White victims, like McCleskey, are the most likely to receive the death penalty in Georgia. The district court dismissed the Baldus Study as flawed and irrelevant. The appellate court found no evidence of discriminatory intent on the part of the jury or trial court and therefore no evidence of unconstitutional discrimination.

MCCLESKEY v. *KEMP*, 481 U.S. 279 (1987)

Justice Powell Delivered the Opinion of the Court, in which Chief Justice Rehnquist, and Justices White, O'Connor, and Scalia joined

Vote: 5–4

This case presents the question whether a complex statistical study that indicates a risk that racial considerations enter into capital sentencing determinations proves that petitioner McCleskey's capital sentence is unconstitutional under the Eighth or Fourteenth Amendment.

II.

McCleskey's first claim is that the Georgia capital punishment statute violates the Equal Protection Clause of the Fourteenth Amendment. He argues that race has infected the administration of Georgia's statute in two ways: persons who murder whites are more likely to be sentenced to death than persons who murder blacks, and black murderers are more likely to be sentenced to death than white murderers. As a black defendant who killed a white victim, McCleskey claims that the Baldus study demonstrates that he was discriminated against because of his race and because of the race of his victim. In its broadest form, McCleskey's claim of discrimination extends to every actor in the Georgia capital sentencing process, from the prosecutor who sought the death penalty and the jury that imposed the sentence, to the State itself that enacted the capital punishment statute and allows it to remain in effect despite its allegedly discriminatory application. We agree with the Court of Appeals, and every other court that has considered such a challenge, that this claim must fail.

A.

Our analysis begins with the basic principle that a defendant who alleges an equal protection violation has the burden of proving "the existence of purposeful discrimination." *Whitus* v. *Georgia*, 385 U.S. 545, 550 (1967). A corollary to this principle is that a criminal defendant must prove that the purposeful discrimination "had a discriminatory effect" on him. Thus, to prevail under the Equal Protection Clause, McCleskey must prove that the decisionmakers in *his* case acted with discriminatory purpose. He offers no evidence specific to his own case that would support an inference that racial considerations played a part in his sentence. Instead, he relies solely on the Baldus study. McCleskey argues that the Baldus study compels an inference that his sentence rests on purposeful discrimination. McCleskey's claim that these statistics are sufficient proof of discrimination, without regard to the facts of a particular case, would extend to all capital cases in Georgia, at least where the victim was white and the defendant is black.

The Court has accepted statistics as proof of intent to discriminate in certain limited contexts. First, this Court has accepted statistical disparities as proof of an equal protection violation in the selection of the jury venire in a particular district. Although statistical proof normally must present a "stark" pattern to be accepted as the sole proof of discriminatory intent under the Constitution, *Arlington Heights* v. *Metropolitan Housing Dev. Corp.*, 429 U.S. 252, 266 (1977), "[b]ecause of the nature of the jury-selection task ... we have permitted a finding of constitutional violation even when the statistical pattern does not approach [such] extremes." Second, this Court has accepted statistics in the form of multiple-regression analysis to prove statutory violations under Title VII of the Civil Rights Act of 1964.

But the nature of the capital sentencing decision, and the relationship of the statistics to that decision, are fundamentally different from the corresponding elements in the venire-selection or Title VII cases. Most importantly, each particular decision to impose the death penalty is made by a petit jury selected from a properly constituted venire. Each jury is unique in its composition, and the Constitution requires that its decision rest on consideration of innumerable factors that vary according to the characteristics of the individual defendant and the facts of the particular capital offense ...

Another important difference between the cases in which we have accepted statistics as proof of discriminatory intent and this case is that, in the venire-selection and Title VII contexts, the decisionmaker has an opportunity to explain the statistical disparity. Here, the State has no practical opportunity to rebut the Baldus study ... Similarly, the policy considerations behind a prosecutor's traditionally "wide discretion" suggest the impropriety of our requiring prosecutors to defend their decisions to seek death penalties, "often years after they were made." Moreover, absent far stronger proof, it is unnecessary to seek such a rebuttal, because a legitimate and unchallenged explanation for the decision is apparent from the record: McCleskey committed an act for which the United States Constitution and Georgia laws permit imposition of the death penalty.

Finally, McCleskey's statistical proffer must be viewed in the context of his challenge. McCleskey challenges decisions at the heart of the State's criminal justice system. "[O]ne of society's most basic tasks is that of protecting the lives of its citizens and one of the most basic ways in which it achieves the task is through criminal laws against murder." *Gregg* v. *Georgia*, 428 U.S. 153, 226 (1976) (White, J., concurring). Implementation of these laws necessarily requires discretionary judgments. Because discretion is essential to the criminal justice process, we would demand exceptionally clear proof before we would infer that the discretion has been abused. The unique nature of the decisions at issue in this case also counsels against adopting such an inference from the disparities indicated by the Baldus study. Accordingly, we hold that the Baldus study is clearly insufficient

to support an inference that any of the decision-makers in McCleskey's case acted with discriminatory purpose.

B.

McCleskey also suggests that the Baldus study proves that the State as a whole has acted with a discriminatory purpose. He appears to argue that the State has violated the Equal Protection Clause by adopting the capital punishment statute and allowing it to remain in force despite its allegedly discriminatory application. But "'[d]iscriminatory purpose' ... implies more than intent as volition or intent as awareness of consequences. It implies that the decision-maker, in this case a state legislature, selected or reaffirmed a particular course of action at least in part 'because of,' not merely 'in spite of,' its adverse effects upon an identifiable group." *Personnel Administrator of Massachusetts* v. *Feeney*, 442 U.S. 256, 279 (1979). For this claim to prevail, McCleskey would have to prove that the Georgia Legislature enacted or maintained the death penalty statute *because of* an anticipated racially discriminatory effect. In *Gregg* v. *Georgia*, this Court found that the Georgia capital sentencing system could operate in a fair and neutral manner. There was no evidence then, and there is none now, that the Georgia Legislature enacted the capital punishment statute to further a racially discriminatory purpose.

Nor has McCleskey demonstrated that the legislature maintains the capital punishment statute because of the racially disproportionate impact suggested by the Baldus study. As legislatures necessarily have wide discretion in the choice of criminal laws and penalties, and as there were legitimate reasons for the Georgia Legislature to adopt and maintain capital punishment, we will not infer a discriminatory purpose on the part of the State of Georgia. Accordingly, we reject McCleskey's equal protection claims.

IV.

A.

In light of our precedents under the Eighth Amendment, McCleskey cannot argue

successfully that his sentence is "disproportionate to the crime in the traditional sense." He
does not deny that he committed a murder in the
course of a planned robbery, a crime for which
this Court has determined that the death penalty constitutionally may be imposed. *Gregg* v.
Georgia, 428 U.S., at 187. His disproportionality
claim "is of a different sort." McCleskey argues
that the sentence in his case is disproportionate
to the sentences in other murder cases.

On the one hand, he cannot base a constitutional claim on an argument that his case differs
from other cases in which defendants *did* receive
the death penalty ...

On the other hand, absent a showing that the
Georgia capital punishment system operates in
an arbitrary and capricious manner, McCleskey
cannot prove a constitutional violation by
demonstrating that other defendants who may
be similarly situated did *not* receive the death
penalty ...

Because McCleskey's sentence was imposed
under Georgia sentencing procedures that focus
discretion "on the particularized nature of the
crime and the particularized characteristics of
the individual defendant," we lawfully may presume that McCleskey's death sentence was not
"wantonly and freakishly" imposed, and thus
that the sentence is not disproportionate within
any recognized meaning under the Eighth
Amendment.

V.

Two additional concerns inform our decision in
this case. First, McCleskey's claim, taken to its
logical conclusion, throws into serious question
the principles that underlie our entire criminal
justice system. The Eighth Amendment is not
limited in application to capital punishment,
but applies to all penalties. Thus, if we accepted
McCleskey's claim that racial bias has impermissibly tainted the capital sentencing decision,
we could soon be faced with similar claims as
to other types of penalty. Moreover, the claim
that his sentence rests on the irrelevant factor of race easily could be extended to apply
to claims based on unexplained discrepancies

that correlate to membership in other minority
groups, and even to gender. Similarly, since
McCleskey's claim relates to the race of his
victim, other claims could apply with equally
logical force to statistical disparities that correlate with the race or sex of other actors in
the criminal justice system, such as defense
attorneys, or judges. Also, there is no logical
reason that such a claim need be limited to
racial or sexual bias. If arbitrary and capricious
punishment is the touchstone under the Eighth
Amendment, such a claim could – at least in
theory – be based upon any arbitrary variable,
such as the defendant's facial characteristics, or
the physical attractiveness of the defendant or
the victim, that some statistical study indicates
may be influential in jury decisionmaking. As
these examples illustrate, there is no limiting
principle to the type of challenge brought by
McCleskey. The Constitution does not require
that a State eliminate any demonstrable disparity that correlates with a potentially irrelevant factor in order to operate a criminal justice
system that includes capital punishment. As we
have stated specifically in the context of capital
punishment, the Constitution does not "plac[e]
totally unrealistic conditions on its use" *Gregg*
v. *Georgia*, 428 U.S., at 199, n. 50.

Second, McCleskey's arguments are best presented to the legislative bodies. It is not the
responsibility – or indeed even the right – of
this Court to determine the appropriate punishment for particular crimes. It is the legislatures, the elected representatives of the people,
that are "constituted to respond to the will and
consequently the moral values of the people."
Furman v. *Georgia*, 408 U.S., at 383 (Burger,
C.J., dissenting). Legislatures also are better
qualified to weigh and "evaluate the results of
statistical studies in terms of their own local
conditions and with a flexibility of approach
that is not available to the courts," *Gregg* v.
Georgia, 428 U.S., at 186. Capital punishment
is now the law in more than two-thirds of our
States. It is the ultimate duty of courts to determine on a case-by-case basis whether these laws
are applied consistently with the Constitution.
Despite McCleskey's wide-ranging arguments

that basically challenge the validity of capital punishment in our multiracial society, the only question before us is whether in his case, the law of Georgia was properly applied. We agree with the District Court and the Court of Appeals for the Eleventh Circuit that this was carefully and correctly done in this case.

Justice Brennan, with whom Justices Marshall, Blackmun, and Stevens join, Dissenting

II.

At some point in this case, Warren McCleskey doubtless asked his lawyer whether a jury was likely to sentence him to die. A candid reply to this question would have been disturbing. First, counsel would have to tell McCleskey that few of the details of the crime or of McCleskey's past criminal conduct were more important than the fact that his victim was white. Furthermore, counsel would feel bound to tell McCleskey that defendants charged with killing white victims in Georgia are 4.3 times as likely to be sentenced to death as defendants charged with killing blacks. In addition, frankness would compel the disclosure that it was more likely than not that the race of McCleskey's victim would determine whether he received a death sentence: 6 of every 11 defendants convicted of killing a white person would not have received the death penalty if their victims had been black, while, among defendants with aggravating and mitigating factors comparable to McCleskey's, 20 of every 34 would not have been sentenced to die if their victims had been black. Finally, the assessment would not be complete without the information that cases involving black defendants and white victims are more likely to result in a death sentence than cases featuring any other racial combination of defendant and victim. The story could be told in a variety of ways, but McCleskey could not fail to grasp its essential narrative line: there was a significant chance that race would play a prominent role in determining if he lived or died.

The Court today holds that Warren McCleskey's sentence was constitutionally imposed. It finds no fault in a system in which lawyers must tell their clients that race casts a large shadow on the capital sentencing process. The Court arrives at this conclusion by stating that the Baldus study cannot "*prove* that race enters into any capital sentencing decisions or that race was a factor in McCleskey's particular case." Since, according to Professor Baldus, we cannot say "to a moral certainty" that race influenced a decision, we can identify only "a likelihood that a particular factor entered into some decisions," and "a discrepancy that appears to correlate with race." This "likelihood" and "discrepancy," holds the Court, is insufficient to establish a constitutional violation. The Court reaches this conclusion by placing four factors on the scales opposite McCleskey's evidence: the desire to encourage sentencing discretion, the existence of "statutory safeguards" in the Georgia scheme, the fear of encouraging widespread challenges to other sentencing decisions, and the limits of the judicial role. The Court's evaluation of the significance of petitioner's evidence is fundamentally at odds with our consistent concern for rationality in capital sentencing, and the considerations that the majority invokes to discount that evidence cannot justify ignoring its force.

III.

A.

It is important to emphasize at the outset that the Court's observation that McCleskey cannot prove the influence of race on any particular sentencing decision is irrelevant in evaluating his Eighth Amendment claim. Since *Furman* v. *Georgia*, 408 U.S. 238 (1972), the Court has been concerned with the *risk* of the imposition of an arbitrary sentence, rather than the proven fact of one. *Furman* held that the death penalty "may not be imposed under sentencing procedures that create a substantial risk that the punishment will be inflicted in an arbitrary and capricious manner." ... This emphasis on risk acknowledges the difficulty of divining the jury's motivation in an individual case. In addition, it reflects the fact that concern for arbitrariness focuses on the rationality of the system as a whole, and that a system that features a significant probability that sentencing decisions are influenced by impermissible considerations cannot be regarded as rational. As we said in *Gregg* v. *Georgia*, 428 U.S. [153,] 200 [(1976)], "the petitioner looks to the sentencing system as a whole (as the Court did in *Furman* and we do today)": a constitutional violation is established if a plaintiff demonstrates a "*pattern* of arbitrary and capricious sentencing."

Defendants challenging their death sentences thus never have had to prove that impermissible considerations have actually infected sentencing decisions. We have required instead that they establish that the system under which they were sentenced posed a significant risk of such an occurrence. McCleskey's claim does differ, however, in one respect from these earlier cases: it is the first to base a challenge not on speculation about how a system *might* operate, but on empirical documentation of how it *does* operate.

The Court assumes the statistical validity of the Baldus study, and acknowledges that McCleskey has demonstrated a risk that racial prejudice plays a role in capital sentencing in Georgia. Nonetheless, it finds the probability of prejudice insufficient to create constitutional concern. Close analysis of the Baldus study, however, in light of both statistical principles and human experience, reveals that the risk that race influenced McCleskey's sentence is intolerable by any imaginable standard.

B.

The Baldus study indicates that, after taking into account some 230 nonracial factors that might legitimately influence a sentencer, the jury *more likely than not* would have spared McCleskey's life had his victim been black. The study distinguishes between those cases in which (1) the jury exercises virtually no discretion because the strength or weakness of aggravating factors usually suggests that only one outcome is appropriate; and (2) cases reflecting an "intermediate" level of aggravation, in which the jury has considerable discretion in choosing a sentence.

McCleskey's case falls into the intermediate range. In such cases, death is imposed in 34% of white-victim crimes and 14% of black-victim crimes, a difference of 139% in the rate of imposition of the death penalty. In other words, just under 59% – almost 6 in 10 – defendants comparable to McCleskey would not have received the death penalty if their victims had been black.

Furthermore, even examination of the sentencing system as a whole, factoring in those cases in which the jury exercises little discretion, indicates the influence of race on capital sentencing. For the Georgia system as a whole, race accounts for a six percentage point difference in the rate at which capital punishment is imposed. Since death is imposed in 11% of all white-victim cases, the rate in comparably aggravated black-victim cases is 5%. The rate of capital sentencing in a white-victim case is thus 120% greater than the rate in a black-victim case. Put another way, over half – 55% – of defendants in white-victim crimes in Georgia would not have been sentenced to die if their victims had been black. Of the more than 200 variables potentially relevant to a sentencing decision, race of the victim is a powerful explanation for variation in death sentence rates – as powerful as nonracial aggravating factors such as a prior murder conviction or acting as the principal planner of the homicide.

These adjusted figures are only the most conservative indication of the risk that race will influence the death sentences of defendants in Georgia. Data unadjusted for the mitigating or aggravating effect of other factors show an even more pronounced disparity by race. The capital sentencing rate for all white-victim cases was almost *11 times* greater than the rate for black-victim cases.

Furthermore, blacks who kill whites are sentenced to death at nearly *22 times* the rate of blacks who kill blacks, and more than *7 times* the rate of whites who kill blacks. In addition, prosecutors seek the death penalty for 70% of black defendants with white victims, but for only 15% of black defendants with black victims, and only 19% of white defendants with black victims. Since our decision upholding the Georgia capital sentencing system in *Gregg*, the State has executed seven persons. All of the seven were convicted of killing whites, and six of the seven executed were black. Such execution figures are especially striking in light of the fact that, during the period encompassed by the Baldus study, only 9.2% of Georgia homicides involved black defendants and white victims, while 60.7% involved black victims.

McCleskey's statistics have particular force because most of them are the product of sophisticated multiple-regression analysis. Such analysis is designed precisely to identify patterns in the aggregate, even though we may not be able to reconstitute with certainty any individual decision that goes to make up that pattern. Multiple-regression analysis is particularly well suited to identify the influence of impermissible considerations in sentencing, since it is able to control for permissible factors that may explain an apparent arbitrary pattern. While the decision-making process of a body such as a jury may be complex, the Baldus study provides a massive compilation of the details that are most relevant to that decision ...

The statistical evidence in this case thus relentlessly documents the risk that McCleskey's sentence was influenced by racial considerations. This evidence shows that there is a better than even chance in Georgia that race will influence the decision to impose the death penalty: a majority of defendants in white-victim crimes would not have been sentenced to die if their victims had been black. In determining whether this risk is acceptable, our judgment must be shaped by the awareness that "[t]he risk of racial prejudice infecting a capital sentencing proceeding is especially serious in light of the complete finality of the death sentence," *Turner* v. *Murray*, 476 U.S. 28, 35 (1986), and that "[i]t is of vital importance to the defendant and to the community that any decision to impose the death sentence be, and appear to be, based on reason rather than caprice or emotion," *Gardner* v. *Florida*, 430 U.S. 349, 358 (1977). In determining the guilt of a defendant, a State must prove its case beyond a reasonable doubt. That is, we refuse to convict if the chance of error is simply less likely than not. Surely, we should not be willing to take a person's life if the chance that his death sentence was irrationally imposed is *more* likely than not. In light of the gravity of the interest at stake, petitioner's statistics on their face are a powerful demonstration of the type of risk that our Eighth Amendment jurisprudence has consistently condemned.

C.

Evaluation of McCleskey's evidence cannot rest solely on the numbers themselves. We must also ask whether the conclusion suggested by those numbers is consonant with our understanding of history and human experience. Georgia's legacy of a race-conscious criminal justice system, as well as this Court's own recognition of the persistent danger that racial attitudes may affect criminal proceedings, indicates that McCleskey's claim is not a fanciful product of mere statistical artifice.

The ongoing influence of history is acknowledged, as the majority observes, by our "'unceasing efforts' to eradicate racial prejudice from our criminal justice system." These efforts, however, signify not the elimination of the problem but its persistence. Our cases reflect a realization of the myriad of opportunities for racial considerations to influence criminal proceedings: in the exercise of peremptory challenges, *Batson* v. *Kentucky*; in the selection of the grand jury, *Vasquez* v. *Hillery*, 474 U.S. 254 (1986); in the selection of the petit jury, *Whitus* v. *Georgia*, 385 U.S. 545 (1967); in the exercise of prosecutorial discretion, *Wayte* v. *United States*, 470 U.S. 598 (1985); in the conduct of argument, *Donnelly* v. *DeChristoforo*, 416 U.S. 637 (1974); and in the conscious or unconscious bias of jurors, *Turner* v. *Murray*, 476 U.S. 28 (1986), *Ristaino* v. *Ross*, 424 U.S. 589 (1976).

The discretion afforded prosecutors and jurors in the Georgia capital sentencing system creates such opportunities. No guidelines govern prosecutorial decisions to seek the death penalty, and Georgia provides juries with no list of aggravating and mitigating factors, nor any standard for balancing them against one another. Once a jury identifies one aggravating factor, it has complete discretion in choosing life or death, and need not articulate its basis for selecting life imprisonment. The Georgia sentencing system therefore provides considerable opportunity for racial considerations, however subtle and unconscious, to influence charging and sentencing decisions.

History and its continuing legacy thus buttress the probative force of McCleskey's statistics. Formal dual criminal laws may no longer be in effect, and intentional discrimination may no longer be prominent. Nonetheless, as we acknowledged in *Turner*, "subtle, less consciously held racial attitudes" continue to be of concern, 476 U.S., at 35, and the Georgia system gives such attitudes considerable room to operate. The conclusions drawn from McCleskey's statistical evidence are therefore consistent with the lessons of social experience.

IV.

The Court cites four reasons for shrinking from the implications of McCleskey's evidence: the desirability of discretion for actors in the criminal justice system, the existence of statutory safeguards against abuse of that discretion, the potential consequences for broader challenges to criminal sentencing, and an understanding of the contours of the judicial role. While these concerns underscore the need for sober deliberation, they do not justify rejecting evidence as convincing as McCleskey has presented ...

V.

At the time our Constitution was framed 200 years ago this year, blacks "had for more than a century before been regarded as beings of an inferior order, and altogether unfit to associate with the white race, either in social or political relations; and so far inferior, that they had no rights which the white man was bound to respect." *Dred Scott* v. *Sandford*, 19 How. 393, 407 (1857). Only 130 years ago, this Court relied on these observations to deny American citizenship to blacks. A mere three generations ago, this Court sanctioned racial segregation, stating that "[i]f one race be inferior to the other socially, the Constitution of the United States cannot put them upon the same plane" *Plessy* v. *Ferguson*, 163 U.S. 537, 552 (1896).

In more recent times, we have sought to free ourselves from the burden of this history. Yet it has been scarcely a generation since this Court's first decision striking down racial segregation, and barely two decades since the legislative prohibition of racial discrimination in major domains of national life. These have been honorable steps, but we cannot pretend that in three decades we have completely escaped the grip of a historical legacy spanning centuries. Warren McCleskey's evidence confronts us with the subtle and persistent influence of the past. His message is a disturbing one to a society that has formally repudiated racism, and a frustrating one to a Nation accustomed to regarding its destiny as the product of its own will. Nonetheless, we ignore him at our peril, for we remain imprisoned by the past as long as we deny its influence in the present.

It is tempting to pretend that minorities on death row share a fate in no way connected to our own, that our treatment of them sounds no echoes beyond the chambers in which they die. Such an illusion is ultimately corrosive, for the reverberations of injustice are not so easily confined. "The destinies of the two races in this country are indissolubly linked together," and the way in which we choose those who will die reveals the depth of moral commitment among the living.

Justice Blackmun, with whom Justices Marshall and Stevens join, and with whom Justice Brennan joins in all but Part IV-B, Dissenting

IV.

B.

Like Justice Stevens, I do not believe acceptance of McCleskey's claim would eliminate capital punishment in Georgia. Justice Stevens points out that the evidence presented in this case indicates that in extremely aggravated murders the risk of discriminatory enforcement of the death penalty is minimized. I agree that narrowing the class of death-eligible defendants is not too high a price to pay for a death penalty system that does not discriminate on the basis of race. Moreover, the establishment of guidelines for Assistant District Attorneys as to the appropriate basis for exercising their discretion at the various steps in the prosecution of a case would provide at least a measure of consistency. The Court's emphasis on the procedural safeguards in the system ignores the fact that there are none whatsoever during the crucial process leading up to trial. As Justice White stated for the plurality in *Turner v. Murray*, I find "the risk that racial prejudice may have infected petitioner's capital sentencing unacceptable in light of the ease with which that risk could have been minimized." I dissent.

1. What role does the *Washington* v. *Davis* (1976) principle of intentionality play in the majority decision?
2. If the majority's interpretation prevails, how is structural racism to be excised from the criminal justice system?
3. In what ways do the dissenting opinions perceive that the death penalty in Georgia could be transformed to be racially fair? Where do they disagree?

As we try to address the manifestations of the social construction of race in the twenty-first century, the question of the relevance of intentionality is significant. The law focuses on the actor's intention in causing illegal racial discrimination, as opposed to the impact of the policy or governmental action under review. As political actions and governmental behavior becomes racially neutral, how do we address the desperate racial impact of these policies. Should the focus of the court be on the intent of the actors or on the impact of the policies? When do you believe the courts should intervene? Which kinds of action should be unlawful? If we return to the metaphor of the tree in the Introduction, the ratification of the post-Civil War Amendments (Thirteenth, Fourteenth, and Fifteenth) and the mid-twentieth-century civil rights laws (Civil Rights Act, 1964, Voting Rights Act, 1965, and Fair Housing Act, 1968) resulted in the removal of the fence of formal legal oppression on the basis of race. However, the scars on our democracy remain. As the nation tries to move toward racial equity and substantive equality, the limitations of our legal process to aid in this endeavor become more obvious. One reason for this is found in the increasingly complex understanding of identity.

7.2 Intersectionality

The concept of intersectionality was introduced by Black women in the nineteenth century as they challenged the dual barriers of sexism (coverture, patriarchy) and racism (slavery, White supremacy). As the early anthology of Black women's studies *All the Women are White, All the Blacks are Men, But Some of Us are Brave* illustrated, intersectionality acknowledges differences and challenges the notion of essentialism (the idea that all women share a common experience that unites them; all who identify with a shared racial community have more in common with each other than those outside that community), contending that our unique perspectives allow us to experience our shared realities distinctly.

Unfortunately, our legal process was based originally on the understanding of single identities, not the intersectional assumption of multiple identities. We have laws that prohibit discrimination on the basis of race and on the basis of gender, as well as on gender identity, and on disability. But the laws do not address discrimination based on multiple identities. Consider, for instance, a woman of Filipino descent who is the lone woman of color in her office. She is condescended to by supervisors and colleagues, assigned less significant responsibilities, passed over for promotions, and when the organization has a budget crunch, she is let go. She cannot sue under gender discrimination because none of the other women are treated so disparagingly, and if she sues under racial discrimination the defense will note all of the men of color who have been promoted into leadership roles. Instead, the law assumes she was treated poorly but not illegitimately discriminated against.

While there have been some accommodations in the law – sex-plus discrimination protections in the Civil Rights Act of 1964 recognizes women with children who were treated poorly compared with men with children – it has not been expanded broadly (Deardorff 2016). An early federal District Court case in Missouri demonstrates this problem. In *Degraffenreid* v. *General Motors Assembly* (1976), a group of Black women who worked at General Motors sued because of a "last hired-first fired" policy that disproportionately impacted them, compared with White women and Black men. The court sought to place them in one of the distinct legal categories defined by the law.

DEGRAFFENREID v. *GENERAL MOTORS ASSEMBLY*, 413 F. SUPP. 142 (E.D. MO) (1976)

District Judge Wangelin

This matter is before the Court upon its ... reconsideration of its Order of September 30, 1975, which denied the cross motions of the plaintiffs and defendant General Motors Corporation for summary judgment on the grounds that questions of fact and law then existed. The Court is of the opinion, for the reasons stated below, that the then existing questions of law and fact have been resolved, and that this matter is now ripe for partial summary judgment as delineated in the accompanying Order of this date.

This action was filed by the plaintiffs seeking a determination that the "last hired-first fired" lay off policies of the defendants discriminate against them as black women, and are therefore a perpetuation of past discriminatory practices. Jurisdiction is alleged to be found in the Civil Rights Act of 1964, 42 U.S.C. § 2000a et seq. and the post Civil War Civil Rights Acts, 42 U.S.C. § 1981.

The initial issue in this lawsuit is whether or not the plaintiffs are seeking relief from racial discrimination, or sex-based discrimination. The plaintiffs allege that they are suing on behalf of black women, and that therefore this lawsuit attempts to combine two causes of action into a new special sub-category, namely, a combination of racial and sex-based discrimination. The Court notes that plaintiffs have failed to cite any decisions which have stated that black women are a special class to be protected from discrimination. The Court's own research has failed to disclose such a decision. The plaintiffs are clearly entitled to a remedy if they have been discriminated against. However, they should not be allowed to combine statutory remedies to create a new "super-remedy" which would give them relief beyond what the drafters of the relevant statutes intended. Thus, this lawsuit must be examined to see if it states a cause of action for race discrimination, sex discrimination, or alternatively either, but not a combination of both.

Sex-Based Discrimination

The Court now turns to the question of whether or not the plaintiffs have asserted a cause of action alleging discrimination based upon sex. Initially the Court notes that the post Civil War Civil Rights Acts, 42 U.S.C. § 1981 do not allow a recovery for sex discrimination.

The Court is of the opinion that, as a matter of law, defendant General Motors is not guilty of sex discrimination. This is especially true when the impact of the Missouri Protective Law, § 290.040, R.S.Mo., 1969, is considered in light of the hiring practices of defendant General Motors.

It must also be noted that affidavits furnished by defendant General Motors indicate that the defendant has hired female employees for a number of years prior to the enactment of the Civil Rights Act of 1964. The hiring of female employees clearly indicates to the Court that the "last hired-first fired" seniority system of the defendants in this lawsuit does not perpetuate past discrimination. The Court also notes that the affidavits furnished by the plaintiffs do not comport with the requirements for stating a cause of action

elucidated in the recent decision of the Supreme Court in *Franks* v. *Bowman Transportation Co., Inc.*, [424 U.S. 747] (1976) in that the plaintiffs state that they did not apply for employment at the defendants' operation because they knew that they would be discriminated against. Such conclusory allegations do not state a cause of action in the opinion of this Court.

... [I]t must be noted that defendant General Motors and the Equal Employment Opportunity Commission entered into a consent decree on January 9, 1973, with respect to the hiring of female employees. That consent decree was approved by the Honorable Roy W. Harper, Senior District Judge of this District, and was reaffirmed by Judge Harper in an Order dated April 16, 1976. To the Court, this is a further indication that the seniority practices of defendants do not discriminate on the basis of sex.

For the foregoing reasons, it is clear that the plaintiffs are barred from alleging a cause of action against defendant General Motors on the grounds of sex discrimination.

Racial Discrimination

An examination of plaintiffs' complaint indicates that they have stated a claim with regards to racial discrimination on the part of the defendants. The claim of racial discrimination alleges that the past illegal discrimination of the defendants, combined with the "last hired-first fired" seniority provisions of the labor agreement between the defendants perpetuates past discrimination and is therefore violative of Title VII of the Civil Rights Act of 1964.

Broad allegations of racial discrimination have been raised with regards to defendant General Motors employment facilities in St. Louis in case No. 72 C 551(4), *Nathaniel Mosley, et al.*, v. *General Motors Corporation, et al.*, now pending before the Honorable John F. Nangle of this District.

It is clear that judicial economy would be served if the allegations of the plaintiffs in the instant action were combined with those now pending in the *Mosley* lawsuit. When the prospect of consolidation with the *Mosley* lawsuit was raised during oral arguments regarding the pendency of this action as a class action, counsel for plaintiffs asserted that the present case at bar was not one of purely race discrimination as is the *Mosley* lawsuit, but rather was an action of both race and sex-based discrimination. It was asserted that this action was brought on behalf of "black women" a separate sub-category under Title VII of the Civil Rights Act of 1964. As the Court has stated above, counsel for plaintiffs, and the Court's own research, have failed to discover any case holdings which allow the creation of a new sub-category within Title VII that would generate such a new protected class of minorities. The legislative history surrounding Title VII does not indicate that the goal of the statute was to create a new classification of "black women" who would have greater standing than, for example, a black male. The prospect of the creation of new classes of protected minorities, governed only by the mathematical principles of permutation and combination, clearly raises the prospect of opening the hackneyed Pandora's box.

So that the goal of judicial economy will be served, the Court will dismiss without prejudice the race discrimination claims of the plaintiffs in the present action at bar, and suggests that they consolidate this action, or seek to intervene with the lawsuit now pending before the Honorable John F. Nangle, *Mosley, et al.,* v. *General Motors, et al.*

Thus, for the foregoing reasons, it is clear that the plaintiffs have asserted a claim of discrimination based upon race. As stated in the attached Order, summary judgment will be granted to the defendants with regards to sex-based discrimination, and to foster judicial economy the allegations of race discrimination in this case will be dismissed without prejudice so that the plaintiffs may either consolidate their claims or intervene in the present suit of *Mosley, et al.,* v. *General Motors, et al.,* No. 72 C 551(4) now pending in this District.

1. What is the impact on the plaintiffs being placed in one specific category?
2. Why has the law been able to address intersectionality? How might law change to address this more sophisticated understanding of identity?
3. What would have to change for intersectionality to be recognized by law: new precedent? Adopted statutory law? What are the barriers to and possibility of both?

The judiciary's common law rules regarding the sanctity of precedent in judicial decision-making, the expectation of intentionality to demonstration racial discrimination, and the exclusive nature of the categories of "race" and "gender" as forms of unlawful discrimination, have been embedded into our legal process. Both intentionality and the discrete category of race have come from judicial interpretations from the mid-twentieth century and have survived and been embedded into our legal process, despite deep changes in our understanding of the nature of racial identity and the concept of equality. How can the law address these barriers to racial equality, given our legal system's precedential structure? Have we reached a limit to the U.S. law?

7.3 Potential Remedy

The issue of increasingly complex identities has stumped members of the judiciary and scholars. In a precedent-based common law system, how do we alter hundreds of years of set law to prod it in a different direction? While the Supreme Court and federal appellate courts could interpret the law in new ways that adjust for changing understandings of race and identity, that has not happened. More often, our courts are self-restrained by the historic values of common law and precedent, which did not always recognize the full humanity of all and defined individuals by set categories of race and gender.

One potential remedy comes from legal scholars Catharine A. MacKinnon and Kimberlé W. Crenshaw, both of whom have written extensively on how the law has excluded people based on protected characteristics like race and gender. According to their 2019 *Yale Law Journal* article, "Reconstituting the Future: The Equality Amendment," they believe a new constitutional amendment is necessary to correct the failures of "language and interpretative canons rooted in an unjust past, and imagine a fully functioning democracy as the inheritance of future generations" (344). They frame their proposal as providing substantive equality, expanding beyond the constitutional promise of formal equality. For them, equality was a "foundational problem" of the Constitution because of the many people excluded from its initial construction. They continue that the Fourteenth Amendment and similar attempts at equality were interpreted so narrowly by the Supreme Court that it could not disrupt the status quo of oppression of race and gender in meaningful ways. The authors note that the expectation of a demonstration of intentionality has resulted in racial and gender discrimination continuing unabated. They find that the Court's decisions in sum pull toward a definition of equality that supports neutrality – the treatment of people the same or color-blindness. The consequence being, according to MacKinnon and Crenshaw, that "[t]he Court shields the rights and entitlements of those whom the Constitution has historically privileged and disarms the aspirations of those it has historically excluded" (350).

For these scholars, the law's inability to perceive inequality or discrimination except when it is intentional or carefully parsed by legally defined categories of "race" and "gender" has made it incapable of meeting its stated claims of equality. They continue with an argument that the laws have created a hierarchy in the United States that is based on sex and/or race and it is politically constructed, claiming "[t]he law's participation in obscuring the fact that the existing system is one of imposed social hierarchy rather than natural difference ... has rationalized and legitimated inequality" (357). This is a very difficult assertion. For the law to have participated in structural inequality by not only allowing inequities, building them into the law by precedent over time, but also by creating legal categories of race and gender, means that undoing these structures demands engagement by the law.

The authors recommend ratifying an Equality Amendment to the Constitution, that in part includes:

> Section 2. Equality of rights shall not be denied or abridged by the United States or by any state on account of sex (including ...), and/or race (including ...), and/or like grounds of subordination (such as ...). No law or its interpretation shall give force to common law disadvantages that exist on the ground(s) enumerated in this amendment.

If you look at this proposal, it addresses intersectionality by using "and/or" instead of the current Civil Rights Act of 1964, Title VII construction of "or." This would allow individuals to sue on grounds of "sex," in that the language of the proposed amendment also includes "sexual orientation" and "sexual identity," and/or race, including ethnicity and color – we have not addressed colorism yet – and/or similar forms of subordination. In this last category, they give an incomplete list starting with disability and faith. This allows for additional aspects of intersectionality to be included over time. By including the states, it insures it is immediately applied to state laws. But this raises questions left over from the Fourteenth Amendment (Chapter 4): does it apply to private acts of discrimination or only by the government and its entities?

The authors also note that their language "does not imply or permit an intent requirement" (361). They hope this constitutional phrasing, along with language about "common law disadvantages," would end the replication of historic practices of inequality by making prior precedent that does such invalid.

---

1. Do you think that such a constitutional amendment could correct the limits of the law in promoting inequality?
2. What concerns remain unaddressed?
3. What new difficulties and inequities might be introduced by such a new framework?

Historically, the courts have ruled specifically on intentionality, providing clear precedent that requires its demonstration, and the law has been written as generally requiring plaintiffs to choose between protections based on race or on gender/sexuality. On other issues regarding race, the Supreme Court has been mostly silent. One such area of law not addressed is the surprisingly complex issue of multiracial people.

7.4 Multiracial People Under the Law

As noted in the Introduction, the law has historically been written to force people to choose between racial identities, with the default being the one-drop rule. Children of families of multiple races were generally classified as identifying with any community of color, but not designated "White." This prioritization has its roots in a desire to maintain White supremacy, control the sexuality of White women, and expand the population of enslaved peoples. Thus, children who were of more than one race, especially if one was Black, were defined by the percentage of Black descent – hence, terminology such as "Maroon," "Quadroon," and "Octoroon" was developed to indicate what percentage of ancestors were not White – and consequently placed within the societal hierarchy. For Native peoples, the state's desire for assimilation similarly ran into conflict with White supremacy, leading to the creation of "blood quantum" as a means of determining identity (see Chapter 5).

7.4.1 Interracial Marriage

Many of these conflicts between the values of White supremacy and federal policies of assimilation are revealed in early cases addressing the so-called anti-miscegenation laws which banned cross-racial marriages. If you carefully review the arguments in these decisions, the competing values are revealed. The 1948 California Supreme Court case of *Perez* v. *Lippold* addresses a challenge against the 1872 California Civil Code §69, implementing §60, which forbade the provision of a marriage license of a White person to "negroes, Mongolians [Asian], members of the Malay [East Asian] race or mulattoes." It also determined that all such marriages were voided and illegal in California, even if they had been legitimately married elsewhere. This case was brought by Andrea Perez, who identified as White, and Sylvester Davis, who identified as Black. They sought to compel the county clerk of Los Angeles County to issue them a marriage license. As members of the Catholic Church, the petitioners claimed that §69 violated their religious freedom to enjoy the sacrament of marriage in their Church, which did not forbid their marriage. The state claimed that racial classifications are "reasonably designed to protect the general welfare and the interests of individual members of the races mentioned, and that the regulation is there a proper exercise of the police power of the state."

PEREZ v. *LIPPOLD*, 32 CAL. 2D. 711 (1948)

Justice Traynor Delivered the Opinion of the Court

The regulation of marriage is considered a proper function of the state. It is well settled that a legislature may declare monogamy to be the "law of social life under its dominion," even though such a law might inhibit the free exercise of certain religious practices. *Reynolds* v. *U.S.*, 98 U.S. 145, 166 (1879). If the miscegenation law under attack in the present proceeding is directed at a social evil and employs a reasonable means to prevent that evil, it is valid regardless of its incidental effect upon the conduct of particular religious groups. If, on the other hand, the law is discriminatory and irrational, it unconstitutionally restricts not only religious liberty but the liberty to marry as well.

The right to marry is as fundamental as the right to send one's child to a particular school or the right to have offspring. Indeed, "We are dealing here with legislation which involves one of the basic civil rights of man. Marriage and procreation are fundamental to the very existence and survival of the race." *Skinner* v. *Oklahoma*, 316 U.S. 535, 541 (1942). Legislation infringing such rights must be based upon more than prejudice and must be free from oppressive discrimination to comply with the constitutional requirements of due process and equal protection of the laws.

I.

Since the right to marry is the right to join in marriage with the person of one's choice, a statute that prohibits an individual from marrying a member of a race other than his own restricts the scope of his choice and thereby restricts his right to marry. It must therefore be determined whether the state can restrict that right on the basis of race alone without violating the equal protection of the laws clause of the United States Constitution.

A state law prohibiting members of one race from marrying members of another race is not designed to meet a clear and present peril arising out of an emergency. In the absence of an emergency the state clearly cannot base a law impairing fundamental rights of individuals on general assumptions as to traits of racial groups. It has been said that a statute such as section 60 does not discriminate against any racial group, since it applies alike to all persons whether Caucasian, Negro, or members of any other race. The decisive question, however, is not whether different races, each considered as a group, are equally treated. The right to marry is the right of individuals, not of racial groups. The equal protection clause of the United States Constitution does not refer to rights of the Negro race, the Caucasian race, or any other race, but to the rights of individuals. In construing the equal protection of the laws clause of the Constitution, the United States Supreme Court has declared that the constitutionality of state action must be tested according to whether the rights of an individual are restricted because of his race. Thus, in holding invalid state enforcement of covenants restricting the occupation of real property on grounds of race, the Supreme Court of the United States declared: "The rights created by the first section of the Fourteenth Amendment are, by its terms, guaranteed to the individual.... It is, therefore,

no answer to these petitioners to say that the courts may also be induced to deny white persons rights of ownership and occupancy on grounds of race or color. Equal protection of the laws is not achieved through indiscriminate imposition of inequalities" *Shelley* v. *Kraemer*, 334 U.S. 1 (1948) ...

In determining whether the public interest requires the prohibition of a marriage between two persons, the state may take into consideration matters of legitimate concern to the state. Thus, disease that might become a peril to the prospective spouse or to the offspring of the marriage could be made a disqualification for marriage. Such legislation, however, must be based on tests of the individual, not on arbitrary classifications of groups or races, and must be administered without discrimination on the grounds of race. *Yick Wo* v. *Hopkins*, 118 U.S. 356, 373 (1886). It has been suggested that certain races are more prone than the Caucasian to diseases such as tuberculosis. If the state determines that certain diseases would endanger a marital partner or offspring, it may prohibit persons so diseased from marrying, but the statute must apply to all persons regardless of race. Sections 60 and 69 are not motivated by a concern to diminish the transmission of disease by marriage, for they make race and not disease the disqualification. Thus, a tubercular Negro or a tubercular Caucasian may marry subject to the race limitation, but a Negro and a Caucasian who are free from disease may not marry each other. If the purpose of these sections were to prevent marriages by persons who do not have the qualifications for marriage that the state may properly prescribe, they would make the possession of such qualifications the test for members of all races alike. By restricting the individual's right to marry on the basis of race alone, they violate the equal protection of the laws clause of the United States Constitution.

II.

The parties, however, have argued at length the question whether the statute is arbitrary and unreasonable. They have assumed that under the equal protection clause the state may classify individuals according to their race in legislation regulating their fundamental rights. If it be assumed that such a classification can validly be made under the equal protection clause in circumstances besides those arising from an emergency, the question would remain whether the statute's classification of racial groups is based on differences between those groups bearing a substantial relation to a legitimate legislative objective. Race restrictions must be viewed with great suspicion, for the Fourteenth Amendment "was adopted to prevent state legislation designed to perpetuate discrimination on the basis of race or color" and expresses "a definite national policy against discrimination because of race or color." Any state legislation discriminating against persons on the basis of race or color has to overcome the strong presumption inherent in this constitutional policy ...

The Legislature therefore permits the mixing of all races with the single exception that white persons may not marry Negroes, Mongolians, Mulattoes, or Malays. It might be concluded therefrom that section 60 is based upon the theory that the progeny of a white person and a Mongolian or Negro or Malay are inferior or undesirable, while the progeny of members of other different races are not. Nevertheless, the section does not prevent the mixing of "white" and "colored" blood. It permits marriages not only between Caucasians and others of darker pigmentation, such as Indians, Hindus, and Mexicans, but between persons of mixed ancestry including white ... In effect, therefore, section 60 permits a substantial amount of intermarriage between persons of some Caucasian ancestry and members of other races. Furthermore, there is no ban on illicit sexual relations between Caucasians and members of the proscribed races. Indeed, it is covertly encouraged by the race restrictions on marriage.

Nevertheless, respondent has sought to justify the statute by contending that the prohibition of intermarriage between Caucasians and members of the specified races prevents the Caucasian race from being contaminated by races whose members are by nature physically and mentally inferior to Caucasians.

Respondent submits statistics relating to the physical inferiority of certain races. Most, if not all, of the ailments to which he refers are attributable largely to environmental factors ...

Respondent also contends that Negroes, and impliedly the other races specified in section 60, are inferior mentally to Caucasians. It is true that, in the United States, catalogues of distinguished people list more Caucasians than members of other races. It cannot be disregarded, however, that Caucasians are in the great majority and have generally had a more advantageous environment, and that the capacity of the members of any race to contribute to a nation's culture depends in large measure on how freely they may participate in that culture. There is no scientific proof that one race is superior to another in native ability ...

Respondent contends, however, that persons wishing to marry in contravention of race barriers come from the "dregs of society" and that their progeny will therefore be a burden on the community. There is no law forbidding marriage among the "dregs of society," assuming that this expression is capable of definition. If there were such a law, it could not be applied without a proper determination of the persons that fall within that category, a determination that could hardly be made on the basis of race alone.

Respondent contends that even if the races specified in the statute are not by nature inferior to the Caucasian race, the statute can be justified as a means of diminishing race tension and preventing the birth of children who might become social problems.

The rationalization that race discrimination diminishes the contacts and therefore the tensions between races would perpetuate the deprivation of rights of racial minorities. It would justify an abridgment of their privilege of holding office, of jury service, of entering the professions. The courts have made it clear that these privileges are not the prerogatives of any race.

Respondent maintains that Negroes are socially inferior and have so been judicially recognized (e.g., *Wolfe* v. *Georgia Ry. & Elec.*

Co., 2 Ga. App. 499, 58 S.E. 899, 901 (1907)) and that the progeny of a marriage between a Negro and a Caucasian suffer not only the stigma of such inferiority but the fear of rejection by members of both races. If they do, the fault lies not with their parents, but with the prejudices in the community and the laws that perpetuate those prejudices by giving legal force to the belief that certain races are inferior. If miscegenous marriages can be prohibited because of tensions suffered by the progeny, mixed religious unions could be prohibited on the same ground.

There are now so many persons in the United States of mixed ancestry, that the tensions upon them are already diminishing and are bound to diminish even more in time. Already many of the progeny of mixed marriages have made important contributions to the community. In any event the contention that the miscegenation laws prohibit inter-racial marriage because of its adverse effects on the progeny is belied by the extreme racial intermixture that it tolerates.

III.

Even if a state could restrict the right to marry upon the basis of race alone, sections 60 and 69 of the Civil Code are nevertheless invalid because they are too vague and uncertain to constitute a valid regulation. A certain precision is essential in a statute regulating a fundamental right ...

The fact is overwhelming that there has been a steady increase in the number of people in this country who belong to more than one race, and a growing number who have succeeded in identifying themselves with the Caucasian race even though they are not exclusively Caucasian. Some of these persons have migrated to this state; some are born here illegitimately; others are the progeny of miscegenous marriages valid where contracted and therefore valid in California. The apparent purpose of the statute is to discourage the birth of children of mixed ancestry within this state. Such a purpose, however, cannot be accomplished without taking into consideration marriages of persons of mixed ancestry. A statute regulating fundamental rights is clearly

unconstitutional if it cannot be reasonably applied to accomplish its purpose. This court therefore cannot determine the constitutionality of the statute in question on the assumption that its provisions might, with sufficient definiteness, be applied to persons not of mixed ancestry.

If the statute is to be applied generally to persons of mixed ancestry the question arises whether it is to be applied on the basis of the physical appearance of the individual or on the basis of a genealogical research as to his ancestry. If the physical appearance of the individual is to be the test, the statute would have to be applied on the basis of subjective impressions of various persons. Persons having the same parents and consequently the same hereditary background could be classified differently. On the other hand, if the application of the statute to persons of mixed ancestry is to be based on genealogical research, the question immediately arises what proportions of Caucasian, Mongolian, or Malayan ancestors govern the applicability of the statute. Is it any trace of Mongolian or Malayan ancestry, or is it some unspecified proportion of such ancestry that makes a person a Mongolian or Malayan within the meaning of section 60?

Section 69 of the Civil Code and section 60 on which it is based are therefore too vague and uncertain to be upheld as a valid regulation of the right to marry. Enforcement of the statute would place upon the officials charged with its administration and upon the courts charged with reviewing the legality of such administration the task of determining the meaning of the statute. That task could be carried out with respect to persons of mixed ancestry only on the basis of conceptions of race classification not supplied by the Legislature.

In summary, we hold that sections 60 and 69 are not only too vague and uncertain to be enforceable regulations of a fundamental right, but that they violate the equal protection of the laws clause of the United States Constitution by impairing the right of individuals to marry on the basis of race alone and by arbitrarily and unreasonably discriminating against certain racial groups.

Chief Justice Gibson and Justice Carter, Concurring

It is my considered opinion that the statutes here involved are the product of ignorance, prejudice and intolerance, and I am happy to join in the decision of this court holding that they are invalid and unenforceable. This decision is in harmony with the declarations contained in the Declaration of Independence which are guaranteed by the Bill of Rights and the Fourteenth Amendment to the Constitution of the United States and re-affirmed by the Charter of the United Nations, that all human beings have equal rights regardless of race, color or creed, and that the right to liberty and the pursuit of happiness is inalienable and may not be infringed because of race, color or creed. To say that these statutes may stand in the face of the concept of liberty and equality embraced within the ambit of the above-mentioned fundamental law is to make of that concept an empty, hollow mockery.

In the face of these authoritive [sic] pronouncements the matter of race equality should be a settled issue. It is, at least, a settled issue so far as the fundamental law is concerned. And the only question before us is whether the Legislature may enact a valid statute in direct conflict with this fundamental law. It seems clear to me that it is not possible for the Legislature, in the face of our fundamental law, to enact a valid statute which proscribes conduct on a purely racial basis. Such are the statutes here involved. The wisdom of the broad, liberal concept of liberty and equality declared in our fundamental law should be apparent to every unprejudiced mind.

It is, of course, conceded that the state in the exercise of the police power may legislate for the protection of the health and welfare of the people and in so doing may infringe to some extent on the rights of individuals. But it is not conceded that a state may legislate to the detriment of a class a minority who are unable to protect themselves, when such legislation has no valid purpose behind it. Nor may the police power be used as a guise to cloak prejudice and intolerance. Prejudice and intolerance are the cancers of civilization.

It is my position that the statutes now before us never were constitutional. When first enacted, they violated the supreme law of the land as found in the Declaration of Independence. It is further my position that the Fourteenth Amendment to the Constitution of the United States invalidated the statutes here involved …

In this case, there are no decisions of either this Court or the Supreme Court of the United States which uphold the validity of a statute forbidding or invalidating miscegenous marriages. As has been pointed out, even if there were precedent, it would not necessarily be binding in this case. The cases from other jurisdictions are, of course, not binding here …

We may take judicial notice of the fact since it is a political and historical fact that steady inroads have been made on the myth of racial superiority and its outgrowths.

The rest of the world never has understood and never will understand why and how a nation, built on the premise that all men are created equal, can three times send the flower of its manhood to war for the truth of this premise and still fail to carry it out within its own borders.

In my opinion, the statutes here involved violate the very premise on which this country and its Constitution were built, the very ideas embodied in the Declaration of Independence, the very issue over which the Revolutionary War, the Civil War, and the Second World War were fought, and the spirit in which the Constitution must be interpreted in order that the interpretations will appear as "Reason in any part of the World besides."

Justice Shenk, Dissenting

I dissent.

The power of a state to regulate and control the basic social relationship of marriage of its domiciliaries is here challenged and set at nought by a majority order of this court arrived at not by a concurrence of reasons but by the end result of four votes supported by divergent concepts not supported by authority and in fact contrary to the decisions in this state and elsewhere.

... [S]uch laws have been in effect in this country since before our national independence and in this state since our first legislative session. They have never been declared unconstitutional by any court in the land although frequently they have been under attack. It is difficult to see why such laws, valid when enacted and constitutionally enforceable in this state for nearly one hundred years and elsewhere for a much longer period of time, are now unconstitutional under the same constitution and with no change in the factual situation. It will also be shown that they have a valid legislative purpose even though they may not conform to the sociogenetic views of some people. When that legislative purpose appears it is entirely beyond judicial power, properly exercised, to nullify them.

Moreover, the right of the state to exercise extensive control over the marriage contract has always been recognized. The institution of matrimony is the foundation of society, and the community at large has an interest in the maintenance of its integrity and purity ...

It is apparent from what has been said that if the law under attack bears a substantial relationship to the health, safety, morals or some other phase of the general welfare of the people of this state, it would not be invalid because incidentally in conflict with the conduct and practice of a particular religious group. Similarly if there is a rational basis for the law, if it is reasonable, and all within a given class are treated alike, there is not violation of the due process or equal protection clauses of the Fourteenth Amendment to the United States Constitution.

The prohibition of miscegenetic marriages is not a recent innovation in this state nor is such a law by any means unique among the states ... A law declaring marriages between white persons and Negroes to be illegal and void was enacted at the first session of our Legislature. Section 60 of the Civil Code declaring certain marriages invalid has existed since the advent of our codes in 1872, at which time it extended only to intermarriage between white persons and Negroes or mulattoes ...

Twenty-nine states in addition to California have similar laws. Six of these states have regarded the matter to be of such importance that they have by constitutional enactments prohibited their legislatures from passing any law legalizing marriage between white persons and Negroes or mulattoes. Several states refuse to recognize such marriages even if performed where valid, particularly if an attempt has been made by residents of a state to evade the law. The infrequency of such unions is perhaps the chief reason why prohibitive laws are not found in the remaining states.

The ban on mixed marriages in this country is traceable from the early colonial period. For example, Maryland forbade the practice of marriage unions between Negroes or Indians and white persons as early as 1663. Laws forbidding marriages between Negroes and whites were passed in Massachusetts in 1705, in Delaware in 1721, in Virginia in 1726, and in North Carolina in 1741. In 1724 it was decreed in France that no Negro-white marriages were to take place in Louisiana. Most of the remaining states enacted similar legislation in the period between the formation of the United States and the Civil War.

[Looks at evaluation of such laws]

The foregoing authorities form an unbroken line of judicial support, both state and federal, for the validity of our own legislation, and there is none to the contrary. Those authorities appear to have passed upon all attacks on such legislation on constitutional grounds, but notwithstanding their unanimity it is declared by some of the majority that there is a sort of racial discrimination which solely formed the basis for the enactments and by another of the majority that the constitutional guarantee of freedom of religion has been infringed. However, it is the law that if there is some factual background for the legislation, that circumstance forms an appropriate reason for the enactments, and it is then proper to consider the rules of law which govern the courts in that connection.

Some of the factual considerations which the legislature could have taken into consideration are disclosed by an examination of the sources of information on the biological and sociological phases of the problem and which may be said to form a background for the legislation and support the reasoning found in the decisions of the courts upholding similar statutes. A reference to a few of those sources of information will suffice.

On the biological phase there is authority for the conclusion that the crossing of the primary races leads gradually to retrogression and to eventual extinction of the resultant type unless it is fortified by reunion with the parent stock.

Those favoring present day amalgamation of these distinct races irrespective of scientific data of a cautionary nature based upon the experience of others, or who feel that a supposed infrequency of interracial unions will minimize undesirable consequences to the point that would justify lifting the prohibiting upon such unions, should direct their efforts to the Legislature in order to effect the change in state policy which they espouse as was done in Massachusetts in 1843, Kansas in 1859, New Mexico in 1866, Washington in 1868, Rhode Island in 1881, Minnesota and Michigan in 1883, and Ohio in 1887.

Finally, it is argued that sections 60 and 69 are too vague and uncertain to constitute valid regulation in that they lack definitions of descriptive terms, such as mulatto, and are uncertain as to the mode of proof of race. After almost one hundred years of continuous operation of the present and pre-existing similar laws, the claimed obstacles to the application of the statute are more theoretical than real. In any event the contention is not a matter for consideration in this proceeding. In the application for a marriage license the petitioner Perez states that she is a white person and the petitioner Davis states that he is a Negro. The petition for the writ contains allegations of the same facts. There is therefore no indefiniteness in the code sections that can avail the petitioners; nor is there here any problem of proof. It is the well-established rule that a charge of unconstitutionality can be raised only in a case where that issue is involved in the determination of the action, and then only by the person or a member of the class of persons adversely affected.

1. What exactly is being contested in this case?
2. How is the existence of the children of these unions relevant to the majority and dissent? Consider the language of "miscegenous marriages" and what that might imply?
3. Why were legislatures so concerned about the potential of children from these marriages?
4. Do you see the tension between values of White supremacy and assimilation within these opinions? If so, where and how?
5. What do the anti-miscegenation laws tell us about the relation of the law to the definition of race?

The Supreme Court would finally address this issue nationally in the 1967 decision in *Loving* v. *Virginia*. The state of Virginia had a law similar to California's which Mildred Jeter, who identified as Black, and Richard Loving, who identified as White, challenged. They were legally married in Washington, D.C. in June 1958, moving to Virginia soon after the wedding. In January 1959, they were indicted, charged, pleaded, and sentenced to one year in jail for violating the Virginia anti-miscegenation statutes. The trial judge suspended the sentence, dependent upon whether the Lovings left Virginia and did not return for 25 years. In rendering his decisions, he noted:

> Almighty God created the races white, black, yellow, malay and red, and he placed them on separate continents. And but for the interference with his arrangement there would be no cause for such marriages. The fact that he separated the races shows that he did not intend for the races to mix.

The Lovings returned to the District of Columbia and in 1964, appealed the constitutionality of the statute and their sentence to the Virginia appellate courts. Eventually, the Virginia Supreme Court upheld the statutes and affirmed the Lovings' convictions; the Supreme Court of the United States agreed to hear their appeal.

LOVING v. *VIRGINIA*, 388 U.S. 1 (1967)

Chief Justice Warren Delivered the Unanimous Opinion of the Court

Vote: 9–0

This case presents a constitutional question never addressed by this Court: whether a statutory scheme adopted by the State of Virginia to prevent marriages between persons solely on the basis of racial classifications violates the Equal Protection and Due Process Clauses of the Fourteenth Amendment. For reasons which seem to us to reflect the central meaning of those constitutional commands, we conclude that these statutes cannot stand consistently with the Fourteenth Amendment.

Virginia is now one of 16 States which prohibit and punish marriages on the basis of racial classifications. Penalties for miscegenation arose as an incident to slavery and have been common in Virginia since the colonial period. The present statutory scheme dates from the adoption of the Racial Integrity Act of 1924, passed during the period of extreme nativism which followed the end of the First World War. The central features of this Act, and current Virginia law, are the absolute prohibition of a "white person" marrying other than another "white person," a prohibition against issuing marriage licenses until the issuing official is satisfied that the applicants' statements as to their race are correct, certificates of "racial composition" to be kept by both local and state registrars, and the carrying forward of earlier prohibitions against racial intermarriage.

I.

In upholding the constitutionality of these provisions in the decision below, the Supreme Court of Appeals of Virginia referred to its 1955 decision in *Naim* v. *Naim*, 197 Va. 80, 87 S.E.2d 749 (1955), as stating the reasons supporting the validity of these laws. In *Naim*, the state court concluded that the State's legitimate purposes were "to preserve the racial integrity of its citizens," and to prevent "the corruption of blood," "a mongrel breed of citizens," and "the obliteration of racial pride," obviously an endorsement of the doctrine of White Supremacy. The court also reasoned that marriage has traditionally been subject to state regulation without federal intervention, and, consequently, the regulation of marriage should be left to exclusive state control by the Tenth Amendment.

While the state court is no doubt correct in asserting that marriage is a social relation subject to the State's police power, the State does not contend in its argument before this Court that its powers to regulate marriage are unlimited notwithstanding the commands of the Fourteenth Amendment. Nor could it do so in light of *Meyer* v. *State of Nebraska*, 262 U.S. 390 (1923), and *Skinner* v. *State of Oklahoma*, 316 U.S. 535 (1942). Instead, the State argues that the meaning of the Equal Protection Clause, as illuminated by the statements of the Framers, is only that state penal laws containing an interracial element as part of the definition of the offense must apply equally to whites and Negroes in the sense that members of each race are punished to the same degree. Thus, the State contends that, because its miscegenation statutes punish equally both the white and the Negro participants in an interracial marriage, these statutes, despite their reliance on racial classifications do not constitute an invidious discrimination based upon race. The second argument advanced by the State assumes the validity of its equal application theory. The argument is that, if the Equal Protection Clause does not outlaw miscegenation statutes because of their reliance on racial classifications, the question of constitutionality would thus become whether there was any rational basis for a State to treat interracial marriages differently from other marriages. On this question, the State argues, the scientific evidence is substantially in doubt and, consequently, this Court should defer to the wisdom of the state legislature in adopting its policy of discouraging interracial marriages.

Because we reject the notion that the mere "equal application" of a statute containing racial classifications is enough to remove the classifications from the Fourteenth Amendment's proscription of all invidious racial discriminations, we do not accept the State's contention that these statutes should be upheld if there is any possible basis for concluding that they serve a rational purpose.

The State finds support for its "equal application" theory in the decision of the Court in *Pace* v. *State of Alabama*, 106 U.S. 583 (1883). In that case, the Court upheld a conviction under an Alabama statute forbidding adultery or fornication between a white person and a Negro which imposed a greater penalty than that of a statute proscribing similar conduct by members of the same race. The Court reasoned that the statute could not be said to discriminate against Negroes because the punishment for each participant in the offense was the same. However, as recently as the 1964 Term, in rejecting the reasoning of that case, we stated "*Pace* represents a limited view of the Equal Protection Clause which has not withstood analysis in the subsequent decisions of this Court." *McLaughlin* v. *Florida*, 379 U.S. 184, at 188 (1964). As we there demonstrated, the Equal Protection Clause requires the consideration of whether the classifications drawn by any statute constitute an arbitrary and invidious discrimination. The clear and central purpose of the Fourteenth Amendment was to eliminate all official state sources of invidious racial discrimination in the States.

There can be no question but that Virginia's miscegenation statutes rest solely upon distinctions drawn according to race. The statutes proscribe generally accepted conduct if engaged in by members of different races. Over the years, this Court has consistently repudiated "(d)istinctions between citizens solely because of their ancestry" as being "odious to a free people whose institutions are founded upon the doctrine of equality." *Hirabayashi* v. *United States*, 320 U.S. 81, 100 (1943). At the very least, the Equal Protection Clause demands that racial classifications, especially suspect in criminal statutes, be subjected to the "most rigid scrutiny," *Korematsu* v. *United States*, 323 U.S. 214, 216 (1944), and, if they are ever to be upheld, they must be shown to be necessary to the accomplishment of some permissible state objective, independent of the racial discrimination which it was the object of the Fourteenth Amendment to eliminate.

There is patently no legitimate overriding purpose independent of invidious racial discrimination which justifies this classification. The fact that Virginia prohibits only interracial marriages involving white persons demonstrates that the racial classifications must stand on their own justification, as measures designed to maintain White Supremacy. We have consistently denied the constitutionality of measures which restrict the rights of citizens on account of race. There can be no doubt that restricting the freedom to marry solely because of racial classifications violates the central meaning of the Equal Protection Clause.

II.

These statutes also deprive the Lovings of liberty without due process of law in violation of the Due Process Clause of the Fourteenth Amendment. The freedom to marry has long been recognized as one of the vital personal rights essential to the orderly pursuit of happiness by free men.

Marriage is one of the "basic civil rights of man," fundamental to our very existence and survival. *Skinner* v. *State of Oklahoma*, 316 U.S. 535, 541 (1942). To deny this fundamental freedom on so unsupportable a basis as the racial classifications embodied in these statutes, classifications so directly subversive of the principle of equality at the heart of the Fourteenth Amendment, is surely to deprive all the State's citizens of liberty without due process of law. The Fourteenth Amendment requires that the freedom of choice to marry not be restricted by invidious racial discriminations. Under our Constitution, the freedom to marry or not marry, a person of another race resides with the individual and cannot be infringed by the State.

These convictions must be reversed. It is so ordered. Reversed.

1. Compare the decisions in the California Supreme Court and the U.S. Supreme Court to overrule these state laws. Where do you see similarities and differences?
2. Is the fact that this decision is unanimous significant? In what way?
3. How does the Supreme Court understand the existence of multiracial children as influencing the creation of these laws?

It took time, but by the early twenty-first century the stigmas around interracial relationships had begun to fade and the children of these unions became a larger identifiable segment of the population. However, the question of the law's ability to protect against racial discrimination toward individuals who identify as multiracial remains unsettled.

7.4.2 Multiracial Identities

The U.S. Census changed its format to allow residents to note their racial identity as a race "in conjunction with" another race or as "two or more races" in 2000. The growth in this population exploded after a decade of measurement. The multiracial population self-reported as 9 million in 2010 and by 2020 had increased by 276 percent to 33.8 million individuals. This was the largest overall change in racial identity. Those who identified as Hispanic and multiracial similarly grew from 3 million in 2010 to 20.3 million (Jones et al. 2021).

By 2015, the Pew Research Center found that the number of people who identified as multiracial were growing three times as fast as the U.S. population. They found that "69% of [those who claim an origin from Black and White parents] say most people would view them as [B]lack or African American – [with] a set of experiences, attitudes, and social interactions that are more closely in line with the [B]lack community" (Parker et al. 2015). The opposite was true with those who were biracial and of White and Asian or White and Native descent – they typically identified more with the White community. While those of Native American and White descent are the largest self-reported multiracial population "ties to their Native American heritage are faint," as only 22 percent note a sense of commonality with people who identify as indigenous (Parker et al. 2015).

The reasons for these changes are numerous: the U.S. population identifies as more racially diverse; the stigma regarding interracial relationships has faded; Americans are now more likely to embrace their diverse racial identities and not seek to pass as White; and the revised census forms allows people to express their identity (Tavernise, Mzezewa, and Heyward 2021). While this population has grown, the law remains based on an understanding of mono-racial identities and on a precedential basis – the one-drop rule. For racial justice to occur in the twenty-first century, is the current legal structure sufficient to incorporate these new identities or does the law surrounding racial discrimination need to explicitly incorporate multiracial people?

Because of the current legal framing of race, in racial discrimination cases the courts redefine plaintiffs with multiracial identities as being from a single minority group – most typically as "Black" or "African American." "Multiracial" is not yet seen as an independent racial identity politically or legally, although there are many who advocate for this type of formalization. Those who seek this kind of legitimization fear that the current status of law makes it "highly unlikely that a multi-racial individual could convince a court that he or she is wrought with disabilities, politically powerless, or has been subjected to a history of purposeful and unjust treatment" (Myers 2020, 71) all attributes required by the courts to be given protected status. Scholars who advocate for multiracial legal protections argue that the current structure obscures the discrimination faced by multiracial people based on their identity. Their argument is very similar to the challenges made regarding intersectionality – our current jurisprudence cannot handle this kind of identity complexity. Scholars such as Nancy Leong contend that there is a history of animus against people solely because of their multiracial status, as demonstrated by the history of laws against racial intermarriage (Leong 2010).

On the other hand, scholars like Tanya Katerí Hernández argue that multiracial plaintiffs who claim racial discrimination are never fighting against bias on the grounds of their complex racial identity, but instead a bias against "nonwhiteness." This means their claims are not unique to their racial identity but instead are shared by all perceived to be members of communities of color:

> ... [T]he increase in the number of individuals identifying as mixed-race or multiracial does not present unique challenges to the pursuit of political equality inasmuch as the cases are mired in a long-existing morass of bias against nonwhiteness and its intimate connection to white dominance. Rather than point to a need for a shift away from the existing current civil rights laws, the cases instead indicate a need for further support of the current structures. (Hernández 2018, 6)

There are few cases that contain explicitly identified multiracial plaintiffs and have been decided by the courts, but in relying on precedent these decisions do not clearly address the multiracial identity of the claimant, even if such identity is at the heart of the discussion.

In the federal District Court case of *Callicutt* v. *Pepsi Bottling Group, Inc.* (2002), the court was confronted with a racial discrimination case in which five men, who worked at a Pepsi Minnesota warehouse as loaders, claim that they were discriminated against by Pepsi on the basis of their race, in terms of promotion, segregated working environment, hostile working conditions, and retaliation. One of the five men, Gentry McQuiston, who identified as biracial, noted that his experience with racial bias reflected his lighter complexion: he was called "FUBU," a reference a Black-owned clothing line FUBU ("for us by us") and "Sinbad," a reference to a lighter-skinned Black comic. He also made similar claims as the other plaintiffs noting the racially hostile work environment and retaliation. After filing with the EEOC, their claims were deemed viable and they were given "right to sue letters" and filed their claim in the District Court. Does the Court's treatment of McQuiston as African American under the law demonstrate a need for a multiracial classification or would it not change the outcome of the decision?

CALLICUTT v. PEPSI BOTTLING GROUP, INC., CIVIL NO. 00-95 (DWF/AJB) (D. MINN.) (2002)

Judge Donovan W. Frank, Wrote the Decision of the Court

The above-entitled matter came on for hearing before the undersigned United States District Judge on March 1, 2002, pursuant to Defendant's Motion for Summary Judgment. Plaintiffs allege racial discrimination in the form of a racially hostile work environment and retaliation ... Plaintiffs also raise common law claims of intentional infliction of emotional distress, invasion of privacy, and negligence. For the reasons set forth below, Defendant's motion is granted in part and denied in part.

Discussion

B. Issues

Plaintiffs allege racial discrimination in the forms of a racially hostile work environment and retaliation in violation of Title VII of the Civil Rights Act of 1964, Sections 1981 and 1981a of the Civil Rights Act of 1991, and the Minnesota Human Rights Act (MHRA). Plaintiffs also raise common law claims of intentional infliction of emotional distress, invasion of privacy, and negligence. By its current motion, Pepsi moves for summary judgment on all claims.

Although Plaintiffs raise separate MHRA claims, the Court conducts its analysis of these claims pursuant to Title VII case law.

2. Hostile Work Environment

Title VII provides that it is "an unlawful employment practice for an employer ... to discriminate against any individual with respect to his compensation, terms, conditions, or privileges of employment, because of such individual's race, color, religion, sex, or national origin." 42 U.S.C. § 2000e-2(a)(1). "The phrase 'terms, conditions, or privileges of employment' evinces a congressional intent to strike at the entire spectrum of disparate treatment of men and women in employment, which includes requiring people to work in a discriminatorily hostile or abusive environment." *Harris* v. *Forklift Systems, Inc.*, 510 U.S. 17, 21 (1993). Consistent with this congressional intent, discrimination is defined "in the broadest possible terms," not confined to specific acts of discrimination or defined types of illegal activity. Consequently, a plaintiff may establish a Title VII hostile work environment claim based on racial discrimination.

To succeed with their claims, Plaintiffs must make a prima facie showing that: (1) they are members of a protected group; (2) they received unwelcome harassment; (3) there is a causal nexus between the harassment and their status as a member of a protected group; (4) the harassment affected a term, condition, or privilege of employment; and (5) Pepsi knew or should have known of the harassment and failed to take prompt and remedial action. The evidence of a racially hostile environment presented by Plaintiffs "must not be compartmentalized, but must instead be based on the totality of the circumstances of the entire hostile work environment."

The Court rejects Pepsi's argument that incidents involving a racially hostile work environment occurring in 1998 are not relevant in the case at bar. The Court agrees that Plaintiffs cannot maintain a claim arising solely on hearsay evidence, or events occurring prior to their employment. However, under the totality of the circumstances, Plaintiffs' awareness of racially discriminatory incidents experienced by others at Pepsi may be relevant as to whether Pepsi maintains a racially hostile work environment. For example, if Pepsi instituted a mandatory diversity and sensitivity training policy in 1998, such evidence of other incidents may serve to determine whether the policy was adequate. However, the Court views evidence relating to events in 1998 for the limited purpose of providing context evidence that, without more, cannot serve as the basis for the current claims.

The parties do not dispute that Plaintiffs are members of a protected class or that they were subjected to unwelcome harassment. However, Pepsi does contend that several of the hostile acts were not directed at Plaintiffs because of their race. More significantly, the primary contentions between the parties are whether the harassment was severe or pervasive enough to permeate the work environment and thus affect a term or condition of employment and whether Pepsi knew or ought to have known of the discriminatory conduct and failed to take appropriate remedial action. Pepsi argues that Plaintiffs rely largely on isolated incidents, involving unidentified perpetrators, that often went unreported to human resources. Pepsi further contends that, on the occasions Plaintiffs

did report incidents to supervisors or human resources, it took prompt and remedial action to end the discriminatory conduct. Plaintiffs argue that they each produced evidence of direct racial slurs and harassing behavior that they experienced throughout their employment with Pepsi. Plaintiffs additionally contend that of the core nineteen incidents reported, Pepsi only took action two times, and in any event, the action taken was ineffective.

a. Protected Class

Plaintiffs must first show that the hostile acts directed at them were because of their membership in a protected class. Plaintiffs are entitled to work in an environment free from racially motivated "intimidation, ridicule, and insult." Racial epithets often serve as the basis for racial harassment claims and may create an inference that racial animus motivated seemingly innocent conduct as well. Accordingly, not "all instances of harassment [must] be stamped with signs of overt discrimination to be relevant under Title VII if they are part of a course of conduct which is tied to evidence of discriminatory animus."

Without question, the racial epithets of "nigger," "blacks," or "boy," qualify as discriminatory comments based on race. Likewise, when viewed in conjunction with blatant, racially motivated incidents, epithets of "nothing," "FUBU," and "Sinbad," may also be determined to have been motivated by a racial animus. It stands to reason that if the same white co-workers who used racial slurs were kicking Plaintiffs off forklifts, playing pranks on them, and singling them out in the break room, these arguably benign occurrences may be found to stem from a racial animus as well. Consequently, the Court finds that a reasonable jury could conclude that Plaintiffs each experienced unwanted harassment directed at them because of their race.

b. Severe and Pervasive

Having established that the discriminatory harassment was because of their race, it is well settled that Plaintiffs must show that the workplace was permeated with "discriminatory intimidation, ridicule, and insult that [was] sufficiently severe or pervasive to alter the conditions of the [their] employment and create[d] an abusive working environment." In order to alter a term or condition of Plaintiffs' employment, the offensive environment must satisfy both a subjective and objective test; it must be hostile and abusive to the reasonable person, and Plaintiffs had to perceive it as such. Factors to consider when determining whether discriminatory activity "is sufficiently severe or pervasive include: [(1)] 'the frequency of the discriminatory conduct; [(2)] its severity; [(3)] whether it is physically threatening or humiliating, or a mere offensive utterance; and [(4)] whether it unreasonably interferes with an employee's work performance.'"

Although a close case, the Court finds that a reasonable jury could conclude that Plaintiffs Callicutt, Gordon, O'Neal and Poindexter were subjected to a racially hostile work environment that was severe and pervasive enough to affect a term or condition of their employment. Callicutt and Gordon each reported multiple instances of "nigger" being used, both directed at them and generally used in everyday work banter. Co-workers told Callicutt that "blacks" were lazy and stole things, and should be taught some manners. Callicutt also reported separate instances of physical harassment in the form of a white co-worker attempting to run him over with a forklift. Gordon, meanwhile, reported an earlier encounter with his union steward, who told him he was "nothing," and then was subsequently terminated ...

O'Neal reported an incident where a white co-worker called him a "nigger." He also reported seeing "nigger" written on the bathroom walls on multiple occasions. Additionally, he experienced situations where his union steward told him he was not worth "shit," had arguments over forklifts, and allegedly was singled out on breaks. Poindexter reported several instances of verbal abuse as well. He heard white co-workers sing a song called "Almighty Whitey," refer to him as "boy," and freely use "nigger" during a smoke break. Poindexter also experienced multiple instances of physical harassment in the forms of unwanted pranks and practical jokes, which, coupled with the other evidence of racially

hostile acts, could be seen as racially motivated. Finally, Poindexter took extreme offense from the donut incident on Martin Luther King Jr. Day as well. While many of these incidents could very well have been non-racially motivated, a reasonable jury could find, under the totality of the circumstances, that such incidents were racially motivated and attempts to intimidate or threaten African-American employees ...

O'Neal reported hearing or seeing racial epithets on only a few occasions, but he also experienced other incidents which may have been motivated by racial animus. These incidents occurred over the entire time he worked in the warehouse. Poindexter reported incidents ranging from when he first began working at Pepsi in late fall through the following summer. None of these Plaintiffs were employed for more than two years.

Indeed, O'Neal and Gordon were only at Pepsi for three months. Within a shorter time frame, such as the tenure of some of the instant Plaintiffs, even a few instances of the use of "nigger" may be found to be severe and pervasive. The Court thus finds that a reasonable jury could find that the racial hostility experienced by Callicutt, Poindexter, Gordon, and O'Neal, was severe and pervasive enough to affect a term or condition of their employment.

In contrast, the Court finds that, as a matter of law, McQuiston fails to make the required showing of severe and pervasive hostility. McQuiston alleged that he was not hired full-time because of his race, but supported this contention with nothing more than his own perception. He was called "FUBU" or "Sinbad" on only two occasions. While the Court recognizes that McQuiston may have been rightfully offended by this and that the behavior of McQuiston's co-workers was wholly inappropriate, the Court does not find that a reasonable juror could find such conduct to constitute severe harassment. Finally, McQuiston offered other incidents that fail to demonstrate severe or pervasive racial harassment in and of themselves, or in combination. He, like some of his fellow Plaintiffs, alleged that white co-workers invoked seniority over him, but he makes no showing that this was race based conduct. He felt he was singled out on lunch breaks, but even if true, he only reports one instance. The Court does not doubt the sincerity of McQuiston's subjective beliefs. However, the Court finds that he has not succeeded in demonstrating that, as an objective matter, racial discrimination, intimidation, and ridicule permeated his workplace, so as to constitute severe and pervasive conduct under Title VII.

c. Remedial Response

Because the alleged racial harassment occurred at the hands of co-workers rather than supervisors, the remaining Plaintiffs must show that Pepsi knew or ought to have known of the racial harassment and failed to take prompt and remedial action. "When assessing the reasonableness of an employer's remedial actions, the court may consider the amount of time that elapsed between the notice of the harassment and the remedial measures taken, including any disciplinary action against the harasser or other options available to the employer such as employee training sessions." "The promptness and adequacy of an employer's response will often be a question of fact for the factfinder to resolve."

At the outset, the Court recognizes that Pepsi responded to some of the reported incidents. It terminated Carney and Frary and suspended Bader and Severson. In addition, Pothen talked to O'Neal and Faith, and told them that everyone needed to work together. Pepsi also investigated the donut incident and had Callicutt look through an employee photo list in an effort to identify who had said "nigger" in the break room. It painted over the bathroom walls when "nigger" was found written in black marker. Pepsi also responded to Plaintiffs concerns that the workplace was segregated by implementing a new bulk loader team selection process where the supervisors assigned the teams, a process which Plaintiffs admit corrected the problem. Pepsi hired Sherman Carter, an African-American, as a senior human resources employee in charge of investigating and responding to claims of racial harassment in the workplace. Since 1998, Pepsi mandated diversity and sensitivity training for all employees. Of the incidents Pepsi did not investigate, some were incidents where no perpetrator was identified, were horseplay or purported invocations of seniority, or were unreported.

The Court agrees that Pepsi took remedial action on some of the incidents reported to it, especially those involving the most offensive racial epithets. However, the Court finds that whether Pepsi's remedial actions were adequate, given the totality of the circumstances, remains a question for the jury. While Pepsi's response could be deemed adequate, the Court finds that the nature of its responses and the continued occurrence of incidents prompting complaints could lead a reasonable jury to conclude that Pepsi should have done more.

Consequently, the Court finds that Callicutt, Poindexter, Gordon, and O'Neal have succeeded in making a prima facie showing of a racially hostile work environment. Although a close case, the Court finds that a reasonable jury could find in favor of Plaintiffs, and accordingly, the Court declines to issue summary judgment in favor of Defendant with respect to four of the five Plaintiffs.

3. Retaliation

... To establish a prima facie case of racially discriminatory retaliation under Title VII and the MHRA, Plaintiffs must show that: (1) [they] filed a charge of racial harassment; (2) subsequent adverse action by [Pepsi]; and (3) the adverse action was causally linked to the protected activity.

The Court finds that Plaintiffs do not make a prima facie showing of retaliation. Gordon and O'Neal did not file their EEOC complaints until they were no longer working at Pepsi. Gordon filed nearly two months after he was terminated, and O'Neal filed his charge over three months after he was terminated. Both therefore fail to meet the second element of subsequent action. Callicutt, Poindexter and McQuiston all filed their EEOC charges while they were working, but all fail to meet the third element by establishing a causal link between the filing of the charge and their respective terminations, or any other alleged adverse action. Callicutt was not terminated for over a year after filing his charge, and he does not refute Pepsi's explanation that he was terminated for theft of company product. Poindexter remained at Pepsi for another eight months after he filed his claim, and then resigned. He does not make a claim of constructive discharge nor does he allege any alternative adverse action which might be causally connected to his EEOC charge. Finally, McQuiston was terminated three months after he filed his EEOC charge for a "no call, no show." He does not dispute that this was a legitimate reason for termination, and, in fact, admits that he had a history of tardiness and absenteeism.

To the extent that Plaintiffs allege their protected activity is one or all of the various reports made to Pepsi personnel; Plaintiffs have also failed to show that any of the alleged discrimination following such reports, or any other alleged adverse action, was somehow related to their complaints. Plaintiffs have made no allegations that the alleged activity worsened following their reports. To the extent that Gordon alleges that his termination was in retaliation for his involvement in the Carney incident, Gordon has offered nothing more than a conclusory allegation. The Court finds that, as a matter of law, Plaintiff has failed to raise a genuine issue of material fact. Indeed, Plaintiffs failed to brief the retaliation issue, and only stated orally that they did not wish to drop this claim. Because none of the Plaintiffs offer any evidence of a causal link between the filing of their respective EEOC complaints, or their reports to Pepsi personnel, and the eventual terminations, Plaintiffs' claims of retaliation must fail.

4. Common Law Claims

Plaintiffs raise common law claims of intentional infliction of emotional distress, invasion of privacy, and negligence. Pepsi argues that the MHRA's exclusivity of remedies provision, preempts Plaintiffs from raising these claims. Plaintiffs agree that the MHRA preempts their common law claims, but contend that their common law claims survive, in the alternative, if the Court grants summary judgment on the MHRA claims. Plaintiffs, however, cite no authority for this contention and essentially support it with nothing more than a conclusory sentence. This Court acknowledges the nebulous state of the case law surrounding this issue, but it agrees "that the MHRA preempts a common law cause of action if: (1) the factual basis and injuries supporting the common law claim also would establish a violation of the MHRA; and (2) the obligations the defendant owes to the plaintiff, as a practical matter, are the same under both the common law and MHRA." Plaintiffs rely upon the same incidents of racial harassment for their common law claims as for their MHRA claims. Although the elements for Plaintiffs' common law claims vary, the Court finds that the same incidents of racial harassment in the workplace would serve to support both the common law claims and the MHRA claims. Accordingly, the current Plaintiffs' common law claims, as pleaded, are preempted by their corresponding statutory claims.

For the foregoing reasons, IT IS HEREBY ORDERED THAT:

1. Defendant's Motion for Summary Judgment (Doc. No. 26) is GRANTED in part, and DENIED in part such that:
   a. The Court denies Defendant's Motion for Summary Judgment with respect to the claims of racially hostile work environment, with respect to Plaintiffs Callicutt, Poindexter, Gordon, and O'Neal. The Court grants Pepsi's motion for summary judgment in all other respects;
   b. Plaintiff McQuiston's statutory claims, Counts I, II, and III are DISMISSED WITH PREJUDICE; however, Counts I, II, and III remain standing with respect to Plaintiffs Calicutt, Gordon, O'Neal, and Poindexter; and
   c. Plaintiffs Calicutt, Gordon, McQuiston, O'Neal, and Poindexter's common law claims, Counts IV, V, and VI, of intentional infliction of emotional distress, invasion of privacy, and negligence are DISMISSED WITH PREJUDICE.

1. How does the judge evaluate the claims made by McQuiston? How is he classified under the law?
2. Was he treated differently as a multiracial plaintiff than the other African
   American plaintiffs who brought a claim?
3. In light of the debate among scholars regarding the treatment of multiracial
   plaintiffs under current racial discrimination law, which position do you find
   more compelling and why?
4. What might be the relationship between colorism (treatment of darker complected individuals more negatively than lighter complected individuals) and
   racial discrimination of multiracial individuals?
5. What would have to change in the law to allow for the explicit protection of
   multiracial people? Is their discrimination distinct from that of other racial
   discrimination?
6. Does this case better support the position of Leong or Hernández?

Our common law system is based on precedent, which means current issues
are defined and interpreted based on courts' past analyses and decisions. While
our understanding of race has become more nuanced and complicated, as well as
our definitions and expectations of equality and equity, our law remains static.
This stability has some value but also means that we use past understandings to
determine current interpretations. As we debate the importance of intentionality in
demonstrating discrimination and the significance of intersectionality in providing equality, we must explore how the law can change and evolve to meet these
new demands. Should the courts revise their jurisprudence, or should statutory law
change to address a changing society? Or are there issues that the law is simply
not equipped to address?

Conclusion
What Do We Owe Democracy?

It is easy to believe that our democracy will never be able to correct the nation's historic and ongoing choices that have alienated many based on their perceived race. Time alone is insufficient to ensure meaningful changes will be made to address the scars of White supremacy as well as ongoing policies, precedents, and values we have not yet reexamined. But just as our nation's legal choices were debated and challenged during the very origins of the United States, they are contested today. We legally constructed the idea and meaning of race in our country, therefore we can redefine these terms and change the meanings. However, this endeavor will require the effort of everyone.

The Metaphor of the Room

Imagine our democratic society as a giant room. There are walls and windows, carpeting or hardwood on the floor, and furniture throughout. Citizens with full constitutional protections are inside the room, and those excluded are barred from entering by a locked door. Individuals and groups who have power allow those without it to enter the room by opening the door for them. The law can serve as a key to provide people outside the room with access, or it can be wielded by those inside the room as a lock to prevent outsiders from gaining entrance. As this book has demonstrated, law is a tool that can be utilized by both the powerful and the politically dispossessed to pursue their own ends. However, there is an inherent bias in U.S. law that favors past interpretations over current needs because our common law system relies on past precedents, and because the people implementing the law already reside within the room and do not share the same perspectives or experiences as those outside. Even so, the Constitution and our statutes also point us toward the values of equality, claiming to prioritize an ideal that we have not yet fully integrated into our laws. As Frederick Douglass argued, this value provides both hope for those outside the room and the legitimacy to press their claim for inclusion.

If you are locked out of your house and you know people are inside ignoring you, what do you do? You begin by knocking on the door, then pounding, then yelling—you escalate your demands. Eventually, you may try to break a window and climb in or do something even more drastic. This is how protest expands. You have a righteous claim because you know you have a right to be in your home. The Constitution and its promises give us the authority to be insiders—equal citizens in our democracy. This is our own righteous claim.

People knock on the door of democracy by exercising traditional means of resistance and protest. They file legal challenges (this book is full of examples of such "knocking" through court cases and organized litigation), using the judiciary to challenge unjust laws and practices. Traditional forms of resistance and protest involve holding the political system accountable to its own rules, as stated in the Constitution and through statutory law. Even those who do not have political clout still have economic leverage; in a free society, they can determine to whom they sell their labor and where they spend their money. People can resist through picketing and boycotting. Individuals can also protest and assemble to challenge the status quo, mobilize voters who share their concerns, and organize communities to challenge unjust rules.

When knocking—even vigorous pounding—is not sufficient to encourage those inside to open the door and let others in, people move to more insistent forms of pressure, including civil disobedience. Those who use these techniques acknowledge the legitimacy of the government, but challenge the validity of an unfair policy. They just want to reside in the room, not destroy the house. When an individual or community engages in civil disobedience, they publicly break the unjust law, but acknowledge the legal authority of the state by accepting their punishment. Protestors want to put moral pressure on people in the room, wakening the powerful to the shameful nature of their injustice and encouraging them to do what is right.

Rebellion, on the other hand, does not accept the legitimacy of the government. It challenges not just unfair policies but the very political structure that allows such inequalities to exist. It seeks to gain attention and power by destroying the previous government and replacing it with one of its own. There are many tools of rebellion, including sabotage and passive economic or property destruction, as well as theft and neglect (Kelly 1994). Not all violence or property damage is political; some rebels may just be people who take advantage of chaos and conflict. Groups may be conflicted over their methods of resistance, and some violent action may be renegade. Sometimes violence is the last refuge of those who believe they are unheard and unseen. Such strategies are responses to the argument that in a capitalist system, protecting private property is more important than protecting the right of the people to protest. Sometimes those in the room focus on the damage to property over the desperation of the protestors, who feel they have nothing left to say that will be heard. The final and most extreme stage of resistance is revolution: pure violence against the state. The room and the democracy are destroyed, and often the politically dispossessed who believe they have nothing left to lose—especially the elderly and children—pay the greatest price.

We achieve formal equality when we allow people into the room, giving them access to the workings of democracy with the promise of treating everyone the same under law. Yet all people are not the same. They may have differing needs that must be addressed in order for them to fully exercise their rights of citizenship. Although formal equality ended slavery, stopped Jim Crow segregation, protected basic voting rights, and statutorily banned race-based employment and housing discrimination, it could not ensure that all people would be treated as human or equal regardless of race. Formal equality ensures that race cannot be a barrier to admittance to the room, *but it does not inherently make outsiders welcome.* Substantive equality asks those more recently included in the democracy whether or not they like the look of the room. Does it seem comfortable? Would you want to live in it? Do you want to change the curtains, paint the walls, rearrange the furniture, pull up the carpet? We must think about what it means when we let people into the room – our democracy – and then refuse them the opportunity to redecorate. If they cannot change policy, elect their own representatives, or contribute to rethinking the values of the nation, are they truly citizens of our society? Are they truly equal?

Today, we still have substantial racially based disparities regarding access to education, housing, pathways out of poverty, and unbiased economic and social structures. Our divides still cut across many sectors, yet many segments of our society define equality as being "color-blind," arguing that if we ignore the role of race, its significance will dissipate. Many of those who have been in the room and decorated it want new citizens to sit quietly, admire the décor, and appreciate their good fortune on being admitted. However, this commitment to stagnation may put our democracy at risk, for these are the historic values of "assimilation," not citizenship. It serves us well to remember that a newcomer who wants to update the décor is not equivalent to an arsonist who wants to burn down the house.

A Final Thought: the Metaphor of the Candy Dish

It is easy to read this history, reflect on our current debates and challenges surrounding race in the United States, and be overwhelmed. Feelings of anger, resentment, guilt, and hopelessness are all understandable. But these are not new problems. They took centuries to fully develop, and people have been protesting, challenging, rebelling against injustice, and debating what justice and democracy demands throughout the lifetime of our Nation, which has persevered. It is hopelessness and despair that threaten us. Our current "American dilemma" has been centuries in its creation and perpetuation, and members of each generation either fight for progress, or, if they have racial privilege, ignore the contradictions between our national ideals and our reality.

My grandmother left me a candy dish when she passed away. It was made of flowered pastel-colored glass that I found unattractive, and it had a lid that hid the ribbon and hard candies kept within. But it was my grandmother's, so I kept it. Our national inheritance regarding race is like an old family candy dish that we have handed down generation after generation, never opening the lid and never dealing with the sticky mess inside.

We did not create the candy dish or choose the design, and we did not ask for it—it was given to us by our forebears. Each generation passed it to the next, acknowledging it as an unwelcome legacy, but not doing much to improve it. Our generation has the opportunity to do something different. Instead of thoughtlessly preserving the past and handing it off to our children, we can lift the lid, confront the mess, and work together to clean it out. Likewise, we can bring debates about our history and assumptions out into the open as a step toward ridding our nation of its continuing contradictions. Many Whites fear such a reckoning. They dread losing power or being denied what little they perceive they possess, as evidenced by the resistance encountered from school boards and state legislatures over critical race theory and the appropriate curriculum at all levels of public education. There is a better alternative, even if it may make many of those with power uncomfortable or fearful. The only other option is to continue as we have—not fulfilling the nation's half-hearted promises or the guarantees many generations of Americans of color clung to, fought for, and deserve.

REFERENCES

Ablavsky, Gregory. 2014. "The Savage Constitution," *Duke Law Journal* 63(5): 999–1089.

Ablavsky, Gregory. 2021. "Two Federalist Constitutions of Empire," *Fordham Law Review* 89(5): 1677–1706.

Akee, Randall K. O., Katherine A. Spilde, and Jonathan B. Taylor. 2015. "The Indian Gaming Regulatory Act and its Effects on American Indian Economic Development," *Journal of Economic Perspectives* 29(3): 185–199.

Allah, Sha Be. 2021. "Black LGBTQ Teen Found Hanging from Tree in Massachusetts," *The Source.* May 5, available at: https://thesource.com/2021/05/05/black-lgbtq-teen-found-hanging-from-tree-in-massachusetts.

Allen, James, ed. 2000. *Without Sanctuary: Lynching Photography in America.* Santa Fe, N.M.: Twin Palms, available at: http://withoutsanctuary.org.

American Civil Liberties Union (ACLU). 2023. "To: Girad USD 248 Re: Hair Length Policy," November 17, available at: www.aclukansas.org/en/girard-usd-248-re-hair-length-policy.

Anderson, Kathryn Freeman, Angelica Lopez, and Dylan Simburger. 2021. "Racial/Ethnic Residential Segregation and the First Wave of SARS-CoV-2 Infection Rates: A Spatial Analysis of Four U.S. Cities," *Sociological Perspectives* 64(5): 804–830.

Anderson, Terry H. 2004. *The Pursuit of Fairness: A History of Affirmative Action.* New York: Oxford University Press.

Arendt, Hannah. 1976. *The Origins of Totalitarianism.* New York: Harcourt: 296–297.

Armor, David J. 1995. *Forced Justice: School Desegregation and the Law.* New York: Oxford University Press.

Barde, Robert. 2004. "An Alleged Wife: One Immigrant in the Chinese Exclusion Era," *Prologue Magazine Spring* 36(1): 24–35.

Bass, Jack. 1981. *Unlikely Heroes: A Vivid Account of the Implementation of the Brown Decision in the South by the Southern Federal Judges Committed to the Rule of Law.* Norman: University of Oklahoma Press.

Bay, Mia. 2009. *To Tell the Truth Freely: The Life of Ida B. Wells.* New York: Hill & Wang.

Bell, Derrick. 2004. *Silent Covenants:* Brown v. Board of Education *and the Unfilled Hopes for Racial Reform.* New York: Oxford University Press.

Berard, Adrienne. 2016. *Water Tossing Over Boulders: How a Family of Chinese Immigrants Led the First Fight to Desegregate Schools in the Jim Crow South.* Boston, MA: Beacon Press.

Berlin, Ira. 2015. *The Long Emancipation: The Demise of Slavery in the United States.* Cambridge, MA: Harvard University Press.

Berry, Mary Francis. 1994. *Black Resistance, White Law: A History of Constitutional Racism in America.* New York: Penguin.

Bilder, Mary. 2021. "Without Doors: Native Nations and the Convention," Research Paper 556, April 20. Boston College Law Legal Studies Research Paper Series.

Blackhawk, Maggie. 2019. "Federal Indian Law as Paradigm within Public Law," *Harvard Law Review* 132(7): 1787–1872.

Blackhawk, Maggie. 2020. "On Power and the Law: *McGirt v. Oklahoma,*" *Supreme Court Review*: 367–421.

Blackhawk, Ned. 2023. *The Rediscovery of America: Native Peoples and the Unmaking of U.S. History.* New Haven, C.T.: Yale University Press.

Blackmon, Douglas A. 2008. *Slavery by Another Name: The Re-Enslavement of Black Americans from the Civil War to World War II.* New York: Anchor Books.

Blight, David W. 2018. *Frederick Douglass: Prophet of Freedom.* New York: Simon & Schuster.

Brooks, Charlotte. 2009. *Alien Neighbors, Foreign Friends: Asian Americans, Housing, and the Transformation of Urban California.* Chicago: University of Chicago Press.

Brooks, Roy L. and Kirsten Widner. 2010. "In Defense of the Black/White Binary: Reclaiming a Tradition of Civil Rights Scholarship," *Berkeley Journal of African-American Law and Policy* 12: 107–144.

Brown, Anna. 2020. "The Changing Categories the U.S. Census has Used to Measure Race," Pew Research Center. February 25, available at: www.pewresearch.org/short-reads/2020/02/25/the-changing-categories-the-u-s-has-used-to-measure-race.

Brown, DeNeen L. 2021. "Lynchings in Mississippi Never Stopped," *Washington Post*, August 8, available at: www.washingtonpost.com/nation/2021/08/08/modern-day-mississippi-lynchings.

Brown, Michael K., Martin Carney, Elliot Currie, Troy Duster, et al. 2004. *White-Washing Race: The Myth of a Colorblind Society.* Oakland: University of California Press.

Brundage, W. Fitzhugh. 2006. "The Ultimate Shame: Lynch Law in Post-Civil War American South," *Social Alternatives* 25(1): 28–32, 29–30.

Buccola, Nicholas. 2012. *The Political Thought of Frederick Douglass: In Pursuit of American Liberty.* New York: New York University Press.

Bush, Jonathan A. 1997. "The British Constitution and the Creation of American Slavery." In Paul Finkelman, ed. *Slavery and the Law.* Madison, WI: Madison House: 379–418.

Calloway, Colin. 2018. *The Indian World of George Washington: The First President, the First Americans, and the Birth of the Nation.* New York: Oxford University Press.

Canellos, Peter S. 2021. *The Great Dissenter: The Story of John Marshall Harlan, America's Judicial Hero.* New York: Simon & Schuster.

Cecelski, David S. 1994. *Along Freedom Road: Hyde County, North Carolina, and the Fate of Black Schools in the South.* Chapel Hill: University of North Carolina Press.

Coates, Ta-Nihisi. 2014. "The Case for Reparations," *The Atlantic*, May 21.

Colby, David C. 1986. "The Voting Rights Act and Black Registration in Mississippi," *Publius* 16(4): 123–137.

Cose, Ellis. 1997. *Color Blind: Seeing Beyond Race in a Race-Obsessed World.* New York: Harper Perennial.

Crepelle, Adam. 2022. "The Law and Economics of Crime in Indian Country," *Georgetown Law Review* 110: 569–612.

Daniel, Pete. 1990. *The Shadow of Slavery: Peonage in the South, 1901–1969.* Champaign: University of Illinois Press.

Daniels, Roger. 2013. *The Japanese American Cases: The Rule of Law in Time of War.* Lawrence: University Press of Kansas.

David, Fiona. 2017. "Modern Slavery: From Statistics to Prevention," *Chance* 30(3): 54–60.

Davidson, James West. 2007. *"They Say"! Ida B. Wells and the Reconstruction of Race.* New York: Oxford University Press.

Deardorff, Michelle D. 1993. "The Supreme Court and the Rights of Political Minorities: Changing Priorities Within a Single Contextual Framework," Ph.D. dissertation, Miami University of Ohio, Department of Political Science.

Deardorff, Michelle D. 2005. Review of *Racial Culture: A Critique* by Richard T. Ford. *Law and Politics Book Review* 15(3): 215–218.

Deardorff, Michelle D. 2014. "Symposium Keynote: Constructing the Franchise: Citizenship Rights versus Privileges and their Concomitant Policies," *Mississippi College Law Review* 33: 161–180.

Deardorff, Michelle D. and James G. Dahl. 2016. "Competing Definitions of Equality: Formal and Substantive Equality," *Pregnancy Discrimination and the American Worker*. New York: Palgrave Macmillian: 39–59.

Decosta-Willis, Miriam, ed. 1995. *The Memphis Diary of Ida B. Wells: An Intimate Portrait of the Activist as a Young Woman*. Boston, MA: Beacon Press.

Dittmer, John. 1995. *Local People: The Struggle for Civil Rights in Mississippi*. Urbana: University of Illinois Press.

Douglass, Frederick. 1857. "Response to Dred Scott," Speech to the American Anti-Slavery Society, Rochester, New York. May 14.

Dray, Philip. 2003. *At the Hands of Persons Unknown: The Lynching of Black America*. New York: Modern Library.

D'Souza, Dinesh. 1995. *The End of Racism: Principles for a Multiracial Society*. New York: Free Press.

Dubois, Page. 2003. *Slaves and Other Objects*. Chicago: University of Chicago Press.

Eberle, Edward J. 1987. "Procedural Due Process: The Original Understanding," *Constitutional Comment* 4: 339–362.

EEOC Guidelines, Section V., Language Issues, available at: www.eeoc.gov/laws/guidance/national-origin-guidance.cfm#_Toc451518821.

Eggers, Andrew C., Haritz Garro, and Justin Grimmer. 2021. "No Evidence for Systemic Voter Fraud: A Guide to Statistical Claims about the 2020 Election," *Proceedings of the National Academy of Sciences* 118(24). https://doi.org/10.1073/pnas.2103619118.

Ehrlich, Walter. 1992. "Scott v. Sandford." In Kermit L. Hall, ed. *The Oxford Companion to the Supreme Court of the United States*. New York: Oxford University Press: 761.

Epstein, Lee and Joseph F. Kobylka. 1991. *The Supreme Court and Legal Change: Abortion and the Death Penalty*. Chapel Hill: University of North Carolina Press.

Equal Employment Opportunity Commission (EEOC), U.S. 2023. "Press Release: Exxon Mobil Corporation Sued by EEOC for Race Discrimination." March 2, available at: https://www.eeoc.gov/newsroom/exxon-mobil-corporation-sued-eeoc-race-discrimination.

Erman, Sam. 2021. "Truer U.S. History: Race, Borders, and Status Manipulation," *Yale Law Journal* 130(5): 1050–1287.

Fehrenbacher, Don E. 2001. *The Slaveholding Republic: An Account of the United States Government's Relations to Slavery*, completed by Ward M. McAfee. New York: Oxford University Press.

Feitlowitz, Marguerite. 2011. *A Lexicon of Terror: Argentina and the Legacies of Torture, rev. and updated*. Oxford: Oxford University Press.

Fine, Doris. 1986. *When Leadership Fails: Desegregation and Demoralization in the San Francisco Schools*. New York: Transaction Books.

Finkelman, Paul. 1992. *Lynching, Racial Violence, and Law*. New York: Garland Science.

Finkelman, Paul. 1996. *Slavery and the Founders: Race and Liberty in the Age of Jefferson*. New York: M. E. Sharpe.

Fisher, Louis. 2019. "Japanese-American Cases," *Reconsidering Judicial Finality: Why the Supreme Court is not the Last Word on the Constitution*. Lawrence: University Press of Kansas: 162–182.

Foner, Eric. 1990. *A Short History of Reconstruction*. New York: Harper & Row.

Fong, Clara, Kelly Percival, and Thomas Wolf. 2023. "The Impact of Reforming Census Questions About Race and Ethnicity," Brennan Center for Justice. March 7, available at: www.brennancenter.org/our-work/research-reports/impact-reforming-census-questions-about-race-and-ethnicity.

Ford, Richard T. 2005. *Racial Culture: A Critique.* Princeton: Princeton University Press.

Formisano, Ronald P. 1991. *Boston against Busing: Race, Class, and Ethnicity in the 1960s and 1970s.* Chapel Hill: University of North Carolina Press.

Francis, Annie M., William J. Hall, David Ansong, Paul Lanier, Travis J. Britton, and Ashley McMillan. 2023. "Implementation and Effectiveness of the Indian Child Welfare Act: A Systemic Review," *Child and Family Service Review* 146: 1067–1099.

Francis, Megan Ming. 2011. "The Battle for the Hearts and Minds of America," *Souls* 13(1): 46–71.

Fredman, Sandra. 2016. "Substantive Equality Revisited," *International Journal of Constitutional Law* 14(3): 712–738.

Garroutte, Eva Marie. 2003. *Real Indians: Identity and the Survival of Native America.* Berkeley: University of California Press.

Gates, Jr., Henry Louis. 1987. *The Classic Slave Narratives.* Mentor Books. Berkeley, CA: Signet Classics.

Giddings, Paula J. 2008. *Ida, a Sword Among Lions: Ida B. Wells and the Campaign against Lynching.* New York: Amistad/HarperCollins.

Glenn, Evelyn Nakano. 2002. *Unequal Freedom: How Race and Gender Shaped American Citizenship and Labor.* Cambridge, MA: Harvard University Press.

Golub, Mark. 2018. *Is Racial Equality Unconstitutional?* New York: Oxford University Press.

Graber, Mark A. 2006. Dred Scott *and the Problem of Constitutional Evil.* New York: Cambridge University Press.

Greenberg, Jack. 1994. *Crusaders in the Courts: How a Dedicated Band of Lawyers Fought for the Civil Rights Revolution.* New York: Basic Books.

Greene, D. Wendy. 2017. "Splitting Hairs: The Eleventh Circuit's Take on Workplace Bans against Black Women's Natural Hair in EEOC v. Catastrophe Management Solutions," *University of Miami Law Review* 71: 987–1036.

Gunderson, Joan R. 1987. "Independence, Citizenship, and the American Revolution," *Signs* 13(1): 59–77.

Hacker, J. David. 2020. "'From 120 and Odd' to 10 Million: The Growth of the Slave Population in the United States," *Slavery & Abolition* 41(4): 840–855.

Hahn, Hayley, Johanna Caldwell, and Vandna Sinha. 2020. "Applying Lessons of the U.S. Indian Child Welfare Act to Recently Passed Federal Child Protection Legislation in Canada," *International Indigenous Policy Journal* 11(3). Doi:10.18584/iipj.2020.11.3.8206.

Hall, Jacqueline Dowd. 1993. *Revolt against Chivalry: Jessie Daniel Ames and the Women's Campaign against Lynching, revised ed.* New York: Columbia University Press.

Hermann, John R. 2019. "A Demographic Shift in College Students: A Preparatory Guide for Political Scientists and the Discipline," American Political Science Association Annual Meeting, August 29–September 1, Washington, D.C.

Hernández, Tanya Katerí. 2018. *Multiracials and Civil Rights: Mixed Race Stories of Discrimination.* New York: New York University Press.

Higginbotham, Jr., A. Leon. 1996. *Shades of Freedom: Racial Politics and the Presumptions of the American Legal Process.* New York: Oxford University Press. not cited.

Howard, John R. 1999. *The Shifting Wind: The Supreme Court and Civil Rights from Reconstruction to Brown.* Albany, N.Y.: SUNY Press. not cited.

Huggins, Nathan Irvin. 1977. *Black Odyssey: The Afro-American Ordeal in Slavery*. New York: Vintage.

Hughes, Coleman. 2024. *The End of Racial Politics: Arguments for a Colorblind America*. New York: Thesis.

Ignatiev, Noel. 1995. *How the Irish Became White*. New York: Routledge.

Irby, Matt. 2023. "The Native Family the Supreme Court Didn't Care About," *Balls and Strikes*. May 31, available at: https://ballsandstrikes.org/scotus/adoptive-couple-v-baby-girl-anniversary.

Irons, Peter. 1983. *Justice at War: The Story of the Japanese-American Internment Cases*. Oakland: University of California Press.

Jacobs, Gregory S. 1998. *Getting Around* Brown*: Desegregation, Development, and the Columbus Public Schools*. Columbus: Ohio State University Press.

Johnson, Mea. 2020. "I Am Not My Hair: Natural Hair Discrimination in Corporate America," *Journal of Race, Gender, and Poverty* 11: 111–133.

Jones, Jr., Augustus, Michelle D. Deardorff, and Michelle Briscoe. 2006. "Splitting the Baby: Media Constructions of *Grutter v. Bollinger* and *Gratz v. Bollinger*," *Journal of Political Science* 34: 118–150.

Jones, Nicholas, Rachel Marks, Roberto Ramerez, and Merarys Ríos-Vargas. 2021. "2020 Census Illuminates Racial and Ethnic Composition in the Country," *U.S. Census*. August 12, available at: www.census.gov/library/stories/2021/08/improved-race-ethnicity-measures-reveal-united-states-population-much-more-multiracial.html.

Jordan, Winthrop D. 1968. *White Over Black: American Attitudes towards the Negro, 1550–1812*. Chapel Hill: University of North Carolina Press.

Jordan, Winthrop D. 1974. *The White Man's Burden: Historical Origins of Racism in the U.S.* New York: Oxford University Press.

Kammen, Michael. 1986. *A Machine that Would Go of Itself: The Constitution in American Culture*. New York: Vintage.

Kato, Daniel. 2016. *Liberalizing Lynching: Building a New Racialized State*. New York: Oxford University Press.

Katznelson, Ira. 2005. *When Affirmative Action was White: An Untold History of Racial Inequality in Twentieth-Century America*. New York: W. W. Norton.

Kelley, J. W. 1929. "Dred Scott and John Elk," 6 *Dicta*: 25–26.

Kelly, Robin D. G. 1994. *Race Rebels: Culture, Politics, and the Black Working Class*. New York: Free Press.

Kendrick, Stephen and Paul Kendrick. 2006. *Sarah's Long Walk: The Free Blacks of Boston and How Their Struggle for Equality Changed America*. Boston, MA: Beacon Press.

Kerber, Linda. 1997. *Toward an Intellectual History of Women*. Chapel Hill: University of North Carolina Press.

Kernahan, Cyndi. 2016. "Raising Awareness and Reducing Color-Blind Racial Ideology in Higher Education." In Helen A. Neville, Miguel E. Gallardo, and Derald Wing Sue, eds. *The Myth of Racial Color Blindness: Manifestations, Dynamics, and Impact*. Washington, D.C.: American Psychological Association: 227–241.

Keyssar, Alexander. 2000. *The Right to Vote: The Contested History of Democracy in the United States*. New York: Basic Books.

Klarman, Michael J. 2004. *From Jim Crow to Civil Rights: The Supreme Court and the Struggle for Racial Equality*. New York: Oxford University Press.

Kluger, Richard. 2004 (rev.). *Simple Justice: The History of* Brown v. Board of Education *and Black America's Struggle for Equality*. New York: Vintage.

Kolnick, Jeff. 2022. "Minnesotanos: Latino Journeys in Minnesota," *MNopedia*. Minnesota Historical Society, available at: www.mnopedia.org/minnesotanos-latino-journeys-minnesota.

"Korematsu and Executive Order 9066: A Reenactment," 1998. *University of Michigan Law School*, Summer: 64–71.

Lane, Charles. 2008. *The Day Freedom Died: The Colfax Massacre, the Supreme Court, and the Betrayal of Reconstruction*. New York: Henry Holt.

Lebron, Christopher. 2013. *The Color of our Shame: Race and Justice in our Time*. New York: Oxford University Press.

Lebron, Christopher J. 2017. *The Making of Black Lives Matter: A Brief History of an Idea*. Oxford: Oxford University Press.

Lentz, Ryan. 2012. "Investigating Deaths of Undocumented Immigrants on the Border," Southern Poverty Law Center. August 26, available at: www.splcenter.org/fighting-hate/intelligence-report/2012/investigating-deaths-undocumented-immigrants-border.

Leong, Nancy. 2010. "Judicial Erasure of Mixed-Race Discrimination," *American University Law Review* 59: 469–550.

Litwack, Leon F. 1998. *Trouble in Mind: Black Southerners in the Age of Jim Crow*. New York: Alfred A. Knopf.

Logan, Rayford W. 1954. *The Negro in American Life and Thought: The Nadir, 1877–1901*. New York: Dial.

Lomawaima, K. Tsianina. 2013. "The Mutuality of Citizenship and Sovereignty: The Society of American Indians and the Battle to Inherit America," *American Indian Quarterly* 37(3): 333–351.

Lopéz, Ian Haney. 1996. *White by Law: The Legal Construction of Race*. New York: New York University Press.

MacKinnon, Catharine A. and Kimberlé W. Crenshaw. 2019. "Reconstituting the Future: The Equality Amendment," *Yale Law Journal of Forum* 129: 343–364.

Malone, Christopher. 2008. *Between Freedom and Bondage: Race, Party, and Voting Rights in the Antebellum North*. New York: Routledge.

Maltz, Earl M. 2007. Dred Scott *and the Politics of Slavery*. Lawrence: University Press of Kansas.

Marshall, Thurgood. 1987. "The Constitution's Bicentennial: Commemorating the Wrong Document?," *Vanderbilt Law Review* 40(6): 1337–1342.

McFeely, William S. 1997. "Capital Cases: A Legacy of Slavery and Lynching: The Death Penalty as a Tool of Social Control," November, available at: www.nacdl.org/CHAMPION/ARTICLES/97nov03.htm, last accessed September 11, 2013.

McGee, Jon. 2015. *Breakpoint: The Changing Marketplace for Higher Education*, Baltimore, MD: Johns Hopkins University Press.

McGuire, Danielle L. 2010. *At the Dark End of the Street: Black Women, Rape, and Resistance. A New History of the Civil Rights Movement from Rosa Parks to the Rise of Black Power*. New York: Vintage.

McMillen, Neil R. 1990. *Dark Journey: Black Mississippians in the Age of Jim Crow*. Urbana: University of Illinois Press.

Meier, August and Elliott Rudwick. 1976. "The Boycott Movement against Jim Crow Streetcars in the South, 1900–1906." In August Meier and Elliott Rudwick, eds. *Along the Color Line: Explorations in the Black Experience*. Urbana: University of Illinois Press: 267–289.

"Memorials of the Cherokee Indians, signed by their representatives, and by 3,085 Individuals of the Nation," March 15, 1830. H.R. Rep. No. 311, 21st Cong. 1st Sess. (1830).

Mickey-Pabello, David. 2020. "Scholarly Findings on Affirmative Action Bans," *The Civil Rights Project/Proyecto Derecho Civiles*. October 26. UCLA, available at: www.civilrightsproject.ucla.edu.

Mill, John Stuart. 1869. *The Subjection of Women*. Harlow, Essex: Longmans, Green, Reader & Dyer.

Molina, Natalia. 2014. *How Race is Made in America: Immigration, Citizenship, and the Historical Power of Racial Scripts*. Berkeley: University of California Press.

Morgan, Edmund S. 1975. *American Slavery, American Freedom*. New York: W. W. Norton Press.

Morgan, Jennifer L. 2004. *Laboring Women: Reproduction and Gender in New World Slavery*. Philadelphia: University of Pennsylvania Press.

Mumphrey, Cheyanne and Annie Ma. 2023. "Black Student Disciplined Over Hairstyle Hopes 'To Start Being a Kid Again,'" *Washington Post*. October 13, available at: www.washingtonpost.com/lifestyle/2023/10/13/locs-hairstyle-texas-crown-act-student/9fe9ab60-69ed-11ee-9753-2b3742e96987_story.html.

Myers, Landon. 2020. "The Gray Area: Exploring the Black–White Binary's Exploitation of the Multi-Racial Identity," *Georgetown Journal of Law and Modern Critical Race Perspectives* 12: 61–77.

Nackenoff, Carol and Julie Novkov. 2021. *American By Birth: Wong Kim Ark and the Battle for Citizenship*. Lawrence: University Press of Kansas.

Neo-Bustamante, Luis, Lauren Mora, and Mark Hugo Lopez. 2020. "About One-in-Four U.S. Hispanics Have Heard of Latinx, but Just 3% Use It," *Pew Research Center*, August 11, available at: www.pewresearch.org/hispanic/2020/08/11/about-one-in-four-u-s-hispanics-have-heard-of-latinx-but-just-3-use-it.

New Yorker Staff, 2019. "Te-Nihisi Coates revisits the case for Reparations?" July, available at: www.newyorker.com/news/the-new-yorker-interview/ta-nehisi-coates-revisits-the-case-for-reparations.

Niemann, Yolanda Flores and Geoffrey Maruyama. 2005. "Inequities in Higher Education: Issues and Promising Practices in a World Ambivalent about Affirmative Action," *Journal of Social Issues* 61(3): 407–426.

Nunn, Lisa M. 2019. *33 Simple Strategies for Faculty: A Week-by-Week Resource for Teaching First-Year and First-Generation Students*. New Brunswick, N.J.: Rutgers University Press.

Oshinsky, David M. 1996. *"Worse than Slavery": Parchman Farm and the Ordeal of Jim Crow Justice*. New York: Free Press.

Oshinsky, David M. 2010. *Capital Punishment on Trial: Furman v. Georgia and the Death Penalty in Modern America*. Kansas City: University of Kansas Press.

Ostler, Jeffrey. 2019. "Locating Settler Colonialism in Early American History," *William and Mary Quarterly* 76(3): 443–450.

Padilla, Mariel. 2019. "Student's Case Leads New Jersey to Enact Ban on Hair Discrimination," *New York Times*. December 23.

Parker, Kim, Juliana Menasce Horowitz, Rich Morin, and Mark Hugo Lopez. 2015. "Multiracial in America: Proud, Diverse, and Growing in Numbers," Pew Research Center. June 11, available at: www.pewresearch.org/social-trends/2015/06/11/multiracial-in-america.

Patterson, Orlando. 1982. *Slavery and Social Death: A Comparative Study*. Cambridge, MA: Harvard University Press.

Patterson, Orlando. 1999. *Rituals of Blood: Consequences of Slavery in Two American Centuries*. New York: Basic Civitas Book.

Payne, Charles M. 2007. *I've Got the Light of Freedom: The Organizing Tradition and the Mississippi Freedom Struggle.* Berkeley: University of California Press.

Penner, Louis A. and John F. Dovidio. 2016. "Racial Color Blindness and Black–White Health Care Disparities." In Helen A. Neville, Miguel E. Gallardo, and Derald Wing Sue, eds. *The Myth of Racial Color Blindness: Manifestations, Dynamics, and Impact.* Washington, D.C.: American Psychological Association: 275–293.

Perea, Juan F. 1998. "The Black/White Binary Paradigm of Race: The 'Normal Science' of American Racial Thought," *La Raza Law Journal* 10: 127–171.

Pomeroy, Sarah B. [1975] 1995. *Goddesses, Whores, Wives, and Slaves: Women in Classical Antiquity.* New York: Schocken.

Ponsa, Christina Duffy. 2015. "When Statehood was Autonomy." In Gerald A. Neuman and Tomiko Brown-Nagin, eds. *Reconsidering the* Insular Cases: *The Past and Future of the American Empire.* Cambridge, MA: Harvard University Press: 1–28.

Pratt, Richard H. 1892. "Official Report of the Nineteenth Annual Conference of Charities and Correction." Reprinted in Richard H. Pratt, "The Advantages of Mingling Indians with Whites," *Americanizing the American Indians: Writings by the "Friends of the Indian" 1880-1900.* Cambridge, MA: Harvard University Press, 1973: 260–271.

Pratt, Robert A. 1992. *The Color of Their Skin: Education and Race in Richmond, Virginia, 1954-1989.* Charlottesville: University Press of Virginia.

Pratt, Jr., Walter F. 1992. "Insular Cases." In Kermit Hall, ed. *Oxford Companion to the Supreme Court of the United States.* New York: Oxford University Press.

Rana, Aziz. 2010. *The Two Faces of American Freedom.* Cambridge, MA: Harvard University Press.

Reséndez, André. 2016. *The Other Slavery: The Uncovered Story of Indian Enslavement in America.* New York: Houghton Mifflin Harcourt.

Rice, James D. 2012. *Tales from a Revolution: Bacon's Rebellion and the Transformation of Early America.* New York: Oxford University Press.

Roediger, David R. 2007. *The Wages of Whiteness: Race and the Making of the American Working Class.* New York: Verso.

Rothstein, Richard. 2017. *The Color of Law: A Forgotten History of How Our Government Segregated America.* New York: Liveright.

Sanford, Victoria. 2004. *Buried Secrets: Truth and Human Rights in Guatemala.* New York: Palgrave.

Saunt, Claudio. 2020. *Unworthy Republic: The Dispossession of Native Americans and the Road to Indian Territory.* New York: W. W. Norton.

Schmidt, Ryan W. 2011. "American Indian Identity and Blood Quantum in the 21st Century: A Critical Review," *Journal of Anthropology* 1(1). doi.org/10.1155/2011/549521.

Schwartz, Joanna. 2023. *Shielded: How the Police Became Untouchable.* New York: Viking.

Scott, James C. 1990. *Domination and the Arts of Resistance: Hidden Transcripts.* New Haven, C.T.: Yale University Press.

Seth, Vanita. 2020. "The Origins of Racism: A Critique of the History of Ideas," *History and Theory* 59(3): 343–368.

Shestack, Jerome J. 1979. *The Case of the Disappeared: Testimony of Jerome J. Shestack, President, International League for Human Rights, before the Subcommittee on International Human Rights, House of Representatives of the United States.* New York: International League for Human Rights.

Shklar, Judith N. 1991. *American Citizenship: The Quest for Inclusion.* Cambridge, MA: Harvard University Press.

Siler, Julia Flynn. 2019. *The White Devil's Daughters: The Women Who Fought Slavery in San Francisco Chinatown.* New York: Knopf.

Silver, Peter. 2008. *Our Savage Neighbors: How Indian War Transformed Early America.* New York: W. W. Norton.

Smith, Rogers. 1997. *Civic Ideals: Conflicting Visions of Citizenship in U.S. History.* New Haven, C.T.: Yale University Press.

Smith, Rogers. 2015. "The Insular Cases, Differentiated Citizenship, and Territorial Status in the Twenty-first Century." In Gerald L. Neuman and Tomika Brown-Nagin, eds. *Reconsidering the Insular Cases: The Past and Future of the American Empire.* Cambridge, MA: Harvard University Press: 103–128.

Sparrow, Bartholomew H. 2006. *The* Insular Cases *and the Emergence of American Empire.* Lawrence: University of Kansas Press.

Stevenson, Bryan T. 2015. *Just Mercy: A Story of Justice and Redemption.* London: One-World.

Strum, Phillipa. 2010. Mendez *v.* Westminster*: School Desegregation and Mexican-American Rights.* Lawrence: University of Kansas Press.

Stuntz, William J. 2011. *The Collapse of American Criminal Justice.* Cambridge, MA: Belknap Press: 202.

Thomas, Brook, ed. 1997. Plessy *v.* Ferguson*: A Brief History of Documents.* New York: Bedford Books.

Thomas, Hugh. 1997. *The Slave Trade: The Story of the Atlantic Slave Trade, 1440–1870.* New York: Simon & Shuster.

Tolnay, Stewart E. and E. M. Beck. 1995. *A Festival of Violence: An Analysis of Southern Lynchings, 1882–1930.* Champaign: University of Illinois Press.

Travernise, Sabrina, Tariro Mzezewa, and Giulia Heyward. 2021. "Behind the Surprising Jump in Multiracial Americans, Several Theories," *New York Times.* August 15, available at: www.nytimes.com/2021/08/13/us/census-multiracial-identity.html.

Treuer, David. 2019. *The Heartbeat of Wounded Knee: Native America from 1890 to the Present.* New York: Riverhead Books.

Turner, Caroline M. 2016. "Implementing and Defending the Indiana Child Welfare Act through Revised State Requirements," *Columbia Journal of Law and Social Problems* 219(4): 501–549.

Tushnet, Mark V. 1987. *The NAACP's Legal Strategy against Segregated Education, 1925–1950.* Chapel Hill: North Carolina University Press.

Tushnet, Mark V. 1994. *Making Civil Rights Law: Thurgood Marshall and the Supreme Court, 1936–1961.* New York: Oxford University Press.

Urofsky, Melvin I. 1997. *Affirmative Action on Trial: Sex Discrimination in* Johnson v. Santa Clara. Lawrence: University of Kansas Press.

Ushpiz, Ada (director). 2015. *Vita Activa: The Spirit of Hannah Arendt.* Documentary. New York: Zeitgeist Films.

Vallely, Richard. 2004. *The Two Reconstructions: The Struggle for Black Enfranchisement.* Chicago: University of Chicago Press.

Villegas, Paulina. 2023. "Mississippi Ex-Officers Plead Guilty to State Charges in Torture of Black Men," *Washington Post.* August 14, available at: www.washingtonpost.com/nation/2023/08/14/mississippi-cops-torture-guilty-goon-squad.

Walzer, Michael. 1992. *What it Means to Be an American: Essays on the American Experience.* Venice: Marselio Press.

Washburn, Kevin K. 2006. "Federal Criminal Law and Tribal Self-Determination," *North Carolina Law Review* 84: 779–858.

Watford, Paul J. 2014. "Hallows Lecture: Screws v. United States and the Birth of Federal Civil Rights Enforcement," *Marquette Law Review* 98(1): 465–485.

Wells, Ida B. 1892. *Southern Horrors: Lynch Law in All Its Phases.* New York: The New York Age.

Wells, Ida B. 1895. *A Red Record: Tabulated Statistics and Alleged Causes of Lynchings in the United States, 1892–1893–1894.* Chicago.

Wilkins, David E. and K. Tsianina Lomawaima. 2002. *Uneven Ground: American Indian Sovereignty and Federal Law.* Norman: University of Oklahoma Press.

Williams, Patricia J. 1991. *The Alchemy of Race and Rights: Diary of a Law Professor.* Cambridge, MA: Harvard University Press.

Williams, Yohuru R. 2002/2003. "Anatomy of an Untruth: The Controversy over 'Picnic' and the True Cause of Lynching," *Black History Bulletin* 65/66: 9–16, 11.

Winterdyk, John. 2019. "Explaining Human Trafficking: Modern-Day Slavery," *Palgrave International Handbook of Human Trafficking*, Chicago, IL: Champaign International Publishing: 1257–1274.

Witkin, Alexandra. 1995. "To Silence a Drum: The Impositions of United States Citizenship on Native Peoples," *Historical Reflections* 21(2): 353–383.

Wong, Edlie L. 2015. *Racial Reconstruction: Black Inclusion, Chinese Exclusion, and the Fictions of Citizenship.* New York: New York University.

Wong, Chin Foo. 1887. "Why Am I a Heathen," *North American Review* 145(369): 170–175.

Wood, Amy Louise. 2009. *Lynching and Spectacle: Witnessing Racial Violence in America, 1890–1940.* Chapel Hill: University of North Carolina Press.

Woodson, Kevin. 2016. "Derivative Racial Discrimination," *Stanford Journal of Civil Rights and Civil Liberties* 12: 335.

Wright, James E., Dongfang Gaozhao, and Meagan A. Snow. 2021. "Place plus Race Effects in Bureaucratic Discretionary Power: An Analysis of Residential Segregation and Police Stop Decisions," *Public Performance & Management Review* 44(2): 352–377.

Wynn, Jr., Judge James A. 2009. "*State v. Mann*: Judicial Choice or Judicial Duty?," *North Carolina Law Review* 87: 991–1005.

Young, Iris Marion. 1999. "Residential Segregation and Differentiated Citizenship," *Citizenship Studies* 3: 237–252.

Zangrando, Robert L. 1980. *The NAACP Crusade against Lynching, 1909–1950.* Philadelphia, P.A.: Temple University Press.

Zug, Marcia. 2021. "ICWA's Irony," *American Law Review* 45: 1–102.

INDEX

Printed by Integrated Books International,
United States of America